THE NEW DICTIONARY
OF PASTORAL STUDIES

THE NEW DICTIONARY OF PASTORAL STUDIES

Edited by Wesley Carr

First published in Great Britain in 2002 by
Society for Promoting Christian Knowledge
Holy Trinity Church
Marylebone Road
London NW1 4DU

Copyright © SPCK 2002

British Library Cataloguing-in-Publication Data

A catalogue record for this book is available from the British Library

ISBN 0–281–05000–7

Typeset by Wilmaset Ltd, Birkenhead, Wirral
Printed in Great Britain by
Mackays of Chatham

The Editors

General Editor

WESLEY CARR MA PhD is Dean of Westminster, a post he has held since 1997. A graduate of Oxford and Cambridge and with a semester in Geneva, he was ordained in 1967. After a curacy in Luton Parish Church, he returned briefly to Ridley Hall, Cambridge, to teach New Testament. Subsequently he was elected Sir Henry Stephenson Fellow in the University of Sheffield, where he was awarded his doctorate. He moved on to Chelmsford Cathedral as Deputy Director of the Cathedral Centre for Research and Training, Director of Training for the Diocese of Chelmsford and a Canon Residentiary of Chelmsford Cathedral. In 1987 he became Dean of Bristol. He has been involved widely in education and training in the Church of England and elsewhere.

Other appointments include an Honorary Fellowship at New College, Edinburgh, where he participated in the Media and Theological Education Project.

Since 1994 Wesley Carr has been associated with the Tavistock Institute Group Relations Programme, and he is currently a member of its Advisory Group. He has directed many group relations conferences, in Great Britain and in the United States, including the Tavistock Leicester Conference.

Wesley Carr is Editor of the New Library of Pastoral Care. He has published a number of books, including six on pastoral studies. With Edward R. Shapiro he jointly wrote *Lost in Familiar Places*, and he edited a collection, *Say One for Me*. In 1992 he wrote the Archbishop of Canterbury's Lent book, *Tested by the Cross*. He has written many articles and reviews. Most address his focal interest, which is the relationship between the human sciences, theology and the Church's ministry.

Editorial Panel

DONALD CAPPS is William Harte Felmeth Professor of Pastoral Theology at Princeton Theological Seminary, Princeton, New Jersey, USA. He holds the BD and STM degrees from Yale Divinity School, the PhD from the University of Chicago, and an honorary doctorate in sacred theology from Uppsala University. He was editor of the *Journal for the Scientific Study of Religion* from 1983 to 1988, and President of the Society for the Scientific Study of Religion from 1990 to 1992. His most recent books are: *Agents of Hope: A Pastoral Psychology*; *The Child's Song: The Religious Abuse of Children* (1995); *Men, Religion, and Melancholia* (1997); *Living Stories: Pastoral Counseling in Congregational Context* (1998); *Social Phobia: Alleviating Anxiety in an Age of Self-promotion* (1999); and *Jesus: A Psychological Biography* (2000). He is also editor of several volumes, most recently *Freud and Freudians on Religion* (2000).

ROBIN GILL is the Michael Ramsey Professor of Modern Theology in the University of Kent at Canterbury. Previously he held the William Leech Research Chair of Applied Theology at the University of Newcastle. Among his books are *The Social Context of Theology* (1975), *Theology and Social Structure* (1977), *Prophecy and Praxis* (1981), *A Textbook of Christian Ethics* (1985, revised 1995), *Theology and Sociology* (1987, revised 1996), *Competing Convictions* (1989), *Christian Ethics in Secular Worlds* (1991), *The Myth of the Empty Church* (1993), *Readings in Modern Theology* (1995), *Moral Leadership in a Postmodern Age* (1997) and *Churchgoing and Christian Ethics* (1999). He is also series editor of New Studies in Christian Ethics for Cambridge University Press. Ordained an Anglican priest in 1968, he continues to be active in pastoral ministry, and is now an honorary Canon of Canterbury Cathedral.

ANTON OBHOLZER BSc, MB, ChB, DPM, FRCPsych is a consultant psychiatrist and psychotherapist, a Fellow of the Royal College of Psychiatrists, and a child and adult psychoanalyst, who trained at both the Tavistock Clinic and the Institute of Psychoanalysis in London. He currently holds the position of Chief Executive of the Tavistock and Portman Clinics in London, is Chairman of the Consulting to Institutions Workshop and a Senior Consultant in the Tavistock Consultancy Service. Dr Obholzer consults and lectures widely on the application of psychoanalytic, psychotherapeutic and systemic ideas in a variety of settings, including management, the public sector, voluntary agencies and the Church. His special interests are unconscious factors that interfere in interpersonal and intra-institutional communication and change.

RUTH PAGE was born in Dundee, Scotland. After taking a degree in English and French from St Andrews University, and a teaching qualification, she travelled the world, landing in New Zealand. There she found herself called to the Presbyterian ministry, and took a divinity degree at Otago, Dunedin, New Zealand. Having won some scholarships she went on to doctoral study in Oxford, returning thereafter to Otago to teach both dogmatic and philosophical theology. In 1979 she returned to Scotland to take up a position in the Faculty of Divinity of the University of Edinburgh. Ultimately she was Principal of New College, and retired in 2000.

DEBORAH VAN DEUSEN HUNSINGER is an ordained minister in the United Church of Christ. She has taught pastoral theology at Princeton Theological Seminary since 1994. A practising pastoral counsellor for nearly fifteen years before she began teaching, Deborah is a Fellow in the American Association of Pastoral Counselors. Her long-standing interest in the relationship between Christian theology and psychotherapeutic theory and practice culminated in the publication of her book *Theology and Pastoral Counseling: A New Interdisciplinary Approach* (Eerdmans, 1995), which explores the intersection between these two fields of study. She is vitally interested in the Christian vocation to prayer and in building up the life of prayer in congregations.

ROWAN WILLIAMS is the Anglican Archbishop of Wales. Brought up in Wales, he has taught theology at Mirfield, Cambridge and Oxford. He is the author of several books, including most recently *On Christian Theology*, *Lost Icons* and *Christ on Trial* (the Archbishop of Canterbury's Lent book for 2001), as well as two collections of poetry. With Geoffrey Rowell and Kenneth Stevenson, he is editor of *Love's Redeeming Work*, an anthology of Anglican writing on holiness. He has chaired the Church in Wales' Division for Social Responsibility and is one of the founders of the Network for Anglicans in Mission and Evangelism. His special interests lie in the historical development of Christian spirituality and in the borderlands between theology, psychology and the arts.

Contributors

Authors of substantive articles are individually credited in the text. Short 'definition' articles are written by members of the editorial panel and contributors, and are unattributed. The following are authors of single short articles:

Glenn Asquith	'Intervention, Pastoral'
Stuart Charme	'Masochism'
Henry Close	'Hypnosis'
Susan Dunlap	'Mood Disorders'
Leland Elhard	'Ego Psychology'
Jeanette A. Good	'Self-Destructive Behaviour'
Jaco Hamman	'Paranoia'
Richard E. Hoffman	'Brain Death'
Richard A. Hutch	'Heterosexuality'
Merle R. Jordan	'Phenomenology'
Christie Neuger	'Empowerment'
Jean Neumann	'T-Group'
Randall Nichols	'Preaching, Pastoral'
Frank J. Stalfa	'Enneagram'
Ralph Underwood	'Positive Regard'
Peter VanKatwyk	'Differentiation'
Peter Van Ness	'Ecstasy'
J. Bradley Wigger	'Educational Psychology'

The Editors have made every effort to provide up-to-date information on contributors, but if there should be any inaccuracies, we apologize.

LeRoy H. Aden is Luther D. Reed Professor Emeritus, Lutheran Theological Seminary, Philadelphia, PA, USA.

Ian Ainsworth-Smith is Chaplain of St George's Hospital, Tooting, London, England.

Carol Rausch Albright is Co-Director Midwest region, John Templeton Foundation Science and Religion Course Program, Purdue University, Hammond, IN, USA.

Richard Stoll Armstrong is Ashenfelter Professor of Ministry and Evangelism Emeritus, Princeton Theological Seminary, Princeton, NJ, USA.

William V. Arnold is Associate Pastor for Senior Adults at Bryn Mawr Presbyterian Church in Bryn Mawr, PA, USA.

Glenn Asquith is Professor of Pastoral Theology at Moravian Theological Seminary, Bethlehem, PA, USA.

John Atherton is Canon Theologian at Manchester Cathedral and Honorary Lecturer at the University of Manchester, Manchester, England.

Ron Baard is a pastoral counsellor and consultant in Phoenix, AZ, USA.

Paul Badham is Professor of Theology, University of Wales, Lampeter, Wales.

Edward Bailey is Rector of Winterbourne and visiting Professor of Implicit Religion at Middlesex University, London, England.

J. Paul Balas is Associate Professor of Pastoral Theology, Lutheran Theological Seminary, Gettysburg, PA, USA.

Paul Ballard is Professor in the Department of Religious and Theological Studies at Cardiff University, Wales.

Stephen Barton is Senior Lecturer in New Testament, Department of Theology, University of Durham, England.

Belinda Barwick is Deputy Headteacher at Tuckswood First School, Norwich, England, and an Anglican lay reader.

David Bell is a Consultant, Adult Department, the Tavistock and Portman NHS Trust, London, England.

Janet Bellamy is a Lecturer in Counselling, University of Birmingham, Westhill, Birmingham, England.

Phillip C. Bennett is Coordinator and Assistant Professor, Graduate Program in Pastoral Care and Counseling, Neumann College, PA, USA.

Derek Blows is the former Director of the Westminster Pastoral Foundation. He is an Anglican priest and Canon Emeritus of Southwark Cathedral, London, England.

Carolyn Bohler is a lecturer. She lives in Dayton, OH, USA.

David W. Bond is Honorary Treasurer, Maidstone Christian Care, and Assistant Priest, Parish of Otham with Langley, Maidstone, Kent, England.

Heather Bond RGN is former Chief Officer, Royal College of Nursing, and Chairman, St George's Nurses League, London, England.

Kenneth Boyd is Senior Lecturer in Medical Ethics, Edinburgh Medical School, Scotland.

Nicholas Bradbury is Vicar of Horfield, Bristol, England.

George Bright is a Jungian psychoanalyst in London, England and Paris, France.

Mary Louise Bringle is Professor of Religion and Philosophy, Brevard College, NC, USA.

Reginald D. Burgess is a pastoral counsellor, Fairfax, VA, USA.

Derek Burke CBE DL is retired vice-chancellor, University of East Anglia, Norwich, England.

Rupert Bursell is an Anglican priest, a Circuit Judge, Chancellor of the dioceses of Durham and St Albans, and Deputy Chancellor of the Anglican diocese of York, England.

Mary Butterton is a lecturer and teacher of music psychotherapy, formerly in the NHS, now in private practice, Derby, England.

Alastair Campbell is Professor of Ethics in Medicine, University of Bristol, England.

Donald Capps is William Harte Felmeth Professor of Pastoral Theology, Princeton Theological Seminary, Princeton, NJ, USA.

Wesley Carr is Dean of Westminster, London, England.

Stuart Charme is Professor of Religion, Rutgers University, Camden, NJ, USA.

Dana Charry is a psychiatrist in Richard Hall Mental Health Center, Bridgewater, NJ, USA.

Rosemary Chinnici is Professor of Pastoral Theology, Graduate Theological Union, Berkeley, CA, USA.

David Clark is an Honorary Lecturer, University of Birmingham, Westhill, Birmingham, England.

William Clements is Edna and Lowell Craig Professor, Pastoral Care and Counseling, Claremont School of Theology, Claremont, CA, USA.

Howard Clinebell is Professor Emeritus, Pastoral Psychology and Counseling, Claremont Theological Seminary and University Graduate School, Claremont, CA, USA.

Henry Close is a counsellor in Atlanta, GA, USA.

Chris Clulow is Marital Psychotherapist and Clinical Lecturer in Marital Studies, and Director of Tavistock Marital Studies Institute, London, England.

Mary Anne Coate is a chartered clinical psychologist, Westminster Pastoral Foundation Counselling and Psychotherapy, London, England.

Allan Hugh Cole is Visiting Lecturer in Pastoral Theology at Princeton Theological Seminary, Princeton, NJ, USA.

Robert M. Collie is a pastoral counsellor in private practice, Fort Wayne, IN, USA.

Chris Cook is Professor of the Psychiatry of Alcohol Misuse, Kent Institute of Medicine and Health Science, University of Kent at Canterbury, England. He is a non-stipendiary curate in the Church of England.

Niall Cooper is National Co-ordinator for Church Action on Poverty in Manchester, England.

James Cotter is a presbyter, writer and publisher in the Anglican diocese of Sheffield, England.

Pamela Couture is Associate Professor of Pastoral Theology, Crozer Theological Seminary, Rochester, NY, USA.

The late Revd John Dalrymple was a Roman Catholic parish priest and author.

Tim Dartington is a group and organizational consultant in London, England.

Douglas Davies is Professor in the Study of Religion, University of Durham, Durham, England.

David E. Demson is Professor of Systemic Theology, Emmanuel College, University of Toronto, Toronto, ON, Canada.

James Dittes is Professor of Pastoral Theology and Psychology at Yale Divinity School, New Haven, CT, USA.

Carrie Doehring is Professor of Theology, Boston University, Boston, MA, USA.

Susan Dowell is a theologian and Christian feminist writer.

John Drane is Professor of Practical Theology, University of Aberdeen, Aberdeen, Scotland.

Martin Dudley is Rector of St Bartholomew the Great, Smithfield, City of London, England.

Ann Dummett is a writer in Oxford, England.

Susan Dunlap is Professor of Pastoral Theology, Duke University Divinity School, Durham, NC, USA.

Gordon R. Dunstan is a former Professor of Moral and Social Theology, and a former Chaplain to Queen Elizabeth II. He lives in Exeter, England.

Robert C. Dykstra is Associate Professor of Pastoral Theology at Princeton Theological Seminary, Princeton, NJ, USA.

Leland E. Elhard is Professor of Pastoral Theology at Trinity Lutheran Seminary, Columbus, OH, USA.

J. Harold Ellens is a psychologist and pastoral counsellor, and Research Scholar in the Department of Near Eastern Studies, University of Michigan, Ann Arbor, MI, USA.

Michele Elliott is a child psychologist and writer. She is the Founder-Director of Kidscape, London, England.

James Emerson Jr is Chair of the Editorial Board, *Pastoral Psychology Magazine*. He is Pastor

Emeritus, Calvary Presbyterian Church, San Francisco, and adjunct faculty to San Francisco Theological Seminary, CA, USA.

Abigail Rian Evans is Charlotte Newcombe Professor of Practical Theology, Princeton University, Princeton, NJ, USA.

Frank Field MP is Member of Parliament for Birkenhead, House of Commons, Westminster, London, England.

George Fitchett is Associate Professor and Director of Research, Rush-Presbyterian-St Luke's Medical Center, Chicago, IL, USA.

Heather Formaini is a Jungian analyst and writer in New South Wales, Australia, formerly a religious affairs correspondent in London, England.

Duncan Forrester is Emeritus Professor of Christian Ethics and Practical Theology, University of Edinburgh, Edinburgh, Scotland.

Leslie Francis is Professor of Practical Theology at the University of Wales, Bangor, North Wales.

Judith Freedman is a consultant psychiatrist at the Portman Clinic, London, England.

George Furniss is a retired hospital chaplain and adjunct theological seminary faculty member, Eugene, OR, USA.

Caroline Garland is a consultant psychotherapist in the Adult Department of the Tavistock and Portman NHS Trust, London, England.

Robin Gill is Michael Ramsey Professor of Modern Theology, University of Kent, Canterbury, England.

Nicola Glover-Thomas is Lecturer in Law at the University of Liverpool, Liverpool, England.

Miriam Anne Glover-Wetherington is Professor at Duke University, Durham, NC, USA.

John Goldingay is Professor of Old Testament at Fuller Theological Seminary, Pasadena, CA, USA.

Jeanette A. Good is a counsellor in Massachusetts, USA.

Howard Gordon is Community Health Care Chaplain at George Eliot Hospital, Nuneaton, and North Warwickshire NHS Trust, England.

Tim Gorringe is Professor of Theological Studies, University of Exeter, Exeter, England.

Larry Kent Graham PhD is Professor of Theology and Care at Iliff School of Theology in Denver, CO, USA.

Robin Greenwood is Ministry Officer for the Church in Wales.

Elif Gurisik is a consultant psychotherapist and psychoanalyst at the Portman Clinic, London, England.

John Hall is Head Clinical Psychologist, Oxfordshire Health Authority, and Senior Clinical Lecturer in Clinical Psychology, University of Oxford, Oxford, England.

Jaco J. Hamman is Assistant Professor of Pastoral Care and Counseling at Western Theological Seminary, Holland, MI, USA.

Archibald Hart is Professor of Psychology, Fuller Theological Seminary, Pasadena, CA, USA.

Nicholas Peter Harvey is a moral theologian and writer, Suffolk, England.

David Haslam is Minister of Herne Hill United Church, and Christ Church, East Dulwich, London, England.

Barbara Hayes is an industrial chaplain in Oxford, England.

David Healy is Senior Director, North Wales Department of Psychological Medicine, University of Wales, Bangor, North Wales.

Margaret Hebblethwaite is a theologian, writer and mother.

Daniel A. Helminiak is Assistant Professor of Psychology, State University of West Georgia, Carrollton, GA, USA.

Savitri Hensman is a justice and peace worker in and outside the Church.

Richard L. Hester is Senior Staff Counselor and Supervisor, Triangle Pastoral Counseling, in Raleigh, NC, USA.

Philip Hewitt is School Counsellor at Westminster School, London, England.

Richard E. Hoffman is Chaplain and Director of Pastoral Care, Saratoga Springs, NY, USA.

Judith Hubback is a retired analytical psychologist and training analyst, and a writer, London, England.

John M. Hull is Professor of Religious Education, University of Birmingham, Birmingham, England.

Victor L. Hunter is Pastor of Evergreen Christian Church (Disciples of Christ), a retreat director, and adjunct faculty, Phillips Theological Seminary, Colorado, USA.

Richard A. Hutch is Professor, Department of Studies in Religion, University of Queensland, Brisbane, Australia.

Martin Israel is a writer, Senior Lecturer in Pathology at the Royal College of Surgeons, London, England; priest-in-charge, retired 1996.

Michael Jacobs is an independent consultant in psychotherapy and counselling, Dorset, England.

David Jenkins was Bishop of Durham, retired 1994, and is Honorary Assistant Bishop of Ripon and Leeds, Yorkshire, England.

Malcolm Johnson is the Bishop of London's Adviser on Pastoral Care and Counselling, St Martin-in-the-Fields, London, England.

Merle Jordan is Professor Emeritus of Pastoral Psychology at Boston University School of Theology, Boston, MA, USA.

Brett Kahr is Senior Lecturer in Psychotherapy and Counselling at Regent's College, London, England.

Israel Kestenbaum is ACPE Supervisor and Director of the Jewish Institute for Pastoral Care of the Health Care Chaplaincy in New York, NY, USA.

Mary Kirk is former Director of the Church and Community Trust, a relationships counsellor, and author of books on relational and marital issues, Suffolk, England.

Robert B. Kosek is Associate Pastor at St James Church in Oakville, ON, Canada.

Una Kroll is a former medical practitioner, a priest in the Church in Wales, and a counsellor in Monmouth, Wales.

Christopher Lamb is Rector of four rural parishes in South Warwickshire, and Canon Theologian of Coventry Cathedral, England.

Ryan LaMothe is Associate Professor of Pastoral Care and Counseling, St Meinrad School of Theology, St Meinrad, IN, USA.

Roy Lawrence is Honorary Consultant to the Churches' Advisers in Healing, Liverpool, England.

Raymond Lawrence Jr is Director of Pastoral Care, New York Presbyterian Hospital, New York, NY, USA.

Dave Leal is Lecturer in Philosophy at Brasenose College, Oxford University, Oxford, England.

John Leonard is a consultant physician, Withington Hospital, Manchester, England (retired).

Andrew Linzey is Senior Research Fellow, Mansfield College, Oxford, England.

Pat Logan is Social Responsibility Adviser in the diocese of Southwark, London, England.

Brid Long is Assistant Professor of Pastoral Theology, the Catholic University of America, Washington, DC, USA.

Alan Luff is Canon Emeritus of Birmingham Cathedral (retired) and Vice-Principal of the International Fellowship for Research in Hymnology.

Lyman T. Lundeen is Professor of Religion at Pacific Lutheran University, Tacoma, WA, USA.

David Lyall is Senior Lecturer in Christian Ethics and Practical Theology, University of Edinburgh, Edinburgh, Scotland.

Gordon Lynch is Professor in the Department of Theology, Birmingham University, Birmingham, England.

H. Newton Malony is Senior Professor, Graduate School of Psychology, Fuller Theological Seminary, Pasadena, CA, USA.

Ian Markham is Liverpool Professor of Theology and Public Life at Liverpool Hope University College, Liverpool, England.

Ian McDonald is Professor, Faculty of Divinity, University of Edinburgh, Edinburgh, Scotland.

Lynda Miller is Consultant Child and Adolescent Psychotherapist, Adolescent Department, Tavistock Clinic and Enfield Child Guidance Service, London, England.

Jolyon Mitchell is Lecturer in Communication and Theology, and Director of the Media and Theology Project, University of Edinburgh, Edinburgh, Scotland.

Christopher Moody is Team Rector of Market Harborough, Leicester, England.

David M. Moss is Director of the Coventry Association for Pastoral Psychology in Atlanta, GA, USA.

Lesley Murdin is Head of Training at Westminster Pastoral Foundation of Counselling and Psychotherapy, London, England.

Derek B. Murray is Chaplain, St Columba's Hospice, Edinburgh, Scotland (retired).

Gordon Mursell is former Provost, then Dean of Birmingham Cathedral, Birmingham, England.

Christie Neuger is Professor of Pastoral Theology, United Theological Seminary, New Brighton, ME, USA.

Jean Neumann is Senior Consultant Researcher, Tavistock Institute, London, England.

George Newlands is Professor of Divinity, University of Glasgow, Glasgow, Scotland.

Randall Nichols is Director of the Doctor of Ministry Program and Lecturer in Theology and Communications at Princeton Theological Seminary; and Senior Psychotherapist at Trinity Counseling Service, NJ, USA.

Michael Northcott is Senior Lecturer in Christian Ethics, University of Edinburgh, Edinburgh, Scotland.

Rachel Nugee is former Central (international) President of the Mothers' Union, and a Justice of the Peace with a practice in the Family Division.

Wayne E. Oates was a writer and Professor of Pastoral Theology in Kentucky, USA. Professor Oates died in 1999.

Paul Oestreicher is Canon Emeritus and International Consultant at Coventry Cathedral, England.

Robert Orchin is a priest-in-charge in the Anglican diocese of Portsmouth, England.

Judith L. Orr is Professor at St Paul School of Theology, Kansas City, MO, USA.

Ruth Page is former Principal of New College, University of Edinburgh, Edinburgh, Scotland (retired).

Paul P. Parker is Associate Professor of Theology and Religion, Elmhurst College, Elmhurst, IL, USA.

Susan Parsons is Director of Pastoral Studies, the Margaret Beaufort Institute of Theology, Cambridge, England.

Stephen Parsons is a parish priest, and Adviser on the Ministry of Healing to the Bishop of Gloucester, England.

Stephen Pattison is a former Lecturer in Pastoral Studies at Birmingham University and honorary curate, Moseley St Mary, Birmingham, England.

John Patton is Professor of Pastoral Theology at Columbia Theological Seminary, Decatur, GA, USA.

John Peirce is the Founder of Church Action on Disability, and a consultant in private practice, London, England.

Martyn Percy is the Director of the Lincoln Theological Institute, University of Sheffield, Sheffield, England.

Catherine Pickstock is a Lecturer in Philosophy of Religion, Faculty of Divinity, University of Cambridge, Cambridge, England.

James N. Poling is Professor of Pastoral Theology, Care, and Counseling at Garrett-Evangelical Theological Seminary in Evanston, IL, USA.

Val Potter is Deputy Chair, British Association for Counselling and Psychotherapy, and Head of Counselling, Westminster Pastoral Foundation, London, England.

Harry Potter is a barrister at law, Gray's Inn, London, England.

Mark Allan Powell is Professor of New Testament at Trinity Lutheran Seminary, Columbus, OH, USA.

Peter Price is Bishop of Kingston, Southwark diocese, London, England.

Mark Pryce is Dean of Chapel and Tutor, Corpus Christi College, Cambridge University, Cambridge, England.

Andrew Purves is Professor of Theology, Pittsburgh Theological Seminary, Pittsburgh, PA, USA.

Lewis Rambo is Tulley Professor of Psychology and Religion at San Francisco Theological Seminary, San Anselmo, CA, USA.

Richard Randolph is Instructor of Christian Ethics, St Paul School of Theology, Kansas City, MO, USA.

J. Bill Ratliff is Professor of Pastoral Theology, Earlham School of Religion, Richmond, IN, USA.

Hillary Ratna is a registered practitioner with the British Association for Counselling and Psychotherapy in London, England.

Lawrence Ratna is Consultant Psychiatrist and Lead Clinician, Barnet General Hospital, London, England, and Associate Professor of Psychiatry, St George's University, Grenada.

Martin Reardon OBE is former General Secretary, Churches Together in England, retired.

Alastair Redfern is Bishop of Grantham in the Anglican diocese of Lincoln, England.

Bruce Reed is President and Senior Consultant, the Grubb Institute of Behavioural Studies, London, England.

Robert Reiss is Archdeacon of Surrey, diocese of Guildford, England.

Harold Remus is Professor of Religious Studies, Wilfred Laurier University, Waterloo, ON, Canada.

Foy Richey is a clergyman, of the Disciples of Christ, and President, Rocky Mountain Pastoral Care and Training Associates, Inc., CO, USA.

Martha Robbins is the Joan Marshall Associate Professor of Pastoral Care at Pittsburgh Theological Seminary, Pittsburgh, PA, USA.

Nicholas Sagovsky is William Leech Professorial Research Fellow in Applied Christian Theology, Newcastle University, Newcastle upon Tyne, England.

Cicely Saunders is the founder of the hospice movement, and a writer.

Betty Saunders is a Health Service administrator, retired.

Carroll Saussy is Emerita Professor of Pastoral Theology and Care at Wesley Theological Seminary, Washington, DC, USA.

Charles J. Scalise is Associate Professor of Church History at Fuller Theological Seminary, Seattle, WA, USA.

Peter Sedgwick serves on the Church of England's Archbishops' Council Board for Social Responsibility (Home Affairs) in London, England.

Joanne Silove is a counsellor in the Adolescent Department of the Tavistock and Portman NHS Trust, London, England.

Valerie Sinason is a child psychotherapist and adult psychoanalyst, and Director of the Clinic for Dissociative Studies, London, England.

Peter Speck is Health Care Chaplaincy Team Leader at Southampton University Hospitals NHS Trust, Southampton, England.

Bernard Spilka is Professor Emeritus, Department of Psychology, University of Denver, Denver, CO, USA.

Frank J. Stalfa is Associate Professor of Pastoral Theology at Lancaster Theological Seminary, and staff therapist at the Samaritan Counseling Center, Lancaster, PA, USA.

Jeanne Stevenson-Moessner is Associate Professor of Pastoral Theology and Christian Formation, University of Dubuque Theological Seminary, Dubuque, IA, USA.

Philip Stokoe is a community care expert, London, England.

Elizabeth Stuart is Professor of Christian Theology, King Alfred's College, Winchester, England. She is editor of the academic journal *Theology and Sexuality*.

Sharon Swain is a religious education expert, and a priest in the Church of England.

David K. Switzer is Emeritus Professor of Pastoral Care and Counseling, Perkins School of Theology, Southern Methodist University, Dallas, TX, USA.

Ekman P. C. Tam is Spiritual Director of Tao Fong Shan Christian Centre in Hong Kong.

Charles W. Taylor is Professor of Divinity, Church Divinity School of the Pacific, Berkeley, CA, USA.

Douglas Thorpe is Director of Pastoral Counseling, Center for Pastoral Counselling, McClean, VA, USA.

Lorraine Tollemache is Senior Clinical Lecturer in Social Work at the Child and Family Department, Tavistock Clinic, London, England.

Shirley Trickett is a counsellor in Newcastle upon Tyne, England.

P. Robin Turner CBE is Chaplain of Dulwich College, London, England, and Archdeacon Emeritus of the Royal Air Force, former Captain-in-Chief, Royal Air Force.

Ralph Underwood is Professor, Austin Presbyterian Theological Seminary, Austin, TX, USA.

Peter J. van de Kasteele is an Anglican clergyman, former General Director of the Clinical Theology Association, retired.

Deborah Van Deusen Hunsinger is Associate Professor of Pastoral Theology, Princeton University, Princeton, NJ, USA.

Peter VanKatwyk is Director of Pastoral Counselling Programmes, Waterloo Lutheran Seminary, Waterloo, ON, Canada.

Peter H. Van Ness PhD is a Postdoctoral Fellow in Epidemiology in the Department of Epidemiology and Public Health, Yale University School of Medicine, New Haven, CT, USA.

Chad Varah is the founder of the Samaritans, and Prebendary of St Paul's Cathedral, London, England.

Patrick Vaughn is a counsellor in the USA, formerly in Waxhaw, NC.

Margot Waddell is a consultant child and adolescent psychotherapist, Adolescent Department, the Tavistock Clinic, London, England.

John Wall is Assistant Professor of Religion, Rutgers University, Camden, NJ, USA.

Sue Walrond-Skinner is former Advisor in Pastoral Care and Counselling, diocese of Southwark, London, England.

Tony Walter is Director of the MA programme in Death and Society, University of Reading, Reading, England.

J. P. Watson is Professor of Psychiatry, Guy's Hospital, University of London, London, England.

Lovett H. Weems is President, and Professor of Church Leadership at St Paul School of Theology, Kansas City, MO, USA.

Gordon F. West is Director, Department of Pastoral Care, Eisenhower Medical Center, Rancho Mirage, CA, USA.

Wendy Weston is a therapist in London, England.

Merold Westphal is Distinguished Professor of Philosophy, Fordham University, Bronx, NY, USA.

J. Bradley Wigger is Associate Professor of Christian Education, Louisville Presbyterian Theological Seminary, Louisville, KY, USA.

Rowan Williams is Archbishop of Wales, Newport, South Wales, and an author.

Lala Winkley is a liturgist in London, England.

Isca Wittenberg is a consultant analytic psychotherapist, Tavistock Clinic, London, England.

Christine Roy Yoder is Assistant Professor of Old Testament at Columbia Theological Seminary, Decatur, GA, USA, and an ordained minister in the US Presbyterian Church.

Frances Young is Pro-Vice Chancellor of the University of Birmingham, Edgbaston, Birmingham, England.

Administration
Joanna Moriarty, SPCK
Linda Hurcombe, SPCK

Introduction

There are varieties of dictionary. Some offer long and original articles, often making a new contribution to the field. Others provide concise definitions but little explanation other than a word's derivation and use. This volume occupies a middle ground. It is designed for students who are beginning pastoral studies and need help with unfamiliar technical terms, and for other readers who may have forgotten the meaning of a word or who wish to check their understanding. The articles are all written to the same structure: concise definition followed by explanation and discussion.

In 1987 SPCK published *A Dictionary of Pastoral Care*, edited by Alastair Campbell. It soon became a standard reference work and remains such. When, however, there was thought of reprinting it with some revised content, it soon became clear that a rewriting of the existing articles would not be a sufficient response to the enormous developments that have taken place in pastoral studies since its publication. Many of the articles are still valuable; indeed some have been slightly rewritten and incorporated in this dictionary. Others have inevitably dated. But even more significantly, the discipline of pastoral studies itself has moved on. It has become more technical and involves an ever-widening range of approaches. Today's students are expected to be familiar with psychology and sociology, but, in the case of pastors, without forsaking their basic theology. They need a different type of help.

The New Dictionary of Pastoral Studies is a working dictionary. When enquirers look something up they should rapidly be able to find a succinct definition and some comment. There are more than 700 entries by 200 contributors, and extensive cross-referencing. The interested reader can pursue a serendipitous trail of learning.

It can be said of any such volume that the criteria for inclusion and exclusion are unclear. Some may discover that important topics, often their favourites, are missing. Others may consider articles misleading. All are likely to question the relative weight given to certain words or disciplines. The co-ordinating theme is 'pastoral'. This dictionary is for those who may, for instance, have some theology yet need some sociological ideas – and naturally vice versa. There are, therefore, many articles on topics from the social and behavioural sciences. This does not represent the denigration of theology. But today in pastoral education and practice the interchange between theology and the social sciences is central. What is more, these are the terms which the pastor and new student are mostly likely either not to know or to be unsure about, and on which they may need instant help.

All entries have in common that they are addressed from the pastoral perspective. To experts in their fields some definitions will, therefore, appear oversimplified. But the dictionary is not designed for experts: it is for readers to whom the languages of this range of disciplines will be largely unfamiliar. Where matters are disputed (and that is not infrequent in this field), the aim has been to avoid taking sides and to outline the issues.

The editors have attempted, so far as possible, to harmonize style. Each author has allowed his or her piece to be edited. Cross-references are extensive and crucial. They are indicated by under-lining. They are designed to take a reader through a range of articles that together will provide substantial background information. References to literature can date rapidly. So the contributors have been invited to mention books that they reckon may be available for some time to come, if not in bookshops then at least in libraries. Journal articles are for most people inaccessible and have been excluded. Books are only listed in their English-language editions and as they are cited by the authors of the articles: there may be different publishers in the

UK or the USA. Citations within articles are to author and date of publication (and occasionally a page reference). The bibliography gives the full details of the publication.

The Dictionary is being published in the UK and the USA. In each country there are different church traditions, separate legal systems and varying assumptions about pastoral studies. So far as is possible, attention has been paid to different backgrounds, but care should be taken always to check technical matters.

The editors, both those from the UK and those from the USA, have been generous with their time and knowledge. Joanna Moriarty, Editorial Director of SPCK, has been involved with the project from its inception. Jon Pott, Editor-in-Chief of William B. Eerdmans Publishing Company in the USA, co-ordinated necessary transatlantic input. But above all I must record thanks to Linda Hurcombe. She joined the team at a difficult moment and took on the relentless and onerous work of assembling texts, writing to contributors, keeping the material flowing and on occasion undertaking the hard task of telling someone that an article for some reason would not suit. That the volume has appeared at all is due to her perseverance.

The great lexicographer Samuel Johnson remarked that 'to make dictionaries is dull work'. It has not been dull editing this volume but stimulating and educational. It has been a pleasure as well as a learning experience to work with my fellow editors and all involved. My fellow editors and I are grateful to everyone who has contributed to this collaborative enterprise.

Wesley Carr
2001

A

ABORTION
1. The termination (which may be spontaneous) of a pregnancy after implantation of the blastocyte in the lining of the womb but before the foetus has attained viability.
2. More popularly, the deliberate termination of a pregnancy, whether for therapeutic or other reason.

Historically, attitudes to abortion have varied. Despite the Hippocratic Oath of 'I will not aid a woman to procure an abortion', the Graeco-Roman world did not prohibit abortion. The semitic peoples were much more strict in their attitudes, though the Bible itself has little to say on the subject. Exod. 21.22–24 is often interpreted as having relevance. While it does not deal directly with abortion, but rather with miscarriage as a result of violence, this passage has been interpreted to imply a difference in status between mother and child. The weight of Christian tradition from the Apostolic Fathers through the Reformation right up to major sections of the contemporary Church (notably Roman Catholic and conservative evangelical) has been resolutely opposed to abortion.

Legally, the situation has changed dramatically within the past 30 years. The 1967 Act of the UK Parliament decreed that doctors would not be prosecuted for performing an abortion in four situations where there was risk (1) to the life of the mother; (2) to the health of the mother (physical or mental); (3) to existing children (the so-called social clause); and (4) of physical or mental handicap in the child. In 1990, the legal limit was reduced from 28 to 24 weeks but all time limits were removed in situations of either risk to the mother or of foetal handicap (in fact a tiny minority of the grounds for abortion). In the USA the case of Roe v. Wade (1973) radically widened the provision for termination of pregnancy, and worldwide there has been a huge increase in the number of abortions performed.

Ethically, opinions are polarized even within the Christian community. A major statement of the 'pro-life' position is found in the papal encyclical *Humanae Vitae* (1968), which states that 'the direct interruption of the generative process already begun ... is to be directly excluded as a means of regulating birth'. Pro-life arguments include (1) the conceptus is as much a human being as the mother; (2) the wilful destruction of the foetus is murder, i.e. abortion is a criminal act as well as an immoral act; (3) abortion encourages promiscuity; (4) a compassionate society should care for the handicapped. The 'pro-choice' lobby is of much more recent origin and some of its arguments are considered by some to be related to the rise of the feminist movement. These include (1) a woman has a right to control her own body; (2) the foetus is not to be equated with the woman in terms of status as a human being; (3) only wanted children should be born; (4) legalized abortion is needed to avoid social discrimination; and (5) the right to perform abortions protects the autonomy of the medical profession. Much of the ethical discussion relates to the status of the foetus. Daniel Callahan (1970) has identified three positions.

1. The *Genetic School* identifies personhood with the establishment of the genetic code, i.e. the foetus is fully a person from the moment of conception, a position congruent with outright opposition to abortion.

2. At the opposite extreme, the *Social Consequences School* sees personhood as relational and beginning at birth, a position clearly acceptable to proponents of abortion on demand.

3. The *Developmental School* is less easy to define precisely because some process of development (undefined) is considered to be necessary before one can speak of personhood. Yet perhaps there is some virtue in the essential ambiguity of this position because it reflects the actual context in which human decisions have to be made (Callahan, 1970).

Pastorally, situations involving abortion require to be handled with great sensitivity and here, above all, pastors and counsellors need to be aware of their own prejudices. It has been argued (largely by secular counsellors) that in a pastoral context the kind of value-free approach in which a woman can make her own decision is not possible. This is not necessarily so. A compassionate pastoral relationship may be as helpful as secular counselling. It is important in a pastoral context to become aware of the expectations which the pregnant woman brings with her. There are obvious distinctions between pre- and post-abortion pastoral care. In the former, it will be important (1) to help the woman take a considered decision based upon her own needs, feelings and realities, and not simply the wishes of the father (though he will have his needs) or of her family; (2) to make sure that she is aware of and has considered all the options open to her; (3) to promise to provide ongoing support no matter what decision she takes – and to deliver on what has been promised. Post-abortion pastoral care may be characterized by the kind of grieving manifested by any woman who has lost a baby. While these may be complicated by a sense of guilt, the pastor should not assume that this is the case. One must listen to what the woman is saying, not to what one thinks she ought to be saying (Tong, 1997).

Special attention must be given to the needs of women who lose a baby in pregnancy when they would dearly have wished for a different outcome, whether through spontaneous abortion or because of foetal abnormality or risk to the health of the mother. For the mother (and the rest of the family) the loss is a real one and the reality of that loss may need to be affirmed, sometimes, according to the needs and wishes of the mother, mentioning the child by name in prayer. Again feelings of guilt, no matter how irrational, may need to be taken seriously. [David Lyall]

ABREACTION
The emotional discharge of feeling associated with a particular event.
As a technical term, abreaction is mostly employed by psychoanalysts. It is a normal reaction to an event which has been emotionally disturbing as the strong affect or emotions associated with it are discharged. This may be an immediate response to some powerful experience or, particularly in therapy, it could be the release of feelings that have long been pent up.

ABSOLUTION
The pronouncement of God's forgiveness of sins, customarily following confession.
For many Christians (chiefly in the Catholic tradition) it is the Church's privilege, through its authorized ministers, to pronounce God's absolution. For others (mostly Protestant) absolution is the saving power of the gospel that the minister proclaims. The divergence largely depends on the prevailing understanding of sin. Absolution is not forgiveness, which is the prerogative of God. General absolution is pronounced in the liturgy. Personal and specific absolution may follow individual confession and assigning a penance.

ABUSE
The normal professional term for physical, sexual or emotional violence towards another.
The first use of this term, which lasted from the medieval period right up until the twentieth century, carried a meaning of 'misuse' or deliberate misrepresentation of someone. The term was a symbolic one and did not initially mean something done directly to another human being's mind, body or soul.

From the 1970s in the USA and the 1980s in the UK and Europe, the term 'abuse' became the formal professional term to cover physical maltreatment of a child (physical abuse), physical maltreatment of an adult partner (domestic abuse, wife abuse), sexual violence towards a child (sexual abuse), emotional damage done to a child through negligence or direct mental cruelty (emotional abuse), and violation of a child or adult's religious beliefs (spiritual abuse). Abuse towards elderly persons by their middle-aged children or carers is now known as elder abuse. From the 1980s onwards the term has also been used in relation to addictions that are damaging to the person – e.g. drug abuse, alcohol abuse.

Physical abuse. This is sometimes also defined as non-accidental injury, physical maltreatment or child-battering. Hobbs and Wynne (1990) found that one in six physically abused children had also been sexually abused. Until the work of Kempe in America in the 1970s, children with signs of injury were thought to be 'clumsy'. At a point where it was legal within the West for teachers to use physical instruments of punishment it is not surprising that it was culturally harder to notice further signs of physical violence from adults. Once physical abuse could be seen, diagnosed, and culturally accepted as a fact, it was possible for other forms of abuse to be noticed.

Emotional abuse on the active side. This can take the form of sadistic withholding of nurturing adult behaviour, teasing, victimizing and threatening, and, on the apparently passive side, lack of provision for the child's physical and mental health, which is also called neglect. Failure to thrive is often a sign of emotional abuse.

Emotional deprivation, lack of affection and failure to protect are seen as acts of 'omission' rather than 'commission', but psychoanalytically they can be seen as very 'active'.

Sexual abuse. In psychoanalytic history, although Freud wrote much about the child who suffered 'seduction', this and 'incest' were the key terms. Only after the work of paediatricians and psychologists in the 1970s and 1980s did psychoanalysts followed suit with the same linguistic terms.

The most commonly accepted definition of sexual abuse is 'the involvement of dependent developmentally immature children and young people in sexual activities which they cannot fully comprehend, to which they cannot give informed consent, and which violate the social taboos of the culture and are against the law'.

Over a century ago Freud (1896) correctly delineated three categories of sexual abuse that remain the most common today. The first group is the smallest and involves isolated instances of sexual assault by a stranger. The second category involves adult care-takers, from relatives to nursery-maids and governesses. The final group is sibling abuse. Freud made the important point that where an older sibling uses force to sexually abuse a younger there has usually been abuse by an adult against that perpetrating child.

Psychoanalysts and child psychotherapists working with abused children who have been abused by attachment figures become particularly concerned at the emotional consequences. Where the person to whom the child needs to turn for help is also the person hurting the child there is often a psychic fragmentation in which the child desperately tries to preserve the concept of a good parent. Often this is achieved by turning all rage for the abusing parent on to the self. 'If I was a good enough child my stepfather would never have hurt me, so it is all my fault.' Such mental reframing also allows an illusion of being in control that takes away from the terrible feeling of helplessness.

Other internal consequences can include powerful feelings around betrayal and lack of trust in authority figures or a corrosive linking of love with being hurt.

Substance abuse (drugs, glue, drink). One factor in the linguistic success of the term 'abuse' is that these different categories of abuse all have important links. Homes where there is domestic abuse, drug or alcohol abuse also include a worrying cross-over with regard to emotional abuse. The vulnerability and lack of self-esteem it causes in children can also make them more vulnerable to sexual abuse.

The effects on children *in utero* of maternal substance abuse are also significant, with learning disability, growth failure, facial anomalies and physical abnormalities also caused by foetal alcohol syndrome.

All of these addictions can also be seen as means to try and deal with human mental pain which do not succeed.

In work with perpetrators of sexual abuse, most have been found to have experienced a variety of abusive environments themselves in their childhood. *[Valerie Sinason]*

ABUSE, CHILD
The maltreatment of children, resulting in harm.

The maltreatment of children has been widespread in the past and continues today. Historically, unwanted or deformed babies were either killed or left to die. Children, kept in appalling conditions, were used as slave labour and still are in some countries. They were pushed up chimneys and down mines, working long hours for little or no pay, often ending up crippled. In some countries children are mutilated in the name of custom or religion or so they can be more effective as beggars. Child abuse covers a wide spectrum from the extreme of murder, poisoning, burning, starvation, beating and rape to the more subtle deprivation of withholding love. Abuse is commonly divided into four categories: physical, sexual, emotional and neglect.

Neglected children are deprived of the basic needs to live, usually through a lack of supervision, knowledge or judgement on the part of the parent or carer, but sometimes from deliberate neglect. The chronically neglected child may have poor weight; failure to thrive; poor hygiene; constant tiredness and hunger; a poor state of clothing; compulsive eating habits, or be constantly scavenging for food; and untreated medical problems. They also experience serious difficulties with social relationships and may display destructive tendencies. Their physical and mental development can be severely affected.

Emotionally abused children are the victims of rejection, hostility and verbal abuse to the extent that their natural development is impaired. They may have physical, mental and emotional development lags; have speech disorders; exhibit neurotic behaviour such as rocking, hair-twisting, self-mutilation; and show extreme passivity or aggression. Children who have been emotionally abused will often constantly self-deprecate. They feel themselves to be unlovable because they have been emotionally starved and lack all self-esteem. This may also prevent them from learning to interact with others, so they become even more isolated.

A child being physically abused may have unexplainable injuries such as burns (e.g. from a cigarette or from scalding water); black eyes, cuts, bites, marks from belts or whips; bruising on soft tissue, such as pinched ear lobes; or less obviously, internal and/or head injuries. They may wear inappropriate clothes, and make improbable excuses to explain injuries. They may also shrink from physical contact and have self-destructive behaviours.

Sexually abused children may have medical problems such as genital infections or even venereal diseases; be overly affectionate or knowledgeable in a sexual way, which is inappropriate for their age; compulsively masturbate; and draw sexually explicit pictures. They may also have extreme reactions such as depression, suicide attempts, drug overdoses, anorexia or self-mutilation. They may try hard to cover up the abuse, sometimes by being the 'perfect' child so no one will question what is happening.

Abused children are often victims of more than one form of abuse. [Michele Elliott]

ABUSE, CHILD SEXUAL
The exploitation of a child by an adult or significantly older person for their own sexual pleasure, gratification or profit.
Sexual abuse may range from indecent exposure and taking pornographic photographs to intercourse, buggery (sodomy) and rape. Incest and involving children in sex rings or prostitution are also often involved. It can consist of a single incident or events that occur over a long period. Sexual abuse happens in every class, race and cultural background. Statistics indicate that most abused children are abused by someone they know and that abuse by total strangers is rare. Girls and boys are both at risk of becoming victims.

Children often are frightened that they will not be believed if they tell, or that something terrible will happen. This is particularly true if the abuser is someone they know and may like. The abuser may threaten children, tell them the abuse is their fault or say that he will end up in prison or that the family will be destroyed if the abuse is revealed.

It is important that those who care for them be aware of some of the possible signs of abuse. These signs are a guide and could also be indicative of other problems. However, it is a good idea to check if a child is showing several of the following signs: behaving in a sexual way inappropriate to age; attempting to abuse another child; compulsive masturbation; soreness, infections or bleeding in the throat or genital area; repeating obscene words or phrases (said by the abuser); hinting about secrets they cannot tell; fearful of or refusing to stay with a certain adult for no apparent reason; developing eating disorders; dramatic change in personality or behaviour; depression, withdrawal, aggression; attempting suicide.

The majority of reported sexual abusers of children are male, though there are increased reports of female abusers. Some experts say it occurs because many abusers were themselves sexually, physically or emotionally abused as children and are taking out their own need to control others, and their anger and frustration, on children. What is not clear is why so many children who have been abused do not become abusers. Many abusers say they 'love' children and that what they are doing is all right because 'children are sexual'. They are denying the damage they do and imposing their needs and desires on the child. Children normally develop their sexuality at their own pace; sexual abuse interferes with that natural process.

The adult survivors of child sexual abuse report that their lives have been dramatically affected by the abuse. Some have problems with drug and alcohol abuse; relationships; self-mutilation; anorexia or bulimia and suicidal feelings. Because of the suffering of children and the possible lifelong consequences of child sexual abuse, it is essential to report any suspected abuse to the authorities. In the UK this is required by educational and church authorities. [Michele Elliott]

ABUSE, SUBSTANCE
See: ADDICTION

ACCEPTANCE
One of three core conditions commonly considered necessary to facilitate change in counselling or psychotherapy.
Fundamental to the client-centred (or person-centred) therapy of Carl Rogers

(1951), and supported by the research of Truax and Karkhuff (1967), is the proposition that three conditions are necessary (and sufficient) for the psychotherapeutic relationship to effect change in the client. These are (1) congruence, (2) empathy and (3) acceptance (sometimes also referred to as unconditional positive regard or non-possessive warmth). Acceptance is a consistent valuing or 'prizing' of the client and his or her experience throughout the therapeutic relationship, even when they cannot find worth in themselves and even when the counsellor finds it difficult to like the client and/or cannot approve of the client's behaviour. If the client no longer feels the need to be defensive, fear diminishes, openness and trust increase. Acceptance by the counsellor leads in turn to self-acceptance on the part of the client, and the client becomes that more free to move towards more constructive ways of living and relating.

There has been debate within pastoral counselling as to whether acceptance is no more than a therapeutic technique or whether the accepting relationship points to something of deeper significance. Thus Paul Tillich (1949), a major theological influence upon pastoral counselling, points in a famous sermon ('You Are Accepted') to acceptance being at the very heart of the way in which God relates to humanity. Thomas Oden (1966) has argued that 'just as the precondition of self-understanding is being understood, the precondition of *self-acceptance* is being accepted. There is a significant analogy between the radical divine acceptance which is the subject of the Christian kerygma and the radical therapeutic acceptance which enables the client to accept himself.' Oden, however, in line with Tillich, moves beyond analogy. 'The psychotherapeutic injunction that the basis for acceptance for others is self-acceptance has its deeper ontological root in the Christian proclamation that the basis for the freedom to love the neighbor is the forgiveness of God.'

While there is general agreement among most therapeutic approaches that a degree of acceptance of the client as a person is a necessary precondition for therapeutic progress, there is less unanimity as to whether it is a sufficient condition. Other approaches, such as the Gestalt techniques of Fritz Perls and the rational emotive therapy of Albert Ellis, can be much more confrontational in their approach to clients. Within pastoral counsel-

ling Howard Clinebell (1981) has highlighted a weakness in the Rogerian approach – an unwillingness to confront behaviour which is damaging to the self and others. Such confrontation, however, can only be effective in the context of a relationship in which trust has been established. [*David Lyall*]

ACCOUNTABILITY
The process of being answerable for actions, the discharge of responsibility or role.
The specification of a clear accountability pathway is seen as fundamental to effective operational management. But the issue of who is accountable to whom or what often involves other salient 'stakeholders', e.g. investors in businesses, MPs' constituents, the recipients of professional services. It is also possible to be accountable to non-human agents, e.g. codes of conduct, or to an overarching entity such as the democratic principle.

These dimensions of accountability all feature in pastoral care, but often in the reverse order of prominence to the above.

Overarching accountability to God has been paramount, though it has often not gone by that name. Implicit exemplars include: (1) the responsibility given to humankind for the rest of creation (Gen. 1.28; 2.15); (2) the OT understanding of the king as accountable to God for the people; (3) the marriage service: e.g. 'The vows you are about to take are to be made in the name of God who is judge of all' (*The Alternative Service Book 1980*); (4) confession of sin; (5) such concepts as stewardship (talents), apostolate and priesthood (*The Alternative Service Book 1980*, Ordination).

There is also accountability relative to Scripture and tradition including the Ten Commandments, the Creeds, the Thirty-Nine Articles, and various interpretations of church order, e.g. celibacy, apostolic tradition, different emphases on word and sacrament. Delineation of 'primary' and 'secondary' accountabilities in this area can be a source of conflict.

At the human level there is accountability most obviously in the area of ministry (Jacobs, 1989), although it is inconsistent in its structure and operation. Bishops and priests share the cure of souls; yet priests in the Church of England have historically been self-employed (or the employer has been identified as God), and until recently consistently enjoyed 'the parson's freehold'. Free Church ministers and rabbis have been more obviously 'hired' by, and accountable to, their congregation.

The oldest process of accountability is probably spiritual direction. Systems for work consultancy, professional development and appraisal are more recent. Overall, development has tended to be slow, possibly because:

1. Accountability to God has been seen as in tension or conflict with accountability to human beings. The supreme place accorded to conscience epitomizes this.

2. Many secular systems of accountability and appraisal require assessment against measurable objectives. This is perceived to be difficult in the areas of pastoral care and ministry; what would an effective ministry actually look like – increased church attendance, faithful provision of the liturgy, accessibility to those in need or something else? It is difficult for people to know that they are doing a good job (Coate, 1989).

3. Systems of accountability are often viewed with distrust as inevitably judgemental; their potential to raise self-esteem and to relieve stress is not recognized.

4. The process of accountability can become confused. Bishops, for example, are cited as being 'fathers in God'; but how possible is it to combine their supportive and (potentially) disciplinary functions? [Mary Anne Coate]

ACTING OUT
The expression of an unconscious impulse from the past through action in the present as a way of relieving tension.
Acting out is a defence mechanism described in Freudian theory as a resistance to therapy, usually expressed through aggression or sexual impulse (Freedman, Kaplan and Sadock, 1972). Acting out is used more broadly to characterize any behaviour that masks repressed feelings or thoughts. Teenagers who knew little warmth in childhood may act out their hunger for affection through indiscriminate sexual activity. Adults may act out their anger through compulsive spending.

ACTION RESEARCH
Addressing specific practical issues that people are facing and at the same time extending the general understanding of them for wider learning and application.
In action research the researcher is a trained agent and the subjects of the research are participants in creating scientific knowledge. Programmes of action research were developed after the Second World War, when social scientists were wanting to apply the same urgency to social problems in peacetime as had been applied in the war effort. The phrase 'action research' was coined by Kurt Lewin, who said 'there is nothing more practical than a good theory'. It is also associated with the stance of the social scientists who founded the Tavistock Institute of Human Relations in London. This approach in the social sciences sits uncomfortably with the aspirations of scientific method, of which double-blind trials would be an example. However, once it is accepted that the presence of an observer affects the phenomena being observed, pretensions to fly-on-the-wall neutrality carry much less weight. Action research offers the opportunity to acknowledge and work explicitly with the values and perceptions of the researcher. Psychoanalytically informed researchers may also use transference and counter-transference phenomena in the consultant–client relationship as data.

The approach was applied to such issues as race relations, industrial democracy, regional economic development, community development, the implementation of public policy at a national level. The principles of action research invite examination of power relations and the use of language and communication, even within the research project itself (Miller, 1993).

It follows that those whose interest has been to pursue empowerment and participation as values in themselves are especially attracted to action-research methodologies. For example, community-operation research takes methodologies that were originally devised for planning and control in large and complex systems and applies them to small voluntary organizations and collectives. It also involves local people in participatory democracy projects in response to community care.

Action research may be thought to have a reforming objective – e.g. to achieve organizational change – or one that is transformational, e.g. to empower the oppressed. These have been called 'First World' and 'Third World' approaches. [Tim Dartington]

ADDICTION

The habitual use of any chemical substance, legal or illegal, which can harm the spiritual, emotional, mental, physical or social well-being of users and/or those around them.

No level of society or class of persons, including ministry, is exempt from the addiction process. Addictive substances routinely include drugs such as narcotics, amphetamines, barbiturates, anti-anxiety agents, and hallucinogens, usually obtained (and perhaps manufactured) illegally. Common addictive substances that society tolerates, even encourages, include caffeine, tobacco and alcohol. Not included among the addictions are various compulsive behaviours that do not necessarily involve chemical substances, or physical withdrawal symptoms, such as gambling or sexual activity.

Addiction involves an overwhelming craving for a substance, characterized by disregard of negative consequences associated with its use. Symptoms may include: dependence; tolerance; preoccupation; and reduction or modifications in social, occupational, familial or spiritual roles due to substance use. Cessation of use frequently causes symptoms of withdrawal, which vary with the particular substance being withdrawn, but usually include subjective symptoms of discomfort or increased anxiety. Most persons do not desire to become addicted, but experience addiction as an unintended consequence. Addicts lose the capacity to choose freely use or cessation, but are physically and emotionally compelled to use the substance for the desired effect or to delay withdrawal symptoms. They may demonstrate polydrug use, consuming whatever substances are available that produce the desired effect or delay withdrawal. Persons may become cross-addicted, i.e. addicted to more than one distinct substance, such as alcohol and an anti-anxiety agent (Valium, Librium, Dalmane, etc.).

Pathways to addiction are widely varied, yet often involve attempts to seek solace from physical and emotional pain such as loneliness, existential emptiness or alienation from self, others and God. Recovery from addiction frequently involves social support, self-introspection, interpersonal honesty, and the development of skills that enable coping with existential anxiety without the use of chemical substances.

Ministry may contribute to recovery in several ways. First, normal pastoral care can be given to persons involved in various stages of the recovery process. Frequently, before undertaking recovery, addicted persons have been absent from the spiritual community. The numbing effect of the chemical substance has masked dependence on God (often referred to as a 'higher power'). Guilt associated with the chemical dependency (a consequence of self-deception and lying to associates and loved ones) has contributed to alienation. In addition, pastors can address various social, economic and psychological issues associated with addiction by participation in public meetings intended to discuss solutions. Following specialized study, clergy may make helpful information available through bulletin inserts and brief pastoral paragraphs addressing discrete aspects of the addiction process. They can also sponsor education programmes that inform without becoming morally condemnatory. Most pastors need never become expert regarding addiction and recovery processes, but all need to be knowledgeable about the basic symptoms of addiction and the potential relationship between spiritual growth and wholeness that can be a beneficial part of life while recovery is undertaken and thereafter.
[William M. Clements]

ADJUSTMENT DISORDERS

A group of mental disorders characterized by emotional and/or behavioural symptoms developed in reaction to identifiable sources of stress.

Adjustment disorders are of particular interest because they are caused by psychosocial stressors. Symptoms, which may include depression, anxiety, disturbance of conduct, or any combination of the three, develop soon after the onset of the cause of stress. Normal grief and other non-pathological reactions to stress do not constitute adjustment disorders. They usually signal a crisis. Pastoral intervention should include emotional support and assistance toward developing better strategies for dealing with the precipitating factors.

ADOLESCENCE

A normal, though often turbulent, developmental process, the central task of which is that of maturing into an adult state of mind with a separate sense of identity.

Initially the difficulties are those of adapting to the physiological and emotional changes of puberty: namely, the development of secondary sexual characteristics, the onset of menstruation and ejaculation, the change in endocrinological and hormonal levels, and the increase in sexual and aggressive drives. Such changes constitute biological sexuality. They may be accompanied by swiftly fluctuating states of mind as the young person struggles to discover and establish a new position in relation to the family and the outside world. Anxieties are often intense, especially around gender identity, masturbation and sexual experimentation.

A psychological regression takes place towards infancy, and feelings of love and hate which belonged to early relationships, particularly with parents, are re-aroused. The adolescent often undergoes a renewal of primitive states of mind, characterized by extreme feelings and the tendency to idealize and denigrate both the self and others (Anderson & Dartington, 1998). Anxiety about the self often takes precedence over concern for others. Disregard for parental values is characteristic, often involving excessive rejection in the attempt to establish an independent identity. This, in turn, may arouse feelings of emptiness and guilt, and fears of loss.

In addition to these pressures are the ordinary psychosocial tasks of adolescence: separating from parents, exam and career choices etc. Solutions to the problems are often sought in trying to evade them through various forms of denial, e.g. of the thinking self (drugs, substance and alcohol abuse); of the independent and therefore vulnerable self (group activities, conformity to ephemeral fashion); of the childlike and known self (anti-parent, anti-authority and delinquent activities). A more positive aspect of each of these enterprises is that they may involve a degree of self-exploration. Individuation and merely oppositional stances are often difficult to tell apart.

Delinquent activities are expressions of impulses to act externally when an internal conflict becomes too intense. Acting out tends to be especially marked in early adolescence when group allegiances are particularly strong. As the holding function of the family lessens, most adolescents become enmeshed in group-life with friends who now tend to be all-important. This can be supportive and helpful if benign, or more gang-like if hostile behaviour is the cohering factor.

During the middle and later years of adolescence the groupings usually become less pronounced and the experimenting less extreme. The young person begins to consolidate the early fragile sense of identity into an increasingly consistent way of being and behaving. There is often both the need and the readiness to embark on a couple relationship which is more lasting and committed than the early rather shifting and changing relationships. Personal strengths and weaknesses, talents and aptitudes will become more focused. Depending on the nature and degree of the early experimentations, a more definitive separation will be felt to be possible so that the adolescent can embark on adult life. [Margot Waddell]

ADOPTION

The means by which a child is transferred from the birth parent(s) to a new adoptive family and all legal links are severed with the first family.

The nature of adoption changes constantly and reflects the changing nature of society. Its form can vary from 'closed' adoption, in which an adoptive child's break with his or her birth family is total, to a more 'open' practice when links are retained in varying degrees. Adoption is a way of meeting the needs of the child and giving him or her the best developmental opportunities; it can also be a means of meeting the needs of childless couples.

Changes in practice come about for a variety of reasons. For example, in economically developed countries a drop in the number of babies available for adoption has meant that people have been more willing to consider older children ('older' meaning anything from a few months to teenage). It has also meant an increase in the number of babies adopted from overseas, often from Third World countries. This means the nature of adoption varies. Late-placed or institutionalized children often have troubled histories and can make considerable demands upon the adopters. This in turn can lead to the recruitment of a wider range of adopters, including single people or families who have successfully raised birth children. Ideally adopters should be self-selected, but also carefully informed and prepared. It is now recognized that post-adoption support is crucial.

The intrinsic differences between families that come about by adoption and those that come about by birth should also be recognized, even in the case of 'baby adoptions'.

Birth parents retain a psychological presence in the minds of adoptees and adoptive parents. It is natural for some adoptees to wish to trace birth parents, a process eased by the development of contact registers and the provision of counselling. Closed adoptions have been the norm. A more controversial development is that by which birth parents retain contact with the child throughout the adoption. Views vary as to the value of this for all involved. Retaining contact with siblings, where they cannot be placed together, is less controversial. Further controversies surround the policy of making only 'same race' placements, although the general importance of fostering a child's racial identity is less questioned. The practice of gathering information for a child in the form of a 'life story book', so that it may gradually make sense of its experience and consolidate a sense of identity, is considered sound practice by many social workers.

Adoption is of relevance to pastoral studies as members of the adoption 'triangle' (the birth parents, the adoptee, and the adoptive parents) frequently present themselves for help at some stage of family life. It is important that the complexities of their situations are recognized, as well as the length of time it can take to become a family, and the speed at which such a family can unravel. Though practice varies and numbers of adoptions rise and fall, it can be a satisfactory way by which many childless people and children needing parents can find each other. [*Lorraine Tollemache*]

ADULT EDUCATION
The learning which takes place during adulthood in so far as this is the result of an intention to be educated.
Adult education should be distinguished from the incidental learning of daily life. While institutions of further and higher education do offer education to adults, adult education usually refers to a wider range of formal and informal learning which may or may not be publicly funded. Expressions such as 'continuing education' and 'lifelong learning' are similar.

Historically, education has been directed mainly towards children. However, in the twentieth century there was increased interest in the education of adults. Rapid technological change requires continuous retraining, and the various psychologies of human development have revealed adulthood as passing through a series of transformations. It is no longer regarded as a stable period which follows adolescence. While the liberal tradition of adult education, stemming from such nineteenth-century figures as F. D. Maurice, still continues, much contemporary adult education is more utilitarian. This practical character is emphasized by describing the process as training: assertiveness training, anti-racist training, etc. Modern industries often emphasize personal skills such as learning to co-operate with others, listening more effectively, time management and dealing with stress.

Within the churches, all forms of preparation for public ministry may be thought of as adult education, although they are more frequently described as theological education. Adult education often refers to lay people. Nevertheless, it is increasingly recognized that ministerial education must include more than traditional theological knowledge, and must include personal and group developments such as are dealt with in humanistic and transformational approaches to adult education. The urgent need to help Christian adults to reinterpret their faith under the conditions of modernity has led to a rapid expansion of adult education. Most Anglican and Catholic dioceses have adult training or education officers and nearly all denominations offer such expertise from their headquarters. The local church as a whole may be thought of as a learning community. Adult learning may be focused into midweek groups or weekend conferences, and many adults benefit from participation in the several distance-taught programmes now available.

Although there is interest in the methods of adult education (Craig, 1994), the field is of concern to many because it involves assumptions about the nature and future of Christian faith. The questions of what it would be to become a mature Christian adult today and how to become a truly educated church involve the adult educator in central theological issues (Hull, 1991).

Adult education is related to pastoral care in that many apparently pastoral problems may be regarded as learning issues. On the other hand, adult education is offered to adults who are experiencing no more than normal levels of confusion and stress, while psychotherapy and the more specific situations of counselling may be directed towards those who are passing through unusual experiences of stress and loss. [*John M. Hull*]

ADULTERY
Sexual relations between a married person and someone who is not that person's husband or wife.

In many countries adultery is a crime. Under some systems, such as Islamic law, it may carry the death penalty. Generally speaking, however, it only constitutes a ground for divorce. This was the case in English law until 1971, when a 'matrimonial offence' had to be proved before divorce was normally possible. Since then it has continued to provide the evidence for 'irretrievable breakdown', the current basis of divorce, and especially for women petitioning against their husbands. Adultery ceased to feature in divorce law when the 1996 Family Law Act came into operation in 1998. Adultery disappeared from divorce law in the United States under the 'no fault' divorce revolution of the 1970s and 1980s (unless one counts the new 'covenant law' system recently enacted in a small number of states which allows for fault-only divorce as an option if the couple so choose).

Adultery differs from infidelity in its social significance. Traditional patriarchal systems of marriage were based on the assumption that a woman surrendered her separate identity and belongings to her husband on marrying him. In effect, she became his property. The economic contract was paramount, and had significance beyond the confines of the married couple. It was especially important that the progeny of a marriage were legitimate: they established the line of descent through which family property would pass. If women had sexual relations outside marriage the property contract was endangered by the risk of pregnancy. Adultery was theft. However, this clarity of perception with regard to female sexuality did not carry over in the same degree to male sexual behaviour.

This double standard for sexual behaviour was encoded in English law until the middle of the last century. Observers from a psychological perspective have commented that it had the additional function of protecting the male psyche against anxiety about female sexuality. Adultery continued to constitute a ground for divorce in the UK until 1971, and its significance lay in the fact that the offence was regarded not only as being committed against the spouse but also against society. This attitude increasingly came into disrepute as evidence was staged to enable marriages to be terminated and, more recently, to provide a fast track to divorce.

Infidelity is a more private matter than adultery. It implies a betrayal of trust within the marriage but carries less social significance. As marriage has become an increasingly private arrangement (the relationship being valued above the role and status ascribed by the institution), adultery is a less commonly used word than once it was. It is becoming redundant as a legal concept, and changes in sexual behaviour may also have contributed to the wane in its usage. There is now social tolerance of premarital and non-married sex, and many opportunities for sexual liaisons outside marriage. The indications are that many marriages have one or more unfaithful partners, and that women are behaving more like men in this respect (Lawson, 1990; Reibstein and Richards, 1992). However, marital fidelity is still prized very highly, despite discrepancies in practice. Current psychological thinking represents fidelity as a moral achievement rather than compliance with social code (Colman, 1993). *[Christopher Clulow]*

ADVANCE DIRECTIVE
An umbrella term that refers to all written instructions about end-of-life health-care choices.

The purpose of an advance directive (AD) is to make as unambiguous as possible treatment preferences. This is necessary for four reasons: (1) to assure medical decisions which are consonant with one's values, shorten the period of possible suffering and improve outcomes for patients; (2) to avoid conflict or legal suits where ambiguous patient preferences exist which the family, hospital or state try to interpret, as in the Nancy Cruzan case (Steinback and Norcross, 1994); (3) to lessen a family's anxiety about doing the right thing and a physician's burden of having to decide on cessation of treatment without sufficient information; (4) to reduce high financial expenditures for unwanted treatment.

AD may include detailed instructions concerning types of treatment or non-treatment specified in particular circumstances. Popularly it includes 'Do Not Resuscitate Orders' (DNR), or refusal of artificial nutrition and hydration, dialysis, chemotherapy or other life-prolonging procedures in the event of terminal illness, permanent unconsciousness or mental incompetence. However, it does not necessarily refer to a request for cessation of treatment, but can also indicate a desire for aggressive and prolonged treatment. To be legally binding, ADs generally need to be written and signed by competent persons and witnessed by two persons who would have nothing to gain from the person's death.

In lieu of detailed instructions, a proxy decision-maker (Durable Power of Attorney (DPA)) may be appointed when one is unable to speak for oneself. ADs are now legal in all fifty United States. In England and Wales an advance refusal of medical treatment is legally binding, subject to certain safeguards. Living wills have the support of the British Medical Association and the form used has been designed to provide a document on which most doctors are willing to act. Similar schemes are emerging in most developed countries where modern medical methods, e.g. life-support machines, are in use. Under the Patient Self Determination Act, health-care institutions in the United States are required to ask whether a DPA or living will is present upon patient entry. If not, the hospital may provide information and assist with filling one out. The patient, however, can refuse all of this if he or she wishes. Only 28% of Americans have signed any type of advance directive. Religious organizations, health-care institutions, legal societies and state agencies have sample forms. Some religiously worded forms can be ambiguous. However, most religious groups encourage AD and affirm the individual's right not to prolong dying, but oppose active euthanasia.

Some people confuse these health-care requests with euthanasia, and either direct or indirect, physician-assisted suicide or refusal of treatment. An AD, of course, is used when the patient is not competent to make a decision. The central issue at stake concerns choices about how to live while dying, not choosing death itself. A person weighs the benefits and burdens of a particular treatment and the quality of life which is acceptable. Care should be conveyed when cure is no longer possible.

Public support for AD is tied to the historical shift from dying at home surrounded by loved ones to dying in a depersonalized hospital setting. The phenomenal advances in technological medicine many times prolongs dying and suffering rather than improving the last days of living. AD becomes a form of self-advocacy. It is a continuation of patients' rights (Ramsey, 1978).

Certain standards for making advance directives morally valid have been suggested. These include the provision of sufficient information about the procedure, competency on the part of the decision-maker and involvement, where possible, of interested parties so that extrapolating to diverse circumstances can be discussed ahead of time. Patient preference, stability and consistency may be hard to measure but are important aspects of clear advance directives (Verhey and Lammers, 1993). [Abigail Rian Evans]

AFFECT
The feelings or emotions associated with events in a person's life.
For Freud every event in life has an associated affect, which may be held unconsciously. When recall of the memory of that event occurs, as for example (though not only) in therapy, the affect that was originally associated with it may revive. In therapy this revival is an essential part of effective treatment. Today the term is more loosely used to describe any <u>emotion</u> attached to ideas.

AFFIRMATIVE ACTION
See: POSITIVE DISCRIMINATION

AGAPE
1. Love, particularly as exemplified by Christ's self-giving. 2. A love-feast.
In the New Testament and the Christian tradition, agape has been vested with particular significance. Following septuagintal practice, the Gospels use it to express love to God and neighbour, love to enemy, the love of God for the world and Christ's self-giving and example. Paul uses it in the celebrated hymn of love (1 Cor. 13), as well as of the love of husband and wife, the love of Christ for the Church, the goal and ethos of community life and the love which sums up the commandments (Furnish, 1972). It thus brings together the two motifs of God's covenant love and Christ's ministry (Outka, 1972). The love-feast, which was to promote agape among the participants and thus unite them with Christ, was a religious meal of uncertain origin. It was subsequently assimilated to the <u>Eucharist</u> and then increasingly detached from the sacrament. It was a real meal, not a symbolic one, held in private homes or churches. In modern times the love-feast has been revived by such groups as the Moravians, Mennonites and some other Christian bodies. [Ian McDonald]

AGEING

A process that takes place throughout the human lifespan, involving a person's physical and psychological systems in a complex series of changes.

The concept of ageing is frequently associated with old age but, in practice, it is not limited to it (Bromley, 1988). From childhood and adolescence onwards a process commences in which ageing and development are balanced. Towards the end of the lifespan the effects of ageing eventually predominate. A person in their fifth and sixth decades of life is increasingly likely also to have experienced the death of one or both parents and of contemporaries. Some indicate their growing awareness that there is now no generation between them and their death. Such an insight may lead to a rethinking and examination of issues connected with basic spirituality, as expressed in a need to hold one's past, present and future in some sort of cohesion and continuity. The boundaries between middle age and old age are not necessarily clear. The period surrounding the end of a person's active working life and the first decade of retirement in developed countries has been called the 'Third Age'. The later phase, which may include increased infirmity and dependency is similarly known as the 'Fourth Age' (Oram, 1997). Retirement from active working life and a career may be preceded for some by working at full capacity well into the seventh decade of their life. For others, retirement will begin earlier, with many entering retirement bringing latent, emergent and potential skills. Increasingly, however, due to a decline in traditional sources of employment, others may not have worked in a paid capacity for many years prior to reaching retirement age. Some people, again, will simply continue to use their skills of home-making and childrearing in the role of grandparent or carer in their family. Even with the extensive changes which have taken place in family structure, related to increased family mobility and different work patterns and expectations for women, research suggests that the role of the family is crucial. The family typically provides a setting where support can both be given and received for an ageing person. Retirement may also involve the loss of role and a social grouping which went with active paid work.

Physical ageing may involve all the organs and functions of the body, with the possibility of illnesses brought about by degenerative disease or other causes connected with ageing. Many of these illnesses may exist together as a person ages. Physical ageing involves the wasting of muscle and decrease in bone density, especially in women. (Some of the effects of ageing may be offset by the use of drugs and medication, for example hormone replacement therapy (HRT) in post-menopausal women which may reduce the risk of diseases such as osteoporosis. Significantly the sexual and emotional needs of people who are ageing have received little attention until recently. Sexual functioning in men and women may be enhanced by the use of HRT and drugs such as Viagra. The efficacy of these treatments is still being debated.) Others may experience reduced respiratory capacity and some decline in the acuteness of the senses of taste, smell, sight and hearing. An increased time may be taken to recognize and process what is seen and heard. Ageing may also bring an increased tendency for fatigue and a reduced ability to concentrate on and remember written and spoken material.

Ageing is, however, affected by many variables, biological, psychological, social and cultural. (Blythe, 1981). The issues raised are very significant, especially in societies where a large proportion of members survive well over twenty years beyond what is sometimes seen (quite arbitrarily) as the end of their productive lives. In the United Kingdom approximately 16% of the population is currently aged over 65. The proportion of people over 85 will have doubled between 1981 and 2001 to constitute approximately 3% of the population. Autonomy and the freedom to make decisions about how an ageing person orders their life and relationships, and eventually their own death, needs to be stressed, however difficult and painful this may be in practice. In that a very high proportion of all health-care and social support resources, possibly as much as 45%, are deployed during the last five years of life, the implications for planning and organizing services for an ageing population are considerable. Over one-half of all admissions for orthopaedic, medical and psychiatric problems are connected with ageing. While there is a higher incidence of depression as ageing progresses, a distinction needs to be made between depression, typically associated with an absence of feeling, and appropriate and very natural sadness at some of the life events experienced.

Women tend to have a longer life span than men, leading to a population of elderly people in which women outnumber men by three to one beyond the age of 75.

The concept of 'ageism', discrimination on the grounds of age in employment, housing and medical resources, has come into prominence recently. Assumptions made about the needs of elderly people have to avoid generalization and presupposition. The purpose of care for an ageing population is to improve the quality of life and not longevity as an end in itself. Ageing is not simply about decline and loss. Life experience and learned, mature life skills are frequently a resource to others, especially in a wider family or social group. The losses which characterize ageing, of livelihood, health, spouse or partner are in terms of human growth and development a natural preparation for the final loss of facing one's own death with as much dignity and autonomy as possible. [*Ian Ainsworth-Smith*]

AGGRESSION
1. Malign: deliberate violence towards others.
2. Benign: energetic pursuit of a goal without intentional harm to others.

By derivation (Latin: *ad* & *gradi*) 'going towards or against', the term 'aggression' is ambiguous. Fromm (1977) has characterized it as malignant or benign.

Benign aggression has obvious personal and social utility, and it presents problems only when it is unmoderated by awareness of the needs and goals of others. But malign aggression, often demonstrated in acts of gratuitous and cold-blooded violence unique to the human species (Storr, 1970), is puzzling in its origins, of no obvious social function and hard to modify or contain. It is found in notorious historical figures, such as Hitler and Stalin, but equally in 'ordinary people' in domestic and urban settings. In war conditions, gratuitous violence erupts in massacres of non-combatants and in deliberate acts of genocide, such as 'ethnic cleansing'.

Theorists differ about the origins of excess human aggression. The two main types of explanation are: (1) biological, e.g. the 'death instinct' theory of Freud and more sophisticated neurological and biochemical theories based on laboratory experiments, which trace excess violence to a genetically determined chemical imbalance; (2) social/ environmental, e.g. cultural conditioning and role modelling; harsh and inconsistent parenting; social deprivation and anomie – the breakdown of normal social constraints in depersonalized urban contexts. Recent debate has focused on the influence of violence in the media.

None of these explanations has proved adequate to explain all instances of destructive aggression, and it appears likely that the causes are complex and related to both heredity and environment. Thus practical solutions will include improving social conditions, teaching parenting skills, providing better support for families, and encouraging non-destructive outlets for aggression (e.g. sport). A better understanding of how to acknowledge and express anger may also reduce destructively aggressive acts such as 'road rage' and domestic violence. Changes to the 'culture of violence', for example through stricter gun laws, may also be effective, but whether this should include a reduction in violent imagery in films, TV and computer games is unclear. It is possible that fantasy violence provides a safe outlet rather than dangerous role models.

Clearly the main pastoral task is to oppose all forms of malignant aggression and to encourage conditions in family and community life that will reduce or prevent it. There are, however, many unfortunate historical and contemporary associations between religion and violence, and it is therefore imperative that churches confront the abuses within their own congregations and families and repudiate totally the use of religion as a justification for war and terrorism. [*Alastair V. Campbell*]

AIDS/HIV
A condition of impaired immunity which is diagnosed by a number of criteria, including infection with the Human Immunodeficiency Virus (HIV). Acquired Immune Deficiency Syndrome (AIDS) is a specific condition which has strict criteria involving at least (1) HIV infection; (2) low counts of the CD4 lymphocytes; (3) the presence of certain opportunist infections such as pneumocystis, CMV etc., or certain malignancies such as Kaposi's sarcoma. These change from time to time.

HIV is the virus itself. It is possible for a patient to be HIV positive and not have AIDS (or at least meet the criteria for

AIDS). Normally in a viral infection antibodies are produced which can neutralize the virus. With HIV antibodies are produced but they are ineffective and do not destroy the virus. When these antibodies are present a person is 'HIV positive'. Pastoral care is needed for those considering a test – although hospitals always advise a talk with a health adviser or counsellor before testing is carried out. The HIV antibody test reveals the status of a person as it was three months previously. Some might want to know their status so that drug therapy can begin; others may not feel they can live with a positive result.

AIDS is usually diagnosed when the immune system is so damaged by the virus that the person becomes susceptible to a range of specific infections and to certain types of cancer. The commonest symptoms are severe diarrhoea, profound fatigue, weight loss, night sweats and swollen lymph glands. The diseases commonly found are tuberculosis, HIV-related dementia, Pneumocystitis Carinii Pneumonia (a lung infection) and Kaposi's sarcoma (a cancer of the skin and lymph node). The course of the illness is variable, unpredictable and dependent on many factors, which include the psychological state of the person, their previous health record, access to an adequate diet and warm, dry housing, and use of antiviral medications.

The virus cannot be acquired through ordinary social contact (such as sharing plates or cutlery). Infection occurs by the transfer of body fluids – blood, breast milk, seminal and vaginal fluids – from an infected person into another's bloodstream. Hence unprotected penetrative sexual intercourse or sharing needles or syringes are high-risk activities. When the disease surfaced in the early 1980s, people receiving blood transfusions were at risk through contaminated blood supplies, but these are now screened in most countries.

More than 22 million people now (as of 1999) have the virus, the vast majority in sub-Saharan Africa, Latin America and Asia, and the infection rate in some countries is accelerating to epidemic proportions. Five million are affected in India and over 10% of the population in Uganda. In the United Kingdom 8,000 have died and over 25,000 have been diagnosed. In the USA 430,000 have died, and 733,000 have been diagnosed. In Canada 11,700 have died and 16,900 have been diagnosed. AIDS/HIV has been branded a gay plague but this is misleading: worldwide it is estimated that 60 to 70% of HIV transmission is by heterosexual intercourse. This does not preclude the possibility that transmission can be the result of homosexual or drug related activity.

There is at present no cure. A variety of medical treatments are available, so that AIDS/HIV is not now an automatic sentence to an early death. The drug AZT is used in certain situations but more success is achieved by combination therapy, which includes pairing AZT and 3TC, blocking the HIV enzyme called reverse transcriptase. Combination therapy that includes the new protease inhibitors can have dramatic results. They do not eliminate HIV but they can reduce the amount of the virus in the body to below detectable levels. Much support is needed because the side effects are mostly unknown. This cocktail of drugs is costly and causes financial problems not just in the Third World but in Western countries where medical care is now being prioritized.

Those tested positive now live longer, but they live lives of uncertainty and anxiety. Help is needed for them to live, not die, with HIV/AIDS. Some viruses, such as CMV, Hepatitis B and the herpes viruses, may help HIV to invade cells that were previously unaffected, causing them to deteriorate more quickly. Reinfection with other strains of HIV might also be a possibility after unsafe sex. It is now known that there are different strains of HIV and some are more virulent than others. Because this is a mutating virus, new forms are developing constantly, and some have already developed a resistance to drugs such as AZT.

In the USA and the UK the disease struck just as a gay lifestyle was beginning to receive some recognition. Suddenly gay men were plunged into a health crisis as profound as any in their history: gay sex was once again thought to be dirty, diseased and lethal. However, homosexuals soon achieved a measure of admiration for the way they raised funds, founded hospices, buddy groups etc., surrounding the illness with compassion and love.

AIDS/HIV is different from other diseases because most of the taboos in modern society are associated with it – death, disfigurement, drugs, disablement, mental illness, sexual minorities and sexually transmitted diseases. Add to this self-oppression and the guilt often generated by a religious upbringing, and the load to be carried is almost intolerable. It is difficult to tell parents, people at work and friends, so that the situation is often cloaked in secrecy. Much help is needed to help people understand what an HIV diagnosis really means. If parents or friends are not told they can feel extremely hurt when they find out the truth after a death has occurred.

There is no solution to AIDS/HIV, only a response. In the early 1980s, panic and paranoia prevailed and shaped political, scientific and religious responses. Now we only occasionally hear that the disease is God's judgement. Most people realize that the God and Father of our Lord Jesus Christ does not punish by sending disasters and disease to God's creation. People with AIDS/HIV have been victimized and abused at work and home. Often they find it difficult to obtain life or health insurance, so protecting the rights and dignity of people with the virus is vital to successful prevention and care. At present the condition can best be tackled by modifying behaviour that leads to its incidence, which means continuing the AIDS/HIV education programme. Awareness and responsibility are still the most effective weapons against this scourge. To that any pastor can contribute. [*Malcolm Johnson*]

ALCOHOLISM
A physical, progressive, addictive illness that is frequently fatal unless the compulsive, chronic cycle of addiction to alcohol is interrupted by abstinence from all substances containing alcohol.
In most developed societies alcoholism is a leading cause of premature death and disability, ranking with heart disease and cancer as scourges that decimate society. Unlike heart disease and cancer, however, alcoholism frequently thwarts the afflicted individual's quest for spiritual wholeness. Destructive behaviours associated with alcoholism are well known. Alcoholism frequently accompanies spousal and child abuse. Alcoholics are at greater risk than non-alcoholics of automobile accidents and domestic mishaps. They commit suicide in greater numbers, have higher divorce rates and are more likely to be imprisoned. Men have a higher rate of alcoholism than women, though women's alcoholism is more likely to remain hidden for longer periods.

Certain warning signs are characteristic: tolerance; withdrawal symptoms; preoccupation with drinking; and changes in social, occupational, recreational or spiritual activities due to alcohol. Non-alcoholic spouses, parents, workplace supervisors or law-enforcement agents typically recognize these warning signs before the alcoholic does. Alcoholics themselves are usually the 'last to know' the secret of their illness since denial is a hallmark. Because of the mechanism of denial, alcoholics may recognize symptoms in others yet remain oblivious to the same symptoms within themselves. The occurrence of even one blackout associated with excessive drinking is an ominous sign. Blackouts are episodes in which alcoholics may appear to function normally but retain no memory of what happened during the period of the blackout, which may be an hour, a day or longer. Alcoholics may experience considerable remorse for behaviour during drinking. Unfortunately, renewed drinking often follows remorse, in part to dull the guilt feelings and in part to deal with early experiences of withdrawal that may include increasing anxiety and nervousness.

Alcoholics often sincerely desire to stop drinking, and do stop for various periods, only to return sooner or later. Others attempt to control drinking by limiting (unsuccessfully over a period of months or years) the number of drinks ingested during a day or week. Others shift from one form of alcohol to another, such as from whisky to vodka. Thus, during the illness the alcoholic gradually becomes preoccupied with matters relating to alcohol. As the illness unfolds, alcohol plays a greater and greater role in the individual's life and social network.

Ministers are themselves not immune from the illness of alcoholism. Neither they nor physicians have demonstrated astuteness at recognizing alcoholism until its later stages. Physicians may confuse symptoms of alcoholism with other valid health problems, such as hepatitis, high blood pressure or depression. Pastors may encounter the alcoholic without recognition in pastoral care of the hospitalized, in marital or family care and counselling, or following the alcoholic's gradual withdrawal from the faith community. Some pastoral experts have theorized that in the life of the alcoholic, alcohol has at least anaesthetized normal existential anxiety and at most become a substitute for the spiritual quest. [*William M. Clements*]

ALIENATION
Estrangement from God, self or others.
In the New Testament, alienation is concerned with humanity's relation with God. Augustine believed alienation corrupts the whole being of humanity and is particularly evident in concupiscence, or sexual passion. According to Aquinas the alienated person retains the potential for good as well as evil, but in a state of privation, a sickness of nature, which requires healing by divine grace.

Modern writers locate alienation more in the mind and in society than in the body or the soul. Freud identifies alienation with a psychic split between the conscious and unconscious mind. Kierkegaard and Sartre see alienation as an inevitable feature of human consciousness of finitude in an infinite universe, and of powerlessness in the face of death. For Marx alienation is a social condition; workers are alienated because they have no control over the product of their labour.

ALTRUISM
A regard for others as a guiding principle for one's actions.
Altruism is highly valued in most religious and secular ethical systems. In addition, the subordination of individual need, in the short or long term, to a perceived greater good has an important value in preserving the cohesion of a family, group or society. The degree of choice and autonomy exercised in choosing an altruistic course of action is significant. There is always the possibility that real or perceived expectations of others may affect a decision which may seem purely altruistic. The principle of altruism has important benefits in practice. For example, patients with advanced incurable disease may choose freely to participate in medical research which will not affect the outcome of their illness but which may help others in the future. In addition they may derive a sense of meaning and purpose from their decision.

ALZHEIMER'S DISEASE
See: DEMENTIA

AMBIVALENCE
1. The psychological term describing the feeling of internal conflict when a person is torn between two contrary emotions.

2. One of the three 'insecure' attachment systems, i.e. ambivalent attachment.
The word 'ambivalence' was first used by the Swiss psychiatrist Eugene Bleuler to describe a state of emotional oscillation. Ambivalence is therefore that feeling of emotional turmoil experienced when a person is torn between two very different sets of feelings for another person or situation. Sometimes the feelings are as extreme as love and hate and threaten to distort the real relationship which exists. A person who lives with such ambivalence will feel alternately secure and insecure in quick succession.

Ambivalence is also used by the British psychiatrist and attachment theorist, John Bowlby, to characterize one of the three 'insecure' systems of emotional attachment. An 'ambivalent' way of relating may develop in early childhood, depending upon the quality of care shown to the child. A child who has a parent who oscillates in their own feelings towards the child, or who is alternately caring and harsh to the child, may experience ambivalence in attachment. Uneven emotional behaviour towards a child may result in the child feeling both insecure and ambivalent about the parent and unable to internalize a secure environment. The child's internal boundaries will not be firm and flexible. The internal conflict then experienced by the child may produce frustration, and feelings of desire for closeness quickly followed by anger. These feelings may then be followed by guilt.

If the child is lucky enough to become 'secure' through attachment to another care-giver it may be possible to grow up with a capacity to contain the contradictory feelings internally rather than display them in 'ambivalent' and contradictory behaviour. If the emotional conditions for the child are poor then the child will very likely suffer from anxiety and guilt, and may feel unsure about the important relationships in life.

In love relationships the ambivalently attached person may feel a need to please the loved one to the point of extremity. This very likely stems from a feeling of being unlovable and therefore needing to give to the relationship much more than the other.

When mourning the loss of an important figure the ambivalently attached person may mourn with ambivalent holding to the relationship with the person who has died.
[Heather Formaini]

AMNESIA
Inability to remember.

Amnesia may be partial (the loss of either long- or short-term memory) or total. Sometimes it is retroactive, as when someone cannot recall what was happening just before or at the time of a shock. Amnesia is today also associated with Alzheimer's disease. There is also a form of amnesia which is used unconsciously to defend against painful recollection. When an otherwise normal person in counselling or confession claims to forget, it is worth holding on to the possibility that they are denying a distressing memory.

ANALYTIC PSYCHOLOGY
The Jungian term for psychoanalysis.

In 1913 Jung left Freud's psychoanalytic movement to establish his own form of analysis. He called this 'analytic psychology'. He moved away from the emphasis on sexual instincts or drives as the core of a person's being. His analytic psychology took into account not only the world of both the personal and collective unconscious, but also aspirations and hopes.

ANDROGYNY
A condition of balance between male and female characteristics.

Androgyny occurs in the plant world where some plants, such as plantains, have male and female flower spikes. In the animal world the word can describe an animal or person of one sex but where male and female characteristics are held in balance.

Christ has been described as androgynous in the belief that since he could only redeem what he had assumed, he must have taken on female nature as well as male nature (Irenaeus, second century CE). Such views depend on sexual dualism and are today rejected by most theologians.

ANGER
An emotion provoked by frustration or threat.

The physiology of anger is virtually indistinguishable from fear. The body is put in a state of arousal in preparation for flight or fight through an adrenaline surge which contracts muscles, heightens blood pressure and halts digestion. The experiencing of this arousal as anger depends on the individual's perception of the situation in which the arousal occurred, and for humans loss of self-esteem can constitute a powerful threat.

Traditionally Christian teaching has viewed anger as dangerous and sinful, in light of Matt. 5.22 (equating anger with murder) and of various references in the epistles (Col. 3.8; Eph. 4.26; Jas. 1.19) to its detrimental effects on character. Yet Jesus is described as angry with the Pharisees and with his disciples (Mark 10.13–16), and the anger of God features in both Testaments in over four hundred references. This paradox has led to attempts to distinguish between righteous and unrighteous anger, with the implication that virtually all human examples will be unrighteous. But both pastorally and theologically anger is better viewed as morally neutral, an inevitable concomitant of the vulnerability and mutual dependency of human life. Anger – whether human or divine – is one of the costs of love, and apathy or indifference when relationships go wrong is a clear sign that love is dying or dead. Both the anger of God and anger at God, strong features of the Old Testament depiction of the covenantal relationship, portray a living if stormy faith (cf. Jesus' cry of dereliction, quoting Ps. 22).

Thus the main moral and pastoral concern must be not whether people feel anger, but what they do with it. In the Church there is a tendency to 'chronic niceness' (Augsburger, 1979), which merely conceals resentment. Increasingly evidence is emerging of emotional, physical and sexual abuse in church homes, including the homes of clergy, hidden below the veneer of niceness. Moreover, when anger is denied, the physiological responses do not disappear, but often re-emerge as depression or psychosomatic illness.

A more positive and creative approach entails four steps (Campbell, 1986): acknowledge the emotion; identify the true source of frustration or threat (often anger is displaced); try to understand why the threat to oneself is so great; seek to remedy the breakdown in relationship through direct and honest communication with the instigator (cf. the exhortation of Eph. 4.25 that as members of one body we should 'speak the truth in love'). Clearly this is a statement of an ideal. Communication may be impossible or ineffective, and some situations appear irremediable and therefore must be avoided or endured as best we may. But the potential for a healing anger often exists in both personal and political settings. Anger can lead to a reconciling love or to destructive aggression. Often, though not always, people have a choice. [Alastair V. Campbell]

ANIMA/ANIMUS
In Jung and Jungian psychology, the soul; the mostly unconscious, contrasexual, inner personality.
This portion of the psyche complements the conscious persona or outer personality, and contains sexual qualities which the persona lacks. In males, it is called the 'anima' and exhibits feminine characteristics. In females, it is called the 'animus', and is characteristically masculine. The anima/us functions primarily through projection, in relationships with persons of the opposite sex. Understanding its content and effects has the potential of fostering psychic and relational wholeness and balance. It may be an appropriate issue to be included in pastoral discussions of gender and sexuality.

ANIMAL RIGHTS
The concept that all sentient creatures possess intrinsic value, dignity and moral rights, and are deserving of human moral solicitude.
Although ethical concern for animals is not new, animal-rights thinking has acquired momentum in the context of socially progressive thinking during the last 30 years. The use of the word 'rights' as distinct from 'welfare' or 'protection' signifies a change from appeals based on fellow-feeling or kinship to one based on justice. Animal-rights thinking rejects the idea that sentient creatures can be properly classed as machines, tools, commodities or resources here for us. Each individual sentient being should be treated as an end in itself and not simply as a means to human ends. Modern animal advocates seek to end all forms of exploitation involved in the commercial use of animals, notably in entertainment, farming and science.

Animal-rights theory is sometimes held to be in conflict with Christian theology. The notion of 'rights' is itself held to be problematic since creation is grace and creatures can have no 'rights' against their creator (Webb, 1998). This view is consistent if all rights – human and animal – are disallowed. Others hold that the notion of rights both for humans and animals can be defended on the basis that God as creator has rights to have

creation treated with respect (Linzey, 1987). Rights language is one way of expressing God's own interest in what is created. What animal advocates find difficult is the current widespread acceptance among Christians of human rights but the rejection of any analogous right for animals.

Perhaps the debate is best approached by asking, what does it mean to accept that animals have rights? In practice, the issue turns on whether there are strong – as opposed to weak – moral limits to what humans may do to animals. Some Christians have difficulty with the idea that what is owed non-human creatures is in any way analogous to moral obligations to humans, since they are made in the image of God and are especially valuable. But the notion that there are limits to how humans may treat animals is firmly embedded within the Judaeo-Christian tradition (Murray, 1992). For example, animals were clearly included within the Noachian covenant and various injunctions in Hebrew law concern the treatment of animals. Many saints befriended animals and extolled kindness and respect for other creatures. The foundation of the RSPCA in 1824, and the subsequent anti-cruelty movement, was largely Christian in inspiration. Arguably the concept of animal rights develops notions of moral limits already present within the Jewish and Christian traditions. Animal-rights thinking poses three challenges to traditional pastoral theology.

1. A *conceptual challenge*. Pastoral theology is exclusively humanocentric whereas animal theologians are concerned to see notions of care and ministry extended to all suffering creatures. These theologians argue that it is precisely because humans are made in God's image and given 'dominion' over animals that we should care for them as God's own creatures. According to animal theology, humans are not to be the master species but the 'servant species'. Human uniqueness is defined as that ability to become 'co-participants and co-workers with God in the redemption of the world' (Linzey, 1994).

2. A *moral challenge*. Animal advocates are increasingly vocal about the need for a reappraisal of traditional theological attitudes. Church practice worldwide still supports or acquiesces in cruelty. For example, in Norway clergy bless whaling ships, in Spain church authorities condone bull-fighting, in Canada bishops support fur-trapping, and in England clergy still go hunting with hounds.

Specifically commended is the need for a cruelty-free lifestyle and a vegetarian diet. Churches need to understand this new moral sensitivity and recognize the implicit theological insights which undergird it.

3. A *liturgical challenge*. The Church has not yet found a way of incorporating wider concerns for creation – and animals in particular – into its liturgy. Despite the example of the saints, the idea that Christians should pray for suffering animals is still regarded as eccentric. There are a few rites for animal blessing, healing or burial, though an increasing number of churches hold 'animal services' on St Francis' Day (4 October), which is also designated World Day for Animals. Pastorally sensitive worship is required which enables individuals to celebrate and give thanks for the lives of other creatures.
[*Andrew Linzey*]

ANOINTING
The ritual application of oil.
Anointing is an ancient custom to mark and effect transitions such as puberty, consecration of priests, setting aside a building for divine purposes and coronations. It is commended in the Epistle of James. In the Christian tradition three main oils are used: (1) oil of the catechumens for baptism and consecration of churches and the coronation of Catholic monarchs; (2) chrism for baptism, confirmation and ordination; and (3) oil of the sick for use in healing. They are blessed at the Chrism Mass on Maundy Thursday. In the Catholic or Orthodox tradition anointing is a sacrament. While other churches may not agree on this, anointing is nevertheless becoming more widely recognized as part of the healing ministry of all churches (Dudley and Rowell, 1993).

ANOMIE
Social or psychological conditions arising from the breakdown of social stability.
The French sociologist Emile Durkheim believed that the loss of social stability and shared values consequent on rapid social change in modern societies resulted in a condition of lawlessness, rootlessness or anomie. Anomie gives rise to a lack of social and psychological integration, a fact which he sought to prove by contrasting the high incidence of suicide in modern societies undergoing rapid social change with the low incidence of suicide in the stable, face-to-face communities of aboriginal societies.

ANTHROPOLOGY OF RELIGION
The study of human nature, both physical and social, with specific reference to the contribution and function of religion.
Anthropology emerged in the 1870s under the influence of evolutionary ideas. Throughout the twentieth century increasing numbers of detailed studies of human societies generated vital information on the nature and variety of human life. Various theories interpret descriptions and may contribute to pastoral studies in the areas of ritual, the significance of the human body, and merit-generation associated with salvation (Davies, 1990).

The Scottish Old Testament theologian William Robertson Smith helped foster early anthropology. He explained how sacrificial meals bonded kinsfolk together and conferred a sense of hope. His work influenced Sigmund Freud's psychology of religion and Emile Durkheim's sociology of religion, both of which affected theories of the mind and of community. Subsequent theories of ritual have been widely influential.

Arnold van Gennep identified as rites of passage a widespread pattern of ritual surrounding changes in social status. A rite of separation from the old status led to a period of apartness, in which new values were learned, before the final rite of incorporation placed the person into a new social status. Depending upon the total purpose of the rite, one of these phases would be stressed, funeral rites stressing separation, marriage stressing incorporation into a new family. These three phases were also called the pre-liminal, liminal, and post-liminal stages of change of status, after the Latin word for threshold (*limen*). Victor Turner explored the dynamics of liminal periods, arguing that those undergoing a status-change together experienced a shared sense of oneness or *communitas*. He contrasted this unity with the hierarchical structure of everyday life. He coined the word 'liminoid' to describe a similar shared humanity experienced in modern, urban societies during periods of festivity, carnival, holiday or pilgrimage. This accounts for the unity felt by people sharing educational or life-development training when everyday status is dropped as each sees the others as fellow brothers and sisters given to the task in hand.

Robert Hertz showed that funeral rites often involve two separate phases of activity. One deals with the decaying body and the other with the finally dry remains. Rites associated with the first phase symbolically remove the dead from their social bonds with the living. The dry remains are used to mark the new status of the dead among the ancestors or in a heavenly realm. This is especially important for cremation and should prompt good pastoral practice in performing rites for the cremated remains in addition to the preceding cremation service.

Maurice Bloch's theory of rebounding violence or rebounding conquest explored changes in the individual fostered by rites of passage. The ordinary facts of life move from birth through maturity to death. Society transforms this in rites which begin with a symbolic death and speak of a symbolic rebirth into a new life of religious power. This newly empowered life then sets out to conquer the old nature wherever it is to be found. This important development has many applications for pastoral life, especially in terms of religious conversion, evangelistic missions and movements of spiritual renewal.

The mystical career of spirit-influenced people has, in turn, been much analysed by anthropologists. Ioan Lewis showed how possessed people were often marginalized or relatively powerless individuals. This is not only important for charismatic contexts but for the pastoral aspects of social theology involving justice and oppression.

Within the French tradition Marcel Mauss brought to light the power of reciprocity in general, while Claude Lévi-Strauss specifically showed how the giving and receiving of women in marriage bonded groups together in kinship. Many sorts of gift-giving underlie social life and are of great importance for pastoral studies, because such reciprocity also provides a model for ideas of merit, grace and salvation. S. J. Tambiah coined the term 'ethical vitality' to describe the Buddhist belief that a life lived according to strict religious rules could generate merit which could be transferred to others and aid their salvation. This theory of merit-making is widely applicable to Christianity in the Catholic tradition's view of the treasury of merit of the Church. Since the Reformation, renewed emphasis focused on the merit of Christ, whose obedience to divine commandments generated enough merit to save all people. Faith acknowledges that human acts of gift-giving do not generate merit and cannot earn salvation. Instead, divine grace overturns the system of reciprocity. Pastoral problems emerge when people still hold to very human ideas of cause and effect, of gift and repayment, instead of grasping the divine system of grace. Some, incorrectly, even think that misfortune is the payment for some bad deed, or wonder why a good person suffers what they do not deserve. Christianity demands a different classification of the world.

Studies of particular societies show how each describes and classifies its own world. Many follow a dual classification, setting various pairs in opposition to each other, as with day and night, men and women, land and sea, Jew and Gentile, life in the flesh and life in the spirit. Others follow much more complex patterns of classification. Classifications underlie the rules and behaviour of social life and mark boundaries which help establish the identity of a group. Mary Douglas argued that creatures which straddled different categories symbolized a confusion of identity; they were deemed an abomination in the Old Testament and could not be eaten. The idea of ritual purity is often invoked to defend these identity-conferring boundaries (Geertz, 1993).

Practical studies of religion have shown the difference between the formal systems of doctrine developed by professional elites and the realm of actual practice of ordinary believers. This distinction is important for priests, who form elite groups ministering to those whose life-interpretations may differ widely from their own. In practical terms, studies of myths, especially in Claude Lévi-Strauss's structuralist interpretation, show the power of descriptive narratives to resolve deep problems of existence in a non-philosophical way. Here there is a close link with narrative theology and the life of Christian communities. Some anthropologists also think that the actual performance of ritual in itself exerts a positive effect on people (Girard, 1986). [*Douglas J. Davies*]

ANXIETY
An emotional state aroused by happenings, both from within and without, that seem to threaten physical or mental stability.
The Latin derivation of 'anxiety' means 'worried about the unknown'. This, however, describes a very small part of the

state of anxiety. The Greeks, who said the word means 'to compress or strangle', are more accurate. This is exactly what anxiety does to every part of the being – physical, emotional, mental and spiritual.

Humans and animals are born with an innate system that their bodies use when they are threatened, the 'flight/fight syndrome'. A surge of adrenaline (a chemical which works on the autonomic nervous system) is released, enabling the pursued to move quickly if they are, for example, in the path of a bus or if a mugger leaps out at them. But in the minefield of childhood children do not have the experience to know when it is inappropriate to be anxious. They are very sensitive and react to what they feel and see in their environment. Many experience horrific abuse. Chronic anxiety in childhood and later life can be well understood, if this is the experience. But there are also children of loving parents who suffer the same long-term effects because they grow up with overanxious people around them. Children cannot discriminate – they do not have the knowledge to say 'Mother is making rather a lot of fuss about that wasp/thunderstorm/stranger', but feel the fear to such an extent that they become chronically anxious adults, with phobias, obsessions, or a multitude of symptoms, including deep depression. Often the sufferer has no clear idea of what they are anxious about – a 'free-floating anxiety'.

1. *Physical symptoms*. These range from palpitations, 'butterflies in the stomach', to a severe, debilitating illness, where the person is no longer able to function and is unable to leave the safety of the home because of panic attacks and agoraphobia.

2. *Mental effects*. A great deal of energy is used when a person is anxious. Preoccupation with the pain of the condition leads to confusion, and memory loss. A person might have made a cheque out for the milkman for fifteen years and yet, when in this state, be incapable of remembering his name, or they may forget very familiar telephone numbers and names. Loss of identity and feelings of unreality are very common.

3. *Emotional effects*. Relationships suffer and there is often a feeling of distance from those we love. There is usually accompanying guilt but anxious people feel unable to express this because their own suffering so overwhelms them.

4. *Spiritual effect*. Anxiety is the precursor of depression. In this state people cannot 'hear God' and, when the pain becomes too much, they retreat to a depressive state in an attempt to block it. If help is not sought (and sometimes even if it is), this can progress to psychosis. This is one stage further in retreating from the world, often in a desperate struggle to get on a spiritual path, connect with God, Universal Love or however the divine is perceived. Depression is also an illness of the spirit. While there is do doubt that some people respond to medication and find themselves again, many do not. This will continue until the difference between a nervous breakdown and a striving for a spiritual breakthrough is clarified. *[Shirley Trickett]*

APATHEIA
A Greek word meaning mastery over the passions.
The passions may be regarded as neutral or as intrinsically evil. The former view is Aristotelian; the latter Stoic. Both find their place in the Christian spiritual tradition. The aim is not to suppress desire but to purify it. This ancient approach contributed to the sense of repression from which nineteenth-century dynamic psychology thought it should release people. But apatheia is more positive (Ware, 1983). It should not be confused with the modern sense of 'apathy'. The word is also sometimes used with reference to God's absence of passions.

APATHY
Impassivity; indifference; a lack of emotion of any kind.
A low energy level leads to lack of motivation, listlessness and disinterest. Apathy may be, and often is, a symptom of depression, but the two states are not synonymous. Apathy is caused by physical or psychological factors or a combination of both, such as the aftermath of physical illness; a response to bereavement; or the failure to achieve an expected hope or ambition. It may also be part of the natural rhythm of creativity, when a considerable output of energy is followed by a period of retraction and stasis.

APOLOGETIC THEOLOGY
The argument for faith in general and Christian faith in particular.
Christians are required to 'have a reason for the hope that is within them' (1 Pet. 3.15). Apologetics is the study of those reasons which are to be used as a defence of the gospel. The nature of apologetics changes

according to the cultural and intellectual context within which the Church is set. In pastoral studies the apologetic side of the gospel is especially important. In much pastoral work the minister will not occupy a shared frame of reference of belief with the client yet the encounter itself will have come about, however tangentially, because the pastor represents the Church and its beliefs. These he or she will both utilize as part of the interpretative frame and in so doing will elaborate an applied defence (*apologia*) for the gospel (Carr, 1989).

APPLIED PSYCHOLOGY
The practice and profession of the application of psychological knowledge and theories to human needs and problems.
Applied psychology describes both a constellation of concepts and procedures, and a number of professions. The theoretical underpinning of applied psychology both comes from experimental psychology and is derived from analysis of the applications themselves. The procedures encompass (1) psychometrics – the statistical analysis of psychological ability and attainment tests, personality and other measures; (2) the psychological analysis and assessment of everyday and industrial tasks, both for occupational and rehabilitative purposes; (3) psychological formulations of a range of conditions of social or health concern; (4) designing effective learning programmes in many different settings; (5) and both individual and group psychological interventions designed to improve functioning and social and health status. Most areas of applied psychology have developed since the Second World War, arising from research done then in the fields of manpower selection, specialist skill training, and psychological treatment (Butler and Hope, 1995). There are four main applied psychological professions.

1. *Child, or educational psychology*. This is concerned with the assessment, remedial education and treatment of children and young people. Child psychologists work in school and clinical settings with parents and teachers, as well as the identified child.

2. *Clinical psychology*. This is concerned with the assessment and treatment of primarily psychological disorders, and also of the psychological consequences of physical illnesses. Most clinical psychologists work in the mental health field, treating, for example, adults with anxiety disorders or with addic-

tive behaviours. Others work with children and adults with learning disabilities, children with emotional and behavioural difficulties, older adults, and with patients with neurological or physical disabilities.

3. *Occupational psychology*. Sometimes called industrial psychology, this is concerned with fitting people to jobs, and with adapting jobs and tasks so they can be done more effectively – a good example being the design of aircraft instrument and control arrays.

4. *Forensic, or criminological psychology*. This is concerned with the assessment and rehabilitation of offenders.

There are other smaller fields of applied psychology, such as traffic psychology, and growing areas are sport psychology and counselling psychology.

Some applied psychology is included in the training of many professional groups, such as nurses and social workers, and there is a high psychological content to many aspects of personnel work and management studies. Many topics in applied psychology have some potential pastoral implications, such as work on group functioning, understanding the reactions of victims of serious crime, and counselling and caring for those with serious mental health problems. Applied psychologists may be employed by a statutory or voluntary agency – in Britain most clinical psychologists work in the National Health Service – or may work in private practice. In either case, they should be registered or chartered by a registration body, which in the UK is the British Psychological Society and in the USA is the American Psychological Association, both of which establish professional standards, indemnity requirements, and complaints procedures. [*John Hall*]

APPLIED THEOLOGY
Study of the social, political and ethical aspects of theology, especially as they are invoked in the pastoral context.
This branch of theology holds its place alongside other academic disciplines. It does not imply that theological learning is somehow applied to human situations. It emphasizes the explicit use of theology to inform the work of the pastor and the way in which that work enlivens other theological disciplines. The contemporary interest in praxis has shown how important applied activity is to the discernment of truth. The term is quite new and relates closely to 'practical theology' (Ballard and Pritchard, 1996).

APPRAISAL
The reviewing of someone's work and performance of it.

The regular appraisal of ministry is now a well-established practice in many churches. Adapted largely from the secular world, it has proved a useful tool for enabling ministers to reflect on their work, thus contributing to the care of ministers themselves (Eastell, 1994). It also provides a system for pastors being accountable for their work. Theological justification is found in the notion of the mutual accountability and interdependence of the members of the whole Body of Christ (Jacobs, 1989).

Appraisal should be distinguished from work consultancy, which normally focuses on a specific piece of ongoing work, from evaluation, which normally concerns reviewing a piece of work or programme after it has ended, and from assessment, which is more conveniently used of assessing a person's suitability for a role or job.

The focus of appraisal may be primarily on the person or on their work, or on a combination of the two by looking at the person in their role. Preparatory work normally includes a written self-appraisal by the appraisee, and may include written reports to the reviewer from those who know his or her work. The heart of the review is an interview by the reviewer, and this will normally consider the achievements and failures of the period under review, agree on objectives for the next period of work, and outline any personal objectives including any in-service training that may be desired.

The frequency of reviews may vary from every three years to every year. Some schemes allow for major reviews every two or three years, but with a briefer review, normally in the form of a written report from the pastor, in the interim period.

Reviewers may be more senior than the person being reviewed, or appointed to carry out the task on behalf of someone more senior (both such reviews sometimes being called hierarchical reviews), or by a fellow (peer reviews). Which type is adopted in a church may reflect its ecclesiology: episcopal or quasi-episcopal churches are more likely to have hierarchical review systems, while congregational churches are more likely to invite representatives of the congregation to review their minister's work as peers.

While practice in the secular world has influenced ministerial review, there are factors that make it different. There is little formal line-management in the Church and the contact between the reviewer and the person being reviewed is usually less close than in secular organizations. In the Church it is difficult to find agreed criteria for 'performance'. These criteria are often fought over theologically. The highly personal nature of pastoral work also means it touches on not merely the minister's competence but also their character, and it is this which makes ministerial appraisal particularly sensitive. *[Robert Reiss]*

ARCHETYPES
Psychological instincts, i.e. structural components of the psyche.

Archetypes are universal and recurrent forms and ideas, without specific content. They are in themselves irrepresentable; they are experienced in psychic and somatic ways, usually with strong affect, as images or symbols of the stages and themes of human life and personality traits. The concept derives from that of Plato's ideas; in modern terms they are to some extent comparable to programmed patterns of behaviour.

ART THERAPY
The use of a variety of art forms to enable the exploration of intense or painful feelings within a supportive and therapeutic environment.

Art therapy involves using a wide variety of art materials: for example paint, collage and clay, and the collection and arrangement in patterns of many varied objects. Self-expression not artistic skill is the objective, enabling feelings and inner conflicts to become more visible and therefore manageable.

The term 'art therapy' was introduced by Adrian Hill in Britain during the 1940s and the method was developed out of his work with tuberculosis patients. Art therapy has both diagnostic and treatment potential. It is used either as an adjunct to other forms of counselling or psychotherapy, or as a therapy in its own right. Children's drawings made during play therapy or in a family therapy session fall into the first category. Many individual therapies encourage the patient to express him- or herself through art, and Jung, for example, viewed drawing and painting as important adjuncts to analytical psychology (Waller and Gilroy, 1992).

When used as a therapy in its own right, the meaning of the artistic production itself is the primary focus of attention, with perhaps opportunity being given to develop the picture or model over a sustained period of time. The art therapist may subsequently discuss the latent meaning and symbolism of the picture with the patient and encourage the use of a sequence of pictures painted over some months to examine emergent themes and changes in the patient's feelings, fantasies, self-concept and perceptions of the outside world. Art therapists who use a psychoanalytic approach stress the need to interpret the artistic production alongside the patient's associations to it, if unconscious theme and phenomena such as transference are to be fully understood. Other approaches put more emphasis on the healing processes of catharsis and sublimation.

Art therapy may be conducted on a one-to-one basis or in groups. When used with a group, the therapist will encourage group members to develop a picture together, helping them to handle as they arise the difficult feelings and behaviours that may occur over sharing in the production of the art work with others. The process of creation is as important as the product that is ultimately created (Case and Dalley, 1997).

Art therapy has been used successfully with people suffering from a range of mental health problems: people experiencing stress within organizations; people with learning difficulties; and children and young people who may be exhibiting behaviour problems or who have internalized painful feelings following bereavement or other severe stress. It can also be used more informally in a variety of group situations where the object is to enable members of the group to learn more about themselves, to get in touch with less conscious feelings and to explore other means of self-expression. [Sue Walrond-Skinner]

ASCETICAL THEOLOGY
The study of the methods and process by which individuals and communities, in response to the call and experience of God, seek to foster spiritual growth.

The word 'ascetic' derives from the Greek *askein*, meaning 'to train or exercise'. It appears only once in the Bible (Acts 24.16), though a similar word, *gumnazein*, appears more often. It means literally 'to train naked', as classical athletes used to do. Ascetical theology has always been concerned with stripping away all that is illusory or trivial, with going narrower in order to go deeper,

with the (often costly) willingness to let go of certain possibilities in life in order to embrace or aspire after what matters most. A modern Orthodox theologian has described this process as 'an awakening from the sleep-walking of daily life', its purpose being to dissolve 'all the hardness of the heart, so that it may become an antenna of infinite sensitivity, infinitely vulnerable to the beauty of the world and to the sufferings of human beings, and to God who is Love, who has conquered by the wood of the cross' (Clément, 1993).

Ascetical theology has been subjected to some significant critiques. The Protestant tradition has been suspicious of a process that can appear to give greater stress to what human beings do in fostering spiritual growth than to what God does. More generally, the pervasive Greek influence on early Christianity led to asceticism being associated with a fierce hostility to everything physical. And modern psychology has exposed the dangers of repressing what should rather be acknowledged. Yet ascetical theology carries a prophetic charge of its own. In arguing for the paradox that spiritual growth is attained precisely by a radical unpossessiveness, it questions the link between economic growth and human happiness. In insisting that personal fulfilment is found only through an unselfish attention to others, it subverts the narrowly individual scope of much psychotherapy and spiritual direction. Above all, it seeks to school people in a pattern of what seventeenth-century writers called 'practical divinity': truth that could be lived, that integrated every aspect of life, and whose goal was an inner freedom rooted in compassion for others and in the challenge of Christ's words: 'Those who want to save their life will lose it, and those who lose their life for my sake, and for the sake of the gospel, will save it' (Mark 8.35). [Gordon Mursell]

ASSERTIVENESS TRAINING
Preparing persons to express their thoughts and feelings directly and honestly in making their wants and needs known, as opposed to using either negative aggression or avoidance behaviours.

People with low self-regard tend to avoid expressing themselves to others, either because they do not think they have anything worth saying or because they do not think others are interested in what they think or feel. Years of such avoidance can result in their losing touch with their genuine feelings and desires. Others, operating out of comparable low self-esteem, may lash out in destructive or inappropriate ways. Women with low self-esteem tend to be passive and non-assertive; men struggling with self-esteem issues are more apt to act out with destructive aggression. In such cases women need to be more aggressive; men, less.

Assertiveness training involves step-by-step attempts at clear articulation of one's thoughts and feelings, making it less likely that a person will either avoid confrontation or act out hostile impulses. A formula frequently used in parent effectiveness training as well as assertiveness training is this: 'When you ... [a person's behaviour is stated in concrete detail] I feel ... [again, a specific feeling is named] because ... [the value behind one's felt response to the behaviour is specified].' For example: 'When you are consistently late for class I get angry because your entrance is distracting and a mark of disrespect for both me and your classmates.'

While many theorists perceive aggression as negative, viewing it as on one end of a continuum, with non-assertiveness on the other, and assertion at the ideal centre (Augsburger, 1979; Miller and Jackson, 1995), Kathleen Greider offers a far more nuanced and useful notion of aggression, recognizing it as a desire to live with satisfaction (Greider, 1997). Her reinterpretation of aggression highlights the bipolarity of this fundamental drive that results in emotional expression and behaviour ranging between violence and assertiveness. At its best, aggression is basically lively energy that adds passion and endurance to life. While love tells us who we care about or desire, Greider points out, aggression moves us toward that which we seek. The challenge is to find creative, constructive ways to use aggression. Greider's work is particularly important to women who struggle with asserting their opinions and needs, much less aggressively moving toward self-chosen goals. It also provides a model for groups of persons who want to use their anger and rage at injustice in ways that can move communities toward their goals and reduce injustice. In other words, aggression at its best is assertiveness.

With assertiveness training within a respectful relationship with a skilled person, both non-assertive and hostile people learn to speak their truth to others in such a way that it can be heard. *[Carroll Saussy]*

ASSESSMENT
The assessing of someone, usually with a view to deciding their future.

While closely related to appraisal, assessment has overtones of making judgements about people, and the most obvious context where assessment occurs is in selecting candidates for a particular post.

The key to greater objectivity lies in clarity about criteria. These necessarily vary. When a specific post requires a clearly defined task to be done, it is relatively easy to identify the qualities needed. It becomes more difficult when a job or role may be carried out in a variety of ways, depending on the skills and personality of the person concerned. However, it is still normally possible to identify key qualities needed, and then to list other desirable qualities of greater or less importance.

In assessing those qualities in a person the best guide to the future is normally the past. Careful investigation of the person's past record, aided where possible by reports from those who have known the candidate well, should help to determine where their strengths and weaknesses lie. It may be more difficult where a person is young, and where the emphasis is more on potential than achievements, but even in a person's school career there is evidence to be sifted.

The Church has always needed to make such decisions. In the past, methods of assessing candidates have varied from the random to the rigorous, and from essentially intuitive judgements to ones based on objective evidence. Mainly under the influence of developments in the secular world, the trend has been towards a more objective and rigorous approach to selection and assessment, with clear job descriptions and person specifications produced.

While students are training for ministry there is usually some continuing assessment of their suitability. The trend has been to include the candidate's perception of themselves in the process and to set that self-assessment in the context of reports that are open to the students. As more clergy enter the ministry through that process, their experience of open assessment and reporting may influence other areas of church life where assessments have to be made.

One area of growth in this field has been the use of psychological testing. Measurable qualities, such as verbal reasoning, are tested in some selection processes, while psychometric tests producing a personality profile are widely used to help candidates reflect on their own characters and so understand better their responses to people and situations.

Such developments feed the trend towards increased self-assessment. Organizations committed to providing pastoral care need to take that trend seriously. However, it can never ultimately remove the need for others in authority to make their own assessments of an individual's actual performance when making decisions about future appointments. [Robert Reiss]

ASSESSMENT FOR CARE
The process of assessing both a person's treatment needs and personality with a view to providing appropriate care.
When an individual is considered to be in need of help, or is seeking help for his or her difficulties, a careful assessment of their personality and treatment needs must be carried out by a suitably qualified and experienced diagnostician. This may be a psychiatrist, psychologist, psychoanalyst or other working in the mental health field. Two kinds of questions are asked: what kind of patient is in trouble, and what kind of trouble is he or she in? A medical/psychiatric diagnosis implies a set of symptoms, a category of illness, a prognosis and a treatment. A psychotherapeutic diagnosis also attempts to categorize a range of symptoms and to predict and prescribe treatment, but goes on to differ from a medical diagnosis in a number of ways (Holmes, 1991). Unlike a psychiatric diagnosis which is descriptive, it contains a view as to the origin of this particular patient's difficulties (for example, the way certain kinds of relationship in childhood affect adult development), and concentrates on the patient's relationships within his particular history. Some of this information and a subsequent formulation will be made on the diagnostician's sense of the nature and intensity of the actual interaction in the room between patient and diagnostician. Decisions about treatment (whether involving admission to hospital, medication, type of psychotherapy, frequency of sessions) will take the psychodynamic formulation into account as part of good psychiatric practice. Medical, social and psychological factors thus all have a part to play in arriving at a diagnosis and treatment plan suitable for a particular patient at a particular point in his life.

A psychotherapeutic assessment involves a careful history taking, with special attention paid to certain features of early life as well as the quality and quantity of relationships in the present. Prolonged or frequent separations from primary care-givers, changes of primary care-giver, deaths in the family (including stillbirths), and the patient's view of the nature of his or her parents' relationship are all important. The patient's internal world – the kind of figures that populate his or her thinking and imagination, both conscious and unconscious, and the ways in which they are perceived to relate to each other – is as critical for the diagnostician in arriving at a dynamic formulation as the patient's history and current circumstances. Only by taking both internal and external into account can a picture be gained of the patient as a three-dimensional figure in the landscape of his or her life. [Caroline Garland]

ASSOCIATIONAL CHURCH
See: CONGREGATION; PARISH

ASSOCIATIONISM
A psychological theory that association is the key principle of mental life.
A now largely outmoded approach, associationism examined pieces of the psychological elements in behaviour, such as experiencing or sensing, by connecting them with one another in various categories. By this means the higher thought processes are to be explained. Its empirical approach was especially congenial to English psychologists.

ASSURANCE
Confident knowledge of salvation.
The understanding of assurance always reflects the understanding of faith. The medieval Church, for example, invited faith in its creeds and teaching; the corresponding assurance was found in trust in the teaching authority of the Church. The Reformers, recovering a more dynamic understanding of faith, regarded assurance as an experiential aspect of that faith. The doctrine of assurance is a distinctive mark of John Wesley's teaching: it is every believer's privilege. Although a core theme of the gospel, if assurance becomes separated from the idea of faith as movement or pilgrimage, with its necessary uncertainties and doubts, it may become euphoric, leading to complacency and a grandiosity that is at odds with Christian self-understanding.

ATONEMENT
See: CROSS

ATTACHMENT
See: SEPARATION

AUTHORITY
1. The power and the right to command or to demand obedience.
2. A person who has superior knowledge of a subject and who can therefore influence the opinions or beliefs of others.
Authority is difficult to define precisely: its meaning depends very much on the context in which it occurs. It often implies a moral or legal supremacy, with the ability to make final decisions that others must respect. It can refer to a group or individual who wields this kind of power in a given context, as, for example, the authority of the Church. In medieval times authority was vested in the Church hierarchy and was largely unquestioned. The Church exercised temporal as well as ecclesiastical power. One of the tenets of Protestantism, however, was that authority lay in the Word of God, which in the minds of many simply equated with the Bible, rather than with any human being. Papal authority was replaced by the idea of the Bible as the authority in matters of faith.

Pastoral authority is defined as spiritual power used to influence opinion, encourage belief and lead people to moral actions. In pastoral counselling, pastors try to lead an individual or group to accept the ultimate authority of God in their lives without becoming authoritarian themselves. By using a client-centred approach, the pastor can focus on the belief system of the client and avoids imposing his or her own beliefs. The issue of authority in pastoral care is complex. The pastor is at the same time under authority (authorized), being an authority (learned and trained), and affirming authority to others (inviting them to take their own authority). He or she is under the authority of the religious body that endorses his or her ministry, and is accountable to that body. Ministers, being educated in their faith and ordained, are also authorities themselves. They have something within them that can inspire and support others; this of course varies from one person to another. Pastoral duties may also include supervising the ministry of others, which involves conveying authority. Dealing effectively with these different aspects of authority is part of learning

to identify with the pastoral role, so that it becomes part of one's identity. *[Hillary Ratna]*

AUTONOMY
The achievement of personal responsibility and functioning.
The notion of the autonomously functioning individual is given great prominence in contemporary thought. It is often regarded as the aim of counselling. It is one of the main pillars of modern thinking that emerged from the Enlightenment. A version of it continues in postmodern thought. Autonomy is sometimes confused with independence, as if it were the opposite of dependence. The latter is held to be malign; the former state something desirable and to be achieved. Technically 'autonomy' means 'functioning independently'. Whether this condition is possible for human beings is a matter of continuing debate. It might be better to see persons as those who oscillate between dependence and independence.

AUXILIARY MINISTRY
Lay and ordained ministry assisting the parochial clergy.
An older term for non-stipendiary ministers in the Church of England was 'auxiliary pastoral ministers'. Most dioceses also run schemes for licensed lay pastoral auxiliaries or pastoral assistants who might also have fallen under this term, especially, paradoxically, if they were paid. Both were defined by their relationship as 'assistants to' rather than 'sharers in ministry with' parochial clergy. That has changed, with a more collaborative view of ministry emerging. As the balance in ministry shifts, some reckon that the stipendiary clergy may become the professional auxiliaries to locally based teams of lay and ordained ministers.

B

BAPTISM
The rite of entry into the Christian Church.
Baptism uses a natural symbol, water, to build upon the physical and psychological dimensions of a universal human experience. Pre-Christian and similar non-Christian rites also used water and the experience of social and spiritual refreshment that it confers to

signify the desire to lead a new life and the opportunity to enjoy a new relationship with God. St Paul vividly describes the transformation that he underwent at his conversion and baptism. The rite, however, became and has remained a point of controversy, although most churches recognize any baptism conducted in the name of the Trinity. Many of the doctrinal difficulties with baptism have arisen from attempting to turn Paul's retrospective reflections upon his own changed life into descriptions of the status of infants who had no such history. For them, the meaning of baptism necessarily lies in the future. This is customarily explained in the preparation of the parents in the case of infant baptism that most ministers and local churches now undertake (Carr, 1994).

The essential components of the rite are the use of water and confession of faith in the triune God. To these should be added the office of the one administering the sacrament and the desire of the one receiving it. The parents and godparents or sponsors express this, in the case of infant baptism, on the candidate's behalf. However, exceptionally, the right of anyone to administer baptism in an emergency (or the validity in the case of martyrs of 'baptism in one's own blood') has long been recognized.

There is similar agreement among the churches regarding both the desirability of baptism and the rejection of attempts to repeat it. Confirmation appropriates its benefits rather than duplicating its effects. The traditional renewal of baptismal vows on Easter Eve is not sacramental. Some Baptist or Baptist-based churches insist on adult baptism by immersion, denying validity to any baptism in infancy (WCC, 1982). The main exceptions to this consensus are the Society of Friends (Quakers) and the Salvation Army. The former deny all particular sacraments, insisting that everything is sacramental; the latter originated as a special-interest group (for poverty and evangelism) within the membership of the existing churches.

Many have expressed concern over the pastoral wisdom, theological propriety and moral rectitude of baptizing infants. Discussion usually concentrates upon the children of non-churchgoers. In England, for example, Anglican parish priests are obliged to baptize all those brought to them. They therefore now usually insist upon preparation and on following up the children, for example with a view to confirmation. They also customarily observe parochial boundaries, so that joining a worshipping community is a real possibility. The responsibility for deciding is left with the parents. There is also a service of Thanksgiving for the Birth of a Child that may be offered. With this option and preparation, more clergy seem willing again to treat baptism as an evangelical opportunity. To that end it is now often administered during public worship, usually the main church service on a Sunday. [Edward Bailey]

BAPTISM PREPARATION
Arrangements made by a church to help parents and godparents get ready for a baptism within the family.

Virtually all infant baptisms involve some preparation since the vast majority of clergy regard this as an important responsibility. In 1963, 98.35% of the Chelmsford diocesan clergy (Church of England) expressed this view. Adult baptism, however, raises the questions of catechesis and Christian formation and is tied in some denominations with confirmation. Its implications go beyond the normative connotation of baptism preparation as associated with infants. The continuing desire of parents in countries with a Christian heritage for infant baptism is a cultural fact.

The decline of institutional religion draws churches to seize on this as a rare evangelistic opportunity. They commonly respond in one of three ways. (1) Some churches refuse baptism to families unwilling to become churchgoing Christians. They write off as folk religion what appears to them such a casual and unchurched request. Applicants must first become church members and receive instruction. (2) Some churches insist on a little church attendance and a modest course of instruction. They do not want to pass up the chance to teach what they judge to be the basic essentials of faith. Neither do they want to lose their potential new contact by being too demanding. Their policy is to demand as much as they think they can get away with. They retain control of the agenda and the teaching syllabus. The applicants must come and learn what Christian tradition has to say. (3) Some churches are generally willing to baptize infants on request. Without avoiding or minimizing the importance of Christian teaching, they do not demand church attendance or specific instruction. They see preparation as a process of dialogue, interpretation and shared learning. The task is to respond imaginatively and creatively to what underlies the applicants' request for infant baptism. This approach aspires to start with the applicants' agenda. It seeks to build bridges between their experience and Christian faith. It recognizes and accepts the applicants' confusion and affirms their desire 'to do what's best for the child', whatever that may mean in the context of ultimate concern.

This third approach is of particular interest to pastoral studies because it acknowledges cultural, social and psychological realities as well as doctrine. It takes seriously the significance of rites of passage, symbol and ritual. It includes awareness of unconscious needs and projections (Carr, 1994). In all approaches it is customary to meet parents and godparents once or twice specifically to go through the service of baptism. In many churches lay people are involved as sponsors who offer a welcome and make a visit. Sometimes they participate in preparation sessions drawing from their own experience.

Baptism preparation as a concept has been criticized as misleading (Carr, 1994). It implies that the rite of baptism is the end result. A deeper exploration, however, is likely to surface significant meaning with spiritual potential. [Nicholas Bradbury]

BASE COMMUNITIES
Small, self-directed Christian groupings seeking the radical renewal of Church and society.
The development of base communities was a mark of the churches in Latin America, Asia and Africa during the late 1950s. They were known there as 'basic ecclesial unities' and grew rapidly in Latin America and the Philippines, though they were less numerous elsewhere. This movement had later influence on aspects of church life in the West, where similar communities emerged gradually, although they were never very numerous. The style of base communities owes much to their origin (Clark, 1977).

Basic ecclesial communities, especially in Latin America, were dominantly Roman Catholic. Their aim was to renew the Church at the grass roots and specifically to pursue the 'option for the poor' as a theme of social justice. At the heart of the worship was the Eucharist and out of this developed liberation theology. Bible study was the foundation

of thinking, and theologians themselves were marked by active advocacy of causes in social and political contexts. The members were the economically poor, and most of these communities were found in the poor neighbourhoods within and on the edges of cities, although some were established in poor rural areas. The communities met frequently, at least weekly, in homes or huts and sometimes in church halls. The movement was largely lay-led, assisted by travelling priests and religious. There was little ecumenical perspective, largely because of the dominance of the Roman Catholic Church in those areas. In its early days the movement was encouraged by the church authorities, but criticism and suspicion of the radical political nature of the movement was always present and later became more prominent (Hebblethwaite, 1993).

The Christian communities which formed in the West were different. They were religiously plural. The aim was to find new forms of Christian community and secular engagement. Worship was marked by experiment and the theology was a theology of the Kingdom, although professional theologians showed only limited interest. Most of the groups were small and based themselves upon liberal Christian studies. Socially they were middle class and were to be found in the inner city and some rural areas. This movement was also strongly lay, but ordained ministers were more commonly involved than in South America. At a local level the ecumenical perspective was considerable, but there was little contact with or support from the mainstream churches. Networks of these communities, however, are growing with occasional regional, national and European (rather than international) focus (Hinton, 1995).

The future of such movements is not clear. Since the 1980s the South American basic community movement has been taken over by a growing Pentecostal presence. In Europe the charismatic links are in evidence, but at present there are no obvious alternatives emerging. [David Clark]

BEFRIENDING
The offering of friendship to people in need, known or unknown.
The meaning of this word was transformed in 1953 when the Revd Chad Varah founded the Samaritans in London. He offered his counselling skills to the suicidal or depressed

but found that his volunteer assistants offered a listening therapy in a friendly non-judgemental way and consequently seven out of eight callers did not then need to see him. Today other caring organizations have befriending schemes. The most important difference between this and counselling, psychotherapy and psychiatry is that the latter demand qualifications and have an agreed objective, whereas befriending needs qualities and, as Chad Varah says, 'is deliberately, beautifully aimless'.

BEHAVIOUR THERAPY
The treatment of mental disorders or problematic behaviour through the use of stimuli and reinforcements.
Behaviourism involves a scientific approach to understanding behaviour through objective observation of actions and reactions. Behaviour therapy (also known as behaviour modification therapy) is the practical application of treatments developed in accordance with this theory. B. F. Skinner and J. B. Watson, working independently in the early twentieth century, are considered the founders of behaviourism theory, a term coined by Watson in 1913. Behaviourists proposed that consciousness was comparable with ideas of the soul and that human behaviour was purely the product of stimulus-response mechanisms that had been either positively enforced with rewards or negatively enforced with punishments. By the mid-twentieth century behaviourism dominated theories of psychology in America. The term behaviour therapy was coined by Skinner but its development is also attributed to Joseph Wolpe and Hans J. Eysenck.

Therapies based on behaviourism use the belief that all behaviour is the result of internal stimuli, such as hunger, paired with external stimuli, such as the sight or smell of food, to create a response that becomes learned through repetition. This learning of responses necessitates reward. Behaviourists also believe that personality is created by a collection of responses that have yielded the greatest rewards for the person in question. More complex forms of behaviour can be understood by breaking them down into behavioural building-blocks which can be explained in terms of more basic learning principles. By developing an understanding of learning processes it becomes possible to manipulate them and change behaviour through applying learning principles. Beha-

viour therapy involves the re-education of the client in order to improve problem behaviour. The therapist first carries out a behaviour analysis to ascertain what precedes or reinforces certain symptoms of the client's behaviour. He or she then utilizes various techniques, such as positive thinking, to encourage the client to think and behave differently. Through the repetition of techniques based on learning principles, the client can unlearn or modify 'bad' responses to create more beneficial behaviour. This approach has been particularly successful in the treatment of phobias, by presenting the relaxed client with increasingly frightening stimuli (Wolpe defined this as 'reciprocal inhibition psychotherapy') and with rewards for 'good' behaviour. Other treatments developed in accordance with behaviour therapy include assertiveness training, social skills training, aversive therapy and systematic desensitization. Cognitive behaviour therapy, developed by Aaron Beck, examines the nature of the thought processes associated with adverse feelings such as depression. These thoughts are monitored and counter-thoughts and strategies are evolved in a dialogue between therapist and client. Cognitive therapy has been shown to be as effective as antidepressants in the treatment of depression in a number of randomized trials. [Lawrence Ratna]

BELIEF
Anything that a person thinks is true.
There are two major areas of controversy surrounding belief, which are important for pastoral theology. The first is the general problem of whether it is possible to talk about some beliefs as true (i.e. they accurately describe the way the world really is) or false (i.e. they are mistaken in the way they describe the world). The second is the more particular problem for pastoral theology. What is the precise relationship between beliefs and actions? Do beliefs determine behaviour or is behaviour largely unrelated to beliefs?

With respect to the truth and falsity of beliefs, much depends on the extent to which the human mind can formulate beliefs that are true descriptions of reality. Some philosophers call themselves 'critical realists' because they believe that it is possible to judge the truth and falsity of a belief by the way the world really is. 'It is raining' is true if, in reality, there is precipitation falling from the sky. And 'There is a God' is true if God exists in reality. Other philosophers, called anti-realists, argue that such 'reality' is inaccessible. When we see, touch, hear things, such experiences need to be interpreted by language. These interpretations are determined by our culture and there is no way of knowing which interpretation corresponds with reality. So, for example, a person having a fit in Europe during the twelfth century will be interpreted as suffering demon possession; a person having a fit today will be interpreted as suffering epilepsy. The culture will determine the interpretation: neither interpretation is true or false; they are just different.

There is a growing consensus of philosophers, influenced by the work of Alasdair MacIntyre (1998), who argue that, although complete certainty about reality is impossible, the human mind does have the capacity to formulate beliefs about the world that are better or worse. So, for example, European culture moved from Ptolemaic views of the universe to a Copernican one because the latter had greater simplicity and coherence. It made more sense of the data.

When it comes to beliefs and actions, there are three main models. The first involves our beliefs being integrated with our actions. This means that our behaviour flows from our view of the world. Certain religions make this a central requirement: you cannot be an Orthodox Jew unless you attempt to be Torah observant (i.e. you behave in ways required by the Jewish law). Or, to take a different example, Nietzsche believed that our post-Enlightenment world had not come to terms with the 'death of God'. Given that God has gone, our conventional morality no longer makes sense. We should, argued Nietzsche, behave in ways compatible with our growing atheism. The combination of integrated beliefs and actions is the ideal because it ensures that our behaviour is considered and consistent with our view of the world. However, there is some evidence that many find themselves operating with the second model. Here our actions are being undermined by our beliefs. Some commentators (Bellah *et al.*, 1985) have argued that although we continue to behave in ways that stress the need for community, our individualistic beliefs are undermining our community behaviour. The third model is often implied by some on the right in British and American politics. They believe that, on the whole,

beliefs are not a significant factor in behaviour. The significant factors are much more basic: emotions, feeling and prejudice. They argue that most people don't have a worldview, but just live in the world – watching soap operas, playing soccer and paying rent. Their behaviour is determined by a whole host of non-rational factors that need careful cultivation and protection.

Anyone involved in pastoral theology must form a view about the significance and nature of belief in human behaviour. On this decision, other issues are then determined. [*Ian Markham*]

BENEVOLENCE
The attitude of goodwill towards other people and towards nature.
The Christian faith affirms that benevolence is the nature of God. Some regard benevolence in men and women, therefore, as a natural quality that needs nurture; others see it as a specific gift of the Spirit. Benevolence through charitable giving is a mark of many religions that has permeated society. But the intensity of the resulting contemporary demand on people's benevolence is challenging the concept itself. Unable to be, as they see it, sufficiently benevolent, people may fall into compassion fatigue.

BEREAVEMENT
The consequence of personal loss.
Bereavement is usually associated with the death of a loved one, but can also describe other losses. The most obvious consequence of bereavement is grief, the painful emotion that accompanies loss. The two words are often used interchangeably. In recent decades bereavement literature has multiplied and studies have added to our understanding of this natural human condition.

For the pastoral carer there are some key guidelines. Bereavement is a universal experience that can be studied and mapped. But each person grieves in a unique way. A knowledge of the stages of bereavement is useful but they should not be treated as essential information but rather as signposts towards understanding. Bereavement counselling, whatever form it takes, may be useful for some, but not necessarily for all. Many people have inner resources with which to handle this inevitable experience.

Bereavement is part of biography. Other people's stories can be used to relieve the feelings of isolation that may accompany grief, and as a mirror for personal experience. Reactions to bereavement are also different at various stages of human development. But with due attention to these caveats, the stages of grief as Parkes (1986) and others have distinguished them may be helpfully outlined.

1. At first there may be denial, which may persist in various forms, such as laying a place at table for the dead person.

2. There may follow a period of searching and yearning, when old photographs are examined, places visited, and when there can be auditory and visual hallucinatory experiences, e.g. a voice on the phone.

3. Anger is very often present, and may surprise the bereaved person as much as anyone. It may also result in social isolation.

4. Guilt and fear may also remain. So many unspoken words and unresolved resentments remain after any parting that it is not surprising that bereaved people tend continually to rehearse the last days of a relationship.

5. Eventually, when a range of emotions has been lived through, the grief ends in resolution. This may simply be quiet acceptance, or it may be a new start, as in remarriage, or a total change of location or employment.

However, the emphasis on grief as a task that must be undertaken has recently been challenged (Walter, 1994). The 'grand narrative' of grief has to be seen as giving way to a diversity of postmodern narratives. The identification of 'normal' grief has also been questioned, and a new weight has been put on telling the story. Reading or listening to the stories of others and telling one's own story are key therapeutic activities. It is seen to be important that the biography of the deceased is drawn up, discussed with family and friends, and that, in this sharing of information, the deceased is taken into the continuing life of the bereaved person.

Although there are no 'normal' reactions to bereavement, there are several indicators when grief has gone wrong.

1. The bereaved person may not be moving on at all, but may be continually rehearsing the same stories.

2. They may neglect themselves, abuse alcohol or drugs, or withdraw from their familiar society.

3. He or she may develop, or appear to develop, symptoms of the illness of the person who has died.

4. He or she may behave obsessively, e.g. cleaning the house in the middle of the night, or spending much time at the cemetery.

5. There may be talk of suicide.

6. Questions of religious faith may arise. Some people seek the consolation of religion and find comfort in returning to church. Indeed they may be free to take on new tasks. Others find the atmosphere unhelpful, and cannot return to the pew where they sat, for example, with their father for so many years.

Ministry to bereaved people will inevitably be a large part of every pastor's work. He or she needs to be aware of abnormal signs and learn to recognize when referral to specialized care is necessary. It is also important to realize that most people are bereaved in some way. It may be far in the past. The loss of a parent in childhood, for example, may be accepted for many years until another loss brings back memories and questions, and raises unresolved issues. The death of a baby, or a miscarriage in early adulthood can still be a painful memory for an elderly woman. The carer will be available to listen, to ask judicious questions, to be interested and alert, and to respond as necessary and useful. Regular contact is usually appreciated by the newly bereaved. After the funeral the bereaved person is often expected too soon to return to normality. Most employers, for instance, do not consider bereavement as a reason for staying off work for more than a few days. There is no right period for grieving. The literature speaks of one or two years as the norm. But in fact bereaved people are never the same again. Anniversaries are important. Three months, six months, and particularly the annual anniversary of a death are days of sadness, and merit a visit or phone call. Wedding anniversaries, birthdays and major social festivals (e.g. Christmas and Easter) can be especially difficult times. Some have found comfort in writing about their experiences, but for most people talking suffices. The pastor will learn mostly through experience when to encourage reminiscence and when to offer diversion and new opportunities. [Derek B. Murray]

BIBLE, USE OF IN PASTORAL CARE

The normative function of the Bible in the belief, witness and service of the Church, including pastoral care.

The Bible is the primary witness to salvation history, culminating in the life, death and resurrection of Jesus Christ, and to the life and faith of the aspostolic Church. The question, however, of how it is to be used pastorally is complex and contested. Two important factors have to be noted in relation to contemporary practice: (1) critical, historical scholarship has both changed the approach to the texts and raised the problem of authority and status; (2) pastoral care has turned to the modern human sciences and related professions for fresh insights and skills. This, it has been argued, has introduced new authorities which can and have usurped theological perspectives. There is a movement to redress the balance and to bring the two together in a creative and authentically Christian relationship (Challis, 1997).

The use of the Bible in pastoral care, therefore, is part of the wider debate about how the gospel as gift and claim is expressed in pastoral practice. This is most dramatically found in the tension experienced between the imperative of proclamation and the widely accepted therapeutic models, such as client-centred therapy. Some see these as irreconcilable, while others find more or less overlap in the way the gospel includes freedom, respect and the security of love, giving the other a legitimate autonomy.

The use of the Bible pastorally can be thought of in two ways. First, in what ways is the Bible properly introduced and referred to in the pastoral situation? In general terms this can only be as and when thought appropriate. Such uses range from shared Bible reading to making allusions and citing quotations in the course of pastoral conversation. How this is done will tend to reflect the answer to the second question: How does the Bible, as a source of Christian insight, inform and mould pastoral practice? It is possible to discern four models.

1. The first solves the issue by claiming that the Bible contains all the necessary resources for pastoral counselling. Modern psychology and therapy is more or less dismissed as humanistic intrusion. A prime example is 'nouthetic' counselling. This approach attributes all non-physical disease to sin, the biblical response to which is repentance and obedience.

2. The second recognizes the value of the human sciences and therapeutic insights but the Bible remains central and normative. Pastoral practice takes place within a biblical understanding of the human condition in relation to God and the divine purposes for creation as found in Christ. This provides the primary patterns for human relationships. The Bible's text can illuminate our fears and

joys, hopes and desires and direct us back to our true being. But how care is offered is enriched by all that the caring professions can offer. It is a mark especially of Protestant orthodoxy and conservative evangelicalism (Hurding, 1992).

3. The third model, using the method of critical correlation, attempts to give due weight to both Bible and the human sciences. Such an approach is almost always exploratory and perhaps tentative. Three illustrative examples can be given. In the first, attention is given to the self-understanding of the pastor as rooted in the biblical tradition. This gives direction and priorities to the pastoral task. The second seeks to provide biblical justification and context for pastoral care. It points to the varied genres of biblical literature that can offer support to different modes of counselling. The third turns to the great themes of covenant, reconciliation, resurrection and so forth which give a framework for pastoral care. The pastor's work will reflect the biblical dialectic of saving initiative and free response.

4. The fourth model, which has been dubbed tokenism, uses the Bible simply to confirm the insights and practices of modern counselling with the field more or less left open to secular theory.

The Bible, however, is at the heart of the worshipping community as its Scripture, the witness to revelation and faith. There it is read, contemplated, proclaimed and dramatically re-enacted sacramentally. The primary pastoral use of the Bible, therefore, is the way it moulds the corporate life of the Church and the personal life of the faithful. Through worship and Bible study, prayer and meditation, the biblical perspective enters into the fabric of the community of faith and the lives of the faithful, and which then becomes part of the natural resource for nurturing and caring for those within and without. The Bible becomes alive and normative in the shared meditative listening to the Word of God in the midst of praise and concerned intercession. [Paul Ballard]

BIGAMY
The offence of being married to more than one spouse at a time.

Bigamy is an offence in law for those societies that legitimate monogamous marriage. It is most prevalent in communities where there is strong social pressure to marry and few, if any, legal exits from marriage. The tolerance of cohabiting unions and ready availability of divorce makes bigamy redundant.

BIOFEEDBACK
Using biological instruments to monitor responses of the body with a view to learning control over these responses.
Developed in the 1960s after it was discovered that certain beneficial brainwave states could be learned through feedback, it has now become an established scientific procedure for treating a wide variety of stress disorders. For example, profound relaxation can be achieved through muscle feedback with instructions on how to lower muscle tension. Biofeedback, therefore, has become a recognized scientific technique for treating such disorders as high blood pressure, headaches, pain, tachycardia and teeth-grinding.

BI-POLAR DISORDER
See: MOOD DISORDERS; DEPRESSION

BIRTH
The moment when a child leaves the womb and is said to enter the world, whether by normal delivery or caesarian section.
1. *Care of the child.* In the last few decades increased attention has been paid to the child's psychological and emotional needs around the time of birth, so that its entry into the world is gentle and the physical closeness of its mother's body is continued, through close holding and breast-feeding.

No matter what views are held on abortion, all Christians seem agreed that every child has full human rights at least from birth onwards, even if it is severely disabled; some hospitals, however, have sometimes sedated and withheld food from the most severely disabled newborn babies. If urgent surgery is needed to save the life of a handicapped child, the parents' consent has to be asked.

Most Christian churches administer baptism to babies. There is a move to make baptism more of a public, liturgical event and less of a private affair than it is in some traditions, in order to emphasize the importance of the entry into the Christian community. Some act of welcome by the local parish (a card or present, for example) can give additional expression to this. In case of danger of death, anybody (a parent or nurse, for example) can baptize.

2. *Care of the mother.* Before the birth the mother needs preparation. She needs to know what to expect from the medical staff. She needs information about the physical events of labour, the emotional experiences of other mothers and the means of pain control that are available (whether through relaxation or medical intervention). During the birth the wishes of the mother should be attended to as fully as possible, so that she is in a comforting environment. It is now normal practice to allow the father of the child to be present throughout the labour and delivery.

For the mother, birth is often a peak experience, and can be followed by a period of great excitement, renewed understanding of the meaning of life, physical exhaustion and emotional fragility. A time of upset and weeping is perfectly normal two or three days after the birth. (Post-natal depression is a later phenomenon, showing more long-term difficulties in adjustment.) The mother needs gentle, respecting care during the early period, because she is in a special time of suffering, grace and the beginning of new love. She can expect to experience at least some ambivalent feelings about the new demands upon her.

Many mothers are now seeking early discharge from hospital, largely because they feel more emotionally secure at home; others, however, find that their stay in hospital gives them a chance of rest that they would not find amid the pressures of home life.

Early bonding between the mother and child is of great importance, and can be hindered if the mother is not able to hold her baby much. Sometimes this is unavoidable, as when a baby needs to be in an incubator, but everything possible should be done to recognize, support and confirm the new mother–child relationship. The now obsolete rite of 'churching' was one way in which the woman's new maternal state was recognized after her confinement; it has largely dropped out of use, since it implied an impurity after birth which would not now be recognized.

3. *Theological dimensions.* Since baptism is spoken of as essentially a new birth (John 3.5), the experience of birth is an opportunity for a deeper understanding of what Christian initiation means. It also provides a uniquely privileged way in which a man and a woman can experience their co-operation with God in creation (Hebblethwaite, 1984). The specialness of the mother–child relationship, particularly at the peak moment of birth, has led some writers of spiritual classics to speak

of God as a mother: e.g. St Anselm – 'So you, Lord God, are the great mother ... for you have brought it about that those born to death should be reborn to life'; Julian of Norwich – 'Our true Mother Jesus, he alone bears us for joy and for endless life, blessed may he be.' [*Margaret Hebblethwaite*]

BIRTH ORDER
A person's chronological position among the siblings within the nuclear family or as an only child.
While Freud noted that a child's position in the family held consequences for a lifetime, Adler considered it a major variable in the development of personality. Following their lead, Austrian psychologist Walter Toman conducted extensive research among thousands of families to explore the significance of birth order or sibling position. The result of his work appeared in the classic book, *Family Constellation* (1969).

Family systems theorist Murray Bowen (1978) incorporated Toman's research into his work, convinced that sibling position provides key information about patterns of relationships among extended family members across the generations. Sibling position is also a useful predictor of the compatibility of persons joining in marriage or committed relationship.

While the focus is often on the oldest, youngest, middle and only child, birth order is far more complex in families with more than three children, and is further shaped by the gender of the child in each position, the gender and birth order of the other siblings, and by the age differences between or among the various siblings. Children closer in age generally have a greater influence on one another.

The oldest child is typically the responsible one, a person who takes charge, likes to be in control, and is a high achiever with perfectionistic tendencies. Oldest children seek the central recognition they knew as only children; they try to win back their place, and therefore find it hard to receive criticism. They can be harsh critics of others.

Second or middle children do not feel as special as they perceive the first-born or youngest to be. When the second child is of the other sex, she or he may feel special and the older does not feel as displaced. Consequently less competition usually develops between the siblings. Middle children turned adults tend to take less initiative and are less

independent than first and youngest children. At the same time they are often friendly, peaceful people and make good negotiators.

Youngest children remain the baby of the family long beyond early childhood. They are cared for by the whole family and live with fewer expectations within the family. They tend to be friendly and charming, less ambitious and go through life expecting to be cared for by others.

Only children never know displacement and tend to have higher self-esteem. They expect a lot of themselves and generally meet their expectations. Unused to living intimately with persons near their age, intimate relationships can be difficult for them.

Sibling position is further complicated by the presence or absence of older brothers and sisters and younger sisters and brothers. For example, the oldest sister of sisters plays a role quite distinct from the oldest sister of brothers (Richardson, 1995).

When a youngest child marries an oldest child, behaviours learned in their family of origin readily transfer into compatible adult family relational patterns. When people couple with persons in their same sibling position, conflict often follows. Each expects to function as the responsible one (oldest child), as the one to be cared for (youngest child), or as the special one to be recognized as such (only child). [*Carroll Saussy*]

BISEXUALITY
A state of being in which an individual is sexually attracted to members of both sexes.
Bisexuality does not require equal attraction or gender-blindness. Rather, the term defines an individual's basic sexual orientation, and it may change over time. Bisexuals may express their sexuality primarily through heterosexual marriage or they may have a homosexual partner. One common misconception is that it is a stage in the coming-out process; another is that it is an attempt to hang on to a heterosexual privilege. This may be true for only a few. Bisexuals in fact often feel unwelcome by both heterosexual and homosexual groups.

BLACK STUDIES
Investigation of the experience of people of African descent, and sometimes of other communities descended from non-European peoples.
There are now many college courses and publications in the USA, Britain and elsewhere

focusing on black studies. These draw on various disciplines – such as history, sociology, political science, the arts and philosophy – to examine the background of, and issues facing, black people in the West and elsewhere in the world. Religious experience is also sometimes included. In North America, the term 'black' is used mainly for African-American, African-Caribbean and African people. However, in Europe, Asian and Latin American people and the original inhabitants of North America and Australasia are also sometimes described as 'black'.

The interest in this subject today is to some extent a reaction against a long period when it received little attention. It was widely assumed – in the West and sometimes in other parts of the world which were, or had been, colonies – that white people were mainly responsible for human progress. Anthropologists sometimes studied the customs, beliefs and social patterns of non-European peoples, and the achievements of ancient civilizations such as those of ancient Egypt, India and Peru were sometimes recognized. But often black people, especially those of African descent, were regarded as culturally – and sometimes biologically – inferior, and they themselves believed their progress relied on learning from white people.

By the twentieth century, anti-imperialist movements were gaining strength, as well as actions against discrimination in the West. There was renewed interest in uncovering black history, which was a source of inspiration (though accounts of the past were sometimes oversimplified), and celebrating more recent accomplishments. It was less uncommon for white scholars, artists and political and religious leaders to express respect for, and interest in, what black people had created. Oral traditions were written down or recorded, and a growing amount of academic and creative work was published exploring different aspects of black people's lives and changes in which they played a part, from colonization and slavery to struggles for emancipation and independence.

Though Christianity had largely come to be associated with the West, there was greater awareness of the critical role of Asian and African communities in the early Church, and of the different cultural forms in which the gospel could be embodied. The importance of theology developed within black-led churches, and by black people in predominantly white denominations, was more widely recognized, including the impact of biblical narratives such as the Exodus story and the death and resurrection of Jesus, as a source of hope for people facing oppression and suffering. There was also a revival of interest in other faiths, and the role which they played in the lives of black communities.

In recent decades, the wider adoption of black studies by academic and other institutions did not mean a unified approach. As with other fields of study, perspectives varied. For instance, some have emphasized the continuity of traditions among people of African descent across time and place, while others have explored the adaptation of communities to different social and economic conditions, and the ways in which they have influenced and been influenced by their neighbours. Ethnic communities are sometimes treated as cohesive groups, while elsewhere gender, class and other differences may be more fully examined.

There is a risk that the development of black studies may be used to justify the ongoing tendency to marginalize the experience of black people, often unintentionally. It should not be assumed that 'literature' is 'literature written in English or other European languages and within a Western aesthetic tradition', that 'pastoral theology' is what has been developed by white theologians, while everything else can be covered under 'black studies'! It should also be noted that black struggles for survival and liberation have not taken place in isolation. Martin Luther King, for example, not only championed civil rights for African-American people but also challenged Christians of all communities to work for social and economic justice and peace; and the role of the Church in South Africa in challenging apartheid and assisting in the transition to a multi-racial democracy also has wide-ranging implications.

Nevertheless, black studies can help black people to understand their own experience and take constructive action, for instance around poverty, ill health and alienation, and can assist white people in building positive relationships with their neighbours. The issues raised and insights gained can throw light on some of the factors shaping the modern world, the dangers and possibilities facing humankind and the questions and challenges for Christians today. [*Savitri Hensman*]

BLAME
The attribution to oneself or another of responsibility for wrongdoing.

The legitimacy and degree of blame depends, not on the seriousness of the actual or potential consequences, but on the extent of the wrong-doer's personal culpability and moral awareness. Acceptance of appropriate blame is a mark of moral maturity. Unjustified or excessive self-blame may indicate an over-sensitive conscience or even neurotic disorder. Persistent unfair blame by others may produce low self-esteem, reluctance to exercise trust, and anti-social behaviour (Gough, 1990), and in severe cases depressive illness.

BLESSING
The bestowal of happiness or good, by a divine being (God), upon a person, object or place.

In a religious context a blessing is usually understood as being divine in origin and bestowed authoritatively through the ministers of that religion. Therefore, to bless someone is to express the hope that they will receive only good things as a consequence. The opposite of such an activity is to invoke a curse, with the intention of ensuring only harmful things happen to that individual. In the Bible there are many instances of both blessings and cursings in both Old and New Testaments (Neh. 13.2; Mal. 2.2; Acts 13. 9–11; Luke 6. 27–36). The priestly blessing of the Israelites by Aaron and his sons (Num. 6. 22–26) is still used at the end of some acts of Jewish and Christian worship. Blessings may also occur over food and places such as the consecration of Solomon's Temple (1 Kings 8. 14, 54).

When human beings seek to act as mediators of God's action it is important that such activities are not misused as a means of imposing one's own will and purpose in a manipulative way. Thus the blessing of objects and places can sometimes be mixed with superstition and magic, and otherwise helpful aids to prayer and devotion, such as a medallion or a crucifix which has been blessed, can be abused as a means to ward off evil rather than as a reminder that the individual is held within the love of God from which nothing can separate them.

Liturgically a blessing is used at the end of worship to bestow God's favour on people as they go out to witness to their faith. In Christian sacraments acts of blessing may happen over water (baptism), bread and wine (com-munion), oil (anointing), rings and people (marriage).

Within a pastoral context a form of blessing can be a way of bringing a sense of peace in the presence of emotional distress, physical pain or illness. The purpose of this blessing is to assure the person of God's ability to strengthen, heal and restore. The blessing may be through a form of words (usually trinitarian) or accompanied by an outward sign or symbolic act such as making the sign of the cross, the laying on of hands or anointing with oil. An especially solemn form of blessing in the Catholic tradition is the Benediction of the Blessed Sacrament in which the priest makes the sign of the cross over the congregation with a consecrated host (bread). This practice grew out of a fourteenth-century custom of exposing the host for public adoration. But Benediction was and remains unacceptable in Protestant and Orthodox circles.

A blessing is not, however, a holy sticking plaster to cover doubts and conflicts, but is intended for the strengthening of faith and hope. Thus a pastoral contact may conclude with a blessing as an expression of the person's worth and value in the sight of God. *[Peter Speck]*

BODY
The physical organism which constitu-tes the material part of a person.
The human body is a highly complex system which contains such components as our skeletal structure, organs, tissues, glands, ducts and the outer sheath of skin. Particularly remarkable in the operations of the body is an intricately balanced system of electronic, chemical and mechanical functions. Two systems of bodily function are of more central interest in pastoral studies and psychology than most other physical characteristics. First, the endocrine system is significant because of the intricate relationship between its biochemistry and our psychological and spiritual states. Second, the brain is crucial because of the manner in which it apparently generates mind by means of its electrochemical processes, and thus is central to the mind-body problem. In addition, human psycho-spiritual states are affected by and expressed in our body images and body language.

The endocrine system is that interconnected network of glands, ducts and organs which produces and regulates the chemistry of the entire body. It includes the hypothalamus, pituitary and thyroid, as well as the numerous subordinate hormone- and enzyme-producing components which they control, such as the adrenal glands and the ovaries or testicles. Recent research has confirmed that the endocrine system both significantly affects and is affected by a person's psycho-spiritual states. Numerous effective synthetic medications have been developed in the last two decades which can be used to supplement a person's deficient body chemistry with those normally present chemicals, thus relieving the affected person of serious psychological or spiritual suffering caused by such deficits. Many forms of anxiety and depression, as well as obsessive-compulsive disorders, and other forms of human suffering, are the direct result of dysfunctions in the chemistry-producing or -regulating operations of the endocrine system.

Body image is also crucial in psycho-spiritual health. Human beings spontaneously develop a mental concept of their bodily form and function. Whether this body image is objectively accurate or inaccurate, it fundamentally affects how we perceive ourselves and each other as persons. For example, in the mid-nineteenth century the ideal image of a man in Western culture was that of a portly and prosperous figure. At the beginning of the twenty-first century the ideal is that of a slim, athletic figure. Our perceptions of how we compare with the cultural or societal ideal influence our self-concepts, how we think and feel about ourselves.

Moreover, our own personal attitudes or assessments regarding various physical characteristics also affect our concept of ourselves in important ways. The images of our bodies which we have developed have important psycho-spiritual consequences. Thus it is of considerable significance for persons to understand how their views of their physical characteristics influence their psycho-spiritual attitudes and feelings, whether these perceptions are realistic or healthful, and what the developmental influences were which shaped their body images. Most people seem to adjust their body images as they age, thus retaining a stable self-concept while appropriately modifying their sense of the importance of the body image ideal. A healthy and healthful body image generally conforms to the cultural and social ideal, with great allowances for individual uniqueness.

The general shape of a person's body is largely influenced by genetic inheritance. Attempts have been made to link body shape with behaviour and temperament. William Herbert Sheldon proposed a system for body-typing. He suggested that there are persons who are endomorphic whose bodies are large, fleshy and spherical; mesomorphic people whose bodies are muscular, angular and athletic; and those who are ectomorphic whose bodies are slender, linear and thin. He thought endomorphs love physical comfort, need approval and seek affection or social relationship; mesomorphs are self-centred and independent; and ectomorphs are secretive, inhibited and prone to solitude. This categorizing approach to the relationship between our bodies and our psycho-spiritual states has not proved useful or accurate.

We articulate our psycho-spiritual states through the way we use our bodies. Our posture, facial expressions, gait, blushing, body odours, tone and intensity of voice, and gestures, intimate or overtly communicate how we feel about ourselves, others or an issue that is being addressed. This body language, as it is called, is non-verbal communication that frequently indicates to others our meanings, feelings and intentions as clearly as does verbal language (Lowen, 1958). In fact, our body language is a more direct expression of our inner states, particularly our unconscious responses to people and situations, than are our words. When we formulate verbal messages in communication with each other we process them through our reflective thought system and so we edit the emotional as well as the cognitive content in the way we sense the situation requires for our best advantage. Our body language, however, is a direct expression of our inner worlds and thus what we express bodily is not edited for effect upon the situation. Thus we often feel that a person's actions speak louder than his or her words. We sense that posture, facial expressions and gestures tell us more about how he or she really feels about an issue than do his or her words. Body language is important in the processes of social intercourse, as well as in our personal perceptions and assessments of our own psycho-spiritual states. Frequently we surprise ourselves when our body language, tone of voice and gestures express intense emotion which we were not aware of having regarding an issue or situation. Such body language can make us aware of inner dynamics which need attention but which we have carefully edited out of our conscious awareness and out of our verbal expressions (Lowen, 1967). Significant attempts have been undertaken to utilize this human characteristic in therapeutic interventions such as the various body-centred therapies (e.g. bioenergetics and martial arts). These techniques attempt to employ the body and body language for assessment of a client's psychological state and mental life. They assume that a split between the functions of the body and the mind is resposible for psychological illness, particularly character disorders. The functional dynamic of these therapies is the achievement of self-awareness through movement and touch.

This raises the mind-body problem. Are the mind and body different functions of a person or are they extensions or expressions of each other? If they are distinct and separate operations or aspects of human beings or of humanness, how are they related or connected? A strictly materialist approach would suggest that the mind is merely a type of function of our physical organism and thus is a dynamic expression of the body's existence. A strictly psycho-spiritual model would claim that the mind is an entity in its own right and functions objective to, alongside, or over against the body. The truth seems to be illumined more specifically by models which suggest that consciousness, self-awareness, self-consciousness, and such primal operations of the mind, are functions of a person in which the interface of body and mind are intimately and intricately connected.

The measurable electrochemical functions in the brain have manifest and measurable relationship with the operations of the mind in cognition and self-expression. The formation of our thoughts, ideas, conscious awareness and reflections, as well as our feelings and sensations, are all possible because of the physical function of our brains. These are all shaped and conditioned for good or ill by the healthy or pathological state of the electrochemical operations of our brains. Moreover, the state of our feelings and thoughts seems to influence the state of our brain chemistry as well. So the human organism is not a dualistic system of separation between mind and body, but a unitary system in which our minds and bodies function in virtual enmeshment and dynamic interface with each other. We are more than our bodies but our transcendent and transpersonal qualities of spirit and psyche are, nonetheless, crucial operations of

personhood that arise from, express and depend upon the function of our bodies.
[*J. Harold Ellens*]

BOREDOM
A condition of restlessness or lack of interest in life.
Augustine identified restlessness as the spiritual disease of those who are alienated from God. The modern origins of the term boredom and its French equivalent, ennui, indicate that it is a characteristically modern condition. Its provenance is often identified with the division of labour which condemns many workers to the uncreative servitude of machines, or to the material, psychic and social impoverishment of unemployment. It may also be a consequence of the anonymity of modern mass societies and social systems.

BOUNDARY
See: LIMIT-SETTING

BRAIN DEATH
The irreversible cessation of all functions of the entire brain, including the brain stem.
Brain death can result from traumatic injury to the head, stroke or cardiac arrest. Unlike cardiac death, brain death is irreversible. It is medically recognized as a cause of death. There are two major pastoral care issues to consider: organ donation, and the possibility of biological functions continuing after brain death. It is incumbent on pastoral care givers to be supportive of the bereaved as they decide about consenting to organ donation, and also to help them accept brain death as 'real' death.

BRAIN, PHYSIOLOGY OF
The human brain co-ordinates the functions of the body; provides sensory awareness; controls motor activity; produces thought; holds the key to personality.
1. *Structure*. Slightly larger than a medium melon, weighing about three pounds, the human brain is walnut-like in its wrinkles and grooves, and something like putty in appearance. Its top layer, the neocortex, is actually a thin sheet of cellular tissue about a yard across, intricately folded so as to fit within its bony confines. It is divided into two halves or hemispheres, left and right. Generally speaking, the left has chief responsibility for language and for step-by-step opera-

tions, while the right thinks of 'the big picture' and relationships.

Each hemisphere has four sectors, or lobes. The paired frontal lobes lie behind the forehead and occupy most of the front half of the neocortex. These are involved in making plans and carrying out goal-directed behaviour, and they help to co-ordinate the functions of other parts of the cortex. Behind the frontal lobes, across the top of the head, are the parietal lobes. These handle general sensory information. On the sides of the head and behind the frontal lobes are the temporal lobes. These deal with sounds, spatial discrimination, memory formation and other tasks. The occipital lobes, in the back of the head, process visual information. All these sectors have functions besides those listed, and they do not act independently, but interact continually; to assign a function solely to one area is to oversimplify, except for highly specific operations.

If we were to flip our specimen brain upside down, the part on top would be the brain stem. It connects the brain to the spinal cord and handles life-maintenance operations such as circulation, respiration and temperature control. Next to the stem is the bulbous cerebellum, which primarily co-ordinates motor activity.

Still more structures are sandwiched between the neocortex and the brain stem. Some (which have correlates in all reptiles, birds and mammals) handle such survival behaviour as feeding, establishing dominance and guarding territory, and they also regulate reproductive behaviours. Others, found only in mammals, form the limbic system, which generates emotions and emotional behaviour, including attachment, nurturance, and playfulness. The limbic system plays a role in memory formation, and it contributes emotional evaluation and motivation to the logic, planning and insight of the neocortex. Several nerve-tissue bridges carry information from one side of the brain to the other; the most important is the corpus callosum, which connects the right and left hemispheres of the neocortex (Ashbrook and Albright, 1997).

2. *Operation.* Information is received and transmitted by brain cells called neurons. There are billions of them in each human brain, and a typical neuron communicates with thousands of others. Neurons send outgoing messages through axons – long fibres extending from the body of the neuron. Neurons also sprout bushy structures, known as dendrites, that receive incoming messages. An axon from one neuron and a dendrite from another meet at a junction called a synapse. There, signals cross from one to the other, mediated by chemicals called neurotransmitters. (Most drugs used to treat anxiety or mental illness work by changing the balance or activity of neurotransmitters.) Within each neuron, information is transmitted and integrated by electrical means. Many neurons have a coating of myelin, an electrical insulator produced by cells called glia, which also provide the neurons with nourishment (Kandel *et al.*, 1992).

Genes have a major influence on the design of the connections among the brain's neurons. However, the fine-tuning of functional circuits is heavily influenced by their repeated use – and, of course, the environment and personal choice have major impact on which circuits are used repeatedly. Circuits initially formed by genetics but not reinforced by use do not persist well. In this way, experience, especially during childhood, helps to shape not only personality but also the brain itself. Although adult brains are less malleable than children's, experience can also affect adults' 'circuitry'. All things being equal, a well-used brain will develop and maintain more connections throughout life than one that is relatively idle (Kandel *et al.*, 1992).

3. *Disease and trauma.* Despite protection by the skull and its lining, the brain is a vulnerable organ. Lack of oxygen due to interruption of respiration or blood circulation can, in a few minutes, cause brain cells to die. Other threats include brain haemorrhage or blood clot (two types of stroke), chemical poisoning, traumatic injury and degenerative diseases.

It may readily be seen that damage to different parts of the brain will have different sorts of effects. For example, a stroke that damages certain brain centres may have a greater effect on the ability to speak than on the ability to understand. In multiple sclerosis, destruction of myelin sabotages neurons' electrical information-processing. In Parkinson's disease, degeneration of cells that secrete the neurotransmitter dopamine leads to the tremor and unsteadiness that characterize that disorder. Alzheimer's disease involves the formation of abnormal structures in the brain called 'plaques and tangles'; these often affect centres where new memories are encoded and progressively disable many areas of the brain. More subtle are the changes in persons with damaged frontal lobes; such persons may retain all their linguistic and mathematical abilities and their memories, yet consistently fail to carry out plans or to act as reliable, considerate individuals (Damasio, 1994). Ageing by itself is less likely to impair brain function than was once thought, although it may slow the processes a bit.

In 'brain death', there is complete absence of brain function due to death of the brain cells, from which recovery is impossible. 'Brain dead' individuals lack all cognition, including pain, thought and emotion, and they cannot independently maintain the basic bodily processes, such as breathing, that are controlled by the brain stem. Previous definitions of 'brain death' required complete absence of cerebral electrical activity as measured by an electroencephalogram (EEG). In many jurisdictions, this definition has been superseded by clinical criteria, making the EEG unnecessary in many cases. [*Carol Rausch Albright*]

BUDDYING
In Great Britain an arrangement whereby trained volunteers befriend and support people with an illness (usually AIDS and symptomatic HIV) on a one-to-one basis.
Buddies are committed to confidentiality, regular contact, and helping people help themselves by keeping control of their situation. A buddy's activities might include chatting, cleaning, cooking, shopping and helping someone in their relationships with statutory and voluntary agencies. Asking for a buddy may mean acknowledging a diagnosis/prognosis and accepting a certain invasion of privacy so buddies will need support, particularly if family and friends feel threatened by them. The relationship can continue or end by mutual agreement.

BURIAL
Deposition of the corpse in the ground.
Burial is the mode of disposal historically preferred by Judaism, Christianity and Islam – world religions that affirm resurrection of the body. The symbolism of the body resting in the ground and rising on the last day is powerfully represented in medieval art and sculpture. Muslims bury in a shroud, as was also typical at certain times in Christian Europe. The British place a simple coffin

directly into the earth. North Americans are first embalmed, and then placed in a strong casket, possibly made of steel, which is typically placed in a concrete-lined grave.

BURNOUT
A general description of severe physical, emotional, psychological or spiritual exhaustion.
In pastoral studies the term 'burnout' is normally used to describe the fatigue, frustration and loss of energy and interest among caregivers, especially the clergy. The condition has been noted in many studies, describing varying degrees of emotional breakdowns, shutdowns, crack-ups, and cessation of functioning.

Burnout manifests itself in one or more of three losses: the loss of control, the loss of challenge, interest and energy, and the loss of faith and commitment. The downward spiral toward burnout is usually experienced in the following stages: frustration, stress, chronic frustration, depletion, depression, helplessness, burnout, hopelessness. While stress is the excitement of the adrenal system, burnout is the depression of that system.

Contributing factors to burnout among clergy are: too much work; too long a day; too varied a complex of issues, problems and duties with which to deal; too unrelenting a drain on emotional and mental resources; repressed anger; insufficient opportunity to get away; inattention to self-care; and being caught in a crossfire of conflicting or contradictory expectations within the institutional Church. Work-related issues often become intertwined with personal life and family-related issues. Joseph Sittler once referred in a lecture to these dynamics in the ministerial vocation as the 'maceration of the minister' – being chopped into small pieces. Clergy, called and ordained to the ministry of word, sacrament and order, end up in the parish focusing on many tasks unrelated to these central commitments of the pastoral vocation. This leads to a sense of vocational guilt (not doing what one is called to do), vocational confusion (not knowing what the pastoral calling actually is in the confusion that abounds in the contemporary Church), or vocational defeat (the interpretation of one's ministry as a failure). The experience of shame accompanies both the sense of failure and the condition of burnout (Davey, 1995).

Burnout and accompanying depression are likely to require both spiritual and medical attention. Since the effects of clergy burnout can be destructive not only to the minister, but also to the minister's family and to the church, steps should be taken to prevent burnout. These steps should address not simply the symptoms, but the underlying issues of pastoral vocational clarity (Capps, 1997). For most pastors, the vocation is not simply a profession but an identity. When burnout is experienced in the vocation, depletion is experienced in personal identity and the sense of self.

Attention to self-care is of utmost importance in the prevention of burnout. Unfortunately, misguided understandings of Christian asceticism have militated against self-care in favour of self-denial and self-renunciation. Since clergy have a fiduciary responsibility to care for others, the practice of self-care becomes an ethical mandate. Self-care is the foundation of caring for others and, therefore, a foundation for ministerial leadership.
[Victor L. Hunter]

C

CANCER
A lay term applied to a wide group of conditions which have in common the uncontrolled progressive development of new tissue (a tumour or 'growth').
Tumours may be benign and localized, in which case they are purely of local significance, and are not included in the term cancer. Malignant tumours (cancers, carcinomas, sarcomas) spread remorselessly locally, and often also to distant parts of the body. Thus a cancer arising primarily in the breast may spread locally via the lymphatics, and via the bloodstream may spread (metastasize) to bone, brain, liver and other organs.

The fundamental cause of cancer is not known, but there are several well-known predisposing factors, such as smoking in the case of lung cancer. Cancers may arise at any age, though they are fortunately rare in children and young adults. After the age of 40, the incidence of malignant disease begins to rise, and this increase persists until old age. Growths may arise in almost any organ – in North America and Western Europe, the commonest sites are stomach, bowel, lung and brain in both sexes; and in women, breast and uterus; and in men, prostate.

Cancer has acquired a dreaded reputation because it is such a common cause of death, being responsible for about a quarter of all deaths in developed countries. Nevertheless, the prospects for survival have significantly improved in some patients, often depending on whether the condition is diagnosed early when the growth is still confined to its primary site: once the tumour has spread to distant organs, the prospect of successful treatment is less good, except in certain rare circumstances. If the tumour is confined to its original site, then the condition may be successfully treated by surgical excision. Prospects for this are best in bowel cancer, which may be cured in up to about half of all patients. For tumours that have spread, surgical treatment may be supplemented by drug treatment (chemotherapy), hormone treatment in the case of cancer of the breast, prostate and thyroid, or X-ray treatment (radiotherapy).

Until recent years, it was relatively uncommon for the patient to be informed directly of the diagnosis, such was the dread that the term 'cancer' evoked; but of course the patient's relatives were informed. This was a very unsatisfactory practice, often leading to tensions and lack of mutual confidence in the family at a time when family support was required more than ever. Further, the practice led to a loss of confidence by the patient in his or her medical advisers, and often engendered more anxiety and uncertainty than disclosure of the diagnosis. Nowadays, the general practice is to inform the patient, unless there are special factors making this an unwise move. It is very important that the information is tactfully and sympathetically given, and that the confidence of the patient is secured so that the best possible plan of treatment may be devised. Many patients with cancer dread above all the prospect of severe pain; this is a lay misconception – severe pain is exceptional, and where present it should nowadays be possible for effective treatment to be given.

Psychological support for the patient and the patient's family is an essential component of care, and one that is often poorly undertaken. When both the patient and the professional adviser share a common, strong religious faith, such a bond may be of enormous benefit to the sufferer. Where religious faith is lacking, the situation is more difficult; the carer must avoid foisting religious beliefs on the patient, but nevertheless much help can be given by sympathetic discussion of the issues, by such reassurance as is possible, and by counselling in an unhurried manner.

For the patient who is dying of cancer, the choice is usually between arranging for extended nursing and other care to be given at home, or for admission to a hospice for terminal care. The choice will largely depend on the patient's family and economic circumstances, and on his or her medical condition. The hospice movement has made tremendous improvements in the field of pain relief and nursing care, and many hospices (whether or not they are religious foundations) now provide an ideal supportive milieu for the dying patient. [John Leonard]

CANON LAW
The legal rules applicable within Churches of the Roman Catholic, Orthodox and Anglican traditions.
Theologically, canon law is based on divine law as mediated through the Old and New Testaments and thereafter through the Church: see Matt. 18.18; Luke 22.28–30; 1 Cor. 5.2. As a human institution the Church requires regulation, including on matters of liturgy. The needs of the Church were first met by local custom and episcopal direction. Thereafter, to obtain uniformity, regulations (called 'canons') were made by regional or ecumenical councils.

In the Western tradition, collections of canons and decretals (namely, papal letters setting out particular decisions and ruling) were made, some of which were well-intentioned forgeries. As the body of church law grew, jurisprudential harmonization became essential; the most influential such harmonization was Gratian's *Decretum*, c. 1140 CE. Interpretation and further decrees followed, which in turn were formed into other collections. By the end of the fifteenth century the formal body of canon law, the *corpus iuris canonici*, was completed.

In the Roman Catholic Church the *corpus iuris canonici* remained the basis of canon law until a further codification and revision in 1917. In 1983 this code was replaced by another code of canon law which reorganized the Church's discipline and accommodated the teachings of the Second Vatican Council (Coriden, 1991).

As elsewhere throughout Europe, the canon law, known as the *ius commune*, had been applied in England subject to local variation based on custom. Local canons continued to be made by local synods. By far the most influential book on this pre-Reformation canon law was Lyndwood's *Provinciale Angliae*. At the Reformation, however, only such parts of the *ius commune* as were not 'repugnant, contrariant or derogatory' to the laws or statutes of the realm, nor to the prerogatives of the Crown, received statutory recognition. This church law (often referred to as 'ecclesiastical law') became part of the national law, enforced primarily within the separate church courts known as 'consistory courts'. The Church of England continued to be able to make canons; but these now could bind only the clergy. However, the general ecclesiastical law still continues to bind both clergy and laity alike, although it is now primarily unenforceable against the laity. It can be altered both by statute and, within particular bounds, by 'measures' having statutory authority made by the General Synod (Briden and Hanson, 1992).

Within the Anglican Communion outside England the ecclesiastical law's enforceability depends upon voluntary membership and contractual consent. Jurisprudentially the canon law of the Roman Catholic Church has the same basis both within England and elsewhere.

The canon law has always been concerned with the souls of the faithful. The need for flexibility by which to meet particular pastoral needs was at first met by local custom and dispensation. Custom now has little legal relevance in either Church. Flexibility is provided to a greater or lesser extent by judicial interpretation, although less in Anglican ecclesiastical law because of statutory rules and judicial precedent. Dispensation now has little place in the Anglican ecclesiastical law. [Rupert Bursell]

CARING
To be anxious for, provide for, look after, watch over, be compassionate, be concerned professionally as in medicine, social work, nursing, pastoral care or guardianship.
The word 'care' derives from the Latin *cura*, which has a wide range of meanings. Increasingly, however, caring has come to mean the help given by charitable agencies or professional/statutory bodies to those deemed to be in need. Effective caring necessitates the ability properly to assess need, whether physical, emotional, psychological or spiritual.

Such care may be offered in the individual's own home or social setting by the family, the primary health care team, meals-on-wheels service, local church or other community carers. However, the needs of the individual may necessitate the person entering a caring institution, temporarily or permanently, such as a hospital, old persons' residential home or nursing home. *Informal caring* may, therefore, be offered by family and friends in a variety of settings ranging from the individual's own home, support groups in the community, or caring visits to those who are hospitalized. *Formal caring* is usually undertaken by professional carers (e.g. health-care workers) or others who have undergone training in order to work in a voluntary caring agency. In the Western world people tend to live longer and frequently outlive their friends and so may face a lonely old age with a lack of carers when their health begins to fail. The impact of this has been added to by the fragmentation of the nuclear family, in the UK and elsewhere, which has necessitated the development of a variety of statutory and voluntary agencies to offer the care that would usually have been available within the family network. The demands on volunteers have increased as statutory services struggle to maintain a caring service in the face of increased demands following legislative changes, coupled with low staffing levels as a result of economic constraints.

Needs and wants are not the same and carers can be under great pressure to meet unrealistic expectations of clients. In addition to proper assessment of need, effective caring also requires an assessment of one's own ability to meet some or all of the person's needs, or to recognize that collaboration with other carers is required. A balance also has to be maintained between being and doing. The fussy and over-busy carer can easily add to the dis-ease of the person being cared for. Training can help the non-professional carer to be more aware of their limitations and help them avoid inappropriate involvement. However, training should not over-professionalize the amateur lest it remove their most valuable asset – their vulnerability.

Empathic, compassionate caring can be very costly for the carer, particularly in emotional terms. There is now a greater readiness to acknowledge that carers (formal and informal) require a measure of support if they are to be able to go on caring. For example, for too many years single children have cared for elderly, infirm relatives or severely handicapped children without any respite or adequate support for themselves. Health-care professionals are themselves often expected always to be nice and loving towards those they care for, even when the cared for may respond in a negative way. While a period of respite may be valuable and supportive for some carers, the opportunity in a safe setting to work through some of the emotional and psychological effects on themselves of their caring role can be crucial to their own well-being. In particular the effects of unconscious, as well as conscious, processes which can affect the quality of care or the ability to go on caring, can be potentially damaging to the carer in the long term. Some of these unconscious processes are present in multi-professional carer groups as a result of competitiveness and rivalry, or the unrewarding nature of some aspects of care which can arouse strong and often primitive feelings in the carer and the cared for (Speck, 1994).

The essence of the caring role is when the carer communicates to the cared for the ability to listen and enter into the situation of the other person in a non-judgemental and accepting way. This affirms and values the person being cared for, avoids paternalism, and is reflective of a counselling relationship. For carers motivated and informed by a belief system, this quality of care may reflect the carer's understanding of the nature of God and of a requirement to demonstrate the loving aspect of God in relationship to other people. Thus in Judaism it is especially meritorious to visit and care for the sick and, in Christianity, the early Christians gave expression to their belief through sharing together and caring for each other.

Some belief systems can have the effect of creating the expectation that believers will become perfect carers, and much guilt can develop when this is not achievable, or the carer represses any negative thoughts and feelings concerning those cared for. To 'love your neighbour as yourself' (Matt. 19.19) implies a requirement to first love yourself and to take care of yourself and recognize your limitations. Support and a safe exploration of the consequences of caring may be especially important for those seeking to be perfect carers. They may need help in recognizing that most belief systems are primarily calling on believers to become good enough carers to good enough clients. This shift in understanding may enable them to sustain their caring role and not become victims of their own belief system. [*Peter Speck*]

CATHARSIS
A psychoanalytic term which explains the release of unconscious energy from a hidden or forgotten memory.
The 'cathartic' method was used in a number of forms in psychotherapy during the nineteenth century. This was in order to find the underlying psychological problem in an individual. It was in 1895 that the Viennese physician Josef Breuer first observed that symptoms of 'hysteria' vanished after a session of hypnosis. Freud then turned from catharsis to psychoanalysis or, as Anna Q, a gifted young female patient of Breuer's termed it, 'the talking cure'. Catharsis not only releases unconscious psychic energy, allowing that energy to return to consciousness, but also brings a sense of peace.

CATHEXIS
A Freudian psychoanalytic term meaning 'investment', specifically investment of energy in an idea or an object.
Freud never gave a theoretical definition to the term cathexis, possibly because he did not like technical terms. He was, however, very concerned with 'libidinal' energy and the way in which that energy 'cathected' (attached) itself to an idea or an object. It is very obvious that people with certain phobias have made a cathexis in a particular idea or object and that the level of energy is maintained in relation to the idea. 'Cathexis' is translated from the German verb 'besetzen', which has a number of meanings including 'to occupy'; hence the energy, the cathexis, occupies the idea or object. Some psychoanalysts think that a cathexis has its origin in the 'instincts'.

CELIBACY
Originally the state of being unmarried; now public commitment to the single state for religious reasons.
For most of Christian history the practice of religious celibacy has arisen from the conviction that purity of soul and union with God are best pursued without sexual, marital and familial involvements. The notion of 'eunuchs for the kingdom of heaven' has a long history, whether or not Matt. 19.12 is really about celibacy. The view that only the

celibate can give undivided attention to the Lord is supported in 1 Cor. 7.

Within that broad assumption celibacy has meant different things in different settings. For many people it has been a step into freedom, in face of the alternative of being handed over to oppressive versions of marriage. For Ambrose of Milan, consecrated virgins represented with minimal ambiguity the boundary between the Church and the world, exemplifying most starkly the transcendence of sexual appetites. Gregory of Nyssa also commended consecrated virginity, holding that the institution of marriage, understood as essentially procreative, had come into being only as an attempt to fend off human anxiety about mortality. Since Christians have the risen Lord, said Gregory, they are not ruled by this anxiety and therefore have no need of any such expedient (Brown, 1988).

Christian advocates of celibacy have proceeded by way of downgrading marriage, sex and procreation. Sixteenth-century Protestant Reformers attacked celibacy for their own reasons and did something to rehabilitate marriage. But within Catholicism the commendation of celibacy retained its power. It is only nowadays that the dominant modes of Christian thinking unequivocally affirm the goodness both of sexuality and of marriage understood as the fullest and most enriching form of relationship. Once sexual awareness and activity are explicitly seen as graced, celibacy loses its traditional meaning as the gateway to a fully Christian life. Those who commit themselves to celibacy are taking on something which has lost meaning. This is not to say that professed celibacy could never again have meaning, but that no new meaning has yet appeared. That way of thinking has lost its power that saw sexual interest and sustained focusing of emotional energy on a partner as obstacles to further conversion. Those who in relation to compulsory clerical celibacy say that what is needed is better preparation of ordinands do not register this loss.

A shift may be observed from a Christian tendency to downgrade sex to one that downgrades celibacy, at least by implication. Modern theology's newly positive perception of human sexual bodiliness may already be in danger of replacing one overly restrictive image of what it is to be human with another. Experienced pastors say that there is in any case much de facto celibacy, within and outside marriage. Exploration of the human possibilities of this celibacy is a task as yet unaddressed by the Church. [*Nicholas Peter Harvey*]

CHAPLAINCY
Ministry in and to an institution rather than to a church or parish.

Chaplaincy work (e.g. hospital, industrial, prison, college) tends to be more specialized than ministry in a parish or a gathered congregation. Chaplains are understood as having a ministry to the institution as such as well as to the individuals who are involved in the institution. They often exercise the normal functions of clergy – leadership in worship, pastoral care, counselling, preaching, education, etc. – but there are often different emphases from the 'normal ministry'. Industrial chaplains, for example, rarely conduct worship in the businesses to which they are attached and sometimes emphasize the prophetic role in their calling. Chaplaincy may be a part-time occupation to which stipendiary or non-stipendiary clergy are appointed. There are advantages in part-time chaplaincy work, particularly in 'total institutions' such as hospitals or prisons, where the chaplain's coming and going may provide a significant link with the broader community. But there are also difficulties in part-time chaplains gaining a deep enough knowledge of the structures and processes of the institution to be able to exercise a fully effective ministry to the institution as such.

Chaplaincy is usually more specialized than parochial ministry. It is hard, for instance, to operate as a pastor and chaplain in a psychiatric hospital unless one knows enough of psychiatric practice to be able to relate intelligently both to patients and staff, and understand their difficulties and dilemmas. Similarly, effective school or college chaplaincy demands a knowledge of the educational process and of the tensions and pressures to which staff and students are subject. In some educational institutions the chaplain is also a teacher. While this gives inside knowledge of the educational process and brings the chaplain into day-to-day contact with a range of people in the institution, it also means that the chaplain is regarded by some as part of the authority structure of the institution. This can limit the chaplain's pastoral effectiveness. Similarly, in hospitals sometimes the chaplain is seen as having a role which involves a stance firmly on the side of the institution and its authority structures. This can inhibit patients from seeing the chaplain as an independent figure. There is much discussion about who appoints and pays chaplains. Industrial chaplains, for example, commonly regard it as important for an effective ministry that they are acceptable to both management and trade unions but not seen as financially or otherwise dependent on either. This kind of independence is seen as a prerequisite for effective ministry.

The popular idea that a chaplain should be minister to a whole institution and to all its members has not gone unchallenged. The worker-priest movement in France and other countries was based on the belief that in a polarized industrial situation ministry was only possible for those who took sides unambiguously with the workers and their struggles, identifying themselves as workers as well as priests. The need for neutrality has also been challenged by Pattison (1994). As a consequence of his own chaplaincy work in a psychiatric hospital, Pattison was forced to ask himself the question, 'Whose side am I on?' He discovered that many patients felt that they were victims or objects of treatment, and were acutely suspicious of a chaplain who was part of the institutional establishment. Effective ministry to patients was only possible, he argued, when one abandoned the effort to justify and explain the treatment patients received and unambiguously took their side. This, he argued, enabled both pastoral ministry to patients and prophetic ministry to the hospital and the health-care system.

In chaplaincy work, as in other spheres of ministry, there are often problems in fulfilling both the pastoral and the prophetic offices of the minister. In some situations chaplains are subject to military discipline or expected to give an unquestioning loyalty to the institution in which they work. The prophet as whistle-blower is often not appreciated or tolerated. Many chaplains see their role as primarily the pastoral care of individuals and try not to concern themselves with issues of the power structures in which they work. Particularly in industrial chaplaincy the experience, analysis and critiques of chaplains have helped the churches to address issues of modern industrial society in an informed and perceptive way.

Chaplaincy work was often developed as a response to the increasing secularization of society. Thus many forms of industrial, urban and rural chaplaincy see their primary task as mission in a world profoundly alienated from the Christian Church, where the traditional congregation and parish often seem an inadequate agency of evangelism. The model of chaplain-as-missionary suggests that the chaplain is not 'at home' in the institution nor part of its authority structures; the chaplain's activities are all in some way or another the proclamation of good news to the institution and those who work in it (Northcott, 1989).

Heiji Faber (1971) developed the model of the hospital chaplain as a clown: the chaplain takes part in the life of the institution but is unique and different; an amateur among professionals. The chaplain's activity is spontaneous and apparently naive in offering something different from all the others. The role of chaplain-as-jester merges into the prophetic role. As the chaplain gives support, care and encouragement there is also a questioning of values, assumptions and structures which can be painful but is in fact constructive. [*Duncan B. Forrester*]

CHARACTER
In virtue ethics a key concept of what is universally human.
Influenced by Aristotle and Aquinas, this usage is offered as an alternative to moral theories centred on notions of law. What kind of character would we expect in a virtuous person? This question assumes that there is a universal description of the truly human which is already in some sense implicitly known. There is therefore the same danger of idealization as in law-based theories, especially as this form of discourse is largely innocent of modern psychology (Hauerwas, 1981).

CHARISMATIC RENEWAL
A twentieth-century movement found across the denominations that seeks renewal by recovering the presence of the Spirit as its proponents believe it to have been in the churches of the New Testament.
Although many centuries within Christian history have witnessed revivals – of ritual, tradition, devotion to saints, pilgrimage, liturgy or spirituality – 'charismatic renewal' is arguably the largest and most global of them, perhaps influencing up to one-fifth of the world's Christian populaton. Primarily a twentieth-century phenomenon (and arguably entirely post the Second World War), it

has tended to concentrate on the 'charismatic' gifts of the Holy Spirit identified in Acts and the writings of Paul (e.g. 1 Cor. 12.8–10). These include speaking in tongues, deliverance, healing, prophecy and miracles. Charismatic renewal has undoubtedly grown out of Pentecostalism, but earlier influences may include Edward Irving and Charles Finney from the nineteenth century. Charismatic renewal, understood as a movement, has affected virtually all the major Christian denominations worldwide. It has also spawned new churches and denominations, many of whom believe themselves to be 'restoring' the principles and powers of the original Apostolic age (Walker, 1995). In the history of charismatic renewal, it is now commonplace to distinguish it from Pentecostalism, insofar as most of those within the movement have tended to remain within their denominations, thereby hoping to 'revive' them.

The character of charismatic renewal defies generalization. The phenomenon expresses itself differently from country to country, and from denomination to denomination. The boundaries between Pentecostalism and charismatic renewal in Protestant and Roman Catholic churches in South America are not as apparent as they are in Western Europe. The type of influence charismatic renewal generates in a typical evangelical Church of England congregation is likely to be quite different from that of any neighbouring Baptist church.

Those involved within charismatic renewal would see the focus on new types of praise, spiritual gifts, with manifestations of epiphenomenal and ecclesial power as the key marks of the movement. Critics have tended to emphasize the pastoral problems that may be linked to an overemphasis on rational or social abrogation (in order to experience the liberation of praise), which may be more cathartic than spiritual. They also point to the problems associated with stressing an arbitrary list of 'gifts of the Spirit' over and against tradition or reasoning, and giving undue prominence to power-related phenomena as a 'sign' that God is both demonstrably and conclusively present or immediate (Butler, 1990).

Despite the enormous influence of charismatic renewal in the latter half of the twentieth century, its future looks increasingly fragmented at the turn of the millennium. A number of studies indicate that the volatile nature of charisma makes institutionalization unpredictable. Equally, the attractiveness of the movement lies in its immediacy, and in the aspiration of access to power. Some charismatic groups have become communitarian (popular in the 1970s), others millenarian, sectarian, esoteric, libertarian, postmodern, post-evangelical or post-charismatic. The lasting legacy of charismatic renewal may be that it has become an acceptable ecclesiastical prefix in recent years, joining 'high', 'liberal', 'catholic' and other titles. This suggests that, at the very moment of its inculcation into many churches and denominations, its institutionalization and routinization also arrive. This perhaps indicates that the charismatic 'movement', like many kinds of revival before it, has already done its main work, and will be a more diffuse force within the mainstream denominations in the twenty-first century. [Martyn Percy]

CHILD ABUSE
See: ABUSE, CHILD

CHILD PSYCHOLOGY
See: APPLIED PSYCHOLOGY

CHILDHOOD
The period of human development from birth to maturity.
Childhood in Western culture spans the age range from birth to puberty, although adolescents, especially those in the younger age group from thirteen to sixteen, continue to be dependent upon their parents in many respects. From an adult perspective they can still be regarded as children. Broadly speaking, it is useful to consider childhood in phases: infancy, the pre-school years, latency (which corresponds approximately to the years spent at primary school from age five to eleven), puberty and early adolescence.

1. *Infancy.* The first period of childhood, infancy, begins at birth, although it can be argued that the foetus has a capacity for experience in the womb which begins to shape the personality. The new-born infant is dependent for its survival upon a caring adult, usually the mother. It is a widely held view, supported by extensive research evidence, that the experiences of a baby in the first months of life are highly significant in terms of future development. It is well known that babies and small children need the consistent, loving attention and care of their parents (or parent) if they are to grow

up with an inner sense of value. Some writers on infancy have taken the view that the mother, or permanent mother-substitute, should stay at home with her baby throughout the period of infancy if healthy emotional development is given the priority it deserves. This may not be possible for many reasons, economic reality being one. But it is clear that the human infant is vulnerable and totally dependent upon caring adult attention for a prolonged period of time. The baby only gradually moves on from the safety of an intimate one-to-one relationship to a sense of relative autonomy. The desire to explore and master the world around becomes stronger and heralds the toddler phase.

2. *The pre-school years.* The toddler period of childhood is characterized in healthy development by an increase in the sense of individual identity, distinct and separate from the parents, yet still in constant and intimate relation to them. This phase can be conceptualized in the context of the young child gaining an increasing sense of mastery over his or her world: they can move independently and rapidly gain skills from walking to running, climbing and exploring the physical universe. Cognitive skills develop at a rapid rate, evidenced in language acquisition. Toilet training is usually achieved by the beginning of this period, as is the capacity to feed themselves. When this urge to gain control over the world is thwarted, as when a parent says a firm 'no' to demands, the child's frustration can be intense and loudly expressed in tantrums. The years from two to five are a time when the young child will experience powerful emotions and will need help from parents in learning to manage extreme feelings of anger and jealousy. The latter can be provoked by the birth of a sibling, when the young child is usurped from the position of being the first and only child. Learning to manage anger and jealousy is integral to development in the toddler years. Successful negotiation of this period relies on the understanding of the parents and the provision by them of firm boundaries. This enables small children to develop the capacity to tolerate these strong feelings in themselves and in others as they grow up. The Oedipus complex, a term coined by Freud (1905), comes to the foreground in this phase, as the male child struggles with strong feelings towards his parents as a couple. A successful negotiation of the Oedipus complex

involves the child coming to terms with the reality of his parents' sexual life, an intimate relationship between them from which he is excluded. Cognitive and emotional development proceed rapidly in a conducive environment, one in which the parents continue to love and protect their child, yet encourage curiosity and exploration. Gradually small children move towards a position in which they feel secure enough within themselves to spend many hours of the week away from the family in school.

3. *Latency*. The latency period, according to classical Freudian theory, spans the years when children in Western culture attend primary education. This period culminates in the beginning of puberty. From the Freudian point of view, the latency years are characterized by repression. This implies a relatively quiet period in which intense emotions are 'latent'. This enables children to make friends, acquire a vast amount of new knowledge, play organized co-operative games which are bound by rules, and develop social skills. Children usually become involved in hobbies and activities, especially those which involve swapping and collecting. This is a world of social interaction outside of the family home, with peers and with other adults. It requires compromise and conformity, yet it can be argued that 'repression' in the Freudian sense can be a misleading term, implying a dampening down of the strong impulses and emotional needs of early childhood. In reality, children in the latency period often have rich imaginations, and the deep emotional ties to the parents continue. If parental love and support is withdrawn during these formative years, children can suffer serious emotional problems. Melanie Klein (1921), a pioneer of psychoanalytic work with children, writes about the rich internal world of childhood that underlies all aspects of observable behaviour.

4. *Puberty and early adolescence*. Childhood comes to a close in some respects during the pubertal years and early adolescence. This is a complex transitional period and children have to encompass changes in their bodies and in their emotional states which can for some be overwhelming. The peer group takes on increasing importance as young people strive towards finding an identity which is distinct from that of being a child in relation to the parents.

When engaging in pastoral work with adults it can be useful to remember that infantile, childlike and adolescent parts of the personality coexist with more adult and sophisticated ways of functioning in everyone. [*Lynda Miller*]

CHILDLESSNESS
The absence of children in a relationship or community.

The widespread availability of reliable methods of birth control has brought about significant shifts in the management of, and hence attitudes to, human fertility in the industrialized West. It would be rare, for example, to hear a sexually active single woman who had never conceived or carried a child to term described as 'childless', more rarely still a single (presumed fertile) man. The predominant assumption would be that they had taken appropriate 'responsible' steps to avoid conception.

The formation of a committed permanent partnership or marriage is, however, commonly taken to signal a readiness to bear, or consider bearing, children at some point. When an explicitly Christian form of marriage is undertaken, this expectation is given the added weight of traditional church teaching in which the bearing and nurture of children is one of the three purposes for which marriage was ordained. Many couples, though, including committed Christians, continue to seek control over their fertility by deciding if, when and how many children they will bear. The pattern is reinforced by: (1) increased educational and employment opportunities for women, with significant numbers of women entering professions formerly thought the preserve of males; (2) an expectation that women will continue to pursue the work for which they have been trained after marriage.

Thus while an established couple's continued childlessness cannot automatically be presumed to be by intent, it is only when they declare themselves to have tried and failed to conceive that direct assistance, pastoral and/or medical becomes appropriate. Pastoral care and thought is, however, appropriate in assessing the unease inherent in and arising from the decision-making process, as experienced both by the individuals concerned and the communities in which they are situated.

The difficulties of combining career and family life should not be minimized and there is evidence, official and anecdotal, to suggest these difficulties can be so overwhelming as to appear to offer no real alternative to continued childlessness. Nor should the additional burdens, psychological and material, placed upon women in this situation be underestimated. With responsibility for childcare still falling mainly upon mothers, the female partner is most likely to have her working life and earning power curtailed and/or disrupted. Given too the finiteness of female fertility (unlike that of men, who can father children well into old age), they experience greater anxiety about delaying conception – the 'biological clock' syndrome.

Additional pressures can be brought to bear by: (1) friends and family: parental disappointment in the non-appearance of grandchildren is a commonly reported phenomenon; and (2) by the wider church and society, where concern is expressed about the declining birth rate. The average number of children born to European women has dropped from 2.6 in the early 1960s to around 1.54 at the end of the twentieth century. This has led some to equate chosen childlessness with hostility – e.g. Pope John Paul II's reference at the time of the 1994 Cairo Conference on population control to a 'culture of death'. More general fears for the future of traditional marriage can become fastened onto the childless: doubts about how 'Christian' a childless (whether intentionally so or not) marriage can be continue to be expressed by church leaders.

The decline in birthrates is by no means worldwide and the most significant falls (below replacement level) have occurred among groups whose options, professionally and in terms of access to effective birth-control, have expanded most rapidly, i.e. the middle classes of the more prosperous nations. The anomaly of providing incentives to breed for one section of society while promoting population control among the world's majority needs to be more openly and critically acknowledged. [Susan Dowell]

CHILDREN, CHURCH WORK WITH
The education and nurture of children (usually under 12 or 14 years) by the Christian Church.
For many churches, work with children starts at birth with infant baptism or dedication. In the West this may include work with parents and godparents, regular mother-and-toddler services, or the establishing of a church crèche. Initial follow-up may be through the minister, the Sunday school or crèche, the

Mothers' Union, or other suitably appointed person.

The majority of work with children carried out by the Church is now conducted through its Sunday school (sometimes called by other names, e.g. Junior Church), which may be held either on a Sunday or midweek. The emphasis here is on the church rather than the home. Children are taught in small groups, and nurtured into the Christian faith, until they are deemed ready to receive confirmation or adult baptism. At this time the young people join the adult church at worship, though numbers sometimes drop radically as teenage years approach.

Many churches in both the UK and USA have good contacts with members of the uniformed organizations, for example the Scouts and Guides, Brownies or Cub-Scouts. In England, children belonging to these organizations often attend family services. Children may also be encouraged to join other church groups, for example the choir, bell-ringers, Girls/Boys Brigades or the Girls' Friendly Society. All of these organizations continue the work of nurturing the young person in the Christian faith.

In the United Kingdom the different denominations also work with children through their church schools (voluntary-aided and church voluntary-controlled schools). These schools find a parallel in the US in an array of Christian day schools, some directly controlled by denominations and some controlled directly by local churches or by parents. Many clergy in the UK are involved in conducting the daily act of collective worship (i.e. assembly); in creating the religious education syllabus; or in serving on the governing body of a school. Local communities may also be responsible for funding some aspects of their church voluntary-aided school. Accordingly, there is usually a close relationship between church and church school.

Since 1988 an emphasis has been placed on all-age learning and worship within many Anglican church communities as a result of the report *Children in the Way.* The pilgrimage model preferred in this report has been adopted by churches throughout the world, and children are now encouraged to learn alongside adults on their lifelong journey. One result has been the desire to aim the family service at adults as well and the subsequent dropping of the title 'family service' for other names which emphasize the all-age aspect. Another result has been the emphasis on all-age learning, and on ways that adults and children may learn together.

Debate continues over the following: (1) the wisdom of nurturing children apart from their family; (2) the difference between nurture and indoctrination; (3) the question of when a child becomes a full member of the Church; (4) whether children should receive communion before confirmation.

The subject of child protection has become very important to all those working with children. Groups working with children are required to conform with local or national guidelines in order to offer both children and adults greater protection. *[Sharon Swain]*

CHRISM
Oil used in religious ceremonies.
Traditionally the chrism (from the Greek for 'anointing') is a mix of olive oil and balsam which the bishop blesses. It is then used in baptism, confirmation and ordination. The oils are customarily blessed at the chrism mass of Maundy Thursday.

CHRIST
See: JESUS; INCARNATION

CHRONIC ILLNESS
A state of long-lasting ill-health.
Chronic illness leads to a different level of adjustment to that needed for an acute illness. The nature of the illness may bring a variety of losses in its wake, and a grief for what one might have been. This may be reawakened during 'flare-up' of symptoms, or deterioration in function, depending on the body system affected. The most commonly affected are: vision, hearing, breathing (asthma, chronic bronchitis), the nervous system (disseminated sclerosis, Alzheimer's disease, senility, ME, or the epilepsies), the cardio-vascular system (stroke, chronically high blood pressure), the connective tissue (chronic arthritis in its many forms) and chronic forms of mental illness.

Whatever form the illness takes there will be an impact on various aspects of life. There is the dominant theme of uncertainty in that the person may not know how they will feel from one day to the next, what they can plan to achieve or how long they can remain independent. There is an impact on the family in that the illness may impose lifestyle restric-

tions as well as psychological and social effects on the family as a whole.

Age is an important factor. Chronic illness in early life can have marked effects on the person's social and mental development. While some of these effects will be negative, many people seem able to adopt a very positive approach to life and make a significant contribution to the lives of others. The coping strategies that people have developed are important, together with the inner resources which sustain a sense of purpose and existential meaning. A growing body of research shows that a belief system can be significant in predicting how someone will cope with chronic illness (Koenig *et al.*, 2000; King *et al.*, 1999).

Pastorally the support of people with chronic conditions entails providing a reliable, regular and accepting ministry that is able to stay alongside the individual and the family through the peaks and troughs. Platitudes cut no ice and the best teacher is usually the individual with the illness. The fact that there is often no cure need not extinguish hope, provided the hope is realistic. Some chronic conditions may respond well to palliative approaches to symptom management which may provide hope for some control in the person's life. Pain can isolate and make communication difficult. The pastoral carer may need to develop a relationship that can explore ways of relating and communicating at such times, through listening and learning when the pain is reduced or controlled. The individual needs to feel able to say 'go away' as well as 'stay' without offence. Because of the isolating effect of pain the local church, in visiting, can help to mitigate loneliness. However, with an increased number of elderly people who are not mobile, they can quickly drop out of church life. Visiting by the Christian community (not just the ordained members) can provide a vital link, minimize possible deterioration in mental health, and maintain a sense of well-being. *[Peter Speck]*

CHURCH
1. A building for public worship.
2. An ecclesiastical organization.
3. A local gathering of Christians.
1. *Church as a secular term.* In the Roman empire the political and social welfare of cities was organized through meetings of free citizens. The gathering was known as *ecclesia*, which

became the word 'church'. Although such meetings often had religious overtones, *ecclesia* means an assembly of people gathering for ordinary, secular activities. The term *ecclesia* was applied to voluntary associations, early universities, schools of philosophy and rhetoric, patriarchal households, and synagogues. Jewish synagogues were more than places of worship: 'The synagogue is a house of prayer, the place of counsel, "parliament" even the university' (Hoornaert, 1988).

2. *Church in Jewish and early Christian usage.* The synagogue has represented the primary gathering place for Jews from the exile into Babylon, through the time of Christ to the present day. Synagogues are autonomous, each defined by its community and congregation rather than locality and buildings. As a model of *ecclesia* the synagogue was particularly appropriate to communities experiencing persecution and exile, who, in order to maintain distinct identity, might need to regroup and relocate. Two key elements – those of 'family' and 'household' – defined the shape of synagogue practice. Communal activities such as offering prayer, reading scriptures, teaching the patriarchs and prophets, as well as sharing food, were associated with observances such as the sabbath, Passover, and the Feast of the Atonement. Early Christianity seems to have been influenced by synagogue practice, including the formation of household-based churches. The celebration of the common meal and Eucharist was in homes. Such households were composed of landowners, tenants, servants, slaves and sojourners and their respective dependants. Christian gatherings were groups of people who held in common the experience of faith and baptism, in Jesus Christ: 'one began a new life, reorganizing the whole of one's existence in terms of a new project. The whole Christian body took shape and form around the rite of baptism, articulating the whole of its community life in reference to it – its liturgy, the catechumenate and catechesis, its Eucharist, its penance, its fasting and prayers' (Hoornaert, 1988); and for a short while in the earliest days, the sharing of possessions.

3. *Church as organization.* In cities such as Antioch, Rome and Corinth a number of congregations formed and increasingly required organization and co-ordination. Early leadership seems to have been that of apostles and deacons, and later bishops or presbyters. Apostles had the groundbreaking task of

teaching and speaking prophetically in the founding of new faith communities. Deacons were initially called to pastoral service in the early church communities. Early on, however, deacons also assumed a more liturgical role. Bishops, or presbyters, began to oversee groups of congregations, and increasingly directed or presided over church affairs and liturgy. Personal and moral qualities remained important. During the third century, Rome politically reorganized its empire into territories. The Church too began to organize territorially into provinces and dioceses, creating areas of episcopal authority that were often coterminous with government. Constantine the Great (274–337) was the first emperor publicly to espouse Christianity, and he sought to tie church structures into those of the state.

4. *'Catholic.'* The term 'catholic' was first applied to the Church by St Ignatius of Antioch in 110 CE: 'Where the bishop is, there the multitude gathers, just as where Christ is, there is the catholic church.' The word 'catholic' is from the Greek, meaning 'full', 'entire', or 'throughout the whole'. Churches such as the Roman Catholic, Orthodox, Anglican and Lutheran all describe themselves as 'catholic', although the use of the term has come to be equated with the spread of Christianity throughout the world. The twentieth century has witnessed the expansion of the Christian Church in its various forms into all parts of the world. This expansion mainly reflects historical divisions. The Orthodox Church, based on Constantinople and divided from the Roman Church in 1054, is strongest in Greece, Russia and the Slavic countries. Missionary enterprise has made Roman Catholicism the largest communion. The Reformations in Europe, between the fourteenth and seventeenth centuries, created a Protestant tradition reflected variously in Lutheranism, Calvinism and, in Britain, Anglicanism. Anglicanism defined itself as both Catholic and Reformed. Nonconformist churches, such as Congregationalists, Baptists, Mennonites and eventually Methodists, and dissenting groups such as Quakers, became so defined in England because of their refusal to conform to the doctrines or jurisdiction of the Established Church.

5. *Church unity.* The World Council of Churches was formed in 1948 as a sign of a growing desire for a recovery of visible unity among the churches. It is today composed of

the mainstream traditions within Western Protestantism, the Orthodox Church, and significant numbers of new churches, notably those within the Pentecostal tradition. The Roman Catholic Church is a full member of the Faith and Order Commission, but not of the World Council itself.

The Christian Church continues to be innovative. This has been marked in Protestantism by the influence of evangelical and pentecostal movements, and in Roman Catholicism and other catholic churches by the formation of basic ecclesial communities, particularly among the poor.

The pastoral activity of a church depends to a large degree on its self-understanding. A gathered community, for example, will tend to offer care and support chiefly to its members. Churches in the Catholic and Orthodox traditions have been accustomed to seeing all citizens as 'members' and therefore those to whom pastoring is available. The former have tended to create self-sustaining pastoral systems; the latter to look first to the authorized minister or priest. One effect of the ecumenical movement has been to draw churches with different ecclesiological traditions closer together in social and pastoral work, so that the differences are less obvious. [Peter Price]

CHURCH MEMBERSHIP
See: MEMBERSHIP OF A CHURCH

CHURCH PLANTING
A mission strategy involving a number of committed members of one congregation choosing to become the nucleus for another.
In a non-technical sense church planting has been a key element in Christian history from the earliest days, through the Middle Ages, the nineteenth-century world missionary expansion, and the endeavours of patrons and benefactors, offering church buildings in new housing areas over the past two centuries. Church planting has been more specifically identified in evangelical initiatives of recent decades. Two complementary elements are: (1) the transfer of part of a congregation into a new place deliberately to bring Christian faith and renewed spirituality to others; (2) the setting up of new faith communities to further the mission of the Church to bring to reality God's Kingdom in different geographical and cultural contexts.

CIVIL RELIGION
Basic beliefs that hold a society together and have their own seriousness and integrity.
Rousseau listed four dogmas of 'civil religion' that were essential to social harmony: the existence of God, the life to come, the reward of virtue and punishment of vice, and the prohibition of religious intolerance. Bellah (1967) used the term 'civil religion' to identify 'an elaborate and well institutionalized civil religion in America [which] ... has its own seriousness and integrity and requires the same care in understanding that any other religion does'.

Bellah himself was careful to distinguish civil religion from simple nationalism. So at its best civil religion is not merely a celebration of the American collectivity or thanksgiving for the blessings which that society has received (or bestowed). Civil religion is capable of standing in prophetic judgement on the extent to which the nation is, or is not, fulfilling its true calling. Thus, any valuation of America as another 'Israel' becomes similarly provisional: what is 'chosen', can be changed. Distinguishing between 'religion' and 'Christianity', for instance, he insisted upon the continuing importance of 'civility'. So he was able to focus attention upon the link between society and religion without, in the view of some, disturbing the constitutional separation of Church and State. Bellah analyses Presidential inaugural addresses as examples of formal, societal, 'civic theology' (Greeley, 1973). Others put a lower value on civil religion. Outside the USA, the concept has also proved fruitful for pastoral analysis. [Edward Bailey]

CLASS
A type of social stratification measured as occupation, but also income, lifestyle, status and power.
Class is a phenomenon of industrial capitalism that still elicits debate between functionalists and conflict theorists. It has been affected by contemporary developments, including the changing nature of employment in post-industrial societies, the decline of work as the determinant of attitudes and identity, and the growing importance of women in the workforce. Is class now outmoded? Employment still largely determines life chances. Attitude surveys also still reveal class as central for understanding social differences and inspiring social justice. As an issue,

therefore, it will remain central for Christian social thought and practice.

CLIENT
A person who contracts to receive pastoral counselling.

Calling a person who receives pastoral counselling a client implies a certain kind of relationship between that person and the pastoral counsellor. A client contracts formally for the services of a professional and typically pays for those services. The relationship between client and professional is narrowly defined and focused, and often governed by codes of professional ethics and legal statutes. In pastoral counselling, as in other counselling professions, laws and ethical codes may require that clients give informed consent to any treatment they receive, that all information revealed by clients in counselling sessions be bound by standards of confidentiality, and that relationships between clients and counsellors outside the contracted counselling relationship be minimized.

This terminology of client and counsellor is the dominant language in secular counselling and mental health disciplines other than psychiatry. As pastoral counselling has adopted this language it has signalled its emergence as a speciality within the counselling professions. It has also differentiated itself from pastoral care and other forms of pastoral ministry that do not involve formal, contractual client–counsellor relationships.

Other possible terms for one who seeks pastoral care and/or pastoral counselling include 'counsellee' or 'patient'. 'Counsellee' refers to one who seeks advice or counsel. It implies an ongoing relationship rather than a one-off conversation, but does not necessarily connote the high level of definition and focus entailed by a client's relationship with a professional. By contrast, the medical term 'patient' spotlights the illness or dysfunction of the person seeking 'healing', 'cure' or 'treatment'. Its connotations are foreign to pastoral ministry, and its use outside the medical profession is not recommended.

Although in most cases it is perfectly obvious who the client is, confusion about the identity of the client can arise, especially when the person receiving counselling services is not the one paying for them. When parents bring children to therapy, for instance, questions of goal-setting, confidentiality and informed consent become more complicated. Pastoral counsellors who are paid by judicatories to do psychological evaluations of candidates for ordination may also face complications in identifying the client and the rights and responsibilities of all parties involved. In these sorts of complicated situations counsellors do well to clarify in advance the nature of their relationship with each party. [Douglas M. Thorpe]

CLIENT-CENTRED THERAPY
A non-directive approach to counselling which is warmly affective.

Client-centred therapy is especially associated with the work of Carl Rogers – indeed it is sometimes known as Rogerian. It is marked by a positive regard for the client. It has been influential on the Church's pastoral ministry, making clergy and ministers in particular more aware of the person with whom they are dealing.

CLINICAL PASTORAL EDUCATION (CPE)
An interdenominational (interfaith) approach to professional pastoral care education.

Clinical pastoral education (CPE) brings together clergy and laity and students of theological education for the purpose of supervised encounter with persons in crisis. Students develop new awarenesses of themselves and of the needs of others out of an intensive involvement with persons in need. Students of CPE are encouraged to reflect theologically and dynamically on the nature of the human condition so as to better understand and respond to a diversity of human situations. An understanding of professional interdisciplinary team work is stressed in CPE training as a way to bring co-operation in ministry with other professional disciplines.

Anton T. Boisen, Richard C. Cabot and Helen Flanders Dunbar were early leaders in the CPE movement that began in 1925. The early organization of Boisen, Cabot and Dunbar, situated in Boston, was called the Council for Clinical Training of Theological Students (later to become simply the Council for Clinical Training (CCT)). In 1931, a critical break between Boisen and Cabot led to the geographical movement to New York City and, subsequently, the organization of the Cabot-inspired Institute of Pastoral Care (IPC) in Boston. The latter took a more skills-approach to training of ministers whereas Boisen's followers were generally more focused on the development of the person of the minister. Boisen's emphasis was also anti-textual, a posture revealed in his focus on the 'living human documents'. Boisen's approach was more inductive, emphasizing the importance of the client setting the agenda in the pastoral conversation and the trainee setting the agenda and objectives for learning. Both New York and Boston centres relied on learning borrowed from psychology, especially psychoanalytic theory.

During the 1940s and 1950s, Lutheran and Southern Baptists created their own denominational clinical training group, competing to some extent with the CCT and the IPC. In the late 1960s these four groups united into one organization to form the Association for Clinical Pastoral Education, Inc. (ACPE). Meanwhile the pastoral counsellors split off to form their own organization, the American Association of Pastoral Counselors (AAPC), and the Roman Catholics created the National Association of Catholic Chaplains in order to ensure that clinical training included appropriate Catholic teachings. Clinically trained institutional chaplains formed the College of Chaplains, later to be renamed Association of Professional Chaplains. Several other smaller groups organized around clinical pastoral practice. During the 1980s the ACPE sought and received endorsement from the US Department of Education for recognition of its training programmes as graduate theological education.

In 1990 the College of Pastoral Supervision and Psychotherapy (CPSP) was formed by a committee of 15 persons, most of them significant leaders in the ACPE and AAPC. They were reacting to evidence of the dehumanizing bureaucratization of the old organizations and seeking to create a covenantal community based on respect for persons and attention to theology as well as psychology. CPSP is structured as a grass-roots community, with power and authority vested in small groups and a Governing Council that holds the small groups together around a Covenant and Constitution. CPSP certifies pastoral counsellors, pastoral psychotherapists and clinical pastoral supervisors. All certification must be renewed annually, based on a continuing relationship with a peer group.

CPE is offered in diverse settings, such as hospitals, jails, prisons, hospices, missions, mental health clinics, and parish churches. Trainees in clinical pastoral care and counselling bring case material for small group consultation sessions with the intention of deepening their pastoral skills and self-awareness. Group and individual supervision of ministry events is mixed with interdisciplinary interaction of other service-care professionals. Clinical and theological reflection is the centrepiece of learning about how to minister to the human condition. Formal and informal didactic seminars focus on the integration of practical/theological issues with clinical/dynamic understandings of assessment and intervention strategies in ministry. Trainees learn by doing ministry under close group and individual supervision.
[*Foy Richey/Raymond Lawrence*]

CLINICAL PSYCHOLOGY
See: APPLIED PSYCHOLOGY

CLINICAL THEOLOGY
A pastoral discipline which correlates psychology and theology.
Clinical theology was originated by Frank Lake, medical missionary and psychiatrist, in the 1950s. He was inspired by the Swiss theologian Emil Brunner, who directed him towards the dynamics of the adult Jesus, portrayed in St John's Gospel 'for a model of man's understanding of himself. . . acceptable to a Christian theology'. The usual scientific assumption is to take an average of human behaviour as the norm. Alternatively, 'one must, as an act of faith, set up a certain pattern as normal, and proceed to examine existing human specimens in the light of it. The clinical theology model of interpersonal relationships – the dynamic cycle – regards the adult Jesus as the norm.

Lake died in 1982. His book *Clinical Theology* (1966) contains the essence of the discipline and shows how responsible pastors must be attentive to primal feelings, both in themselves and others. He also reported how memories in need of healing can be traced to early life experiences including the pre-verbal and those of the womb. Clinical theology was defined by Lake as 'substantively theology, putting faith, ultimately, not in human wisdom but in the love and power of God, yet meticulously observant of the sound practice of psychiatry and psychotherapy'. 'Clinical' is not used in a primarily medical sense but rather in that of being attentive to, and learning from, the holistic needs of a troubled person. 'Theology' means the intention to be explicit about assumptions, values and meanings of Christian faith. Respect for faith other than Christian is implied. Clinical theology, with its emphasis on an experiential dimension and its aim to improve pastoral practice by developing self-awareness, was for many in Great Britain the entry to this dimension of pastoral studies. It has had less impact, however, in the USA.

The practice of clinical theology is a Christian service of accepting unconditionally other people, listening at depth, and engaging in pastoral dialogue which believes that God both speaks and hears through his Son. The pastoral person who believes that God's love is efficacious listens long and hard to the person who has no experience of love but who deeply desires to love and be loved. 'If we believe in truth, we shall need to listen at one and the same time right down to the truth of this desperate person's history, and right down to the Truth himself . . . crucified upon his cross' (Lake 1981). [Peter J. van de Kasteele]

CLOSED SYSTEM
A system that ignores the significance of its environment for the way that an organization functions.
A system is described as closed when it seems to function without reference to its context. This contrasts with an open system, in which the interchange between a system and its environment is taken into account in its organization and functioning. Some have regarded religious institutions as by definition closed because there is no output: belief is open-ended. But this has been challenged by some research that has examined the functioning of churches in society. They can be seen as open systems (Reed, 1978; Shapiro and Carr, 1992; Carr, 1997).

CO-COUNSELLING
A form of mutual self-help in which two individuals take on, in turn, to be the counsellor and the client, with the client always in charge.
Co-counsellors join a fundamentals class to learn to listen and respond helpfully, in pairs. They then go on to counsel as many different partners as possible. Normally there are rules about socializing outside the co-counselling relationship, to preserve safe boundaries. The movement was formed in reaction to conventional counselling, in which the counsellor holds the balance of power, being identified as the 'expert' who is paid. The best known

form of co-counselling is re-evaluation co-counselling, started in the USA.

CO-DEPENDENCE
The painful reality experienced by spouses, children and friends of an alcoholic or an addict to another form of substance dependency.
The concept of co-dependence evolved gradually in the last quarter of the twentieth century as a specific term in the field of chemical dependency. It attempts to name the complex reality that an alcoholic or an addict is not the only person affected by her or his disease process. Close family, including spouses and children, along with friends and associates, are also deeply affected.

Some time after Alcoholics Anonymous emerged in the 1940s as a self-help group for alcoholics, persons living in close relationship to alcoholics began forming new self-help groups under the name Al-Anon. In these groups the term 'enabler' was often used to describe the person, usually the spouse, whose energy was focused on changing the alcoholic, yet who, in covert ways, was perhaps helping to support the destructive habits of the addicted partner. It was not until the late 1970s, however, that the term co-dependence surfaced to describe this syndrome. [Ron Baard]

CODES OF CONDUCT
Lists of statements which codify the expectations of a group concerning the conduct of group members.
All groups, from families to nations, develop implicit or explicit codes of conduct. The more organized and formal the group, the more likely these codes are to be set in 'tablets of stone' – laws which must be obeyed. Failure to keep to a code usually leads to the imposition of sanctions. There are certain situations when it is especially important to establish clear codes of conduct: (1) when a group, such as a new nation, needs to establish solidarity among its members; (2) for groups that provide services which care for or protect individuals, to reassure those who seek members' services of their trustworthiness; (3) to make manifest the high moral calling of those who follow faith or a vocation.

In pastoral situations it is clearly important to set and maintain high standards of conduct. If a pastoral role is set in a professional context it is often easier to be clear:

churches set guidelines for their pastors, professional associations set codes of conduct for their members. Services are monitored and complaints investigated. If the pastoral worker has an informal role in the community, the group may rely on the individual's personal integrity to ensure good behaviour. It could, however, be argued that the looser boundaries of such a role make it *more* important to establish a clear code of conduct. Good will is not always sufficient to guarantee good behaviour.

There are inevitable tensions between different concepts of the proper ethical basis for conduct. Some codes are based on the assumption that moral law is universal and eternal (laid down by God), and should be obeyed without question. Codes based on this premise literally lay down the law (for example, the Ten Commandments). A righteous individual is seen as someone who conforms, who behaves as the law dictates. Other codes of conduct see the basis of moral standards as personal integrity. Codes based on this premise list the characteristics of the virtuous individual and affirm their freedom to act as their conscience dictates. The focus is on right attitudes and intentions in the care-provider and on the rights of the individual. 'You have heard that it was said, "You shall love your neighbour and hate your enemy" but I say to you, Love your enemies and pray for those who persecute you' (Matt. 5.43–44).

Ideally, as St Paul teaches, the law and the spirit inform each other and lead to right action. Since we do not live in an ideal world, we need to build in safeguards, to guard against codes of conduct protecting the interests of the carers at the expense of those of the recipients of care, and to balance the rights of the individual with responsibilities to society. This is particularly important in our pluralist society where there is little agreement about the proper ethical basis for conduct. *[Val Potter]*

COGNITION
The faculty, process and product of knowing, including conscious thinking, problem-solving, imagining and reflecting.
Philosophers explore the nature of cognition by studying the relation between thought and word. The pastoral relevance of cognition arises from the interest of psychologists, who are increasingly adopting a cognitive approach to human development (leading to major revisions of Piaget's theories) and to language, and applying cognitive models to a range of psychological disorders. Most relevantly, cognitive explanations of distorted thinking in depression, for example, have led to a set of cognitive therapy and cognitive behaviour therapy techniques of proven effectiveness.

COGNITIVE DISSONANCE
A theory that assumes that a drive to maximize consistency between two or more cognitions will press for the reduction of inconsistency.
This social psychological theory was developed by Leon Festinger (1957). There is a natural drive to maximize consistency between two or more cognitions, so the existence of inconsistency motivates a person to reduce the inconsistency by harmonizing the cognitions. The theory predicts that engaging in behaviour counter to a person's attitudes creates dissonance to change the attitudes so they are consistent with the behaviour. The theory can also incorporate thoughts and beliefs, and has been important because of some counter-intuitive predictions in fields such as racial prejudice.

COGNITIVE THERAPY
A clinical intervention based on the theory that emotional disorders result from negative and distorted thoughts (cognitions).
Concerned with conscious thought processes, the goal of cognitive therapy is to help persons become aware of how thoughts, perceptions and motivations collectively influence their emotions and functioning. It seeks to ameliorate distortions of reality by helping one understand and evaluate one's own thoughts as they relate to the 'objective' world. This allows negative thoughts to be replaced with more realistic and adaptive ones. Cognitive therapy is best described as a 'school of thought' rather than as a particular theory, with the work of Alfred Adler and Aaron T. Beck being seminal. Therapists may vary with regard to specific clinical techniques and emphases. However, all cognitive therapy assumes that both what and how one thinks greatly influence one's emotions and behaviours. Cognitive therapy teaches one to apply the techniques of thought identification, understanding and modification on one's own. Thus, a disciplined monitoring of

thought processes and corresponding emotions, and the capacity for self-reflection and analysis, are required. An approach that can be used with persons aged ten to adulthood, it has proved particularly effective with depression, self-defeating thoughts, low self-esteem, anxiety and panic disorders (Freeman *et al.* 1990).

Proponents of this approach cite the following as its strengths (Gurman and Messer, 1995). (1) It is cross-culturally relevant as the focus is not on understanding a predetermined thought content but rather on understanding thought processes and their relationship to emotional functioning. (2) Empirical studies have shown it an effective treatment which often results in more enhanced functioning than that prompted by other psychotherapies and even medication. (3) Its focus on preparing one for ongoing work after conclusion of therapy is believed to be responsible for a lower rate of recurrent problems. (4) It is intentionally goal-directed and can be utilized in time-limited therapy.

For those contending that unconscious drives take precedence over conscious thoughts, cognitive therapy's focus on thoughts, perceptions and motivations puts the cart before the horse and thus misses the root cause of a particular problem. Thus, cognitive therapy is said to treat symptoms of a problem and not the problem itself. What is needed instead, it is argued, is a focus on the unconscious drives giving rise to particular thoughts, perceptions and motivations. There is, however, increasing rapprochement between these two approaches.

Cognitive therapy is relevant for pastoral studies in that its empirical bent and goal-directedness allows for progress to be measured by one receiving therapy. This fosters a feeling of empowerment and accomplishment, and in turn promotes a sense of hope consistent with the heart of the Christian message. Since these developments are utilized after therapy ends, such hopefulness also may be a source of lasting recovery. This approach further lends itself to the time-limited work most suitable for the parish setting. It also may be used in conjunction with prayer and appeals to Scripture. These may serve as means for disciplined self-examination in light of God's promises to and desires for humankind, thereby fostering a faith and optimism conducive to ameliorating problems. [*Allan Hugh Cole Jr*]

COHABITATION
A primary intimate relation between an unmarried heterosexual couple who also share a home.

Cohabitation has enjoyed a complex history. Before the Reformation, cohabitation and marriage were not distinguished by civil law because marriage did not enjoy the kind of public legal status it has today (Witte, 1997). Prior to the introduction of civil marriage in the UK in 1837, cohabitation probably continued to be the norm for those who could not afford the high costs of marriage. Up to the beginning of the twentieth century, cohabitation between couples intending to marry was socially sanctioned under the rubric of 'betrothal'. For centuries, betrothal was recognized by Church and society alike as a legitimate arena for sexual relations and living together, so long as betrothal included the intention of marriage (Thatcher, 1999).

The 1950s and 1960s saw an increasing valuation of marriage itself, and especially youthful marriage. Dormer (1992) calls it a 'golden age' of marriage: 'rarely have marriage, sex and childbearing been so tightly bound together'; 'premarital sexual activity, extra-marital childbearing and cohabitation fell to very low levels.'

However, between 1979 and 1987 in the UK there was a threefold increase in the number of women cohabiting (Kiernan and Wicks, 1990). In the US, there are now nearly six million cohabiting households, an eightfold increase since 1970 (Waite and Gallagher, 2000). In both countries, nearly half of all couples cohabit prior to marriage, up from around 7% in the early 1970s. Some long-term social and cultural changes are probably responsible for these trends, including the relative emancipation of women, the increasing availability of contraceptive methods, the gradual improvement in the legal status of children born out of wedlock, rising affluence, and greater emphasis on transience and freedom of individual choice.

Currently, two broad kinds of cohabitation can be identified: marital and non-marital cohabitation. The former involves an intention to marry and is close to more traditional forms of betrothal. The latter does not involve an intention to marry, being either a temporary arrangement or a long-term alternative to marriage. Some family researchers view cohabitation among the young as now an institutionalized part of the mating process (Kiernan and Estaugh, 1993). Other researchers claim cohabitation is not generally the healthiest arrangement for any children that may be involved, and view the experimental nature of non-marital cohabitation as harmful to any subsequent marriage (Popenoe and Whitehead, 1999).

The churches have responded to cohabitation in a variety of ways. The Roman Catholic Church condemns cohabitation as a 'free union' akin to adultery, divorce, polygamy, and incest. The Presbyterian Church of the USA, on the other hand, welcomes cohabitors openly into its membership. In *Something to Celebrate* (1995), the Church of England seeks out something of a middle ground in which cohabitation is counter to the ideal commitment of sexual unions but still treated sympathetically as an understandable aspect of modern life. A truly useful theology of cohabitation would connect it to the intention to marry, perhaps by reclaiming older traditions of betrothal and ideas of marriage's positive and sacred possibilities. [*Sue Walrond-Skinner and John Wall*]

COLLECTIVE UNCONSCIOUS
The primordial archetypes, patterns and images buried deep in the psyche of each individual and common to humanity.
The term was introduced by Carl Jung, for whom the psyche consists of three subsystems: the conscious, having to do with intelligence and mental activity; the personal unconscious, which consists of repressed and neglected elements that are acquired; and the all-important collective unconscious, which is inherited, innate and morally, intellectually and aesthetically neutral. The archetypes of the collective unconscious (like the myths of creation) are inherited predispositions, which are powerfully influential in human behaviour.

COLLUSION
A relationship in which those involved unconsciously conspire to avoid confronting some aspect of that relationship.
The term describes an unconscious joining between two parties around a shared need. For example, an abuser and the abused person may unwittingly collude in sustaining a relationship that brings both some gratification. Such collusion is less obvious but is also possible between client and therapist, minister and congregation, or priest and penitent.

Consultancy, by drawing people's attention to unconscious collusion, may enable them to break the cycle of such behaviour.

COMMON RELIGION
Religious beliefs and practices that are not expressed through a prevailing religious institution.
'Common religion' means neither 'common to society as a whole' nor 'common among many members of society', but 'of the common people' (Williams, 1951). The phrase 'civil religion' has largely superseded it (Towler, 1974). It refers to those pointers to transcendence that are often associated with fate or luck. Orthodoxy tends to ignore (or even tries to dismiss) these as mere superstitions. 'Common religion' technically differs from 'folk religion' and 'popular religion' by its interpretation of the status of such phenomena. It draws attention to the lack of control over belief exercised by religious bodies.

COMMUNAL CHURCH
See: CONGREGATION; PARISH

COMMUNE
A small intentional community usually pursuing some form of alternative lifestyle.
A historical phenomenon reflected, among other contexts, in the life of the Christian Church down the centuries, communes were given a new impetus by the hippie movement beginning in the USA in the late 1960s. They have developed in secular and Christian form worldwide since then, with their members taking up a diversity of concerns: alternative forms of family life, ecological self-sufficiency, healing and therapy, arts and crafts, anti-war protests, care for the marginalized, radical approaches to spirituality, and more. Much networking occurs but there is little overall organizational form.

COMMUNICATION
The act of imparting, transmitting, disseminating or sharing information, messages or meaning.
Communication lies at the centre of human experience. It takes place at a number of levels.

1. *Intra-personal communication.* This is sometimes described colloquially as 'talking to ourselves'. Past and present experiences of words, images and events can shape this

internal dialogue. The communication process within the individual not only provides resources for, but also creates barriers to, spiritual growth, healing and change.

2. *Inter-personal communication*. This refers to basic human interaction between individuals. In face-to-face encounters non-verbal signals may speak more loudly than the specific words being used. Eye contact, gesture, touch, as well as tone of voice, contribute to the communication of meaning. The art of comprehensive listening, which is sensitive to both verbal and non-verbal communication, is foundational for pastoral care. The development of the telephone, portable phone and fax has complicated and extended interpersonal communication. These inventions raise questions about the importance of physical presence for pastoral care and counselling.

3. *Group communication*. This can take place in groups of varying sizes. In both small and large group meetings, non-verbal signs may also point to the levels of involvement and feelings of inclusion among all the participants. In many church settings, small groups such as Bible study and discussion groups supplement larger gatherings for worship and other public meetings. Smaller groups operate with different communicative dynamics from larger gatherings, and can encourage interactive, vulnerable and honest communication. Larger gatherings in church settings are liable to focus attention on one speaker (e.g. the preacher) or one act (e.g. holy communion). They may encourage attempts to communicate and interact with God through prayer, singing, communal silence, listening and taste. The layout of the church, the dress and the form of the 'liturgy' employed by those involved in leading the services communicate as much as the words spoken.

4. *Mass communication*. This is normally communication with many or multiple audiences. The rapid evolution of mass communication techniques in the last hundred years has transformed how humanity communicates. The invention and development of the radio, phone, television and video has transformed work and leisure practices. Digitalization is leading to the convergence of these technologies through the use of computers, which are connected by the telephone, fibre-optic cables and communication satellites. The subsequent growth of the Internet and interactive television provoke new ethical dilemmas concerning censorship and the control of information. Barriers of space

and time have been also eroded through the ability to communicate instantaneously across what Marshall McLuhan famously described as the 'global village'. These transformations raise a range of vital issues for all those involved in pastoral studies.

Alongside these technological developments, communication breakdown remains a regular experience. This occurs in intimate relationships, in local groups and between nations. Micro-communication problems in families are still paralleled by international macro-communication difficulties. Technological excellence in communication has not prevented marital breakdown, violence in the home and community, isolation of the elderly and infirm, ethnic conflicts and even genocide. Some argue, controversially, that there is a direct causative link between these communication breakdowns and the development of communication media. It is asserted, for instance, that graphic depictions of violence and sexual exploitation on film, video and television encourage, and even directly cause, 'copy-cat' acts of degradation. The ability to form realistic electronically created images has supposedly led to the shattering of traditional values and the polluting of the imagination. From this critical perspective, communication technology has opened a Pandora's box leading to an increase in intrapersonal, interpersonal, group and global communication breakdown. On the basis of this negative view, it is argued that pastoral studies must seek approaches by which to undermine the technological causes of these communication breakdowns.

Such convictions are hotly contested. Opponents argue that this is too simple an analysis, as it ignores the fact that communication breakdown has been part of the human condition since records began. They contend that it is important to acknowledge how the communication technologies have also connected nations, peoples and individuals. These links have highlighted various aspects of the human experience: the plight of disaster-ravaged communities, the suppression of human rights by oppressive regimes and the achievements of pioneers in many fields. The Band-Aid concerts in the mid-1980s, for example, relied upon global communication technology. They raised more than US$110 million for famine relief. On the basis of this more positive view, it is argued that pastoral studies must acknowledge how the sharing and dissemination of information through the electronic mass media can inform, entertain and educate.

A third more judicious approach seeks to make sensible use of the developments in communication technology and to face the continuing reality of breakdowns within human communication. In short, communication technology has the potential not only to complicate, but also enrich the work of pastoral studies. Videos, overhead projectors and multimedia, for example, are now commonly used in theological education, and to a lesser extent in worship. The use of these tools illustrates the growing belief among some faith communities that oral discourse, 'chalk-and-talk' style communication, has limited effectiveness within our communicative context. Some go further and argue that the increasingly audio-visually dominated climate makes activities such as preaching outdated. Recent texts within homiletics have defended this traditional form of communication. They argue instead for the importance of recognizing how listeners used to television presentations now hear oral discourse. The answer is not to replace the pulpit with a video screen. It is rather to create pictures with words, to form visual 'movie-type' scenes in sermons and to encourage the listeners to use their imaginations in recreating vivid images from the biblical texts.

'The Word became flesh' remains a foundational text for an understanding of God's communication and for those involved in the work of reconciliation in intrapersonal, interpersonal, group and mass communication. [*Jolyon Mitchell*]

COMMUNION
See: EUCHARIST

COMMUNITY
1. A group of people living in a locality and sharing a culture.
2. Interdependence within a society.
3. Participation in love of God and neighbour.
These definitions indicate the difficulty of defining the term 'community' in spite of the fact that it is widely used. Many commentators on Western society in the late twentieth century are agreed that the fabric of society is under considerable strain. Symptomatic of this are the failure of both collectivist and individualist approaches to political economics and the breakdown of a sense of belonging to

a common life beyond the bounds of the nuclear family. That is why there is a call in many quarters for the renewal of community, a call associated in recent politics with what has become known as 'communitarianism'. Here, community is understood as 'any voluntary association of people larger than the individual and smaller than the State ... [including] such diverse phenomena as charitable organizations, religious congregations, neighbourhood watch schemes, local race-relations groups and parent-teacher associations' (Sacks, 1995).

In theological perspective, however, community is more than this. Community is that participation in the triune life of God which makes possible truthful, just and enduring encounter between human beings in all their diversity. As such, community is not an end in itself, nor is any model of community given a privileged position. Rather, community is an outworking of something more important: love of God and love of neighbour in a militant communion on earth which will be triumphant in heaven (Ford and Stamps, 1996).

1. *Threats to community*. The factors contributing to the breakdown of our common life are profound and far-reaching. One has to do with the cultural and intellectual revolution of the Enlightenment, with its roots in the Renaissance, the Reformation and the Wars of Religion. In its quest for universal values and objective knowledge, the Enlightenment disparaged epistemologies which gave a privileged place to revelation and tradition. It also disparaged institutions like the Church, the courts and the monarchy, which claimed to mediate revelation and tradition from one generation to the next. It did so in favour of an epistemology based upon the exercise of pure reason by the unencumbered self operating according to the universal principles of scientific method. In the process, it undermined much of what provided the ethos and particularity of both national and local communities, and laid the foundation for the strongly individualistic understandings of the self characteristic of modernity.

A second and related factor has been the loss of a shared sense of what constitutes the common good under the impact of the increasing privatization of morality and religion. Indeed, the very category 'religion' understood as something distinct from the state, the judiciary, the market-place and education, is itself symptomatic of the marginalization of those people, practices and institutions which have in the past contributed significantly to sustaining community life. This is what sociologists refer to as secularization; and a good case can be made for the view that the widespread acceptance of the idea that religion and morality are matters of individual choice related only to personal lifestyle shows how fragile the bonds holding communities together have become.

Another factor is the impact of globalization on national and local economies and on popular culture. Here, the interests and values of international corporations and the 'global village' are so powerful that they are able to transform and even undermine identities, traditions and commitments at more local levels. Thus, unrestrained market forces create huge areas of debt which threaten traditional economies and cause poverty and social breakdown, especially in the new nations of the Third World. Similarly, a massive trade in arms encourages the violence and terrorism so inimical to the peace and stability of communities around the world.

There are other factors as well. In some countries, the life of communities is threatened by the decline of nation-states into ethnic groups whose vulnerability finds expression in outbreaks of ferocious 'ethnic cleansing'. In others it is threatened by the fear and polarization commonly associated with the rise of religious fundamentalism. In the urbanized and industrialized West, analysts point to the deleterious impact on communities of high divorce rates – high residential mobility, long-term unemployment, changes in gender roles and expectations, racial intolerance, increases in crime, and so on. There are, therefore, many grounds for concern and many justifications for positive action.

2. *Building community.* Countering threats to community and building communities which allow all people to attain their full humanity as children of God are central Christian concerns. Indeed, the vocation of Israel according to the Old Testament and of the Church according to the New is so to share in the life and love of God that it becomes the people and the place where the virtues and skills for life together among the nations are known and practised. The truthful and just encounter between human beings in all their diversity which constitutes community is dependent upon true worship of the truthful and justifying God. This means that true community is a gift of divine grace; and its quality as gift means that it is not something which we can presume upon or determine in advance. In the end, it is not a matter of human calculus or rational planning. Like happiness, it often occurs in its most profound forms when and where we least expect it. It occurs when heaven and earth touch: which is why Jesus taught his disciples to pray, 'Thy kingdom come, Thy will be done on earth as it is in heaven.'

But what are the virtues and skills for life together which come from being people who share in the life and love of God? In the Old Testament, they are summarized in the Ten Commandments, which provide the foundation for covenant community with God and neighbour, whether kinsfolk or stranger (Exod. 20.1–17). In the New Testament, they are summarized both in Jesus' prescription for communities of the Kingdom, in the Sermon on the Mount (Matt. 5—7), and in Paul's teaching on the fruit of the Spirit as what makes possible a common life which crosses traditional ethnic and social divides (Gal. 5.22–23). Such virtues and skills are by no means for the Church only. They are what make possible the building of true and just community anywhere (Jones, 1995). But it is the case, nevertheless, that the Church is called and gifted to witness in a special way to the life together of people of every kind and condition, which is the will of God. It does so by being itself: one, holy, catholic and apostolic. By its unity, the Church witnesses to the oneness of God and to the possibility of the unity of all humankind in all its diversity. By its holiness it witnesses to the disciplines and virtues which make community possible. By its catholicity, the Church witnesses to its loyalty to the whole human race past, present and future, a loyalty vital for the preservation of humanity. By its apostolicity it witnesses in word and sacrament to the source of both its own life and the life of the world. That source is the forgiveness of God through the death and resurrection of the divine Son. There can be no community without atonement and there can be no atonement without sacrifice. [*Stephen C. Barton*]

COMMUNITY CARE
1. In the UK, provision of health and social care (especially mental health) within the community and not in a

hospital or institution. (In the USA the comparable concept is 'home-based care'.)

2. In the USA, the use of community-based and patient facilities or clinics to provide medical care.

Erving Goffman's book *Asylums* was published in the USA in 1961. In this collection of essays he drew attention to the situation for patients in large psychiatric hospitals. He made available to the general public the idea of institutionalization, i.e. the process by which the institution (the mental hospital) creates an impact on long-stay patients which prevents them from feeling able to take on responsibility for themselves. They become totally dependent upon the institution. The idea that such large institutions which offered treatment away from the general public were damaging the patients they were there to treat, led to a growing pressure on both sides of the Atlantic to move mental health provision back into the community. It is significant that this thinking was supported by politicians on the right as well as on the left. It is also a significant fact that no real move to close the large mental hospitals in the UK was begun until various committees suggested that provision in the community would be cheaper. The National Health Service and Community Care Act 1990 provided the legislation needed to allow for a different way of funding services so that local authorities (through social service departments) could form partnerships with local health authorities and voluntary and private organizations to provide services at a 'local' level.

Care in the community has become controversial because it has proved difficult to provide integrated care for people who are severely mentally ill. Significant numbers of the population, who had originally been long-stay patients in large hospitals, have ended up homeless or without organized care. The result is increased public awareness of such people, not only because of those who are homeless but because they now appear publicly 'in the community'. This, combined with a handful of high-profile and disturbing acts of violence by seriously ill patients, has generated major concern that the provision of services to the mentally ill in the community is not adequate. It is becoming clear that the logic that care in the community is cheaper rested on some assumptions which do not apply to those with serious mental

health problems. For instance, the majority of care-givers in the community in the general health field are members of the family; but this does not apply to such patients. More important still is the misunderstanding about the difficulty of providing treatment for mental illness. It seems that the general feeling that large institutions were damaging patients led to the important skills and expertise which such hospitals possessed being discounted. There developed a belief that these skills could be provided by less qualified people. The consequence is that the seriousness of the illness is often underplayed and the patients are lost.

Three major reports form the background to the legislation in the UK. The 1986 Audit Commission Report, *Making a Reality of Community Care*, took the line that there was a bias towards residential care for those with care needs because the supplementary benefit system made money available for such expenditure without drawing on the resources of local authorities. It argued that it would be less expensive to keep people in their own homes.

The Griffiths Report, *Community Care: Agenda for Action* (1988) was the result of a brief to 'review the way in which public funds are used to support community care policy and to advise ... on the options for action that would improve the use of these funds as a contribution to more effective community care'. Griffiths recommended that people should be helped to stay in their own homes as long as possible, so that institutional care would be reserved for those whose needs could not be met in any other way. He also recommended that people who are able to should pay the full economic cost of services provided in their own homes. The local authority was seen as an enabler, acting as the designer, organizer and purchaser of non-health-care services. This report was the basis of the White Paper and subsequent Act.

The third report was also produced in 1988; this was the Wagner Report, *Residential Care: A Positive Choice*. Its author emphasized the positive choices to be made by residents entering care and in care. She also distinguished between needs for care and needs for accommodation, saying that people should not have to move just because their care needs have changed. The principles which should form the basis of good practice in residential care were defined as: (1) provision of personal caring; (2) opportunity for individual choice; (3) continuity; (4) opportunities for change; (5) clarity about common values underpinning practice.

The Government prepared the ground for the act in the White Paper, *Caring for People* (1989), in which its stated aim was to

[provide] the services and support which people who are affected by problems of ageing, mental illness, mental handicap or physical or sensory disability need to be able to live as independently as possible in their own homes, or in 'homely' settings in the community. The Government is firmly committed to a policy of community care which enables such people to achieve their full potential.

The White Paper produced six key objectives which were reflected in the Act: (1) provision of services for people at home, targeting those whose need is greatest; (2) services for carers; (3) assessments for care, as the cornerstone of practice; (4) a mixed economy of care by promotion of the independent sector; (5) a clear demarcation of responsibilities; (6) better value for taxpayers' money by ensuring that social security provisions should not provide any incentive in favour of residential and nursing home care.

In general, community care represents a preference for home life over institutional care. This ideal, however, although widely supported in principle, has effects which are now beginning to emerge. For example, one result is that 'informal carers' provide most of the community care. In 1990 a survey identified 6.8 million such carers, of whom some 3.9 million (58%) were women. There are signs that the realities of this situation are now beginning to be noted, and the theory and practice are likely to be modified. For pastors and churches it is likely that they can make a significant contribution by providing support for the carers rather than engaging directly in the work of professional caregiving. [*Philip Stokoe*]

COMMUNITY DEVELOPMENT
A process of self-help neighbourhood regeneration.
This has taken various forms, notably: the confrontational Saul Alinsky approach pioneered in Chicago in the 1930s; the 'non-directive' method associated with the work of T. R. Batten in Central Africa from the 1950s; the professionalized community work approach, given impetus by the Home Office projects in the UK in the late 1960s and early 1970s; and the new 'community organizing' (or 'broad-based organizing') method which started in the USA in the mid-1980s and moved into the UK in the early 1990s, reflecting Alinsky's philosophy but in a milder form.

COMPASSION
1. Being moved by the suffering of others.
2. Entering another's suffering with a view to relieving it.
Compassion is a key theme for all pastoral activity. To be compassionate is to focus on the other and his or her needs. It is not to generalize feelings, but to be specific and so to channel the emotion generated by someone's predicament into an active response to it. Such compassion is often almost inadvertently exercised by neighbours and friends when someone is in distress. It is not the prerogative of the minister. But pastors are both expected to be and usually look to themselves to be compassionate, whatever professional training they may have. And since their ministry is offered without the therapist's defences of control of time, limited space and payment, they especially need to be aware of the emotional drain of such availability.

COMPLEMENTARY MEDICINE
See: SICKNESS

COMPULSION
Behaviour that, when not carried out, causes acute anxiety.
The compulsive person is dominated by some internal force that makes them act in a certain fashion, even against their own will. 'Repetition compulsion' is a Freudian theme. At the heart of his understanding of psychoanalysis lies the compulsion to repeat past history through recollection and working through in the transference.

COMPULSIVE BEHAVIOUR
See: OBSESSIONS

CONFESSION
1. Profession of Christian faith.
2. Acknowledgement of sins before God, privately to a priest or publicly.
3. More recently, a denomination.
In the early Christian tradition the word signified the profession of faith of martyrs or

other persecuted believers, and especially the avowal that 'Jesus is Lord'. From this usage it came to apply analogously to the tombs and shrines of martyrs or other confessors. In the medieval period the practice of auricular confessions arose in which an individual privately acknowledged sins before God and in the presence of a priest who had authority to forgive sins in God's name. Confession here was an element of the sacrament of penance. Collective liturgical confessions of sin also had a long history in Christian worship following the example of Jewish practices on the Day of Atonement (Yom Kippur). Reformation Christian communities composed and published communal professions of faith, the first being the Confession of Augsburg in 1530. From this communal usage originated the practice of describing religious communities themselves as confessions.

In contemporary North American Christianity the notion of confession has gained a distinctive meaning suggested by its use in the phrase 'confessional theology'. Associated with the Lutheran and Calvinist traditions, and especially with the Reformed theologian H. Richard Niebuhr, this conception of theology acknowledges that Christian language about God occurs relative to particular historical, social and epistemological contexts. A confession of faith in this context has several traits that distinguish it from an assertion of fact. A confession of faith is a public and communal affirmation of theological belief that is characterized by trust, hope, metaphor and mystery. Christian confessions of faith bespeak a trust that God has spoken authoritatively to previous generations of believers. Therefore, to some extent they adopt traditional language that might not be chosen were a similar affirmation composed today. The trinitarian affirmation of God as Father, Son and Holy Spirit (Matt. 28.19) uses gendered language that may not be completely felicitous but can still be meaningfully affirmed.

Christian confessions of faith express a hope that God will fulfil divine promises recorded in the Bible and received by early Christians. Therefore, to some extent they assert not what is known to be true but what they hope will become true. The christological affirmation that Christ is the saviour of all persons (1 Tim. 4.10) is not an accomplished fact but a hoped-for reality. Christian confessions of faith are metaphorical in the sense that they appeal to worldly images that inadequately capture divine reality. Therefore, to some extent they always indirectly convey what they sometimes explicitly confess – that human beings are finite and fallible creatures. The christological affirmation that Jesus is Lord (Rom. 10.9) successfully acknowledges power and authority but also suggests distance and arbitrariness. Christian confessions of faith are mysterious because they announce a meaning that their confessors do not entirely comprehend. Therefore, to some extent they speak a new and strange language so as better to understand that same language when it is spoken to them. The theological affirmation that God is love (1 John 4.16) intends to make both confessor and hearer more attentive to God's love.

The pastoral importance of the confession of sin is that it engenders the humility befitting the Christian life; the pastoral importance of the confession of faith is that it instils the courage necessary for Christian living. *[Peter H. Van Ness]*

CONFIDENTIALITY
The moral or legal responsibility to preserve privacy in respect of information about another person.

Confidentiality is rooted in the philosophical concept of the right to privacy. In Western traditions individuals generally are believed to have the right to keep certain information about themselves secret and to dispense that information at their sole discretion. Pastoral care and counselling require that people disclose and discuss personal information of an intimate, sometimes painful nature. Confidentiality prevents the release of that information to anyone else by a pastoral professional without the permission of the person concerned.

Confidentiality is so vital to establishing a safe, trustworthy helping relationship that the duty to maintain confidentiality is a central tenet of all codes of ethics in the helping professions. The *Code of Ethics* of the American Association of Pastoral Counselors (1994), for instance, states: 'We respect the integrity and protect the welfare of all persons with whom we are working and have an obligation to safeguard information about them that has been obtained in the course of the counseling process.' In many jurisdictions, legal statutes further reinforce the obligation of helping professionals to uphold confidentiality.

Related to both privacy and confidentiality is the concept of privilege. Privilege allows individuals to block the release, in a legal action, of information revealed in a pastoral conversation. Privilege is a legal right of an individual, who alone can waive it, while confidentiality is an ethical obligation on a professional. The obligation to protect confidentiality is binding but not absolute. The most dramatic exception to confidentiality comes in the 'duty to protect', first clearly articulated in the USA in the court case 'Tarasoff v. Board of Regents of University of California'. The duty to protect requires helping professionals who become aware of a threat of physical harm to an identifiable individual or individuals to attempt to protect the intended victim from their clients. In the related 'duty to report', the professional is required to inform designated authorities of the threat, but is not required to make further attempts to protect the potential victim. The duty to report is established most clearly in cases of suspected physical or sexual abuse of children. Some jurisdictions also require reporting of 'elder abuse'.

Ethically and legally complicated confidentiality issues can arise when dealing with families. While children do not generally have a legal right to confidentiality, they do have a limited ethical right to privacy. The pastoral professional must balance the child's privacy with the parents' right and obligation to know what goes on between their child and a professional adult.

Subpoenas by courts can pose ethical difficulties around confidentiality. Although courts have considerable power to compel the disclosure of information, their power to override privacy is not absolute. As in all situations where the legal and ethical dimensions of confidentiality overlap, it is the pastoral professional's responsibility to know the relevant legal statutes in that jurisdiction and to seek legal consultation when needed (Haas and Malouf, 1995). [Douglas M. Thorpe]

CONFIRMATION
An ecclesiastical rite that confirms what was done in baptism.

Teaching in the churches about confirmation varies. Anglican thinking emphasizes both the Church and the individual, the objective matter of the sacrament and the subjective faith involved in its reception. The laying on of hands by a bishop signifies confirmation of baptism. The candidate's personal profession of the Christian creed is seen as confirming that confession of faith that accompanied the original washing. For much of the Christian era the arrival of a bishop was rare and confirmation sporadic. During the nineteenth century, however, the ceremony tended to be held at the onset of adolescence and it became almost another rite of passage into puberty. The majority of Lutherans in Scandinavia are still confirmed after thorough preparation in their fifteenth year. In the Roman Catholic Church, since the later Middle Ages, the baptized person has been admitted to holy communion through a rite of confirmation. The bishop or priest anoints the candidate's head with oil (in the sign of the cross), taps their cheek and extends his hands in blessing. This takes place when the child is about seven years old. In the Orthodox Churches the link with the bishop was retained through the use of the chrism (oil and balsam) that he had blessed. The parish priest administers baptism, confirmation and communion in a single rite that occurs in infancy. Among the Free Churches the Methodist form, for example, contains a personal affirmation and a symbolic shaking (rather than imposition) of hands with the circuit superintendent or district chairperson. The ceremony takes place following the attainment of an age of 'reason'. In all cases confirmation both picks up what was promised at baptism and admits to holy communion.

Pastorally, many ministers have seen confirmation as a specific opportunity to engage with young people. However, there is an increasing feeling that the natural disarray of adolescence is not the best stage in life for such teaching and commitment. In addition, the modern emphasis on the Eucharist and family worship has made the age of admission to communion a point of dispute. Discussion about the 'proper' or 'best' age for confirmation (from the point of view either of the individual's right to choose or of the Church's mission) continues. Although in most churches confirmation involves teaching and preparation, it is today acknowledged that the Spirit can rest upon those with severe learning disabilities. Perhaps age can no more be regarded as guarantor of spiritual development than can education or ability to learn. [Edward Bailey]

CONFIRMATION PREPARATION
An educational programme of the local church to help adults and adolescents decide whether to be confirmed.

According to the Acts of the Apostles the first Christians received some instruction in the Christian faith before their baptism. Having thus joined the Church, their availability for deeper instruction in the content and consequences of faith could initially be assumed. The widespread endorsement of infant baptism, however, led to a distinct rite of confirmation being institutionalized. Preparatory instruction for this rite has long been set forth in catechisms, rote learning and repetition, which have constituted the major part of confirmation preparation.

With the spread first of literacy and then of education theory, confirmation preparation in most churches has moved away from learning a catechism towards discussion (involving laity as well as clergy), experience of community living (e.g. at a youth centre or retreat), and incorporation into the local church practically, liturgically, socially, sacramentally, administratively and spiritually. The current trend is towards hearing what the Spirit might have already been saying to, and might have to say through, the candidates themselves. This process of questioning and answering was always involved in catechizing, but it is now seen as applying to the teachers as well as the taught.

Confirmation preparation and catechizing have often been given a high priority by the Church, because they are simultaneously pastoral, missionary and evangelistic. The head of the Catechetical School in Alexandria in the third century was regarded as one of the most important offices in the Church. Today a simple scheme of a meal and video-led discussion (Holy Trinity, Brompton's 'Alpha Course') has been used worldwide. The popularity of this focused approach, which is targeted towards adults, reflects the decreasing supply of adolescent candidates from among those baptized in infancy.
[Edward Bailey]

CONFLICT
Opposition between impulses or desires that produces emotional tension.

Conflict may be social, interpersonal or intrapersonal. Social conflict occurs where different factions in a society have interests that are deeply opposed to one another. Examples would be, in Marxist thought, class conflict; or in everyday political life, the struggle between the government and opposition. Interpersonal conflict seems essential as part of the process of growth and self-definition. It is especially found in family life. Intrapersonal conflict occurs when different parts of the structure of the ego are in imbalance. Maturity is about coming to terms with this and being able to establish relationships by giving and receiving affection. Conflict, therefore, is an inevitable component of human interactions. It may be destructive but can also be constructive. Conflict not surprisingly also lies at the heart of the gospel, the scheme of redemption linking the conflict between good and evil with personal salvation.

CONFRONTATION
A technique by which the counsellor challenges the client's assumptions by pressing on them a consideration of reality.

In counselling, confrontation is not an emotional response. It is a deliberate stance adopted to enable the client to rediscover some reality which they are denying by living with a wilfully false sense of themselves and their responsibility for their behaviour. The counsellor draws the client's attention to an obvious piece of behaviour or emotion which the client seems to wish to avoid.

CONGREGATION
In general usage, those who habitually attend a particular place of worship or the membership of a local church.

The word 'congregation' carries a range of meanings which need to be distinguished. These include: (1) any gathering of people or animals; (2) secular uses, e.g. as in a university; (3) in Roman Catholicism, formally for (a) departments of the Papal Curia, (b) certain orders, (c) groupings of monastic houses within an order; (4) in Protestantism the term can stress the corporate nature of the Church in contrast to hierarchical models, e.g. historically (the sixteenth century) the congregation constituted the universal Church. Informally it may refer to all those associated with a local church, sometimes in contrast to full members. In the USA and other parts of the world the word is often synonymous with 'parish', both referring to a gathered group of worshippers. The congregation of local fellowship is the normal vehicle for Christian belonging. It is the primary public expression of the Church. Being part of the Church is experienced in terms of worship and community, people are built up in the faith, and from it flows the mission of proclamation and service. However, there is an immense diversity in congregational life affected by theology, history and culture.

The New Testament term *ecclesia* means to be called out or together. The stress is on God's initiative in gathering together a people for himself. This is true of the Church universal and of the local congregation which is a microcosm of the whole. There has, however, historically been a tension between the universal and local which has been traditionally expressed in two contrasting patterns of polity. The episcopal and presbyterian traditions stress the wider belonging and see the local as essentially part of a wider structure. In practice this means a greater degree of centralization, making the congregation more dependent and less responsible. The congregational polity, on the other hand, understands the local as the primary unit and final seat of authority which relates to the universal through more or less formal forms of association. This can degenerate into anarchic independency.

Other theological factors also affect the life of congregations. For instance, highly formalized liturgical worship produces a different sense of community from a more homely participatory expression of the priesthood of all believers; similarly, models of ministry and authority determine patterns of effective belonging. In response to rapid social change there has perhaps been more change and diversification in congregational life in recent decades than ever before. These can be characterized briefly: (1) innovations in worship, revised liturgies, new music, including for example folk or rock music, and greater freedom has meant increased diversity in services, not least in mainstream denominations; (2) the growth of ecumenical projects has produced the need for congregations to create their own, often idiosyncratic, styles of working; (3) new congregations have come into existence outside the existing structures, notably in the 'house churches'; (4) liberation theology has stimulated interest in building 'base communities' around issues concerning the poor or other special interests; (5) awareness of inculturation has encouraged the development of local forms and structures (van der Ven, 1996).

Another diversity is between congregations that see themselves as 'parochial' or 'communal' in orientation and those that are 'associational' in attitude. The former, relating to the sociologist's 'church' type, understand the wider locality (the original sense of parish) or community as their responsibility, providing a living reminder of God's presence in and for the world. Membership, therefore, tends to be more open, including those who may only have nominal allegiance, seldom using the church except for rites of passage (birth, marriage, baptism and burial) and other occasional offices. The latter, closer to the 'sect' type, differentiate more carefully between faith and non-faith, seeing mission more in terms of building up the community of faith. In a pluralistic society the latter becomes increasingly normative. There are, however, many congregations that try to hold the two in creative tension, exploring both a strong sense of faith commitment and community service.

Pastorally, too, there has been a rediscovery of the congregation. With a greater emphasis on the corporateness of the people of God and the diversity of gifts in the community, pastoral care has shifted from the ordained leadership to the fellowship itself and has produced a wide range of both recognized and informal ministries. Every aspect of the congregation's life has its pastoral dimension, from house groups and Bible study to catechism, worship and liturgy. Moreover there is a greater sense of using plant and persons as resources for the wider community.

There is now, therefore, a very diverse and often disturbing variety of expressions of congregation. The inherited patterns have been significantly eroded and the new are often detached from any sense of tradition. Yet the situation can equally be regarded as creative and challenging. These concerns have not unnaturally stimulated an interest in how congregations function with a view to better fulfilling their mission. Hopewell (1988) suggests that these studies may be divided into four kinds: (1) *contextual*, looking at the external relationships of the congregation in its wider community. This is exemplified by the 'parish audit' or community survey; (2) *mechanistic*, or managing the resources efficiently. There is a growing interest in patterns of management and their appropriateness to the Church; (3) *organic*, which focuses on building fellowship and enabling personal growth; (4) *symbolic*, using anthropological or ethnographical tools to understand a congregation's corporate tradition, its history, culture and belief structures. To these we may add (5) the *sociological*, or how the congregation is caught up in and affected by wider social changes. Together, perhaps with others, these can help provide a rounded picture of congregational life. [*Paul Ballard*]

CONGRUENCE
In client-centred therapy, the integrity in the way that counsellors present themselves.
Carl Rogers identified four conditions for sound counselling: genuineness, empathy, congruence and non-possessive love. These constitute the basis of client-centred (sometimes called 'Rogerian') therapy. It also describes the way in which, while listening and responding positively to the client's perceptions, the counsellor should not collude by conforming to their expectations. As a result congruence also refers to the way in which, through the emerging counselling relationship, the client's 'real' self becomes increasingly compatible with their 'ideal' self – a harmony between outward expression and strongly felt inner meaning.

CONSCIENCE
An independent source of moral insight.
Within the Christian tradition two perennial issues arise around conscience: (1) what authority does it have? (2) what exactly is it? There are also two broad answers: (1) conscience emerges as the normal human ability to reason is applied, especially from past experience; (2) conscience is a moral sense that may be compared with the physical senses, which acts intuitively. The former position allows more for fallibility, human reason being suspect; the latter has a stronger sense of the voice of God. In moral theology, however, there is a long tradition that the rights of the individual's conscience are to be respected and taken into consideration in any moral judgement. In the twentieth century, thought about the individual's conscience has been augmented by attention being paid to the way in which institutions also might develop a conscience and a corresponding sense of responsibility (Schweiker, 1995).

This long debate about conscience has been augmented in the twentieth century by the findings of psychology. In psychoanalytic theory the conscience is a product of the super-ego, which is formed through early relations with parents. If this development does not go well, then excessive attention to conscience might mark the adult's life as someone who is obsessed with inappropriate rituals and a permanent sense of guilt. Another aspect is a person's self-image and his or her aspirations. Only those who can cope with both of these can be, it is argued, free to be responsible (Polanyi, 1958). It is possible to reconcile the theological tradition of conscience as the voice of God with these positions. But the overall impact of life in the twentieth century has been to make people wary of claims to invoke conscience as the sole justification for any act. The corruption of the will is returning to the theological agenda, coupled with the psychological questioning on altruism and any idea that there might be no self-interest in any action.

CONSENT
The voluntary informed agreement of a mentally competent patient which a doctor is obliged to ascertain before commencing treatment.
1. *Ethical Considerations*. It is a generally accepted principle that a doctor must respect the autonomy of the patient, for the patient has the right to self-determination. However well-meaning a doctor may be, any violation of a patient's autonomy affronts society's notion of personal bodily integrity. From this principle can be derived the legal and moral necessity for consent. Consent has a number of functions: (1) it affirms the idea of respect for persons; (2) it confirms the right to self-determination; (3) it assists therapy as patients feel their views are respected; and (4) it prevents abuse.

These functions act as safeguards, which protect the patient's right to self-determination. Where consent has not been forthcoming the doctor cannot administer treatment. Instead he or she must respect the patient's decision irrespective of the possible consequences. It is for the doctor to obtain consent (Veatch, 1989).

2. *Elements of a valid consent*. In order to ensure the consent (or indeed, refusal of consent) is real, and thereby valid, the doctors must make sure that: (1) the patient's decision was made of his or her own free will, with no duress or undue influence; (2) the patient

was given sufficient information about the proposed treatment; and (3) the patient had the necessary mental capacity to make the decision.

The consent must be given voluntarily. The patient must not be subject to any obvious force or duress. Difficulty in determining whether a patient's decision was made voluntarily arises when subtler pressures are exerted. Is the patient merely consenting for a quiet life, to satisfy someone else or because the advice and persuasion to which he or she has been subjected is such that he or she can no longer think and decide for him- or herself?

The consent given by the patient must be the result of an informed choice. Being informed indicates that consent given in ignorance cannot be relied upon. In relation to the validity of the consent to medical treatment, it is only necessary that the patient understand the broad nature of the treatment proposed. On this basis, the doctor's duty amounts to the provision of elementary facts about the treatment. It could be argued that in order for the patient to be informed they must have much more information to make an informed choice. While equally, the patient cannot be told (and fully understand) all that the doctor knows. For the doctor to fulfil his or her duty of care towards the patient, they must provide adequate information so that the patient can make up their own mind. The provision of such information allows the patient's autonomy to be respected. Some would argue, however, that the notion of truth-telling might prove harmful to the patient. The doctor's duty to inform can be excused when the patient waives the right to know. It will also be absolved when there is clear evidence which suggests the imparting of further information would harm the patient's mental or physical state – the law recognizes this as 'therapeutic privilege'.

Before a valid consent to treatment can be given the patient must be mentally competent. The test for determining mental capacity has been laid down as a functional test where the assessor asks whether the individual is able, at the time when a particular decision has to be made, to understand its nature and effects.

In English law the explicit formulation of capacity to consent has three stages. Does the patient (1) take in and retain treatment information, (2) believe it, and (3) are they able to weigh that information, balancing risks and needs?

Where the patient is found to be incompetent the doctor must obtain consent from another. The person who provides the proxy consent must act in the patient's best interests. Where the patient is a child who is under 18 and is not considered mature enough to be competent, the doctor must obtain consent from the child's parents. When the patient is an adult, generally the doctor will approach the court for a declaration absolving him or her of any liability in battery. The doctor cannot rely on the proxy consent of a relative or next of kin, as it has no effect in law. Proxy consent is justified on the basis that the incompetent patient's autonomy is enhanced because the doctor will not be tied to following the ill-judged decision of the patient. [*Nicola Glover-Thomas*]

CONSOLATION
The provision of solace and comfort, cheering those in distress.
In Christian tradition various arguments were developed and elaborated from a common literary form in antiquity, the *consolatio*. This provided philosophical reasons for not despairing. Biblical perspectives, such as the notion of resurrection, enhanced the tradition. Later spiritual writers focused on the consoling presence of God, contrasting the periods of spiritual desolation when the Spirit of Jesus seemed to be absent. Ignatius of Loyola, for example, offered rules for the discernment of spirits.

CONSTRUCTION
A reconstitution of childhood history in both real and fantasy aspects.
A construction is built by a therapist from the evidence provided by the patient. It is then offered back with the intention of freeing repressed or blocked memories. Sometimes called a 'construct', the idea has been difficult to define and to handle. Recent questions about false memory, especially in terms of childhood abuse, have made the idea of construction even more problematic. The term 'construct' is often used simply as an alternative to 'concept'.

CONSULTATION, PERSONAL
The practice of seeking the wisdom of others in response to specific pastoral situations.
This seeking of guidance implies granting at least limited authority to the consultant's tradition of meaning. The consultation

process can involve skill development, deepening of insights, or personal growth. Personal consultation is a general term, but examples of consultation topics might include: discerning God's leading; growth and formation; reactions to a parishioner's suffering; ministering to a difficult parishioner or counsellee. Someone may explicitly agree to serve in the role of consultant or supervisor. Often, however, people talk informally about a situation. Consultants might include peers, Christian leaders, parishioners wise about their faith or community, and other specialists (e.g. therapist, nurse).

Consultation relates to the communal nature of Christian faith. To disparage consultation is to assume individual self-sufficiency. The need for consultation is grounded theologically in human finitude, sin and the incompleteness of human transformation. Consulting parties seek to compensate for distorted perspectives rooted in deformed development, unconscious self-interests, and social location. Consultation promotes interdependence within the body of Christ. Intense consultations, touching on the core of personal identity, incorporate confession of sin and identification and nurturing of gifts.

Consulting has been integral in relationships throughout the Church's story: e.g. nurturing disciples, pastoral shepherding, care of souls, spiritual direction, mentoring, prayer groups and clinical pastoral supervision. Examples include: John Cassian, who studied with the fourth-century Egyptian monks; Richard Baxter (seventeenth century), who formed a monthly pastors' group; and Asian Christian women, who have created ecumenical dialogues in which to struggle against oppression.

In twentieth-century cultures, where psychology plays such a prominent part, pastoral clinicians have defined 'professional consultation' in comparison to clinical pastoral supervision. A supervisor shares responsibility for the outcome of the ministry. A consultant usually does not. Consultation typically is voluntary and non-binding. Yet despite support for the idea of consultation, its practice is controversial. Christians differ about which aspects of their complex tradition to emphasize. In addition, consultations occur amid overlapping (complementary and conflicting) systems of meaning (Pryser, 1976). Controversies in consultation have focused on how to combine theology and the clinical

psychologies. Each psychology, clinical movement and pastoral community functions as a web of meaning, a culture that shapes both individual identity and experiences. Instead of borrowing appreciatively but judiciously from among the psychologies, too often Christians have credited twentieth-century therapeutic culture with presenting 'objective truth'. So authorized, psychology's nature as a cluster of philosophical and quasi-religious cultures functions invisibly (Placher, 1989; Murphy, 1990). Absorption with psychology has accompanied a neglect of rich pastoral resources: Cassian, Gregory the Great, Baxter, African-American womanism, the spiritual ferment in the two-thirds-world churches, etc.

In addition to addressing specific pastoral problems, personal consultation serves two roles. First, intense consultations are, to some extent, formations of individuals into the psychological or theological traditions of the consultant. Consequently, forethought is needed about implicit assumptions and goals in the consultant's convictional culture. Second, for Christians, quality personal consultation is the art of faithfully developing the traditions of a living community, constituted by God's story and moving into God's future. [*Miriam Anne Glover-Wetherington*]

CONSULTATION, POLITICAL
The engagement of various interest groups in the political process through representation, focus groups and other types of enquiry.

The idea of political representation has developed with the changing nature of how politics works in Great Britain. At the beginning of the nineteenth century British politics was seen as the representation of group interests, largely landed. This group's supremacy was challenged by the rise of industry. Politics was run on an agreed framework with politicians not putting forward a programme until after an election when they were called into office; the budget was to be balanced; and governments were to act even-handedly in judging competing interests. Free trade and the Bank Charter Act put most economic decisions beyond party politics and the new Poor Law settled social policy.

This approach could not survive electoral reform and the move towards a universal franchise. A mass electorate required organizations to mobilize a mass vote. Modern political parties were the result. The modern political party in Britain began with the developments pioneered by Joseph Chamberlain in Birmingham. Party programmes were put forward before elections with the electors choosing accordingly. Slowly the membership began to have a say on what these programmes should be. Ideas could be put forward by local branches feeding their views into party discussions, through and into the party leadership or via the party conference. In time, the annual party conference determined the main outline of a party's programme.

At first political parties were controlled from the centre: the Conservatives used it as a rallying ground; the old Whig establishment fought the new politics of Chamberlain; and Labour adapted a form of democratic centralism, i.e. everybody was bound by a party decision once it was made, irrespective of their views prior to that decision taking place. Only in the twilight of what looks like the age of the political party has power truly been shared, with the final move coming as party members gained a decisive say in the selection of candidates and of the party leader.

With the decline of the importance of the party to the working of British government has been the rise of interest groups. The major industrial, financial and social interests now employ considerable talent to shape policy their way. To help decide in outline what an opposition party likely to win an election will do in office is one key objective. Once in office a government will usually consult widely on the outline of a reform, often working with some specialist groups in deciding the detail of that policy.

In addition to the responses requested to government Green and White Papers, means of consultation come from select committee hearings, royal commissions, official departmental committees of inquiry, and unofficial committees staged by the voluntary sector. More recently, the rise of the focus group, allegedly representative groups of voters, has led not merely to changes in the presentation of policy, but to the choice of policies themselves. Consultation is also held locally by local authorities and by the official committees listed above taking local evidence for their inquiries. [Frank Field]

CONTRACEPTION
The prevention of pregnancy.
The safest method of preventing an unwanted pregnancy is by total abstinence from sexual intercourse. All other methods fail in varying degrees. In human beings conception can only occur if sexual intercourse takes place within three or four days on either side of actual ovulation. In some women the time of ovulation can be determined by the onset of acute abdominal pain on the day the egg is produced and starts its journey down the fallopian tube. In other women alterations in basal temperature combined with alterations in the consistency of vaginal secretions can give a reasonable prediction of ovulation. Abstinence from sexual intercourse during these seven or eight days each month may be a successful method of contraception, but it does not take into account unpredictable spontaneous ovulations. Total abstinence from sexual intercourse and the use of the so-called 'safe period' are the only forms of contraception currently acceptable in official Roman Catholic teaching.

Some other methods of contraception rely on preventing sperm from ever reaching the ovum. A form of contraception practised for many generations before any barrier methods were developed was coitus interruptus, the withdrawal of the penis from the vagina before male orgasm. This method is highly unreliable. The sperm can be prevented from reaching the vagina through the use of male condoms. Sperm can be killed through the use of chemicals applied either to the condom or within the woman's vagina. Physical barriers (vaginal and cervical caps) between the sperm and ovum can be inserted into the woman's vagina with or without the addition of spermicides. These methods of contraception carry virtually no risk to people's health, but can be unreliable.

Sterilization, either of men or women, the tying off and/or severing of the vas deferens in men and the fallopian tubes in women, is an effective and possibly permanent way of achieving long-term contraception. Since it is intended to be permanent (even though it is sometimes surgically reversible), it permits the pleasure of sexual intercourse without fear of conception. Such divorce between the duty of procreation and pleasure is not acceptable to many people of faith, especially to Roman Catholics. The chief objection to sterilization among other people is its permanency and the slight risk associated with anaesthesia.

Hormonal suppression of ovulation became popular in the second half of the twentieth century. It allows women to take control of their own fertility and does not require immediate application before sexual intercourse, as the barrier methods do. It is an effective method of birth control and is more acceptable to many women than methods that depend upon stopping a fertilized ovum from developing. Hormonal contraception, either by oral or injection methods, carries health hazards for some women, and a small mortality rate. Doctors and nurses need special training to prescribe all the above methods of contraception.

The methods of contraception hitherto discussed are generally acceptable to most Christians and to some peoples of other faiths. Methods of contraception that allow fertilization of an ovum but prevent implantation, such as intrauterine devices and the 'morning-after' pill are less acceptable as they involve the destruction of a fertilized ovum and potential human life. Therapeutic abortion has saved the lives, health and sanity of many women, but is unacceptable to many people of all faiths, and none, as by the time pregnancy is terminated actual life has to be destroyed. The moral problems associated with contraception have been exhaustively discussed, particularly in the last hundred years when the rise of population, especially among the poorer peoples of the world, has had serious economic consequences. The availability of effective contraceptives in the last forty years has made choice possible for women whereas before the advent of oral contraceptives they had very little or no choice.

The teaching authority of the Roman Catholic Church, and the strongly held opinions of many people of other faiths, maintain that the prime function of human sexual intercourse is the procreation of children. Pleasurable sexual contact between husbands and wives is a secondary consideration and should not be allowed to interfere with the possibility of procreation. This attitude was consistent in earlier times when the world population was small, the workload in any family was considerable and where infant mortality was high. It was then highly desirable to promote birth so as to ease the workload and maintain and increase the population. In a world that is now heavily overpopulated and where many people in the poorest countries of the world (where birth rates are high) die of malnutrition and related diseases, it is hard to see how a totally negative attitude towards contraception

and sterilization can be maintained in the absence of very determined efforts by all concerned to redistribute the wealth and resources of the world. If contraception is used properly, the population can be reduced, although at the cost of potential rather than actual life. If contraception is not permitted then the inevitable result is the loss of actual human life unless all Christians and others who object to contraception are successful in the redistribution of land, wealth and resources.

Hopes for an alteration in the teaching of the Roman Catholic Church about contraception were raised by a papal commission on birth control following the conclusion of Vatican II. Many Western educated Roman Catholics, who anticipated change, began to use contraceptives ahead of the expected decision in favour of some safe methods of contraception. The publication of a papal encyclical, *Humanae Vitae*, by Pope Paul VI in 1968, in which he condemned birth control, other than abstinence and the use of the 'safe period', led to a widespread disregard of this injunction and a breakdown in the authority of the Roman Catholic Magisterium, a breakdown which has since spread to other areas of life. [*Una Kroll*]

CONTRACT, THERAPEUTIC
See: THERAPEUTIC CONTRACT

CONTRITION
Interior repentance in the face of God's love.
The classic expression of contrition remains Ps. 51: 'Have mercy on me, O God: wash away my offences and cleanse me from my sin; create a pure heart in me; then I will teach sinners the way of righteousness; my sacrifice is a broken spirit.' From both a sense of God and his or her own unworthiness the penitent cries to God, seeks forgiveness and absolution and promises a new life marked by teaching others (i.e. the sinner intends not to offend again). Contrition is grounded in God's love, as both Catholic and Protestant theologians emphasize. An act of contrition is a short prayer that includes the basic elements outlined above, although their use remains a point of issue between Catholic and Protestant. The pastoral importance of seeing a penitent as such and not as someone necessarily to be offered or given counselling is usefully emphasized by the notions of contrition, penitence and penance.

CONVERSION
1. To return or repent on the part of one who has violated their relationship with God.
2. To turn to God as a decisive change from an old way of life to a new.

The primary meaning of words translated 'conversion' is 'to turn, return or to turn again'. The two definitions above are roughly those associated with the Old and New Testaments respectively.

The conversion of Saul of Tarsus is the paradigmatic conversion narrative in the New Testament. The sudden, dramatic and total transformation of Saul into Paul the Apostle often leads people to assume that all authentic conversions must follow the same pattern. Peace (1999) argues, however, that the New Testament provides validation for conversions nurtured over time as well as radical, instantaneous transformations.

Previously the Christian community believed that conversion was a profound process of transformation triggered by an emotionally charged environment. Today, however, the phenomenon is seen as a process that involves a person's intellect, will, emotions and a turning from a way of life that may be destructive or empty to a life that is centred on a relationship with God and the community of faith. While dramatic experiences may be included in the meaning of the term today, conversion is currently understood as the ongoing process of reorienting one's life in the direction of finding the wellspring of meaning and purpose in a relationship with God (Gelpi, 1998).

One of the most fascinating and vexing issues confronting psychology, in particular, and the social sciences, in general, is how and why people change. That issue is intensified in the religious or spiritual realm: how and why do people convert? From the earliest days of the psychology of religion, conversion has elicited much interest. Contemporary studies of conversion include the investigation of conversion from one religion to another, recruitment to new religious movements, detailed historical studies of the encounter between missionaries and indigenous people in the colonial period, and experiences of spiritual transformation in urban, secular environments (Lamb and Bryant, 1999).

In the current religious environment, pastoral care-givers must be aware of several crucial issues. At what stage is the individual in terms of the conversion process? Is the person just beginning the process of change? Is that person being unduly influenced by pressures being brought to bear on that individual within a religious community? What are the conscious and unconscious motivations energizing the person's experience?

Another important issue involves the person's stage in life. Even though there are many different models of the process of human development, the pastoral care-giver needs to be alert to 'where the person is' in his or her life journey. Is this individual going through major changes because of the normal processes of adolescent adjustments or is it a mid-life crisis of a person in their 40s or 50s? For some people a conversion is initiated by a transitional process in the life-cycle and for others it is shaped by the cognitive and emotional capacities inherent in a particular stage in life. Knowledge of these issues can enable the pastor to engage the convert in meaningful conversation.

The pastor must, first of all, carefully listen to and observe what is happening in the life of the convert. What emotional, cognitive, spiritual and other needs are being met in their desire for religious and spiritual change? In some cases, a pastor needs to discern if distinctly emotional, rather than spiritual, needs are propelling the transformation. In that case, the pastor should guide the person to seek therapy to confront those issues before undertaking the arduous journey of spiritual transformation.

While it is true that some conversions may be characterized, or even be constituted, by a dramatic event or experience, most students of conversion see conversion as a process (Rambo, 1993). Various stage models have been developed to assist in understanding the complex, multifaceted nature of conversion.

Rambo's stage model of conversion should be seen as a heuristic device rather than a universal or invariant sequence of stages. The first stage, *Context*, is the dynamic force field in which religious change transpires. The context provides the ecology of conversion in which different factors foster and hinder the process of change. The second stage, *Crisis*, points to the common experience in most conversions of an incident, experience or insight that disrupts, challenges or erodes a person's common pattern of living. The crisis may be triggered by internal issues or by an externally imposed event or experience.

Whatever the cause, the person begins to search for ways to organize life.

The disorientation or disruption motivates most people actively to *Quest* for new options. Many scholars of conversion stress the active agency of the potential conversion in this stage. During the Quest stage some people actively seek religious or spiritual people or institutions that provide alternative methods of living or new interpretations of the nature of the self, life and the Divine. For some converts, the sequence of the stages may begin with an *Encounter*. An Encounter may provide a situation in which life may be redefined or even a crisis may be triggered by a person who embodies a new way of life that may question the other's taken-for-granted foundation of life. The nature of the Encounter stage is important in determining the nature of the relationship. In the missionary setting the advocate may, because of economic, political or other form of power, exert too much control so that a potential convert is, to some degree at least, coerced into a new religious institution.

The *Interaction* stage involves a series of exchanges between the potential convert and the advocate. Should the potential convert find the alternative attractive, he or she continues to learn new theologies, new methods of constructing one's life, and new religious vocabularies. Crucial dimensions of conversion are manifest at this stage, with the most crucial being the quality of relationship established. One of the few things about which researchers on conversion agree is that conversions take place through existing or created networks of family and friendship. Relationships provide a growing sense of trust, affection and confidence in the new option. Ritual enhances the learning process by enabling a person to develop methods through which to enhance and sustain the religious life.

The *Commitment* stage involves a crucial turning point in the conversion process. Most religions require a public ceremony that marks the transition from one status to another. In Christianity, baptism, at least for most denominations, symbolizes the death of the old, sinful self and the rebirth of a person as a child of God. The rituals involved at this stage are designed to assist the person in setting aside an old way of life and taking on a new set of beliefs and practices which transforms the person.

The *Consequences* of the conversion process vary from person to person and group to group. Assessment of the nature of the changes that triggered conversion requires a willingness to be as objective as possible. Some people experience conversion as a life-transforming and healing experience, while others may see the process as constricting a person's life and even fostering regressive modes of coping.

Ideally, a pastor – whether minister, priest or rabbi – should nurture and guide a person through the journey of transformation for the welfare of the person. Mere recruitment for the benefit of the organization is an unworthy goal. What should remain paramount is the enhancement of a person's relationship with God, other human beings and one's self.

Ultimately, turning to God is a mysterious process in which a person is touched profoundly by the Spirit of God and makes major changes in his or her life in response to that gift. Care-givers must, with humility and respect, bring their knowledge and skills to bear as they serve as midwives in this conversion process. Conversion is often a confluence of the deepest region of the human personality and the tender, or in some cases, shocking intervention of the Divine in the most unsuspecting person who experiences God for the first time or in unexpected, disconcerting ways. [*Lewis R. Rambo*]

CORRELATION
See: INTEGRATION

COUNSELLING
A therapeutic approach, similar to psychotherapy, usually based upon talking through issues in the context of a focused relationship between counsellor and client(s).

Counselling is closely linked to psychotherapy, and like psychotherapy takes different forms. Common to all counselling is the centrality of the relationship between the counsellor and the client, which at the very least in all approaches provides a co-operative partnership, in which the counsellor encourages the client to take equal responsibility for the work they do together. This is known as the working alliance. Most counselling approaches also stress the personal relationship of counsellor and client (or client and client in group work) as a means of expression and change (Jacobs, 1993).

Building upon that common base, different

counselling approaches emphasize particular features in the counselling relationship. Person-centred counselling, for example, stresses the necessary conditions which the counsellor must provide: genuineness, immediacy, congruence, and a non-judgemental attitude, all of which can provide the right milieu for the client's natural growth and development. Psychodynamic counselling, largely adapted from psychoanalysis, emphasizes the reflection and repetition in the counsellor–client relationship of earlier and other significant relationships in the client's life, so that these are worked through in the here and now of the counselling relationship. Cognitive behavioural counselling sees the counsellor's role more as a teacher, assisting the client to challenge ways of thinking and behaving, so as to learn new patterns of reacting and thinking. Co-counselling emphasizes the peer relationship of two people, who give time and attention to each other for equal periods of time. Although talking is the main means of communication, some counsellors may suggest use of painting, physical exercises or role-playing as additional ways of helping clients to express themselves.

The different approaches to counselling are all linked to similar approaches in clinical psychology and psychotherapy. Indeed in some schools the terms counselling and psychotherapy are synonymous, their usage depending largely upon the context in which the counsellor or therapist works. Thus there tend to be school counsellors, or family therapists, marriage counsellors or sex therapists. Other approaches, such as the psychodynamic school, believe there are distinctions between counsellors and psychotherapists, largely based upon the training and type of clients with whom they work. But these distinctions are not easy to make, and disputed even then. In any case, in some countries these particular distinctions are immaterial – in the USA for example, counsellors, psychoanalysts and psychologists would be the more usual professional distinctions.

Counselling can be offered to individuals, to couples (couple counselling), to families (family therapy), or in groups (group therapy, growth groups). It may take place in particular contexts, such as schools, the workplace (through employee assistance programmes), in doctors' surgeries, in youth counselling and advice centres, in voluntary agencies or in private practice (see the series *Counselling in Context*, Open University Press,

1993 onwards). Pastoral counselling refers to counselling in church contexts (Jacobs, 1993). Counselling is also applied to specific work such as post-traumatic stress counselling. It even appears in the commercial world as 'financial counselling', 'colour counselling', etc., although often this usage describes advice work rather than counselling as it has been generally understood. For that reason there is a move to describe counselling as it is used here as 'therapeutic counselling'. An important distinction is also to be made between the use of counselling skills and therapeutic counselling itself. Counselling skills can be used effectively in many caring situations, leading to more attentive and sensitive listening, without carers seeing themselves specifically as counsellors.

Counselling skills include careful listening, both to the obvious words and the hidden messages, being emphatic, not giving advice, not making judgemental or moralizing remarks, allowing space, responding carefully through the use of non-threatening questions, open questions, and summarizing and paraphrasing what the client has been saying. Therapeutic counselling builds upon these skills, which remain central to the work, but in addition sets clear boundaries to meetings, such as regular (mainly once-weekly) times and a neutral meeting place, with a clear sense of contract about the number of sessions offered. Counselling is defined by the British Association for Counselling (1985) as follows:

> People become engaged in counselling when a person, occupying regularly or temporarily the role of counsellor, offers or agrees explicitly to offer time, attention and respect to another person or persons temporarily in the role of client. The task of counselling is to give the client an opportunity to explore, discover and clarify ways of living more resourcefully and toward greater well-being.

As already stated, most counsellors make intensive and often explicit use of the relationship between the counsellor and client, seeing this as one of the most important factors in the process. For this reason counsellors do not like to see clients in any other role, where strong emotions evoked in counselling carry the risk of being inappropriately expressed. Whereas pastors, for example, may use counselling skills in the pastoral care of a person who wants to discuss an issue with them, and is also the leader of that person's congregation at worship, a counsellor should be someone who will not see the client in any other context.

Counselling can be short term or long term. Much of the counselling offered through agencies working for employers, or in the health-care setting, is limited to a short number of sessions. This work requires particular skills if it is to be effective, including accurate assessment of potential clients before embarking upon a counselling contract. Long-term counselling is offered by counsellors in independent practice and some agencies where the resources can meet the growing demand for help. All counsellors have regular supervision for their work with clients. Counselling has become very attractive as a concept and as an occupation, with many people wishing to call themselves counsellors. This work is therefore increasingly becoming regulated by national and international professional bodies, so that a thorough training is required, including the student's own personal counselling, before accreditation or registration. [Michael Jacobs]

COUNSELLING, COUPLE
See: COUPLE COUNSELLING

COUNSELLING, SEXUAL
See: SEXUAL COUNSELLING

COUNSELLING SKILLS
The methods and procedures learned and employed in carrying out the task of counselling.
Counselling is a multi-phase process: establishing a relationship, exploring and clarifying the problem, developing new perspectives on the problem, setting goals, facilitating action to meet goals, evaluating the counselling process, and termination. Each phase requires particular skill competencies. For example, the initial phase of establishing a relationship requires skills in attending, observing, listening, conveying warmth and understanding, questioning, giving feedback, orienting to the counselling process, and planning for termination.

Studies in cross-cultural counselling confirm the historical and cultural contingency of counselling techniques and the absence of one universal expression of any given skill (Augsburger, 1986). Additionally, particular skills may be more or less utilized depending on the theoretical perspective of

the counsellor. The wise use of religious resources such as Scripture, prayer and ritual in counselling are important skills for pastoral counsellors to develop in living out the Church's mission of spiritual formation and faith development (Egan, 1982). [Judith Orr]

COUNSELLING, TERMINATION OF
See: TERMINATION OF COUNSELLING

COUNSELS OF PERFECTION
See: MONASTICISM; PERFECTION

COUNTER-TRANSFERENCE
The feelings generated in the analyst or anyone who is the object of transference.
Counter-transference has received increasing attention as developments in psychoanalysis and group relations have occurred. The term describes the feelings that someone has who is being used tranferentially. If they attend to them, they may pick up what it is that the client, patient or group are doing. It is an essential dimension to effective ministry, where the question 'What is happening to me and why?' gives the pastor clues to what he or she is dealing with (Carr, 1997). They may then guide the pastor to a point of interpretative interaction.

COUPLE COUNSELLING
The process of addressing issues affecting adult couples through the counselling relationship.
As more couples live together outside marriage, the term couple counselling is becoming increasingly synonymous with marriage counselling. In this context, one or both partners will have identified a problem in their relationship for which they want help. The defining features of the counselling process are then the same as those described under marriage counselling. However, the term is more all-embracing than marriage counselling in that it includes the process of counselling homosexual couples.

Couple counselling differs from marriage counselling when it describes interventions that do not depend upon the couple having identified a problem in their relationship. Context becomes an important defining feature in these circumstances. For example, genetic counselling may be requested by couples who are considering starting a family, and where one partner has, or may have, a genetically transmittable adverse condition. Counselling in this context involves obtaining specialist information and advice as part of a decision-making process. The counsellor may pay little attention to the couple's relationship. Only their joint presence in connection with a matter that concerns them both defines the encounter as couple counselling.

A further differentiating feature occurs when the counselling process is initiated by the counsellor, or by the agency for which she or he works. This may happen as part of a broader programme of intervention being offered to and affecting the couple. Assisted conception schemes are required to offer a counselling session to couples before commencing fertility treatment. Adoption agencies may offer counselling before placing a child with a couple. An emphasis on providing information, the element of compulsion and an often accompanying hint of assessment distinguishes this form of counselling from couple counselling based on marriage-counselling models. It is a matter of debate whether such activities properly fall into what is commonly understood as a counselling activity. [Christopher Clulow]

COVENANT
A contract or agreement between two parties involving mutual obligation and trust.
Moral seriousness characterizes a covenant, as individuals or collective bodies enter into a voluntary agreement with due solemnity. In a religious context a covenant implies a special relationship with God, entered into through baptism or belonging to a specific religious group. For example, Jews believe in the covenant of God with the descendants of Abraham, which makes them the chosen people. Its outward token is the Old Covenant, while the relationship of God to humankind brought about by Jesus is called the New Covenant.

However, a covenant differs from a legal contract in an important way. The contract is an equal, bilateral agreement such as a treaty or a business deal; it is conditional upon both parties observing the terms of the agreement. If one party breaks the agreement, it is in effect ended, and the 'innocent' party is then released from any further obligation. Sometimes the innocent party will proceed legally against the party who has

broken the contract, becoming an adversary rather than a partner.

In contrast, a covenant is an unconditional agreement which is intended to survive imperfections and mistakes on one or both sides, overcoming them through forgiveness and renewal. The theological basis for this commitment is the grace of God, who binds himself to humanity in the Hebrew Testament, especially to the 'chosen people', promising unilateral fidelity despite human weakness. The Christian Testament affirms that God reconciles sinful humanity to himself through Christ, thus restoring and fulfilling the covenant which on his side was never broken.

This pattern provides a model of commitment for human relationships. The concept of marriage is grounded in analogies to God's covenant. In Scotland, the National Covenant was signed in 1638, defending the Presbyterian Church against the episcopal system brought in by James I. A church covenant is the establishment of a distinct religious society, as in the case of the Congregational Church in New England.

The concept of covenant remains a fundamental dimension of pastoral care, the aspect of mutual trust undergirding all counselling. [Hillary Ratna]

CREATION
The Christian doctrine that refers to: (1) the conditions in which all life exists; (2) the divine origin and destiny of all living things; (3) the ongoing relationship between creator and creature.
The concept of creation identifies those physical, intelligible, moral and spiritual conditions which God has established for life in all its forms, human and non-human. In humanity God is said to have created a being with a unique capacity to change and manipulate these conditions. Thus the Book of Genesis identifies human responsibilities to name and steward creation, while it also refers to the event which Christian theologians characterize as the fall, whereby a human challenge to the boundaries and moral ordering established by God undermines the original goodness of creation.

A central issue in the development of the Christian doctrine of creation over the centuries is the relation of creator and creation. Lynn White has argued that the traditional Christian doctrine of creation evacuates creation of the sacred by setting

God apart from the world in a way that other religious traditions do not. The consequent desacralization of nature is said to have provided a cultural milieu in which rationalistic, technological and industrial manipulations of nature have come to the fore, eventuating in the abuse and destruction of nature, and the contemporary environmental crisis. However, Northcott and others argue that the desacralization of space in post-Enlightenment philosophy and theology (as instanced in the deist image of creation as clock and creator as clock-maker) is a consequence of the iconoclastic efforts of the Protestant Reformers to obliterate sacred space(s) from Christian thought and practice, rather than something intrinsic to the Christian creation tradition (Northcott, 1996). Before the Reformation, biblical, patristic and medieval accounts of creation allowed for a deep and ongoing relationality between creation and creator which is given characteristic expression in the Hebrew Psalms (for example Psalm 139), and in the offices and liturgies of Jews and Christians through the centuries. This also finds expression in the practices of prayer and mysticism which address God as present and active within God's creation, not as a distant spirit or absentee landlord (McClendon, 1994).

This ongoing relationship finds definitive historical and material expression in the incarnation, crucifixion and resurrection of Jesus Christ in Palestine in the first century for in these events God visits the creation as flesh and blood, and reclaims the creature for God's original purposes. It is essential to the integrity of the Christian doctrine that the redemptive purposes of God for creation, as revealed in the incarnation, are not separated from the account of creation as matter, life and condition for human existence. For Christ is revealed as the mediator between God and creation, as the original principle or *logos* by which God gave life to that which is not God, and as the form in which God appears materially within creation to make known God's original purpose in creating, and the ultimate destiny of all creatures (Gunton, 1998).

This understanding of the relation between creation and redemption is central to the import of this doctrine for contemporary Christian and pastoral practice. The conditions of life in modern societies are largely those that have been invented and ordered by purely human purposes and technologies without reference to the transcendent origin and destiny of all living things and of matter itself. In very many ways modern lifestyles no longer conform with biblical and traditional Christian conceptions of created order and created life. For example, modern working and living patterns have all but obliterated the practice of sabbath from modern society, and this has significant consequences not only for worship of the creator but also for respect for creation: humans, other animals and the land itself have biophysical needs to rest from labour and production, the neglect of which produces ill health and bad environments. Modern life also ignores natural rhythms such as those of light and darkness, and the natural function of animals (modern farming has made cannibals of many farm animals with deleterious consequences for both animal welfare and human health) with the consequence that many urban dwellers experience little relation with creation as that which is larger than, and other to, the human technologically manufactured and ordered world which they mostly inhabit.

Practitioners of what has become known as ecopsychology find that this growing distance between modern humans and the non-human world is a major factor in the high incidence of mental ill health, alienation, and relational dysfunction in modern urban cultures. Clinebell argues that the modern alienation between humans and nature is not only responsible for the ecological crisis, but also for a growing psychological crisis in modernity (Clinebell, 1996). This crisis can only be challenged by efforts to reconnect human life with its biophysical location and ordering. Ecopsychological practices include nature meditation, wilderness journeying, and the development and practice of rituals in daily living that reincorporate natural symbols and cycles into urban life.

Insights derived from the doctrine of creation indicate the collective as well as individual consequences of ecological alienation for modern societies and communities. In particular the growing maldistribution of increasingly scarce resources such as water, clean air, fertile land, quiet and safe space is a major feature in the injustices which lie at the heart of the global environmental crisis. The Hebrew prophets identified ecological alienation – verdant pasture turning to desert, rivers drying up and vineyards becoming infertile – with the abandonment of the worship of God, and of God's original design for human society and especially the just distribution of natural resources (Northcott, 1996). They saw in other words a hidden law, or 'deep magic', at work in the natural order, such that when human societies abandon God's design, then the whole creation, and not just humanity, suffers. In the same way the psychological effects of ecological alienation cannot be viewed apart from the social and environmental consequences of the maldistribution of resources – both within and between nations – that increasingly characterizes modern global capitalism. [*Michael Northcott*]

CREMATION
Incineration of the corpse.
In the West, cremation is practised most in secularized Protestant countries, and least in religious, Catholic and especially Orthodox countries. Great Britain (72%) and Sweden (63%) contrast markedly with Eire (4%) and Italy (3%). The USA has a relatively low cremation rate of 24% (1997 figures). Cremation has historically been avoided by religions affirming resurrection rather than reincarnation. The process emerged in the late nineteenth century; cremation societies were founded in England in 1874 and in the USA in 1876. Christian liturgists are still developing appropriate rites for a form of disposal that has developed in the West for pragmatic rather than spiritual reasons.

CRIME
An offence in the public domain, as opposed to a private injury.
As such, crime is an action committed or omitted in violation of a law. Legally, the offender must intend (*mens rea*) a criminal act. Recent sociological and theological discussions have concentrated on why people commit certain acts (*see* Criminology) and how society can enable them to make reparations (Maguire *et al.*, 1997). Another recent definition of crime is 'acts of force or fraud undertaken in pursuit of self-interest'. Crime has come to the top of the political agenda in most Western countries since 1980, and the debate on the level of crime is intense.

CRIMINOLOGY
The systematic study of how criminal laws are enacted; why some people break these laws; how society and the state react to the breaking of law; and the methods of dealing with convicted offenders.
The discipline began in the eighteenth century with the classical definitions given by Cesare Beccaria, the English philosopher Jeremy Bentham and in the nineteenth century Cesare Lombroso. Bentham's theory of crime in 1789 gave an explanation of why people committed crime, but his interest was not simply theoretical. He was deeply involved in the design of the Panopticon, or inspection house, where prisoners could be observed by a few guards at the hub of a circular prison. This design influenced the building of the first national penitentiary (or prison) at Millbank, London in 1816. The use of Christianity in this system was crucial: the chaplain had a central role in promoting repentance and godly discipline, with convicts kept in the quiet of their solitary cells to study the Bible, interspersed with hard physical labour. There is a graphic description of this world in Michel Foucault's *Discipline and Punish* (1979).

Contemporary criminology is based on an analysis of why people commit crime, especially the deprivation often found in the background of offenders. One movement in criminology, which has interested theologians, is that of 'restorative justice' (Burnside and Baker, 1994). Here crime is seen as a breakdown in relationships, between offender and victim. Other relationships affected include offender–family, victim–family, and the relationship with the local community. The central idea is that of reintegrating an offender back into the community by 'constructive shaming', rather than by shaming as stigmatization. The offender should be helped to make reparation to the 'victim' in ways which restore the relationship broken by the crime. Elements of this approach are found in the criminal legislation of the British (Labour) Government from 1997 onwards. They follow earlier pioneering approaches in Australia, New Zealand and Canada.

Theological discussion of criminology is mainly confined to two areas. One is the study of the working of the prison system, as in the study by the Church of England's Board for Social Responsibility (1999), *Prisons: A Study in Vulnerability*. Such studies demonstrate the effect of prison on particular individuals, such as those with mental illness, young people and families. They describe the challenges which chaplains face in prison. A different approach is given as a response to theoretical criminology, and relates this to Christian understandings of punishment. In turn this can lead to reflections on theories of atonement in Christian doctrine. How does the understanding of punishment relate to the meaning of the cross? One recent study by Gorringe (1996) takes this argument further and asks if the development of theories of punishment in Western societies was itself influenced by Christian theories of the atonement. Put bluntly, did theories of penal substitution enable the death penalty to be retained? *[Peter Sedgwick]*

CRISIS INTERVENTION

A form of brief psychotherapy used to aid individuals in a state of flux following either a psychosocial change which may be developmental (such as adolescence or retirement) or accidental (such as bereavement or a disaster).

Crisis is seen as offering the possibility of change. The Chinese symbol for crisis is an amalgam of the symbols for danger and opportunity. Crisis therapy aims to maximize growth in the state of transition induced by the crisis, and to minimize the risk of deterioration. Gerald Kaplan described four stages of crisis intervention and went on to develop a model of preventative psychiatry. In America it has been applied in social work and counselling. In Britain the concept has been developed into broad-based psychosocial programmes of psychiatric care for the seriously mentally ill.

CROSS

The central symbol of redemption and of God's paradoxical strength in weakness.

Crucifixion was the Roman means of death by torture reserved for slaves and guerrillas. Its function was to enforce the 'peace of the empire' (*Pax Romana*) by terror. The early community, and above all Paul, seized on Jesus' death by crucifixion as the hallmark and sum of God's redemptive purpose. In an extreme paradox Paul talks of the crucified Christ as 'the wisdom and the power of God' (1 Cor. 1.24). The history of theology is the attempt to fathom this insight, which cannot be reduced to a set of theories.

Feminist theologians are right to insist that some of these attempts have taken sadistic and life-denying forms (Soelle, 1976). Sacrificial and penal understandings of the atonement have especially been open to this misunderstanding. The claim that the cross is redemptive is not, however, to place a positive value on suffering or death, nor to preach submission to the oppressed. To understand the cross as good news it is essential to retain Paul's dialectical usage. The cross is 'good news':

1. *As the wisdom of God.* The cross as God's identification with the victims of history takes up the theme of the Exodus in tracing the working out of God's purpose in the humble and unnamed rather than in 'the makers of history'. In this sense Nietzsche understood Paul, and, although his view of the cross is a caricature, it is also a perceptive commentary on its real significance (Nietzsche, 1990).

2. *As the power of God.* Placing the story of the crucifixion at the centre of the gospel represents a perception about the nature of power. Imperial power, today as in the first century, always claims to keep the peace and always does so through crucifixion. The cross exposes the fraudulence of these claims. Over against this the gospel places the power of forgiveness and love of the enemy: in forgiving his executioners as he dies Jesus refuses their logic and claim to ultimacy. The cross proclaims the inauguration of the messianic age of non-violence (Isa. 11).

3. *As providing light in the darkness of history.* The cross takes its place as part of an endless catalogue of state terror. 'Only that historian will have the gift of fanning the spark of hope in the past who is firmly convinced that *even the dead* will not be safe from the enemy if he wins' (Walter Benjamin). The cross is good news to the victims because it is the promise that they have not passed into darkness but that God, the source and heart of all reality, is alongside them and therefore their guarantor (Job 19.25).

4. *As the emblematic affirmation of Jesus' teaching about the Kingdom in which the first will be last, and the least the greatest.* It inaugurates a radical alternative: 'It shall not be so amongst you' (Mark 10.42). It represents Jesus' rejection of the ways of the lords of the Gentiles and his option for God's domination-free order. *[Timothy Gorringe]*

CULT

1. A description of a particular faith or religious practice.
2. A label for a group deemed by 'orthodox' churches to be deviant.

3. A sociological classification of certain religious groups.

The word 'cult' is so spongy and pejorative as to have almost lost its definition. The etymology of the word in English lies in the Latin term *cultus*, meaning 'worship' or 'ritual'. Virtually every major religion has spawned its own cults. Hare Krishna is a Hindu cult; the Mormons are a Christian cult; Messianic Jews originate from Judaism.

The study of cults has come to prominence in recent years, not only in the social sciences, but also in confessional spheres. The definition, analysis and interpretation of a cult is often determined by the outlook adopted in the method. Saliba (1995) notes three of the main approaches: (1) *theological* – but prone to be dogmatic, usually 'anti-cult'; (2) *psychological* – but prone to focus on mind control; (3) *sociological* – but prone to focus on structure as expression of value. Saliba also notes that 'cults', like any religious system, have strengths and weaknesses. Negative features might include the demand for total allegiance, the discouragement of rational thought or of engaging critical faculties, and excessive communitarianism (in some cases). These features may be exacerbated by tyrannical leaders, a stress on proselytizing, or an appeal to a rigid, all-embracing religious system. On the other hand, positive features of cults may include close 'family-type' relations between members, the offering of a disciplined life, and the chance to explore new vistas of religious and social experience. Clearly, many religious groups, not just those classified as 'cults', could share any of the features identified above (Melton, 1992).

The boundaries between 'cults' and new religious movements (NRMs) are increasingly hard to define and justify. Moreover, several Christian denominations that have had sectarian movements operating within them have often experienced those groups as operating in a 'cult-like' way. The word 'sect' comes from the Latin *secare*, meaning 'to cut', but although such groups are separatist, they can also have strong reformist tendencies, aiming to transform the very group that they are apart from but related to. Some Roman Catholics would regard a movement like Opus Dei as sectarian, and perhaps possessing cult-like tendencies. In the same way, Baptists and evangelical groups in Britain have struggled with organizations such as the Jesus Army.

Pastoral concerns in relation to cults normally arise when individuals join such groups, and then change radically. However, allegations of 'brainwashing' are rare, and it should be noted that the overwhelming weight of scholarly research undermines any notion that cults can somehow control and alter the minds of ordinary people. Furthermore, research shows that anyone can join a cult – members do not have to be vulnerable, suggestible, alienated, disaffected or deprived. Cults and NRMs appeal to the curious and the fully self-aware as much as to anyone else. Cults are by no means necessarily destructive. They can be therapeutic and provide helpful accounts of life for people. Some see joining a cult or NRM as a kind of rite of passage – something you do once in your life, for a few years or less. The majority of people who join a cult or NRM will leave within two years.

A move by an individual towards a 'new' religious movement or a 'cult' can often pose more of a problem for the family and friends who are left behind than it does for the initiate or convert. Yet very few religious groups can be deemed to be abusive, manipulative or dangerous. What 'cults' often have in common is that they bind people together in a new form of community. Inevitably, those who join change: themselves, their ideals, goals, lifestyle and relations. It is worth remembering that Jesus was no less demanding on the disciples: they were required to abandon their families, jobs, and even the dead, to embrace the coming Kingdom. Religions, by definition, upset existing social order and offer alternatives that are either competitive or complementary. Invariably, religion reshapes minds and hearts.

One of the major pastoral considerations in addressing families, cults and new religious movements is keeping a sense of proportion. Those who are concerned about the dramatic conversion of, or in, someone – of lifestyle, character or behaviour – may find that the adjustment is akin to a kind of temporary bereavement. However, it must be remembered that for the convert who embraces a new faith, the trauma can be as great for them as for those who somehow feel they have lost someone. In such circumstances, support is vital. The fact that someone embraces a new faith need not be read as a definitive rejection of their past, even though, in the early stages, it may appear to be so. Dialogue remains a vital key to fostering empathy and understanding, so that as many channels are kept as open as possible. From here, communication can be developed that will lay the foundation for new relationships, irrespective of whether the choice to join a new faith turns out to be a passing phase or a decision that lasts a lifetime. *[Martyn Percy]*

CURE OF SOULS
The responsibility of the pastor to treat people's lives in the setting of eternity.
The 'cure of souls' is handed by church leaders to local pastors. For example, a bishop in the Church of England shares this cure with his parish priests. The old word 'cure' is today usually translated as 'care'. But the Latin word *cura* carries stronger overtones than either 'cure' or 'care'. It indicates the pastor's responsibility to counsel and to put his or her ministry with individuals or groups into a divine context. The classical tradition of care is found in such theologians as Cyprian, Tertullian, Chrysostom, Augustine and particularly Gregory the Great. The Reformation and post-Reformation classics would include Luther and Calvin, as well as Richard Baxter, George Herbert and Jeremy Taylor. Most of these were practising bishops and pastors (Oden, 1984). Their pastoral theology, therefore, is both rooted in experience and hammered out against their major theological preoccupation. To some degree their authority has been subverted in late twentieth-century pastoral thinking by greater reference to psychologists and psychotherapy. But the recovery of a sense of the cure of souls is beginning as pastors find that they are expected to offer more than psychological counsel (Carr, 1989).

CURSING
Uttering words against a person or thing that consigns them to evil.
People have believed in the efficacy of cursing since earliest times. Today the argument is whether a curse 'works' parapsychologically or psychosomatically. The capacity of a cursed person to believe that they are cursed is part of the curse's power. Many otherwise rational people can be trapped into believing that they are somehow afflicted. The influence of witchcraft and the migration of people from various cultures and religions have both contributed to a wider belief in curses. The pastor should be especially careful not to collude with the frame of reference of someone claiming to be cursed. Nevertheless this is often a field in which chaplain

and psychiatrist can work well together (Perry, 1996).

D

DANCE
1. An ancient form of praying.
2. An art form in which physicality is used to communicate the fullness of humanity.
Dance gives form and shape to our thoughts and feelings through rhythm, movement and stillness. Three forms may be useful in pastoral work: liturgical dance – dance as worship; contemplative dance – meditative prayer in movement; and circle dance – set-step community dances derived from an international folk tradition.

1. *Liturgical dance.* This is performed in sacred places as a gift offered by those dancing to the other worshippers. The theme of the liturgy must determine the choreography and structure for the worship. It can offer another level to understanding the good news and the gospel values we are called to follow. Spiritual and scriptural sources, often with complex inherent contradictions (e.g. dying/living), can unfold their meaning more clearly by using 'contrasts' in the language of dance (e.g. lifeless/energized). Narrative storytelling in mime, choreographed prayer gestures or dance-drama may be appropriate on occasion. But in Western cultures, much of the possibility of using dance in and as worship has arisen from the modern dance movement. This development and progression into 'dance in education' with its more natural style, expressive of feelings, has enabled keen, non-professional dancers to perform with grace, poise and meaning.

2. *Contemplative dance.* This acknowledges our sacramental nature as revealed in the incarnation. Our creator is in the beauty of our being. In a physical language we ourselves embody that transfiguring transcendence that makes holy our humanity. For many, an act of reconciliation must come first, eradicating discrimination. The movements are motivated from the core of the dancer's being, emerging naturally to communicate in person and in community, celebrating the mystical gift of our physicality, which images our creator. Of its nature this form of dance is a meditative search, unplanned, instinctive,

never a performance. It gives form to our feelings, finding God's affirmation of our human experiences in all their diversity, especially moments of deep personal significance. It is a theological and pastoral activity offering moments of insight and experiential understanding applicable to biblical reflection and to our own lives. It requires centred concentration, attentive to self and aware of everyone around, actively involved, not being a spectator, listening in inspirational readiness and prepared to accept an element of risk.

3. *Circle dancing*. All participate, emphasizing mutuality. Simple repetitive motifs are danced in unison, to a wide variety of music. It is as a danced prayer, symbolic of a community in harmony. Its simplicity is such that it can easily be taught by demonstration just prior to the dancing, making it possible for a whole congregation to contribute to a liturgy. It needs a clear, gentle, confident facilitator. *[Lala Winkley]*

DARK NIGHT OF THE SOUL
The apparently total lack of any sense of consolation or meaning in prayer and Christian life generally.
Christian writers on the subject of prayer have often described it as being, at some levels, a journey into darkness as much as a journey into light. Serious prayer takes you beyond images and concepts, beyond a state in which you can 'see' or make sense of God as if God were an object confronting you. Such writers also – but less often – speak of the sense which may accompany this of abandonment, anxiety or numbness. However, it is not until the sixteenth century that this is formalized and explored in detail in the work of the Spanish friar, John of the Cross. With Teresa of Avila, he was the leading figure in the reform of the Carmelite order.

The most extended treatment of the subject is in the two-part treatise *The Ascent of Mount Carmel*: the incomplete second volume is entitled *The Dark Night of the Soul*. John begins from the basic premise that God must be experienced by human beings as 'night'; that is, God's reality is such that every human capacity will be frustrated when confronted with God. It feels as though we are encountering nothing in particular, no object that we can contain or 'process' in any way. Faced with this frustration, our only way through is to allow God to transform our capacities: memory, intelligence and will must change into hope, faith and love. But in

this process, they must wholly let go of their ordinary ways of working, and this letting go is experienced as a moment of total darkness (Louth, 1991).

The detailed discussion of how this darkness operates leads finally to a sobering account of the loss even of 'spiritual' comfort. It may be relatively simple to give up material ease, even to purify one's thoughts about God; but the ultimate test is when the very thought of God makes no sense whatever, and one's sense of security and self-worth seems to disappear. This is when darkness reaches right into the depth of the spirit – hence 'the dark night of the soul'.

Later writers (Augustine Baker, Jean-Pierre de Caussade, John Chapman and others) develop this, often in the context of pastoral guidance (O'Donoghue, 1989). A discerning spiritual director will know when someone is entering this experience and will not try to force a directee to meditate or to produce artificial feelings of confidence. Someone in the 'night' must simply trust and endure. Great damage can be done if they are made to feel that their doubt or misery or numbness are not acceptable or marks of failure. A modern director will need also to be able to distinguish this from clinical depression. This is not always easy, but the salient point is that the 'night' is (paradoxically) something that is grasped as a consequence of conscious commitment to God. *[Rowan Williams]*

DATA PROTECTION
Maintaining computerized personal data in accordance with legal and ethical requirements.
The advent of the computer has rapidly introduced new ethical issues concerning the acquisition and use of personal data. In the UK the 1984 Data Protection Act places legal requirements on anyone who stores data about people in computers. The user must register on the Data Protection Register. The pastor who keeps personal material about members of the congregation or others should remember that they have legal access to what is recorded.

To date, the USA does not have such an act, and the US Commerce Department has had to establish a 'safe harbor' programme in order to enable US companies to trade in compliance with EU privacy rules. Ethical considerations are important outside of legal requirements.

DEACON
An ordained or elected minister, as distinct from a priest, performing a recognized service.

In the developing order of the churches of the New Testament, *diakonia* (service) was shared by the whole community. It described a way of living with each other and in the world brought about by the revelation of God in the ministry of Christ as the 'one who serves' (Mark 10.45) and in the outpouring of the Spirit to equip God's people for proclamation, service of the Kingdom, and the ministry of reconciliation. The term can be applied to any individual ministry in its relation to the whole Church and to the whole Church in relation to its service to the world (2 Cor. 3—5). The diaconate is therefore a powerful sign of the true nature of the Church. This understanding has led, latterly, to a renewed interest in its function as a distinctive calling, rather than a halfway house between lay and 'fully' ordained ministry. The Lima Report (WCC, 1982) states that by struggling in Christ's name with the myriad needs of societies and persons, deacons exemplify the interdependence of worship and service in the Church's life.

In the New Testament churches the function was associated with the fellowship of the common meal. This included not only serving at table but also the collection and administration of food and other material possessions in the service of poorer members (Acts 6). The importance of this function and its association with the material needs of the Church is preserved in the title 'archdeacon' for the bishop's chief administrative officer (usually today a senior cleric). The range of activity of a deacon, however, seems to have originated in earliest times. Stephen, for example, is noted for his preaching and martyrdom rather than for any administrative ability. In Phil. 1.1, 1 Tim. 3.8–13 and elsewhere it is already recognized as a separate order in distinction from the 'overseers' or 'elders' (Collins, 1990).

The influence of the diaconate diminished considerably during the Middle Ages. As its hierarchical inferiority to the priesthood became more emphasized, so it became increasingly in the West merely a stage of transition between lay and ordained ministry. Only in the Orthodox Churches did the permanent diaconate survive with its own definite liturgical function. In Anglican and Roman Catholic churches the term 'deacon' describes those episcopally ordained to a pastoral ministry which includes preaching, teaching, baptizing, marrying and leading worship but excludes presiding at the Eucharist, blessing and absolving. The diaconate usually lasts only a short time before ordination to the priesthood. The Second Vatican Council allowed for the diaconate to become a permanent state for older married men, and there have been experiments with a permanent diaconate in both churches. In the Lutheran Church the term applies to all assistant parochial ministers, 'fully' ordained or not. In several Protestant denominations it is a lay office associated with the pastoral and material needs of the church to which members are elected by the local congregation. In this way the various denominations reflect the New Testament diaconate in fragmentary form. It may be, however, that the way forward is not a return to a permanent diaconate as a separate order of ministry, but a greater recognition of the diaconal nature of all forms of ministry and a greater openness of all church life and structures in service to those who remain outside its fellowship.
[Christopher Moody]

DEAD, PRAYER FOR THE
See: PRAYER FOR THE DEAD

DEATH
The end of present bodily existence.

Death is an issue of growing importance in pastoral studies. The idea of death as a taboo subject is breaking down and it is coming to be recognized that there can be positive good in the open acknowledgement of terminal illness. The ending of a conspiracy of silence enables the dying person to talk through with relatives, nurses, clergy and counsellors his or her worries and concerns. They often reflect on their past lives and sometimes seek a last opportunity to put right damaged relationships with others. Thanatologists are being trained to help people affirm the life which is now ending, and to see their dying as a significant experience. Such discourse often implies an underlying spirituality in which death is not seen as the final end. This attitude is supported by the claim that whatever philosophy a person may have held during life, they almost always approach their own dying with an implicit conviction that in some sense 'they' will go on. Clergy and ministers should recognize that their role may become increasingly important within such a process, provided that they realize that in this context it is not their own beliefs that need to be affirmed but rather the somewhat inchoate and tentative hopes and fears of those to whom they are ministering.

Within the wider society death is often thought of as simply 'the end', 'the horizon that closes off the future'. Such attitudes are encouraged by a reductionist 'scientism' that affirms that human beings are no more than complicated psycho-physical organisms; by an anti-dualist trend in contemporary philosophy; and by theologians who endorse the Hebrew insistence that human beings are irreducibly physical beings whose only possible life is on this earth. Such attitudes pose a significant challenge to belief in the Christian hope. The dominant trend in contemporary theology is to insist that death must be taken seriously as the ending of individual existence. Resurrection is then seen as a new creation by God which transcends all that we can think or imagine. In this perspective the resurrection of Jesus Christ is seen as the one foundation for future hope. In his resurrection 'end-time entered our time' and in the light of what happened to Jesus then we can look forward to what we may expect for ourselves. Philosophically this position raises issues concerning the continuity of personal identity through such change. Scientifically there are problems with integrating talk of this dramatic eschaton with what we know of likely developments within the cosmos. Pastorally this view is a problem in that fewer Christians find it believable. Hence if the Christian hope is to find any ongoing credibility the grounds for it must be re-examined.

Belief in life after death has always been at the heart of Christianity. For St Paul it was axiomatic that 'if for this life only we have hoped in Christ, we are of all people most to be pitied' (1 Cor. 15.19). Throughout the Christian centuries all the main themes of theology and worship revolved around the hope that death was not the end. There is no accident about the primacy of such belief, for the coherence of any real belief in God depends upon it (Davis, 1989). For the Fathers, the Schoolmen and the Reformers it was axiomatic that Christian hope consisted of two elements: the immortality of the soul and the resurrection of the body. This belief continues to be Catholic orthodoxy. According to Pope John Paul II (1979), 'the Church affirms that a spiritual element survives and subsists after death, an element endowed with consciousness and will, so that the

"human self" subsists, though deprived for the present of the complement of its body. To designate this element the Church uses the word "soul".' Catholic theology does of course make clear that a permanently disembodied soul would not be a suitable vehicle for the expression of human personhood and so resurrection continues also to be a key component of the Christian hope. But it recognizes that for resurrection to happen to 'me', the concept of the soul remains essential as the bridge between the two worlds.

Belief in the immortality of the soul has recently received encouragement from two sources: (1) from a revival of interest in religious experiencing, often outside mainstream religion; (2) from the reports of people resuscitated from a close encounter with death about what they experienced during the time when their hearts had stopped beating and their lungs had stopped breathing. In most cases 'they' claim to have gone 'out of their bodies' and to have looked down with interest on the resuscitation attempts. Many also had experiences of a transcendental kind which profoundly changed their attitude to life. A survey of 344 British cases (Badham and Ballard, 1996) shows that the biggest change is that 82% said they now had less fear of death and most of them had developed a strong conviction that their consciousness or soul can exist independently of the body and continue in being after death.

Historically such experiences have been rare but deemed of great significance. For St Paul it was on the basis of such an experience that he sought to defend his own spiritual authority (2 Cor. 12.1–7). Near-death experiences also appear to have had a significant impact on many mystics. It seems that today a historically significant experience has been 'democratized' by modern medical technology and is now giving an important input into contemporary thought about the nature of death. [Paul Badham]

DEATH INSTINCTS
Instincts which, according to Freudian theory, drive people back towards an earlier, inorganic state.
This is a much disputed area of Freud's thought. In another typical dualism he proposed that there were death instincts running counter to the life instincts. They are a drive to avoid stimulation and so aim at death and dying. By contrast the life instincts are focused in eros.

DECEPTION
Telling an untruth in order to make someone believe as true what is false.

Disciples are to say what they mean and mean what they say. According to Jesus, 'Let your word be "Yes, Yes" or "No, No"' (Matt. 5.37). Paul said to the Corinthians concerning his intended visit to them, that his word was not 'Yes and No', for 'the Son of God, Jesus Christ . . . was not "Yes and No"; but in him it is always "Yes"' (2. Cor. 1.15–20).

In Christian pastoralia deception marks the opening to John Chrysostom's *Concerning the Priesthood*, where he cheats his friend Basil to avoid ordination. Gregory the Great, however, counselled a contextual sensitivity to the appropriateness of truth-telling (*Pastoral Care* 111.11).

Self-deception is well known to pastors and counsellors. It usually needs addressing in terms of reality, sometimes through confession, penitence and absolution. But pastors need to be alert to persistent self-deception which denies reality, and which may be a sign of possible psychological disturbance for which professional help is required.

DEFENCE MECHANISM
The means through which a psychological defence is given specific expression.

The term is Freud's but it has widespread use in technical and popular thinking and has been developed (A. Freud, 1937). Defence mechanisms are unconscious processes that individuals mobilize to defend themselves against the feelings associated with uncomfortable situations. All defence mechanisms have one aim – to reduce any anxiety that psychological conflict might generate. They are therefore the work of the ego and correspondingly aspects of normal functioning. They may become pathological, but are not inevitably so. The mechanisms include repression, regression, isolation, projection, turning against the self and sublimation, as well as others. Klein, for example, adds primitive defences – splitting, projective identification, omnipotence, and rationalization or the denial of any psychic reality.

Obviously these various defences do not have the same quality or status. But the key point for the pastor is that resistance, whatever form it takes, is not something to be overcome. Like any behaviour it is to be interpreted, thus leading the client to better understanding.

DELIVERANCE MINISTRY
Freeing people from bondage, usually to Satan, and offering Christ's liberation from human sinfulness or the demonic.

The Church has a long history of involvement with the demonic and its exorcism. Today pastors and counsellors are likely to come up against similar instances. But in some traditions the ministry of freeing people from any bondage, not necessarily to the demonic, is generally called 'deliverance'. This is a wider word than 'exorcism' (Perry, 1996). There is dispute in the churches about the nature and practice of this ministry. Some of its proponents seem more interested in demons and the devil than might be judged healthy. Others, however, tend to emphasize the positive and healing aspects of the ministry of deliverance.

The issues raised are essentially threefold, and concern (1) the source of the deliverance; (2) the nature of this deliverance; (3) the benefits of the ministry.

1. *Source of deliverance.* The rudimentary meaning of deliverance adopted by the Christian tradition refers to the sacrifice of Jesus on the cross. This is God's supreme act of love and an 'eternal sacrifice' which, surpassing any other sacrifice, becomes 'the source of eternal salvation for all who obey him' (Heb. 5.9). Through the new covenant that the cross establishes between God and humans, all may be delivered from the power of evil and thus be 'justified by [God's] grace as a gift' (Rom. 3.24). Thus Jesus Christ is the source of the ministry and through his power any deliverance is achieved.

2. *Nature of deliverance.* Deliverance is from all that extinguishes the life of God in us. It means abandoning one's old self in order to live with Christ as a new creature. This new creation brings people a new freedom, which is rooted in the freedom of God. To live in such freedom means to be delivered from all that enslaves. The ministry of deliverance is exercised through guidance and teaching people about the full sense of Christian freedom. A fundamental indication of this is when people's relationships show a commitment to reflect the divine love which enfolds all.

3. *Benefits of this ministry.* How can the ministry of deliverance be applied to the case of a person impoverished of love? Drawing upon the stories of Jesus' love, the minister begins to introduce his healing power into the cycle of the human wounds and injuries. Through the power of Jesus' deliverance the person begins

to experience the gift of divine love, which in turn will be brought into other human relationships. Whenever a person claims the right to receive love while excluding any responsibility towards other persons, he or she denies the healing power of divine love. However, since God loves us, we in turn should love ourselves. When this happens people can begin to heal and make progress on the road to well-being. In such broad terms, as well as in the narrower emphasis on the demonic, we can say that the minister of Jesus' grace is practising the ministry of deliverance.

Today it is recognized that the demands for exorcism may be rare but the need for deliverance remains an important pastoral function. One difference is that while exorcism is supposed to be practised only by priests who carry special authority from their churches, deliverance can be offered by any Christian. The popularizing of the demonic in film and television seems to have led to an increase in fears about the occult and demons. But this ministry and the phenomena with which it deals raise many questions of theology and psychology. Most churches, therefore, advise pastors who find themselves dealing with people who are disturbed to consult advisers and not act alone. Roman Catholic and Anglican dioceses have special advisers who may be consulted. [Robert B. Kosek]

DELUSION
A pathological state in which a person constructs an idiosyncratic, untestable world.
A delusion is a false opinion that cannot be altered by reason. The language used may have its own unfamiliar logic. Whether delusion is a form of insanity is therefore disputed. Delusion can be contrasted with 'illusion'. This describes the normal range of fantasies through which people live. The words are often used interchangeably, especially in discussions of religion. It is a characteristic of religious belief that it seems to be located where illusion meets delusion – hence the popular assumption that religion may at times approach madness (Meissner, 1984).

DEMENTIA
The name of a syndrome (collection of features detectable on clinical examination) due to brain disease which is usually chronic and progressive.
The brain disease interferes with memory, orientation in time and space, thinking and language use, emotional control, social behaviour and motivation. As the disease progresses, self-care and the activities of daily living become difficult and sometimes impossible. The person may become unable to recognize loved ones and totally dependent on others. In progressive dementia, the outcome is fatal, though survival may continue for several years (rarely more than ten) from first diagnosis (Jacoby and Oppenheimer, 1997).

Any pathological process causing lasting interference with brain function may cause dementia. Hence the causes include infections, injuries, tumours, vascular problems and a wide range of general medical illnesses. Also, specific pathological processes, of which the most important is Alzheimer's disease, may cause dementia. Dementia in general can occur at any age, but is much commoner in later life, particularly over the age of 80. Varieties of dementia common among the elderly are dementia of Alzheimer type; vascular dementia (where blood vessel disease harms the brain through circulatory failure); and a mixed type with features of both diseases.

Characteristic early symptoms of dementia are memory disturbance, with short-term and recent memory much more impaired than distant memory, and disorientation, in clear consciousness. It is however important not to jump to the conclusion that someone with these symptoms has some form of dementia, because acute and recoverable brain impairments, called 'confusional states' or 'delirium', also cause recent memory problems and disorientation. Sometimes delirium accompanies an acute or subacute physical illness so that the cause of the delirium is obvious; at other times physical illness can present with mental symptoms and a confusional state. Mental symptoms suggestive of the possibility of acute or chronic brain disease warrant medical assessment.

Problems of depression and anxiety are common at all ages, and depression is frequent among the elderly. The relationship between depression and dementia is complex, and important, because treatable depression should not be missed. Depression may be the first sign of a developing dementia, but itself causes (temporarily) impaired brain function which may mimic dementia. It is often difficult to distinguish between depression due to environmental stresses, for example retirement or bereavement, and depression attributable to brain disease. A clinical rule of thumb is that failure to respond to antidepressant medication may be due to concurrent dementia or other physical illness.

Expert assessment of medical, psychological and social functions should be made whenever dementia is suspected. Often an assessment at home gives invaluable information about the individual's difficulties and the extent to which they can manage and be managed at home. A minority of patients are placed in residential or hospital care, most individuals remaining at home, often with massive and multiple problems and disabilities. Often a complex of interventions can be helpful, including contributions from professional medical and social care staff working as possible with family members and other local people.

Most carers of individuals with dementia are relatives, most often spouse or daughter. Most undertake the caring task more or less willingly, but may not realize how extremely burdensome carer responsibilities may become. Some devoted carers experience a sense of inadequacy in the task, which arises from their own devotion to the ill person rather than from the reality. Sometimes the problems associated with caring are family relationships. Behavioural manifestations of dementia may pose particular problems: aggression, repeated questioning, incontinence, disoriented wandering, and reversal of day/night sleep rhythm (sleeping during the day and wandering awake at night) are often especially hard to cope with. To cope with unremitting exposure to the declining conditions of a loved one is one of the hardest tasks with which anyone may be faced. It is common experience that family and friends 'rally round' when a person becomes ill, but that the continuing caring task falls upon one or very few people.

Pastoral attention should be directed both to the individual with dementia and to those caring for them. One can feel uneasy about conversing with a dementing person whose conversation is difficult to follow, repetitious, and indicates impairment or absence of conversational niceties and the inability to retain any new information. It is always helpful to respond to parts of conversation which are coherent. Often, the person can recall and talk about past events and this can be pleasurable and rewarding for them. At the same time, helping with ordinary life tasks, such as feeding, washing and toilet,

with as little fuss as possible, can greatly help patient and carer. Frequent short visits may be especially helpful, rather than infrequent longer ones.

Carers may appreciate simple sharing of their concerns and burden with pastorally involved colleagues as with friends or relatives. Opportunities for 'respite' may be welcome; 'elderly sitting' may be a practical service which is not difficult to provide. Pastoral attention may contribute to carer decisions about their loved one moving to residential care, should this be necessary and available, and also to the making of representations to relevant authorities about service deficiencies when it is not. Specifically religious activities, for example providing the sacrament or saying prayers with the dementing person and their carers, may be very helpful with people to whom these have been meaningful in the past. Careful planning of funeral arrangements after the demented person has died should acknowledge that carers may have gone through a process of 'anticipatory grief' so that relief of their burden becomes paramount after the death. All involved may be greatly helped by emphasis on the celebration of the life of the dead person as remembered when they were well.

Support groups (such as that run by the Alzheimer's Disease Society) may be very helpful. [James Watson]

DEMONIC
A belief in superhuman beings or spirits that can be beneficent or malevolent.

In the context of pastoral theology, it is vital to recognize that conceptualizations of the demonic are widely dispersed, with a variety of histories. 'Demon' derives from the Greek word *daimon*, meaning 'power'. In the early Greek world-view, there were no devils or demons. *Daimon*, as a notion, was linked either to an attribute of God (an unidentified force), or to the fortune and character of an individual, whether good or bad. In the fourth century BCE, Plato began the process of reconstituting *daimon* into demon, by suggesting that what affected people's character was not just internal or given, but could be a particular category of beings that were intermediary between gods and humans.

Demons are acknowledged to occur in virtually all religions. Some of the earliest literate cultures such as those of Egypt and Mesopotamia reveal belief in supernatural beings who are feared as hostile and intrusive. However, recognition of demons does not always lead to a personification of <u>evil</u> in one supreme being, such as the <u>devil</u> or Satan. In Taoism, Mesopotamian and some primal cultures, evil spirits exist without a devil. They may be linked to natural objects such as rivers, rocks, animals and trees, or possibly ancestors. These demons may be malevolent or beneficent. In Christianity, Judaism, Islam and Zoroastrianism, demons are regarded as a separate class of beings and minions of the devil. As such, they provide an account of evil that is neither the direct responsibility of God nor under immediate human control.

Conceptualization of the demonic in Christian cultures has varied, as has the practice of <u>exorcism</u>. The early Church had to respond to an overemphasis on evil spirit from Manichaeism. In medieval Christendom, demons began to be features in Christian paintings and sculptures, symbolizing all types of evil and disaster. During the Reformation, and subsequently, demons were more personalized, and linked to heresy, witchcraft and sorcery. The number of trials, purges and witch hunts rose correspondingly. The Enlightenment, with its emphasis on empiricism and rationality, signalled a period of decline for the stress on the demonic. However, the twentieth century (a modern and postmodern era) has seen a resurgence of interest in demons, evil spirits and angels. This has partly arisen through the influence of African and West Indian animism that was partially absorbed into some expressions of Pentecostalism. Some new religious movements (NRMs) have also encouraged an interest in 'magic' and in superstition, with renewed regard for pagan religious practice.

In the last fifty years, charismatic renewal has absorbed many Western contemporary cultural obsessions with evil spirits and demons. Some <u>deliverance ministries</u> can be dualist, and propose novel hierarchies of demons, including 'territorial spirits' and demons linked to certain conditions, or charged with certain responsibilities (Percy, 1996). Other revivalists suggest long lists of activities that expose Christians and non-Christians to demonic affliction. Films have worked their way into the consciousness of contemporary revivalism. In this sense, many revivalists are reaching back into the realms of medieval imagination. Few theologians in the last century have paid much attention to the demonic. Barth was an exception, as was Tillich. More generally, Freud,

Jung, Rollo May and others have tended to treat the demonic seriously without necessarily assenting to its reality. They see it as either deeply repressed evil wishes or desires, a good account or metaphor for the struggle between good and evil, or perhaps psychosis. However, some serious mental illnesses (such as multiple personality disorder, also known as dissociative disorder) lend themselves to the vocabulary of possession, with sufferers perceiving of themselves as having been taken over by an alien force that is compelling them to evil or harm. Anthropological and psychological studies tend to cast the demonic and possession as genres that have a liminoid function. Deliverance becomes a rite of passage, in which the dysfunctional or antisocial person is restored to the community. More recently, some theologians have suggested that Jesus' deliverance ministry was highly selective, and was offered only to the marginalized and poor as a mechanism for social reintegration and as a judgement on society. A person alleged to have a demon may in fact be 'demonized' in some sort of drama engendered by a hostile community that cannot come to terms with mental illness (cf. Luke 8.26–39).

Demons are held to be responsible for all manner of things: temptation, oppression, physical illness, misfortune and disaster, mental illness and actual 'possession'. Yet each of these problems is capable of being described in other ways which may be more appropriate. Those engaged in the exercise of deliverance need to act with great care and discernment. Where possible, professionals with other expertise such as psychiatrists or counsellors should be invited to give an opinion and participate in treatment and care. The explosion of deliverance ministries in the late twentieth century has brought a number of pastoral problems. People with genuine problems may find some temporary comfort and relief in projecting their difficulties into complex and constructed demonic cosmologies. However, the same ministries often lack a breadth of pastoral resources, specifically in offering an appropriate depth of diagnosis, prognosis and long-term care for those who think they are possessed or afflicted.

Studies of the demonic show that, whether real or imaginary, the naming and embodiment of evil is an evolving concept in the history of religion and human consciousness. Theologians and experts in religious studies can show that experience of the demonic is often a combination of artefact, projection and contemporary cultural constructs, as well as evil or illness. Generally, it is vital that perceptions of the demonic are taken seriously in the first instance. Whether the evil spirit is ultimately 'real', or subsequently turns out to be a form of projection, is something that can only be tested and handled within the context of a mature, constant, consistent and caring community. [Martyn Percy]

DENIAL
Refusal to recognize the reality of some traumatic perception.
Denial may be a defence against facing the feelings generated by an unpleasant reality. But care needs to be taken with such expressions: they may be instances of good self-management. For example, a client who avows that they are not worried by being fired or forced to resign, may, unknown to the pastor, have another job lined up and not be worried. Nevertheless, denial of feelings is usually a defence against reality, which requires sensitivity in response. In English, 'denial' carries strong overtones. The process is better thought of as 'disavowal'.

DEPENDENCE
A relationship with the potential to give support and the hope, desire for or even expectation of that support.
The apparently neutral concept of dependence is so surrounded and coloured by ethical debate, psychological theory and political philosophy, that it may seem to emerge as not neutral at all: dependence bad, independence good. For example, dependence may be linked with a patriarchal model of family and other relations, where feelings of impotence are associated with a fear of and dependence on authority. It is helpful, therefore, in thinking about the meaning of dependence in human relationships, to make the distinction between primitive and mature dependence.

In its primitive sense, dependence derives from a frightening and frightened state of mind, where the immature organism looks desperately in its environment for a reliable object to save it from unimaginable danger. This is true, say, of the crying infant, who receives comfort and reassurance as well as food from the mother's breast. Later comes the process of weaning, through which the child learns to tolerate a degree of independence. However, weaning is never complete. As individuals and as members of social groups in different contexts, people tend at times to put aside their own competences to deal with a situation and invest all competence in others. In this dependent state, where gratification is sought rather than doing what has to be done, it is difficult to be creative or productive. Anyone who has been in a meeting that seems to go on for ever and is unable to make any decisions has experienced this phenomenon in everyday life. There is, moreover, a tendency in an unrealistic and often unconscious way to invest authority in a leader who will take away fears and gratify wishes.

Dependence in this sense has been regarded as pathological and destructive. Social institutions that are thought to encourage such dependence have themselves come under attack. A welfare state is described in derogatory terms as a 'nanny state', maintaining people in a state of infantile dependence rather than encouraging an appropriate reliance on one's own capacities to cope. Critiques of traditional institutional care have demonstrated that a system that only allows for the meeting of dependence needs – perhaps the need for help with dressing, eating, toileting of a person with disabilities – denies the capacity of the individual to take an independent decision-making role in relation to these dependency needs and all other activities. Care of elderly people, for example, is complicated by the challenge to carers to respond appropriately to dependency needs without infantilization.

It is important, therefore, also to have a sense of mature or healthy dependence. Without such a concept, a dismissive rejection of dependence in general as weak or pathological may be thought to lead to rampant individualism and a narcissistic egocentric view of the world. Mature dependence starts from a socio-centric perspective, where 'No man is an Island, entire of it self'. It is as if the infant, having first made the painful distinction between what is 'I' and what is 'Not-I', has to continue the equally painful learning of how to make connections. Dependence in this sense is a necessary recognition of the limitations of our own fantasies of omnipotence. It also avoids the perils of counterdependence, a denial of dependency needs, a frustrated kicking against the constraints of reality, that hinders independent thought and action. Mature relationships are grounded in the individual's developing capacity for attachment (originating in the bond between parent and child), trust, reliance on others as well as self-reliance. John Bowlby (1971) preferred these terms to those of dependence and independence, which look as if they are mutually exclusive.

The recognition of dependence, even if it is not overtly acknowledged, is essential to evolving processes of social behaviour, including the division of labour and the establishment of trading relationships. It is through the tolerance of mutually dependent relationships that social structures are formed and maintained. An example of mutual dependence would be the institution of marriage. A mature dependence is not then about the simple gratification of needs, passively demanded of an often-absent leader. It is an interactive process, requiring both thought and action, in which difference is recognized as is use of that difference to achieve mutually agreed ends. One aspect of dependence, therefore, is a capacity for followership, for responding in a purposeful way to the leadership being offered.

Nevertheless, the distinction between primitive dependence and mature dependence is not so clear-cut when it has to be worked out in everyday social interaction. This may be seen in a helping relationship, where a certain amount of regression to an infantile state of dependence is to be expected. Indeed, it is arguable that the development of any relationship of trust requires the surrender of some personal autonomy. This is why trust, as developed in a dependent relationship, is always open to abuse. Dependence therefore puts a particular onus of responsibility on the person in a leadership role. The leader, receiving projections of omnipotence from others, who are experiencing a certain regression, is therefore in a powerful position. This does not mean that the leader should summarily reject the dependence of others. That is likely to leave them confused and angry, and at a loss to know what to do. Rather the leader may be working over a period to make their role redundant.

An example of that approach is found in some consultancy relationships. 'The intervention will be successful if clients have transformed the dependence on me into fuller exercise of their own authority and competence' (Miller, 1993). Dependence is therefore not a chronic but a transitional state, evident at the beginning and end of life, and a neces-

sary element in the management of transitions throughout life, where the individual is temporarily dislocated from the certainties of previous experience and so more than usually reliant on the experience of others.

The theme has also been extensively examined in studies of the task of the Church and the role of the clergy (Reed, 1978; Ecclestone, 1988; Carr, 1997). Natural human dependence is the material with which churches work: it is seen as a fact of humankind's desirable mature dependence on God. The danger of reinforcing immature dependence is particularly acute where such necessary dependence is transformed into an infantilizing and debilitating holding of people in a collective form of weakness. [Tim Dartington]

DEPRESSION
Depression is a word that is probably at present undefinable.
At the end of the twentieth century, a World Health Organization survey suggested that depression is one of the commonest disorders of humankind, accounting for a greater amount of disability than any other disorder except cardiovascular disorders. It was estimated that in all likelihood it would outstrip even cardiovascular disorders in the early years of the twenty-first century as the greatest source of disability on earth. Given that depressive disorders were all but unrecognized a century previously, this is an extraordinary development. It suggests that any definition of depression must take into account a range of social and cultural factors, in addition to the biological underpinnings that are traditionally used to define a disease state (Healy, 1997).

Depression is now thought of as being a mood disorder. However, this helps us very little in terms of trying to define it in that no one can define what a mood disorder is. Unlike a motor disturbance or a visual disturbance, which affect discrete brain areas, at present there is no agreement on the existence or whereabouts of a mood centre in the brain. The classic manic-depressive disorders involve gross motor disturbances in a manner that makes it possible to argue convincingly that these are motor rather than mood disorders. Other disorders defined as depressive involve states of general nervousness or anxiety with concomitant distress and dysphoria, which for most of the twentieth century were defined as 'nerves' or anxiety rather than depression. All of these very disparate states are at present classified under the heading of a mood disorder, but it would seem improbable that they are varying manifestations of a common disturbance.

The Greeks had recognized melancholic and manic states, but until the late nineteenth century melancholia was a term that could be applied to any underactive form of insanity. People with obsessive compulsive disorders or any other condition that inhibited activity, such as schizophrenia, social phobia or even Parkinson's disease, might all be classified as melancholic. There was no suggestion that this was a mood disorder as this term would now be understood. Mania in contrast was any overactive insanity. It was a state that could be brought about by delirium as well as many overactive delusional or schizophrenic states. Clearly, given these definitions of mania and melancholia, the ancients were referring to something very different from what we now understand by mania or depression, even though, for example, the portrait of Job in the Bible makes it indubitable that what would now be thought of as profound mood disorders occurred in the classical period.

The term depression was first used by Samuel Johnson around 1753 to refer to a general state of debility, lowered spirits and nervousness. However, reading Johnson's account of his own disturbances suggests a condition more like what would now be called obsessive compulsive disorder rather than depression.

The first person to suggest that there was a mood faculty in the brain and that this might be disordered in ways that would give rise to something like the modern idea of depression was Esquirol, one of the greatest of the early French psychiatrists in the nineteenth century. Disorders of the mood faculty, Esquirol argued in the 1830s, gave rise to lypemania (*lupos* = Greek for sadness).

The next step in the shaping of modern mood disorders lay with the description in the early 1850s by two of Esquirol's successors in Paris, Falret and Baillarger, of a condition where individuals could cycle from a low to high motor or mood state. This bipolar disorder was the first delineation of what was in 1896 in the hands of the German psychiatrist Emil Kraepelin to become manic-depressive disease. Kraepelin included recurrent states of depression, now termed a unipolar mood disorder, along with swings of mood, a bipolar disorder, in his concept of manic-depressive disease.

In 1905, Adolf Meyer, then emerging as the leading American psychiatrist, suggested discarding the terms manic-depressive, melancholia and mania and replacing them in the case of patients who had lowered spirits and retardation of activity with the supposedly neutral term depression.

All of these terms referred to conditions found in or likely to lead to admission to asylums. At this time the nervous problems experienced by individuals in the community were more likely to be seen as neurasthenia (literally weakness of the nerves) or as anxiety. These conditions were the province of physicians with an interest in psychosomatic medicine, neurologists and later psychodynamic psychotherapists.

Rates of admission to asylums through the nineteenth century and first half of the twentieth century for depressive or bipolar disorders remained extremely low – much lower than admissions for schizophrenia, for example.

Starting in the late 1950s a series of drugs were discovered that have since evolved into what are now termed the antidepressant drugs. When initially discovered, pharmaceutical companies were reluctant to develop these agents for depression as the size of the market appeared to be too small. Initially also these drugs were termed psychic energizers or thymoleptics rather than antidepressants, as the concept of an antidepressant had not been born. Through the 1960s and 1970s, sales of antidepressants remained low. This was an 'age of anxiety' and tranquillizers such as Librium and Valium were thought of as the appropriate treatment for these disorders. The age of anxiety came to an end with the public crisis of involuntary dependence on benzodiazepines in the early 1980s. The benzodiazepine tranquillizers gave way to a new generation of antidepressants, termed the selective serotonin reuptake inhibitors (SSRIs) of which Prozac is the best known, and the 1990s saw the emergence of an 'age of depression'. Estimates of the prevalence of depression in the year 2000 show a one or two thousandfold increase since 1950.

As of the turn of the millennium, there is no general agreement as to what causes depression, no agreement on what happens in the brains of people who are depressed and no agreement on whether one or more different

conditions lurk under the name depression.
[David Healy]

DEPRESSIVE POSITION
In Kleinian thinking, the stage of integration of hitherto separated feelings.
According to Melanie Klein (1963) this is the second stage in human development. It occurs in infancy but recurs in adult life, both in individuals and institutions. It emerges from the paranoid-schizoid position, which is marked by splitting and projection. In the depressive position the person generates a more integrated whole. For example, instead of seeing mother as either good or bad and oscillating between these perceptions, the child integrates her into a whole object. It is called 'depressive' because Klein saw it as a move from the comfortable simplicities of splitting and projection to the demanding work of integration. The depression, therefore, is the result of unconscious mourning for the time when the world was simple, of guilt and general sadness. The word 'position' is used rather than 'phase' because this behaviour is not confined to childhood but recurs in adult life (Obholzer and Roberts, 1994).

DEPTH PSYCHOLOGY
A general term for any psychological approach that employs the notion of the unconscious mind.
The phrase is chiefly associated with Freud's and his successors' theories of psychoanalysis. It is no longer an especially useful term in the light of developments, although it is still sometimes employed. It is a reminder that although psychoanalysis and psychology have moved into many separate disciplines, they share the same roots. The essential facet of depth psychology is willingness to acknowledge and work with the concept of the unconscious mind.

DESERTION
The legal ground for divorce.
Desertion has been a ground for divorce in England since 1937. The desertion of a partner for three years or more constituted sufficient evidence for divorce when it depended upon the petitioner being able to prove a 'matrimonial offence'. The significance of this new ground for divorce being introduced must be understood in the context of an unfolding legislative process

that gave women access to divorce on the same terms as men (Stone, 1992). Technically, desertion ceased to be a ground for divorce once the 1969 Divorce Reform Act became operational in 1971. However, it could still be used to demonstrate that a marriage had irretrievably broken down. This situation ended in 1998 when the Family Law Act came into operation. In the US, while grounds for divorce are no longer required in those states which have enacted no-fault divorce laws, desertion continues to have an impact on other legal issues surrounding divorce, including decisions about property division, custody, child support and alimony.
[Christopher Clulow]

DESPAIR
A malignant condition resulting from total loss of hope.
People who are under sentence of death, whether from execution, a desperate situation, or from terminal illness, are unlikely to despair so long as they continue to hope for life, even if their hope is, to the observer, unrealistic. They may die without ever having experienced despair. By contrast, if despair sets in, people seem to become more vulnerable to illness and death. This may account for the fact that some people survive terrible injuries and illnesses while others succumb to lesser assaults on their bodies.

Loss of hope does not always result in despair. A criminal on the way to execution may walk towards the death chamber with a sense of justice being done. A man trapped underground, or in a submarine, may face the total loss of hope with equanimity, knowing that death is inevitable. Such people are not subject to despair as we understand the condition, even if they are not people of religious faith.

When people despair, however, they lose all sense of purpose in life and all sense of the possibility that their condition may improve in the future. They feel profoundly depressed and may come to believe that they and/or their families might be better off if they were dead. Suicide is one way out, but some people who are in despair do not have sufficient energy to kill themselves. They may then just take to their beds, refuse to eat or drink and eventually die of inanition or a related infection.

Despair is not easy to diagnose, even in people who are overtly depressed. Some people are clever at concealing the disappearance of hope.

Despair is not often cured by an injection of hope from outside. Empathic listening, together with an ability to admit to the awfulness of such an experience, is the most helpful attitude to adopt. Trying to sort out the evident problems too soon sometimes worsens the situation. Watchfulness for sudden suicidal attempts is needed. Those who care for people in despair should not lose hope themselves. They need to continue to state their belief that hope may return, but not try to impose it. When hope does return it will appear only as a glimmer. Patience needs to be exercised if that glimmer of hope is to be fanned into a flame.

Some say that Jesus experienced despair on the cross when he felt abandoned by his Father. His plight may help some people of faith to feel that Christ is close to them in what they are experiencing. It may encourage them to hold on since they know that at the end of his life Jesus did surrender his spirit trustingly into the hands of God. Those who have pastoral care for people in despair should be careful not to invoke this incident quickly. But speaking about it can help some faithful Christians in a remarkable way. [Una Kroll]

DETACHMENT
1. Lack of involvement with personal concerns, people and surroundings.
2. Dissassociation from reality.
3. A sense of emotional freedom.
Winnicott (1958) defined detachment as the capacity to be alone, a kind of self-confidence that was the end product of having had secure attachments early in life and feeling secure in oneself. However, it is also one of the stages that a child experiences when it is separated from its mother in infancy. The stages are protest, despair and denial (which was later changed to 'detachment'). This last was considered to be of adverse prognostic significance in the child's development of social functioning. Karen Horney's theory, on the other hand, was that detachment is a kind of defence mechanism that prevents the individual from forming close relationships or attachments to others. This results in their becoming emotionally aloof, unable to empathize and lacking in sensitivity towards other people. Though Horney labelled this aloofness 'neurotic', it can also be seen as a rational choice not to get involved in some

situations, and therefore could be a reasonable stance, depending on the circumstances.

Considered within the psychiatric framework of the *Diagnostic and Statistical Manual of Mental Disorders IV*, detachment, also called 'depersonalization', is described as 'estrangement from oneself'. The individual can experience emotional or even physical numbness, actions or reactions being in some way divorced from his or her own perception. Detachment can involve the individual feeling that they are a passive observer of their own life which, in some cases, is so unrecognizable that the individual is unable to identify him- or herself reflected in a mirror. The experience of detachment has been likened to a dream state.

Detachment can occur independently as a symptom of a physiological medical condition such as temporal lobe epilepsy or can also be drug-induced. The experience of detachment can be brief, episodic or prolonged. [Lawrence Ratna]

DETERMINISM
The view that all aspects of life are the inevitable results of previously existing material conditions.
That all phenomena derive from previously existing conditions is a central part of Freud's original theory. The debate therefore ensued on issues of determinism and free will. The behavioural sciences were, at least in the popular mind, marked by a determinist stance: there is an inevitability about human development and behaviour which can, in theory, be discovered by the scientific collection and interpretation of evidence. But with subsequent developments the range of factors contributing to development is recognized (Rycroft, 1985), with consequent diminishing of the sense of determinism in the behavioural sciences.

DEVELOPMENT, FAITH
See: FAITH DEVELOPMENT

DEVELOPMENT, MORAL
See: MORAL DEVELOPMENT

DEVIL (OR SATAN)
In the Christian tradition, a created being or fallen angel held to be the personification and instigator of evil.
The name 'Satan' has sometimes been connected with a Hebrew verb meaning 'to roam', implying that Satan is God's spy.

More commonly, the etymology is linked to concepts of plotting and opposition. The term 'devil' is derived from the Septuagint translation of 'Satan'. The terms are used synonymously, although devils, in the plural, can be linked to the demonic. In the Old Testament Satan is an adversary of humanity charged with testing faith and prosecution, but specific connections with evil are tenuous.

Christianity synthesized Greek, Persian and Jewish concepts of the devil. In the New Testament the character and personality of Satan is developed into the personification of evil. It shows Satan being opposed to Christ and the intentions of God. It also theorizes about Satan's origins and discusses his distinctive defeat. However, Christianity is generally imprecise in its identification of the devil and (his) tasks. 'Satan' may simply be a metaphor for evil and rebellion against God that has been personalized and mythologized. Moreover, it is not clear from Scripture to what extent the world, the cosmos or Hell (Hades) are under (his) control. Satan, Lucifer ('prince'), Beelzebub ('lord of dung') and Beelzebul ('lord of flies') are parallel concepts that derive from various sources.

In medieval Christianity, Satan started to become a popular figure in folklore. The acquired visual identity (horns, cloven feet, tail and three-pronged fork) seems to be linked to antipathy towards paganism and gods of fertility (Russell, 1977). But as early as 1218, Gervase of Tilbury argued that our knowledge of the devil may be hallucinatory, and linked to ordinary fears. Many modern scholars have suggested that humanity 'manufactures' the devil out of personal and collective neurosis (Ricoeur, 1967). Renewed interest in deliverance ministries from charismatic and fundamentalistic churches has led to speculative and exotic portrayals of the devil. While the presence of evil cannot be denied, tracing the cause to an unverifiable spiritual personality can over-complicate any issue, and may turn a crisis into a drama. [Martyn Percy]

DIET
A regimen for food and drink consumption.
Food is one of the primary needs and pleasures of the human creature; eating is one of our primary ways of relating to our natural environment. For both these reasons, regulating food consumption has been a frequent focus for religious observance. Jains and Buddhists practise vegetarianism; Orthodox Jews follow laws of Kashrut. Although Jesus proclaimed all foods clean (Mark 7.18), his earliest disciples engaged in fasting as a form of spiritual discipline (Acts 13.2–3), even as many contemporary Christians still undertake some special abstinence during Lent.

In a secular rather than sacred context, diets serve a variety of purposes, from 'cleansing the system' to controlling cholesterol, insulin, blood pressure and the like. In popular parlance, however, the term 'diet' most commonly implies a regimen of food restriction for the purpose of losing weight. Such weight-loss dieting raises controversial questions within both medical and pastoral communities.

1. Do weight-loss diets work? Generally speaking, no. Statistics from the USA suggest that the vast majority of dieters fail to achieve lasting results. 'Set-point' theory offers an explanation for their failure. This theory, first proposed in 1972 and popularized a decade later by Bennett and Gurin (1983), hypothesizes that every human body has a 'natural' homeostatic weight range which it defends against extreme changes in either direction by adjusting its basal metabolism to the amount of food consumed. Decreased food intake results in increased metabolic efficiency, so that the body requires fewer calories for basic fuel. When food restriction ceases or pre-diet eating patterns are resumed, the more metabolically efficient body quickly converts excess calories to fat in an attempt to return to its earlier set-point.

2. What kind of diet has the greatest likelihood of success? The greatest lasting success comes from a gradual transformation of overall lifestyle to emphasize good nutrition and a balance of physical exercise with careful food and drink consumption; indeed, such lifestyle transformation is health-promoting, whether it results in significant weight loss or not. On the other hand, the obsession with 'quick weight loss' encourages imbalanced eating, restricts essential nutrients, and leaves underlying food and exercise habits unchanged. Thus, it is as unhealthy in the short term as it is unsuccessful in the long.

The obsession with weight loss to the detriment of health constitutes an issue of pastoral as well as medical concern. The growth of the diet industry in affluent nations manifests a cultural fetish with body shape and size. Bringle (1992) has identified this fetishization as a form of idolatry with acute spiritual as well as physical costs. Near epidemic incidence of eating disorders such as anorexia nervosa and bulimia underlines the gravity of the problem. From a Christian theological perspective, food is one of the blessings of God's good creation; not anxious preoccupation, but grateful and responsible enjoyment constitutes the spiritually fitting response. Pastoral care-givers are challenged to help people with weight-loss obsessions and body-image distortions to rediscover embodiment – incarnation – as a gift rather than a burden. [*Mary Louise Bringle*]

DIFFERENTIATION
A crucial process in human development from dependency and fusion towards the integrity of self-definition.
In psychoanalytic studies differentiation is linked with the concepts of separation and individuation. After a physical separation from the mother in biological birth, the infant needs to separate from the mother psychologically in a birthing or 'hatching' (Mahler *et al.*, 1975) process. Bowen family systems theory emphasizes the ongoing and never-ending task of self-differentiation from the family of origin. Friedman (1985) defines pastoral counselling and spiritual leadership as the ability to self-differentiate: to be both separated and connected through a 'non-anxious presence' with people and their problems.

DIRECTION, SPIRITUAL
A helping relationship in which one Christian assists another or others to grow towards a mature Christian life.
Spiritual direction traces its roots to the ministry of Jesus. Scripture reveals Jesus as a wise and compassionate guide in one-to-one relationships with persons from different walks of life, such as Nathanael, Nicodemus, the Samaritan woman and the rich young man. The apostles, following Jesus' example, provided pastoral guidance to Christians of the early Church. They stressed the importance of the discernment of spirits and saw it as the sign of a developing spiritual life (Phil. 1.9–10; 1 John 4.1). A mature Christian is one who can recognize the signs of the Spirit, which are 'love, joy, peace, patience, kindness, generosity, faithfulness, gentleness, and self-control' (Gal. 5.22–23). The fourth-

century desert fathers and mothers were keen to exercise this gift of discernment.

By the sixth century, with the rise of monasticism, spiritual direction took on an institutional form. As the centuries passed, spiritual direction became a ministry of and for the religious and clergy. They were concerned with vocation and ministerial life. A contemporary understanding of spiritual direction, however, is quite different from the institutional model. The ministry of spiritual direction is a response to the widespread need of people from all walks of life, who search for a deeper relationship with God. It concerns one's spiritual life as lived in the context of everyday life (Barry and Connolly, 1982).

Contemporary theology and insights of modern psychology clarify the term 'spiritual direction'. The word 'spiritual' refers to the whole person, not just the inner person. Its usage in the Pauline letter (1 Cor. 2.14–15) does not refer to a contrast between spiritual and physical, but rather speaks of a life opening to the Spirit ('spirit') and a life resisting the Spirit ('flesh'). The 'spiritual' person is not someone who rejects material reality but rather someone led by the Spirit of God. There is no rift between one's spiritual life and one's physical and emotional life. Human development and spiritual growth go hand in hand. In a word, one's spirituality is reflected in one's whole lifestyle.

The word 'direction' should not be taken to justify superiority and authority. Spiritual direction is to be done with an egalitarian spirit. A spiritual director has no authority to command or persuade a directee to follow a certain way of prayer or a particular mode of life. The role of the spiritual director is not overly directive; the basic attitude is one of listening, supporting and discerning. The following metaphors help understand the director's role and the helping relationship: (1) a host provides a guest with a resting place for deeper self-exploration; (2) a friend accompanies a confidant on the contemplative journey; (3) a teacher shares with a student the wisdom of spiritual and human development; (4) a guide assists a believer in avoiding the pitfalls often found along the journey; (5) a midwife assists a birth-giver to go through periods of desolation and celebrates with her the birthing of a new life.

Spiritual direction facilitates the directee's continuous actualization of what it means to be a human person created and called by a gracious God. The director may expect to encounter the reality of sin in the facilitation process. Sin is a regression from growth. To deal with spiritual growth without addressing spiritual regression is similar to a physician attempting to promote wellness but never mentioning illness. However, spiritual direction should not be confused with confession or preaching; nor should sin be understood in purely moralistic terms. While avoiding legalism, the director assists the directee to discern counter-movements to growth. The desert wisdom concerning the seven deadly sins is insightful. One is far from maturity if one is overcome, for example, by 'greed', which is a consuming desire for wealth or affluence, causing one to think of little else. Nor is someone led by the Spirit of God when the person constantly entertains the pleasure of 'pride', a feeling of moral superiority over others and the showing-off of one's knowledge, possessions, status, accomplishments, or even one's children (Guenther, 1992).

Spiritual direction is different from counselling. While both are helping relationships, they have very different orientations. Spiritual direction seeks to aid people to understand the working of the Spirit within them, whereas counselling endeavours to help people achieve their psychological well-being. The two, however, are not mutually exclusive. In fact, the difference is always blurred in actual practice. It is therefore a challenge for the spiritual director to recognize what is and what is not properly within her or his role. Most directees are emotionally balanced and behaviourally adaptive, but there may be some who come for spiritual direction burdened with serious emotional conflicts and difficulties in coping with life trials. When counselling is found to be more helpful for the directee, at least for the moment, referral to other helping professionals should be made.

Spiritual direction as a helping relationship may also have the danger of undue emotional involvement or transference. It is not easy to handle transference creatively. Regular supervision may sensitize the director to avoid unethical practices. The director should be aware of her or his unfulfilled needs and desires. It is not unreasonable to expect a spiritual director to be psychologically and spiritually mature.

The contemporary practice of spiritual direction is rich in its approach (Liebert, 1992). While one-to-one direction remains the popular model, direction provided in a group setting is not uncommon. Spiritual direction is not necessarily provided by clergy or done within a church. Many retreat houses are offering the service too. And some pastoral workers have been exploring the prospect of the ministry in schools and other communities. With the availability of training programmes, more and more lay people become life-enriching directors. Some directors integrate dream work or personality testing into spiritual direction. Others develop models of spiritual direction with women or with a specific age or social group such as mid-life adults and people living with AIDS. Finally, the cross-cultural perspective in spiritual direction is of concern to contemporary directors. [Ekman P. C. Tam]

DISABILITY
The effect of an antipathetic environment upon an individual with an impairment.

Impairment might be of the body, the senses or the mind. Antipathetic environments relate to inaccessible buildings, adverse attitudes of people or exclusive structures of institutions. Examples include: someone with limited reading ability becomes disabled when full participation involves extensive use of printed material; someone with a hearing loss, who uses a hearing aid, becomes disabled in a public building which is not fitted with an induction loop system; someone with restricted mobility who uses a walking stick or wheelchair becomes disabled where an alternative to stairs is not provided. Yet, while the international wheelchair symbol has done much to heighten awareness about disability, it has been unhelpful in equating limitation of movement with disability. In fact a minority of people with impairments use wheelchairs.

It is estimated that about 10% of the population of economically developed countries live with at least one major impairment. Impairments might be genetically inherited or result from the processes of birth; however, a large number are the consequence of accidents. Some impairments result from medical conditions, from substance abuse or from the consequences of poverty; many others result from violence or war. A lot of impairments therefore are preventable and anyone might find themselves impaired and so disabled. Many people eventually experience disability as an effect of advancing years.

Various models of disability are identified including 'the medical', which assumes that with treatment a cure is possible, and 'the moral', which supposes disability to be a sign of divine disapproval or punishment requiring forgiveness or healing. These and other models assume the person with impairments is dependent, in need of help: an impression often heightened by the use of inappropriate language.

On a 'social model' of disability, however, it is assumed that disability arises from society's assumptions and facilities, policies and priorities. Changes in the social environment would reduce disability and its effects on the individual. The Church as a social institution is inevitably involved in this process.

It is important not to speak of people with impairments as an homogeneous group (e.g. 'the disabled') or as 'them' (as opposed to 'us') and to avoid circumlocutions (e.g. 'less able') and patronizing language. Language shapes attitudes. This is as true of religious and liturgical as of secular language. Language also portrays underlying attitudes.

The general principle that all people need to be able to define themselves applies equally to those with impairments, from whom an acceptable language around disability needs to be learnt.

The Bible, at least on a superficial level, presents negative approaches to disability. The seeming correlation there of disability with demon possession, sickness and the fall are not helpful in responding to today's question: 'What has the Bible to say about disability?' More progress is possible starting from: 'What has disability to say to religious belief?' Disabled theology is likely to be just that, while a theology of disability aligns with some (at least) of the principles of liberation theology (Pailin, 1992). Starting from this basis the Church could make a positive and prophetic contribution to the current social and political movement for the removal of disabling barriers.

The foregoing is reflected in pastoral practice. Inaccessible or poorly equipped buildings, reactionary attitudes of people and the disablist assumptions of institutions disable perhaps 10% of the population. This also is as true in the Church as in the rest of society. Anyone aspiring to offer pastoral care to people with impairments will need to begin with a sense of repentance and a willingness to learn from those they seek to help.

Increasingly, equality of opportunity is being required by legislation. Those institutions, their premises and even their pronouncements that exclude or disadvantage people with impairments will find themselves subject to prosecution. The Church ought not to seek privileged exemption from the terms or spirit of this legislation. There are parallels here with issues of race and gender.

A start to appropriate pastoral practice at national, regional or local level might begin with a disability audit. This could lead on to a statement of aims and objectives relative to disability and thence to a long-term practical plan for teaching and for improved accessibility of buildings and other facilities. Specialist church organizations exist in most countries to help with this process and reference needs also to be made to secular and statutory bodies and the services they offer. An important principle here is the involvement of those most affected in the whole process of audit, planning and execution. People who have the best experience of disability are those who have impairments: their contribution to the formulation of church policy (at any level) is vital. This might also prove to be the starting point for involvement of people with impairments in the giving, as opposed to the receiving, of pastoral care.

People with direct experience of impairment have particular contributions to offer to the churches' theology, pastoral work and ministry. Those responsible for the provision of pastoral care need to consider first what gifts candidates have to offer, what training needs there are, how potentially effective any person's ministry might be. This is as true in considering the calling of a person with impairments as of anyone else. The Church needs to experience ministry by people with a range of impairments if it is not itself to be disabled.

One of the main disabling difficulties in the way of ministry by those who are perceived to be disabled is the fear of difference from a supposed normality. A welcoming of the rich variety of pastoral gifts opens up new possibilities not only for marginalized minority groups but also for the mainstream Church. Without that welcome there remains the risk of a projection of overbearing care on to people with impairments which perpetuates dependence. [*John Peirce*]

DISASTER
Any circumstance which causes the believed-in, safe world to break apart and disappear.

Many events in life are disastrous to individuals. It is part of the human condition to experience, even momentarily, a feeling of being lost and alone in a world too large and difficult to understand or control. This experience may be caused by a natural force such as a fire or flood or by the more private individual experience of the death of a loved one or the loss of one's health. At times like these it is not unusual for an individual to have a significant faith crisis, to call into question her or his belief system, to feel abandoned by God.

Pastoral literature presents a variety of suggestions regarding responses during times of disaster. These suggestions start from reminding the pastor to be present with the individual, to listen to them, and to help them grieve. Such grief may be for the death of a loved one, for a lost home, for health problems, the loss of treasured mementoes, or the death of a pet.

There are, however, important areas to keep in mind when attempting to provide pastoral care to someone who has just experienced a disaster. First, because the person may be in the middle of a profound faith crisis, they may reject the offer of help. If this happens, there may be little to do but offer to be available when they are ready and continue to remember them in prayer.

Second, the person may be experiencing a loss of contact with her or his established community support and, if this is the case, the pastor's desire to perform regular ceremonial functions may increase their feelings of loss. Ministers need to be imaginative in designing rituals that speak to the individual's personal needs.

Third, in the case of a natural disaster, pastors may also be victims. Their own faith life and beliefs may be challenged at exactly the same time as parishioners'. If this happens and the minister attempts to pretend that everything is normal, others are done a disservice. Sometimes the best pastoral care is found in admitting doubts and misgivings and indicating a willingness to stand with another in darkness.

Finally, particularly in a natural disaster, it is important to remember that the normal procedures of providing care do not work. People often cannot come to the pastor's office: he or she must go to them. Sometimes their most immediate need is as simple as helping them to remove the fallen tree in front of their house. Many unchurched people may be affected by the disaster. Limiting visits to those specifically from the pastor's own denomination can create division instead of a building up of the community. [*Rosemary Chinnici*]

DISCERNMENT
Keenness of insight.

Although not a technical term, 'to discern' is often found in pastoral studies. It describes the process of empathetic listening, not just to the person encountered but also to the resources of the Christian gospel and tradition. In a person-to-person encounter it is recognized that God also may be discerned. The theme is sometimes connected with 'wisdom' (Carr, 1997).

DISCIPLINE
1. The control and training of children in family or school.
2. A system of rules as in a monastic order.
3. The maintaining of order in a church.

The word 'discipline' comes from the same root as disciple or learner and has a wide range of meaning. It is not simply a system of formal requirements, goals or sanctions, but denotes a control which, when internalized, creates the possibility of moral freedom and personal autonomy. It has to do with recognizing the parameters within which acceptable behaviour lies. It is also concerned with the shaping of attitudes, the quality of relationships, and community ethos. It is thus closely related to pastoral concern.

1. Since the family is a primary group, it can express the sense of belonging, of connectedness and of security which provides the conditions in which a well-disciplined personality may be shaped. Much depends, of course, on the quality of relationships which are expressed in the family group, the examples of good self-control which are present within it, and the extent to which it can sustain the pressures of modern life. It is desirable that home and school should co-operate and be mutually supportive in the ethos they provide. Home–school contracts are becoming an accepted practice. Self-control is based on self-awareness. Harsh discipline may produce emotional isolation and alienation. Children – and sometimes adults too –

need help to control anger, jealousy, greed, frustration or hostility. Bottled-up anger is liable to be vented on siblings, companions, teachers, or other scapegoats, or find expression in bigotry, racism or violence. Or it may be turned against oneself. One way of dealing with such pent-up emotion is to seek a legitimate outlet for it. Another way is to identify the feelings involved and to talk about them openly; or to explore why one may feel angry with another. Discipline is therefore not just a matter of regulating behaviour through punishment or praise. Schools often struggle with the breakdown in relationships and feelings of rejection and failure on the part of the pupil. Unwise handling of the situation may make matters worse, leading too early to the final resort of sanctions or exclusion. This practice contributes little, if anything, to the release of 'negative feelings' and the internalizing of moral controls. Good discipline allows good principles to be worked into one's character. This involves the emotions and will; it is concerned to influence what people want to do, not merely what they actually do. In this process lies the secret of moral freedom.

2. A similar approach is to be found in monastic discipline. Monks have their lives regulated by rules, the most notable probably being the *Rule of St Benedict*. This links a system of organization and authority with personal obligation, i.e. vows, and sets the whole in the context of prayer and worship. In the Protestant tradition a similar form of discipline sometimes arose in congregations. Notable among these is that laid down within the Calvinist tradition. This took distinctive form in Scotland in 1560, when the *First Book of Discipline* was drawn up by John Knox. In practice, however, the approach was resisted by the civil authorities, which were needed for its enforcement, and it remained an interesting example of a severe approach to discipline rather than an effective one.

3. The third sense of 'discipline' is the sum of ecclesiastical laws and customs which regulate the life, both religious and moral, of a church. In an episcopal context this would be exercised by the bishop in relation to his clergy. The clergy, however, were also historically responsible for disciplining the congregations. An example may be found in the opening rubric to the order for Holy Communion in the Book of Common Prayer (1662). In general, however, the absence of sanctions made external discipline difficult or impossible. Church teachers have tended more to emphasize the place of self-awareness and self-discipline in the spiritual life. *[Ian McDonald]*

DISCIPLING
Training and directing the newly converted.
The term is used mainly in evangelical and charismatic churches for a system whereby new converts are taught the faith and the ways of the congregation by elders. In some cases it may be as explicit as direction about money and sexual life in marriage.

DISPLACEMENT
The redirecting of one's feelings and thoughts from their actual target to a less threatening person or thing.
Freud observed that people isolate disturbing ideas and feelings from their source and reattach them to safer objects through displacement. Displacement is a defence mechanism that attempts to release a feeling, deal with a threatening thought or find a solution to a perceived problem by separating the feeling from the relationship out of which it emerged and projecting it onto an unknowing target. The emotional attention is shifted to something or someone more manageable. For example, the child terrified of his own rage may shift that fear onto thunderstorms or fierce animals. The adult who is unable to react in anger towards a partner may take out that anger on a child, a salesperson in a department store, a pet, a piece of furniture. Much of the rudeness and unpredictable behaviour of drivers on crowded motorways is a displacement of frustration felt elsewhere (Valliant, 1977). *[Carroll Saussy]*

DISSOCIATION
A state in which a person removes herself or himself from reality by splitting off or disconnecting from the present moment and entering an altered awareness of her or his context.
Dissociation is considered by some to be a healthy defence mechanism as long as it does not impair functioning; others define it as a disorder. Dissociation is a state of relative unreality ranging from simple daydreaming or forgetting what happened in moments of trauma, to assuming a distinct personality, referred to as multiple personality. Some dissociation is normal, such as daydreaming, consciously entering meditative states, or

having no recall of a horrendous accident; multiple personality is a disorder most often related to early childhood trauma.

The *Diagnostic and Statistical Manual of Mental Disorders IV* defines a dissociative disorder as 'a disturbance or alteration in the normally integrative functions of identity, memory, or consciousness. The disturbance or alteration may be sudden or gradual, and transient or chronic.' Included among the dissociative disorders are dissociative identity disorder (multiple personality), psychogenic fugue, psychogenic amnesia, and depersonalization disorder.

In dissociative identity disorder at least two distinct personality states assume control of the body at separate moments, resulting in at least partial memory loss for the personality not in control. In psychogenic fugue, a person is unable to recall a previous identity; similarly, in psychogenic amnesia, one is unable to recall personal information. Both are short-lived states that typically follow extreme stress or natural disaster. Depersonalization disorder, also stress-related, describes a persistent or recurring shift in self-perception. The person feels like a detached observer of her or his actions or has a sense of being in a dream state. Treatment for dissociative disorders that cause serious impairment is long term yet frequently successful. [*Carroll Saussy*]

DIVORCE
The legal dissolution of marriage.
The grounds on which divorce has been permitted by church and society in the West has a long and varied history. Medieval canon law permitted divorce in restrictive circumstances like consanguinity, bigamy and proof of non-consent. The primary reasoning here was that marriage is both a consensual and natural relation. The Protestant Reformers in the 1500s made divorce a 'civil' rather than 'sacramental' issue, and so permitted divorce under wider circumstances such as adultery, desertion and lengthy separation. They also insisted that divorce be made publicly, since it relates to the larger social order (Witte, 1997). The Reformed Protestant view of divorce predominated both ecclesiastically and legally until the middle of the twentieth century, when divorce laws were revolutionized to permit one spouse to end a marriage for any reason they chose.

Where divorce is perceived as social deviance marriage can only be ended by proving the commission of a 'matrimonial offence' (for example, adultery, unreasonable behaviour and desertion). The procedural emphasis is on establishing the ground for divorce and publicly adjudicating on its consequences. Where divorce is perceived as a family transition it may be achieved by a statement from one or both partners asserting that the marriage has irretrievably broken down. The procedural emphasis is then upon encouraging informed choices, addressing the consequences of divorce and supporting the private ordering of contentious matters, always subject to the proviso that vulnerable parties are protected. The 1996 Family Law Act (implemented in England and Wales in 1998) reflects public acceptance of divorce, treating it as a process to be accomplished over a period of time by the parties concerned.

In the US, all fifty states have since the 1970s adopted variations of so-called 'no-fault' divorce laws, in which parties do not have to provide reasons for legally ending a marriage. However, some states have recently adopted legislation enacting a two-tiered marriage system in which couples can voluntarily enter a 'covenant marriage' having stricter requirements for divorce such as marriage counselling, a waiting period, and some kind of 'fault' clause. These states are responding to concerns primarily over the effects of divorce on children, who have been shown on average to suffer serious short- and long-term consequences from divorce. They are also responding to the effects of divorce on social issues like crime, worker productivity, and mental health.

While divorce is a legal process, it interacts with psychological and socio-economic processes that together define how divorce is actually experienced by individuals. [*Christopher Clulow/John Wall*]

DO NOT RESUSCITATE
See: ADVANCE DIRECTIVE

DOUBT
The withholding of personal assent from particular beliefs or even from the faith as a whole.
Doubt must not be confused with critical questioning, which seeks better and fuller knowledge and understanding, in order to integrate into it the knowledge already gained and retained. However, faith that seeks understanding will normally have to cope with doubt during that search. Various

feelings such as anxiety or hesitation are associated with doubt, especially when they arise in relation to questions of belief.

A distinction is made between intellectual doubt and personal doubt. Intellectual doubt hesitates to accept something as true. The attitude of Thomas towards the resurrection of Jesus (John 20.24–29) is an example. Personal doubt refers more to a lack of trust, such as that experienced by the disciples whom Jesus rebuked in the episode of the storm at sea (Matt. 8.23–27).

Doubt, in the theological sense, is present only where there is faith. Jesus' disciples 'believed in him' (John 2.11) yet he reproached them as 'foolish ... and slow of heart to believe' (Luke 24.25) and 'upbraided them for their lack of faith and stubbornness' (Mark 16.14). Faith is linked to love of the truth (2 Thess. 2.10), which on the personal level implies that assent is by way of attraction and love rather than clear evidence.

On the spiritual level, reasons for doubt can vary. Faith is lived and developed in society and in the community of Church and family. If the social milieu is not favourable to faith development, it is easy to experience a sense of isolation and doubt. It is important that faith development keep pace with intellectual development so that an adult relationship with Jesus Christ is fostered. If faith development does not match intellectual development and if the milieu is in any way hostile to religious development, doubt can arise. Doubt can also be fostered when the baptized have an insufficient understanding of the truths of faith when they are known. Reason for doubt can also be of a moral order. If moral conduct is not in conformity with the demands of faith, justification is often sought in principles foreign to faith and the way is thus prepared for doubt.

It is recognized that temperament plays a role in doubt especially in persons who suffer from anxiety, uncertainty and excessive worry. Doubt can also become obsessive if there is a tendency towards scrupulosity. In these cases, the doubt is generally considered to be apparent doubt rather than real doubt, which refers to a specific proposition such as the real presence of Jesus in the Eucharist.

Spiritual direction can help uncover the cause and origin of doubt as well as be a support in the life of faith. Such accompaniment, patiently offered and sustained, may help the person of faith to develop a clear sense of self, a lively spirituality, and a habit of ongoing discernment of where the Spirit of God is leading. [Brid Long]

DREAMS
Remembered imaginative mental events which occur during periods of rapid eye movement (REM) sleep.
Dreams have been subjected to interpretation in most, if not all, civilizations. Such interpretation has served a variety of purposes, chiefly hermeneutic (i.e. to elicit meaning from the dream or impute meaning to it) or predictive. The biblical canon, in common with much ancient literature, contains a wide variety of different treatments of dreams. Within the past century, the approach to dreams has changed considerably, first as a result of the development of psychoanalytic ideas and practice, and second through the scientific study of dream sleep.

Contemporary systematic interpretation of dreams in the context of psychological help can be dated to Freud's work *The Interpretation of Dreams* (1900). Freud described dreams as 'the royal road to the knowledge of the unconscious activities of the mind'. His theory states that during sleep, we experience a lessening of the waking inhibition on mental impulses, resulting in their expression in the form of dreams. Rycroft (1979) likens dreams to poetry, in that they are 'not a human effort to express emotions, but emotion's expression of itself'. Hence dreams have been given special value within psychoanalysis and psychotherapy as expressions of the dreamer's truth.

However, it would be incorrect to suppose that psychoanalytic theory has provided tools which make it possible for dreams to be analysed and understood in isolation – that is, outside the context of the analytic relationship and set-up. The focus in psychotherapy and analysis is on the relationship between analyst and patient, including its unconscious aspects. In analysis, dreams are therefore discussed mainly against the background of the dynamics and possible meanings inherent in the relationship between analyst and patient. Psychoanalysis is not, therefore, so much interested in the interpretation of dreams as in the interpretation of the dynamics of the analytic relationship, to which patients may bring dreams as they also bring many other expressions of their mental and emotional lives and experiences.

From an analytic point of view, dreams cannot therefore be interpreted or discussed except within the context of an analysis. Psychoanalysis does not offer a general theory of dreams, nor guidelines to the interpretation of their contents. The popular 'self-help' literature guiding individuals on the interpretation of their own dreams or those of others should therefore be treated with caution, as it tends to draw on psychoanalytic insights but lacks the binding core context of the analytic relationship as the basis for interpretation. An exception to this is *Ariadne's Clue* by the Jungian analyst Anthony Stevens (1998), which acknowledges the problems in interpreting dreams outside the analytic setting, yet manages to produce a tentative alphabetical list suggestive of common associations to specific dream images.

Taken as part of the whole communication of a patient to his or her analyst, dreams can be subjected to interpretative guesses and discussion which may help to develop an understanding of the psychological situation of the dreamer. Jung describes the process thus: 'The dream is a living thing ... a living situation, it is like an animal with feelers or with many umbilical cords ... while we are talking of it, it is producing ...' (Jung, 1928). Within analysis, this process of relating to the dream is termed 'association'. However, the emphasis within analysis is not primarily on developing an understanding or diagnosis of the patient's psychology, but on facilitating the processes of the patient's development. Hence dreams are used analytically not so much for hermeneutic purposes but rather to support the developmental and individuating processes.

Physiologically, dreams occur when the body is in a state of arousal during sleep. This state, which appears common to all mammals, includes irregularities in pulse, blood pressure and respiration, rapid eye movement and sporadic activity in certain fine muscle groups. This state is generally termed REM (rapid eye movement) sleep. It occurs throughout the night, on a cycle of about ninety minutes, and lasts for increasing periods of time, from about five to forty minutes. When subjects are experimentally deprived of REM sleep, they deteriorate into confused mental states more rapidly than subjects deprived of non-REM sleep. Freud believed that dreams serve to safeguard sleep, by converting alarming and disturbing memories, impulses and experiences into less frightening and more disguised narrative form. On the basis of sleep research,

however, Freud's belief would have to be reversed, as it appears from it that we sleep in order to dream, rather than, as Freud thought, that we dream in order to remain asleep. The most recent work in neurophysiology suggests that during dream sleep, the brain is ordering and storing the disparate memories and experiences of waking events. The dreaming brain is, on this model, not trying to disguise coherent but unacceptable thoughts, but is rather trying to make sense of an array of chaotic feelings, memories and imagery.

The common thread shared by psychoanalytic and sleep laboratory research is the importance of the dream as a way of establishing meaning. This links with the ancient hermeneutic approach to the interpretation of dreams.

The use of dreams within pastoral work is currently limited to the contexts of the psychodynamic psychotherapies (e.g. psychoanalysis, analytical psychology, psychotherapy and psychodynamic counselling). In these contexts, the practitioner is trained to use the relationship with his or her client or patient as the main tool in helping to resolve the client's difficulties. Discussion and analysis of the client's dreams form a subsidiary part of discussion and analysis of the relationship. There is no scientifically developed basis for analysing dreams in isolation or within other pastoral contexts. However, dreams will always be a source of fascination and challenge, and inevitably, some of the insights from psychodynamic practice have found their way into the self-help pastoral literature. [*George Bright*]

DRUG ABUSE
See: ADDICTION

DRUG THERAPY
The treatment of disorders, especially psychiatric problems, by medication, as opposed to counselling, psychotherapy or psychosocial interventions.
Over the past fifty years, many new medications have been developed for treatment of schizophrenia, major depression, bipolar disorder (manic-depressive illness), panic disorder, and other psychiatric conditions. The effects of this medical revolution have been enormous. Countless numbers of people previously considered untreatable have been able to recover and lead productive lives. The most obvious large-scale effect has been

the dramatic decline in long-term hospitalization of the mentally ill and the consequent closing down of many hospitals.

A more subtle effect has been a shift in thinking about the root causes of these illnesses. Prior to the creation of Thorazine in the 1950s, the dominant theories of aetiology were psychoanalytic. These posited that these disorders were the result of traumatic early childhood experiences. From this hypothesis, there was a tendency among mental health professionals to attribute blame to parents and other care-givers of the ill individual and to separate the patient from these important sources of support. Once it was seen that these patients responded dramatically to medication, it also became obvious that they were the victims of physiological brain malfunction. In practice, drug therapy is often given in combination with one or more of the other modalities. So, for example, early family experience is still considered an important factor in forming the personality of the ill individual, but these conditions are now also thought of as biochemical brain diseases. This change is parallel to the understanding of diabetes as a biochemical pancreatic disease and hypertension as a biochemical disease of blood vessels and kidneys. This shift in thinking has decreased the stigma of mental illness (although not by any means eliminated it), brought psychiatry into closer relationship with the rest of the medical profession, and allowed family members to resume their status as important care-givers and part of the treatment 'team'.

The pastor or counsellor does not need to know the details about the mechanisms by which these medications act or their side effects. Yet there are some general characteristics of modern medication treatments that need to be understood.

There is no medication which does not have the potential for causing side effects, but individual persons vary greatly in their susceptibility. With any given drug some people will experience no problems, while another small group may have strongly adverse reactions; the majority of patients will fall somewhere in between these two extremes. The patient's age, sex, medical health status, other drugs being taken, and other factors can influence the likelihood of side effects. This is why it is always best to refer patients with questions about side effects back to their prescribing physician.

A note of caution may be sounded: it is usually not helpful for individuals to acquire their information from the *Physician's Desk Reference* (PDR), which is widely available in the USA. The PDR is a compilation of manufacturers' package inserts, and these companies are required by law and by liability considerations to list every single side effect ever reported, even if it is rare. The prescribing physician can interpret this data to the patient and advise him or her about which side effects are most likely to occur.

Most side effects are annoying but not disabling or life threatening. They frequently occur early in the treatment, as the patient's body adjusts to the new drug, and subside within the first two weeks. Anything that appears to be a severe side effect should be reported immediately to the prescribing physician. But in most cases, the patient will need to persevere through the initial stage of treatment, and the support and encouragement of the pastor or counsellor can be very helpful.

At present, many medications are available for treatment of each disorder. It is impossible to predict with certainty exactly which drug will work best for each individual patient. An experienced psychiatrist can narrow the field to a handful, but in the end there is no alternative but to do a careful process of trial and error. Sometimes the first medication tried is not effective or causes an intolerable side effect, but in the great majority of cases, a successful medication is eventually found. The pastor or counsellor can be very helpful in supporting and encouraging the individual not to give up and refuse treatment after an unsuccessful medication trial.

Medications used in the treatment of depression have a slow onset of action – one to two weeks is the average time for the patient to begin feeling the therapeutic effects. Unfortunately, side effects often occur right away. Furthermore, some drugs are started at a lower dose and gradually increased. This minimizes the initial side effects, but it can delay the onset of therapeutic action even further. Here again, the support of the pastor or counsellor can be very important in encouraging the patient to 'hang on' and not leave treatment.

Most of the psychiatric illnesses which are treated with medication cannot be cured but can be effectively controlled with long-term treatment. In this respect they are similar to other widespread chronic medical diseases, such as hypertension, diabetes and arthritis. With all of these disorders, the patient must accept the situation and make a commitment to co-operate with long-term medication therapy. For many psychiatric patients this acceptance is very difficult. These individuals either view their disorders as signs of personal weakness and failure, or they continue to have intense angry feelings about their lot in life. To escape such feelings, they deny their illness, discontinue medication and drop out of treatment. This frequently leads to relapse and hospitalization, which then sets off another round of shame or anger.

The resolution of these conflicts has become all the more important now that effective drug treatment is available. When the simple act of taking pills every day can mean the difference between chronic hospitalization and a productive life, it becomes critical to remove inner barriers to treatment. Many patients who struggle with these problems express their conflicts in spiritual terms, and seek out pastors and religious counsellors. The challenge to the counsellor is to articulate a theology which takes illness seriously but also frees the sufferer from anger, guilt and shame. [Dana Charry]

DYING
The process of moving from life to death.

This process is capable of many definitions, philosophical, theological, medical and legal. Here the emphasis is on the process and the human reaction to it. Dying can be almost instantaneous, as in a road accident or a sudden heart failure, or it can be almost imperceptible, as when an elderly person ceases breathing or when someone with terminal illness enters a coma and loses vital signs. Definitions of clinical death are helpful, and they illuminate the dying process. But to the observer dying is always mysterious, although it is recognized as natural and inevitable in all forms of life.

In recent literature, much deriving from the pioneer work of E. Kübler-Ross (1970), dying has been researched and rediscovered as a subject for multidisciplinary pastoral care. Her account of the stages of dying was based on evidence acquired in discussion with patients and staff. The stages have been criticized as making a process too simple, or as being too prescriptive, but they are still, with due modifications, useful in describing what happens.

1. There is an uneasy suspicion in the sick person, when relatives appear, doctors murmur just out of earshot, and the minister becomes attentive, that the illness is serious.

2. There is, or often can be, denial, which may persist to the end. It takes many forms, and may be the best way the patient can deal with bad news.

3. There may well be anger, with the medical profession, life itself, the family, God and God's representatives.

4. Sometimes there is an attempt to bargain, to win time.

5. Depression, turning the face to the wall, is a phase that causes great concern among relatives.

6. Acceptance in some form may finally come.

This is only a rough guide to dying and it only applies to prolonged and expected death. It is by no means a universal pattern. Nevertheless such a scheme goes some way towards making sense of the human experience of this mystery.

Pastoral care of dying people has certain key aspects (Ainsworth-Smith and Speck, 1999). All are dying; but those facing known death are not a special category to be treated differently from others. Many of them can feel, laugh, argue, be kind or obnoxious. But they are also weary, sleepy, enfeebled, and emotions and responses can be on a lower scale. The dying person must be respected. They may hear the conversation, even if they look asleep. They need therefore always to be addressed. The carer is often an interpreter. Dreams and hallucinations can be disturbing and they need to be listened to. Requests may be hard to understand, and perhaps the pastor may have more time to listen and find out meanings.

There are some almost standard questions that may be asked: 'Why me?' 'What have I done to deserve this?' To such questions as these there is no direct answer. Even to have asked them may be enough. Complex explanations are too hard to understand when the patient is having difficulty breathing and focusing. 'Why am I taking so long to die?' is a more difficult question, because it can be bound up with guilt, and a fear of having offended God. Dying persons may need to be affirmed. They may feel that their life has had no shape nor meaning and that they have hardly achieved anything. Patiently eliciting a life story may uncover forgotten deeds, and help to give a sense of achievement. Dying people often have a fear of being alone, and especially of dying alone. There will be opportunities to reassure and to organize company. Dying people are more often afraid of the process than of death itself. Reassurance about choking and the loss of bodily and mental control can be given, and many people's dread of dying alone can be addressed. For many, dying means reunion with loved ones, or with one particular person who has been especially close or significant. Sometimes pastors find this attenuated version of the communion of saints hard to handle, but it is safe to say that the dying are not usually able to enter into theological discussion, and the reinforcement of deeply held hopes is valuable.

The pastoral care of the dying can be a satisfying ministry in which most pastors are likely to be involved. To be a helpful carer a person must have at least thought about their own death. It is not possible to experience death consciously, but close observation of the dying, undertaken with patience and imagination, can begin to give some indication of what the dying process might be like. There is, in poetry and fiction, material to stimulate the understanding. It is also of course important to confront fears and apprehensions about one's own death, and to have a clear view of what that might entail. Caring for the dying demands attention and alertness. It can be draining of the emotions. This may lead to a sort of depression, or, as a defence, to callousness and a loss of sensitivity towards the dying person. It is a mark of wisdom to know when to withdraw, as for example when the carer has suffered a personal loss, and when to seek diversion. [Derek B. Murray]

DYNAMIC CYCLE
In clinical theology the cyclical process of movement away from and back to maternal resource.
The dynamic cycle of interpersonal relationships undergirds clinical theology (Lake, 1966). It originated from Frank Lake's study of St John's Gospel and object-relations theory. The infant's 'being' and 'well-being' arise from its relationship with mother as resource for unconditional acceptance and sustenance. These two phases of the infant's dependency are followed by status and achievement during which effort is expended. The infant is renewed by return to its source of acceptance and sustenance, thus completing the cycle before it begins again. The model also demonstrates degrees of loss of 'being' and 'well-being'.

E

EATING DISORDERS
Health-endangering disturbances in eating behaviours, resulting from obsession with weight and body size.
Eating disorders, among which are included anorexia nervosa (self-starvation), bulimia (bingeing and purging) and binge eating disorder, are a by-product of media-saturated cultures which prize slenderness as an ideal of beauty. While most sufferers are adolescent females, the disorders are not limited to any gender, age, economic or ethnic group. Weight-loss dieting is not itself an eating disorder, nor is occasional over- or underconsumption of food in response to stress. However, such episodic behaviours can become disorders if they grow into entrenched patterns, interfering with physical health, social relationships or normal functioning at school or work.

Anorexia nervosa manifests itself in intense fear of weight gain and distortion of body image: sufferers see themselves as 'fat' no matter how thin they are. Anorexics practise unusual rituals involving food and avoid eating in public; many exercise compulsively. Medical complications include irregular menstrual cycles, low blood pressure and body temperature, cardiac problems, kidney damage, hair loss, brittle bones. Anorexia has the highest death rate of any psychiatric illness.

Bulimia is characterized by recurrent out-of-control eating to a point of uncomfortable fullness, followed by attempts to 'undo' the binge through vomiting, laxative abuse or compulsive exercise. Bulimics often hoard food and eat in secret. Purging activities produce medical complications: tooth damage, electrolyte imbalance, digestive and intestinal problems. Mood swings frequently occur.

Binge eating disorder is similar to bulimia, without the compensatory behaviours. While feelings of numbness accompany a binge, intense shame and self-disgust follow. Alcohol or other substance abuse may coexist. Medical complications include diabetes, elevated blood pressure and cholesterol, risk of stroke, and sleep apnoea.

Eating disorders respond best to early diagnosis and multi-pronged treatment. Medical evaluation assesses and responds to potential physical complications, determining if hospitalization is required; medication, including antidepressants, can be useful. Nutritional counselling helps restore healthful eating habits. Psychological treatment includes individual, group and family therapy; combines cognitive and behavioural interventions; teaches ways of dealing with feelings which trigger disordered behaviours; and assists patients in discovering sources of power and worth other than control over eating or embodiment of a 'slenderness' ideal. Support groups help sufferers and their families; relapse often figures in the long recovery process.

Pastoral care-givers need to know the medical and psychological resources in their communities to make appropriate referrals. Further, they can critique cultural values and address personal issues underlying eating disorders. Biblical theology promotes balanced attitudes toward food and body: Christians pray for daily bread (Matt. 6.11), yet do not live by bread alone (Matt. 4.4); they are not to be overly concerned or anxious about their bodies (Matt. 6.25), yet they are temples of the Holy Spirit (1 Cor. 6.19). Hungering hearts are ultimately better fed by God's love than by compulsive eating or dietary control; pastoral care-givers are prime ambassadors of this love (Bringle, 1992). [*Mary Louise Bringle*]

ECOLOGY
See: ENVIRONMENT

ECSTASY
A trancelike state in which a person experiences something other than an ordinary or rational orientation towards the world.
Classically ecstasy was associated with astonishment but today with intense pleasure. The Greek word *ekstasis* literally signifies the state of being put out of place or outside oneself. It occurs in Acts 10.10 to describe Peter's vision of four-footed creatures. Despite this and other biblical precedents, experiences of ecstasy became suspect among early Christians (e.g. Clement of Alexandria) because of their association with Dionysian rites and their incompatibility with the indwelling of the Holy Spirit. 'Rapture' is a nearly synonymous word that is more common in theological discourse. The closest approximation

to religious ecstasy likely to be experienced by many contemporary Christians is intense participation in devotional music.

EDUCATION
1. The process of rearing children.
2. The systematic schooling or training given to the young and, by extension, to adults.
The word is derived from the Latin *educare*, which includes the senses of 'to bring out' and 'to nourish'. It recalls the classical myth of existence which implies that all capacities are already innate and simply need to be brought out. Modern educators tend to think of it as realizing human potential. It has to do with the person: with the acquiring of knowledge, understanding and skills; with the quest for personal meaning; with the formation of character. It is therefore directly related to pastoral concern. Throughout history various models have influenced theory and practice.

1. *Ancient education.* Plato envisaged education as a tool for the creation of a just society, based on the idea of truth. It prepared people for the role they would play in society, but emphasized character and intelligence. Nevertheless, his plan for education contained elitist and oppressive elements. Emergent Christian education, combining Christian belief with classical insights, emphasized that fallen human nature needed to be turned to the light of truth, whose source is divine. It also combined instruction for the immature and uneducated (the catechetical method) with more creative procedures for advanced students. Augustine's curriculum, centred on religious education but encompassing the main realms of meaning, was influential in Christian schools. The use of catechisms continued for many centuries, eventually falling into disfavour as excessively mechanical and a form of indoctrination. But used creatively and in a supportive context they were productive educational tools.

2. '*Natural*' development. In the aftermath of the Renaissance and especially the Enlightenment, educators reacted against divisive dogmatic structures; Rousseau's *Emile*, for example, was characterized by a hatred of civilization. More positive emphases included freedom of enquiry, rationality, a return to nature, discovery methods and readiness for learning. Kindergarten work was encouraged

and to this was added social enterprise and project work, including practical problem-solving. Child-centred education placed emphasis on growth and development towards maturity, through stages involving cognitive dissonance and the regaining of equilibrium, or through interaction with the environment. Developmental psychology, as it emerged strongly about the mid-twentieth century (e.g. Erikson, 1950), reinforced the child-centred approach, making it a dominant stance in twentieth-century thinking about education.

3. *Liberal education*. Under the guidance of Matthew Arnold and John Henry Newman, a liberal education embodied 'the best that has been thought and said'. Hirst and Peters (1981) related it to the development of the rational mind and induction into the forms of knowledge, about which there has been a continuing dispute. Essentially optimistic about human nature, it also assumed that education was to be acquired for its own sake. To balance what is sometimes seen as an overly intellectual approach, attention has had to be paid to education and the emotions, and to relating understanding and skills to the needs of society.

4. *Pre-vocational and vocational education*. Education should fit the student for work or profession, both in terms of general educational competence and in terms of specific skills acquisition. Even in traditional areas such as law, medicine and divinity, practical experience is now seen as an integral part of the learning process for those entering professions. More generally, emphasis is placed on links with industry, work experience, professional induction and training for employment. There is also renewed demand that basic skills such as literacy and numeracy should be reinforced. Others emphasize the importance of scientific understanding and moral education. To confuse education with training, however, involves a grave reduction in its quality and scope.

5. *Multicultural education*. This approach takes the pluralist context of society as the key to the nature of education, placing a premium on toleration and the acceptance of cultural difference. It is designed to promote unity through diversity, counter ignorance, prejudice and educational disadvantage, and thus further community relations and educational achievement. Weaknesses include the imposition of a bland secularism that mishandles important factors such as religion, which tends to be seen as a factor of division; and the adoption of a stance of relativism in matters of value and truth.

Finally, some creative modern perspectives may be noted.

1. *Liberation perspectives*. Here the emphasis is on 'the pedagogy of the oppressed', associated in particular with Paulo Freire (1972). Important elements include the rejection of a 'banking' view of education, where an elite uses education as a means to power; and emphasis on motivating the victims of the system to find their voice and acquire skills, such as literacy and critical reflection. These will then enable them to take charge of their own lives ('conscientization'). 'Base communities' and interactive group learning make an important contribution. The movement is of great moment for development education and has had an important influence on 'life-long education' and on adult education generally.

2. *Feminist perspectives*. An important movement, feminism has already challenged male dominance and associated prejudice in many areas of education. Its influence is seen in such diverse areas as equal opportunities for employment and inclusive language as the accepted mode of communication. It has had notable effects in the area of moral education and challenges underlying assumptions by affirming ecological perspectives and valuing connectedness over against competition (Gilligan, 1993).

3. *Critical Christian perspectives*. Christian thinking, so fundamental to the origins of the Western tradition, has contributed to the various historical phases. Schleiermacher responded to Enlightenment thinking, Newman to the liberal movement, and Tillich to twentieth-century debate. The complexities of the modern situation, in both Western and global contexts, require the Christian perspective to emphasize 'education for critical consciousness'. This includes the critiquing of dominant cultural assumptions, the promoting of critical openness in the area of religion (not least the Christian religion), and a concern for a just society. It relates directly to the aims of education, the understanding of person and community, pastoral concern, moral education and the interpretation of value, global and environmental concerns, religious studies, science and religion, moral issues in politics and economics, and the idea of tolerance and neighbour love in a plural society. *[Ian McDonald]*

EDUCATIONAL PSYCHOLOGY
The branch of psychology generally concerned with teaching and learning.
Educational psychology is particularly relevant to religious education. The assumption is that the better educators understand human knowing – for example, how people think, what cultivates knowledge, what motivates learning – the better teachers can design educational situations. Historically, educational psychology has concentrated on such subjects as learning theory, teaching methods, the 'mind' and its relation to the body, memory, consciousness and thinking, perception, communication and intelligence. Philosophically, educational psychology can be considered part of the general field of epistemology, the 'study of knowing'.

EDUCATION, RELIGIOUS
See: RELIGIOUS EDUCATION

EGO
1. The individual's experience of self.
2. The rational, conscious part of the self which is also self-conscious.
Much discussion has taken place over the translation of Freud's German term 'Ich' by the Latin 'ego'. This, it is suggested, has made the concept, especially in the USA and UK, too clinical and scientific. Other languages do not have this problem and some modern writers in English now simply use 'I'. Such a general word inevitably means different things according to the context. But put simply, Freud came to see the individual as having three dimensions: (1) the id, which is the unconscious area of human make-up, where instincts and impulses are located; (2) the ego (or 'I'), which is largely the part of the self which is self-aware and rational; (3) the superego, which is conscience. Several aspects of the individual fall under the general heading 'ego'. The self is a complex phenomenon, a mix of causal, moral and structural dimensions (Freud, 1923). The context is also important in determining which aspect is being invoked.

EGOISM
Thinking or acting in a selfish or self-serving manner.
Freud's term 'Ich' was translated as 'ego'. He used it to denote the component of the mind that was conscious and most aware of the external reality. The term 'egoism', however, predates Freud and was used in philosophy and ethics, in which self-interest is regarded as the basis of moral behaviour. The psychoanalytic use of 'ego' has reinforced this stance. The ego is responsible for self-preservation and advancement. Freud argued that it is basic human nature to think and behave in a manner that is of the greatest benefit to oneself. Egoism, however, normally has a negative connotation.

EGO PSYCHOLOGY
A psychological scheme that gives priority to the development of the intentional self.
Freud shaped his psychoanalytic view of the person around three terms: id, ego and superego. Late in his career he increasingly focused on the ego, and H. Hartmann, E. Erikson and others continued that emphasis. Ego psychology attends to the strength of the thinking, imagining and willing of the person to deal somewhat successfully with reality without crippling self-deceptions. The ego is not just a helpless pawn pushed around by the unconscious struggle between the body's relentless drives (the id) and the stern internalized, civilizing demands of society (the superego). This organizing function of the ego has both unconscious and preconscious dimensions. It is not egoistic self-awareness of one's experience. The individual's ego-identity is shaped by the social habits, memories and relationships within which personal awareness occurs.

ELECTRA COMPLEX
A Jungian term for the feminine Oedipus complex.
Freud's discovery of the Oedipus complex was a key aspect of his work. Among other issues he considered whether it was only a male phenomenon or whether there was a female Oedipus. That discussion continues today. Controversy arose between Freud and Jung over female sexuality and its capacity. It was driven by Jung's proposal that there was a distinctive female version of the Oedipus complex, according to which the daughter was attached to her father and aggressive towards her mother. This he called 'the Electra complex', something that Freud resisted. Interest in the issue of the female Oedipus has been recently revived.

ELECTRO-CONVULSIVE THERAPY (ECT)

A treatment for severe depression, in which a minute electric current is passed through the brain of the patient. Passing a current through the brain causes an epileptic seizure, and – for reasons still not completely clear – this can lead to a rapid and dramatic remission of depression (Kaplan, Sadcock and Scheele, 1996).

ECT technique has been significantly refined in recent years to minimize the patient's discomfort and the risk of injury to the brain and other organs. In practice, memory loss is the only significant side effect, and memory usually returns within weeks after treatment. But because of the risk that still remains, ECT is usually recommended only when life-threatening depressive symptoms are present, and medication has failed or cannot be used for medical reasons. Those who counsel individuals with severe depression who have been advised to receive ECT, should bear in mind that ECT is one of the most rapid and effective treatments of depression available. The understandable apprehensiveness of patients and their families must be balanced against the fact that severe depression can be fatal, from starvation or suicide, if left untreated.

EMPATHY

A process whereby one person enters into the deepest possible awareness of what another person is experiencing at a given moment. Empathy includes intellectual understanding and shared information as well as fellow-feeling. It has long been recognized that empathy is an important quality in a caring relationship. St John of the Cross identified the importance of 'loving attentiveness'. In this century existentialist philosophers, notably Martin Buber, in his description of the 'I–Thou relationship', have stressed the importance of empathic dialogue in shaping our awareness of both our individuality and our relatedness to others. Empathic awareness is at the heart of the psychoanalytic concept of 'transference', the appreciation of unconscious patterns of relationship formed in childhood. Along with respect and genuineness it is one of a triumvirate of 'core values' identified by Carl Rogers as essential to a therapeutic relationship.

Empathic understanding of another requires us to seek to see the world through their eyes. In order fully to empathize it is also necessary to tune in to each individual's unique way of giving form to their experience. Paul Tournier (1957, p. 22) describes this process. After stressing the importance of seeing each individual in his or her historical, cultural and social context he says:

> There suddenly awakes within me the certainty that I am no longer learning, but understanding. It is quite different. It is not the sum of what I have learnt. It is a light which has suddenly burst forth from our personal contact ...
>
> A characteristic feature is that he has experienced this inner certainty at the same time as I ... We become fully conscious only of what we are able to express to someone else ... it is as if I had discovered him, not now from without, but from within.

Empathy is important because it communicates understanding and deep personal concern, both of which are vital in promoting self-esteem. The healing ambience of an empathic relationship helps to encourage the exploration of difficult feelings. This is important in all pastoral situations, and crucial in traumatic situations.

It is questionable whether empathy can be taught, but we can take steps to deal with factors which impede it. Preconceptions of any kind interfere with empathy. The pastoral visitor who said to the widow, 'If your husband has been dead for three months you must be up to anger by now', cannot have helped her to deal with complex feelings of grief. Self-consciousness is an even more insidious problem; if I am preoccupied by the urge to sort things out for someone, or even to make them feel better, I may miss the full import of the feelings they express.

Responding with empathy is emotionally both costly and rewarding. Openness to the feelings of others entails deep awareness of their experience and resonates with my feelings and memories. It is important that I am in touch with the effect this has on me, if I am to guard against being resentful of the drain on my feelings, or seduced into 'compulsive caring' to enhance my own self-worth.
[Val Potter]

EMPOWERMENT

The process of gaining the necessary resources for individuals, groups or communities so that they become

better able to exercise increased agency for their own well-being.

The resources required may be psychological, spiritual, relational, political or material. Empowerment requires both an analysis of power and the commitment to a just distribution of power. It involves a de-centring of outside leaders and external authorities so that people and groups can better initiate and take responsibility for their own decisions and directions. Both a responsibility for self-empowerment and a commitment to the empowerment of others are central for justice. The notion of empowerment is grounded in theological concepts of justice, vocation, and the centrality of the *imago dei*.

ENCOUNTER GROUPS
A particular form of group work emphasizing personal growth as well as the development and improvement of interpersonal communication and relationship through an experiential process.

Especially popular in the United States in the 1960s and 1970s, encounter groups provide a way of dealing with the feeling of distance and separation between people and address the need for intimacy – for relationships that are close and honest in which feelings can be expressed and accepted, experiences can be shared, and new behaviours risked and practised.

Kurt Lewin originally developed the idea of groups for training in human relationships. After his death his students and supporters held the first sensitivity training in 1947. Around the same time Carl Rogers developed training for the counsellors of hospitalized soldiers returning from the Second World War with a focus on personal and therapeutic growth. But the popularity of encounter groups spread as a grass-roots movement rather than through any central leaders or institutional financing. They were a response to an impersonal culture among the more affluent. Encounter groups assume many of the tenets of humanistic psychology such as human holism, the human potential for growth, and self-determination. They emphasize both education and growth in the history of their development (Lieberman, Yalom and Miles, 1973).

Typically encounter groups provide a high-intensity focus on feelings as opposed to a focus on ideas or actions, and the expression of such feelings is assumed to unblock barriers to relationships and personal resistance to

growth. This high intensity is promoted through a short-term intensive format, e.g. groups meet 20 hours for a weekend or 40+ hours for a week. Membership is kept small at 8 to 18 members, and the format is relatively unstructured. Members choose their own goals and personal direction. The group focuses on the process and the dynamics of immediate personal interactions, and it is assumed that members will trust the group to develop its own potential and that of its members. The leader sets the climate of safety and is directive in facilitating the expression of meaning or feelings, but does not plan exercises or an agenda for the group and avoids interpretation of member contributions. The leader is as much participant as facilitator. Group process focuses on the present and on expression of one's own problems, to which the group responds with levelling (acceptance and confrontation) towards greater authenticity.

Most encounter group members benefit from participation, but not all. Some found the changes they made were only temporary. Some felt they were stripped of their defences and then left with no resources to address the problems which still remained. Some reported nude marathons within encounter groups which were offensive and misguided, if not abusive, quests for intimacy. These matters raised questions about adequate preparation of group leaders. Rumours of encounter groups being part of a communist conspiracy circulated but were never proven.

Substantial educational research on encounter groups, especially during the 1970s, indicated that 'changes do occur in sensitivity, in the ability to manage feelings, in the directionality of motivation toward self-actualization, in attitudes toward self and other, and in interdependence' (Rogers, 1970). The decline in popularity of encounter groups is, therefore, not because they are not effective, but because they no longer address the most pressing problems of Western cultures. Personal boundaries may no longer be too constricting and rigid, but rather too permeable and weak. Nonetheless many group skills honed in encounter groups continue to be used by ministers and by group leaders in other settings. *[Judith L. Orr]*

ENDINGS
Completion, conclusion or termination.
Ending may refer to a piece of work, and hence fill one with a sense of achievement, but more

usually endings are associated with loss. It may refer to the loss of a phase of one's life, like the advantages of infancy, of childhood, of youth or of one's working life. Or it may be associated with the loss of what is familiar, like the loss of one's home, country, citizenship or one's job. It may refer to the loss of health, limb, the functions and independence through ageing, and finally the ending of one's life on earth. All losses are painful and, as Freud (1917) pointed out, lead to a state of mourning. Even changes which are associated with progress, such as completing a course of study, getting married, moving to a better job, moving house or the end of pregnancy, may involve painful feelings. What is familiar is lost and the unknown has to be faced. The frightening and sad feelings associated with these endings are usually overlooked by others. They tend to stress only the positive aspects of change. This leaves the person who experiences the loss feeling not understood and lonely. Mostly, endings are associated with the loss of a close and important relationship, be it with a partner, a friend, a mentor, doctor, social worker, or indeed any person who is being relied upon for a sense of security, care and development. This may arise through separation or death. It leaves the child, or the child within the adult, feeling abandoned, unloved, uncared for or afraid. He or she feels that without this person they will be unable to manage their life. Such feelings of neediness, which have their origin in dependency on parents or carers in infancy and childhood, may also be transferred to others, who are felt to be important father or mother figures. Mass grief might be shown at the death of a monarch, a political or a spiritual leader. The death of one's child is possibly the most difficult loss to overcome. It is felt to be against the natural order and to take away the hope that one's future will be continued via one's offspring.

Endings evoke powerful feelings of mourning. The immediate reaction, especially if the loss is sudden and unexpected, is shock. There are physical manifestations, such as coldness, loss of appetite, insomnia, as well as an inability to take in mentally the reality of what has happened. There is a preoccupation with the loved, lost person, and a withdrawal of interest in the outside world. In order to protect the dead person, anger at feeling deserted by the departed is turned against others. The bereaved person inevitably feels guilty at not having done enough, having neglected the deceased or harboured death wishes. Such guilt may be projected onto others such as doctors, who could have saved life or protected the beloved from pain, or pastors, who might have prayed more effectively. In the effort to preserve one's love, the departed person is often idealized. This may give way to grief and yearning and a more realistic picture of what has been lost. The painful work of mourning takes many months. If in the long run love and gratitude for the good gained in the past supersede, this may be used to invest in creative new ventures. [Isca Wittenberg]

ENLIGHTENMENT
A movement in Western culture that emphasized the importance of reason over faith and of the individual rather than the community, and which questioned traditional doctrines of the Church.

The Enlightenment describes intellectual developments from the late seventeenth century that were so dramatic that people came to think of themselves as being in an entirely new era. History was viewed as having three main stages: ancient, medieval and modern. The modern era developed from the rise of humanism in the fifteenth century, as a new confidence to value human abilities and achievements began to upset the relationship between revelation and reason carefully propounded by Aquinas to preserve the priority of the former. In the eighteenth century the work of Newton, Voltaire, Locke and Franklin asserted the clear primacy of reason, and proclaimed the end of superstition and slavery to myths and mysterious rituals. Now all claims to truth, including those of Christian revelation, were to be submitted to the judgement of human reason.

The key features of the Enlightenment as an intellectual movement are:

1. Reason is the tool for determining truth. There was an assumption that 'reason' is a faculty common to all human beings, and thus the seed of potential harmony and progress. The task of theology became the process of reflection on experience in the light of Scripture and tradition. The method is empirical and experiential. Scripture and tradition are subject to criticism and evaluation at the bar of reason. Objectivity and scientific method are crucial.

2. Human experience is a primary ingredient to the discernment of truth. Again, Scrip-

ture and tradition are subject to criticism and evaluation by this criterion.

3. Nature provides an essential model and key to understanding the purposes and processes of the world. What is 'natural' is assumed to be right. Miracles are suspect.

4. Progress provides the pattern for human life. The present is assumed to be superior to the past, and this gives confidence that human judgement is ever improving. Even when the reality of suffering and failure is recognized, thinkers such as Teilhard de Chardin have been able to advocate an overall sense of progress and improvement. This is the basis for much optimism in the processes of pastoral practice. Similarly the great emphasis upon education and the possibility of better performance and perspective in the future. The key is process rather than any established pattern by which to measure.

5. Tradition has a limited value: its philosophies and practices are liable to be outdated, limited and inaccurate. This has led to a widespread collapse of confidence in Scripture and doctrine being easily accessible resources for the Christian enterprise, and a corresponding shift of emphasis towards pastoral practice and institutional organization as more defining forces.

6. There is a hermeneutic of suspicion. Whatever has been formulated is always capable of improvement by new insight. Thus everything can, and should, be constantly challenged.

7. This leads to a process of change being seen as normative. Institutions easily become repressive. Individuals need space and opportunity to grow and develop. Individualism has a primary importance.

8. Utilitarianism becomes a key factor in evaluating any course of action or understanding of truth.

The outcome of these shifts has been to promote atheism as a direct consequence of placing complete confidence in human abilities and potentialities. Christian theology has become more rational and more clearly focused on the agenda of this world. The result has been increasing pre-eminence for pastoral practice and social issues, and widespread debate and exploration about the nature of divinity and its relationship to the human enterprise. Religion tends to become reduced to morality and the sphere of private life.

In the late twentieth century there was a movement to question these features of Enlightenment, and a sense of moving into a different, 'postmodern' era (postmodernism). However, the thinking of Western culture is still deeply immersed in Enlightenment presuppositions, which serve to separate it from the rest of the world. Similarly there is a strong tension within Christianity between a Western, Enlightenment model, and the more spontaneous, charismatic, biblical faith advancing in other cultures.

The discipline of pastoral studies in the Western Church is a child of the Enlightenment. It is rooted in: (1) the empirical; (2) an optimism about progress and human potential – for clients and communities and for those who help them. Hence the importance of supervision and planned progression; (3) a confidence in a basic coherence that can be found through human reason; (4) a trust in therapeutic, growth models of behaviour and belief; (5) a focus on personal experience; (6) a method based on the hermeneutic of suspicion – there is always more to discover, and skilled help is the best way of making such discoveries; (7) belief in the value of training and continuing training; (8) a concentration upon individuals, often with a presupposition that the 'institutional factors' are unhelpful or at least limited in import; (9) a sense of distance from Scripture and tradition as primary rather than occasional resources; (10) a desire for the natural person to set the agenda and take priority.

It is important to put these features into perspective. They are valuable as expressing the reality of how contemporary culture is seen to operate. They are dangerous in their tendency to marginalize (1) the place of revelation; (2) the classic resources of Scripture and tradition; (3) the role of the Church as community; (4) the importance of symbol and ritual; (5) the persistence of sin and human imperfection; (6) the significance of mortality. Each of these issues deserves increasing attention from pastoral studies as it grows into a more developed discipline. [Alastair Redfern]

ENNEAGRAM
A word meaning 'nine point[s]', representing the number of personality types described in this system.
The Enneagram is a personality typology which is thought to have originated in Sufi mysticism during the fourteenth century. Towards the end of the twentieth century the Enneagram established itself as a method of

introspection widely used in various contexts, including spiritual direction, clinical psychology, psychiatric diagnosis and pastoral care. Each of the nine personality types expresses a distinctive world-view characterized by a struggle between its 'virtue' and its 'vice'.

ENVIRONMENT
The natural and humanly constructed context of biophysical existence.

The environment is the surface of the planet earth, which environs or envelops human life. The word 'environment' is a conceptual and linguistic device which distinguishes human consciousness and existence from this biophysical envelope. It indicates the human capacity to imagine the world as a biophysical sphere separate from the human body and human consciousness. This imaginative capacity, which is uniquely human, may be said to be a hazardous one. The human body, the human brain and human identity are all constituted and sustained by constant exchanges of nutrients, gases, organisms and sense impressions generated in the environment. The tendency of urban industrial societies to obscure these biophysical exchanges may be implicated in the growing evidence of damage to the earth's surface that modern human activity has created (Simmonds, 1979).

The earth's surface from ocean floor to upper atmosphere is no more than three miles deep. It is relatively thin compared to the earth's surface area, and relatively fragile. It is the only planetary surface in the known universe capable of supporting organic life. Scientific observations reveal that modern industrial and agricultural activities are making significant impacts on this environment.

1. Chlorine from refrigerants and aerosols has thinned the ozone layer in the upper atmosphere, which protects plant and animal life from harmful ultraviolet radiation.

2. Deforestation is creating a mass extinction of species, reducing biodiversity.

3. Carbon dioxide and other gases produced by industry, heating, transport and agriculture are warming the earth's surface, melting the polar ice caps and changing climate patterns.

4. Inappropriate agricultural techniques on fragile soils are destroying topsoil and extending deserts on every continent.

5. Global industrial fishing is wiping out whole species of fish and destroying fishing grounds.

6. Chemicals used in agriculture and food processing and packaging are reducing the male sperm count and increasing immune problems and cancer rates in humans, and endangering many species of insect, bird, fish and mammal.

7. Industrial and agricultural effluents are acidifying lakes, poisoning rivers and ground water, and polluting the air.

Environmental concern and protest are growing in both advanced industrial societies and developing societies. Ideas and movements concerned with nature preservation, and especially with the conservation of wilderness, emerged as part of the Romantic reaction to industrialism in the nineteenth century. Resistance to animal hunting, factory farming and animal experimentation became prominent in the twentieth century. Animal-rights philosophers and activists argue that animals have intrinsic rights which humans must respect. The science of ecology has identified interconnections and balances between different inhabitants of the ecosystem. Environmentalists argue that agricultural, industrial and residential developments should be designed so as to minimize harms to whole ecosystem communities, as well as to individual species.

Ecological philosophers and theologians argue that the environmental crisis is related not just to modern industrial or agricultural techniques or to the increasing size of the human population, but also to modern ideas about nature and the cosmos. Christian ecotheologians propose that we are more likely to care for the environment when we identify the natural order with the purposes of a beneficent divine creator instead of seeing it as the product of random chemical or organic events (Northcott, 1996).

Environmental concern is sometimes regarded as conflicting with the collective quest for economic security and well-being. However, environmental disasters are more often generated by human greed than human need. Many of the most fragile environments are inhabited by the earth's poorest people. They are also frequently the first victims of climate change, desertification or other environmental problems. Traditional nomadic and subsistence agricultural practices are often better suited to exploiting and conserving the resources of fragile lands or forests than commercial mono-cropping and industrial development. Protecting the land rights of poor nomadic peoples or subsistence farmers also helps to conserve the environment.

Environmentalists also point to the denatured, polluted, hazardous and unstimulating urban environments in which many poor people are forced to live in modern cities. Studies have found connections between social and psychological pathologies in inner cities, including increased delinquency and crime, and poor environmental conditions. Social justice and access to cleaner and healthier environments are not opposing but related social and moral objectives in both developed and developing societies. Theologians and feminists have coined the term eco-justice to indicate the connections between the exploitation and degradation of the environment and oppression, injustice and poverty in human society. [Michael Northcott]

ENVY
A powerful emotion aroused through comparing oneself unfavourably with another.

The comparison may be with the other's qualities, possessions or even behaviour, and may lead to malice and resentment. Envy involves two people; where three are concerned the comparable state is jealousy – the response to disloyalty or rivalry. Both can produce destructive behaviour, but envy more so. It relates to hating and not possessing and can destroy the envious person's life.

Covetousness, the actions resulting from envious desire, is condemned in the tenth of the Ten Commandments (Deut. 5.1–21). For many centuries those commandments established behavioural norms for Judaeo-Christian societies. Envy, if allowed to be put into action, can cause great distress in families and communities. Guilt over envious actions can be difficult to assuage. It is one of the seven deadly sins, because in the desire for self-esteem the envious person puts down another.

With the decline of religious and moral influences in many communities, envy has crept insidiously into most modern and post-modern societies, and now sometimes presents itself as a natural ambition and desire for self-improvement. It is sometimes difficult to distinguish between envy and the proper desire for improvement in living standards that prompts individuals and societies who are disadvantaged to seek parity with their more affluent neighbours. Considerations of justice will normally enable the distinction to be made.

Envy is a word that is often weighted with negative images, but holy envy can and does exist. The desire to enter or possess the Kingdom of heaven, the desire to acquire the mind of Christ, has often prompted the disciples of Jesus to desire to acquire the virtues they envy in him and some of his followers. What makes the difference between a deadly sin and a holy desire is that those who truly desire to enter the Kingdom of God also desire everyone else to find their place in that Kingdom. They do not desire to deprive others of their rightful birthright, or of natural justice. Rather they desire that everyone shall find justice and be able to enter into the Kingdom of God and they are content to work towards that end. [Una Kroll]

EROS
1. In classical Greek, sexual passion and the God of love.
2. In Freud, the life instinct in contrast with the death instinct.
3. In a philosophical sense, the desire for truth.

The absence of the word eros in the New Testament has led to an exaggerated distinction between eros and agape (Furnish, 1972). The Fathers used it both of God's love for humankind and human love for God, as well as of the bringing together of what is separated. Subsequently, however, this use went into decline. In the nineteenth century Freud revived the notion, seeing it as very close to what he understood by sexuality. At times it is not very different from his term 'libido'. This intensity of use, together with the Fathers' understanding, is also found in Tillich's notion of creative justice, which involves the reunion of what is separated or alienated (Osborne, 1994).

EROTICISM
In psychology a general term for that which arouses sexual excitement.

The term 'eroticism' has only recently entered the vocabulary, although the underlying Greek word eros (love) has a long history. Eros plays a key part in Freudian theory as the life instinct, the source of drives that encourage the individual to reproduce and seek self-preservation. The instinctual aspect of eroticism was emphasized throughout the twentieth century. In the Christian tradition eros has often been contrasted with, and even differentiated from, agape. The former is sexual, self-actualizing and erotic love; the latter is sacrificial, agapaic love (Batson, Shoenrade and Ventis, 1993). This distinction, however, will not strictly hold in the New Testament, where eros is not used and other words for 'love' cannot always be distinguished. Ethicists have also used this distinction, although care is needed. In medieval Christendom the structure of the social order controlled eros (sexual love) and compared it with affection, friendship and agape or charity. One outcome of the Reformation was that eroticism was slowly regained as part of the Christian tradition. Nevertheless, when issues of eroticism arise the churches seem from the first to have been uncomfortable (Brown, 1989; Lawrence, 1989). [Raymond J. Lawrence]

ETHICS, PROFESSIONAL
Moral obligations which govern the practice of vocational groups and their members in making the specialized knowledge or skill professed available to the public.
Professional ethics include, but extend beyond, professional etiquette, namely the conventions governing mutual relations within the profession. The marks of a recognized profession are: (1) common possession of a body of knowledge and skill which practitioners are expected to develop, enhance and transmit to new aspirants; (2) extensive autonomy under the law, conditional upon the exercise of oversight and discipline over identified members; (3) recognition of a corporate ethics of conduct, both between members and between each of them and the client or public; (4) entitlement, in return, to social satisfaction in status and material reward (Bond, 2000). Despite individual lapses and the swellings of corporate self-interest which have provoked cynics from Aristotle (*Nicomachaean Ethics* V. vii. 13) to George Bernard Shaw ('All professions are conspiracies against the laity'), professional ethics are among the sinews of a free society. They sustain and extend (when they do not abuse) reliance on trust; they limit coercive regulation and state control where human interests are best served by free and privileged communication. However, this classic position on professionalism is becoming more fragile with the proliferation of ideas of human rights and the consequential turning

to the law to regulate relationships. It is difficult at present to discern which course future developments will take. The current enthusiasm for public accountability is said to put a serious query against the concept of a profession and the need for codes of professional ethics.

Professionals are made distinctive by the knowledge or skill which they possess, and which they are both expected and authorized to exercise, undeflected by self-interest or personal idiosyncrasy. The ethics are a complex of obligations: primarily to the client; generally to society as a whole, with its conventions and reliance upon trust to sustain the professional relationship with the client; internally to colleagues in the profession, to maintain their corporate integrity and repute; and overall to the canons of truth proper to each scientific discipline or skill. The ethics are first a corporate possession of the professional body, whether coded or conventional; and thence in the keeping of each practitioner, informing his or her conscience when occasion requires. They presuppose a relationship of covenant with the client: a commitment on the one side to serve the client's interest to one's utmost ability, and, on the other, to observe the discipline of the accepted regimen. Within this relationship there may exist a contractual factor when a consideration, normally a fee, is interposed. But in its ethical aspects the professional relationship is not contractual. Some obligations, therefore, stand, whether they are reciprocated or not (Bond, 1994).

Among the common features are these: (1) the client's interest is paramount up to the point where its promotion would gravely threaten an interest vital to society; (2) confidences are to be kept inviolate, in that there must be no improper disclosure; (3) there must be no betrayal, or improper personal advantage taken, of a position of trust; (4) no private or sectional advantage may be taken of the power which the professional worker has over clients in their vulnerability or dependency; (5) a professional adviser is answerable for the advice he or she gives; (6) the induction of new members requires them to gain experience with actual clients – those responsible for their induction have a duty of care for those who may be at risk of harm from such inexperienced attention; only those capable of discharging that duty should be entrusted with the responsibility of induction.

Clergy and ministers, though traditionally constituting a profession, imperil their pastoral relationships if they succumb to the formal distancing of themselves, the detachment, which is a mark of some other professional relationships. This is true, but they also risk their pastoral standing and their order if they neglect the distinctive ground of their professional standing or calling, which is theology. Despite the elements of professional ethics held in common, professions are discrete disciplines. Practice and the ethics of practice attach to role and context. Hybridization, or the uncritical lifting of norms out of one context into another, can only weaken and confuse. It is as improper for the priest to ape the role of the doctor or social worker as it is for these to assume the functions specific to a priest. Co-operation in good pastoral care assumes not interchangeability but difference, in a mutual trust based on respect for the competence of each in their own professions. *[G. R. Dunstan]*

EUCHARIST
The sacrament of holy communion.
Pastorally the Eucharist has throughout the Church's history been associated with healing. In the Anglican Book of Common Prayer the connection is explicitly made between physical healing and communion in the Prayer of Humble Access and the words of administration. This approach is also found in the Roman Catholic and Orthodox Churches and the higher traditions of the Anglican and Lutheran Churches. The Eucharist has also been used in exorcism. In spite of the risks of magical associations, there continues to be a pastoral use of the Eucharist in confirming the restoration of a penitent. Although originally a distinctive mark of the Catholic tradition, in recent years such eucharistic awareness has become more widespread.

EUTHANASIA
Intentional ending of a person's life by action or inaction when that life is reckoned not worth prolonging.
The definition of euthanasia, like its practice, is controversial. Surveys indicate that many members of the public seem to want it. The medical profession is divided. All mainstream churches oppose it, although a few theologians and church leaders argue for it. The law generally is becoming less clear. In Holland, for example, it has been legalized (2001). The issues involved are central to the pastoral care of the terminally ill.

Opponents of euthanasia offer a series of arguments: that it is an infringement of God's sole right to determine the hour of our death; it is an offence against the commandment not to kill; dying is an important experience; suffering may lead to spiritual growth and readiness for eternity; above all, permitting euthanasia will further undermine the sanctity of life – the 'slippery slope' argument. It can lead to pressure on people – such as the elderly, those with disabilities, those suffering chronic pain, and some with psychological disorder, who may feel that they are a burden on others and ought to ask for their death. Medical opponents agree that most requests are really for relief of pain which can be provided by palliative care. There is, however, also the longing to be relieved from suffering in general. Finally, if euthanasia were legalized, it would damage doctor/patient trust and there is a real fear that legislation intended for a few hard cases would rapidly lead to euthanasia on demand and then to involuntary euthanasia.

On the other side, the case for euthanasia is that, despite the claims made for palliative care, every newspaper death-column commonly shows that death comes 'after much suffering bravely borne'. Nuland (1994) provides medical documentation that some suffer inescapably in the normal process of dying. It is sometimes noted that doctors commit suicide more often than the general public because they know what terminal illness and death involve and they have the means and knowledge to bring their own suffering to an end. In fact, however, most doctors who commit suicide do not seem to have terminal illness: there is a particularly high incidence of depression among them. If assisted suicide were legal, doctors could help their patients make their own preferred response to the prospect of terminal illness. This might be regarded as fulfilling Christ's injunction to love your neighbour as yourself. From a theological perspective Badham (1996) argues that we do not passively leave issues of life and death in God's hands. We wage war against disease, with all the resources of modern medicine. If a doctor can be an agent of God's love in fighting illness, so too can the doctor be a channel of God's love in bringing the struggle to a painless end when further resistance is pointless.

The hospice movement has contributed to a new approach towards death, dying and terminal suffering. This has developed an approach to pain control with use of drugs and surgery, even if life is occasionally shortened. It is becoming more widely agreed that doctors should also avoid medical interventions which simply prolong the process of dying and should use the resources of medicine to help improve the quality of the final stage of life. [Paul Badham]

EVALUATION
Judgement of the worth of a project or programme.

Any programme or project benefits from examination of its effectiveness and whether it can be improved. Although evaluation also inevitably uses scarce resources, whether of time or money. Judging a project's value therefore becomes an essential task when looking for improvements and when deciding where future resources should be applied. Increasingly institutions with a pastoral focus have found the need to evaluate their programmes for these reasons or when seeking resources from an outside body.

Evaluation should be distinguished from an 'audit'. An audit normally involves assessing the needs of a whole area such as a parish and then looking at the Church's response; evaluation would normally have a narrower focus. It will also include a strong element of judgement, and in this it differs from appraisal. Unlike assessment, evaluation normally looks at specific pieces of work rather than at the person carrying out the task.

Central to the process of evaluation is the identifying of clear criteria for what constitutes success. For some projects these are stated at the outset, yet in pastoral work such criteria are often notoriously difficult to define. In, for example, evaluating a pastor's ministry, would 'success' count as large numbers coming to church, or the pastor being 'crucified' by a congregation because of standing for unpopular truths? Indeed criteria may even be the subject of disagreement and conflict between those engaged in a particular piece of work. Simply bringing to the surface such disagreements can be a positive outcome of an evaluation.

An evaluation may vary from a low-key affair, simply asking people what went well and less well, to something much more thoroughgoing involving detailed questionnaires. It may be carried out by someone within the organization or by someone external. External evaluation may be more objective and will be particularly useful in any major evaluation. An insider may bring to the process a more detailed knowledge of the matter under review and this may be sufficient for a more low-key process. The evaluator will normally seek objective evidence from the intended beneficiaries of a project as well as listen to those who are engaged in its delivery. An effective evaluator will need listening skills when sitting in at meetings of the project, and skills in designing appropriate questionnaires and processing the information gleaned.

While there are justifiable reasons for evaluations there can also be suspect ones. Warren Feek (1982) suggests that they can be used for avoiding making decisions, ducking responsibility or producing a rosy picture for the sake of another funding body. Any evaluation process can itself be evaluated to check if it meets its purpose, and its own purposes can, of course, be critically evaluated. [R. P. Reiss]

EVANGELICALISM
A movement within Christianity that emphasizes biblical authority, the centrality of the gospel message, and personal religious experience, and that often de-emphasizes institutional affiliation and formal creeds.

Evangelicalism has its roots in the Reformation, pietistic revivals in Protestantism and Catholicism, Puritanism, as well as fundamentalism in the United States. Evangelicalism includes members in every Christian body, although it has largely been identified with Protestantism.

The initial use of 'evangelical' referred to sixteenth-century monks who advocated personal conversion and Bible reading (McGrath, 1995) – proposals which led to the emergence of a vigorous lay religious movement in the late Renaissance. Unfortunately, this institutional support for evangelicalism paled when the term became associated with Protestantism in the Reformation. In the late seventeenth century evangelicalism re-emerged in Puritan and Anglican writings. Pietistic revivals of the last several centuries have also contributed to evangelicalism through their concern for personal, heartfelt religious experience.

In summary, McGrath lists the following as the central affirmations of contemporary evangelicalism: '(1) the supreme authority of the Bible as a source of knowledge of God and a source for daily life; (2) the majesty of Jesus Christ as both incarnate God and Saviour of the world; (3) the lordship of the Holy Spirit; (4) the need for personal conversion; (5) the priority of evangelism; and (6) the importance of the Christian community for nourishment, fellowship, and growth.'

Currently, evangelicalism is most apparent in England and North America. The National Association of Evangelicals (NAE) was organized in the United States in 1942 with the twofold agenda of distinguishing evangelicalism from fundamentalism and from liberalism. Although the NAE began as an outgrowth of the fundamentalist movement, evangelicals came to disagree with its cultural separatism, biblical literalism and premillennialism. However, they were at one with fundamentalism in strongly opposing modernism's assertions about social reconstructionism, environmental determination, scientific imperialism, radical biblical criticism and religious universalism. Instead evangelicals have advocated personal evangelism, individual religious transformation, biblical authority in faith and practice, the finality of the gospel revelation, and evangelism.

In the USA Billy Graham became the personal embodiment of these evangelical affirmations. Although found in many churches, most self-identified evangelicals are members of churches in the Anabaptist tradition. Nevertheless, a significant percentage of the general public in the English-speaking world identify themselves as 'born-again' Christians – a central tenet of evangelicalism. The NAE continues to be influential and *Christianity Today*, evangelicalism's major publication, is well respected. In England a key personification of evangelicalism has been John Stott, Rector of All Souls, Langham Place, London. He provided an atmosphere for young evangelicals that propelled the movement into the mainstream of Anglican life. He led resistance to the recommendation of others that evangelicals form their own denomination at the time of John Robinson's *Honest to God*. In spite of some who perceived the movement as anti-intellectual, there now exists a significant proportion of clergy and a number of seminaries that identify themselves as evangelical.
[*H. Newton Malony*]

EVANGELISM
Communicating the good news of the Christian gospel.

The word 'evangelism' derives from the Greek word meaning 'good message' or 'good news'. The corresponding Anglo-Saxon word is 'gospel' (god-spell). Evangelism, therefore, is the act of 'good newsing' people. The content of the good news historically is the *kerygma* (Greek 'proclamation') that Jesus Christ died for our sins, was raised from the dead and offers forgiveness to those who repent and believe. However, the fuller content and the way this news is communicated are sources of controversy among Christians. For that reason evangelists themselves feel the need for their own expanded definitions to reflect their individual views of the who, what, why, when, where and how of evangelism. Evangelism should be distinguished from proselytism. The latter is a recruiting activity of a religious body; evangelism is telling the good news of the gospel. This may involve words, but also requires matching deeds.

In modern pluralistic societies it can be argued that evangelism is best done in dialogue rather than by proclamation. On this, however, Christians differ. For some evangelism is described, for example, as proclaiming in word and deed the good news of the Kingdom of God and calling people to repentance, to personal faith in Jesus Christ as Lord and Saviour, to active membership in the Church, and to obedient service in the world. Sometimes the term 'evangelization' is employed, but this has different meanings in different churches. In the Roman Catholic tradition it tends to mean recovering lapsed Catholics to their former faith. Evangelicals, however, use it to describe the evangelistic task of the Church, within which service and social action are partners (Stott, 1975).

The biblical mandate for evangelism is found in the Gospels. Each of the Synoptic Gospels has a version of the 'Great Commission' (Matt. 28.18–20; Mark 16.15; Luke 24.47–48), in which Jesus lays upon his disciples the responsibility for making further disciples and communicating the good news to the world. Viewed as a stewardship obligation, therefore, evangelism is an obligation of the Church and every church member can do something to help the Church fulfil its evangelistic mission. Evangelists vary in their effectiveness. Most acknowledge the need to suit methods to the intended recipients, all of whom do not respond to the same approach. Door-to-door calling, sensitively and caringly done, for example, in most contexts is still an effective way for a congregation to reach everyone in the neighbourhood, which is the Church's local mission field. Some churches encourage their members to invite their friends, neighbours and other acquaintances to church, on occasion for special services. Some congregations have found that small fellowship groups are effective with some unchurched people. In Great Britain the Alpha course is a well-known example. Some congregations distribute tracts, flyers, pamphlets, door-knob hangers, and other kinds of literature. Others have employed telemarketing techniques, the mass media and display advertising; evangelistic crusades and preaching missions; streetcorner, market-place, shopping-mall and other on-site witnessing; spiritual retreats and religious conferences. But the effectiveness of some of these approaches is questioned by some people.

Since the gospel has both personal and social implications, evangelism and social action are partners in the Church's mission. Evangelism, therefore, must be service-oriented and contextual. In a pluralistic world sensitive Christians know they have to win the right to be heard by living the faith they profess. [*Richard Stoll Armstrong*]

EVIL
In theological usage the reality of destructiveness, pain and suffering in the created universe.

Two fundamental questions undergird most definitions of and discussion about evil. First, if human beings are created in the image and likeness of God (*imago dei*), why do they contribute to suffering and harm in human existence? Second, if God is good and omnipotent then what is the relation between God, creation and human suffering? The first question points to issues of human freedom and responsibility for suffering in human life and falls under the category of moral evil. The second question, which usually comes under the category of natural evil, addresses the harm that results not from human actions but from common events such as storms, disease and other natural disasters. In the Judaeo-Christian tradition many of the myths (Gen. 1. 2), narratives (Luke 4, 1–13), doctrinal statements, and

theological works are, in part, attempts to answer these questions.

St Augustine was a major contributor to Western Christianity's conceptualization of evil. His formulation emerged from his eventual disagreement with the dualistic (or Manichaean) view of creation (a bad and a good creator) and in his disputes with Pelagian rejection of original sin. Briefly, Augustine argued from a profound doctrine of God as creator that evil, which he treated as 'non-being', emerges from those parts of creation that reject God and the good, which is 'being'. This proclivity for disobedience (original sin) was inherited from Adam and is thus a part of human nature that required God's redemptive grace. Human evil is not a force or substance but rather a disordered passion and an inordinate desire for the material world, which means turning away from God and the good.

Some contemporary theologians (Farley, 1990; Niebuhr, 1941; Tillich, 1963) have posited evil as the human tendency to absolutize the relative and contingent. The source of this tendency is neither an internal predisposition nor an external force, such as Satan. Rather, it emerges from the tragic structure of creation and God's creative activity, which is characterized by indeterminacy, openness, uncertainty, change and ambiguity. These aspects of creative activity evoke human anxiety, fear and disappointment. The tendency to absolutize the relative, then, is a response that attempts to avoid experiences related to indeterminacy, change and ambiguity, but which in so doing denies the reality of God's creative activity. The consequences of individual and communal inclination for idolatry are suffering and harm. In this contemporary understanding of evil God is not its source. Evil is an outcome of the human response to creation and God's creative activity.

At present in pastoral care and counselling the conceptual tools and theories of the human sciences have expanded and, to some extent, dominate our understanding of suffering and harm in human life, placing theological concepts such as evil and sin in the background. But the contributions of the human sciences do not imply that theological perspectives regarding evil are not helpful in understanding and responding to persons' suffering and difficulties in living. Many of the difficulties in living encountered in pastoral ministry result from diverse acts of omission and commission which may be understood, in part, as attempts to absolutize the relative. [*Ryan LaMothe*]

EXCOMMUNICATION
Ecclesiastical censure that excludes from communion, often with other deprivations.
Chiefly associated with the Roman Catholic Church, this form of discipline of the Church's members has been employed since earliest times. It is essentially a human discipline: a person can be excommunicate and remain in a state of grace. And no excommunication can separate someone from God. An excommunicate person, for example, cannot be denied the last rites. In the Book of Common Prayer excommunication is threatened, but in practice it has been rarely used in the Church of England. This discipline of exclusion is now being found in some of the newer sectarian churches.

EXEGESIS
See: BIBLE, USE OF
OLD TESTAMENT
NEW TESTAMENT

EXHIBITIONISM
Extravagant behaviour designed to attract attention.
Exhibitionism is chiefly associated with inappropriate sexual display. In infants such behaviour is normal. When, however, adults manifest such infantile activity, it becomes a perversion. The aim is to stimulate sexual impulses or even to give sexual gratification by, for example, indecent exposure. Pastors and counsellors without special training can do little or nothing for an exhibitionist. There are also obvious legal problems. The condition can only be treated by specialist therapy.

EXORCISM
The expulsion of malevolent spirits from possessed persons, objects or places.
Exorcism was part of the ministry of Jesus and of the Church for many centuries following. Today it is often called 'deliverance' (Perry, 1996). The world was believed to be inhabited with demons, headed by a prince – the devil, Satan, Lucifer etc. These could be expelled from people or places that were possessed by means of adjuration and a series of ceremonies, which were gradually codified. In the medieval Church the minor order of exorcist witnesses to the pervasiveness of exorcism. In a world where people believed in demons, success in the struggle between the power of Jesus and other powers was a significant missionary witness.

The revival of interest in the demonic and the occult towards the end of the twentieth century was probably in part a response to the prevailing secular assumptions. Exorcism should never be attempted by unskilled people. Most churches have an adviser on the subject who should always be consulted (Richards, 1974). Those who ask for exorcism are likely to be emotionally disturbed. To accept their interpretation or to resist it will have a profound psychological effect, apart from the question of whether there are such beings as demons to be cast out. Medical co-operation is customary today, as is proper wariness about media publicity.

EXPERIENCE, RELIGIOUS
See: RELIGIOUS EXPERIENCE

EXTROVERSION
The mark of a type of personality which is directed outwards.
The extrovert (sometimes 'extravert') directs his or her interest towards other people or the world around. This contrasts with the introvert, who is more self-referential (introversion).

F

FAITH
A response of trust and confidence in someone or something.
In the Judaeo-Christian tradition, faith is an empowerment from God that enables a person to believe in, and to rely upon, the graciousness of God. The Church distinguishes between faith as right belief and faith as personal commitment. Both understandings are important aspects of a believer's life, but a heavy emphasis on the first understanding, which happened in the second century, makes faith a matter of orthodoxy rather than a matter of holding on to God's promises.

For the Church, the only proper object of faith is God's forgiving love as manifested and brought to fulfilment in and through Jesus Christ. Any other object is a form of idolatry. True faith is seen as a work of the Holy Spirit and is awakened in persons as they experience the power of God in their lives. Thus faith rests on the conviction that God is trustworthy and is faithful to God's Word, even as it prompts the believer to be faithful to God's Word. Faith is distorted if it is made into a meritorious accomplishment that earns the believer God's favour. On the contrary, faith is an antidote to all human striving. It is a holding on to an acceptance that is freely and divinely given, an acceptance that then motivates the believer to do works of love out of gratitude to God.

Towards the end of the twentieth century, pastoral studies have focused on faith as a human response – faith development. By seeing it as a developmental phenomenon, they have illuminated both the dynamics of faith and how the believer grows in faith. *[LeRoy Aden]*

FAITH DEVELOPMENT
The study of faith as a developmental phenomenon and the application of these insights in nurture and education.
Focusing on faith as a human response, pastoral studies have in recent years turned attention to faith development. The chief proponents have been J. H. Westerhoff (1976) and J. W. Fowler (1981).

Two different, though complementary, approaches may be found. The first uses life-cycle theory and maintains that faith takes different forms, depending on the developmental stage in which the individual is currently immersed. For example, faith takes the form of trust when the individual is struggling with the existential task of trust v. mistrust. The advantage of this approach is that faith not only becomes an apt response to a particular developmental crisis but it also becomes an ultimate and life-giving answer to that crisis.

The second approach uses Jean Piaget's study of a child's sequential patterns of thinking and reasoning to illuminate the structural forms of faith. Fowler is a leading proponent. For him, faith, which is itself a way of knowing and valuing the world from an ultimate perspective, is shaped and in part determined by the cognitive development of the individual. Fowler distinguishes six stages of the development of faith, ranging from a child's intuitive-projective faith, which functions in a fluid and novel-filled world, to a seldom-achieved universalizing faith that

spends itself to bring about love and justice in a transformed world. This approach to faith has attracted criticism, but it has been a heuristic force in the study of the nature of faith and in linking between faith and cognitive human development. *[LeRoy Aden]*

FAITH-HEALING
The popular name given to any form of healing which involves religious and spiritual means to effect a cure for a physical or mental condition.
The term 'faith-healing' is one that no practitioner of healing, whether from a Christian or an alternative spiritual tradition, would use to describe their work. Some Christians involved in healing would claim that the term applies to non-Christian practices, where there is a need to have 'faith' in the practitioner for his or her treatment to be effective. This is contrasted unfavourably with faith in God as the basis for true healing. The non-Christian practitioner would claim that 'healing' does not involve faith in anyone or anything but is an objective technique which can be taught (S. Parsons, 1995).

Although the expression 'faith-healing' finds no favour with those who practise healing, it remains a useful term to describe the phenomenon which has been observed in every culture, that some people seem to have a gift of healing touch. It can be observed that a mother is able to calm an infant by the act of stroking and holding the child. In certain individuals this gift is more focused, so that a touch can relieve pain in another. At this level no religious or metaphysical explanation is sought or offered. Those who practise this kind of healing in a more systematic way will normally tend to explain their work using a number of metaphysical or quasi-religious explanations. The models offered will often involve ideas of light and energy being given and received, and such light and energy is normally seen ultimately to have a cosmic source (Benor, 1993).

Most people, even in a Western secular society, have come to accept the existence of gifts of touch and healing at some level even if no coherent framework of explanation is forthcoming. The realm of the psychic is part of the common assumptions about the way human beings function. In spite of widespread credulity, the responsible pastor, prepared to review the evidence, should have little reason to resist the possibility that healing gifts may be found in a variety of people inside and outside the faith communities. The mechanism of such psychic and healing gifts is outside present scientific paradigms, but this in itself is not a reason for rejecting the phenomenon as having no reality. [*Stephen Parsons*]

FALSE SELF
An individual's interaction with their world when it is shaped compulsively by the demands of others, rather than by the individual's own experiences and needs.

Donald Winnicott (1958, 1965) suggested that the healthy psychological development of a baby rested on two things being present in its relationship with its mother, or primary care-giver. First, the care-giver needs repeatedly to give the baby a 'moment of illusion', when the care-giver provides the baby with a nurturing object (e.g. breast, bottle) just at the point when the baby experiences the desire for such an object. This experience enables the baby both to relate its inner desires to real objects in the outer world and to preserve a sense of omnipotence which serves as the foundation on which to build a healthy sense of self. Second, the care-giver should be able to allow the infant to be themselves and not to interfere with the baby when it is not experiencing any needs. This allows the baby to get used to its experience of 'going-on-being' and to develop a sense of comfortable solitude.

If the care-giver fails to provide these qualities, by failing to respond to the baby's needs or by interfering with its experience of being at rest, then the baby can experience this as a terrifying attack upon its very self. The baby recognizes that something more powerful than itself is making demands on it (e.g. that it should not cry, even though it is hungry) and it is forced to respond to these demands. As a consequence, the infant develops a 'false self', whereby it interacts with its world on the basis of the demands of those around it, rather than on the basis of its own experiences and needs. The 'true self' of the infant therefore becomes overlaid by a 'false self' characterized by compliance to the needs and demands of others. This false self can be carried into adulthood and is evident in the case of an individual who seeks compulsively to attend to others' needs, while being unaware of their own.

Two significant implications arise out of Winnicott's notion of the false self for pastoral care. First, this concept indicates that attending to the needs of others can, for some involved in caring work, have a compulsive and pathological dimension to it. Second, Winnicott believed that individuals could recover more of their true selves in adult life through being in relationships with others who demonstrated reliability, attentiveness, responsiveness, recollection and durability. This highlights qualities which might usefully be embodied in pastoral relationships. [*Gordon Lynch*]

FAMILY
A social group, usually bound by blood kinship, the nucleus of which may assemble under one roof the parent[s] and the dependent child(ren), and whose primary function is to ensure the emotional and material security of its members.

The family is a universal element and the basic cell of human society, which presents many different forms according to period and culture. It is therefore more useful to speak of types of family rather than 'the' family, for there will be marked differences in such areas as marriage, authority, rearing of children, care of the elderly, division of labour and the link with previous generations.

Whereas in Western society the word refers mainly to the 'nuclear' family (a couple with children), the term 'family' may also be extended to include grandparents, aunts, uncles and cousins. It can also mean ethnic or tribal families whose identity is bound up in belonging; or those sharing a home or community or belief (the 'church' family or the 'village' family, the workplace as family). These latter categories are of immense importance to those without, or estranged from, close blood relations.

Western culture encompasses an increasing number of variants on the nuclear family: childless couples; one-parent families (where the parent is widowed, divorced, separated or single); adoptive or fostered; reconstituted or 'blended' families mixing children of the current and previous unions of the partners; homosexual couples living with children.

Ideally, the organized network of familial relationships provides a social foundation where each member belongs, is named and identified. Its functions can be defined as: (1) *biological* – reproduction and child care; (2)

psychological – provision of emotional security, communication and exchange, learning to negotiate interpersonal relationships, and the rhythm of aloneness and togetherness; (3) *social and cultural* – enabling social insertion by giving a name, by educating; (4) *moral* – transmitting values and standards, by demonstrating the consequences of actions and choices; (5) *economic* – ensuring the means of subsistence of its members, sharing resources, solidarity.

Family communities are further defined by their habits, shared language, rules, rituals, history and systems. The family therefore means the individual members plus the relationships between them. Family systems are the patterns of behaving and interacting, mainly unconscious on the part of the members, which have evolved gradually, possibly through several generations. In these, family members may unwittingly collude with one another, perhaps to avoid dealing with emotions they find frightening, painful or unacceptable. Sometimes they will 'project' these all onto one person, who will act them out on behalf of everyone; sometimes they will tacitly signal that these emotions are taboo, which may result in emotional dysfunction. Children growing up with a particular 'system' will often select a marriage partner who will continue this collusion, and so it goes on through the generations, causing the family to fail in some of its functions.

Often it takes an outsider to discern these systems, which may pervade a whole family group but deeply affect the behaviour of a particular member. Pastors need to be aware how easy it is for outsiders to be drawn into a system or manipulated by dysfunctional families. Family therapy may be necessary to dismantle the repeated patterns, the obstructions to communication, the shared attitudes and defences which prevent the needs of members being met.

Western society has seen rapid and significant change in family structure and function during the last century: from extended to nuclear; from autonomous to socialized (the family has been dispossessed of many of its functions by the state); from economic to affective unit (from the family founded on patrimony and hierarchy to one based on affectivity, whose principle aim is the relational reciprocity of its members). Where society becomes impersonal, anonymous and conflictual, and where so much of daily life is carried out in seemingly trust- and value-free zones, the state tends to attempt to invest emotionally in the family, which is seen as offering security against the aggression of society, and as the fount of moral values and standards. This increases the pressure of expectation on family units that may be fragile.

Christians believe that the vocation of every human person is love. Ideally a child's primary experience and expression of love are within the family. It is here too that a child is grounded in social values: respect, dignity, solidarity, sharing, honesty, communication, disinterest, tolerance, generosity, pardon and forgiveness, and these are the basis of spiritual values as well. The Roman Catholic Church has coined the phrase 'domestic church' for this communion of persons in relationship, a living sign of the Trinity. The Church may often appear to extol an ideal of family life which seems increasingly unattainable with the shift away from the 'traditional' family with father as breadwinner and mother as homemaker in a stable domestic environment. However, Christians believe that, whatever the circumstances, God is present in all acts of love and self-giving.

Though there is much that brings joy in family life, it can also be a place of hurt, conflict and failure, where power is abused and sexuality desecrated. Uncared for themselves, adults may not have the resources to care for others, and the downward spiral continues unless help and support are forthcoming. Support of the most practical and concrete kind is vital for families before they reach crisis point. Often these small units are fragile, unable to withstand crises, or the constant pressures of material and emotional poverty. The churches need to train helpers to have some understanding of the dynamics involved, that families are living organisms, and that they do not all respond identically to life events and stresses.

The family is the place where we are made into social human beings, where ideally we learn to look outward to the needs of the larger human family. If the family is endangered, so is the health of the whole of society. *[Mary Kirk]*

FAMILY THERAPY
A form of psychotherapy which draws on an understanding of the whole family in order to perceive and resolve

an individual's problems, and promote optimal functioning.

In seeking to treat individuals presenting with psychological, emotional or behavioural problems, family therapists view the family as a social system – the sum of the individual members and the complex dynamic of their relationships within the family and with the outside world. Within this system one or more members may express the pain and dysfunctionality on behalf of the whole unit. This approach can excavate the root causes of difficulties, which often span several generations. It can promote understanding within the family group both of these and of how they are perpetuated by ingrained patterns of interaction, and it can provide models of more effective behaviours. Often relatively small practical changes can bring swift results and greatly increased happiness.

By seeing the unit as a whole the therapist can discern what is happening, and who fulfils what function within it. The 'what' can be more important in the therapeutic process than 'why'. The tasks of the family therapist are: (1) *To listen* – who speaks, and the order in which information is given, are as important as what is said. (2) *To watch* – unconscious, non-verbal signals between family members (often picked up by an observer or video camera) will often reveal how they interact, and what are the 'taboo' issues or emotions. (3) *To receive* – emotions and transferences 'projected' onto him or her without being taken over by them. He or she must get within the family system but not collude in it. (4) *To be a defined presence* – with clear boundaries, in the face of often turbulent family communications. (5) *To give feedback* – negatively on unhelpful interactions; positively to promote change. (6) *To model* – different methods of dealing with individuals inside and outside the family (e.g. supportiveness, nurturance, effective communication) that the family can internalize.

The main schools of family therapy are:

1. *Object-relations*. This identifies one member as carrying the unacceptable emotions and impulses for the whole family, which may have been passed on over generations.

2. *Family systems*. This analyses the visible patterns of family behaviours and teaches the family to *respond* (by making rational choices, based on the needs of the whole unit) rather than *react* (in purely emotional and selfish ways). Thus they learn to be both 'self' and members of the system.

3. *Structural*. This works on the boundaries/fusion between family members so that each has a clearly differentiated concept of self and his or her function.

4. *Strategic intervention*. This seeks to redress the power balance and to restructure the whole system within the family by identifying the controlling element(s).

Some knowledge of the dynamics of family systems is indispensable where pastors are working with families, in order to facilitate understanding and avoid the danger of unconscious collusion in the system, with its concomitant blurring of professional boundaries. [*Mary Kirk*]

FANTASY
An imaginary scene in which the subject is active, being an unconscious wish-fulfilment.

The term is widely used in counselling and therapy, where it has a stronger sense than in its everyday use, which tends to be dismissive – fantasy as imaginative compared with what is real. The alternative spelling, 'phantasy', was once proposed in an attempt to differentiate the technical sense of the word in psychoanalysis, but has not caught on. Fantasy may refer to a particular imaginative activity most of which is harmless. If, however, a person is worried and mystified by feelings associated with fantasy, it may be desirable to explore the unconscious motivations behind them. Dreams are notably one way of addressing such aspects of someone's life (Freud, 1900). A second reference is to the whole imagination of the individual, conscious and unconscious alike. Here primitive desire and instinct intertwine. However, it should also be noted that some, following Winnicott (1971), use the term to refer to day-dreaming as a use of the imagination, thus bringing the word again back towards its non-technical sense.

FEAR
The anxiety and agitation felt at the presence of danger.

Fear has been of longstanding interest to psychologists. In his study of the origins of the emotions, Charles Darwin described its physiological features, including widely opened eyes and mouth, quick and violent beating of the heart, paleness of skin, hurried breathing, clenched or twisting hands and protruded arms. Global reactions are either immobilization or flight. Herbert Spencer also noted the accompanying mental or cognitive features of fear, including mental representations of certain painful consequences and of counter-attack, the latter precipitated by the emotion of anger which frequently follows the initial reaction of fear. Thus, since the nineteenth century, psychologists have recognized that fear is a complex of physiological, cognitive and emotional reactions to actual or perceived threat.

It was also recognized that the instinct of fear is one of the earliest shown by the human child. William James' (1890) list of the causes of fear in infants includes noises, strange persons and strange animals (especially ones that are perceived to be advancing towards the child), dark places and high places. James also discussed pathological fears, citing the catatonic or crouching immobility of some melancholiacs and the agoraphobic's terror of open places and broad streets. The fact that these emotions have no utility in the adult suggest earlier antecedents in the human child (e.g. making oneself invisible through immobility) and in less developed mammals (e.g. the tendency of rodents to cling for cover, then dash across the open space as a desperate measure). Pathological fears are termed phobias, an unreasonable, excessive and persistent fear of some particular thing or situation.

The relationship between anxiety and fear has been more recently discussed by Erik H. Erikson (1950), who has suggested that the anxieties of adults are directly related to the fears they had as children. In childhood, fears and anxiety are so close to one another that they are indistinguishable. In adulthood, the anxious reaction is no longer so clearly associated with the precipitating fear, and becoming independent of it, magnifies and even creates the illusion of an outer danger, without identifying appropriate avenues of defence or mastery. Such misplaced anxieties also leave one vulnerable to real dangers, and hence inhibit the development of a judicious frame of mind. Anxieties of individuals may also be transmitted to others, as in the mother–infant relationship, and may also create susceptibility to group panic, which may in turn be exploited by political leaders.

An enduring issue, predating the emergence and largely independent of psychology as a science, is the role religion may play in reducing or even eliminating fear. Oskar

Pfister (1948), the Swiss pastor and lifelong friend of Freud, argued that the true religious response to fear is love, for 'perfect love casts out fear' (1 John 4.18). He brought psychoanalytic insights to bear on the issue of fear, especially focusing on the compulsions and obsessions resulting from an excessively self-punitive conscience. Simultaneously, he highlighted Jesus' message of love, and noted that Christianity has consistently violated this message by actively promoting fear, usually in the interests of maintaining doctrinal purity or social exclusivism. Current research and theorizing on fear focuses on the dominance/submissive systems within all social groupings, and proposes that fear is a response to the threat (more likely status-related than overtly physical) the system poses, and manifests itself in anticipatory anxiety. Therapeutic approaches, such as those of Richard Heimberg (1995) and his associates, are paying greater attention to the cognitive features of fear, while not discounting the emotional and physiological, emphasizing the revision of the anticipatory cognitive representations (especially self- and other-images) that individuals bring to feared social situations. [Donald Capps]

FEELINGS
A general term for the affective dimension to experience.
The term is so general as to be almost meaningless. Yet it is widely used in pastoral thinking because of its vagueness. It draws attention to the significance of this dimension to human experience, which has often been ignored or defended against, not least by religious bodies. To bring feelings and reflection on them together is a way of creating a hypothesis which can help others, individuals or groups, to develop.

FEES
Money (or gifts in kind) contracted with, or offered by, the client to the helper.
Whereas in pastoral care it is often assumed there is no financial transaction – pastoral care being freely offered in the course of ministry – fees are requested for many of the services offered by the Church. This is most clearly the case where they are charged for weddings or funerals. But it is also true of pastoral counselling centres where donations or fees might form part of the contract (sometimes on a sliding scale to take account of financial hardship). Less obviously, but just as significantly,

people sometimes offer gifts by way of thanks for the help they have received, or in the course of receiving help. Unless fees or other gifts in kind have been agreed beforehand as part of the contractual arrangements, it is wise not to accept fees or gifts personally. If a person insists on wanting to give something it is best given to the Church or the employing organization as a whole.

The request for fees can evoke different feelings, and similarly the offer of fees or gifts may indeed be a way of expressing very different feelings. Some people resent having to pay for a service which they believe should be offered free of charge. Congregations of course often express their appreciation or criticism of their church or their ministers by the amount of their giving. Some believe that churches need to learn to value what they offer and not to be ashamed of charging, since in a market economy many people have come to connect money and worth. At the same time, churches have the opportunity to show the merits of voluntary giving, whether by volunteer pastoral assistant or counsellor, or indeed by the client.

Some people who receive help want to express their gratitude by giving to the helper or the Church, sometimes excessively so, as if they feel a debt to the person who has assisted them. This may need to be talked through, especially if the gift is a sign of lack of self-esteem on the part of the giver. Sometimes gifts can be a way of expressing the need for more help, or as an unspoken need for some special attention, perhaps even as a type of bribe. Gifts may even be a way of trying to make unconscious reparation for the fear of having damaged the helper by one's demands. Withholding of or delay in settling contractually agreed fees can be understood sometimes as an expression of hostility or discontent which cannot be voiced, or is even unacknowledged. It is of course possible that where help has been freely given, the offer of fees or gifts (whether to the helper or to their organization) is to be seen simply as a way of expressing gratitude. The subtle meanings of fee-paying and gifts cannot be divined without careful listening to the client, both in terms of the overt intention and the underlying message. [*Michael Jacobs*]

FEMININITY

1. A set of qualities believed to be characteristic of the nature of women.

2. A set of cultural prescriptions for the lives of women.

3. The symbolic representation of all that is believed to be ideal in and for women.

The variety of definitions of femininity indicates the controversial nature of the subject. In the first, femininity is linked with the physical make-up of women. It is believed that a woman's body determines her character, making her naturally more caring and sensitive, less intellectual and aggressive. There has never been a consensus on precisely what these characteristics are. The many attempts to provide either empirical or logical proof of them have encountered numerous difficulties. Nevertheless, the presumption that women share a common essence has been a feature of biological accounts of humanness since Aristotle.

In the second definition, it is recognized that femininity is an ideological construction. Here, feminine qualities are merely rules for women's behaviour provided by the wider society. Different cultures will have different roles and expectations for women. These may change as wider political and economic factors change. Therefore, women are made into women by the society to which they belong. The process of conformity to cultural prescriptions is reinforced by the message that this is a woman's natural role, or even that this is the will of God. Rejecting the notion that there is really any essence of womanhood, femininity is instead a cultural script for the writing of women's lives.

The third definition emphasizes the symbolic nature of femininity. The finest qualities of womanliness are projected onto an ideal woman. She is sometimes represented in art or literature, and is often believed to be the inspiration of great artistic and cultural achievements. There may be an emphasis on the 'eternal feminine' which transcends any cultural regulations or historical manifestations of particular women. In this form, the feminine is elevated to a higher spiritual or metaphysical plane. This has been important in some forms of Christian theology, for example those which emphasize the Church or the Wisdom of God as feminine. It has played a major part in the psychology of Jung, for whom 'the feminine' and 'the masculine' are complementary principles in the human psyche.

Debate continues regarding the notion of femininity (Graham, 1995). Many women have rejected essentialist determinism, pressing instead for recognition of their responsibility for shaping their own personal identity. Descriptions of femininity also reveal a fundamental inequality, which presumes man to be the normative being and woman an inferior derivative. Many women are suspicious of this dualism of higher and lower, claiming that this distorts all attempts at making the two sexes 'complementary' to one another. Some would argue, following Jung, that women and men need to discover the opposite qualities within themselves in order to achieve human wholeness. Others would argue that dualisms of all kinds should be transcended, recognizing the multiple possibilities of human identity which defy categorizations. [*Susan F. Parsons*]

FEMINISM
A political and intellectual movement that takes seriously the concerns of women's lives, the analysis and critique of their conditions of life, and the ways in which their lives may become more fulfilling.
Feminism emerged during the Enlightenment in Western Europe and North America, dating from the eighteenth century. It was allied with the new humanism which began to appear and which continues to be the prevailing ideology of the modern era. It reflected the widespread concern for the dignity and sovereignty of human beings and the new confidence in human reason to change society in positive ways. Feminism thus played a part in the formation of the modern period, and thereby brought with it new theological challenges and insights. Feminism has developed into a complex phenomenon, comprised of three interwoven strands.

1. Feminism may be understood as a political movement, the primary concern of which is justice for women. It is affirmed that women and men share a common human nature. Therefore women justly deserve the same fundamental human rights. Women and men are considered to be equally free to make decisions about their lives, and equally responsible for their own actions and relationships. Feminism insists on political recognition of this full humanity being granted to women. This motivates the work of women for social and political justice throughout the world. The hope is for equality of opportunity, of access and of treatment throughout the

structures of society. Women from different backgrounds and contexts may share concerns for human rights and freedom. Nevertheless, many women from the Two-thirds World question whether this emphasis on justice may turn out to be another form of cultural imperialism. There is an increasing recognition within feminism of the diversity among women, which may make the possibility of a single coherent political movement for justice more difficult.

2. Feminism may be understood as a social and cultural critique. In this the primary concern is to liberate women from oppressive social structures and prejudice. Feminism questions the dimensions of women's lives that restrict their full human dignity. Institutions dominated by the presence and the concerns of men are challenged because they render women invisible. The fear with which women's bodies and sexuality are treated contributes to their physical and emotional abuse, leaving them with unexpressed anger. The negative ways in which women are pictured in the wider culture denies their intrinsic value. Economic structures built upon the cheap, willing and often desperate labour of women are criticized. Feminists believe that these forms of social construction disempower women, making them victims of forces beyond their control. The hope is that women will be encouraged to recover their power, by naming the sources of their oppression and by speaking from outside the boundaries in which they have been confined. This form of feminism searches for a liberation that requires radical social changes.

3. Feminism is a commitment to the distinctiveness of women's insights. It affirms the ways of knowing and of reasoning that women have developed through their life experiences. This different voice may be a corrective to the devaluation and fear of women in the Western tradition. Women are encouraged to affirm the validity of their intuitions and to take seriously their embodied experience as a source of wisdom and spiritual truth. In this way, women may no longer collude in traditional cultural stereotypes, and may express positively their goodness as persons in their own right. This emphasis upon women's distinctiveness is controversial. Some feminists believe that women are different by nature, since their biological make-up differs from that of men. Thus, because of this 'femininity', women might be considered naturally to be more empathetic, more

capable of caring, more sensitive to the impact of their choices upon the welfare of others. Others believe this interpretation is too simplistic and literal. They believe that women's distinctive insights are the result of the activities in which they engage and of the positions which they occupy in social structures. Thus, women's experiences of work and of relationships, of suffering and of creativity, provide special knowledge. This gives rise to an affirmation of the standpoint of women.

Feminism has highlighted the issue of gender as problematic in understanding human life and society. It is an important question for feminists to ask who is speaking, and to consider the ways in which gendered experience may shape our thought and our language. Feminists also draw attention to the relational nature of human persons. They are critical of the individualism of Western society and of the emphasis on detachment in Western thought. Feminism has challenged various forms of cultural conditioning, while also seeking to discover realistic forms of human community that are liberating and fulfilling.

All of this presents new challenges and insights for theology and for the life of the Church (Ruether, 1983). Many feminists have been and are Christians, who believe that their faith requires them to take their humanity as women seriously. Their concern for women's dignity is motivated by belief in the creator who made human persons in the divine image. Their commitment to the renewal of women's personal lives is inspired by belief in the redeemer who sets people free for fullness of life in Christ. Their hope for social and political transformation is driven by expectation of the Kingdom in which all creation will be reunited in the love of God.

Feminism challenges the Church to question its own collusion in the oppression of women. It invites the Church to consider its theology, its language, its practices and its structures, and to set all of these within the requirement of the redeeming love of God. Feminism presents a hopeful vision of the Church as the beloved community in which Christ's presence may be known among us in our love and respect for one another (Grey, 1989). [Susan F. Parsons]

FETISHISM
Regarding an object with reverence, fear or affection; now used particularly of objects assigned a sexual association.

A fetish was originally an object to which West Africans assigned magical powers. It was used as a protection against the magic of an enemy or as a means of enchantment. More recently, however, the term has been applied to pathological attachment to objects associated with sexual excitation.

FIGHT/FLIGHT
One of the three basic assumptions about unconscious behaviour in groups.
In his study of group behaviour Bion (1961) describes unconscious activity in terms of three basic assumptions: dependence, pairing and fight/flight. A group caught up in the last seems to be trapped into behaving as though only two ways of saving itself were available – either fight or flight. It may feel, for example, that in order to survive it must either confront leadership or escape from it. Thus the underlying assumption is not either 'fight' or 'flight': the two opposite actions have the same believed result – preservation. To run or to stand and fight are both responses to a situation that feels threatening. Other possibilities are ignored or suppressed. If a group is frustrated, it may seek instant opportunity to express its emotion by fleeing or attacking and it will follow almost any leader who gives orders for instantaneous response in either direction. It is a form of panic which, as Freud (1921) pointed out, is best studied in the military.

FIXATION
1. A learning process of memory or action confirmed by repetition.
2. Being attached to an object or to an early stage of development.
The second sense is the more technical. It describes the way in which a person may be so fixated upon a stage of their early development that they cannot form new relationships, either with people or an interest, or sometimes even cannot adapt to changed circumstances. It is a neurotic state that can be helped by psychotherapy.

FOLK RELIGION
The desire for the Church's ministry by those who rarely attend church.
The term was used in the 1970s and 1980s in recognition that the desire for the occasional offices and similar ministry, which became less widespread in the 1990s, was sincere and could be valued. The phrase is also used (e.g. by American students of society on analogy

with 'folk art' or folk lore) to refer to survivals from earlier cultures. Students of Japanese religion particularly use it to refer to that mix of individual or family practices that underlies the named traditions. A more corporatist understanding appears in the Scandinavian and German usage, that reflects the 'folk' (*volk*) memories of the 'barbarian invasions'.

FORGETFULNESS
Failure to recall an experience or to carry out an action that has previously been learned.
Forgetfulness is a common human trait which at times takes on special significance. Loss of memory (amnesia) is to some degree common and often accompanies the ageing process. The physiology of the brain and how memories are stored and recalled is a major contemporary study. But the inability at any time to recall an experience may have psychological significance of which a pastor should be aware. To forget an appointment, for instance, may indicate a person's unwillingness to engage with an experience that needs to be addressed. The more elaborate the excuse, often the more profound the discomfort with that experience and the thought of addressing it. The pastor needs to be alert to such possible significance but at the same time sceptical of his or her own assumptions. The practice in some churches of the 'healing of memories', whereby someone's past experience is 'bathed in prayer' and even treated as an occasion for expelling demons, may lead to false-memory syndrome. According to this the penitent 'remembers' things (often involving abuse) which never happened. Responsible healers recognize the problem and appropriate skills can be acquired by training. Without this, however, the field is very risky and should, if possible, be avoided by pastors.

FORGIVENESS
Release of someone from a just penalty for hurt caused.
Forgiveness does not come easily or cheaply to most people, unless the offence is trivial. When people are hurt they rightly may be angry. If they offer forgiveness prematurely, or at a superficial level, their wounds may get buried. These can later do damage to themselves or to others. People who are deeply hurt often shrink from contact with the person who has hurt them. A period of separation may be helpful before the victim can contemplate forgiveness, or the offender be ready to ask for, and accept it. Relationships may be completely or partially disrupted. Such separation, even if permanent, does not preclude eventual forgiveness. It is possible, though difficult, to forgive someone who will not accept the offer of release from all penalty and/or a fresh start to the relationship.

Sometimes those who are hurt seek justice and the imposition of punishment. Punishment is not incompatible with forgiveness. Those punished may feel they can offer satisfaction for the offence. Those who have gained justice may be able to contemplate a renewal of relationships once the punishment is complete. Matching punishment to crime is a long-established practice. 'An eye for an eye, a tooth for a tooth' (Matt. 5.28) is the basis of the Mosaic law. The teaching of Jesus in the Sermon on the Mount, however, requires victims to go further than the law allows. They are to fulfil the law by taking the penalty on themselves. So those who are struck on the cheek are urged to 'turn the other cheek' (Matt. 5.39). Those who have a right to hate their enemies are told instead to 'love your enemies and pray for those who persecute you' (Matt. 5.44). In the Lord's Prayer, those who have something to forgive are told to recognize their own need of forgiveness (Matt. 6.12), and they are to forgive not once but 'seventy times seven' (Matt. 18.22).

Forgiveness is not a matter of feeling forgiving; it is an attitude, a desire to release another person from penalty so that he or she can either go free or take up an entirely new relationship with the person who has been hurt. The Church continues Christ's work of forgiveness and reconciliation through its authorized ministries which pronounce the assurance of forgiveness. Through its presbyteral ministries it also offers general and private absolution. Individual Christians continue Christ's work through their own attitude towards forgiveness and their willingness for others to be reconciled to Christ and so to other members of the mystical Body of Christ, including themselves. It is sometimes harder for people to accept God's forgiveness for their own sins than to forgive other people's sins against them.

It is not easy to forgive. To do so at all, it is necessary to perceive that there is a real need for forgiveness. It is vital to make a firm resolution to offer that forgiveness. It is also important to understand that the one who forgives may need forgiveness themselves, if not in the original context then in some other context, and to act in such a way that they show willingness to start a new relationship with the person who has caused the original hurt.

People may really struggle to forgive. They may think they have forgiven someone, only to experience a resurgence of disgust at the memory of the offence and its consequences. They may experience powerful feelings of hatred for the offenders, even if those offenders are penitent and have accepted just punishment for the offence. These feelings may persist for years. They can cause great distress. They may even bind a person to a memory in such a way that he or she becomes unconsciously prejudiced and unable to act dispassionately towards anyone who reminds him or her of the original perpetrator. Such binding can be dangerous in people who find themselves in positions of pastoral care towards those who hurt others, or are criminals. Such pastors may need help to work through their negative feelings.

Some people find that their anger at the original hurt fuels a desire to prevent other people from being hurt in the same way. This can be a creative use of anger, but the absence of real forgiveness may lead to an over-identification with victims of abuse or injustice. Those who find themselves in such situations generally need skilled pastoral care if they are to gain sufficient objectivity to act in a just way to victims and perpetrators alike. Pastors, social workers, medical staff and counsellors generally need good training if they are to understand themselves, and their motives, and do their work properly.

The achievement of forgiveness can be recognized by the fact that events which previously caused emotional distress when recalled no longer have power to trap one in turmoil through past memories and attitudes. They no longer restrict one's ability to get on happily with life. Such freedom is precious and worth waiting for. It merits the hard work most people have to put into forgiving and being forgiven. [*Una Kroll*]

FORMATION

See: VOCATION. *See also*: CLINICAL PASTORAL EDUCATION

FORTITUDE
One of the cardinal virtues: endurance.

Fortitude is the willingness to endure whatever life throws at one with courage and perseverance. With justice, temperance and prudence it is one of the four cardinal virtues.

FOSTERING (US FOSTER PARENTING)
The undertaking by a family to look after someone else's child for a few days, months or even throughout their childhood, usually for an allowance or a fee. The relationship is not permanent or legally binding for life.

Throughout history children have been neglected or abused by their parents, and sometimes abandoned, because parents were unable to bring them up themselves. Informal fostering has always existed to help remedy these situations, but state-regulated fostering can be traced back a long way too. For example, Triseliotis *et al.* (1995) point out that it existed in embryonic form in fifteenth-century England. As part of the Poor Law provision, a more widespread boarding-out of children could be found in the eighteenth- and nineteenth-century industrialized societies where it supplemented the institutional care provided for abused and exploited children. Later, families where children were 'boarded out' were selected, paid and nominally supervised. This led to a realization that a family could provide a more satisfactory experience for children than the impersonal care meted out by institutions. In some Western societies children's homes are closing down and being largely replaced by a wide range of specialist foster families. Indeed, foster families now are often mistakenly expected to take any child, irrespective of the severity of his or her problems.

At its most sophisticated, foster care can provide a very differentiated service. It can span a broad spectrum, offering from short-term to permanent placements, the latter almost rivalling adoption. For example, in contemporary Britain, foster care can offer planned respite placements, brief emergency care, short-stay placements (which can include assessment or pre-adoption placement), medium-length placements (which can include 'treatment' by specialist foster carers), or long-term placements for those children who cannot be returned to family situations that have been abusive. Private foster care is also widely used, when families themselves locate carers, sometimes overseas and via advertisement. However, despite the development of increasingly professional foster carers in some countries, it should not be forgotten that informal unpaid fostering is more widespread and helps to hold together the fabric of many societies.

Those involved with pastoral care need to realize that foster carers occupy an ambiguous position and status in even the most developed schemes. They take the major responsibility for a child and bear the day-to-day brunt of often difficult behaviour, sometimes knowing the child better than anyone else. Yet foster carers have little say in the long-term care plans. They have little legal status. A child can be moved from them suddenly. Foster carers can be open to abuse from a number of angles: (1) from the children placed with them; (2) from the families of those children with whom they are expected to work; (3) by the authorities, who may offer them minimal support but place increasing demands on them. The boundaries around foster families can be exceedingly permeable; both they and their own children can suffer. The plight of foster children also needs considering. Poorly supported and regulated placements are liable to disruptions and the foster children are moved frequently. With every move they become more difficult, each time provoking fresh rejection.

The antidote to the damage to both carers and foster children lies in a rigorous selection of carers, a clear demarcation of tasks, good training, respite for carers, and plentiful support for all involved. There is a need to monitor and regulate the number of foster children in each family. Indeed, in some places today, foster carers can find themselves going through a selection and approval process similar to that undergone by adopters. This reflects the difficulty of the tasks with which they can now be faced.

An ongoing debate concerns the relative merits of foster as opposed to adoptive families as a long-term placement for older and more 'difficult-to-place' children. With the closure of institutions, there has been a growing belief that more children previously considered 'unadoptable' (for example, sibling groups or children with 'special needs') could be found adoptive families. Adopters, encouraged by social work departments, have taken such children in a spirit of optimism, only to find the task a daunting one. Some children with difficult histories are incapable of making attachments to new parents. Many feel acute conflicts of loyalty, and some still maintain contact with members of their birth family. Ongoing help is often not available for adopters. The cost of placements is, therefore, both emotionally and financially high for all involved. The result has been that it is now harder to find adoptive families for certain older children. The advantages of long-term fostering are being re-evaluated.

In many ways, foster families are better equipped for the task, because they can share the responsibilities and difficulties with the authorities involved. Foster carers are less of a threat to birth parents; foster children do not have to make choices, but can allow themselves to experience a reparative reparenting which stands them in good stead for the future.

Foster care, both short and long term, can, if it is well organized and provisioned, offer a valuable resource for children who need substitute family care. In conjunction with adoption and residential care, it can be part of a provision which is truly comprehensive. It can often be the most creative way of helping children who have had a very difficult experience of life. [Lorraine Tollemache]

FREUDIAN PSYCHOLOGY
An approach to the psychology of the individual and the development of interpretative ways into the unconscious discovered by Sigmund Freud.
Freud is regarded as the founder of classical psychoanalysis. In his day he was controversial, and his thinking remains so today. Following his own self-analysis, he wrote extensively on such themes as transference, the unconscious, neurosis, repression and sexuality. Later he considered group phenomena, and discussed the origins of society and religion. Throughout his life (1856–1939) he was continually producing new ideas. The long-term impact of his thinking is difficult to determine. He attracted (and still does so) both devotion and rejection. His prolific writings have been rigorously explored and his life investigated. On the whole much psychoanalysis has developed from, and hence moved away from, his original ideas. His theories, however, have been widely employed in Western culture, not just therapy. Nevertheless, however controversial, his thinking has been one of the major forces to have had an impact on the intellectual and pastoral worlds during the twentieth century (Gay, 1995).

Freud's understanding of psychology originated in the study of hysteria, a very nineteenth-century interest. He developed some theories, particularly about word association and dreams, both of which still play an important part in therapy. The underlying understanding that emerged concerned the functions of instinct and drives, particularly (and at that time controversially) sexuality, in both adult and infant. Behind overt behaviour there resides a mass of unconscious activity that is rarely exposed but which can be explored systematically, given the tool of psychoanalysis. The conscious individual is the 'I' (or 'ego'); the unconscious parts are the energies of the 'id'; and the conscience is the 'superego'. These terms have become commonplace, although their meanings remain disputed. Three main themes, however, from Freudian psychology remain central to modern thought and are important for pastoral studies.

1. *The unconscious or the unconscious mind*. This refers to the area exposed, for example, in dreams. Freud emphasizes that this was not just observable but that there were ways into systematic interaction with this dimension. It is now widely acknowledged that human beings, both individuals and groups, have such an unconscious mind.

2. *Transference*. He discovered that through transference memories can be exposed to examination. In classical analysis the relationship between analyst and patient is used as a way of examining the latter's (often repressed) connection with other people. Counter-transference refers to the feelings that are reciprocated by the analyst.

3. *Projection*. This refers to the way in which people dispose of aspects of themselves, usually those that they deny or dislike, into another and respond to them there.

All three themes are not restricted to the analytic situation: they are universal phenomena and have been extensively employed in the study of groups and even society (Obholzer and Roberts, 1994). *[Wesley Carr]*

FRIENDSHIP
A relationship based on mutual benevolence, independent of sexual or family love.
In the classical world and early Christian thought to the time of Augustine, friendship was highly valued and widely studied. As an ethic of duty, conscience and obedience emerged, it declined in significance for human relationships. It was largely displaced into spirituality as a way of conceiving the soul's relationship with God. Today friendship is seen to be based on empathy rather than sympathy. In friendship two different people can enjoy communion, each flourishing in mutual benevolence. Friendship puts no burden on the other person, as its attitude is one of loving concern. But friendship has become problematic with the eroticizing of relationships during the twentieth century.

The pastoral relationship is based upon love for the neighbour and as such may sometimes be thought of in terms of friendship. A pastor may come to admire someone for his or her moral quality and, as happens, discover mutual benevolence in the pastoral relationship. However, the boundary between friendship and inappropriate pastoral relationships needs constant monitoring. It is difficult to remain sufficiently in role as pastor with a friend, and the mark of true friendship in such instances might be to refer the person to another pastor or counsellor.

FUNCTIONAL PSYCHOLOGY
A psychological approach that studies the function rather than the facts of mental phenomena.
As with 'functionalism', this approach studies the way in which the mind works, putting the emphasis on mental states and activities rather than underlying structures. It is, therefore, more concerned with processes than with describing experience or categorizing behaviour. It is one of the dynamic psychologies.

FUNCTIONALISM
A sociological paradigm representing society as a social system and its constituent parts as functions of the system.
This style of sociology, also known as structural functionalism, is associated with the writings of Emile Durkheim, Talcott Parsons and Robert Merton. It represents the social world as an organism which adapts and mutates in order to survive, and whose constituent parts have functions which are dedicated to the organism's survival. This organic metaphor emphasizes the interrelations between the elements which make up the social structure. It generates an interest in the function which each constituent element performs in the survival and mutation of the whole.

FUNERAL
Ritual disposal of a dead human body.

The desire of humans ritually to dispose of their dead goes back a long way, certainly to prehistory though its exact origins are unclear. Disposing of the body without respectful ritual is a symbolic way to punish the dead, as with Holocaust victims or the medieval traitor who was hung, drawn (disembowelled) and quartered (limbs chopped up and various parts hung up on the city gates). Ultimately, funeral ritual is a mark of respect for the human being and/or the group to which the dead person belongs.

A number of ancient peoples ritually placed their dead in a cave (as was the case with Jesus) or under a mound or barrow (as with some European neolithic peoples). This practice finds an echo in modern Italy, Spain and the USA, where the coffin is often placed in a niche within a mausoleum (a building constructed for the purpose of housing human remains). Cremation and burial are the other major forms of disposal used today.

Funeral ritual often reflects social status, but almost always reflects religious concerns. In most religions, the rite's purpose is to speed the deceased's soul on its way. Hindu rites around the funeral pyre ensure that the soul will be satisfactorily reincarnated. Prayers and ritual acts during and after Orthodox and Catholic funerals smooth the soul's passage to heaven. In a number of societies, funeral and post-funeral rites also ensure that the soul does not return to harm the living, as with the European tradition of burying someone who has committed suicide at a crossroads so that the troubled soul gets confused and cannot find its way home.

Protestantism is somewhat unusual in that it insists the prayers of the living can in no way assist the dead. This is central to the Reformers' claim that only Christ's grace, and the faith of the believers, lead to salvation; the posthumous prayers of the Church are of no avail. Ever since the sixteenth century this has left the Protestant funeral somewhat purposeless. The love of God may be proclaimed, and God may be thanked for the life of the believer, but such prayers have no spiritual effect.

Many societies have two funerals: a 'wet' funeral, when the fresh corpse is buried, and a 'dry' funeral some time later when the bare bones are relocated, as for example in rural Greece (Danforth, 1982). With cremation, the time frame is dramatically compressed – secondary disposal of the ashes often follows within hours or days. When months or years separate the two rites, the symbolism carries several meanings: the body has been cleansed of the corruption of the flesh, the soul is well on its way to heaven, and the mourners may have travelled on in their grief. Modern Western, and in particular Protestant, funerals are notable for omitting secondary rites, and current attempts to devise liturgies for the burial of ashes reflect uncertainty as to the relationship of this rite to the primary funeral.

A number of trends may be observed in funerals in several modern urban societies.

1. Reflecting wider social trends, funerals are becoming more commercialized. Originally conducted by local members of the community (Jewish funerals still often are), funerals have over the past three centuries increasingly been sold as a commodity by funeral directors. The funeral industry now comprises three main players: (a) the funeral director; (b) the burial or cremation authority; and (c) the minister or celebrant who conducts the ceremony. The funeral director contracts with the family, thus reducing the other two actors to his subcontractors. Clergy can still exert influence, but only by maintaining good relationships and good communication with the other parties. By the end of the twentieth century, family funeral firms were being bought up by large multinational companies; funerals are now part of global capitalism, though large numbers of small firms still exist in most countries.

2. As people strive to maintain individuality in the face of the mass society, and as they become more secular, the purpose of the funeral is increasingly to celebrate the life of the deceased. This is the explicit purpose of secular funerals, and is also reflected in many Protestant funerals. Clergy wrestle with the extent to which they wish to facilitate or resist this trend.

Funeral reform organizations are active in a number of modern societies. Their main aims are: (1) to resist further commercialization, to provide families with the information to make informed choices, and to push for legislation to regulate the monopolistic practices of large funeral companies; (2) to promote individualized funerals, in the face of standardized commercial practices and conservative religious forces.

What makes a good funeral? A good funeral disposes of the body in a manner that is culturally acceptable. It helps the soul on its way, or at least affirms the faith and hope of mourners. It affirms the social bonds of the living at a time when one of their number has been wrested from their midst. It may help them grieve (Walter, 1990).

Some modern societies are secular, individualistic and unwilling to acknowledge the dead body. In such societies, the bodily, social and spiritual purposes of the funeral wither, leaving its therapeutic effects on individual grief as its main purpose. Yet it is precisely its physically messy, socially supportive and spiritual aspects that give a funeral ritual its force, and it is doubtful that the funeral can ever be reduced just to psychological therapy. Wise funeral officiants will attend to the deceased's body and soul if they are to have any hope of providing psychological comfort to the mourners; such comfort is best regarded as a by-product rather than an aim in itself. [Tony Walter]

G

GAY RIGHTS
Legal equality and social justice for homosexuals.
Many surveys show that gay and lesbian people suffer considerable discrimination in employment, housing and education, and are subject to much violence and harassment. In Great Britain the age of consent is 16 for both hetero- and homosexuals. Under equal rights legislation the armed forces recognize different sexual orientations. The US armed forces maintain a 'don't ask, don't tell, don't pursue' policy, under which openly gay service people may be discharged. The age of consent for homosexual (as well as heterosexual) behaviour varies from state to state; in some states homosexual activity is illegal. Gross indecency, always a consenting offence, also has different penalties. Some same-sex couples are denied rights in the areas of pensions, immigration, parenting, fostering and adoption and may experience discrimination in the provision of services in hotels, estate agents etc. [Malcolm Johnson]

GENDER
The human experience of maleness and femaleness.
Some prominent Christian discourses have always argued for a God-given and natural connection between a person's sex and the roles assigned to that sex by society and Church. In the debates surrounding the ordination of women to the priesthood in the Anglican and Roman Catholic Churches some Christians have argued that women cannot be priests because priesthood was ordained by God to be an essentially male vocation, either because women are not created to be leaders or because females cannot represent a man, Jesus. In this understanding men and women have divinely ordained roles in society (related to their biological difference) and stepping out of those roles necessarily leads to societal and theological disorder.

Under the influence of secular feminism, however, many Christians in the twentieth and twenty-first centuries have questioned the 'natural' connection between sex and gender, accepting that gender is to some degree at least a social construction, that is, that concepts of masculinity and femininity vary across eras and cultures and have been largely informed by patriarchy – by thought-systems and structures which assume the normativity and superiority of the male. The challenge to Christians posed by feminism cannot be underestimated and has raised profound questions concerning the authority of scriptures and revelation which are still being struggled with. At a basic level, Christians have debated issues such as the relative weight to give Paul's declaration that 'there is no longer male and female' in Christ (Gal. 3.28) on the one hand, and his insistence that women should be silent in church on the other (1 Cor. 14.34–35). But much more profound questions have been raised by the claims that Christian doctrine and practice have all been articulated in the context of patriarchy and need to be deconstructed and reformulated taking into account women's experience. For example, Valerie Saiving (1979) suggested that the dominant Christian understanding of sin as pride reflected male rather than female experience because under patriarchy women were not allowed a sufficient sense of self to be easily guilty of such a sin. Women's sin has rather been acquiescence to self-negation and triviality.

The work of the psychologist Carol Gilligan

(1982) has had significant influence upon feminist theology. She argued that men understand themselves to be isolated, independent and enclosed, engaged in competition with others and concerned with abstract principles, while women understand themselves as being relational and deal with concrete realities. In pastoral studies some women have questioned the central icon of the shepherd, arguing that the model of pastoral care it represents encourages a patriarchal male understanding of human nature (with leaders and the led) and a hierarchical approach to pastoral care, rather than a relational one which might better reflect women's experience and needs (Graham, 1993). Other theologians have questioned the dominant image of the servant in Christian pastoral discourse, arguing that it has often been used to justify women's submission to men (Borrowdale, 1989). A feminist approach would tend to prefer communal models of pastoral care, governed by notions of equality, mutuality and reciprocity and focused on embodied reality.

James Nelson (1992) has argued that men have been the victims of patriarchy too, having been expected to behave in ways that have an adverse effect on their physical and mental health. In the figure of Jesus and other biblical characters, such as David and Jonathan, men can find alternative models of masculinity based upon friendship, intimacy and vulnerability.

British and North American theologians influenced by feminism have tended to see gender as a social construction: they argue that certain ways of knowing and being have been associated with the female and it is time to reclaim these for all humanity as being often more compatible with the life and teaching of Jesus than dominant patriarchal models. Such an approach can, however, be accused of ignoring the significance of bodily difference between the sexes even while claiming that women value the body more than men. Here French contemporary feminism is important because it uses women's bodies as a source of knowledge beyond the bounds of patriarchy. Whereas traditional Catholic understanding of the female body would focus on its maternal dimensions and construct an image of womanness from it, French feminism has used the clitoris and the multiple sites of pleasure on the female body as a basis to construct a female symbolic system to stand alongside that of the male 'phallus'.

Most recently, Christian theology and pastoral practice has had to contend with the challenges of queer theory, which claims that sex is no more stable than gender and that sex and gender are performative: there is no such thing as a woman or a man, only a series of performances which we identify as masculine or feminine. We learn to become a woman or a man by following the gender scripts that our culture hands out to us, and each performance reinscribes that gender upon our bodies. It is only when some people throw away the scripts or perform them badly or subversively that the non-natural nature of sex and gender is revealed. Gay and lesbian people, transsexual people, drag queens, all demonstrate that sex and gender are not 'natural'.

Queer theology is in its infancy but already it has produced work which demonstrates a radically different approach to the whole issue of gender. Kathy Rudy (1997) draws upon queer theory to argue that for Christians the only stable identity is that of a member of the people of God, the Church, conveyed by baptism and constituted by God's self. No identity should take precedence over Christian identity and hence within the Church gender cannot be a determining factor in assessing what kind of sex constitutes moral sex. It has also been argued, drawing upon queer theory's notion of parody as repetition with critical difference, that the parodic performance of sex and gender is an essential element of Christian discipleship precisely because sex and gender are destabilized by baptism and decentralized in Christian morality. The performance of maleness and femaleness by the baptized must be strange because it must constitute a cultural critique of gender. The pastoral care of 'gender outlaws', then, need not focus on straightening them out and returning them to particular roles, but supporting and learning from their parodic performances as gospel witness. [*Elizabeth Stuart*]

GENE THERAPIES
The emerging branch of medicine which looks to treat disease by manipulation of genetic material.

New and fast-changing advances in genetic science and technology will have radical moral and pastoral implications. As yet these remain unclear, but among them the pastor may note the following:

1. *The Genome Project.* The international

achievement in mapping the human genome has raised a number of dilemmas including: (a) Who 'owns' the information generated by this project? Those who believe that it is right to patent the information argue that this prevents secrecy (since all those who want to have the information can pay for it) and rewards research. Those opposed argue that it is inappropriate to patent data already present in the natural order and introduce commercial greed into science. (b) Genetic information from the project is obviously vital to long-term genetic therapy, but it is also vulnerable to social and political abuse. There are fears of returning to eugenic abuses or moving into data information abuses parallel to those being raised currently by public computer networks. (c) There is also some doubt about whether the benefits will outweigh the disadvantages. The potential benefits to those who might be 'cured' from serious genetic disorders are obvious. But others with disorders that cannot be 'cured' may be disadvantaged (in terms of employment, insurance and even peace of mind) by a knowledge of their genetic future acquired through screening. (d) In turn this raises the issue of properly informed consent. Since genetic science is still novel and complex, it is not always clear that those being offered genetic screening (especially children) appreciate its implications, including the potential disadvantages in (c) above.

2. *Individual gene therapy.* Clinical trials in the USA and Europe have already begun using a variety of techniques involving gene-transfer experiments – with the aim of replacing defective genes with healthy substitutes. Potentially there could be therapeutic benefit to patients with malignant tumours, cystic fibrosis and many other inherited disorders caused by single defective genes. In February 1993 permission was given in Britain for the first gene-transfer experiment – an attempt to benefit children with adenosine deaminase (ADA) deficiency. Because such therapy is still experimental and potentially far-reaching, it raises a series of dilemmas. (a) While knowledge of the human genome is still developing, can the risks be adequately measured? There may be risks not just to the patients (who initially may have otherwise terminal genetic defects), but also to the medical teams, to the families and contacts, and possibly to future generations (if the changes effected enter the gene line). The use, for example, of viral vectors may carry dangers

of affecting others or of affecting patients themselves in unplanned and damaging ways. (b) As more and more people with genetic defects are enabled to live and reproduce, so the human genetic pool may contain an increasing amount of various defects. If this happens, the long-term deterioration of human genes might be another instance of iatrogenesis – modern medicine producing new problems when it resolves existing problems. (c) Linked to this are questions about resource allocation. How much should society spend on developing genetic therapy rather than on more conventional forms of medicine? (d) Genetic release into the environment is already causing moral concern – e.g. the impact on the environment, the effects on the food chain, the depletion of genetic variety, the over-dependency upon international conglomerates producing genetically modified food, etc. Once genetic therapy becomes widespread, will it not add to fears about 'improving' the natural order? (e) How far should animals be used in the interests of gene therapy? There are likely to be increasing uses of human genetic material in animals, for example to allow organ transplants from animals into humans (xenografts). At what point does this become unethical?

3. *Germ line therapy.* At the beginning of the twenty-first century germ line therapy – the attempt to alter the genetic inheritance of humans before or immediately after fertilization – is probably still a prospect, although it is already taking place in the agricultural world. However, it raises some acute dilemmas. (a) The potential risks are far greater than 2(a). It is possible that by changing the single-cell 'defects' of an individual there may be unforeseen effects upon future generations. Even when a full map of the human genome is produced, the effects of altering genetic inheritance will still be largely unknown. Future generations may be severely disadvantaged by today's experiments. (b) Much medicine takes risks in the early stages, but hitherto these risks have not involved future generations directly. Does the prospect of germ line therapy represent a qualitative change in medicine? (c) Even if some of the dilemmas raised above are reduced with the prospect of germ line therapy, others are considerably heightened. (d) The future prospects of biotechnology raise the overall issue of whether what could be done should be done. But the issue is com-

plicated by the cynic's observation that what can be done surely will be done by someone, somewhere, sometime.

For the pastor, this area is a moral minefield and looks as though it will remain so for at least a generation. People who are offered new treatments based on genetics may particularly seek counsel and guidance as they enter what is new territory both for them and for the doctors. [*Robin Gill*]

GESTALT PSYCHOLOGY
An approach stressing that behaviour cannot be analysed without including specific reference to the whole.
The German word *Gestalt* refers to an organized whole, which as such has a different and additional quality from its discrete components. Gestalt psychologists argue that the nature of the parts is determined by the whole. They, therefore, resist beginning to address a problem or issue by analysing it into parts but approach it by enquiring what the whole context is and what are its natural parts. Then they may address the various elements. The original work was largely into perception. But Gestalt has also been appropriated as a form of therapy. It aims to shift the client to self-support instead of relying upon aspects of his or her environment. The therapist focuses on the 'here-and-now' so as to help the clients explore aspects of themselves (usually polarities) and integrate them.

GIFTS
See: FEES

GLOBALIZATION
Economic, political and technological processes bringing distant human societies into a single world system of commodities and cultures.
Globalization has its origins in European imperialism, which drew the diverse peoples of the earth into common servitude of European civilization and power. It is also related to technological advancements from steam ships and the telegraph to jet planes and the Internet. These technical processes have generated and sustained global markets in finance and commodities, and a global exchange of peoples and ideas. Electronic communication, global free trade and transnational corporations are the strongest contemporary agents of globalization. Resist-ance to the exploitative and homogenizing effects of globalization is increasingly taking the form of civil unrest in Third World contexts. In addition it may be that this process, as the contemporary context for people in the First World, contributes to a sense of being lost and insignificant for many.

GLOSSOLALIA
See: TONGUES

GLUTTONY
Excessive or inappropriate indulgence in food or drink.
The glutton misuses substances taken in through the mouth in an attempt to numb hungers other than the physical. It is a vice, which Gregory the Great divided into five types: eating (or drinking) too early (i.e. before prayer), too eagerly, too expensively, too much, or with too much attention. While the traditional virtue recommended to counter gluttony is temperance, modern pastoral theology insists that effective remedies must address the deeper issues of trust and mistrust underlying the glutton's urge to seek solace in disordered consumption.

GOD CONCEPTS
Ideas and constructs about a supreme being, God.
Ideas about God lie at the heart of most faiths, and may profoundly affect the lives of adherents. They also influence those who profess no faith. For the pastor, the concept of God being presented is more important than technical theological arguments. Since the deity cannot be objectively known, we formulate God images that are products of experience, personality, motives and needs. They also endow our personal world with meanings that help us interpret significant life events.

Concepts of God are complex (Hood *et al.*, 1996). Factor-analytic research has resulted in scales that assess God in traditional Judaeo-Christian terms, as kindly, wrathful, as an omni-conception, loving and controlling, personal-benevolent, deistic, transcendent–imminent, and as creator, healer, friend and redeemer. Hierarchical analyses suggest two major patterns of God concepts: (1) those representing the inherent character of God-power, wisdom, righteousness, divinity; and (2) qualities relating to humanity-love, fatherliness, mercy, compassion etc. God images have also been explored through interviews and projective tests such as drawing or interpreting pictures. The development of these conceptions largely parallels that of cognition, suggesting progress from immature to mature thinking. Ideas about God have been described as initially unrealistic with a fairy-tale quality. Subsequently, more concrete, human characterizations transform into individualistic representations. By adolescence, these have become multidimensional, abstract and personalized.

On the question of possible origins for the idea of God, the Freudian view derives God from conceptions of the father. Other schemes suggest the referent is the mother, preferred parent, or the self. Socio-cultural possibilities have also been examined. Modern sophisticated object-relations, attachment-theoretical and attributional approaches are now common. Individualized spiritual forms that further intimate individual cognitive, emotional and motivational influences in the formation and utilization of God images usually replace concrete undifferentiated images. Such is evident in the different God concept patterns that affiliate with prejudice or its absence.

The place of God images in personality can be seen in the consonance between God characterizations and the types of prayers people use. The perceived efficacy of prayer ties to positive, benevolent and traditional Christian God concepts. Punitive and wrathful images associate primarily with prayers of confession, petition, ritual, habit, intercession and self-improvement. Personal accountability may be discerned in these patterns. God images and self-esteem also vary, together implying a joint role in personal adjustment. This relationship is partly gender-dependent: women showing higher esteem when interacting with a female deity; men with a male deity. A sense of personal control goes with perceiving God as personal and benevolent. A wrathful God associates with a low sense of personal control. Strength of God belief further correlates with trust and the conviction that the world is a just place. This is qualified by the nature of the God images held. Punitive representations relate to self-reproach and guilt. Not surprisingly, distorted and threatening concepts have been found among mental patients. Clearly, God concepts can play important roles in the personality of believers, and may serve as models and guides for either healthy or unhealthy behaviour. [Bernard Spilka]

GRACE
1. The forgiving love and generosity of God.
2. The God-like virtues of the Spirit-filled Christian.
3. The blessing of food before a meal.

These theological meanings of grace are extensions of common usages. The grace of a dancer refers to elegance and beauty. In music a 'grace-note' is one that adorns. Awkwardness or a grudging demeanour we call graceless. 'Grace and favour' residences are those the monarch freely allows favoured people to use. The expression 'free, gratis and for nothing' expresses the sense of 'grace' using an older form derived from the same Latin root. Related words are 'gratuity', 'gratify' and 'gratitude'.

In the Greek of the New Testament the word carrying such connotations (*charis*) was related to the word for 'greeting'. It is interesting how Paul adapted convention to carry larger theological meaning. A letter today opens with 'Dear Jo' and closes 'Yours, Mary'. A Greek, however, would start 'Mary to Jo, greeting', and a Jew would put, 'Mary to Jo, peace (*shalom*)'. Paul wrote (e.g. 2 Cor. 1.1–3), 'Paul, an apostle of Christ Jesus by the will of God, and Timothy our brother, To the church of God that is in Corinth, including all the saints throughout Achaia: *Grace* to you and *peace* from God our father and the Lord Jesus Christ.' This stood as a greeting but clearly meant more. What more? Paul stated that 'we have peace with God through our Lord Jesus Christ, through whom we have obtained access to this grace in which we stand' (Rom. 5.1). 'Grace' here is basically divine favour. The Apostle envisaged God as the sovereign in whose hands lay justice and before whom all would ultimately have to give account. Earlier in Romans he had referred to Scripture to show that 'all have sinned and fall short of the glory of God' (3.23): 'There is no one who is righteous not even one ... All have turned aside, together they have become worthless' (3.10–12, quoting Eccles. 7.20 and Ps. 14.1–3). So everybody is ultimately dependent upon God's grace and favour, on divine mercy. For Paul, that grace and mercy is disclosed in Jesus Christ. People 'are now justified by [God's] grace as a gift through the redemption that is in Christ Jesus' (3.24).

Interpretations of Paul have been contentious over the centuries. The sheer gratuity of God's saving love has sometimes been obscured in the process. Three issues have caused notorious theological debate: faith versus works; predestination; the means of atonement.

At the Reformation debate centred around the question whether we are justified by faith or works. Paul's argument was read as an attack on the idea that people could achieve righteousness or salvation through their own merit, through acts of penance or charity. 'Good works count for nothing' was the Protestant view: 'only faith saves'. Catholics defended good works. The focus on whether good works or faith were required of human individuals shifted attention somewhat from the fundamental role of God's grace. Grace was absent from the simple slogan 'justification by faith'. The Reformation reading of Romans has been challenged by recent scholarship, with its conscious attempt to place Paul in the context of debates in his own time about what was required of Gentiles compared with Jews. Yet the prime issue remains what qualifications Paul thought human beings need to be saved.

Long before the Reformation Augustine got into controversy with Pelagius because he wanted to insist that we humans can do nothing to qualify: everything depends on God's grace. Even the response of faith issues from God's 'prevenient' grace. It is not a kind of 'work', a human achievement. It happens because God, out of sheer divine love, grace and mercy, has elected some to be among the chosen, and has prepared their hearts to receive the Spirit.

The controversy arose because Pelagius found people quoting Augustine's prayer, 'Command what you will; give what you command.' Pelagius felt they were using it as an excuse to avoid more responsibility, simply waiting for God's grace. The prayer came from Augustine's *Confessions*, a work in which he presented his own life as providentially guided by God, through the years of sinful straying like the prodigal, to the time of conversion. Augustine had come to read Paul, and indeed other Scriptures, as meaning that one cannot save oneself. Salvation comes from God's grace alone.

In the course of the debate with Pelagius Augustine was forced by his own logic to argue for predestination. If salvation depends entirely on God, then so must damnation. If men and women make no contribution to their own destiny, then the obverse of God's grace becomes demonic, the arbitrary condemnation of those who are not saved. Furthermore, there is a tendency for 'grace' to seem like a kind of power or medicine with which we are injected or not as the case may be. A typical criticism of Augustine's position has come to be expressed in this way: the element of personal relationship in the concept of grace has been eroded.

Debate about atonement restores the dimension of relationship. Since the Middle Ages there has been a tendency to read Paul as meaning that the death of Christ was a sacrifice that propitiated God's wrath against sin. God's justice meant that a penalty had to be paid; Christ paid it for humankind who are now accepted by God, and the broken relationship is restored. Liberal theology since the nineteenth century has challenged this interpretation, not least on the grounds that it removes all trace of 'grace and favour' from God's forgiveness. Not only in the teaching of Jesus but in Paul's writings, God's forgiveness is not presented as bought, but as free and overflowing, gratis and for nothing.

These theological debates live on. They impinge on pastoral care since the way people conceive of the character and attitude of God has a profound impact on their emotional health. If God is essentially gracious, then the believer can know acceptance. [*Frances Young*]

GRANDIOSITY
Exaggerated ideas of self-importance or of personal power and/or influence.
Grandiose behaviour and speech may occur mildly as a personality trait. It may also constitute an element in certain illnesses such as hypomania or in schizophrenia when it may take on delusional characteristics and, for example, may be associated with the belief that the person is a historical character such as Jesus Christ or the Virgin Mary (Capps, 1993). Kohut (1976) has identified a splitting in what he terms the narcissistic personality, a grandiose self (given to exaggerated self-importance) and a depleted self (given to feelings of shame, humiliation and worthlessness).

GRATITUDE
1. A state of thankfulness which tends to bring forth a reciprocal attitude.

2. An awareness of a 'state of grace', meaning a gratitude to life through God's favour.

Gratitude is inspired by feelings of thankfulness towards another, the natural order or God. A 'grateful' person tends to be an observant person, with an awareness of what is being given. Gratitude follows such an 'aware' experience. Generally speaking, gratitude animates a person to give, thereby making a reciprocal gesture.

Gratitude is also a relevant aspect of the counselling or psychotherapeutic relationship. Aside from professional considerations, it is important that fees are charged to those people in counselling and therapy. This is to avoid the sometimes overwhelming sense of gratitude that may be prompted by a relationship which returns a person's sense of integrity and self-worth.

GRIEF
The emotional suffering, distress and process of adjustment, taking place over a period of time, in response to the death of a significant person or any other major loss.

Grief typically involves facing intense, sometimes painful, feelings and offers the bereaved person the possibility of developing a new set of personal meanings and undertaking new life tasks.

Pastoral care has traditionally stressed the importance of offering support and care to people who are grieving and the attempt to interpret the loss in the context of whatever faith they may possess. Pastors may meet bereaved people in a wide variety of ways in the long and short term. They may be in contact with people who are dying and their friends and relatives as well as their social and work group. Grief is also typically part of the experience of a dying person facing the losses involved in their impending death. Help may be sought in arranging or presiding at a funeral service or rite, which involves contact with the bereaved, both before and after the funeral. Bereaved people, not necessarily of a formal religious affiliation, may seek the help of a pastor in coming to terms with a loss. The impact of past losses may also be encountered in pastoral care and counselling settings which are apparently unrelated. Other events which do not involve actual death, e.g. divorce, separation or loss of job, may also be experienced as having a sort of religious significance.

The feelings typically associated with acute grief have been documented by Parkes (1991) and others. It is useful to recognize these as key feelings rather than a series of chronological stages. Individual members of a family, for example, may experience a death quite differently. Understanding the cultural background of the bereaved person may be particularly important since the behaviour which is seen as 'normal' in one culture may be seen as deviant or as a symptom of mental illness in another. Stroebe and others (1993) have also suggested that the pattern of mourning may vary significantly between men and women. Three considerations in particular may affect the experience of grief: (1) the nature of the relationship with the dead or lost person, whether or not that relationship was experienced as fulfilling or whether the death left areas of 'unfinished business' in the relationship; (2) the circumstance of the death. Sudden or unexpected death may be particularly traumatic when the bereaved person has had no opportunity for 'anticipatory grief' prior to the death. However, grief after a death preceded by prolonged or chronic illness may still be no less difficult to face because the bereaved person may be physically and psychologically exhausted. Where the nature of the death leaves cause for blame of self or others (as after an accident or suicide) the uncertainty may heighten or prolong grief; (3) the bereaved person's previous experience of death or loss. For example, adults who as children were excluded from family and communal mourning when a death took place may be particularly vulnerable when bereaved later in life.

Initial reactions to bereavement are likely to include shock and disbelief, often expressed as 'I can't believe it'. The reality of the death may be denied. Professional helpers, relatives and others may use euphemisms or offer sedation as a way of dealing with their own feelings of helplessness. However distressing the circumstances, a bereaved person is likely in most cases to be helped by the opportunity to see the body of the person who has died, although this should never be forced. Another reaction can be anger, directed typically at the medical profession, another family member or the pastor who may be perceived as representing a God who allows tragedy to take place. Whether or not the anger of grieving persons seems to have any logical basis, their need to be angry should be treated with respect. Anger in these circumstances is a statement of intense distress to be heard, supported and respected rather than an invitation to justify God. Self-reproach, frequently expressed as 'if only', is another way of trying to make sense of loss. Again, premature reassurance may not be helpful whereas sensitive listening can allow the intensity of the feelings to subside in the absence of any simple answers. Sadness and feelings of intense emptiness are part of grief. These feelings too may need expression. People from religious traditions which consider religious doubt to be problematic may need to be reassured that their expressions of grief are not tantamount to lack of faith. Pastoral care offers ritual, scripture, prayer, personal presence and counselling support as potential resources for the bereaved.

Mourning has both public and private aspects which need to be kept in balance if possible. If death takes place in a very public way, especially with media attention, there is a risk that the bereaved person or people may be deprived of the opportunity to mourn in private. The natural process of bereavement, therefore, may be halted or disturbed and those involved suffer accordingly. This is an aspect of the process in which the pastor can often be of help. If the death took place in circumstances which have been difficult to mention or possibly seen as shameful, e.g. miscarriage, stillbirth or suicide, a more public statement of the loss may be necessary at some point.

The ritual of the funeral itself can attempt to address some of these apparently conflicting needs, although it may not speak to everybody in exactly the same terms. In many cases familiarity with religious language and symbols can no longer be assumed. Consideration is sometimes given as to whether the ritual should have a more generally 'spiritual' content with less reference to formal religious practice. This dilemma can be resolved only by the pastor's judgement. However, there is evidence that the role of the pastor and the structure of ritual together can constitute a useful holding context which can help the bereaved come to terms with their new state.

Grief involves separation from the dead person and from the role one had by being associated with them. It also involves separation from the physical body of the deceased. It involves transition from one role to another and the often vulnerable discovery of a new role definition, e.g. as a widow or widower. The last task of grief is reincorpora-

tion – how a bereaved person re-enters the community of which they are a part. Many 'developed' cultures have few ways of helping this take place. Mourning can be delayed and then re-experienced at a time of another death or loss. The links between pregnancy and the inability to mourn are well documented, but other responsibilities and roles at the time of death may also inhibit mourning. Prolongation of grief may involve one particular feeling, e.g. anger, sometimes expressed in litigation, guilt or idealization, persisting over a number of years. It may seem as if the living are being over-affected by the dead. For many people the circumstances of the death may be revisited in pastoral care in a way which can be useful. Pastors should, however, be aware of the need to seek psychiatric help and support for a bereaved person if necessary. The care of bereaved people involves taking their experience of grief seriously. Simplistic answers should be avoided, but the representative role of the pastor may make what is said and done a resource which the grieving person can use. [Ian Ainsworth-Smith]

GROUP COUNSELLING

Counselling offered to a group, emphasizing both personal growth and the development of communication skills.
Originating in the 1940s, group counselling has become widely accepted and is used in a variety of settings. Bion, working at the Tavistock Clinic in London, developed theories on the nature of group dynamics. Group counselling has the obvious advantages of enabling the counsellor to see numerous clients at one time and being less expensive than individual counselling. Sharing experiences tends to be supportive, informative and therapeutic. Confidentiality is of the highest importance. However, people with very fragile egos may do better in a one-to-one setting.

GROUP DYNAMICS

The study of the process of interaction between individuals and groups and the forces that may assist or resist change in groups.
Group dynamics as a formal study originated in the second half of the twentieth century. The ideas about the individual that had emerged from the seminal work of psychologists and psychoanalysts raised questions about the relation between individuals and their social setting (Bion, 1961). It became

apparent that (1) groups have periods when they are dominated by different moods; (2) the group must be conceived as more than a collection of individuals; (3) whatever patterns (if there are any) that govern such behaviour must interpret change as the balance between forces in the group alters; and (4) expression of feeling is not private but a means of communication, particularly at the unconscious level. Seminal work was done by Kurt Lewin and Wilfred Bion. The study of behaviour in groups has since been refined. It can play an important part in the training of ministers whose preoccupation is often with individuals and who tend to overlook the importance of social context. The study of group dynamics also emphasizes the significance of authority and role, whether formally assigned or not – both issues for any religious leader (Carr, 1997). The study of groups for their own sake should not be confused with group therapy in which some of the issues of group dynamics play an important part but with a different task and objective in mind. Therapy is about healing; the study of group dynamics is an educational tool for any who have to exercise leadership and authority in churches and other organizations.

GROUP MINISTRY
The structured encouragement of collaboration between separate parishes.

In the Church of England group ministries are established through the same procedures as those for setting up a team ministry. In a group ministry each parish continues distinct with its own incumbent appointed by its patron, its own churchwardens and its own parochial church council. Experience has shown the value of appointing a group consultant. The pastoral scheme establishing the group ministry may make provision for the establishment of a group council by Bishop's Instrument. Alternatively, a group council can be established under the Church Representation Rules. A group ministry can be altered or dissolved by a further scheme under the Pastoral Measure 1983.

GROUP THERAPY
A form of psychological treatment in which more than one patient is seen and treated simultaneously, usually by either one or two therapists.

Human beings are social animals, spending their entire life in a variety of groupings.

Effective treatment of difficulties within their social world may be carried out in a group setting. Group therapy is a powerful treatment modality in its own right, not merely employed for its cost-effectiveness in terms of patient–therapist ratio. Outpatient analytic groups are usually composed of seven or eight members, with one or, more rarely, two therapists. Members of a group sit in a circle together with the therapist, and meet in a regular setting in terms of place, time and membership, often for several years. Analytic groups work best with a heterogeneous membership in terms of age, class, gender, presenting problem and defensive structure. Among several approaches to analytic group therapy, Wilfred Bion (1961) employed an interpretative approach that treated the group as a single entity, focusing on the group's relation to its leader. S. H. Foulkes (1975), however, took into account the complex network of interaction between the therapist, the individuals and the group itself.

By contrast, single-problem groups with a homogeneous population (for instance those focusing on bereavement, sexual abuse, eating disorders etc.) are more usually run on cognitive-behavioural or cognitive-analytic lines. These are most productively organized in time-limited sequences of perhaps not more than ten sessions with a given population. Longer than this begins to encourage the members to define their identity round the named problem.

In psychoanalytic group therapy, the internal dynamics driving each individual patient's difficulties manifest themselves in the shape and quality of the actual relationships in the room. Members come gradually to engage with increasing depth and emotional truthfulness in the actual relationships of the here and now of the group session itself. The therapist assists the therapeutic process by fostering a climate in which members' curiosity about each other's lives, freedom and depth of expression, exploration of the important events of the past as well as the present, and a growing trust in each other and in the setting are present. In psychoanalytic group therapy, members are helped to take back into themselves (reintroject or 'own') those functions, attributes, impulses and wishes that in the early stages of any group each member parcels out to others in the room, leading implicitly to the creation of 'roles' for each member – the helpful one, the clever one, the rebel, the clown and so on. Roles restrict the expression and development of an individual's full intellectual and emotional potential. By the end of treatment, members should be more fully in possession of their own wishes, fears and impulses, both the constructive and the destructive, leading to a fuller sense of life and an enhanced capacity for living it. [Caroline Garland]

GROWTH GROUPS
Small groups in congregations and other settings that combine educational and therapeutic functions, with the goal of enabling participants to discover and develop their God-given potentialities.
Utilizing group dynamics insights and group education and counselling methods, such groups can enhance pastoral care by providing growth-nurturing and healing opportunities for people of all ages and life situations (Clinebell, 1984). Such groups include those focusing on personal Bible study, prayer and spiritual formation; grief-healing and recovery; marriage, family and singleness enrichment; preparation for marriage (parenthood, retirement, dying etc.); creative divorce; vocational guidance; developmental crises; self-care to avoid burnout; teacher and leadership training etc. The term was coined by Howard Clinebell.

GUILT
Attributed responsibility for wrongdoing: if justified, true guilt; if unjustified, false guilt.
The attribution of guilt may be made externally by one person upon another, or internally by individuals upon themselves. When made externally, the attribution may or may not be accompanied in the 'guilty' person by a sense of guilt, that is, a cognitive awareness of guilt and an affective feeling of guilt.

Guilt is a concept which is given prominence in law, theology and psychology. Broadly speaking, law and theology tend to concentrate on objective guilt, that is, the state of having done wrong, and psychology on subjective guilt, that is, the sense of having done wrong. However, whereas wrongdoing usually (though not invariably) leads to subjective guilt, subjective guilt often cannot be traced to wrongdoing. This anomaly has fascinated not only those who

work in the field of secular psychology, but also those Christians who are involved in pastoral care.

Virtually every human being experiences feelings of guilt, apart from the psychopath who, by definition, is a person who does not feel guilty. Guilt feelings are widely acknowledged to be an essential civilizing and socializing influence. However, while appropriate levels of subjective guilt provide a defence against uncontrolled wrongdoing, in society, guilt feelings become a problem if they are unresolved, excessive or pathological.

Three views have been advanced to explain the origin of the sense of guilt, usually referred to as conscience: the traditional Christian view that it is an inborn faculty; the psychoanalytic view that it develops from the conflicting feelings of affection and aggression which a child harbours towards its parents; and the behavioural view that it is a conditioned response which connects certain actions with punishment. It is likely that all three play their part.

True guilt, both objective and subjective, is resolved through repentance, which may be considered as a process with five stages: the acknowledgement of wrong done, including the recognition of personal responsibility; the offering of an apology which expresses genuine remorse; the making of amends or restitution for hurt inflicted and damage caused; the desire for acceptance and reconciliation with the offended person; and the alteration of attitudes and behaviour to effect a radical renewal of lifestyle.

Inhibitory factors may prevent the process from being initiated or completed: attachment to the wrongdoing, either in fact or desire; projection of the responsibility on to another person, or displacement of the focus on to another and lesser wrongdoing; the desire to be punished, illness often being regarded as an appropriate punishment; refusal to forgive others, thus creating an emotional hardness which fails to receive forgiveness because it fails to offer it; the need for an authoritative pronouncement of forgiveness; the omission of reparation; and a perfectionist outlook which cannot admit or tolerate departures from absolute standards of behaviour.

False guilt feelings occur when, in the absence of wrongdoing, individuals believe that wrong has been done. Two main categories can be identified. *Perfection guilt feelings* arise through failure to achieve the highest possible standards, particularly of academic attainment and spiritual commitment. Its origin is to be found in unrealistic expectations imposed by authority figures at home, school and church. It leads individuals to believe that, because they are not good enough, they are therefore bad and are responsible for their failure, for example through laziness. Workaholism is accordingly a common reaction to perfection guilt feelings. Pastoral care of those for whom such feelings are a problem requires a twofold approach. First, the individual needs to be encouraged to adopt, according to ability, realistic rather than idealistic standards. This procedure is akin to the psychoanalytic recommendation of reducing the severity of the superego. However, the psychoanalytic tradition has tended to minimize true guilt, and this approach should not be used with failure due to wrongdoing. Second, those whom the individual regards as authority figures need to be encouraged to affirm achievements which attain these realistic standards.

Rejection guilt feelings are found in those who have suffered material and emotional deprivation, and verbal and physical abuse. They experience feelings of guilt because they reason within themselves: 'Only those who have done wrong are rejected and treated like this; therefore I must have done wrong.' Although rejected individuals find it difficult to exercise trust and to form stable relationships, the pastoral response to this type of guilt feeling is welcoming friendship. Kafka's guilt, often supposed to have been existential guilt – without cause, form or remission – as portrayed in his novel *The Trial*, can in reality be traced to rejection by a tyrannical father and an unloving mother. Significantly, it began to be alleviated when, in the final year of his life, he entered a loving relationship (Stein, 1969).

There is evidence that the sexes differ in the way they experience guilt. It has been argued that guilt feelings are more likely to arise for men from the breaking of rules and failure to work competently, and for women from the breaking of relationships and failure to care adequately. If this is so, it is possible that when men feel guilty, the reassurance which they desire is that what they have done or failed to do will not be permanently held against them, whereas when women feel guilty, what they hope to learn is that no relationship has been irretrievably broken.

The Christian faith can be presented in ways which create unwarranted and excessive guilt. Two examples frequently quoted in the literature are obsessive denunciations of sin and legalistic demands for holiness. Those engaged in preaching and pastoral care must therefore ensure that the doctrine of sin is always balanced by those of mercy, forgiveness and saving grace, and the doctrine of holiness by those of reconciliation, acceptance and sustaining grace (Narramore, 1984). *[Howard Gordon]*

H

HABIT
A learned instinctive response to particular situations.
Habits are normally acquired through education (beginning with the earliest parental teaching) and repetition. The term is used widely, from almost instinctual movement responses to habits of thought and attitudes. Virtues and vices are in part habitual, as is a Christian character. This dimension of personal development reminds pastors that much of their work is essentially educational.

HABITUS
The practice of developing Christian character.
While a habit may be acquired almost without thinking, 'habitus' refers to the conscious effort to acquire character. The concept derives from Aristotelian and Thomist ethics. It is disposition that can be cultivated, chiefly by worship. In pastoral studies it has been proposed as a model of Christian formation through self-awareness and habitual activity (Farley, 1983).

HALLUCINATION
Perceiving someone or something without actual stimulation of the senses.
Hallucination is a common human experience but one which bewilders many of those who have it. Bereaved people frequently have moments when the deceased is (they believe) heard, seen or even smelled; then 'there is no one there'. Hallucinations are also a side effect of some modern medicinal drugs as well as of some taken for recreational purposes. They are often experienced on the edge of falling asleep or waking. The pastor

needs to be careful in counselling someone with hallucinations. Often it is a matter of reassurance that their experience is not so unusual. Gentle enquiries about medicine may be required. Usually such pastoral counsel is adequate. But if the hallucinations persist, a medical examination should be recommended. Some treatable conditions are marked by hallucination.

HEALING
The restoration to wholeness of a person who is suffering in mind or body. In spite of, or perhaps even because of, advances in medical care, the issue of healing as wholeness is now on the agenda of doctors as well as of churches. It is well known that some patients who receive the right medical treatment do not get well; equally that patients (e.g. in the case of some cancers) who are expected to decline, fight back and, even if they do not fully recover, sustain a quality of life. Throughout the twentieth century there was a developing dialogue between medical practitioners and those interested in the Church's role in healing. However, both parties also showed a certain nervousness about each other.

Some Christians have always believed that it is right to pray for the sick following the example and command of Jesus (Luke 10.9) and the evident pattern of the epistle of James. In the early days of the Church, healing was, if not widespread, a recognized part of the ministry and miraculous healings are recorded then and in every century right up to the present. St Augustine knew healings that occurred at the tombs of martyrs in North Africa and this association of healing with sacred relics was well established in the Middle Ages in England. The sacrament of unction, anointing the sick with oil, was frequently used in the early centuries, but by the end of the eighth century in the West it had become a sacrament of preparation for death. The twentieth century saw considerable interest in Christian healing both in its sacramental forms and in healing ministries practised by individuals with special gifts. Alongside the ministry of individuals there has also been a rediscovery recently of the corporate dimension of healing in which congregations and groups play a full and active part. Popular Christian literature on healing of the last thirty years has, however, largely focused on the work of particular individuals with a gift of healing.

In the practice of Christian healing in the contemporary Church, various styles can be identified. At the catholic end of the tradition healing prayer is normally offered in a sacramental setting involving the use of oil specially blessed for the purpose. The focus is on the role of the priest as Christ's representative in administering this sacrament and there is little talk of healing being a special charism. At the Pentecostal/charismatic end of the spectrum there is a readiness to identify particular individuals as having a gift of healing. Within this tradition healing is often undertaken in the context of special evangelistic events where large crowds are present. But questions have been raised about the theology and practical results of such crusade-type healing ministries. Between these two particular styles, many Christian individuals, groups and congregations have been exploring a variety of different patterns of ministering to the sick. In one recent survey in the Anglican Diocese of Birmingham it was found that as many as 60% of parishes practise some form of public ministry to the sick. This evident increase of interest over the last twenty years would appear to run parallel with a gradual increasing influence of charismatic ways of thinking and practice within the Church as a whole.

The offering of healing in a Christian setting has caused some controversy in recent years – certain commentators doubt that prayers can ever affect the course of a physical disease. Such scepticism seems to belong to a philosophically defined position that emphasizes a dualism between the mind/spirit and body. The position of the New Testament, where the unity of a human being is taken for granted, is coherent. Within this world-view it is natural to see connections between an illness and a person's attitudes, guilt or relationships. The resolution of inner conflicts may well spill over into greater well-being at a physical level. It is widely recognized today that health is a multi-faceted reality – social and environmental factors contribute a great deal to health and ill health alike. Christians are entitled to bring to their understanding of health and healing the rich resources of Scripture which speak of the disorder and dis-ease of human beings on the one hand and their restoration and healing on the other.

Although healing as a ministry in the Church has not been untainted by scandal, it is recognized by many Christian clergy and their people that an environment of prayer and love can do much to help, support and heal the sick. Clearly many problems identified as illness have a social, existential component and the vitality released in love and prayer can do much to meet that aspect of an individual's need. The reliable Christian literature on healing suggests that there are in fact relatively few types of illness which have never been responsive to prayer, though clearly there are limits, as in the case of lost limbs and genetic illnesses such as Down syndrome. Even accepting a degree of exaggeration and hyperbole in the vast literature, it would appear that prayer for the sick may be using a mechanism which is similar to that at work in certain hypnotic phenomena. Here the mind/brain exerts an influence on the body which is extraordinary and powerful. There is also an increasing awareness of the way that the mind/brain controls every physiological process from digestion to fighting infection. A mechanism for extraordinary healing within the human body seems to exist even if it is normally impossible to predict when it will operate (Harper, 1994). But even if we were to have a fuller understanding of the processes involved in effective healing prayer, the Christian would still wish to emphasize the fact that healing in a religious setting involves more than the removal of symptoms. Reconciliation with God and others and forgiveness for past hurts and wrongs will normally be a primary focus of Christian healing prayer. Thus inner spiritual transformation is sometimes achieved even when physical or mental problems are not resolved. Likewise healing prayer is offered to the dying, not necessarily with the expectation of reversing the process, but with the hope that peace and wholeness may be found for the final journey. In short, healing in a Christian context, while never losing sight of the hope of physical or mental cure, is about mediating the shalom or peace of God (Parsons, 1995).

Healing as an aspect of the Church's ministry will always remain controversial. For its proponents it remains an authentic part of the gospel to a broken world. Those who resist or are indifferent to the widespread growth of healing ministries in the churches can point to its abuses and the problems it raises in respect of theology as well as hope and expectations on the part of the sick. The pastor needs with an open mind to sift through the conflicting claims of theology and practice and make an informed judgement about what is happening when the Church claims to be healing the sick in the name of Christ. [*Stephen Parsons*]

HEALING OF MEMORIES
A process through which painful memories are brought into balance with the individual's wholesome experiences.
The distressing memories of past wounds, whether frightening experiences or hurtful relationships, may have a crippling affect upon the person's physical, psychological, emotional and spiritual life (Linn and Linn, 1978). Healing of memories is an approach that has developed largely within the charismatic parts of the Church. The aim is that through prayer, Bible study, laying on of hands and similar actions the patient can begin to look at their pains from Christ's viewpoint. There is always, however, the risk of false-memory syndrome, especially when the period of life being recalled is a long time past.

HEALING, SPIRITUAL
See: SPIRITUAL HEALING

HEALTH
The integration, harmony and unity of body, mind and spirit in relationship to the community.
Health is a journey towards wholeness – a process, not a state, an adventure (Lambourne, 1985). It is more than the absence of disease and includes well-being, well-working, being unimpeded in realizing one's true nature. Health is achieved by adapting to the stresses of living.

The Greeks understood health as a harmony between the parts of the human organism. Democritus defined it as the tranquillity of the body and happiness as the calm of the soul. Aristotle defined health as the 'excellence' (virtue) of the body and one of the components of happiness (Pellegrino and Thomasma, 1981). Boorse (1981) echoed this perspective by interpreting health as well-working. In turn, well-working meant conformity to the excellence of how we are designed as humans and the working of each part according to its function. The two poles of health were represented by the goddess Hygeia and the god Asclepius. Hygeia's name forms the root word for 'hygiene', and means 'living well' or 'well way of living'. In the fourth century Hygeia, the goddess of holistic health, was replaced by Asclepius, the god of medicine, which shifted the emphasis to a less integrated view of health.

Christian theological definitions of health start from what it means to be human – created in God's image to glorify and enjoy God for ever. However, given humankind's fallen nature, complete wholeness – health – is not possible. Man/woman has a three-part nature – the body is the temple of the Holy Spirit, the spirit the energizing and transcending force, the mind the clarifying and defining part. In the Hebrew and Christian Scriptures, the integration of spirit and body is based on the link between health and salvation. These are twin concepts, signifying individual and global wholeness in relation to God. The Greek *sozein* is often translated as 'to save'. But originally it was more inclusive, meaning 'to make whole', 'to heal', 'to save'. God's incarnation in Jesus Christ clarifies the relation between health and salvation by an expanded notion of humankind. Jesus' title, 'Saviour', also means healer. Contrary to the tendency to denigrate the flesh, St Paul referred to the body as the 'temple of the Holy Spirit' (1 Cor. 6.19). His doctrine of the resurrection of the body reflected an understanding of salvation that addressed and comprehended the whole person (1 Cor. 15.35–58). In post-Constantinian Christianity, however, the salvation of the soul began to predominate.

Health and salvation are related but also distinct concepts. Salvation includes the indispensable additional element of God's grace, which results in our faith in Jesus Christ. Works are the signs of salvation, but neither they nor faith are the cause or basis for it. Health, on the other hand, is not free nor does it necessarily result from a strong faith. It requires active personal responsibility for its fullest realization. Health and salvation are also distinguished by the fact that complete health always includes physical well-being, whereas salvation does not depend upon one's bodily condition. However, suffering and healing may be mysteriously intertwined. Salvation does not consist in being freed from disease or achieving society's definition of mental health.

The biblical perspective of health as wholeness is captured in the concept of shalom – not only inner unity but also outer social harmony. Hence the societal, relational and spiritual dimensions of life all presuppose and relate to one another. Shalom is not some-thing that can be objectified and set apart. Nor can it be enjoyed in isolation. Shalom is a social happening, an event in interpersonal relations. It has to be found and worked out in actual situations. Shalom represents bodily health, contentedness, good relations – what happens when God's will is done. Health as translated by shalom entails justice, so that it is a goal for the whole human community – others' health is the first concern.

Health is a value which also includes adherence to a positive value system. It may be considered a relative or absolute value; normative or descriptive; a primary goal or one among many of life's goals.

1. Scientific medicine measures health objectively as the absence of disease as defined by diagnosis. Medicine usually moves from understanding illness to defining health, which is an absolute value within the medical context. However, from the patient's perspective it is a relative term. An ingrown toenail to a ballerina may be more difficult than paraplegia to a physicist.

2. In society health is a subjective value, as society creates its criteria of health and sickness. People may be labelled 'sick' to exclude or blame them, e.g. for mental illness. The goal is a sanitized not a healthy society. The societal dimension to health may also include our relationship to the community and larger environment. It is the quality of our life together. Health involves clean water, nutrition, housing, education, family status. It is not an individual achievement but a community responsibility (Lambourne, 1985).

3. Health is often understood as a fundamental value or even a right – health for all people.

A holistic definition of health helps to underscore an interdisciplinary approach to health care. Hence the pastor forms part of a healing team along with other health-care professionals, family, friends and the patient/client. An integrated approach fosters a response to the full range of needs of a person in crisis. Emphasizing health as wellness highlights personal responsibility and makes the patient a co-adventurer for health. *[Abigail Rian Evans]*

HEALTH PROMOTION
Prevention of ill health through public policy and personal empowerment.
Health promotion includes (1) medical or social policy measures for the prevention or

early detection and treatment of disease; and (2) education designed to empower individuals or groups in relation to health choices. Its activities overlap with those of primary care and community or public health medicine. Its practitioners include doctors, nurses, health visitors, teachers and other health-care workers. It emphasizes that health (while difficult to define) is more than the absence of disease or than physical fitness. Its least controversial activities are those directed against known health hazards in the home, work or wider environment, or against personal habits such as the abuse of alcohol, tobacco or other substances. More controversial are its activities (1) to expand 'access to health' or 'reduce inequalities in health' and (2) to promote 'positive health behaviour and appropriate coping strategies' (World Health Organization). Governments may consider the former too 'political', e.g. when poverty, poor housing or unemployment are targeted as remediable causes of ill health; or religious bodies may object to e.g. the promotion of contraception, 'safe sex', sex education in primary schools, or harm-reduction as a goal of drug abuse programmes. Or again, communities or individuals on the receiving end of the latter may experience these activities as 'paternalist', or at worst as 'victim blaming'. There may be a real conflict here between the beneficent research-based objectives of health promotion, and the perceived need of health education to respect autonomy and empower groups or individuals to make their own informed choices (Downie *et al.*, 1992). Professional education in health promotion and education stresses the importance of assessing and respecting the expressed needs of communities. But assessment may be hindered by public apathy or skewed by vocal minority groups; and what is implemented may be dictated by financial constraints or political pressures at local or national government levels. Professionals engaged in health promotion and education sometimes are criticized for wanting to create a 'healthocracy', in which health will be viewed as 'the ultimate goal incorporating all life' (World Health Organization). But in practice there is little risk of this. The benefits of the more controversial health promotion or education interventions are difficult to establish by research, except on a larger and longer-term basis than most funding agencies normally are willing to support; and the activities con-

cerned are not usually given high priority by governments. Despite the current rediscovery of 'spiritual need' in other areas of health care, there is little sign in the UK that embattled health promotion and education workers aim to incorporate this dimension in their brief. They are therefore more appropriately seen by churches and other religious bodies as colleagues rather than rivals in serving the community. In the USA, however, the disinclination to incorporate this dimension may be perceived by the churches as an example of secularization and hence a threat. [*Kenneth Boyd*]

HEAVEN
The dwelling place of God and the future destiny of all the saved.
The Shorter Oxford English Dictionary defines heaven as 'the realm or region of space beyond the clouds of which the sky is viewed poetically as the floor . . . the celestial abode of God and his angels and of beatified spirits; the state of the blessed hereafter'. Badham (1978) has documented from St Augustine, Rufinus, and even Origen just how literally this view of heaven's location was taken. One problem for Christianity is that the cosmological discoveries of the seventeenth century have banished this schema beyond the realm of credibility. This does not, however, rule out a revised understanding of heaven as existing in an altogether 'other space', since modern physics allows for the logical possibility of plural spaces. Hence there could be a divine realm in another space with which our present world would not be in any kind of relation. This possibility is explored in Hick (1976). However, the heart of belief in heaven does not lie in speculation about its possible location but in the belief that human beings have an ultimate destiny with God in a future life which is beyond our imagining.

Traditionally Christians have believed in a once-for-all division of humanity at the Last Judgement in which the damned go to hell for ever while those redeemed by Christ go with him to heaven (Matt. 25.33). However, during the twentieth century with its millions of deaths in war and its greater knowledge of what is happening in the world at large, there was an increasing tendency to see all humanity as included within the redeemed. God's will is that 'all should find salvation' and hence Christ 'sacrificed himself to win freedom for all mankind' (1 Tim. 2.4 and

2.6). Pope John Paul II has declared (*Redemptor Hominis*, 1979) that 'Everyone without exception has been redeemed by Christ'.

At the heart of the hope of heaven is the belief that in this life we can enjoy a relationship of love with God and that we matter to God as unique individuals. If this is so, we can rely on God to sustain this relationship through death. Moreover if Jesus is right in describing God as like a loving father always ready to forgive and take back his prodigal children, then this universal love, already experienced by the believer, will ultimately extend to all humanity. The hope of heaven is that this will remain true after death.

Pastorally the hope of heaven affirms the reality of God's love. The limitless forgiveness implied by universal salvation means that the burden of sin and guilt need no longer blight our lives and hence we can always make a fresh start. [*Paul Badham*]

HELL
Place where Christians have believed that the damned would be tortured for ever.

For many centuries most Christians believed that all humanity would be divided into two classes: the damned, who would go for ever to hell, and the saved, who would go with Christ to heaven. Some early Fathers located hell in a lake of fire beneath the earth of which volcanoes like Etna and Vesuvius were vent holes. Since what can be seen in volcanic craters appears to burn endlessly without being consumed they supposed this would also happen to the bodies of the damned. How literally the detail of such pictures was taken is disputed. But that hell was believed to be an actual place of torment is not. According to the Council of Trent the tortures of hell comprise 'an accumulation of all punishments', and the torture manuals used by the Inquisition mirrored what was supposed to be in store for heretics after death. Sermons from over fifteen hundred years of Christian teaching show how vividly the notion of hell was etched into the Christian consciousness.

Hell understood as above was not questioned by the major Reformers. If anything it became more pronounced in early Protestantism because their rejection of purgatory removed the possibility of some intermediate state for those who were neither saints nor sinners beyond redemption. Anglicans shared such views in the sixteenth century, but because a draft article affirming hell was not actually included in the published Thirty-Nine Articles, the Privy Council ruled in 1864 that Anglican formularies have never required its clergy to believe that the punishment of the damned was everlasting.

Since the seventeenth century, and particularly since the nineteenth, hell has increasingly faded from Christian consciousness. One popular reinterpretation is espoused by the Church of England Report, *The Mystery of Salvation* (1995), which uses the word 'hell' as a symbol for the total annihilation of the wicked. Another reinterpretation is to think of hell as a temporary state of punishment designed to reform people and fit them for heaven. Currently the most popular reinterpretation is probably that of the *Catechism of the Catholic Church* (1994), which describes hell as a state of separation from God and prays that no one should actually be in that state. This is justified on the grounds that God 'wills all men to be saved' (1 Tim. 2.4) and that for God 'all things are possible' (Matt. 19.26).

Historically belief in hell can be shown to have had morally damaging effects in that it encouraged cruelty and intolerance and caused deep emotional anxiety (Badham and Badham, 1984). It might seem pastorally useful to encourage reflection on the case against this doctrine, which in practice has been discounted by almost all contemporary churches but which continues to linger on in popular belief and attitudes. These are from time to time enforced by outbursts of sectarian certainties about hell which may generate anxiety in some religious people. [*Paul Badham*]

HERMENEUTIC CIRCLE
The process of interpreting a text by posing questions that are reshaped by the text itself.

The hermeneutic circle is a literary device (Thiselton, 1980) that has been extensively used in the field of pastoral studies (Carr, 1997). In textual study it points to interpretation rather than to merely reading or understanding, focusing on the interchange between reader and text. The same approach applies in the pastoral practice of theological reflection through the hermeneutic circle. An action-reflection-change cycle is employed and the emphasis is upon process. The circle is better thought of as a spiral, which allows for the idea of progression. The circle is also the foundation of political action espoused by liberation theology (Segundo, 1977).

HETEROSEXUALITY
Patterns of life structured or motivated by desire towards a member of the opposite sex.

Discussions of human sexuality begin with the premise that biology is to sex as culture is to gender. Whether patterns of sexuality are considered a cultural construction, a biological given, or both, affects the pastoral management of sexuality and gender. The Judaeo-Christian tradition gives cultural primacy to heterosexual behaviour. Sex is to be enjoyed within a relationship and for reproduction. Both of these aspects also have social significance to do with society, property and inheritance. The production of successive generations to ensure an ongoing biological human future is thus paramount. Procreation and upbringing of the next generation remain the primary end of marriage in the Roman Catholic tradition, while companionship and social stability (which also provides for nurture of children) are emphasized by the Protestant churches. Both positions, therefore, affirm heterosexual behaviour as the norm.

HOLDING
1. The way that a mother clasps her baby and remembers the baby's emotional needs and desires.
2. Hence the sustaining of a secure context for learning.

Psychotherapists have maintained a long-standing belief in the idea that adult behaviours develop out of formative infantile experiences. But few mental health professionals have studied the vicissitudes of infancy as thoroughly as Donald Winnicott. He devoted much of his adult life to the study of babies, most crucially to examining the ways in which mothers and other care-givers may or may not facilitate the baby's development. Winnicott hypothesized that the way a mother holds her baby, both physically and psychologically, will prove to be the prime determinant of the child's subsequent mental health. He averred that mothers who hold their babies well will produce psychologically robust offspring, whereas those who hold their children less well, or even poorly, will promote varying degrees of psychological disturbance in their progeny.

Holding involves all the aspects of physical care, including bathing, feeding and toileting and, according to Winnicott, constitutes one of the three primary tasks of motherhood. But it also indicates the mother's state of mind in relation to her infant. A well-held infant will be supported not only physically, but emotionally. This is demonstrated by the parent's continued ability to remember that the infant exists and that he or she might have preferences.

Successful holding is a necessary substrate for the young baby to reach higher stages of development (Winnicott, 1965). Satisfactory holding permits the infant to grow, both physically and psychically, and it will contribute to the flourishing of qualities such as intelligence, mental structure, the capacity to symbolize, and above all, the ability to engage in human relationships. A well-held boy or girl will be protected from the vulnerability and the absolute dependence which characterize the period of infancy.

The concept of holding has been used not only in the understanding of mother–infant interactions, but also in psychotherapeutic work with patients and clients. Although very few mental-health practitioners or pastoral counsellors will provide physical holding for their patients, in contrast to the mother who *must* hold her baby, psychotherapists and counsellors can offer emotional holding nonetheless. Clinicians and pastors can hold their patients by remembering to appear for sessions, being alert and on time, by remembering the details of their patients' histories, and by behaving in a reliable, dependable and professional manner. The concept has been enlarged from its original use of the mother–child care and applied to institutions, such as hospitals and churches, and how they provide a holding context in society and to the role of the pastor. [*Brett Kahr*]

HOLDING ENVIRONMENT
A secure context within which human development is promoted.

The term 'holding environment' was first described by Winnicott (1965). It has two main characteristics: empathic interpretation and the tolerance to contain aggression and sexuality. Such provision is a primary function of the mother. When it is lacking, either in the early stages of growth or at adolescence, insecurity results in correspondingly disturbed behaviour. Provision of such an environment (albeit temporarily) is one function of therapy. The concept is also useful in pastoral studies to describe the security that is necessary for anyone of any age to risk themselves during counsel or confession (Carr, 1989).

HOLINESS
To be set apart, consecrated by God and for God's service.
The Christian understanding of holiness may be seen as the confluence of two different streams of thought, one Hebrew and the other Greek. Superficially they are very close to each other. In the Hebrew Bible the classic understanding of holiness is found in Leviticus 19: 'You shall be holy, for I the Lord your God am holy.' God's holiness may be said to be rooted in two great creative acts: the separation of light from darkness, and the separation of the Israelites from bondage by the crossing of the Red Sea. Leviticus 19 seeks, in the light of these signs, to apply the teaching of the Ten Commandments to every aspect of personal and social life in Israel, from cattle breeding (19.19) to reverencing the elderly and the alien (19.32–34). It involves the careful separation of good and evil, clean and unclean, so that the whole people may be a priestly community whose holiness will help extend God's reign of justice and compassion. Holiness is not an achievement, but a response to what God has already done: 'You shall love the alien as yourself; for you were aliens in the land of Egypt' (19.34).

In the Greek tradition, 'holiness' denotes the separation, not of good from evil, but of the soul from the body. To be holy is to forsake the promptings of the body in order to respond to the soul's longing to share in the divine life. Positively, this gives holiness a dynamic quality that is less prominent in the Hebrew tradition. It becomes not a set of guidelines to live by but a goal of perfection that challenges worldly values and demands all we have to give. Negatively, it involves a radical depreciation of the body: holiness, in the early Christian tradition, came to be associated with celibacy and the monastic life (Nicholl, 1987).

More recently, the insights of psychology have led to a third approach: the association of holiness with wholeness, self-fulfilment, and individual spiritual health. This reflects the Hebrew tradition in refusing to separate the physical from the spiritual; but it runs the risk of a subtler exclusivism by implicitly separating the personal from the political and the individual from the corporate. Any adequate understanding of holiness needs to draw together the best of these three approaches (Sheldrake, 1987). The Benedictus (the song of Zechariah in Luke 2.68–79) is a good starting point, offering a vision of holiness at once scriptural and contemporary. It is a way of life for the whole people of God, which is both a response to what God has already done in creating and setting free, and a future vision of light and shalom for the world. [Gordon Mursell]

HOLISTIC MEDICINE
Integrative health-care practices which within their environment address the needs of the whole person – physical, mental, spiritual and emotional.
Holistic medicine operates from a unitive rather than mechanistic view of the material and spiritual (Weil, 1995). Its history, philosophy and practice owe much to the Eastern tradition's more holistic vision of human nature, which recognizes people's multidimensional and community make-up. Its practitioners, in partnership with the patient, employ alternative (complementary) therapies in conjunction with Western scientific medicine; their goal is to maintain wellness, discover the root causes of illness, and the power for self-healing.

HOLY SPIRIT
In Christian theology, the third person of the Trinity.
Paul tells us in 2 Cor. 3.18 that the Spirit frees us to behold the glory of the Lord. This is an unsettling witness for many in the Christian community, for they do not recognize where this has occurred or occurs in their lives. Others in the Christian community, during nearly all periods of the Church's life, have claimed extraordinary power given them by the Spirit. Those who make this claim today, as well as others, find themselves intrigued by the experience of spiritual empowerment attested by members of native religions in the West and by members of various religions in the East. All of these Christians, but especially those who allege a correspondence between Christian and non-Christian spiritualities, impel the Christian community to ask about a standard of discernment of the Holy Spirit.

Widely diverse people, Christian and non-Christian, claim to be granted spiritual power. And Christians, following Holy Scripture, will not dissociate the Spirit from the notion of power. The *ruach Adonai*, attested in the Old Testament, can be rendered not only as the 'Spirit of the Lord', but also, at times, as 'powerful wind'. Likewise, *pneuma* in the New Testament can, at least at times, be taken as a 'blowing, powerful wind' and at other times as 'Spirit'. Yet, while these usages indicate a coincidence of Spirit and power, their context in both the Old and New Testaments also indicates that these usages do not suggest that the Spirit is sheer or arbitrary or anonymous power. In the New Testament the Holy Spirit is the power that makes effective what God has enacted in the ministry and death and resurrection of Jesus Christ (Demson, 1997). With this knowledge the Christian gains a standard of discernment for the movement of the Holy Spirit.

This standard gains clarity if we think in turn about the death, ministry and resurrection of Jesus. In his death Jesus gives up any claim for himself (Phil. 2); rather, he counted on the action of the Father to maintain right. The Spirit empowers Christians to claim (positively) that the Father's action in vindicating Christ's self-humbling is right (or justice) and to participate in it, and (negatively) to claim no other righteousness for themselves. The Spirit enables the Christian (and prospectively all humans) to recognize Jesus' ministry as the light of life and to hear Jesus' word as truth, freeing its hearers from all other claims to final truth. In his resurrection appearances the risen Christ sent his apostles to the men and women of all nations. The powerful Spirit by whom the Father raised Jesus Christ from the dead and empowered the apostles is the same Spirit who continued to send, and sends today, Christians to their neighbours to attest God's deeds and Word.

While the activity of the Holy Spirit is not confined to the activity of Christians and the Christian community (the Church), the activity of the Spirit is attested by Christians in its relation to the Church. This relation is made evident by the narrative of the Gospels. Jesus gathered the apostles during his ministry, upheld them by his death and sent them out to others in his resurrection appearances. The apostles are the first congregation. By the power of the Holy Spirit Jesus Christ gathers, upholds and sends out those who come after the apostles by including these later Christians in the gathering, upholding and sending of the original apostles. Jesus

Christ accomplishes this by bringing alive the witness of the apostles (recorded in the New Testament) through the power of the Holy Spirit. The Church at base is the witnessing apostolate and the Church in its fullness is the participation, accomplished by the Spirit, of all subsequent Christians in the communion of the original apostles with their Lord.

The Holy Spirit is bestowed on Christians and on the Christian community. Yet it is better not to say that 'we' possess the Spirit and the gifts of the Spirit, such as faith, love and hope. The sense of the New Testament is better preserved by saying that Jesus Christ by the activity of the Spirit possesses us and that we become possessed by our faith, love and hope.

In the Christian community speech about the Holy Spirit always is accompanied by speech about Jesus Christ and about him who sent Jesus, the Father. What is the relation among the three? The Western Church and the Eastern Church have disagreed. The West has followed the rule that the relations among the Father, the Son and the Holy Spirit that appear in the biblical narrative are the truth about God himself. So the Son comes from the Father and the Spirit comes from the Father *and the Son* (John 14.26; 15.26; 20.22). The Eastern Church affirms that the Spirit comes from the Father, but has reservations about adding '*and* [from] the Son' (*filioque*). A major source of the Eastern Church's discomfort is that *filioque* ('and the Son') appears to it to conceive of the Holy Spirit as the *bond* between the Father and the Son and between the Son and his people, rather than conceiving of the Spirit as the Person: God. Indeed, Augustine, a Western theologian, spoke of the Spirit as 'the bond of love' (Jenson, 1997). It may be hoped that the Eastern and Western Churches will increasingly help each other in this discussion. This can only happen, however, by the power of the Holy Spirit. [*David Demson*]

HOMELESSNESS
The lack of secure, appropriate accommodation.

Unless homelessness is seen holistically, homeless people will continue to be stereotyped, stigmatized and patronized. Context must be taken into account. Systems theory can be used to explore the micro-context, i.e. the relationships, institutions and events that make up the particular world and story of each homeless individual may be addressed with the help of systems theory. More neglected is the macro-context, i.e. the economic processes and cultural values that help determine who becomes homeless and why and what the experience means in any particular time and place. The homelessness of the shanty-town dweller in São Paulo is fundamentally different from the homelessness of the lone parent temporarily lodged in a hard-to-let estate in London, while the lack of a house does not make a member of a nomadic tribe feel homeless.

To develop responses to homelessness that are appropriate to Western society in the twenty-first century, it is helpful to locate four models of response that have originated in different historical periods (Logan, 1996).

1. *The charity model – early capitalism.* One of the casualties in the transition from feudalism to capitalism was a rich, medieval notion of charity. With the dissolution of the organic order, the dispossessed rural poor became 'them' rather than 'us', and charity was no longer about mutual bonds and commitment to a common good, but something done by the more privileged to the less fortunate.

With the advance of industrial capitalism, urban homelessness assumed massive proportions. The distorted form of charity came under increasing strain. Octavia Hill, the great housing reformer and a leading light in the Charity Organisation Society, bemoaned the indiscriminate assistance offered by William Booth's Salvation Army. But common lodging houses and night shelters became the norm and with them the further segregation of 'the homeless'.

In the twentieth century, dramatic small-scale attempts were made to revive the original spirit of charity. 'Houses of Hospitality' were pioneered in Canada by Catherine de Hueck. In France, the Abbé Pierre gathered his Emmaus companions while in Britain Anton Wallich-Clifford founded the Simon Community. These experiments in the sharing of life gave striking witness to the reality of our common humanity, breaking down the distinction between giver and receiver.

2. *The rights model – Welfare State.* As part of the struggle for justice, housing eventually came to be recognized as a basic human right. The right to shelter became enshrined in the 1948 UN Declaration of Human Rights and gradually acquired legal force, in the USA largely through the courts, and in the UK through positive legislation.

Christians were not always in the forefront of this movement. In fact some Christian homelessness agencies whose approach to homelessness had largely been shaped by the charity model seemed at times resistant. By the late 1960s, however, Christians were the key movers behind the new housing rights campaign groups such as Shelter and CHAR. One of the most impressive theological expositions of the right to housing came from the Vatican with its publication *What Have You Done to Your Homeless Brother?* (1989), produced immediately after the United Nations International Year of Shelter for the Homeless (1987).

Pastorally, Christians have made good use of the rights-based approach, acting as advisers and advocates for homeless people in pursuit of their rights, and managing projects in ways that respect homeless people's rights.

3. *The social inclusion model – workfare state.* Towards the end of the twentieth century, the apparently successful social compact between labour, capital and the nation state, which had provided the backdrop for the Welfare State, began to show its instability. Compounding this institutional dislocation was a weakening of ties to family and neighbourhood. In this context, the individualism of the rights model was seen by some as part of the problem rather than the solution. Policies of social inclusion often buttressed by communitarian ideology seemed more promising. The advantage of adopting this approach to the problem of homelessness lay in its offering a more holistic approach, defining the need not just in terms of housing and benefits but also in terms of training, employment, work with families and emphasis on citizenship. But assistance took the nature of a contract, with rights seen as conditional on the acceptance of responsibilities. Rejection of the contract gave the green light to more coercive policies resulting in the use of heavy policing against street culture, enforcement orders on people with mental health problems and detention for asylum-seekers.

Social inclusion policies appealed both theologically and practically to many Christians. Theologically, the policies resonated with the central ideal of *koinonia*, community, fellowship. Practically, the churches' community base made them well placed to be part of a holistic approach to homelessness, seeing family and youth ministry as an opportunity to prevent homelessness, and caring and community ministries as a way of helping homeless people reintegrate into the local community. Social inclusion, however, also brought its own challenges. Including people from outside the fold means dealing with difference and facing painful questions as to whose attitudes and behaviour should be expected to change.

4. *Solidarity model – global capitalism.* The increased global mobility of both capital and labour at the end of the twentieth century led to a new scenario of homelessness as part of an emerging 'Fourth World'. Western industrialized countries experienced an influx of economic migrants and refugees as well as the development of an insecure low-paid economy for those left behind in the competition for high-tech skills. One result has been a deepening of solidarity among homeless people and others squeezed by the same forces. Where a more class-based solidarity characterized earlier radical Christian responses such as the Catholic Worker and the Sojourners movements, the new solidarity is global.

Nor is this new solidarity merely a matter of virtual communities linked via the Internet. London's churches invited a deputation from São Paulo to assist them in a theological audit of their response to homelessness. And lived global solidarity is celebrated by initiatives like PRAXIS in east London.

These four models of response to homelessness must not be seen as confined to the periods in which each arose. The point of a contextual approach is to appreciate the importance of taking one's socio-historical context into account and then, having seen the patterns of homelessness and the factors behind it, to decide whether to use the prevailing model of response, to renew models from a previous era or to adopt a counter-cultural approach. That choice is likely to be the more valid and the more effective if homeless people themselves are involved in making it (Pontifical Commission, 1988). *[Pat Logan]*

HOMOPHOBIA
1. Fear of, aversion to, or dislike of homosexual people, activities and lifestyle.
2. In social institutions it is called heterosexism.
As a psychological and sociological phenomenon homophobia is similar to racism and

sexism. It can manifest itself in ways which range from negative attitudes and statements to physically violent and even murderous behaviour. Homophobia can also be internalized by gay men and women resulting in denial, self-loathing, or even self-harm.

Pastoral attitudes about the nature of homophobia remain as diverse as they are on the question of homosexuality itself.

HOMOSEXUALITY
An attraction to or sexual preference for a person of the same gender.
The word 'homosexual' derives from the Greek *homos*, 'same', combined with the Latin *sexus*. It describes a condition which has troubled as well as inspired men and women since earliest times. The term 'homophobia' has recently emerged to describe the reaction of fear and dislike that still the majority of people have in relation to homosexual persons. They, homosexuals, have been branded as deviant, unnatural and wrong.

Many people today believe that homosexual and heterosexual are not two distinct entities but two conditions. These merge, so that all of us have elements of each and are placed on a sexual spectrum. However, by late teens most know their dominant orientation. It is currently estimated that at least 4% of the population are predominantly or exclusively homosexual.

Medical and psychological opinion remain divided about the causes of the condition. Is it nature or nurture? No easy solution to the question of aetiology has been found. Today, unlike thirty years ago, no attempt is made to cure someone or force them to change their orientation by drugs or electroconvulsive treatment. Counselling may still be used. But few changes in orientation are reported unless a person is in the middle of the spectrum. Medical opinion no longer regards the condition as pathological and it is not regarded as an illness needing treatment. Recent research claiming a genetic causation has caused concern because an attempt might be made to abort a foetus with these genes. Genetic factors might predispose individuals towards a particular sexuality, but social mores and family circumstances play their part. Many homosexuals say they were aware of their sexuality at a very early age.

There are three major kinds of sexual activity between males leading to orgasm: mutual masturbation, oral genital (fellatio) and anal intercourse (sodomy). There seems no reason to suppose that males are either predominantly active or passive. Female homosexuals may enjoy mutual stimulation – oral genital, through penis substitutes (dildos) and of the anus. In previous generations the effeminate gay man and the mannish lesbian were the only visible homosexuals. In today's freer society, others have come forward to show that these stereotypes are false. Homosexuals rightly point out that society still often describes them solely in terms of their orientation, which is dehumanizing, degrading and insulting.

The most quoted passages in the Old Testament which condemn homosexual practice are Gen. 18.16—19.29; Deut. 23.17; Lev. 18.22, 23 and 20.13. Other texts witness to the fact that the Jews abhorred it as a feature of pagan lifestyle that contained no hope of continuing the family. In the New Testament the three passages around which controversy has customarily raged are Rom. 1.26, 27; 1 Cor. 6.9 and 1 Tim. 1.10. Since apostolic times the Church's attitude to homosexuals has been remarkably consistent. Homosexual acts were always declared sinful and rigorously punished. Conciliar decrees and the writings of the early church Fathers confirm this judgement. The Church has always taught that God ordained a heterosexual life for humankind and the monogamous union of Adam and Eve is the pattern of God's intention for the human family. According to this view, therefore, the homosexual indulges in an intrinsically wrong and unnatural way of life. The Catholic view is that homosexual acts exclude all possibility of transmission of life. Such an act cannot fulfil the procreative purposes of that faculty. The majority of Christians currently take these views and ask that a homosexual live a celibate life.

This has been challenged over the last few years by those who suggest the Church should listen to recent psychiatric evidence and to the experience of gay and lesbian people who feel that God has created them to love in this way. They point out that biblical texts need to be read as products of a particular time (as they are in relation to other issues) and question whether all prohibitions in the Bible have equal, abiding force. Can the Church change its mind on this subject as it has done on slavery or lending money at interest? They ask that their loving relations be regarded as natural and normal for them.

Celibacy, as for heterosexuals, should only be embraced voluntarily. Some homosexuals used to seek refuge in religious orders, sublimating their sexuality in community living. Today, when same-sex relationships are socially more acceptable, this is no longer the case. However, the Church, sadly, is perceived by many as oppressive, its morality designed solely for heterosexuals. Since they no longer regard their sexuality as a problem, they seek spiritual sustenance elsewhere.

In Great Britain the 1967 Sexual Offences Act legalized sexual acts between males over 21 in private – the age was reduced to 18 in 1994. Christians drawing a distinction between sin and crime supported this, though they were less happy with the reduction to 16 in 1998. In England the 1991 Bishops' Report *Issues in Human Sexuality* states that a welcome should be given in the Christian community to 'homophiles who follow the way of abstinence' and also to those 'who are conscientiously convinced that a faithful sexually active relationship with one other person is the way of life God wills for them'. Homosexual clergy, because of the public nature of their calling and pastoral function are, however, forbidden to have sexual relationships. At present there is no legal or ecclesiastical affirmation for same-sex couples although a few clergy are willing to bless relationships in private. Organizations like the Lesbian and Gay Christian Movement (Great Britain) and Integrity and Dignity (USA) offer support and also campaign to end discrimination and prejudice. *[Malcolm Johnson]*

HOPE

A dimension of the Christian life, individual and corporate, closely associated with faith and love.

The close association between the three is found most often in the writings of St Paul (cf. 1 Cor. 13.13; Gal. 5.5–6; Col. 1.4–5; 1 Thess. 1.3). This association was confirmed in the medieval Schoolmen's distinction between faith, hope and love as the theological virtues, on the one hand, and the natural or cardinal virtues of prudence etc. on the other. This emphasized their nature as aspects of God's gracious activity, rather than as virtues that could be achieved or acquired by individual effort, but robbed them of the communal and eschatological flavour they had in their original New Testament context.

Hope is the eschatological virtue par excellence. In Scripture it includes the idea of the object hoped for as well as the act of hoping itself. Therefore God can be described as 'the hope of Israel', its embodiment and guarantor. In the prophets this form of hope is contrasted with the false hopes generated by merely selfish need and wish-fulfilment. It paradoxically becomes the stronger the more critical outward circumstances appear, and it is characterized by the ability to wait upon God and trust God in the midst of anxiety. Hope is demonstrated by the ability to take positive action in anticipation of the fulfilment in view (as when Jeremiah purchases the field at Anathoth at the point of Israel's exile as a prophetic sign of their eventual return (Jer. 32.6ff)).

In the New Testament, hope is an outward sign of the Holy Spirit's indwelling of God's people which already gives them a foretaste of the good things God has promised. It is a sign of their new birth (1 Pet. 1.3) and their character as the new community founded in his love (Eph. 1.11–12). They are already in possession of 'Christ in you, the hope of glory' (Col. 1.27) and this enables them to wait for the complete fulfilment of God's promises with steadfastness and endurance. Not only that, but their fellowship and witness in adverse conditions is a 'travail' which itself anticipates and hastens the coming of the Kingdom (Moltmann, 1967). In Rom. 8 this is given cosmic proportions. The whole creation waits 'in eager longing' for the revealing of the children of God (Rom. 8.18–25).

It is hope, understood in this way, which stops the Church from becoming too narrowly focused on its own life. It helps it to reflect critically upon its worship, mission and evangelism in the light of its task as sign and servant of the Kingdom. How the Church embodies the changes longed for in the horizon of God's rule – which is always 'now' but 'not yet' – differs from time to time and place to place (Brueggemann, 1978). But without the dimension of hope as the anticipation of a new way of living yet to be fully revealed, the pastoral activity of the Church loses its true significance. [Chris Moody]

HOSPICE
A skilled community working to improve the quality of life of patients facing death.

A number of homes or hospices that made the care of those dying of cancer and tuberculosis their special concern were founded on both sides of the Atlantic early in the twentieth century. Most of them still continue today and the number of such places has increased worldwide. The modern hospice movement derives from those early hospices, but has seen a match between science and spiritual care develop in new ways.

Several surveys carried out in the 1950s and 1960s revealed that dying patients suffered more pain than was either realized or necessary. The need was acknowledged for special accommodation, skilled home care, support for families and the spread of knowledge (especially about alleviating pain) throughout the general field of medicine concerned with the terminally-ill patient. In 1967 St Christopher's Hospice in London, the first hospice to apply the academic model of care, research and teaching to this field, was founded. This proved to be a catalyst for a now worldwide movement.

The challenge to such a development began from attention to the nature of terminal pain and the need better to understand it and therefore to treat it more effectively. The consideration of its psychological, social and spiritual components, as well as its physical complexities and the need for patients to have as much control as possible gave great awareness of what they and their families could still achieve. The hospice multidisciplinary team (which often includes a priest or minister) aims, by skilled awareness of patients' symptoms and their feelings, to enable them to live to the limit of their physical, social and spiritual capacity. It works as a complementary local service, integrated into the whole field of medical care. It also serves both in-patients and outpatients in general and special centres. Most, though not all, are suffering from some form of cancer and are having their pain alleviated and their families supported. One major part of care is carried out in people's own homes.

As this work was developed, initially in the UK, the USA and Canada, a variety of innovations and interpretations under different titles came to be known as 'the hospice movement'. There are now independent units, wards and separate buildings on a hospital campus, and many consulting home-care and hospital teams with no beds of their own. This variety has grown up in response to local initiative and possibilities, with the minimum of central organization. One major reason for this has been the aim of every hospice that its experience, research and teaching should be so accepted that those in the general field will approach all dying patients with appropriate attitudes and skills. The special centres and teams continue to be needed for those with particularly intractable problems; they pioneer in a demanding and rewarding branch of care and are spreading research into provision of end-of-life care more widely.

Contrary to some popular belief, hospices are not morbid places. They are known for the seriousness with which they treat illness, but also for the warmth of mutual support and understanding between patients, families and staff. The chaplain is a key member of the team. Similar conditions apply to those who visit parishioners as are found in hospitals. But with the total treatment programme being worked in a hospice, visiting pastors may have to accept constraints on their visiting. Much spiritual support to both patients and staff will not use religious language, but a search for meaning and self-worth, often inarticulate, is still common. *[Cicely Saunders]*

HOSPITAL
A place or institution for the diagnosis, treatment and care of the sick or injured and for the management of childbirth.
The word 'hospital' is derived from the Latin *hospitalis* meaning 'guest'. Historically hospitals were places of shelter for travellers or refuge for those in need and were largely associated with religious orders. Monasteries had areas set aside for guests and this included those who were sick or injured. Some of the medieval institutions such as the leper hospitals were solely dedicated to care of the sick and also existed to isolate victims of infectious diseases. After the Reformation in England and the dissolution of the monasteries, some hospitals still existed as part of the system of almshouses.

In the nineteenth century three major discoveries changed the course of medicine. These were anaesthesia, antiseptics and X-rays, and they led to the development of the hospital as we know it today, a place where the sick receive not only care but also active intervention to find the cause of their illness and provide a cure. Charitable organizations and private benefactors as well as religious institutions became involved in

funding hospitals which were now housed in dedicated and substantial buildings.

Since the middle of the twentieth century the majority of hospitals in the world have become government-owned, except in the USA, although there are still some private hospitals in most countries. These may be non-profit making, run by voluntary organizations, churches and independent associations, or they may be run as businesses for private gain. In the USA the term 'voluntary' applies to non-profit-making organizations which serve the whole community. Military hospitals exist in most countries and are either permanent establishments for military personnel and their families or mobile field hospitals and hospital ships to deal with casualties in time of conflict. All hospitals provide some training for health professionals but those with specific medical schools are known as 'teaching hospitals' and tend to be the most prestigious.

Modern hospitals fall into two categories, specialist and general. The specialist hospital provides treatment for a specific type or group of conditions. This will include hospitals for mental conditions, infectious or contagious illnesses, those specializing in cancer treatment, orthopaedic hospitals and maternity or children's hospitals. The general hospital accepts all kinds of medical or surgical cases including all the above, usually with the exception of mental illness, although with the closure of the large mental hospitals some general hospitals now have acute psychiatric units. Most general hospitals also have an accident and emergency facility.

General hospitals are now more common than specialist hospitals in the interest of shared technological resources, expertise and efficiency of administration. They will often concentrate on a particular speciality and become known as a centre of excellence in that area. As treatments improve and become less invasive, hospital stays become shorter and all general hospitals now have day-case or short-stay facilities. Many people will be seen and receive treatment entirely in outpatients' departments for conditions which would once have meant a stay in hospital.

Modern hospitals require a huge amount of support services and many areas of expertise to function efficiently. The financial pressures become ever greater as the possibilities of treatment and consequently expectations increase. This has led to hospitals concentrating more on treating acute conditions and less on care for longer-term illness and disabilities than was the case a generation ago. Most long-term nursing care and care of the elderly infirm now takes place either at home or in specialized private nursing homes. There is a worldwide emphasis on health education, screening and immunization in order to prevent illness occurring, create a healthy society and make hospital admission unnecessary.

Pastoral care in hospitals is provided by chaplains, hospital social workers and by voluntary organizations. Large hospitals have a full-time chaplain and are usually assisted by part-time chaplains from the local clergy of various denominations. Social workers are employed by the local authority but are based in the hospital. Their responsibilities centre mainly on the needs of patients when leaving hospital and their families while patients are away. Various voluntary services exist in all hospitals. Usually the hospital will have its own League of Friends or equivalent support establishment; international organizations such as the Red Cross maintain a presence in all hospitals. [Betty Saunders]

HOSTILITY
An enduring negative attitude characterized by a readiness to attack (verbally or physically), which may be directed towards specific targets or may take an unspecific, generalized form.
Unlike anger, hostility appears to have no positive part to play in human interaction. It is seen in its extreme form in paranoia, but is also common in those who feel lonely, isolated or discarded by society (e.g. the unemployed, the elderly). Pastoral care should seek to overcome the isolation and rejection, by action to reform the alienating social structures and by fostering relevant self-help and support groups.

HOUSE CHURCH
A movement of Christian renewal beginning in the UK in the early 1970s.
This movement originated with a loose cluster of conservative evangelical male leaders, influenced by the wider charismatic renewal scene, who began their ministries within homes. As numbers grew, they moved into rented premises and have increasingly purchased redundant churches as their bases. It is now a movement of independ-

ent but networked congregations, many members drawn from older churches, adhering to a Pauline, male-led, church order. Close links exist with similar bodies especially in the USA and Scandinavia. Total numbers in the mid-1990s in the UK were about fifty thousand.

HUMAN NATURE
The characteristic of human beings as material creatures who develop as persons with spiritual capacities.
Human nature is built from the same basic building blocks as the rest of nature. The key question is 'What is so special about it?' It is marked by a capacity for self-consciousness so that human beings wonder about who or what they are, with a hint or longing or faith that they are more than just the natural stuff that rots and is recycled. A main theme in much Western philosophy and religion has been to understand human nature, as experienced, as a mix of spirit-stuff (soul) and matter-stuff. It is then held that 'really' human nature lies on the spiritual/soul side and various stories explain this mix. The main traditions of the East rejected this dualism. They diagnose the root of worries about human nature as lying in self-consciousness itself. The separate self is an illusion, which feeds on its mistaken longing. There is no human nature and the problems of human awareness disappear as one passes beyond all limits and illusions by means of the appropriate psychological, philosophical and religious disciplines. From the eighteenth century in the West various theories have argued that talk about 'otherness' is the real illusion, and human nature must be understood 'scientifically' and in no other way. Sometimes this type of view is argued optimistically – e.g. eighteenth-century beliefs about perfectibility through proper education and social organization; Marxist views about correct understanding of the dialectic leading to the fulfilment of human beings in the classless society; or psychologically better living for the analysed individual and an understanding society. Sometimes the approach is more pessimistic – e.g. reductionism, determinism and behaviourism. The optimistic views seem refuted by what actually happens; the pessimistic views seem persistently to fail to do justice to some of the things we all experience as human beings, such as free will, the glorious value of values, joy, etc. Historically Christian views of

human nature have been strongly influenced by the spirit/matter dichotomy. But belief in creation and incarnation as activities of God seems to tie up with scientific discoveries to make it clear that human beings are material creatures who develop as persons with spiritual capacities. To separate the spiritual from the material is to believe in a different story about God, men and women and the world from the Christian one. Human nature, therefore, cannot be defined or confined. It must be regarded, and treated, as open, emergent and risky (including the actualized risk of sin). It is a matter of relationships between men and women, their environment and God. The optimism/pessimism dilemma is challenged by the gospel. Nothing short of the Kingdom of God is, in the end, good enough for the fulfilment of the possibilities of human nature. [*David Jenkins*]

HUMAN RIGHTS
1. The human right to receive pastoral care.
2. The role of pastoral care in advocating human rights.

Human rights are fully listed in the Universal Declaration of Human Rights and/or in the International Covenant for Social, Economic and Cultural Rights, but a specific reference to the right to pastoral care as a human right is not mentioned. A sufficient ground for the right to pastoral care is necessary in order for it to be universally accepted as a human right. Faithful human rights advocates are vigilant with regard to policing frivolous rights claims because frivolous rights claims undermine the whole system of human rights.

A brief taxonomy of rights helps to clarify what type of rights pastoral care rights might be. Historically, rights have been divided into two categories: individual rights and group rights. Pastoral care is commonly understood to be an activity of healing, guiding, reconciling and sustaining. Usually it is exercised by individuals with individuals, by individuals with groups, and by groups with groups, but it is always an activity on behalf of a religious group. As such, it is an aspect of the practice of religion, and the right to practise religion is a well-recognized right. Accordingly, though not specifically referred to as a human right, it is a practice that is inherent to the practice of religion and therefore should be afforded the high regard accorded to religion under current understandings of human rights.

The famous United States Supreme Court decision, Griswold v. Connecticut, established the concept that precisely defined rights can be protected under the United States Constitution under the 'penumbra' of other broader rights that are incontrovertible. Writing for the majority, Justice Douglas wrote:

We deal with a right of privacy older than the Bill of Rights – older than our political parties, older than our school system. Marriage is a coming together for better or for worse, hopefully enduring, and intimate to the degree of being sacred. It is an association that promotes a way of life, not causes; a harmony in living, not political faiths; a bilateral loyalty, not commercial or social projects. Yet it is an association for as noble a purpose as any involved in our prior decisions.

It would be equally appropriate to regard the right to practise religion as older than any right to privacy. It would also be easy to characterize it as promoting a 'way of life, not causes; a harmony in living, not political faiths; a bilateral loyalty, not commercial or social projects'. And it is no less noble than any other practice or any other right. Accordingly, the right to pastoral care is a 'penumbra' right to be found within the right to practise religion, a right for which there is no controversy as to its status as a human right.

To what extent does pastoral care promote human rights? In recent years, pastoral-care theorists have argued that advocacy is an additional function of pastoral care. Pastoral care seeks to relieve suffering, a goal that may at times involve advocacy, especially if suffering results from victimization or violence. Advocacy may take many forms. Pastoral care may involve helping a victim gain enough sense of self-worth to demand his or her rights. In order to resist victimization and violence, it may require helping a victim connect with those who suffer in a similar manner. Religious advocates may act as a 'voice', as rights-claimants on behalf of those who have little political or economic power, such as children. Therefore, pastoral care may require activities that educate a victim about human rights, that emotionally prepare a victim to demand human rights, or that support a person or group in maintaining their rights.

One last small point remains to be settled. International discourse on human rights would usually require that the right to pastoral care be fitted into one of two categories of rights: positive rights or negative rights. Negative rights are rights in which the state is not constrained to provide the wherewithal for the claimed right to be exercised. For example, it is commonly understood that the state has no obligation to further religion, to provide for temples or priests, or to collect tax money to provide for the same, though particular states, such as countries with state churches, might require such provision by custom. In the United States the right to practise religion is counterbalanced in the Bill of Rights by an inhibition on the part of the state from being unduly entangled in the practice of religion. Thus, all citizens are protected from the state's unwarranted support for the practice of religion. A right to pastoral care would also fit into this pattern as a right to practise religion. Thus it could not be said that the state has an obligation to provide pastoral care-givers, even though, in some cases, government agencies, such as prisons, the military, and childcare agencies, do employ chaplains that represent the ranges of faiths present in the institution. In other cases, religious groups may provide pastoral care in partnership with government institutions. The state has the sole obligation of merely refraining from interfering in the groups' rights to practise pastoral care and also the duty to prevent other third parties from interfering with their rights; this is why such rights are negative rights.

Positive rights on the other hand require the state or some party to provide goods or services that enable rights holders to enjoy their rights. In unusual circumstances, the state would have the duty to assist in the right of individuals to have their right to pastoral care, as in the case of incarcerated practitioners or the military. While it cannot be claimed that the state would have an obligation to hire, train or produce 'ministers' for the general population, in cases where prisoners and soldiers have access to places of worship, access to chaplains must also be provided. [Pamela Couture]

HUMAN TISSUES
Pastoral and moral issues arising from the donation or abandonment of human tissues for use in medicine and science.
The terms 'donated tissue' or 'donated organ' may cover blood, bone marrow, semen, ova, or partial or complete solid organs. In multiple organ transplants a heart can even be donated from a living donor (when the donor, who has a healthy heart but diseased lungs, receives a heart/lung transplant). Here the issue of consent is crucial: in most cases the notion of 'donation' usually implies voluntary consent. However, this is not always the case in, for example, bone-marrow transplants from one infant sibling to another, where consent may be very minimal. However, as children become older, their wishes are given increasing weight.

In Britain and the USA tissue or organ donations have mostly been altruistic. Titmuss (1973) noted that whereas in some countries human blood is sold, not given, the NHS in Britain has relied instead upon unpaid donors. He regarded such action as important evidence of altruism, of giving between strangers. Although he interpreted this gift relationship in secular terms, for many with religious faith it will appear rather as a part of their relationship to God.

Commercialization may seriously distort this altruistic relationship – for example, if it is discovered that blood donated altruistically or by-products from this blood (antibodies, cell-line developments, etc.) are then sold. Commercialization seems to turn a relationship based upon voluntary, altruistic giving into a commercial transaction or, even worse, into a means of commercial gain unknown to the giver. The latter, especially, seems contrary to any notion of 'fair obtaining'.

Tissue abandoned by the living (such as placenta, body wastes, surgically removed neoplasms or growths, diseased or damaged limbs) may require a different ethical response. Why is consent needed here? It could be argued that a requirement for consent to use such abandoned tissue for research shows an excessive concern for autonomy, and may even provoke commercial greed.

However, there are some examples which suggest a rather complicated mixture of both donation and abandonment. In one case, young women working for Marks & Spencer agreed to give samples of their blood for investigation into heart disease. Is it morally right to use these samples for subsequent studies of genetics without additional consent from the donors? At the very minimum this example suggests that, unless such consent is obtained, the samples should be rendered anonymous and unlinked, for otherwise individuals may suffer some of the disabilities associated with genetic screening (e.g. in terms of insurability).

If whole cadavers are donated for research or teaching purposes, then consent is required and also special treatment and respect. So cadavers are eventually buried or cremated. In the case of a foetus or foetal material there must be a clear separation between the treating doctors and the researchers. [*Robin Gill*]

HUMANISM
Views that begin from the value of the human.
1. Secular humanism is anthropocentric, denying any supernatural reality.
2. Christian humanism is theocentric, affirming God's centrality in all human endeavour.
Historically, humanism is chiefly associated with the Renaissance in fifteenth-century Europe, as medieval Scholasticism began to break down. It opposed the view that knowledge was to be acquired through formal, logical reasoning, and introduced a strategy for gaining true, usable knowledge based on the belief that the written text is the source of knowledge, and the scholar's task is therefore to understand the text. Such understanding requires one to know the history of the language in which it is written so that one may interpret each word according to what it meant when written. This approach applied whether one was attempting to understand a scriptural text or a piece of classical literature. Among the fifteenth-century humanists, Desiderius Erasmus of Rotterdam was a notable example of Christian humanism. He believed that the essence of Christianity was contained in the sacred texts (i.e. the Bible and the writings of the church Fathers) and not in the accumulation of traditional teachings and practices. In his *Manual of the Militant Christian, or Enchiridion*, he sought to transform the practice of Christianity from formal ritual into a personal experience. Familiarity with the texts also enabled Erasmus and other humanists to challenge various church practices on historical grounds, showing that these were later developments.

From these origins developed two types of humanism – Christian and secular. A central tenet of Christian humanism is its emphasis that human dignity is based on God's love for every human being. This is especially evidenced by the capacity of the human mind to seek and comprehend truth and the human will to pursue the good. The emphasis on human dignity, the claim that when God made the human mind, God made an instrument that was capable of knowing the truth about God, self and world, has been challenged by traditionalists on various grounds. The debate continues today. Christian humanism is charged with neglecting human sinfulness and the need for redemption, setting human thought above the word of God, minimizing the sovereignty of God over the created world, and isolating humanity from the rest of the natural order. In response Christian humanists contend that the traditionalist emphasis on human depravity normalizes the human situation and fails to attend to its improvement, that the human authorship of scriptural texts is too self-evident to ignore and does not, in any case, diminish the revelatory claims that are made for them, and that relationship with God involves co-operating with God's benevolent purposes in the world, which requires the use of all one's powers of intellect and will.

The American philosopher, John Dewey (1859–1952), notably expounded the case for a religious humanism. He held that religion had power to introduce perspective into 'the piecemeal and shifting episodes of existence', and contended that such perspective is afforded by specific religions, not religion in general. His humanism was a major intellectual force behind the pastoral theology movements of the 1950s and 1960s in the USA, and is especially evident in the writings of Seward Hiltner (1958).

Secular humanists claim to be humanitarian. Some base their approach on existential thinking, which stresses the need for individuals and societies to create their own values and systems of belief. Others have invested in the scientific revolution and see the solution to problems coming through rational thought and experiment as the way forward. They have in common the dismissal of God (and usually religion) from their frame of reference. [*Donald Capps*]

HUMANISTIC PSYCHOLOGY
An approach that emphasizes the individual's innate power to change.
Humanistic psychology has been regarded as 'the third way' between experimental

psychology and psychoanalytic theory. By the 1960s these were beginning to be regarded with less favour because of their supposed pessimism and reductionism. Leading figures in a movement to acknowledge these insights but to move on were Abraham Maslow (1954) and Carl Rogers (1975), the founder of Rogerian therapy. The approach is deliberately optimistic and turns towards questions of the transcendent. It acquired a strong following among religious counsellors.

HUMOUR
A human way of coping with difficulty through playfulness and (usually quiet) laughter.

Humour is a more complex facet of human life than is always obvious. It differs according to context, personality type, developmental stage and culture. It can vary from laughter at oneself (as, for example, when lacking control a child giggles at a 'rude' noise) to practical jokes (which can be cruel). Exaggeration to make a point is a familiar style of humour and is one which the pastor might occasionally use in offering counsel. Laughing with others can generate fellowship. But it is easy to drift without knowing into laughter at others, and what might be beneficial suddenly turns malign. Abreactive laughter is not humour but a release of tension. It needs interpretation. One further aspect of humour is the licensed fool or clown. Such a person as a sort of court jester may in a group or other social situation be given permission to act subversively through caricature and exaggeration in order to discharge unspoken feelings.

HYMNS
Congregational songs in lyrical form, often biblically based but at the same time personal, sung to tunes that allow the singer to be emotionally involved.

The above definition is of hymns as they were developed in English in the eighteenth century by Watts and Wesley. They are vehicles for corporate praise or prayer, mutual encouragement, spiritual nurture and the teaching of Christian truths in a way that fixes them firmly at a deep level in the mind. Earlier hymns, however, were different. The Latin office hymns of the monastic liturgy are more objective and sung to the less emotional plainchant. Many were translated in the nineteenth century and have formed the

basis of Anglican hymnbooks. Few have proved popular; for the most part the ordinary worshipper senses that these are intended to sustain a different devotional life from that of the regular Sunday congregation.

Sixteenth-century attempts to introduce to Britain the hymnody of the Lutheran Reformation failed; no metrical versions of liturgical canticles came into common use. From the later sixteenth century metrical psalms, influenced by the Reformed tradition, were sung, and served an intellectual style of worship. Metrical psalms are represented in current hymnbooks, but are usually sung alongside hymns and have to compete with them for the affection of the congregation.

The hymn was further developed in the nineteenth century, aided by a more romantic style of poetry and music. The richer style of worship introduced by the Oxford Movement was accompanied by more emotional hymnody. There remains tension between the populist tone of such hymns and those of the evangelical revival and more formal styles of worship. A further impetus to populist styles of hymnody came from the evangelical crusades of the second half of the nineteenth century, particularly from the Salvation Army and the touring evangelists such as Sankey and Moody, with both placing much emphasis on styles taken from popular music.

These various strands remain at the beginning of the twenty-first century, accentuated by the great increase in original writing of all kinds since 1960. In the main-line hymnody there has been an emphasis on hymns that serve the new liturgical understanding in the churches. Throughout the twentieth century hymns also emphasized social concerns both local and worldwide. The charismatic movement has used the populist hymn styles of the nineteenth century and developed them into worship songs, with music based on mid-century popular styles. This tends to the highly emotional and intensely personal. Attempts are regularly made to align this genre with contemporary secular styles for evangelistic work among young people.

There has been much editing of older texts to serve new needs and to sit alongside contemporary liturgies. This has led to the removal of archaisms from older hymns. Alongside this there is increasing agreement that the language of hymns should be inclusive.

Traditionally Nonconformist denominations had a better appreciation of the power of hymns than Anglicans and Roman Catholics. There are signs that this is changing and that more care is being taken over the choice of hymns (Watson, 1997). Pastors recognize increasingly that such doctrine and understanding of the faith as many possess is as likely (if not more so) to be derived from what is sung than from the more formal preaching, training classes and even readings from Scripture. Some hymns, such as 'Abide with me' (sung at a football match) or 'Jerusalem', together with one or two familiar ones from early schooldays, often form the sum of a person's knowledge of the Christian faith. This fact may be pastorally very significant, for example when meeting a family for preparation for one of the occasional offices. [*Alan Luff*]

HYPNOSIS
An induced state marked by suggestibility and rapport with the facilitator.
Clinical hypnosis is a natural state of altered awareness, similar to prayer, meditation and daydreaming. One's functioning is based on internal processes – such as a facilitator's suggestions – rather than in response to sensory input. Therapeutic hypnosis may help to build bridges in the inner self between areas of need and areas of strength. Anyone can enter a hypnotic state and subsequently re-orient. Contrary to popular belief, the person hypnotized does not surrender their will to the hypnotizer. Pastoral hypnosis, when properly used by a qualified practitioner, may become a non-intrusive way of helping some people change and grow.

HYSTERIA
A collection of symptoms, which may include convulsions, paralysis and dissociation.
The term 'hysteria' does not have a specific aetiology but refers to a collection of symptoms. Historically, hysteria was attributed to 'delicate nerves' and disturbances of the female reproductive system, such as a wandering uterus. It was considered a gender-specific condition, and still has a higher incidence in women than men. With the growth of psychoanalysis, explanations modelled on psychoanalytical theories were developed by key figures.

I

IATROGENESIS
The generation of disease by activities of doctors. Patients may develop symptoms inadvertently suggested by doctors (*iatros* = Greek for a physician) whom they have consulted – although this risk may be less than that of consulting medical textbooks. Medical treatment also can have unintended or unpredictable side effects, sometimes serious as in the case of the drug thalidomide, HIV infection from blood transfusion, or some complications of surgical operations. The idea that increasing medicalization of life poses an iatrogenic threat to health was popularized by the Catholic educationalist Ivan Illich (1976).

ID
In Freudian psychoanalytic theory, the instinctual aspects of the person.
The id is one of the three agencies that Freud proposed as making up the psyche. The other two are the ego and the superego. Id is the area of the personality where instinct dominates, being made up of unconscious material, some of which is innate and some of which is acquired through life. The id constitutes a powerful spring of energy that operates unconsciously, without regard for moral constraint or correctness. This energy is directed towards the satisfaction of wishful impulses and desires and is modified by the ego and the superego.

IDEALIZATION
A psychodynamic term referring to an individual's unrealistically high estimation of others which may serve a defensive or developmental purpose.
Idealization was initially identified within the psychodynamic literature as a defence against disturbing feelings. Melanie Klein (1921) noted that the creation of an idealized image of a person or object was utilized as a psychological defence from the earliest months of childhood. She proposed that babies strongly differentiate between pleasant feelings of being fed and nurtured and unpleasant feelings of hunger and rage. The baby wishes to get rid of the unpleasant feelings and projects them out on to the image

of a 'bad breast' which the baby then perceives as threatening to annihilate. Against the threat of this persecutory 'bad breast', the baby also constructs an idealized image of a 'good breast', which is a powerful, nurturing force that is able to protect the infant from annihilation. Klein suggested that this step of creating an idealized 'good breast' was thus an important defence that infants used to manage the terrifying nature of their earliest experience.

The defensive use of idealization continues to be evident in adulthood. An individual can idealize another person to avoid recognizing their ambivalent feelings towards them. Alternatively, an individual might put someone else on a pedestal to avoid facing their feelings of envy towards them. For if the other is sufficiently idealized, they become too perfect to be an object of envy. Because idealization is associated with the infantile processes of making very dramatic distinctions between good and bad objects (a process known as 'splitting'), it is often accompanied by denigration of others. One example of such splitting would be a parishioner who idealizes their previous vicar, who could do no wrong in their eyes, while being harshly critical of their current vicar, about whom they can find nothing good to say.

An important development of the psychodynamic understanding of idealization came in the later work of Heinz Kohut (1976). Kohut suggested that idealization of others could also represent an important part of psychological development in childhood. He proposed that one condition for a young child to develop as a psychologically healthy 'self' was that they should be able to have a relationship with a care-giver, in which the child idealized the adult. Over time, if the adult fails in small ways to live up to this idealized image, then the child takes this idealized image into themselves and it becomes part of their own psychological structure. By internalizing this idealized image, the child can develop a healthy capacity to base its life around strongly held ideals and values which can be carried into adulthood.

An awareness of processes of splitting can be invaluable for the pastoral carer, who may be the focus of others' idealization or denigration. Kohut's work also highlights the therapeutic value of a carer's tolerating another's idealization of them, in that this may help the other person to work through unresolved developmental processes. *[Gordon Lynch]*

IDENTIFIED PATIENT
The person who has sought or has been referred for help.
People referred for help frequently identify themselves as having difficulty; or another (e.g. a partner, or parents) has told them (or the care professional) that they are causing problems. In that sense they are identified as the patient. However, this person may be scapegoated, so that it is actually the partner or family which (also) needs help because the couple or the family are dysfunctional. Individual care or counselling may therefore include others in the work. Alternatively, the carer is not misled into concentrating solely on the 'patient', but works towards identifying the part that others are playing in the situation, sometimes thereby helping the patient involve significant others in examining their own roles.

IDENTITY
Sense of individuality, as experienced by the self, and as perceived and described by other people.
A person's identity is at any one point of time determined by their present perception of the self, by their perception of the current views of other people, by their relationships and their role in society, and through the influence of internalized images of the self and others from the past.

At birth an infant's identity is rudimentary, being almost inseparable from that of the mother, although even then the fact that the baby is a boy or a girl evokes response by the mother and family which provides the foundations for a growing sense of gender identity. Within a few weeks the sense of 'me' and 'not-me' gradually forms as babies appreciate a separate existence from mother. This early sense of self is reinforced through the mirroring of the baby by nurturers. There continues to develop through childhood and indeed throughout life an identity or sense of self that is highly influenced by the expectations and projections of other people in the family and in other relationships.

Adolescence is a particularly formative period, according to Erikson, a time when gender identity, sexual identity, career identity, all contribute to the uniqueness of the individual. Nevertheless, a young person's identity is still influenced obviously and unconsciously by the long process of childhood, as well as by peers. Erikson (1994) sees identity as about finding a role, and contrasts this with young people in whom there is a sense of confused identity. He also sees the sense of individual identity as being an important prerequisite for entering into close relationships, although some feminist writers have challenged the notion that such clear distinctions between self and others are possible.

Adult identity is seldom fixed (except perhaps in the most rigid of characters) and even in the normal course of events it is constantly if imperceptibly changing. A personal crisis or major life change (whether it is success or failure, a loss or entering a new relationship, changing or losing jobs, having children, loss or discovery of faith, etc.) means that most people in such circumstances undergo a major shift in their sense of self, both within themselves and in relation to others, sometimes leading to what is called an 'identity crisis'. This period of confusion, in which a person may temporarily lose the sense of who they are ('I'm not myself any more') is also one of plasticity, where pastoral help can support a person as they acquire their new sense of identity.

Similar to identity is the term individuation, a Jungian concept which includes not only finding oneself as an individual, but locating oneself in the larger scheme of life. Jungians refer also to the persona, a type of mask, so that a person may in public situations adopt different expressions of personal identity, in order to fit in with the particular setting. This is a normal part of social interaction, although a more extreme and less healthy form is found in the psychoanalytic concept of the false self where a person's sense of self and of public image is largely the result of conforming to the expectations of the family and society, the true self having never properly developed. [*Michael Jacobs*]

ILLNESS
See: SICKNESS

ILLUSION

A type of perception that tries to make sense of, and/or attach meaning to, experience.
Freud proposed that an illusion is an idea which is based upon a deeply held wish. It may or may not be true – illusions are not the same as errors – although it is a mark of an illusion that it is not capable of verification. Illusions are not the same as delusions, or hallucinations. He uses several examples to

illustrate his definition, such as Columbus, who had the illusion that he had discovered the Indies, because he so much wished to find a route to India by sailing west. Some illusions can come true: e.g. the belief that one is going to marry a princess, as Freud remarks, does occasionally happen.

Freud suggested that religious beliefs are examples of illusions, in that they are based upon deep wishes, and that they are also incapable of being shown to be true (or not true). Religious belief provides people with answers that are largely comforting to them about death and guilt, fulfilling their need, for example, to have a super-parental figure in adult life who can protect them as once their parents did when they were young; or a belief system that can provide answers to the riddles of the world; or a faith that gives reassurance against the fear of death. Freud acknowledges that other ways of making sense of experience are also possible illusions – even his ideas about psychoanalysis, although he claims that he is not incapable of correction and of changing his mind. Nevertheless some of Freud's followers treated his ideas like religious beliefs, and have had their own illusions about psychoanalytic theories, sometimes held with a religious fervour.

Freud thought maturity in adulthood meant giving up childish wishes (the pleasure principle) in favour of what he called the reality principle. Post-Freudian thinking has recognized that discerning reality is very hard, if not impossible. The idea that we construct our realities, in the form of an illusion, is therefore one which is worth pursuing. Freud does not write about religious thinking sympathetically (see *The Future of an Illusion*, 1927); but Winnicott puts a positive gloss on illusion, identifying illusion as one of several transitional phenomena, necessary for adaptation to new experiences, and part of the process of development throughout life (1992). Winnicott suggests that we live by one form of illusion or another from birth to death. Such illusions (as long as they do not become delusions) generally serve a healthy function in providing a third area, between the objective and the subjective. The arts and religion in particular provide this third area of experience, providing both a means of expressing these illusions, and a resource for people who are looking for ways of constructing their own realities. These illusory realities are largely healthy (although they can sometimes become oppressive and negative), since they provide people with ways of coping with life events. The illusion acts as a filter or as a container; it protects, permeates, contacts, translates and prepares us for change, as we shift from disillusion at one way of constructing reality into the illusion necessary for a new one.

Winnicott posits that a baby's first illusion is that she or he has created the mother's breast. A good mother allows this illusion, until such a time as the baby must begin to wean away from the breast. The mother then enables disillusion to be experienced, so that it can then be replaced by a new form of illusion. In one sense the task of weaning remains a perpetual one for parents, educators and pastors. The way of creating illusions can change, as we encounter new experiences which make old forms of knowledge unsatisfactory. Their importance is that they work for a while, until the point where we become disillusioned and turn to new ways of perceiving. These, in turn, give way to yet further, fresh illusions.

Winnicott draws a vital distinction between illusion, which is a personal construction, and a delusion, which if equally personal is held by the deluded person to be universal, and which needs to be impressed upon other people. By that definition some religious (and some political) ideas can be seen to contain that fanatical element, needing to convince others that they are objectively true. But many people live through a series of illusions which they do not seek to force upon others. And if they are given encouragement and permission, through pastoral care, for example, or spiritual direction, they may be able to move from one way of understanding themselves and the world about them to another construction (Jacobs, 2000). These shifts often occur at times of crisis, when old illusions cease to be effective. In pastoral care, it is important to recognize that there are these different forms of illusion, and that people can only move from one illusion, through disillusion, to another when they are ready to. The help and encouragement to engage in disillusionment as a sign of hope and movement, not of despair and guilt, is a vital part of pastoral care and spiritual direction.

It is possible, as has been suggested by Jacobs (1993a), to identify different forms of illusion and knowledge. In summary, these illusions might be described as consisting first of mythical and magical ideas, and intuitive perceptions of reality, largely unconcerned with contradictions or questions of objective truth; second, a sense of certainty about knowledge and facts, often dependent upon the authority of experts, and yet also illusory; third, a more objective sense of reality, which appears to provide answers, but which leaves little room for the intuitive and the poetic; fourth, the multifaceted interpretation of experience, which is capable of suspending disbelief, and draws upon science, poetry, art, music, religious thinking and stories; and finally mystical knowledge, one which passes beyond words and images to the inexpressible. The tradition in Eastern and Western mysticism called the *via negativa* can only describe the state of knowledge beyond illusions through the use of the negative ('not this, not that'). Remarkably this ties in with Freud's belief that all religious language is essentially a projection of human characteristics onto God, and that mature knowledge consists in letting go of illusions. [*Michael Jacobs*]

IMAGINATION
Power of the mind to create images; creative, synthetic power of the mind.

Imagination has come to mean in the widest sense the capacity of the human mind to create. This is often linked with the human capacity to create images, whether in the mind, as in dreams and visual memory, or in the external world, as in art or literature. The relation between such creativity and claims to truth or revelation is of central importance for Judaeo-Christian thinkers (Coulson, 1981).

The early Platonist tradition, which saw the world as containing only images of eternal 'forms', suspected the human capacity to create images. In Plato's *Republic*, artists are to be banished, since they create images of images. Aristotle comes nearer to giving a positive account of the creative working of the mind by which in any particular situation the right course of action may be discerned. Kant presents the exercise of imagination as the indispensable condition for our experiencing as a coherent 'world' the manifold sense-data which come to us. Coleridge follows him, reinforcing the attribution of artistic creation to this synthetic faculty of the mind. He writes of 'my shaping spirit of imagination'. Newman's *Grammar of Assent* traces the working of imagination in the movement of the mind to religious certitude.

Imagining the future is a characteristic human activity. The moral seriousness of such imagining is evident when the imagined future is presented as the consequence of present behaviour. In their critique, the biblical prophets often depict an imagined future, conveying vividly both threat and promise. The teaching of Jesus includes apocalyptic warning. The book of Revelation seeks to encourage Christians under persecution by the presentation of an imagined future which vindicates God as sovereign in tribulation. In contemporary literature, science fiction presents an imagined future, sometimes purely for entertainment, sometimes to generate hope (e.g. of future escape from earth), sometimes as a means of warning.

The exercise of imagination is vital for scientific endeavour. A disciplined scientific imagination will generate cogent and innovative hypotheses to be tested experimentally. The increasing sophistication of artificial intelligence leads us to ask whether computers can or could ever exercise 'imagination'.

For the Christian, there is an inalienable link between imagination and hope. Certain forms of Christian prayer, for example as described in the *Spiritual Exercises* of Ignatius Loyola, make extensive use of the imagination. The fostering of imagination (e.g. in education) is important as a means of sustaining hope that situations can be transformed for the better. The Christian pastor exercises imagination in entering empathetically into the world of others with the aim of renewing and sustaining hope. The Christian tradition judges between imagined possibilities for the future of the individual and for the future of the world (as in Dante's *Divine Comedy*). Such discrimination, in which the hope of heaven or terror of hell is 'imagined', is exercised on the basis of God's self-revelation (McIntyre, 1987). [*Nicholas Sagovsky*]

IMAGO
The unconsciously held idealized figure that continues to have considerable influence in later life.

A Jungian theme, the imago held by the individual is often that of a parent or family relation. It is not a reflection of reality but an imaginary stereotype, often distorted. Someone with the imago of a severe father, for example, may in fact have had a father who was anything but fierce.

IMAGO DEI
The image of God in which humankind was created.

This Latin tag refers to that aspect of God that is intrinsic in human nature. It contrasts with *similitudo dei* (the likeness of God), which may be destroyed by sin and restored by grace. What precisely the *imago dei* consists of is disputed. The catholic tradition stresses that this facet of the human being maintains the soul's capacity to enter union with God. Protestant thought tends to regard the image as damaged, even wholly destroyed, by the fall.

IMITATION
The way in which a living creature copies another's behaviour.

In a loose sense, imitation is fundamental to human growth and behaviour. From the earliest, children imitate their parents and their peers. As they grow, the number of models increases and the selection of them becomes more complex. It is at this point, however, that the pastor or counsellor in particular needs to take care. In a relationship which is marked by dependency, there is always the risk that the person who comes with a need may idealize the pastor or counsellor and believe that to imitate him or her will provide relief or even cure.

Within the Christian spiritual tradition, the idea of Jesus as a model to be copied has been powerful, in ethics, pastoral theology and spirituality. But the emphasis is not on copying so much as absorbing and being absorbed by Christ, so as to share his life and notably his passion. A movement among young people in the USA – WWJD: What Would Jesus Do? – is a modern manifestation of a popular approach with a long history. Imitation retains a strong influence in contemporary spirituality, even though in the light of modern psychology its dangers have begun to be recognized.

IMMANENCE
The indwelling of creation by God.

Immanence has been expressed, often with neo-Platonic or Hegelian philosophical backing, in sacramental views of nature disclosing spirit. Since the nineteenth century God's immanence has frequently been interpreted as the intelligent, creative principle working in and through evolution and history. Yet immanence has been largely distrusted in the history of theology because of its apparent connection with 'pantheism', a doctrine which calls the whole world divine and thus endangers the distinction between creator and creature. Yet modern views of 'panentheism' (Tillich's God as Ground of Being; Hartshorne's Divine Relativity) which hold that God is in, but is not to be equated with creation obviate the difficulty of pantheism while maintaining God's necessary involvement in all-that-is. Panentheists, however, rarely stress the personal nature of God. Helen Oppenheimer (1973) has developed a model of human immanence in the relation of love between two persons who remain distinct and has applied it to the divine immanence of 'Christ in us'.

IMMIGRANTS
People who have recently arrived in another country.

Immigration is a process which is as old as humanity. Prior to modern times it was more neutrally described as 'the movement of peoples'. There are various reasons for such movement. Primarily these are economic – for purposes of expansion, domination or survival. In recent times 'immigrant' has acquired a negative connotation, at least in Western societies. This is due to the perceived threat of foreigners to the standard of living of these societies. Because of this its use to describe second- or third-generation arrivals in Western societies has become offensive. These groups prefer to be described more objectively, such as 'Black and Asian', 'minority ethnic', 'Hispanic-American' or 'Asian American'. Immigrants are sometimes confused with asylum-seekers or refugees. The two are quite different. However, now primary immigration into the USA and Western Europe has largely been halted, seeking asylum may be the only possibility of gaining entry.

Movements of people in biblical times include those of the clan of Abraham westwards into what became known as Israel, Jacob and his sons into Egypt and Moses and the Hebrews back into Canaan. There was the enforced emigration of the Israelites into Babylon, and the return immigration mainly in the fourth century BCE. During Roman times Jews became immigrants in many cities of the Empire. This movement had profound implications for the spread of the gospel.

Bible translations use words like 'aliens' and 'foreigners' for immigrants. Biblical teaching on how to treat such people is clear: 'The alien who resides with you shall be as a citizen among you; you shall love the alien as yourself, before you were aliens in the land of Egypt' (Lev. 19.34). There is, however, an ideological struggle in the Old Testament between the 'inclusive' and 'exclusive' approaches to foreigners. This reached its height in the return from Exile during the fourth century BCE. It is epitomized in the different approaches of Ezra and Ruth. In Ezra the men of Israel and Judah who have married foreign wives are required to 'send them away with their children' (10.44). In the story of Ruth, the Moabitess not only cares admirably for Naomi, her Judaean mother-in-law, but marries Boaz. From this 'mixed marriage' comes David, Israel's greatest king (Ruth 4.17–22).

The tension between 'pure' Jews and 'mixed' descendants of the post-Exile return (e.g. Samaritans) continues in New Testament times. Jesus is least popular when he suggests that the Kingdom is for Samaritans also. The importance of immigration in the spread of the Christian gospel through the Jewish diaspora in Corinth, Galatia should not be overlooked. It is arguable that fulfilling the Great Commission (Matt. 28.19) requires emigration. And emigrants are always immigrants, from another perspective.

The twentieth century saw mass immigration into the USA from Western Europe, Mexico and, more recently, East Asia and Central America. It saw immigration into Western Europe from Africa, the Caribbean, South Asia and, more recently, Eastern Europe. In the context of contemporary church life, immigrants are a creative influence. They have brought new dimensions of theology, worship and church practice into Europe and North America. Where they join traditional churches they create new life, especially in urban areas where the Church is declining. Where they develop their own church communities they act as a catalyst for traditional churches to re-examine their life and activity. Immigrants from Central America, East Asia and the Caribbean have contributed much to the North American church in the twentieth century. Immigrants from the Caribbean, West Africa and South Asia have done the same in the UK, the Netherlands and other Western European countries. Where traditional churches have been willing to listen, these 'reverse missionary' immigrant Christians have provided a dynamic and thought-provoking challenge.

Immigrants create pastoral opportunities both among themselves and in host communities. Some need housing, furnishings, jobs etc. Others have less tangible needs, such as friendship, hospitality and opportunities for worship. Refugees who have arrived from difficult or even traumatic contexts need more long-term pastoral support. The arrival of immigrants may also trigger fears – expressed as anxiety, or anger – among host congregations. Racism is still deep within Western societies. 'We do not have a race problem here' is usually self-delusion. The problem surfaces when immigrants arrive. It is not, however, in the immigrants, it is in the host community.

There is a socio-political dimension to the question of immigrants. Their presence or continued arrival can be used by politicians to stir up fear. The distinction between immigrants and asylum-seekers is often ignored in this context. The stimulation of fear can lead to violence, even sometimes against long-settled minority groups. In such situations a wider pastoral response is required from the churches. This may include questioning or even condemning politicians or media commentators.

Immigrants are now essential to Western Europe and North America. A younger workforce in these ageing societies is needed. Research in the 1990s into the contribution of migrant workers to the German social security system demonstrated that, without their contributions, it would collapse. A study of the Los Angeles garment industry showed Mexican illegal immigrants were ensuring its survival. They protected thousands of American supervisory, sales and transport jobs. American research has also shown that if immigrant controls were removed, workers from the 'Third World' would enter to do the jobs North Americans reject. This would enable a considerable flow of income to poor countries, helping to ameliorate global inequalities.

There are international conventions and laws relating to the treatment of migrants and refugees. These include the Universal Declaration of Human Rights, the International Covenant on Civil and Political Rights and the International Convention on Rights of Migrant Workers and their Families. All governments should abide by these agreements.

Christians need to question the concept of national boundaries. They help to protect history and culture. Mostly, however, they serve to maintain the interests of the wealthy against the poor. All human beings are children of the same God. The ultimate aim should be to phase out the use of the term 'immigrant' with all its connotations of 'outsider', 'alien' or 'foreigner'. [David Haslam]

IMMORTALITY
See: DEATH

IMPLICIT RELIGION
The kind of religion that is contained in secular life.
In sustained use since 1969, the term 'implicit religion' has three definitions: (1) commitments, most of which take a secular form, but some of which may find expression through 'common religion'; (2) integrating foci within the lives of individuals and of groups; (3) intensive concerns with extensive effects, in which the depth of feeling is matched by the breadth of influence. For example, the supporters of a football team are committed to it, which affects the rest of their lives by acting as a focus and having an impact on the amount of money left for living when the football costs have been expended.

The conceptual approach is similar to that in the anthropology of religion. Students of small-scale societies described the religious system, alongside, for instance, the family, legal, political, economic or other systems. They found that peoples did not know they had a religion but simply spoke of their 'way of life'. The same approach may then be applied to the society from which those students have tended to come (Luckmann, 1967). The designation as religious of those who may not see themselves as such was initially questioned. However, the term 'religion' is being increasingly distinguished from 'Christian' and from moral judgement. Ordinary usage of 'religion' has always employed the term in this way, to refer to whatever in the last analysis a person stands for. The splitting of the religious from the secular is increasingly being seen as a peculiarity of ecclesiastical and sociological writers.

The aim of the approach to the study of implicit religion is to treat the motivation of those who are not formally religious with the same seriousness as that of church people. It sees this as a means of understanding and an avenue to dialogue. This recognition of the commitment of others is preferable to the complaint that 'people will not commit themselves to anything today'. Such attention to intentions is treated as a necessary balance in pastoral studies to the empirical emphasis on cause and effect.

Pastoral observation and care tend to be pervaded by this attention to intentionality. Sometimes it leads to specific policies (such as apply to baptism, confirmation preparation and weddings), or to changes of attitude, or to deeper understanding of, for example, the widespread desire to 'keep religion out of politics'. However, the particular contribution of this approach in pastoral ministry and counselling puts implicit religion within the perspective of religion as a whole. Societies may be distinguished typologically as the small-scale, the historical and the contemporary. Similarly the experience of personhood may be seen as unitary, individuated and subjective. The character of 'religious experience' will likewise vary: between the sense of sacredness, the encounter with the holy and commitment to the transcendently human, which is the particular characteristic of the implicit religion of contemporary society (Bailey, 1997). [Edward Bailey]

INCARNATION
The process by which the word of God became flesh in the person of Jesus Christ.

The Christian doctrine of the incarnation affirms that in the person of Jesus of Nazareth divinity and humanity are related in such a way as to weaken neither. The orthodox position was stated at the Council of Chalcedon, 451, which declared that Christ is one person in two natures. His divine nature is of the same substance as God the Father and his human nature is of the same substance as all of us. These two natures are perfectly united and cannot be divided. Any talk about Jesus which downplays his divinity or compromises his humanity or seeks to separate out the two natures is inadequate from an orthodox perspective.

In modern and postmodern pastoral studies the doctrine of the incarnation has functioned as a reminder of God's solidarity with humanity – in particular, suffering and marginalized humanity – and promise through the resurrection of salvation/liberation. This places an obligation upon the Church as the body of Christ on earth to stand in solidarity with those who are broken, suffering and oppressed in specific social, cultural and historical circumstances. This belief was expressed, for example, at the height of the AIDS crisis in the West in the slogan 'Christ has AIDS'.

In an age obsessed with issues of sex and sexuality the doctrine of the incarnation has also served to remind Christians that God became *flesh* and that therefore sexuality and spirituality cannot be divorced from one another, nor are they opposites. In Christ they are held together. Therefore Christians must affirm that bodies matter, that they must be taken care of, respected and listened to. Christianity cannot avoid issues of sexuality, poverty, ecology, medicine etc., because God entered into the fullness of human embodied experience.

Feminist theology has tended to argue that incarnation is not a process unique to Jesus and that all of us are called to live out and manifest the divine in our lives and relationships. Divinity and humanity are not opposites but intimately related. In some feminist theology divinity is identified with the power of right relation, the yearning in humanity for relationships of equality and mutuality (Heyward, 1999). It is then the Church's mission to overcome all obstacles to the incarnation of such power between people and in the world at large.

In some of the work of radical orthodox theologians, on the other hand, Jesus' incarnational nature is unique but forever changes the nature of embodiment and humanness by catching it up in the mystery of the sacred orders (Milbank et al., 1999). In the story of Jesus, notions of embodiment, gender and sexuality are complicated and Christians cannot simply uncritically buy into contemporary notions of embodiment.

Some Christians would wish to stress that the doctrine of the incarnation, along with the doctrines of salvation and atonement, serves to warn Christians against placing all their hope in human projects such as therapies. Only because God assumed human nature is there any hope for ultimate healing and only by laying hold of this mystery can human beings hope to be saved.

Contemporary pastoral studies centralizes the doctrine of incarnation. Humanity is the place where God chooses to dwell and hence all human beings are worthy of reverence and care. [Elizabeth Stuart]

INCEST
A sexual relationship between those whose marriage would be prohibited by law.

From the Latin *incestus* (meaning 'impure'), the term carried a triple meaning from the Middle Ages until the beginning of the eighteenth century. Two of these meanings were directly linked to sexuality. In the first meaning an 'incestuous act' meant an act of sexual wrongdoing such as adultery. In the second it appertained to a sexual relationship between people whose marriage would be prohibited by law, for example, sexual relationships between siblings or parent and child. Third, it involved over-closeness in a corrupt way between two areas of work that should be kept apart: for example, where knowledge from one could be misused to benefit the other.

While most religious texts carefully laid down which relationships were too close for marriage and were therefore prohibited, there have been notable historical exceptions, including the ancient Egyptian royalty. In the West marriage between first cousins is allowed and encouraged by some religious groups while seen as quasi-incestuous by others. These relationships have provided a space in which fears about the products of procreative familial relationships could be explored. There have also been some rational concerns at some genetic problems being transmitted. From the late twelfth century (Gerald of Wales) concerns were expressed that birth defects in babies could be due to incest. Whether these were primitive guilt fantasies projected on to birth defects, which had other causes, or correct observations concerning the dangers of inbreeding, they show the strong feelings such a subject elicits.

The term 'incest' is currently used particularly for parent–child sexual relationships. It remains an offence regardless of the age of the child. However, there is very little prosecution for 'consenting' incest over the age of consent (sixteen), even though such incest had to begin as an act of abuse against the child when young. In other words, despite the new sense of concern for the adult vulnerable witness, there is a wish to consider that free choice has been made for adult incest victims.

Since the 1980s the term 'incest' has been seen as less helpful a term than 'child abuse'. There are several reasons for this. First, it used to be assumed that 'incest' was something that happened in a family and never occurred outside of it. However, it was found that parents (especially stepfathers) who abused their children did not restrict themselves to children in the family. Second, the term took away from the active experience of abuse by prioritizing the 'family' nature of it. Finally, incest between siblings was frequently underestimated or described as sexual exploration. In fact sibling abuse (incest) is one of the major ways abusive experiences are transmitted. *[Valerie Sinason]*

INDEPENDENCE
See: DEPENDENCE

INDIVIDUATION
The part played by psychic processes in the gradual realization of the self over a lifetime.

In Jungian theory individuation is a process, not a state. Through a lifetime individuals make a personal blend between what is universal and collective and their own uniqueness and individuality. It is not, therefore, a description of how each person attains individuality but of a movement towards wholeness as the conscious and unconscious aspects of the person are progressively integrated. This is achieved through dialogue between the individual and the collective unconscious. Today the term is widely used to describe growth in individual identity.

INDOCTRINATION
The implanting in the mind of another of foreign concepts and patterns of thought.

Although the term 'indoctrination' is generally assigned a negative connotation, it also has a positive aspect. It is derived from the Latin *in doctrinam*, signifying instruction in the doctrine of the Church, and it presupposes induction into a given realm of discourse within which understanding can take place. Viewed in this way, it is educationally valid, provided that the context permits church authority to be recognized as fundamental. When such consensus does not obtain, as in Enlightenment thinkers and pluralistic societies, indoctrination is regarded as controversial or objectionable. Historically, its abuse led to caricature and criticism by Rousseau and others. Yet its critics are by no means free of the same charge – liberal, humanist, rationalist and authoritarian approaches impose their own assumptions, often without acknowledging their controversial nature (Mitchell, 1970). It is now more widely accepted that indoctrination is benignly present in much educational activity. Education opens up new worlds and requires that the learner participate in them in such a way as to grasp meaning. Much emphasis is now placed on educational *ethos* and on shared values. No form of education is value-free, and interaction presupposes encountering the ideas of others.

When, however, the instruction violates or is inappropriate to its context, the process is seen as an attempt to capture and imprison people within a closed and heteronomous view of reality. It becomes a form of oppression, akin to propaganda and brainwashing. In a liberal or post-Christian age the term is often applied negatively to the imposition of religious dogma in what is supposed to be an 'open' context. But it applies similarly to the teaching of any subject where a world-view is intentionally imposed on the students. The danger of illegitimate indoctrination raises a variety of questions: (1) about teaching methods: are the pupils encouraged to think for themselves? (2) about teaching aims: is the aim to promote understanding or to impose solutions? (3) about the teacher–student relationship: is the integrity of the students fully respected in the communication process? Is care taken to ensure that they are not induced to accept views imposed by the teacher which the subject-matter does not require? (4) about the nature of education: is it characterized by an openness to truth, or are certain options effectively closed off? even (5) about teachers, pastors or communicators: what degree of self-knowledge do they possess, and how do they view professional integrity?

The appropriate response is not to require neutrality, which represents a dubious claim to objectivity, and tacitly to commend detachment, non-commitment or suspension of belief as a world-view. Rather, it is openness in the quest of truth. To seek it constantly – whether in a quest for self-understanding or for insight into some other specific aspect of reality – requires openness in communication, dialogue, and the willingness to share perceptions and problems. *[Ian McDonald]*

INDUSTRIAL MISSION
See: CHAPLAINCY

INEQUALITY
Differences between people, and their ranking hierarchically according to class, gender, race and lifestyle.

Complex societies are characterized by unequal distributing of rewards, underwritten by systems of explanation and justification. Pre-industrial societies recognized inequalities as natural and divinely ordained. Modern industrial societies have asserted the essential equality of people, including their political rights. Inequalities are more associated with economic structures, with occupation as indicator of levels of material reward and social standing, correlating with factors like infant mortality, morbidity and access to education.

Contemporary change means that class is complemented by status in determining inequalities. So social citizenship reflects non-market material support through welfare programmes. Consumption as against production-oriented activities gives prominence to lifestyles. Women and black people in the workforce reinforce gender and race in the institutionalization of the unequal treatment of people and communities. However, resource maldistribution continues to be highlighted by class structures, the rich getting richer and the poor poorer in the 1980s. The small upper class has disproportionately large purchase on wealth and power in market economies. This is exacerbated by a large underclass linked to long-term unemployment, one-parent families, inner cities, and dependence on welfare. Explanations vary from blaming welfare and the poor for dependency and criminality, to emphasizing structural inequality in marginalizing groups from the labour market.

Since inequality is a constant feature of the human condition and modern societies, is it a necessary feature? Three arguments should be noted. None explain inequality's complexities.

1. The neo-liberal response affirms inequalities for their contribution to dynamic economic growth. This ignores the cost of social divisions for public harmony and efficiency. It is supported by Christian conservatism.

2. The functionalist theory of stratification also rationalizes inequalities as ensuring important positions in industrial society are filled by the most qualified. Rewards reflect training and compensation for risk. Yet high pay can reflect power and privilege rather

than rewards for scarce skills. This theory is linked to Christian social reformism.

3. The radical Marxist response abolishes inequalities relating to the private ownership of production, distribution and exchange. Yet command economies generate their own inequalities, lower economic growth and major discontent. The position is supported by Christian radicalism and utopianism, including liberation theology.

The collapse of radical alternatives focuses interest on a new consensus on inequality, supported by arguments which pastoral care must address: first, the recognition of the contribution of personal and family pathologies to explaining inequality in addition to structural causes; second, the challenge to the targeting of redistributive policies through positive discrimination programmes in favour of disadvantaged minority groups; third, the dominance of the global market economy, and the importance of competition, incentives and, therefore, inequalities.

Yet this consensus will not remove tensions and instabilities associated with substantial inequalities and their divisive effects on individuals, families, communities and nations. Acknowledging this will continue to be important for pastoral theologians, including recognizing class inequalities and conflict, the value of social citizenship through welfare provision, and the marginalization processes of democracy through majority cultures of contentment. [*John Atherton*]

INFANCY
See: CHILDHOOD

INFERTILITY
The inability of a couple to achieve pregnancy.
A couple is considered infertile when they are unable to conceive a child after engaging in unprotected intercourse two to three times a week for a year. In 40% of these situations the basic problem concerns the female partner. This includes ovulation disorders, blocked fallopian tubes or endometriosis. In 40% of infertile couples the basic problem can be attributed to the male partner. Most commonly, this involves a low sperm count or the complete absence of sperm. In 10% of couples a combination of male and female factors are involved. The cause of infertility cannot be determined in the final 10% of cases. Infertility is more than a biological phenomenon. The human desire to have and

nurture children is strong and innate. When couples are unable to conceive they are confronted with several emotional and, indeed, spiritual challenges.

The first reaction that couples often experience is shock. Many find it difficult initially to believe they are unable to conceive. They may even feel dazed and stunned as they begin to grasp the nuances of their particular circumstance. Another characteristic response is grief. Infertility is a form of loss. These couples have lost an ability that they believed they possessed. They have lost an image of who they are and what they intended for their life together. They mourn. They hurt. They weep. Importantly, they also cry out in anger. They may be angry at God, themselves and even other couples who have children. For example, it can be quite painful for infertile couples to see parents tending to their sons and daughters in stores, at family gatherings and at church functions.

As couples struggle with their inability to conceive, they may also experience intense shame. They often wonder, 'What is wrong with me? What is wrong with us?' Their predicament leaves them feeling flawed, deformed, less than human. It comes as little surprise, then, that many couples who struggle with infertility experience a significant degree of stress in their marriage. In addition to their shock, grief and shame the couple will encounter important decisions concerning how they will address their condition. Some will elect to pursue medical treatment. Some will choose to adopt a child. In both cases the couple may face added financial strain.

One woman's struggle with infertility is described in 1 Sam. 1.1–20. Hannah knew loss and grief. Her marriage suffered tension and strife (vv. 6–8): 'She was deeply distressed and prayed to the Lord, and wept bitterly' (v. 10). These emotional and spiritual challenges moved Hannah to seek the comfort and care of her community of faith. Likewise, many couples grappling with infertility will also reach out to their respective communities of faith. In their anguish they will seek reassurance that they are accepted and not alone. They will seek someone to listen to their tearful laments and angry outbursts. And they will seek support for their marriages. [*J. Patrick Vaughn*]

INFORMATION TECHNOLOGY
The systematic electronic collection and organization of information and its

use; also the consequential automatic functioning of machines.

The impact of information technology (IT) on pastoring has yet to be assessed. The possession and manipulation of data raises ethical questions but also seems to feed attitudes. People may live with the advantages of IT (e.g. automation, ease of access to data) and with a corresponding sense of paranoia – who knows what about whom? Most ministers are likely to be part of the IT culture, using a database for record-keeping and a word processor for work. The provisions of privacy laws and, in the UK, the Data Protection Act need to be carefully observed. But the pastor may also need to guard against pastoral work being conducted with a 'computer mentality'. Possession of information is not enough; it is the interpretation that matters.

INHIBITION
A defence mechanism used to suppress primitive instinctual impulses and their manifestations.

The superego acts to prevent basic urges and feelings, emanating from the id, from emerging into consciousness in the ego. Some inhibitions are necessary within society but extreme inhibition can make individuals unhappy by preventing the full expression of their feelings. In Pavlovian psychology, inhibition designates the active suppression of a response during the latent period of delayed reaction. In neurology, inhibition is the halting of processes already in motion, or the prevention of new processes commencing, the inhibition of opposing muscles.

INITIATION
Rites, ceremonies or instruction which induct new members into societies or social groups.

Most societies have procedures by which individuals who join them, whether by birth or choice, are integrated and drawn into the shared practices, beliefs and values of the group. In traditional and pre-modern societies these procedures frequently take religious and bodily form. Jewish and Muslim males are circumcised eight days after birth. Many primal societies require males approaching adulthood to undergo a form of psychic, spiritual and physical privation – being sent off into the bush with no clothes or staying with the shaman – as a rite of passage to adulthood.

In modern societies initiation procedures have a strongly bureaucratic or educational character, as indicated in the formal registration of birth and hence citizenship rights, compulsory vaccinations, compulsory schooling, the prescription of the age of sexual consent, a minimum working age, and the acquisition of voting rights. Some of these modern initiation practices are enhanced by formal rituals such as graduation ceremonies and professional accreditation for certain occupations. Informal initiation rites may also be attached to various of these procedures including physical ordeals for army recruits or new students.

Initiation has taken a variety of forms in Christian history, most of which have mutated over time. The earliest and simplest form of initiation was the practice of baptism by immersion, by which all the members of a household which became Christian, including children and servants, were fully immersed in a river or bath as a sign of their identification with the death of Christ, and their adoption as children of God. The Apostles saw baptism as the appropriate and immediate response to conversion and the confession of faith in Jesus Christ as Lord. However, in the second and third centuries a much more extended initiation procedure developed. Those who professed the Christian faith were inducted into a lengthy period of training and instruction as catechumens which could extend to two or three years. Catechumens would attend church but had to leave before the Eucharist. After various initiatory procedures including exorcism and pre-baptismal anointings, and at the conclusion of their instruction which was brought to a climax in Lent, they were baptized at the Paschal Mass on Easter Sunday.

Another rite of initiation, confirmation, was added around the third century, involving the laying on of hands by the bishop, accompanied by anointing with oil, as a sign of the reception of the Holy Spirit, and as initiation into the eucharistic mysteries. The rites of baptism and confirmation gradually became more distinct, and were increasingly separated temporally, and linked with the age of the individual initiate. This had the consequence that baptism, at least in the Western Church, became primarily associated with the initiation of infants, and confirmation with the initiation of older children or young adults. Confirmation took on some of the traditional functions of the adult catechumenate as periods of instruction in the faith preceded the rite.

In modern Western societies the growing cultural gap between secular initiation procedures and ecclesiastical initiation practices has accompanied the diminution in the practice and social significance of Christian initiation rites. As churches increasingly acquire the character of voluntary societies, Christian initiation ceremonies may be said to recover their earliest significance as rites which mark out the Christian initiate into a distinct community of values and belonging from the wider society. This may explain why a growing minority of clergy require candidates or parents of candidates for initiation rites, including baptism as well as confirmation, to undergo instruction in the faith and tests of their allegiance to Christ and the Church. [*Michael Northcott*]

INNER HEALING
A general term for approaches to counselling and healing that are largely found in the charismatic tradition.
These approaches (including e.g. 'prayer counselling' and 'healing of memories') are claimed by some to lead people to psychological recovery from deep trauma. There are, however, potential problems of which some practitioners are aware. These are both in terms of psychology (possible manipulation, whether deliberate or inadvertent) and of theology (concerning the understanding of prayer).

INSIGHT
1. Knowledge or awareness of the self or others that penetrates appearances or conventional assumptions.
2. The ability to understand the symbolic meaning of things or events.
Much of Jesus' teaching and conversation may be regarded as being concerned to challenge conventional ways of looking at things and to help people to face deeper insight into themselves in order to bring about change. Ascetic and mystical writers have always insisted on the need for self-knowledge, both as a way of overcoming temptation and sin and as an essential step in coming to the knowledge of God (e.g. *The Cloud of Unknowing*, ch. 14). Prayer, meditation, self-examination and retreat can all be used for this purpose. The difficulty of achieving insight on one's own is acknowledged in the tradition that emphasizes the importance of using a confessor or spiritual director.

In analytical psychology, psychoanalysis and those forms of psychotherapy and counselling that are based on them, the achievement of insight is regarded as an important factor in effecting personality change and constitutes a vital goal of such therapies. To bring about real change, insight must be experienced at the level of feeling and not merely known about intellectually. Such 'intellectual insight' will usually be seen as a defence against experiencing true self-knowledge, which may seem too painful to tolerate. Analytical therapy aims at providing the conditions in which resistance to insight may be overcome. Personal insight is regarded as an essential condition of being able to understand other people and, following Jung, all training institutes in the analytical tradition insist on trainees undergoing therapy themselves in order to develop this.

The cultural resources of drama, literature, art and music all have an important contribution to make to the development of both personal and social insight.

The development of insight, both personal and corporate, may be regarded as part of the pastoral task of any Christian community in nourishing the development of its life and that of its members. It should be borne in mind however that individuals vary widely in their ability to accept new insight into themselves. A pastor may need to acquaint himself or herself with counselling methods that do not depend on achieving insight (Clinebell, 1984). Furthermore, the offering of insight may be experienced by the recipient as very threatening and even as an attack, so that it may succeed only in mobilizing his or her resistance. Careful attention needs therefore to be paid to providing favourable conditions for the acquisition of insight, e.g. trust, acceptance and understanding. The pastor's ability to understand and to help others in this respect will depend on the degree of his or her own insight. Growth in self-understanding and awareness should be an essential feature of all pastoral training. [*Derek Blows*]

INSOMNIA
See: SLEEP

INSTINCT
1. A hereditary behaviour pattern.
2. The dynamic process that directs someone towards their aim.
The first meaning is the more popular. It describes behaviour that is common to

members of a particular species and that is reckoned for reasons of evolution to be virtually fixed. The second meaning derives from the work of Freud and other early psychoanalytic thinkers. Today it is mainly used by psychoanalytically informed people. Far from being fixed, instinct is a dynamic process with three facets: (1) the source, which is a bodily stimulus; (2) its aim, which is to release tension; (3) its object by which it may achieve its aim. As will be clear, the connections with sexuality are close and the theory of instincts as process is central to Freud's thought.

INSTITUTION
An entity in itself which is set up to carry out a specific function, often equated (incorrectly) with organization.
'Institution' originally meant the act of establishing or appointing persons to positions in order to perform specific functions, e.g. the institution of an archdeacon to an office. Today they are thought of as such bodies as family, church, business, parliament, the military or charitable trust. The study of institutions is problematic and complex. It is not sufficient to list what can be seen, e.g. buildings, persons, clergy, liturgy or a church. We need to have an idea in our minds of what a church is in order to integrate these objects, if we are to investigate what the 'church' is, what it is for. Documents can only state what it should be for, but even they originate from an idea-in-the-mind of their authors. Hence we can speak of institution-in-the-mind and organization-in-the-mind.

It is important to differentiate between 'organization' and 'institution'. Institution is the idea of 'the whole' entity and its meaning, whereas organization is the idea of how the institution works, how it is structured and resourced by people, technology, finance etc., to carry out the purpose(s) of the institution. Sometimes the organizational structure is set up on presuppositions which do not lead to the achievement of the primary task of the institution. There are frequent examples when an executive, who has been eminently successful in managing a business, after being appointed to run, say, a hospital, has been a disaster in that post. Such a manager is working consciously with the organization-in-the-mind of his previous company but has unconsciously retained the institution-in-the-mind as a business, and interprets the purpose of the hospital in

terms of a business culture rather than that of community health care.

Organization-in-the-mind is a conscious or preconscious construct focused on intellectual and emotional experience of tasks, roles, inputs, outputs, rituals, purposes, accountability, competence, failure, success (Hutton, 2000). It calls for management. Institution-in-the-mind is an unconscious construct focused on the emotional experience of ideas, values, hopes, beliefs, dreams, symbols, birth, life, death. It requires leadership. We can say that organization-in-the-mind can be understood as a metaphor of the body, and institution-in-the-mind as a metaphor of the spirit. Together they constitute a whole. An example is the nuclear family. 'Nuclear' describes the organization-in-the-mind, and 'family' the institution-in-the-mind.

In the organization-in-the-mind, the elements can be described and measured, as organization is necessarily experienced in a specific context. An example of this is a prison, described as an establishment for young offenders aged 16–19, taking a certain number of convicted young men and women from all over the country. The context is the courts which, by sentencing the accused, send them to prisons under specified conditions. In the institution-in-the-mind, the elements are more difficult to describe because they relate to beliefs, emotions, values and assumptions. Such elements defy measurement although some vain attempts have been made to reduce them to a scale of core competencies. The prison, for example, reflects the culture of its environment and those governors and staff who administer it. Their different views of justice, crime and punishment, deriving from a diversity of institution-in-the-mind, leads to debates about the purpose of prison and how society can best cope with criminal behaviour.

Institutionalization occurs when the members of an institution try to express their values and beliefs through rules and regulation, by incorporating them into their organizational structure. There is no longer any incentive for the members to hold these values in their own minds in creating their roles to express the values freely through their own behaviour. Open boundaries are replaced by closed barriers as human systems become mechanized, and power prevails over authority. The institution becomes bureaucratized with the major purpose of being self-sustaining without paying attention to its meaning.

The proliferation of business schools for management and leadership courses indicates the general concern about organizational and institutional performance. Management relates to organization-in-the-mind and its structures in order to achieve efficient and effective performance of stated targets and budgets. Management relies on the assumption of the prevalence of certain values, e.g. in business: competition, customer care, profit, added value. Other values intrude, like those of the trade unions or an Act of Parliament on human rights, which require attention while pursuing the essential business values. This management development is basically one of skill and competency development.

Leadership development relates to institution-in-the-mind, and the values which constitute it. Whereas management values are expressed through professional disciplines, leadership values are expressed through relationships and come from personal beliefs. These cannot be disciplined nor controlled by others. So any leadership development is based on the understanding and acceptance by the person of their own accountability to the institution, to work to achieve its vision even at the expense of one's own. [*Bruce Reed*]

INTEGRATION
The uniting of two or more distinct groups, disciplines or perspectives into a larger whole.

The subjects of integration differ from one another and commonly exist in tension with one another (e.g. 'racial integration'). In pastoral theology 'integration' typically describes the effort to join two disciplines or disparate perspectives into a unified theory or approach.

Through the middle of the twentieth century Euro-American pastoral studies witnessed numerous attempts to integrate various schools of psychology with the range of approaches to Christian theology. More recently, efforts at integration have expanded to include a variety of approaches to spirituality and a wider range of disciplines in the social (human) sciences, including sociology, congregational studies, cultural anthropology, and linguistics.

Effective pastoral action requires a priest or minister practically to integrate information from diverse perspectives into a coherent approach to ministry. For instance, a Christian pastor must typically connect knowledge of the teachings and traditions of the faith with the assessed needs – psychological, social, cultural, religious etc. – of the persons whom she or he is serving.

The formal study of integration seeks to aid ministers in their development of an intentional working theology. Rather than relying upon an eclectic collection of insights gleaned from diverse disciplines or trusting that a proper rationale will emerge spontaneously in the existential moment of encounter, pastoral theology advocates disciplined reflection upon the integration of theology/spirituality and the social scientific disciplines related to pastoral care.

The following rough typology of some contemporary models for connecting Christian doctrine and the practice of ministry indicates only a portion of the wide diversity of recent scholarly attempts at pastoral integration.

1. *Correlational*. Building upon the method of correlation popularized by Paul Tillich, and extended by David Tracy, correlational approaches seek to connect the questions and concerns of human experience with the symbols and traditions of the Christian faith (Mudge and Poling, 1987).

2. *Contextual*. Empirical examination of the 'lived experience' of races, genders, classes and other groups provides the basis for theological reflection (Neuger, 1996).

3. *Narrative*. The Christian story embodied in community is used to unite Scripture and Christian doctrine with narrative (literary, autobiographical, clinical etc.) renderings of human experience (Hunsinger, 1995).

4. *Performance*. The analogy of fine arts performance (usually musical) hermeneutically connects Scripture and practice of the Christian life and ministry (Young, 1990).

5. *Regulative*. A 'cultural-linguistic' model (Lindbeck, 1984) enables a practice-centred approach to ministry, guided by a functional approach to Christian doctrine.

The pastor also needs to be aware of the theory of child development. In that process there are two integrations. First, or primary, integration occurs when the baby becomes aware of his or her body and that it is separate from other objects around it. In analytic theory secondary integration occurs later, when the child grows into a psychosexual unitary being, all the previously present components now being united into a single whole (Guntrip, 1971). *[Charles J. Scalise]*

INTELLECTUALIZATION
A defence against engagement through intellectual detachment.

A person may discuss a situation or issue in their lives, but without the expected sense of feelings: e.g. 'I am angry' said without a hint of passion. They may talk about themselves in a detached fashion, as if inviting theoretical discussion. This is a familiar defence against addressing something significant. Ministers and clergy are often vulnerable to it. They can easily be seduced into a discussion of theoretical theological or church issues and away from the point of importance in someone's life or faith experience.

INTERCESSION
Prayer for the well-being of others.

Intercession, is, like petition, a prayer of request, but for others' well-being rather than our own. (It can also take the form of a curse, wishing a malediction rather than a benediction, but this is a distorted if understandable human desire and hardly to be contained within the dynamics of the love of God.)

Intercession is classically pictured in terms of a plea to the heavenly monarch to intervene in human affairs for the good of the many or for the good of one. Abraham is reported as praying for the city of Sodom, Moses for the people of Israel, Jesus for the tempted Peter, the Church for the imprisoned Peter. Without due care and thought, this picture-language of plea becomes that of the peasant petitioner on bended knee on the rare occasion of the monarch's progress through the realm, hoping against hope that he or she might be noticed. The versicle and response 'Lord, in your mercy Hear our prayer' can be construed in this way. It is apt to keep praying in a mode of fearful and guilty dependence. It is at best sub-Christian: it assumes an aloof deity who may occasionally be persuaded to pull puppet strings if pleaded with long enough, but who will let the vast majority of human beings continue in their pain and wickedness. Intercession then becomes a cry of anguish, a wordless groaning, a barely articulated 'How long, O God, how long?', and hurls the accusation against a loving God who allows sudden or drawn-out cruelty to even the youngest child.

The passionate plea, the heartfelt hammering at heaven's gates, has always been part of human prayer. At the very least it is honestly expressing the sincerity and longing of our concern. It is the human contribution of love, and we hope that it may meet God's contribution of love, greater than anything that we might imagine but as yet only sporadically visible (uniquely in the love that Christ embodied in enduring to the end). A personal understanding of God seems to require a way that respects God's freedom to act as much as God respects humankind's. This still leaves dilemmas and paradox, but faith can but move among them.

And it does seem that the minor contributions of human love, with the energies of prayer and action, can act as the opening of a sluice gate that the water of God's and others' energies may flow to irrigate the fields. In a strange and sometimes wondrous exchange, divine and human love yearn for and depend upon each other's response. A truly personal rather than mechanical God respects us, respects *our* human contribution, lifts us into the truly personal realm of love and away from that of tyranny and fear. Jesus saw the faith and determination of the friends of the paralysed man: his act of healing was triggered by their desire.

Intercession is made in the conviction that 'nothing can separate us from the love of God in Christ'. It is the faith and hope that all shall be well, even though the result of our prayerful desires is unknown. In bearing one another's burdens, we are kept together in Christ, whatever the temporary outcome, cure or not, reconciliation or not. After a passionate and angry mood has eased there may come a time of silent holding of the other, focusing attention on God and on the other, letting whatever energy there is in our small being become available to the love of God, aligning it with the divine will and energy. Such love in prayer does not necessarily expect, let alone dictate, a wonder, a 'miracle', but is always expectant of such wonder however unexpected its character may turn out to be. The pain of a hand scalded by boiling water may be offered for the relief of someone unknown to us whose greater pain has come from the burns of napalm. The effects of such substitutions of love may always remain hidden to us. At the same time, the 'answer' to such prayer should impel us to act in the world in such a way as to reduce the possibilities of such pain being repeated or increased, whether by donations of money or the practice of skills, and so to increase the likelihood of the good we desire.

What is prayed for varies from the very human desire for a particular effect, especially when we are shocked into prayer by unwelcome news, to the silent holding of the other, asking no more (but no less) than a blessing, that Christlikeness may grow in the other, that he or she or they may be transfigured to glory.

The mighty pray-ers, whose vocation is made visible in the hours of prayer through day and night, take intercession as one of their primary concerns. They sometimes become beacons of God's glory, transmitters (you can see it in their faces) of light. It is as if they keep their faces constantly turned towards God, while allowing others to come and go in their presence and in their mind's eye, that something of the warmth and peace of God might be reflected through them. They may alternate between the prayer of silent attention and soaking their prayer in the psalms, through the words of which all the world and every human emotion pass.

Intercession may also take the form of litanies, with their sequence of intentions and repeated refrains. Such refrains give the mind a sop to lessen its distracted flitting from thought to thought, while leaving the deeper levels of one's being free to continue the praying. Such prayer may have its effect across the separations of death as well as across those of distance. Love expressed for a friend on the other side of the world is much the same as love expressed for a friend on the other side of death. And we may well find ourselves asking for their prayers too, perhaps in such form as this: God bless you richly. Grow in grace. Make love. Keep us in loving mind. Guide us. Pray for us.

There is of course much that gets in the way of the flow of the energies of prayer, not least personal and corporate life that is in disarray, turned in on itself, hardened by cruelty and greed, unaware of and insensitive to the pain of others. The substance of the prayer, for ourselves and others, then becomes such as this: Healing Spirit, set us free ... from fearful memories ... from the grip of compulsions ... from illusion, lying and pretence. And when we turn our attention specifically to those others who are engaged in the work of healing, the prayer will be for both grace and skill, that the Spirit of God may heal through the ministry of those who serve the public health, those who listen and counsel, and those who sit calmly with the distressed.

Ultimately our prayer, with Paul, is that 'the creation will itself be set free from its bondage to decay and obtain the glorious liberty of the children of God'. Our prayer must not be so taken up with people that it loses sight of our care for and hope for the transfiguration of all material stuff. The concern of our prayer is as wide as the universe and as deep as the unfathomable mysteries of God. [Jim Cotter]

INTERCHURCH MARRIAGE
Marriage across denominational or cultural boundaries.

The pluralism of modern society has led to an increasing number of mixed marriages between Christians of different denominations or confessions. These tend now to be called 'interchurch' marriages to distinguish them from marriages between people of different religions, which are called 'interfaith' marriages.

Couples who marry across denominational boundaries find many ways of coping with their differences. Partners whose Christian affiliation is largely nominal are likely to encounter difficulties only at their wedding or the baptism of their children. Marriages in which one partner is more committed than the other may settle for membership of the church of the more committed partner, but this should not be assumed to be the best solution by those exercising pastoral care of the couple; the decision should be made by the partners themselves without any coercion. The greatest problems and opportunities face couples where both partners intend to remain faithful members of their respective churches, and who wish also to participate in the life of the church of their partner. The primary cause of difficulty in these marriages is the divisions between the churches; as these have grown less acute, so the problems have eased. A secondary cause of difficulty is the ecclesiastical regulations with which certain churches have tried to protect their own membership. The greatest difficulties exist in marriages between Roman Catholics or Orthodox and other Christians. Roman Catholic regulations eased with the publication by the Vatican of *Matrimonia Mixta* in 1970. Roman Catholics require permission from their church to marry a Christian of another denomination, and have to undertake to do all in their power to bring up any children of the marriage in the Catholic faith. The other partner is no longer required to give such an undertaking. The 1993 *Vatican Directory* shows clearly that the Roman Catholic Church recognizes the upbringing of the children to be the joint responsibility of the parents, each of whom has equal rights of conscience; and inter-church marriages are explicitly referred to as cases for possible, but exceptional, eucharistic sharing.

All the major churches have recognized their responsibility for the *joint* pastoral care of interchurch families, and working groups of churches in several countries have published recommendations on the subject. However, such joint care depends largely on the mutual trust of local priests and ministers, and it is not yet common.

Associations of interchurch families exist in many countries including Australia, Canada, Ireland, New Zealand, the United Kingdom and the United States of America. Their primary purpose is the mutual support of their members, and information and help for other interchurch marriages. *[Martin Reardon]*

INTERCULTURAL PASTORAL CARE
Pastoral care involving people from different cultures.

Cultural differences are often evident among people from different ethnic backgrounds, even if they live in the same area or belong to the same faith community. There can also be other aspects of culture – for instance connected with class, gender, sexuality and disability – which have a significant effect.

Culture influences people's customs, beliefs and practices, how they perceive themselves and how others perceive them, how they communicate, their patterns of family and community life and other important relationships and the choices open to them. What seems 'natural' or 'normal' to one person may seem intriguing, odd or disturbing to another. So encounters across cultural differences can involve the potential for discovery and growth, and also for misunderstanding the conflict. If an interpreter – however skilled – is involved (for instance if someone fluent in sign-language is counselling a hearing person), some of what is said will be impossible to render precisely. And different codes of body language may be used, so that someone who wishes to appear modest and respectful may be thought to be extremely shy or lacking in confidence.

Where one culture is favoured over another – for instance where European customs are assumed to be more advanced than those of non-European peoples or the ways in which men within a particular community tend to communicate are assumed to be preferable to women's usual ways – additional problems can arise. Sometimes social groups with most power are treated as culturally superior, and others may be pressured or encouraged to imitate them, for instance to adopt their ways of speaking, musical taste or forms of worship. This can lead people to regard themselves as inferior, reject aspects of their own identity or feel resentful. And there can be sometimes unconscious fears and tensions on both sides when they come into close contact with members of the dominant group, particularly in dealing with sensitive issues.

The ways in which people seek and offer support in times of trouble, celebrate when they are joyful and make decisions on important issues can vary. Some are comfortable about receiving formal one-to-one counselling, but in other countries it may be customary to seek guidance from an older relative or neighbour or one with a reputation for wisdom, or talk problems through in a family or community setting. So the most effective ways of providing pastoral care, or recognizing and nurturing this in settings where it is occurring, may vary.

Ministers of religion, lay leaders and counsellors tend to be more directive in some traditions, while in others the emphasis is on individuals being assisted in finding their own solutions. Certain cultures emphasize individual self-fulfilment and the realization of potential, while others give more weight to duty to family and community. In Christian circles, the use of one's God-given gifts and proper self-esteem and love of self may be emphasized, or alternatively love of neighbour and self-sacrifice. Members of different faith communities may have different worldviews and moral codes. Or they may express similar beliefs in different ways so that, for example, a shared rejection of greed for money or cruelty may be conveyed through different concepts.

In preparing to offer pastoral care in multicultural settings, it is useful – as far as possible

– to be aware of one's own cultural heritage, including habits and assumptions which usually go unnoticed, and to try to create an atmosphere in which this and other cultures are respected. Expectations may need to be discussed, clarity sought where there is a serious risk of misunderstanding. For instance, a well-educated black male minister counselling a barely literate white male parishioner may try to be conscious of any tendency on his part to snobbery because of his education or clerical status or diffidence because of his ethnicity, and be mindful of what the parishioner may assume or project on to him. The minister may also question his assumptions about 'obvious' approaches – for instance searching the library for information, going on retreat and praying for guidance or asking the advice of a wise mentor or grandparent – and make an effort to help the parishioner deal with the issues in a way appropriate to him, drawing on what is valuable in his own culture. It may be helpful to find out more about the culture of those who may require care, for instance through books or films.

It should be noted that individuals vary, and may not abide by the norms of their cultural group. At the graveside of a close friend, an upper-class Englishman may break down sobbing instead of keeping a 'stiff upper lip', while a Jamaican woman may be tearless and silent, whatever custom may suggest. In any case, people's cultural identity is often complex. And cultures change with time. A monk who arrives from overseas to teach in a church school in a close-knit mining community may find that the mines have shut, many of the parents are out of work and the children are struggling to deal with change and uncertainty.

In addition, injustice and failure to love (such as violence within families) cannot be justified because they are 'part of our culture'; spiritual growth may challenge cultural norms. For example, a peasant may take up arms in the course of a bitter civil war and become a highly aggressive soldier, then leave the war zone and return to civilian life, joining the prayer group in a local church. Other members, from another ethnic group and without experience of armed conflict, may offer support, and try to make sure that the newcomer does not feel pressured to adopt their customs in order to belong. However, all members of the group may need to draw on resources beyond their cultures in order to deal constructively with the aftermath of social breakdown and war.

In today's world, pastoral care often takes place across cultural differences. This can be challenging while rewarding. [*Savitri Hensman*]

INTERDISCIPLINARY ACTIVITY
A determinative and necessary element in pastoral and practical theology as critical reflection on pastoral practice.
There are four reasons for interdisciplinary activity in pastoral studies: (1) theologically, all pastoral action is directed towards the eschatological completion of all things in Christ who draws all things to himself; (2) pastoral work is with people and communities, holistically, at every level of experience; (3) all practical disciplines, not least theology, draw on a range of methodologies and data; and (4) it is part of the definition of pastoral or practical theologies using 'critical correlation', 'liberationist' or 'hermeneutic' models (Ballard, 1986; Browning, 1991).

This is most clearly exhibited in three areas: (1) at the academic level, in the encounter between theology and, behind it, the Christian tradition, and the relevant human sciences or other fields of enquiry – out of this theoretical dialogue new and creative insights are sought to illuminate the ways of God in the world and patterns of faithful action; (2) at the level of practice, there are pastoral methods and skills that can be (not uncritically) borrowed from different professional and other practices; (3) in the field, it is necessary for different professions and other bodies to work alongside each other. In this respect it is becoming more usual to find inter-professional collaboration, cross-disciplinary encounter and various other means of establishing mutual understanding. In some areas the caring professions, e.g. those responsible for law and order, educationalists and clergy, increasingly work as a team. At another level interdisciplinary bodies have from time to time been set up, such as the Institute of Religion and Medicine and the Churches' Council for Health and Healing.

It is necessary, however, to accept that interdisciplinary working is complex and demanding. Proper respect and autonomy has to be given to the academic and practical fields. It means acquiring the ability to cross frontiers into others' expertise. There is the constant seduction of relevance that can lead to over-simplification of issues, a narrowing down of the field of enquiry, the cutting of corners and an impatience with theoretical enquiry in the eagerness to be actively engaged. Such a dialogue has to be aware of both the incompatibilities and the compatibilities between different disciplines each with its own aims, objectives and presuppositions (Graham, 1996). [Paul Ballard]

INTERFAITH MARRIAGE
The union of two people from different religions.

Interfaith marriage is not to be confused with marriage of Christians from different churches or ethnic groups. A Christian/Muslim or Jewish/Hindu marriage may involve differences of ethnicity and culture, but the sharpest differences are likely to be religious. To the couple these may initially seem unimportant, but inherited values and traditions resurface with the birth of children. What names will they be given? Will a boy be circumcised or baptized? Will one partner still attend church, synagogue or mosque? Will the family celebrate Christmas and Easter? Eat pork or beef, drink alcohol? Maintain friendships in both communities? Even if the couple are not ostracized, family pressure often brings the end of religious observance by one or both of them. Divorce is also more likely. Problems can persist even in death, with the decision between cremation or interment, or the need for burial in separate cemeteries.

Most religious communities have maintained strong barriers against interfaith marriage. The prohibition is a constant theme in the Old Testament, and reaffirmed in 2 Cor. 6.14. The Roman Catholic Church has tried to ensure that where one partner is Catholic any children are brought up in that faith. The Orthodox Churches, like many churches in Asia, have traditionally excommunicated members who marry someone of another faith, although some Orthodox Churches now leave the matter open to pastoral discretion. Jewish attitudes to Jewish 'out-marriage' are particularly hostile, with the exception of some Reform rabbis who will counsel couples. Despite the opposition of the Orthodox rabbinate, European and American Jews marry 'out' in large numbers, in some countries over 50%. Hindus traditionally marry within the caste community in preference even to other Hindus. Wherever

the extended family unit is strong and arranged marriages are the norm, there will probably be fierce opposition to interfaith marriages (Romain, 1996).

Islamic law is interpreted differently by each law-school, but the following generalizations hold true. Muslim men are allowed to marry Jewish or Christian women, though Muslim women must marry a Muslim. This is because the husband should determine the character of family life, and to avoid the cultural confusion outlined above. If a woman becomes a Muslim her existing marriage to a non-Muslim is regarded as dissolved. (There are, however, increasing numbers of Muslim women marrying non-Muslims in Europe.) Muslim law-schools understand the freedom of a Christian wife to practise her faith differently, but the children must be brought up as Muslims, and belong to their Muslim father's family. In the case of death or divorce their Christian mother will usually be given custody of them only until the age of seven. They cannot inherit anything from her, and she cannot inherit from her dead husband, unless he has made a will specifically in her favour. While these strict Islamic rules have no legal force outside Muslim countries they have great moral force within Muslim diaspora communities, and will certainly be effective if the couple settle in a Muslim country.

Such information needs to be known by the Christian minister who counsels a couple intending an interfaith marriage. He or she must be theologically alert to the particular faith, and encourage the couple to explore the issues for themselves as far as they can. How much trouble have they taken to understand their future partner's faith? How much does religion mean to them, and what personal faith do they have? Have they visited each other's homes and families, or home countries? (Is it possible that one partner is already married, or planning a marriage of convenience?) Have they talked together about children, and how they will be brought up? Whereas couples from the same background may not envisage their future life together in such detail, it is vital that a mixed-faith couple do so. Sometimes one partner later rediscovers the family faith, to the distress of the other.

It is difficult to generalize about interfaith weddings in church, since church and state law varies so much. The Roman Catholic Church makes separate provision for all-

Catholic marriages, Catholic/other Christian marriages, and Catholic/unbaptized marriages. The consent of the bishop is necessary if the last is to take place in church, and no Eucharist is possible. The liturgy of the word may take account of the theological sensitivities of the non-Christian partner, for example in omitting references to the Trinity. A similar arrangement may be used in the Church of England, provided the legal wedding has already taken place in a civil ceremony. If the legally recognized ceremony is to take place in church, it must be the normal Church of England rite, without omitting trinitarian or other references. The Church of England must marry parishioners and cannot require them to be baptized, but clergy will obviously want to satisfy themselves that the couple intend a lifelong, exclusive, monogamous partnership before God (Church of England Board of Mission Inter-Faith Consultative Group, 1982).

There are obvious difficulties in requiring people to say things they do not believe, for example marriage vows formulated in the name of the Trinity. But the non-Christian partner may be sufficiently sympathetic to Christianity to accept these forms for the sake of the bride/groom and the other family. The Christian minister who conducts an interfaith wedding service will want to include elements which acknowledge the other faith community, which enable them in some way to feel at home in Christian worship, and which are not inimical to Christian faith. This will clearly be easiest in a Christian/Jewish context, although Jews will have other difficulties entering a Christian church. Appropriate passages from the Qur'an and prayers from Muslim sources can be found, as they can from the *Gita* for Hindus.

The wedding is only the beginning. Those who successfully negotiate the hazards of an interfaith marriage may pioneer new depths in interreligious reconciliation. *[Christopher Lamb]*

INTERFAITH WORSHIP
An event with a common order and a common theme, but which draws upon the faith traditions of all present, and in which everyone present is invited to participate throughout.
Interfaith worship has caused much controversy, but its definition is very unclear. Distinctions need to be made between: (1)

Christians visiting places of worship of another faith community; (2) Christians observing the worship of another faith community; (3) Christians participating in the worship of another faith community; (4) visitors of another faith community being welcomed to Christian worship, which may be altered or added to in some way because of their presence; (5) an event in which representatives of different faiths contribute readings or songs from their own faith traditions one by one, but with no expectation of those of different faiths participating; (6) an event which has a common order and a common theme, but draws upon the faith traditions of all present, and in which everyone present is invited to participate throughout. Of these different kinds of occasion only (3), often called 'serial interfaith worship', and (6), often called 'common order interfaith worship', are the real thing, and some would exclude all but (6).

Some Christians have attempted to allay criticism by avoiding the word 'worship' and advertising an interfaith worship event as an 'observance' or a 'celebration', rather than a 'service'. It is doubtful if the change in terminology helps, and the real theological question may be expressed as follows: 'We can come together to pray, but can we come to pray together?' Praying together implies a focus on the same divine being, which obviously creates difficulties for non-theistic Buddhists. Even among monotheists the differences in theological discourse about God may be felt so acutely that, for example, many Orthodox Jews would find it impossible to participate. It is not only Christians who may have difficulties of conscience with interfaith worship. Yet attempts to remove all possible theological stumbling blocks are likely to produce language that is bland and unsatisfying. In support of interfaith worship it may be said that no two believers of any faith hold exactly the same views, and Christians are assured that God 'has not left himself without a witness' (Acts 14.17). If there is only one God we may surely intend to worship the same divine being even if we differ radically in our descriptions of that being. Can we meet friends of other faiths only in debate about what we hold most dear, and never in common prayer? Is God properly greeted only with debate about the divine nature and never with the common offering of heart and mind in worship?

At heart Christian anxieties are about the

one to whom worship is offered, on the possibility of idolatry, and on the potential neglect or denial of the person of Christ and the salvation offered through him alone. Particular Christian hostility has been expressed to interfaith services which claim to include a genuine Christian contribution, but in which Christ has not been mentioned. Interfaith worship then raises fundamental questions about the character of any faith which does not place Christ at the centre of the understanding of God, and about the nature of salvation and the necessity of evangelism. In response one can say that in many faiths, especially in Judaism and Islam, there is a vigorous tradition of focusing on God alone and repudiating idolatry. The Hebrew Scriptures condemn not only idolatrous worship but also formally correct worship carried out by people who practise injustice and deceit. The sayings of Jesus suggest that there will be great astonishment about who will be saved and who will not (Braybrooke, 1996).

Apart from theological difficulties there will be complications with the naming of any event, its location and its rationale. It is one thing to commemorate victims from different faith communities after a fire or aircraft disaster, in a secular venue like a city park, after planning by the mayor with leaders of the city churches, synagogues, mosques and temples. It is obviously very different for members of a local interfaith discussion group to experiment with a common order of service of their own in the church of one of their members. In the latter case it is likely that using English or the common language rather than the sacred language (Hebrew, Arabic, Sanskrit etc.), sitting shod on chairs rather than barefoot on the floor, following a printed order of service rather than participating from memory – all these and other factors will mean that conventional Western Christian styles and practices in worship will predominate rather than a genuine mingling of faith traditions.

The Christian minister or leader faced with an occasion of interfaith worship must ask the following questions (Inter-Faith Consultative Group, 1992).

1. *What kind of occasion is being proposed?* Whose idea was it? Who will take responsibility for it? Who will support it and why? The most natural and successful occasions are those where the participants already know each other well. Where will it be held, and who will make the decisions about what

exactly is to happen? A neutral venue is often best.

2. *How will a refusal to take part be understood?* It should be possible to explain difficulties of conscience without giving offence.

3. *What are the appropriate themes for such worship?* Shared silence is often the most effective mode of prayer together, perhaps preceded by suggestions or bidding prayers. Peace, justice and ecological issues are often an appropriate focus.

4. *What is the role of the Christian leader in the event?* He or she will want to affirm the members of other faiths as valued fellow citizens without identifying the Church with their beliefs and practices. It is possible to convey a common sense of the transcendent while giving a sensitive but distinctive Christian witness.

5. *What will be the pastoral and spiritual impact of the event?* This will depend on the preparation for the event, the care with which it is publicized and explained, and on the local and national media reporting of it. *[Christopher Lamb]*

INTERNALIZATION
The process by which external relations are transformed into internal ones.
The term is widely used in counselling. It refers to the way that someone may take an external relation, usually of power or authority, and make it part of their internal life. The individual takes into him- or herself the perceptions that another has of them. In Kleinian thinking it refers to the way that the fantasy of an external object is taken inside the subject and so affects his or her behaviour. The term is also widely and usually used in a general sense of 'making one's own'.

INTERVENTION
The initiative taken by the pastor in a family or individual crisis.
In Western society, the pastor is the only 'helping professional' who has unsolicited access to the homes and personal lives of people in crisis. In increasing level of interpersonal effect, intervention may take the form of a letter, a phone call, a chance meeting, a scheduled visit, or an unannounced visit. The form, level and timing of pastor intervention are critical to its effectiveness and reception by those being helped. The basic purpose of intervention is to symbolize the presence of God in the midst of human struggle.

INTIMACY
A state of closeness between people in which inmost thoughts and feelings are shared, and behaviour is open and undefended.

Intimacy is an achievement of human relationships when all has gone well, not only in the context of the immediate relationship but also in the past. An absence of intimate relations contributes to the sense of an impoverished life. Intimacy may be conscious and voluntary, as in a trusting relationship between adults, but it is also unconscious and involuntary, particularly with the very young – for example between mothers and infants. Intimacy with others is both a cause and an effect of mental health. Brown and Harris (1978) have shown that the absence of a 'close confiding relationship' makes a major contribution to depressive states in adults. However, intimacy is not an automatic concomitant of a relationship. Relationships can be habitual and yet not intimate: people can live alongside each other without necessarily making the kind of emotional contact which is satisfying and emotionally nourishing to both parties.

To some extent the capacity for intimacy reflects the quality of the individual's own early relationships. Infants are born with a readiness to make physical and emotional contact with others. If that readiness is not met by an ability in the mother (or primary care-taker) to respond to the baby's needs, then his or her own belief in a responsive and benign maternal presence will become blunted and eventually damaged. A mother may for her own reasons be unavailable to respond to her baby's readiness for intimate contact – she may be depressed or otherwise emotionally unavailable, and find the baby's demands overwhelming; or she may be absent for a variety of reasons. Many infants are able to make use of alternative figures as providers of intimate emotional attachment and experience. These might include fathers, siblings, grandparents, other members of the extended family, nannies, au pairs and child minders. Everyone needs someone to love and to trust, that is, someone to function as a provider of good emotional experience around which early development can take place, and the personality begin to cohere. Without this opportunity, the ability to form intimate relations with others may be chronically distorted or damaged. Such is the need and hunger in children for this type of rela-

tionship that occasionally they may be exposed to the risk of accepting some apparent version of 'affection' from adults who exploit the child's hunger in the service of their own, sometimes perverse, needs.

Sometimes substitute attachments are made to institutions rather than individuals. The child who is sent to boarding school at an early age is, for reasons that are incomprehensible to the young child, deprived of intimacy within the family setting. Children may perceive it as a rejection by the parents, and develop a sense that they are no good, even bad, or that their younger siblings are preferred. In later life they may function better within an institutional setting than in the context of close family relations. Intimate relations are felt to expose such children to the risk of a repeat abandonment, which may have been experienced as a betrayal. The workplace, the office, governmental structures and institutions may offer at the very least familiarity in the shape of some of the features of the early experience at boarding school. Similarly, children provided with the television as a substitute for emotional contact with family members may develop an imperfect sense of the contingency of relationships – the sense that 'What I do has an emotional impact on you, and what you do has an emotional impact on me, for good or ill'. The interaction between a child and a television programme is one-way: they cannot affect the emotions or action on the screen, but conversely they may be left filled with turbulent feelings that, if unable to be communicated to a comprehending adult, may be discharged through action with a diminished sense that their behaviour may affect others. This lack of awareness of contingency may provoke others into avoidance, and thus aggravate an already troubled capacity for intimacy.

Thus early life experiences that have provided individuals with a sense of their own goodness and reliability will form the basis of their own capacity for intimacy. Equally fundamental to intimacy is the individual's ability to know something of the truth of his or her own internal states, whether positive and loving, or negative and destructive. This is necessary if the equally complex reality of others' internal states is to be accepted, absorbed and responded to. This toing and froing within a relationship of the emotional consequences of experience both offers trust and generates it.

A gradual awareness in an individual that he or she is cut off from having certain kinds of satisfying experience in a relationship that appears to be available to others may lead him or her to seek help in addressing this difficulty. Psychotherapy is an important source of such help. The psychotherapeutic relationship is one that tries to explore the issues of trust and intimacy, or emotional contact, within a carefully maintained setting. The therapist tries to sustain the intimacy of the relationship by a careful tracking of the shifts in the patient's internal state, or mood. This kind of work, within a reliably sustained setting, maximizes the possibility of exploring the individual's lack of trust in his or her primary figures, which will include coming to a deep understanding of both constructive and destructive impulses. In this way, the basis for trust in the therapy and in the therapist is built up, thus increasing the possibilities for the patient of intimate relationships outside the treatment setting. [Caroline Garland]

INTROJECTION
The process by which aspects of the outside world are taken into the individual.
Introjection is the opposite of projection, but it is employed in different ways. Possibly its most distinctive use is by Melanie Klein, who describes the way in which good and bad objects come and go through projection and introjection.

INTROVERSION
The mark of a type of personality which is directed inwardly to the person's thoughts or feelings.
The introvert contrasts with the extrovert. He or she has a personality which makes them primarily interested in their own thoughts and feelings.

INTUITION
A form of direct and immediate insight.
Intuition is the capacity to sense or understand something without the intervention of logical reasoning. In counselling, intuition serves the important function of helping the counsellor or therapist to understand what the client is NOT saying. In person-centred theory (Carl Rogers), the term 'empathy' is used to denote the ability to see the world from another person's point of view. This involves an intuitive understanding of the client's experiences and state of mind.

I–THOU
The quality of relationship between human beings in contrast with that with other aspects of creation.
The phrase 'I–Thou' is chiefly associated with Martin Buber (1937). There are two forms of human relating. The first is with 'It' (the impersonal relationship between a person and non-human aspects of the world); the other is with 'Thou' (the personal relationship in which the other responds in a human fashion). The latter is more profound and reflects the social dimension to the life of the individual, whether that between man and a woman or on a larger social scale. 'I–Thou' also characterizes people's relationship with God. Through every 'Thou' we meet the eternal 'Thou'.

IN VITRO FERTILIZATION (IVF)
Reproductive technologies that allow women to conceive outside (in vitro fertilization) the womb (in vivo fertilization).
Initially these technologies were developed to enable previously infertile couples to conceive. However, there is now growing awareness that IVF also has important implications for the control of genetic disorders and even for assisting purely social preferences.

The birth of the first so-called 'test-tube baby', Louise Brown, in 1978 was preceded by considerable pastoral concern about the consequences of IVF. The American ethicist Paul Ramsey, for example, feared that IVF might result in children born with serious disabilities. IVF had previously been used extensively in the agricultural world, but its physical and psychological effects upon human beings were unknown. Given these fears there must be some doubt whether present-day medical research committees in Britain and the United States (had they been in place then) would have allowed IVF at all on human beings. However, in the event, these fears have appeared largely misplaced. Louise Brown and many others have now reached adulthood and are apparently unharmed by IVF. In pastoral terms IVF has enabled many desperate people to have a baby of their own.

The Roman Catholic Church has consistently opposed IVF for a number of reasons. Among these are the separation of the unitive and procreative aspects of sexuality and the creation of embryos only some of whom are subsequently implanted. In theory it is possible to fertilize only those embryos who will be implanted, but in practice the difficulties in collecting and storing sufficient eggs from the woman usually result in the fertilization of more eggs than are implanted (to prevent multiple births a maximum of three embryos are implanted at any one time). Christians across and within denominations differ strongly about whether or not they regard an early embryo as tantamount to a full human person.

New techniques of pre-implantation genetic screening are opening up the possibility that IVF will be used increasingly to control genetic diseases in at-risk families. So, a family known to be at risk from Huntington's disease might be encouraged to conceive using IVF with only embryos being implanted who test negative for the disease. Clearly this has major pastoral implications for those families. Some (especially Roman Catholics) will object in principle to the selection and destruction of affected embryos. Others may object because of the implication that children with a serious disability should not be born. However, others, given the distressing nature of this particular disease, may find this to be a prudent way of avoiding it in future generations of their family.

The same techniques could be used to select other characteristics unrelated to serious disease. An obvious example is using IVF to pre-select the gender of a baby for purely social rather than medical reasons. In Britain the statutory Human Fertility and Embryology Authority makes such a practice illegal. Nevertheless it may well soon be practised illegally in Britain or legally elsewhere. Many fear that this could lead to new forms of eugenics and social discrimination. [Robin Gill]

J

JEALOUSY
A complex emotion, based on the fear of being supplanted, either in the affections of another person or in a cherished position.

The word is morally neutral. In the Bible righteous jealousy is generally ascribed to God (Exod. 20.5; 34.14; Deut. 5.9), unright-

eous jealousy to human beings (Gen. 37.11; Acts 7.9; 17.5). Unrighteous jealousy is difficult to manage. It can be offset by forgiveness and renewed love, but it can also lead to disruption of relationships. Pathological jealousy occurs when there is no basis for jealousy but the person afflicted by it believes that there is infidelity. Skilled treatment is needed. [Una Kroll]

JESUS
1. The central figure of the Christian faith.
2. The historical person who lived in Galilee during the first part of the first century CE.
3. The exalted, eternal figure who existed prior to creation and continues to reign from heaven.

Christian faith and doctrine strive to confirm the unity of these three figures, even though theological scholarship often distinguishes them. Martin Kahler spoke of 'the Jesus of history' and 'the Christ of faith'. Marcus Borg speaks of 'the pre-Easter Jesus' and 'the post-Easter Jesus'. Both of these construals are problematic: Kahler has often been interpreted in ways that steer close to the heresy of docetism, implying that the primary object of Christian faith is a non-historical, non-material being. Borg's categories presuppose rejection of the Christian doctrine of the pre-existence of Christ.

1. *The earthly Jesus.* Scholarship often views the earthly Jesus as a person to be investigated with supposedly objective criteria of historical science. Sayings and actions are checked to see if they are attested by multiple sources or by sources that lacked vested interest in the matter at hand. Attention is also given to which traditions are supported by material that displays memorable content or form or by material that is free of anachronism. Following such criteria, twentieth-century scholarship has reached consensus on many matters related to the historical Jesus. Scholars believe the Synoptic Gospels (Matthew, Mark, Luke) offer the most reliable sources for such historical reconstruction. They favour material thought to derive from a now-lost sayings-source called Q, the existence of which is disputed. The Gospel of John, the apocryphal Gospel of Thomas, and the writings of the Roman historian Josephus are also regarded as important, though secondary sources. Much of what the New Testament says about Jesus is now confirmed

through historical scholarship. He was a celibate, Jewish man who taught in parables, befriended outcasts and spoke of God's Kingdom (or 'reign') as a present reality. He gained a reputation as a miracle-worker, proclaimed an ethic of radical love, and was eventually crucified by the Roman government with the approval of Jewish aristocracy. His followers maintained that he rose from the dead and appeared to them alive.

Other matters are disputed. The diversity of first-century Judaism allows various analogies for understanding Jesus: prophet, rabbi, mystic, social reformer. All these models are explored. A few scholars – notably those associated with the American 'Jesus Seminar' – move away from these traditional Jewish categories altogether. They argue that Jesus was sufficiently Hellenized (that is, influenced by Graeco-Roman culture) to become a generic philosopher. Secondly, most scholars think Jesus' concern for justice was more a religious matter than a political one. Others see Jesus as a social revolutionary who challenged the existing order and advocated alternative political agendas and processes. On the nature and extent of miracles most scholars grant that Jesus performed psychosomatic healings and exorcisms. Some claim he was also known for effecting remarkable cures for which there can be no natural explanation. Very few scholars, however, will grant the historicity of the 'nature miracles' reported in the Bible (e.g. walking on water, multiplying loaves of bread). Some say that Jesus announced the imminent end of the world, and that he was proven wrong when this did not occur. Others think Jesus spoke only of some radical transformation of Israel, and that this did come about through the destruction of Jerusalem and the growth of the Christian Church. A few scholars reject the notion that Jesus had any developed view of the future. Finally, on Jesus' self-consciousness, some scholars believe that Jesus claimed to be the Messiah and may even have identified himself as a unique mediator or embodiment of divine presence. Others think he may have considered himself to be a prophet or divinely chosen teacher without interpreting his role as unique or unprecedented in the history of Israel. Some believe he eschewed all honorary titles for himself and that such descriptions came to be applied to him only later.

2. *The exalted, eternal Jesus.* Christians began worshipping Jesus and praying to him soon after Easter. For Paul, Christians were almost definitively 'those who call on the name of the Lord Jesus Christ' (1 Cor. 1.2). Matthew's Gospel pushes this worship of Jesus back into its historical narrative, so that Jesus is depicted as the object of worship during his earthly life (e.g. Matt. 2.11; 28.9, 17). The theme is found throughout the New Testament, with fullest expression in the hymns of Revelation (e.g. 5.6–14). Doctrine followed liturgy in developing the significance of Jesus beyond his temporal, earthly career. He came to be extolled as one who had existed from the beginning and who had participated in creation (John 1.1–3). He also came to be identified as the coming Judge who would distribute recompense at the end of time (Matt. 16.27). His unity with God was first expressed as a relationship of Son to Father, but this metaphor was applied with ever greater intimacy (Matt. 11.27; John 14.8–10). Eventually trinitarian formulas would identify him as 'of one Being with the Father' (Nicene Creed) and as 'fully God and fully man' (Athanasian Creed). Such reflection both stimulated and was stimulated by an ongoing interpretation of Jesus' earthly life, particularly his last days. His final meal came to be understood as the institution of a sacrament, his death as an atonement for sin, and his resurrection as the beginning of a new age of salvation (Powell, 1999).

While Christians continue to read and ponder accounts of Jesus' earthly life, identification with the exalted Jesus remains the hallmark of Christian piety, whether this is individualistic or communal. In personal piety, the tendency is for believers to make Jesus part of their person by claiming that he lives within them, in their hearts. Corporate piety reverses that metaphor so that individuals become part of Christ's body, identified with the congregation. Pastoral leaders need to affirm that faith involves convictions not open to historical verification. At the same time, they should indicate that Christian faith is grounded in history and so lays itself open to historical investigation. *[Mark Allan Powell]*

JEWISH TRADITION
The concept of pastoral care as found in the religious texts and practices of historical Judaism.

Specialization in pastoral care is a relatively new phenomenon in Judaism. Little has as yet been written that integrates psychological theory with the language and concepts of Jewish theology. The tradition is rooted in the *mitzvah* (ordained commandment) of *bikur cholim* (visitation of the sick). Maimonides in his code of Jewish law, *Mishne Torah* (Book of Judges, Laws of Mourning, 14.1) writes: 'It is a positive commandment of the sages to visit the sick ... The *mitzvah* devolves on everyone, even the great visiting the small and anyone who does not visit is as if he caused their death.'

Bikur cholim has both practical and theological implications. The practical dimension is explicated in the various editions of the codes of Jewish law. Guidelines are described for both the context and content of pastoral visiting. Context guidelines include that one should not visit until the third day from the onset of the illness; that one should not visit in either the first three hours or the last hour of the day; and that visiting should be withheld from those with intestinal disease and severe headaches because visits will burden the sick person. The context of the visit is less prescribed. Nonetheless the traditional texts challenge the visitor to ascertain the needs of the ill person and to pray for his or her recovery.

Theologically the *mitzvah* of *bikur cholim* is derived from the principle of the imitation of God. The Talmud (Sota 14a) teaches: '"The Lord your God you shall follow" (Deut. 13.4) ... follow the attributes of the Holy One Blessed be He ... The Holy One Blessed Be He visited the sick so you must visit the sick.' The biblical source for God's visitation of the sick is derived from Gen. 18.1. In the aftermath of Abraham's circumcision the Bible reads 'The Lord appeared to Abraham by the oaks of Mamre'. There is no stated content to the appearance. The Talmudic sages understood the appearance as God's kindness of visitation of the sick. *Nichum availim* (comforting the bereaved) is a *mitzvah* similarly derived from the principle of the imitation of God. Its contents and context are also codified in traditional Jewish texts. In neither case is there any special importance given to the visitation of clergy. The obligation for care devolves on the individual and community. Historically, Jewish communities have established societies devoted to *bikur cholim*.

Pastoral care in the idea of developing an empathetic relationship with the one who is sick or grieving does not find explicit references in Jewish tradition, but it can be inferred from numerous sources. (1) The Talmud (Nedarim 39b) teaches that one who visits the sick takes from them one-sixtieth portion of their suffering. It goes on to say, however, that this is true if he or she is of the same age and station as the sick being visited. The similarity of age and station seems to suggest that the identification with the suffering is necessary for the full effect of the visit. (2) In that same discussion the Talmud (Nedarim 40b) insists that one needs to visit the sick to be able to pray for them meaningfully. Without a personal visit one will not know what the sick person really wants as his or her prayer. (3) The reference for the *mitzvah* of visiting the sick literally translates, 'And to him appeared the Lord' (Gen. 18.1). The unusual sentence structure makes clear not only the requirement to visit the sick but the nature of that visit. It must focus on the other, with the goal of meeting the other's needs and fostering a healing relationship. [*Israel Kestenbaum*]

JUDGEMENT
1. The quality of discernment and wisdom.
2. The declaration of a moral evaluation.
3. 'Divine judgement', the ultimate determination of the value of human actions by God, expected, in Christian tradition, at the end of the age.

In the pastoral sphere, discernment and discretion have been valued as qualities to be sought, while moral judgement has sometimes been thought of as an obstruction to the client's ability to achieve insight and self-understanding. In earlier centuries this was not so: those who heard confessions were expected to have a grasp of moral theology and therefore to evaluate the penitent's life. The sense of guilt was not of as much concern to the confessor as objective judgement according to theological criteria.

However, since the advent of psychoanalysis the pastoral function has been seen to have more to do with enabling understanding and an honest facing of realities which had previously lain concealed. With this have developed non-directive counselling techniques that rely on the suspension of the counsellor's own value stand in order to allow the client to take personal responsibility for feelings and choices. This has given rise to the image of the counsellor as a morally neutral person to whom the client's values were of no personal interest provided that they were self-chosen.

More recently the values inherent in the non-directive approach itself have been recognized, and with that recognition has come the realization that judgement cannot in fact be suspended in pastoral situations (Browning, 1976). It is possible for the suspension of moral judgement to be itself a form of manipulation, in which the counsellor's own aims remain covert, and that any declaration of the counsellor's own values can liberate the client to make personal judgements. The debate about disclosure of values and religious beliefs is also alive among therapists.

Pastoral care takes place in a social and political context and therefore either supports or resists judgements being made by society at large. It is also doubtful whether Christian pastoral care can ever take place without some recognition of values, norms and commandments by which God will judge the world, since that judgement already impinges on the lives of human beings (Selby, 1983).
[Peter Selby]

JUDGEMENT, MORAL
See: MORAL JUDGEMENT

JUNGIAN PSYCHOLOGY
The psychology of the whole person, linking the conscious and unconscious forces which affect our lives and relationships.

Jungian psychology, as distinct from Freudian psychoanalysis, was named analytical psychology by the psychiatrist C. G. Jung after he had broken away from Freud in 1913, principally because of disagreement on the themes of sexuality and religion. Jung argued that the neglect of the religious needs of the psyche may cause as much neurosis as other factors, such as sexuality. One of his major concerns was to reach out towards an understanding of the meaning of life, paying attention to whatever the psyche offers and valuing all its production. He saw that since time immemorial men and women have needed in various ways to respect some reality beyond themselves and relate to it.

In much of our functioning we operate with our sense of personal identity and continuity, our conscious ego, which mediates between outer reality and the instinctual drives (hunger, sexuality, energy, reflection, spiri-

tuality). The personal unconscious parts of the psyche are composed of what has been forgotten, or repressed because of being unacceptable. Most importantly for Jungian psychology, the unconscious also contains all that is potential, what might germinate, grow and develop, given the right dynamic insight or with the help of a trained professional. What is in the unconscious is opposite and compensatory to what is conscious, either positively or negatively: for example, if we think we are great, our unconscious knows we are also small.

While 'archetype' has been in use since Plato's time, for modern people it is particularly associated with Jungian psychology. Briefly, archetypes are psychological instincts, similar conceptually to the ethologists' patterns of behaviour. They are universal forms through which typical themes, myths, symbols, images, personalities, experiences and the stages of life manifest themselves. All 'isms' are archetypal. The presence of archetypal factors engenders strong feelings, positive and encouraging, or negative and fearful. Myths from all over the world and all cultures tell stories with archetypal themes in them. They often have an impressive numinous quality. Examples include: the well-known pictures of mother and infant reproduced on many a Christmas card; the cross in countless art forms and cultures; and the tree of life from earliest antiquity. Among other archetypes are the following: the two contra-sexual ones, the feminine *anima* part of the man (associated with spirit) and the masculine *animus* part of the woman (associated with intellect); the *puer* or Peter Pan kind of boy; the hero and the heroine; the trickster; the old man or woman (wise or not). The most important is the shadow. It is the invisible dark side of every person, composed of the negative parts which he or she wishes they did not have, and try to conceal. They are primitive, inferior, despised or feared – but essential to being human. And all societies have their collective shadows.

Most contemporary Jungians consider that Jung's views on the anima and animus were too simple and are now dated, whereas the other archetypes he named are still valid as concepts. Each of them can over-influence personality or behaviour. Then there is a complex, an emotionally toned cluster of images and ideas, sometimes valuable and creative, but operating independently of the conscious will. A moderate complex affects the psyche in the neurotic area, and is within reach of insight. If it becomes so strong that it takes over the ego, dangerous fragmentation may ensue, even if only temporarily.

Introverts direct their consciousness subjectively in terms of their inner perceptions; extraverts do so objectively in relation to the outer or concrete world. Few people are crudely one or the other, and neither kind is necessarily more narcissistic than the other. As well as those two main orientations, there are four functional ways of viewing things: the thinking-type person asks 'Just what is it and how does it connect with other things?'; the feeling-type one asks 'How do I respond or react to it?'; the sensation-type observes with the senses, and the intuition-type sees the possibilities via unconscious routes, he or she 'has a hunch'. Jung warned against one-sidedness, the over-development of one or other function and disregard of the others.

Dreams are natural phenomena in which the unconscious psyche is trying to communicate something essentially important. Images in dreams, dramatic events and distortions of commonsense reality all carry the possibility of being deciphered with the help of personal associations and, sometimes, reference to myths. He worked with the manifest features of dreams and linked them to their latent and potential meaning. They do not foretell the future, or gratify wishes and illusions. Rather, the images describe the present situation, so that the dreamer can pay attention and alter course if necessary. They contain the real, objective people of the person's past or present life, but they represent, subjectively, different parts of the dreamer. Some dreams come in series, conveying that a problem has not yet been fully addressed.

The symbols which arise in thoughts and ideas, unlike simple signs, are the best possible representations of something as yet unknown. They stem from unconscious levels, or from nearly forgotten mythical, religious or cultural sources, and they often have a body basis. Coming at times of conflict or when chaos feels imminent, they offer a way forward appropriate to working through anxieties.

For modern people the concept of individuation is important although it is a troublesome term: it might suggest selfish individualism, as compared with an attitude of respect for other people and their needs. Jung described it as a process of the second half of life, whereas now we see it as occurring from the early years on. An individuated person is someone who, in searching for values, has matured to the fullest possible extent of which they are capable, has worked on shadow features and accepted that conflicts between opposites will never disappear. If individuation proceeds well there is good flow between ego functioning and the inner sense of self, but it can never be completed in this life. Jung was not a mystic, but he studied the writings of many historical mystics. From personal and clinical experience he saw the self as both the central organ of the individual psyche striving for wholeness, and a greater power, the (capitalized) Self.

Analytical psychology has developed with reference to people whose lives are troubled with difficulties which they cannot resolve on their own. Jung's writings and those of modern Jungians appeal to people at all stages of life whether therapy is indicated or not. It is humane and flexible because it focuses on the one and the many. It is adaptable to people from varied cultures. Jung himself was religious, widely travelled, a deep thinker, while remaining closely in touch with ordinary human needs and emotions. [Judith Hubback]

JUSTICE
One of the cardinal virtues – fairness.
Throughout history the nature of justice has been keenly debated. It is one of the cardinal virtues and in this sense does not refer to rules or law or the regulation of social interactions so much as to the inner-directed behaviour of one who embraces standards of right and wrong. As a virtue it is not so much a legal concept as that of fairness.

JUVENILE DELINQUENCY
Anti-social and/or criminal behaviour committed by young people.
Juvenile delinquency includes: aggression and violence against people or animals; drug, solvent and alcohol abuse; mugging; destruction of property; arson; burglary; stealing; murder. There is growing anxiety in many countries about violence and crime perpetrated by young people. Various studies have shown that there has been an alarming rise in the number of violent

crimes being committed by young men and women under the age of 21. The concern is worldwide.

Sociologists are at odds over the reasons for juvenile delinquency. They argue that the increase in incidents has been caused by: poverty; unemployment; prosperity causing jealousy; the break-up of the traditional family; unhappy families staying together; not enough discipline; too much physical punishment; influence of violent films, videos and music; decline in moral standards; availability of drugs; child abuse; welfare dependency; poor education and illiteracy; youth-dominated consumer culture; genetic disposition to violence; peer influence. In looking at most of the studies, it is clear that there are some distinctive common characteristics in the backgrounds of the most violent and disturbed young people: their families are unstable – there is violence, anger and a lack of support for the children; there is severe, excessive or frequent punishment and other forms of abuse and neglect; adults with whom the young people are in contact are themselves role models of criminality or violence; there is an alienation from society and its norms.

Although there is disagreement among the experts about the reasons for juvenile delinquency, there is agreement that intervention is important if the problem is to be curtailed. Interventions such as: teaching parenting and interpersonal skills; improving education; preventing child abuse; teaching practical skills for jobs; early detection and treatment for anti-social acts such as harming animals or people, bullying, fire-setting etc.; improved inter-agency co-operation; community facilities and activities for young people; consequences for actions which include praise as well as censure; teaching responsibility and sound values.

The causes and treatment of juvenile delinquency are complex. It would be unfair to say that every young person who engages in anti-social behaviour or violence has the problems listed above. Indeed, some delinquency seems to result from boredom and too much affluence. Some juvenile delinquents engage in a few anti-social acts, then outgrow their infantile behaviour and become responsible adults who look back in disgust on their earlier exploits. Others go on to a life of violence and crime, causing untold misery for themselves and others.
[*Michele Elliott*]

K

KEIRSEY TEMPERAMENT SORTER
A self-completion questionnaire designed to identify the Jungian personality types.
David Keirsey and Marilyn Bates (1978) present the Keirsey Temperament Sorter (KTS) as providing an interim approximation of the Myers-Briggs Type Indicator (MBTI). Like the MBTI, the KTS identifies preferences between introversion and extraversion, sensing and intuition, thinking and feeling, and judging and perceiving.

The KTS employs 70 forced-choice questions. This instrument is much cheaper to purchase than the MBTI and is not restricted to qualified test-users. Although there is a lack of empirical evidence regarding the comparability of the two instruments, the KTS seems to distinguish as well between types but may provide a less sensitive measure of the clarity of type preference, compared with the MBTI.

KENOSIS
The self-emptying in which God in Christ declares solidarity with the victims of history.
The term derives from the Greek verb 'to empty'. Paul alone uses it in the New Testament, especially in the 'Christ hymn' of Phil. 2.5f. In the nineteenth century this passage prompted a 'kenotic Christology' which argued that in the incarnation the Word laid aside the metaphysical attributes of divinity such as omniscience. The moral perfection of God was incarnate in Jesus. However, the hymn's reference to slaves and their punishment more naturally refers to Jesus' solidarity with the oppressed and his teaching on greatness as service (Mark 10.42f).

KINGDOM OF GOD
Primarily not a location in space or time but God actively reigning over creation.
The roots of the phrase 'the Kingdom of God' lie in the notion of kingship in the Old Testament. God's sovereignty as creator is affirmed over all creation, as well as over Israel, the covenanted people. The affirmation of divine kingship is a denial of the sovereign claims of earthly kings (Ps. 2). The

controversy over the proposal that Israel should have an earthly king has left its mark on tradition. An underlying question was whether it was rebellion against God (cf. 1 Sam. 8–12). An answer is sought in the notion of the king as God's vassal, but God alone is sovereign (1 Kings 8). The disappointment of Israel's hopes led to a transfer of expectation to a king who should come, the royal messiah (Isa. 9.2–7; 11.1–9). Deeper disillusion espoused apocalyptic hopes, such as the son of man from heaven whose kingdom is indestructible (Dan. 7.13–14, and apocalyptic literature generally).

The focus of attention in the New Testament is on the encounter with the reality and power of the Kingdom in the ministry of Jesus. The crucial question is how far Jesus, through the totality of his ministry, may be held to have redefined or reoriented Israel's understanding of the Kingdom and thus substantially altered the cosmic view of his followers. Three classical positions on this issue are as follows:

1. *Thoroughgoing eschatology.* Jesus expected the Kingdom in the very near future; Schweitzer put much store by Matt. 10.23 – the Twelve will not have completed their mission to Israel before 'the Son of Man comes'. Jesus' moral teaching was thus intended only for the short period before the end time ('interim ethics'). For Bultmann, Jesus' preaching of the Kingdom was essentially a summons to decision.

2. *Realized eschatology.* In *The Parables of the Kingdom* (1935), Dodd argued that the parables taught the real presence of the Kingdom. In Mark's account of Jesus' initial proclamation of the Kingdom (Mark 1.15) the word *eggizein* meant not merely 'is near' but 'has arrived'. Dodd's etymological argument was quickly refuted by J. Y. Campbell but his interpretation of the Kingdom became influential, although he himself eventually modified it.

3. *Eschatology in process of realization.* Jesus spoke both of the presence of the Kingdom and of the coming eschatological crisis; hence Joachim Jeremias' appeal to the notion of process or growth. Some writers speak of 'inaugurated eschatology'. It is impossible, however, to be sure of what was in Jesus' mind. In particular one must distinguish between the perspectives of Jesus' parables and subsequent interpretation of them in the light of the delay in the coming of Christ.

One factor in such disparity of interpretation is the extent to which philosophical presuppositions have affected exegesis (e.g. the Hegelianism of Weiss and Schweitzer, the existentialism of Bultmann and the Platonism of Dodd). Another is the lack of balance: scholars emphasize one group of sayings and play down others. The 'peril of modernizing Jesus' has not always been avoided. Certainly, weight must be placed on those approaches which take full account of first-century Palestinian world-views, in so far as these can be determined. Nevertheless, it would seem that there is a real tension in the Synoptic Gospels between the presence of the Kingdom and its future consummation. A few further points may help to clarify (Chilton and McDonald, 1987).

1. Eschatology is related to protology: God is alpha and omega. Hence the eschatological world-view contains the notion of God the creator working towards the completion of the divine purpose in salvation and judgement. For those still living in the flow of history there is always a future goal, a future reckoning and consummation. Thus at the last supper, Jesus says, 'I shall never again drink of the fruit of the vine until that day when I drink it new in the Kingdom of God' (Mark 14.25). So also with a number of Son of Man sayings.

2. Those who have spoken of the realization of the Kingdom point to sayings such as Matt. 12.28 and Luke 11.20, which concerns exorcism; to Matt. 11.12–13 and Luke 16.16, which suggests that a new age dawned after the work of John the Baptist; and to Luke 19.11, with its suggestion of the Kingdom present in the midst of the gathering (which included Pharisees). All these passages are difficult. It is hazardous to construe them as suggesting that the Kingdom was present in a permanent sense. Rather, the Kingdom is disclosed in the actions of Jesus – in exorcism or healing, in compassionate actions, in prophetic acts and utterances and even through Jesus' confrontation with those who resisted him. Jesus enacted the Kingdom and drew his hearers into an encounter with its reality (Perrin, 1976). One must indeed discern the signs of the Kingdom. It is given to the humble and childlike, to the meek and pure in heart, to know the reality of God's reign. To the rich, arrogant and unrighteous, it comes as judgement. The Gospels close with the notion of the crucified king (Mark 15.26; Matt. 27.37; Luke 23.38; John 19.19). Hence-

forth, the actualizing of the Kingdom in this world is inseparable from the notion of the cross and the Lamb of God.

The characteristic tension between present and future is found also in Paul. A future perspective is presupposed in the notion of 'inheriting the kingdom' (1 Cor. 6.9f.; 15.50; Gal. 5.21); but its present reality is indicated in Rom. 14.17 and 1 Cor. 4.20. The New Testament itself closes on an apocalyptic note of assurance: the Lamb is the lamp of the eternal city (Rev. 21.23); and 'Surely I am coming soon' (Rev. 22.20).

Pastoral care takes place within the tension of present and future, and is redolent with similar ambiguities and presuppositions. Healing, compassion and forgiveness are themselves powerful expressions of the Kingdom, which also manifested itself through suffering. The future hope signals renewal, peace and fulfilment.
[Ian McDonald]

L

LABELLING
The social definition of deviance.
Forms of behaviour which are labelled 'deviant' vary within society between social groups, and across different societies. Drug-taking is a classic instance of the social character of labelling. It is labelled normal or deviant depending on the social acceptability of the drug which is consumed, rather than on its health dangers or frequency of use. Labelling theory focuses on the interaction between deviant persons and those who observe or respond to deviance. Labelling of deviance is strongly associated with class, ethnicity and gender, hence the marked social biases in the practices of incarceration and punishment.

LARGE GROUP
In the study of group relations a group of more than twenty people.
Different sized groups display different characteristics. The quality of the large group is often that of a mob. Individuals find difficulty in holding to their identity. Sub-groups form with striking speed and sometimes violence (Kreeger, 1975). Society itself may be conceived as a large group (though this is not a total description), as can many

organizations, including churches. Even a small congregation may be a large group. Pastors and counsellors may be helped by recalling that this dimension to human behaviour is the context in which they and their clients live.

LATENCY
A Freudian psychoanalytic term applying to a particular period in childhood when psychosexual development is in a state of suspension.
According to classical Freudian theory there is a definite period of 'latency' in child development between the so-called Oedipal phase (three to five years) and adolescence. During this time sexual development is suspended to allow other aspects of development to take place. This is not true in all cultures nor for all time. The term latency can also be used to describe qualities in a person which have not yet been developed: they are therefore in latency.

Different cultures develop according to their own patterns and may not experience latency in the same way. Theories, therefore, which apply to Western culture do not apply to all cultures.

LAW AND PASTORAL CARE
The law imposes special requirements on those who practise pastoral care.
Making appropriate legal generalizations about the relationship between law and pastoral care is difficult. Various jurisdictions and judicatories assessing the nature of care-giving relationships may reach divergent conclusions. Persons not trained in the practice of law should always consult qualified legal authorities concerning specific cases.

Social developments such as a diminishing tolerance for abuse by persons in power and certain high-profile court decisions are two of many factors accounting for increased legal involvement in pastoral care. Publicized incidents of sexual and/or child abuse by clergy have shaken religious denominations. Such abuse often arises out of relationships of pastoral care. Public awareness of legal remedies and distaste for unprofessional behaviour among clergy reduces any inhibition and disinclination to suing them. Landmark court decisions have made it easier for persons to bring claims in circumstances where professional misconduct is at issue. Additionally, courts in the USA are imposing new duties and higher professional standards for clergy and those who supervise them.

The practice of integrating insights and techniques from behavioural sciences with pastoral care undoubtedly improves the professional character of the care provided. Blending those disciplines, however, exposes practitioners to greater legal liability, especially those who practise in specialized settings. Factors like the amount and nature of training pastors receive, and the kinds of responsibilities undertaken, are influential variables in assessing how the courts will treat pastors in determining legal duty and responsibility for harm done to constituents (Bisbing *et al.*, 1995).

There are several areas of vulnerability. Predicting every potential situation in which pastoral care ministry can lead to entanglements with the law is impossible. We may, however, highlight a few areas of concern from past and current experience. We can think generally about responsibility in these categories: accountability for (1) the nature of the professional relationship; (2) the information people reveal; (3) the characterizations of people under care made to third parties; and (4) the faithful provision of care.

1. *The concept of fiduciary duty.* Underlying many tortious acts is the legal concept of fiduciary duty which has been extended to the clergy-parishioner relationship. Essentially, 'a fiduciary relation exists between two persons when one of them is under a duty to act for or to give advice for the benefit of another upon matters within the scope of the relation' (*Moses*, 1993, p. 11). We should note that the ordinary clergy–parishioner association does not necessarily imply the creation of a fiduciary relationship. A court, however, may consider (a) the nature of the relationship, (b) the vulnerabilities of the parishioner, (c) the duties undertaken, and (d) the type of interaction that creates trust and reliance, and conclude that it should hold the pastor responsible for a higher standard of care. Those types of pastoral-care training that place a high premium upon self-awareness by the practitioner might inadvertently and erroneously lead to the impression that such self-awareness is primary in the pastoral relationship. Such self-understanding is unquestionably important for providers to avoid imposing their values or confusing their problems with those of their constituents. The courts, however, consider the interests and needs of the one receiving care as primary.

Failure to place constituent interests above those of the provider can predictably lead to a breach of fiduciary responsibility (see *Moses*, 1993).

2. *Confidentiality.* Responsibility managing confidential information received in the context of pastoral care is important to avoid legal liability. Some denominations require pastors to keep confidential the information communicated in the pastor–parishioner relationship. Breaching confidentiality may thus be a violation of the standards of pastoral practice within one's denomination and by that contribute to a claim of negligence raised by an injured party. Such a breach may also become actionable in a court of law if the offender violated 'clergy–penitent' statutes existing in a given legal jurisdiction. Cases involving a breach of confidentiality sometimes arise from preaching or in social conversation with other members of the pastor's parish. Counsellors under supervision need to take special precautions to protect the information given to them by counsellees and always obtain written permission before discussing their cases. Exceptions to this general rule include those highly specialized situations where the law may require pastors to violate confidences (e.g. where persons are in imminent danger such as suicide or homicide or in cases of child neglect or abuse where statutory authority requires reporting).

3. *Defamation.* Sometimes pastors are called upon to provide information about their constituents to third parties. Even when parishioners give written permission to discuss their lives and the circumstances of their care, pastors must be careful that their representations are fair and factual. Defamation charges (also referred to as 'libel' when written and 'slander' when oral) may be filed when persons claim to be harmed by false or misleading information detrimental to their well-being. For example, because the speaker is a professional, care must be taken to avoid couching 'opinion' statements as 'fact' or 'fact' as 'opinion'.

4. *Negligence and malpractice.* Generally, ordinary negligence arises from those situations where pastoral care providers owed the complainant a duty of care; the duty was breached; the aggrieved party's injury was caused by the breach, and the injured party suffered damages. Professional malpractice may be viewed as a specific subset of negligence arising out of duties owed to persons

under the care of or in relationship to professionals. In situations where claims of negligence or malpractice are likely, pastoral care providers should not undertake the task of determining responsibility without the help of local legal counsel. Such claims are sometimes difficult to prove owing to a lack of consistent standards across ecclesiastical lines. Increasingly, however, trial courts are upholding malpractice claims and they are being sustained at the appellate level.
[Reginald D. Burgess]

LAY MINISTRY
See: MINISTRY, LAY

LAYING ON OF HANDS
The act of touch which accompanies prayer for an individual.
In Christian sacramental usage the laying on of hands on the head is a part of episcopal confirmation and ordination. Laying on of hands, or touch, is also felt to be a natural part of prayer for the sick whether or not such prayer is seen as a sacramental act.

The use of touch and laying on of hands in ministry to the sick is believed to be following the example of Christ. The healing miracles did not invariably involve the use of touch but where it is mentioned Jesus appears to have touched the afflicted part. Sacramental laying on of hands has normally focused on the head or shoulders; this has come to be considered by many to be good practice for all ministry to the sick. Such a suggested restriction has become more common in the context of accusations of abuse and inappropriate touch within the healing ministry. Often, therefore, laying on of hands occurs either in public or, if in private, when there is more than one person present. Christ himself touched the parts of the body that he was healing (Matt. 8.14–15; Mark 8.26) and it is to be questioned whether such a restriction is of benefit to the sick. There may be occasions when it is appropriate for the pastor to touch the part of the body affected by illness, particularly if requested by the sick person. There is certainly anecdotal evidence to support the claim that individuals have sometimes experienced sensation coming through the hands of the person praying, and thus the placing of the hand on the part of the body which is diseased has therapeutic relevance. But clearly the touching of a sick or distressed person will always be a matter involving the highest professional and personal standards

so that prayer ministry is not debased into exploitation of the weak. [Stephen Parsons]

LEADERSHIP
A process in which one or more persons: (1) work with constituents to discover an appropriate vision of a preferred future for the group; (2) marshal those key persons and resources required for the vision to become a reality; (3) gain the co-operation of most in the group, so that movement is made towards the vision.
Leadership studies in the last century have identified the sources, tasks and attributes of leadership. For years, writings focused on learnings about leadership sought from the lives of 'born leaders'. Later, many disciplines contributed to a broader understanding of leadership that can be found and developed in most people. While many theories abound on each aspect of leadership, there are common findings in most research.

Many elements influence leadership potential, including early development, psychological and social sources, personal traits, education and experience. The tasks of leadership include discerning vision, building and motivating a team, communication, discovering and affirming values, embodying the vision, insuring integrity, and managing. Kouzes and Posner (1993) assert that people expect certain attributes in their leaders: character (honesty and consistency), competence (ability and effectiveness), and inspiration (energy and passion). Leaders who combine these elements have the credibility necessary to make change possible.

Some contemporary understandings that often inform pastoral leadership include transformational leadership (James MacGregor Burns), servant leadership (Robert Greenleaf), the learning organization (Peter Senge), and visionary leadership (Warren Bennis and Burt Nanus). For religious leadership, Max Weber's (1922) distinction between 'priest' and 'prophet' has been useful. The priest leads within an established group with particular norms and standards. The prophet is an agent of change who challenges the established normative order. Pastoral leaders function normally in both roles as they seek to lead from the centre of religious institutions (priest) and from the edge of established patterns (prophet).

Weber's concepts of the 'legitimatization

[*sic*] of authority' are also helpful. He described legal, traditional and charismatic bases of authority. There are, as well, multiple sources of legitimization for pastoral leadership. Some religious leaders are wary of authority, but appropriate authority is essential to effective leadership. The first source of authority is the leader's calling from God. Second is the confirmation of that personal calling by the religious body itself. The third source of a leader's authority comes from the leadership context. A person may be designated for a leadership position, but the authority needed to lead must be worked out among the people with whom the leader serves. One might think of these sources of authority as theological, ecclesial and contextual.

From its beginning, the Church and other religious communities have recognized the need for some persons to be set apart for leadership of the community. Pastoral leadership is always exercised on behalf of, and for the sake of, the faith community and its faithful witness. For example, in the Bible, many persons assume leadership roles and offices. However, such leadership positions never belong exclusively to the individuals. Rather, the leadership responsibility remains always with the total community of faith. The community expects faithful stewardship of this leadership. Honour and authority are never separated from responsibility and effectiveness. Leadership is a trust from the larger community.

Mary Parker Follett (1941) spoke of 'multiple leadership' as a dynamic and fluid process in which leadership emerges from different people at different times in different ways. It is not a rigid or arbitrary allocation of leadership tasks. It is a creative way of working together as needed and appropriate to accomplish a shared vision. It is often in times of renewal that whole generations of different leaders emerge. Conventional assumptions about who are leaders and who are not do not stop this multiple leadership from flowering, unlimited by distinctions based on class, gender, race or ordained status. In the last century, pastoral leadership has been expanded through the emerging multiple leadership of laity, women, racial–ethnic minorities and persons from different social classes. The concept of multiple leadership also helps dispel the myth that some are leaders and others are followers. Multiple leadership expects all to function as leaders and followers at different times. An emerging

understanding of pastoral leadership is that power and leadership gifts multiply when shared. Pastoral leaders increasingly understand power not as a fixed sum that must be carefully appropriated, but as an infinitely expandable sum. Different people within the faith community become strong for their particular callings and, at the same time, make sure that all other colleagues are strong for their own callings. A corollary to multiple leadership is the emergence of more inclusive pastoral leadership. Inclusiveness in pastoral leadership combines diversity of people and ideas with an overall unity of purpose, direction and commitment. Without a unifying centre, mere inclusion becomes only a gathering of unrelated differences. Diversity in leadership has been a challenge for many religious communities in practice, though virtually all affirm the value today. Diversity is seen not as something to endure, but rather as something to celebrate.

Leadership is essential for religious communities because it links past and future. All faithful leadership emerges out of the history, beliefs, values and traditions of faith communities. However, the task of leadership is to help the faithful discern what is their calling in the present day to meet the changed circumstances, new realities and emerging needs. To the extent that those called to pastoral leadership are able to accomplish this goal, there is vitality and renewal within the religious community. Pastoral leadership is never finally about personal authority, a leader's style, or a management process, but rather about the faithful future of faith traditions and communities. [*Lovett H. Weems Jr*]

LEARNING COMMUNITIES
Organizations distinguished by educational and communal qualities of a mutually supportive kind.

Interest in 'learning communities' as such first appeared in the Japanese and American business worlds of the mid-1980s (although the term used in the business context is more often 'learning organizations'). Driving this interest was a culture of constant change, which meant that many businesses had to adapt or die. A readiness to live with innovative ideas and encourage risk-taking thus became a key feature of the learning organization. Other institutions, including the educational world itself, have been slow to take the insights of business into their systems. On the Christian scene, the Church in the USA somewhat tentatively led the way (Senge, 1990). By the late 1990s, there was still no agreed definition of 'learning communities'. Much of the literature was still of a 'pick-and-mix' variety, setting out lists of characteristics rather than a coherent model. But some in-depth analysis was being done, not least in relation to the key concepts of 'education' and 'community', and the 'added value' given by drawing these two concepts into a complementary relationship.

Learning communities are not of any particular size or structure. They can be large bodies or small groups, formal or informal associations, and organizations from very different sectors of society (e.g. education, health, industry, law and order, religious life) and, educationally, learning communities are not so much about instruction and training as about 'learning how to learn'. A core feature is openness to a rapidly changing world; to what may disturb as well as surprise the learner. The focus is not on a subject or technique as such, but on life as a whole and how to live it in a more flourishing way. Education is seen as a process of questioning, using the learner's intuitive as well as rational ability, and as an ongoing journey of discovery. Such learning is shared and public, not individualistic and private (Clark, 1996).

Communally, learning communities demonstrate a quality of relationships which adds a powerful dynamic to the learning process. This quality is shown above all in the way people feel about the organization of which they are members; in particular, whether they feel physically secure, have a sense of significance and experience a sense of solidarity. These core sentiments are, in turn, rooted in the values and beliefs on which the organization is founded. By definition, learning communities will be open to learning from and contributing to the life and work of other learning communities. Where this openness exists on a wide scale, terms such as 'the learning city' and 'the learning society' are emerging.

The Church has an enormous amount, theologically and empirically, to give to and gain from the concept of the learning community. But that contribution will depend on whether the churches can become more learning communities than often appeared evident in the late 1990s. [David Clark]

LEARNING DISABILITY
See: DISABILITY

LIBERATION THEOLOGY
A type of political theology that emerges from Christian theological reflection arising from direct engagement on the side of oppressed people seeking social and political liberation in Latin America.

The concept of liberation came into Latin American theological usage in the late 1960s. It denotes: (a) freedom *from* all that inhibits and oppresses; (b) freedom *for* the growth and development of whole peoples who have been oppressed to the point of annihilation. Liberation is not an abstract, metaphysical concept but rather an active, corporate, human, social and political struggle. It has no connotation of being an intra-psychic or individual process, as it might have in the Western practice of pastoral care.

Liberation theology is a secondary activity. It follows a primary concrete option for the oppressed and their liberation struggle. This experience is then placed in reflective dialogue with the Christian tradition. This allows a reconstruction of theology so that it no longer serves the interests of the powerful against the powerless. Liberation theology can be characterized as committed, political, practical, ideologically self-aware, biased, historical, relative, complete and universalistic (Pattison, 1997). Liberation theology emphasizes the socially influenced nature of all human institutions and ideas. Churches and theologies thus reflect their social context and serve the interests of human groups. Where there is conflict and division between groups, theology and ecclesiastical practices are not characterized by a divine neutrality. They serve the interests of a particular group. When neutrality is impossible and bias is inevitable, the Church must make an active option for the struggle of the oppressed against their oppressors. It should not collude, knowingly or inadvertently, with the forces of injustice.

To explore contemporary social reality, liberation theology uses the insights and methods of the social sciences. Sociology, economics and other relevant social sciences are the primary tools for exposing the nature of society and the structures of injustice and oppression and the place of the Church and theology within it. Only then is any attempt made to produce theological insights relevant to the liberation struggle.

Liberation theology is socio-culturally specific and contextual. It does not seek to be universalizable to all parts of the world. However, because it has a strong, well-developed, practice-focused methodology, it is possible to use it to create an illuminating critique of pastoral care in the Northern hemisphere. By adapting Segundo's 'hermeneutic circle' (Segundo, 1977), a methodological spiral can be constructed. This permits the application of some of the insights and methods of Latin American liberation theology to Western pastoral practice without compromising either. The spiral has five stages commencing with (a) the theoretical insights and methods of liberation theology which (b) arise from the suspicion that the practice, theory and theology of pastoral care may have covert social and political effects and implications. This leads to (c), analysis of the context of pastoral care and particularly of matters of injustice and inequality, using social scientific insights and methods. Thereafter, (d) pastoral care itself is analysed and, if found to be colluding with forces of oppression, it is reoriented towards the interests of the oppressed and powerless. This practical reorientation (e) produces new insights and questions. Thus, one cycle of the spiral is completed and another begins.

The insights and methods of liberation theology offer many challenges to pastoral practice with, for example, people with mental health problems (Pattison, 1997). They highlight the need to see all ecclesial activity and thought in their broadest sociopolitical and ethical context and require the integration of social justice with love and care for the individual. They question the political neutrality of pastoral care and direct it towards a bias to the oppressed. Social and political causes of diminishment and suffering are made clear. Pastoral workers are confronted with the necessity for social and political awareness and commitment as well as personal care. Liberation theology thus provides a necessary counterbalancing critique of the individualistic bias that tends to dominate pastoral care.
[Stephen Pattison]

LIBIDO
A key term in Freudian theory of the sexual instinct, but used more generally by others.
Libido, Latin for 'desire', was an important component in Freud's original theory of instinctual drives – especially the channelling of the sexual instinct. Jung used it to refer to general psychic energy. Others have regarded it as object-seeking not pleasure-seeking, with the primary human drive being towards good relationships. The term is best treated with caution. Its use depends to some extent on the school of the user. It remains a core component of Freud's fundamental theory.

LIMIT-SETTING
The setting of boundaries of permissible behaviour in any social activity or relationship in order to define and protect the space in which these may be safely pursued.
In addition to its obvious importance in childcare and penal work, the setting of limits is an essential feature of counselling, psychotherapy and pastoral care.

In counselling and psychotherapy the need for limits arises both from ethical considerations and also from the particular therapeutic method employed. These limits constitute the framework, structure or space in which the therapy is conducted. Some are established explicitly through an initial contract under which practical arrangements such as frequency, duration, times of sessions, fees, confidentiality, the working procedures of the therapist, and possible goals for therapy are agreed. Others may arise implicitly through the modelling behaviour of the therapist, including a clear differentiation of roles between counsellor and client, and the limitation of their relationship to the sessions for the duration of counselling. While the establishment of these limits depends on an explicit request for help by the client, it is the responsibility of the counsellor to establish and maintain them and to ensure that as far as possible changes are only made after adequate consultation (Jacobs, 1993).

Differentiation of roles helps counsellors to keep their own problems from obtruding. The clear boundary between the counselling and a social relationship may help to make it a safe place for dangerous feelings such as envy, greed or hatred to be expressed and explored, particularly as they arise in relation to the counsellor. It also makes transference open to examination. By setting limits to what the client and counsellor may realistically expect from each other, they may both be protected from any tendency to act out collusive fantasies such as that of the omnipotent parent/counsellor rescuing the helpless infant/client.

Limits define not only what does not belong to the client, but also what does, thus enabling clients to take responsibility for the use made of the space that is theirs. Furthermore, the structure provided by limits helps maintain the overall purpose of the work, so that whatever happens, be it silence, play, interaction or introspection, can be understood and responded to in the light of that purpose and not with the meaning that it might have on social occasions.

In contrast to counselling and psychotherapy, pastoral care, apart from occasions of formal ministry, is typically characterized by informal encounters. Needs are often not made explicit; there is often no clear boundary between pastoral and social aspects of the meeting; and the freedom of the pastor to act unasked and to be spontaneous (and even self-disclosing) in a more mutual relationship are important features. Any simplistic attempt to impose the boundaries of a counselling structure puts these at risk. There are, however, drawbacks if limits are not set. These may be obscured by a common tendency to idealize informality, mutuality and lack of structure as 'real' or 'Christian' caring and to regard limits as contrary to the biblical injunction to go the second mile, and therefore to true Christian loving. Among these disadvantages may be a tendency to lose a sense of pastoral purpose in what may then become simply a social encounter (routine visiting becomes pointless); a tendency to superficiality in pastoral relationships due to the inhibition of negative feelings; and finally the possibility that relationships may develop in ways which become inappropriate or unmanageable, usually leading to an abrupt and unhelpful termination.

Limit-setting should be as much a feature of pastoral care as it is of counselling and therapy, but in a manner that safeguards its distinctive features. To the extent that a relationship is pastoral and not simply personal, it will have, in addition to the ethical commitment of the pastor, (1) a pastoral purpose, (2) a need to manage time, (3) a sense of the symbolic meaning of the pastor's role (Jacobs, 1989).

1. The pastor needs to develop clear though flexible goals and, where appropriate, share them with the parishioner. As a result, if the latter agrees to these goals, some simple negotiation of appropriate conditions can be made. 'I have called to see how things are with you' is a statement of pastoral purpose which, if accepted, can enable the pastor to suggest, for example, that the TV be turned off or that it might be more convenient to return another time. Where appropriate, the pastor may suggest a more formal structure for counselling or religious ministry. Often, however, the pastoral purpose will be left unspoken. Someone who is housebound, for example, may gain important pastoral support by regular visits, such as for 'a cup of tea', which may be the overt purpose of the visit. The pastor will then need to keep a clear sense of pastoral purpose inside him- or herself if the disciplines of good listening and supportive counselling are to be maintained.

2. Pastors have to balance the needs of individual parishioners with their own personal needs and those of their families. Limit-setting is thus important in the management of time. Pastoral visits (and committee meetings) may be unduly prolonged or avoided because of a difficulty in ending. To avoid what may be thought to be a hurtful rejection, pastors may find themselves offering excuses for leaving, with the curious but unspoken implication that if it were not for other demands on their time they would not leave at all. Some people are needy and demanding and can make the pastor feel guilty about leaving. Time limits in this case will be particularly important if the relationship is to be sustained without damage to either party or to the work of the pastor. Furthermore, the pastor's need to be loved, to be all-loving and caring, or to be important, might tempt him or her to behave unhelpfully, and supervision from a colleague may be needed in helping the pastor to set appropriate limits. Simple statements such as 'I have thirty minutes for us to talk' and 'I have to go now', though they may occasionally bring protest, may also bring relief in protecting both pastor and parishioner from fantasies of omnipotence.

3. The symbolic and transference significance of the pastor's role for the parishioner (as representing God, the Church, or parental figures) may endow the pastor's presence (or absence) with powerful meaning. There is therefore a need to be aware of the implications for the parishioner of the behaviour of the pastor, e.g. regularity/irregularity, consistency/arbitrariness, giving/withholding, and for pastors to regulate their behaviour and accept appropriate limits accordingly,

including of course any impulse to act out the projection.

Limits are not merely limitations. They are necessary conditions for work to be done, for relationships to be sustained and for space to be explored. They deserve more attention than is commonly given. *[Derek Blows]*

LISTENING
Paying attention and responding with the intent of understanding the speakers' feelings and content.

Paying attention involves heeding verbal content and non-verbal signs, such as vocal delivery and bodily clues. Verbal content means the feelings, experiences, actions and thoughts that speakers describe. Vocal delivery includes such factors as tone of voice, pitch, voice level, intensity, inflection, spacing of words, emphases, silences and fluency. Postures, facial expressions, movements, involuntary reactions (blushing, sweating, crying, etc.) and focuses of attention constitute the bodily clues. These visual and vocal signs indicate the type and depth of feelings that speakers have about the contents of their statements.

Responding skills are ways of replying that draw out speakers' feelings and content. The two basic responding skills are paraphrasing and probing. Paraphrasing means stating the substance of speakers' statements briefly and non-judgementally in listeners' own words. Paraphrasing does three important things: it offers speakers chances to correct listeners' misunderstandings; it invites speakers to clarify their messages; it engages listeners in the insight-generating activity of articulating speakers' feelings and content. Probing means asking speakers for clarification. Short probes such as minimal prompts ('Yes', 'I see', and 'Hmmm') and accents (repetitions of one, two or three words of speakers' statements) should be used frequently. Because longer probes (i.e. statements and questions) tend to focus the conversation away from speakers' agendas, they should be used infrequently.

Consideration of conversations' dynamic, symbolic and social contexts provides information about their meaning. The relationship between speakers and listeners constitutes the dynamic context. For example, a speaker's negative feelings about a listener might indicate that the positive content of her statement was actually sarcasm. The symbolic context consists of meaning conveyed by the environment and the listener's role, attire and actions. The power of these factors is shown by research which indicates that identified pastors counselling in church buildings are more effective than the same persons, identified as counsellors, in secular settings.

The social context includes such group distinctions as gender, sexual orientation, age, ethnicity or nationality, religious affiliation, occupation and social class. The meaning of words (e.g. 'knock one up' = 'awaken' (UK) but 'impregnate' (US)) and non-verbal clues differs in various sociological groupings. Further, people use clues and language differently with those inside their social group than they do with those on the outside. For example, women sometimes call each other 'girl' as a form of endearment, yet many of these will not use the term in mixed company because men sometimes belittle women by calling them girls.

Three barriers interfere with listening: distractions, evaluations and differences. (1) Distractions are listeners' needs and issues that interfere with their listening. Strong feelings about speakers or their stories are a common form of distraction. Though such feelings are normal and unavoidable, it is important that listeners be aware of them, acknowledge them and let them go. Because listening is hard work, physical tiredness is another common distraction. To increase their energy, listeners need to get enough rest and exercise, and limit times of intense listening. (2) Evaluations, both positive and negative judgements, of the truth of speakers' statements hinder understanding of speakers' feelings and content. By contrast, simply accepting speakers' statements as their descriptions of their experience (non-judgemental listening) helps listeners understand speakers. Listeners must be aware of their evaluations, acknowledge that these judgements relate to their needs and issues more than to speakers' problems, and then let their judgements go. (3) Two differences that interfere with understanding are listeners' social groupings and personal filters. Participation in one set of social groupings (e.g. white, male, upper-middle class, heterosexual, Protestant, English) makes it difficult fully to understand the words and feelings of speakers from a different set of groupings (e.g. black, female, lower-class, homosexual, Catholic, Jamaican). Likewise personal filters, such as personality type, values and aesthetics, make communication difficult with those who have different traits. Despite these differences, listening can be improved by taking two steps: listeners must admit their difficulties in understanding; listeners must ask speakers for help.

Overcoming barriers to listening requires two types of exercises in addition to physical exercises: (1) listeners need self-awareness exercises (e.g. daily reflection, journal keeping, supervision, therapy) that help them grow more conscious of their own feelings and needs; (2) listeners need spiritual exercises that relate them to speakers, increase their tolerance for painful feelings, and lessen their judgements about themselves and others. Listeners can develop their empathy with speakers through intercessory prayer. Contemplation, non-discursive prayer, raises listeners' tolerance for their own and speakers' distressing feelings. The sense of God's love grows through meditation on Scripture, tradition and contemporary religious material.

Carl Rogers (1951) demonstrated the importance of listening by showing that three listening conditions were necessary and sufficient for therapeutic change: (1) non-judgemental listening (unconditional positive regard); (2) understanding of speakers' feelings and content (empathy); (3) self-aware (congruent) listeners.

Carkhuff (1969) did research on listening and teaching listening skills. On that basis he: (1) added concreteness as the fourth condition for change; (2) developed the aspects of listening into concrete skills that could be taught and measured; and (3) integrated these listening skills with challenging and planning skills into a helping construct. Taylor (1991) adapted Carkhuff's helping construct for pastoral use by relating it to pastoral contexts, theological concepts and religious resources.

Listening establishes a relationship with speakers. In addition, listening obtains information. Thus, listening provides the basis of effective lay and clerical pastoral work such as: (1) brief conversations at the church door or befriending a new acquaintance; (2) more involved conversations such as teaching classes, preparing persons for baptism, marriage or the burial service, leading groups, evangelism and social service; (3) long-term intense conversations such as parenting, spiritual direction and pastoral counselling.
[Charles W. Taylor]

LITURGY
A formal, ordered act of worship.

A liturgy is to be resilient and profound enough in word and symbol both to enable a disturbing but strengthening encounter with God and also to be worthy of frequent repetition. Its structures take account of history (though earliest is not necessarily best), metaphor, pastorally sensitive sequences of mood and response, and patterns of faith, e.g. a confession of sin, absolution, prayer for healing, the Peace – each a combination of word and gesture, i.e. kneeling, the sign of the cross, hands laid on heads, handclasp.

LIVING WILL
A type of advance directive with instructions about health-care treatment in the event of terminal illness.

A living will, or 'advance directive', is an explanation of one's values and beliefs that shape the instructions. How to deal with disagreement over its interpretation should be included. In the USA, to be legal it needs to be written, dated, signed and witnessed by two persons with no vested interest in the person's death. However, laws vary worldwide regarding living wills. Such a will is implemented when the person is no longer competent to express his or her desires, and should be made available to the attending physician.

LOCAL NON-STIPENDIARY MINISTRY (LNSM)
Ordained ministry limited by licence to a specific locality.

Although many Free Churches have had a similar ministry for some time, LNSM is a recent development in some dioceses in the Church of England. It constitutes a form of ordained ministry that is not transferable in the same way as non-stipendiary ministry under national schemes of selection and training. The development of this ministry has been in two main contexts: one mainly in urban areas where collaborative ministry involving church leaders, ordained and lay, has already been set up; the other in rural settings where few stipendiary clergy may be available and the need for a regular sacramental ministry may be fulfilled by ordaining a local person within a particular community in which they are already known and well respected. The term for this ministry has recently changed in England to 'ordained local ministry'.

LONELINESS
1. The sadness of being without others.
2. The state of being solitary without choosing to be so.

Attachment theory teaches us that becoming and being separate are necessary both for human development and spiritual growth. As the infant gradually detaches him or herself from the mother, so as life progresses a person has to move away from dependency on parents, school, inherited ideas and dependence on the crowd. To achieve autonomy it is necessary to separate. To be alone from time to time is therefore essential for most people. A need for constant company can be a sign of fear or of inner emptiness.

In one form, loneliness is a sense of not mattering to anyone, and a feeling of rejection. To know oneself different from the majority, and to feel rejected, whether because of sexual orientation, appearance or temperament, can lead to a sense of loneliness, even in a crowd. Loneliness can be the consequence of a reclusive personality or the result of an external event, such as the death of a loved one, which can seem like abandonment. To be left by parents or a partner or, in old age, by those who have shared one's life and interests may lead to loneliness. Other possibilities include it being an aspect of a work situation (at the extreme, for example, keeping a lighthouse); the experience of being single in a world and a church where all the emphasis appears to be on family; or a consequence of serious illness, deafness, inability to leave the home and mix with others. In all such situations loneliness is exacerbated by an unfulfilled desire for companionship; a sense that everyone else has companions (life as portrayed in the media and advertising seems to be lived in company); a feeling of stigma, whether because of poverty, disability or even riches; and a sense of 'missing out' on life generally. Loneliness can lead people to desperate and inappropriate actions: alcohol and drug abuse; a desperate search for relationships in a way that repels others; the rush into unsuitable relationships with other vulnerable people; or total withdrawal.

Pastoral carers will meet many who are in some way lonely. The lonely person may be helped by one-to-one befriending, when non-threatening care can be offered and the reason for loneliness can be gently drawn out. Practical help is sometimes useful, if the person is housebound and disabled or elderly. A gentle introduction to a group or an elderly persons' centre, where habits may be quietly changed, trust built up and a wider life revealed, may help some. Children and younger people are sometimes able to make contacts that elude their elders, and pets can break down barriers. And knowing when one should go away and not feel defeated is crucial. It is likely that loneliness will be an increasing problem as society becomes more fragmented. Already there is an increase in the number of people living alone, whether by choice, default or because they have been deserted. The increase in the number of self-help groups for all sorts of conditions bears witness to the desire for people to share knowledge and support one another. But lonely people may well be non-joiners, and can best be helped by patient, unassuming pastoral care.

A distinction must be drawn between chosen solitariness (solitude) and imposed loneliness. Solitariness is chosen by those who prefer their own company to that of others. These people may make a significant contribution to wider society. By contrast loneliness is thrust upon us. It is an imposed, unwanted condition, a form of human deprivation. It is exacerbated by memory of other times and by fear for the future. Solitary people will usually be content as they are. They may well resent any attempt to be drawn into closer contact with other people. Life in a presbytery for a Roman Catholic priest on his own, for example, will include chosen solitude but also contain elements of true loneliness. He is literally alone; and he is differentiated from the rest of the parishioners. Yet there is an extra element of choice. The priest has chosen the solitary life of celibacy. Solitude is specifically chosen by the hermit and anchorite. Temporary solitude as is found on retreat is an increasingly important spiritual experience for many.
[D. Murray]

LOSS
The sense of deprivation experienced when a significant person or object is no longer present.

Loss can be temporary or permanent and can cause distress at many levels. Although usually associated with death and bereavement, it is a more widespread phenomenon. All loss involves losing part of oneself. There is, for instance, the loss of dignity and purpose when a person is made redundant or fired. Far more than money is involved: the victim's place in society is jeopardized and he or she loses confidence and self-esteem. The loss of a partner through divorce or separation can sometimes seem a relief. But despite divorce becoming more widespread and acceptable in society, it can involve a series of losses – loss of confidence in oneself and in others; it can deprive children of support; and it can raise questions of guilt and responsibility. In a recent study (Davies 1997), it was found that the loss of a dog or a cat might lead to profound grief: it evoked memories of previous bereavements. Of the sample studied, 75% said they had been devastated when their pet died. The pastoral carer will inevitably become involved with such examples. Ageing can be construed as a series of losses – of youth, energy, and often faculties and abilities. The pastoral care of the elderly, of whom there is an ever-increasing number, requires an understanding in terms of continuous and increasingly serious losses. The final loss is caused by death. Death is irreversible and real. 'Not lost, but gone before' is scarcely comfort to the bereaved. When a loved one dies the survivor has lost a companion and confidant; a friend and partner; a fixed point in life; a status as a married person, or as a child or parent; a part of his or her own self; a hope and a cause to live for.

The pastoral carer needs strategies to deal with loss in its manifold forms, not least because dealing with those who suffer it awakes similar feelings in the pastor. Everyone will have experienced this sense of deprivation and have found their own ways of dealing with it. Victims of loss need to be listened to and given more than clichés. Pastors, therefore, need to be aware of the risk of confusing their own needs with those of others to whom they are ministering. Losses, whether they appear great or small, are personal, hard to quantify and very real.
[*D. Murray*]

LOVE
1. A liking, fondness, concern, affection.
2. Sexual desire.
Love has meant many things in different cultures, but it usually has these two overlapping meanings. Different words have denoted notions of love, such as the much criticized contrast between *eros* and *agape*.

Although sometimes defined as the absolute ground of being, in the Christian tradition God is often characterized as being, in essential nature, love. Love is not simply another attribute, such as power, wisdom or holiness, but is the central characteristic of God as God and in relation to the created order (Newlands, 1980). In the Old Testament God is conceived of in a variety of ways. Yet God remains the sustainer of creation, looking after his people. All our human experience helps us to recognize the character of God's concern, but the reference to God as creator implies dimensions in God which go beyond our own experience. The basis of Christian understanding of God's love has been an interpretation of the New Testament in terms of God's self-giving in the sacrifice of his son, and in Jesus' self-giving to God and humankind. God is identified with his creation through his presence in Jesus Christ, suffering, sharing in life and death, bringing life and reconciliation out of death and disaster. Through the resurrection, God's love has in a profound and mysterious way overcome evil – hence Paul's comment that nothing can now separate us from God's love (Rom. 8.39).

The understanding of God as love, and of God's purpose for the created order as leading to fulfilment in love, has sweeping implications for individual and social ethics. Love is to be the informing principle in all human social life. Here is the perennial relevance of an impossible ideal.

Christian reflection on love has developed over the centuries in dialogue with philosophical ideas derived from ancient Greece. Eros is a powerful god, the source of unquenchable sexual desire, driving men and women to distraction. Eros is initially created by attraction to the beauty of the form of the human body. From this attraction friendship and philosophical dialogue in the joint love of wisdom may grow. Beauty becomes the means of transition between the material and the ideal world. The spiritualization of love, with its attendant advantages and disadvantages, reached a climax in the neo-Platonic ideal of the highest love as a purely spiritual contemplation of a perfectly incorporeal God. This tradition has had deep influence on Christianity, emphasizing ascetic and monastic love of God at the expense of love between the sexes.

Augustine emphasized the polarization between love with a sexual dimension and love for God. The Middle Ages saw the development of mystical piety, the search of the soul in love for God, and a wide literature on courtly love, selfless devotion of the lover to his beloved. In the writings of the mystics sexual symbolism was transformed to describe the mystical marriage between the believer and God; in Dante earthly love leads on to union with the divine love (Lewis, 1936). Modern literature and philosophy have explored the psychological and moral dimensions of love. Psychology and psychiatry have brought fundamental changes to our perception of the springs of all human feeling and action. It is hard to overestimate the importance of Freud, even though many of his theories are no longer widely held. He understood the libido, or sexual instinct, as the driving force behind much human action (Lear, 1990).

Christianity is concerned for loving relationships between people at every level. It resists devaluation of the material world in favour of ideas. Love between persons is often expressed appropriately in sexual terms. Love for society means feeding the hungry with real food rather than benevolent sentiment. Yet Christianity also has a truly spiritual dimension and does not regard perfect union as always quasi-substantial physicality. Love includes allowing space to the other, letting be, encouraging independence. The clue for the pastor remains the self-giving love of God in Jesus Christ (Vanstone, 1977). *[G. M. Newlands]*

LUST
Insatiable desire for pleasure.
Lust is one of the vices, one of the mortal sins, being contrasted with chastity and temperance. Sexual lust is usually regarded as typical, but there is also notable lust for power or money. Lust exploits people and seeks immediate gratification. Because the emotions associated with sex, power and money are themselves so powerful, there is sometimes a tendency to regard any enthusiasm for these as lust. But healthy longing and desiring is quite different from lust and needs to be distinguished by the pastor. The legitimate pursuit of power can become lust for domination. Healthy and normal sexual attraction can be depersonalized into lust. Earning money can become an end in itself or a means of exercising power.

M

MAGIC
The art of producing extraordinary effects by supernatural, often occult, means.
Serious problems beset even this barest of definitions. One dictionary prefaces 'art' with 'pretended'. To its definition of 'thaumaturgy' (the supernatural working of the extraordinary effects labelled 'miracles') another dictionary appends *'specif.* Magic'; to 'thaumaturgist' it adds *'esp.* Magician'. Who decides what is 'magic' and what 'thaumaturgy' – or what is 'magic' and what 'religion'? Much of the literature on magic, ancient and modern, seeks to distinguish 'magic' from 'miracle' or 'religion'. These efforts do not withstand scrutiny.

1. 'Magic', it is claimed, employs manipulations and material means, whereas 'miracle' does not. The so-called magical papyri discovered in Egypt in the nineteenth century and dating from the second century BCE to the fifth century CE do indeed swarm with incantations, recipes for potions, and instructions on bodily movements and gestures, as do the cursing and binding spells extending over four millennia of human history (Gager, 1992). However, miracle accounts in religious traditions also report manipulations and material means: for example, in Judaism (Elijah and Elisha; 1 Kings 18.42; 2 Kings 4.34), or in Christianity, Jesus puts his fingers in a man's ears, spits, and touches his tongue in an act of healing (Mark 7.33). Touch or laying on of hands figure in many New Testament healing accounts and material means in others. In medieval Christianity relics appear in numerous accounts of miracles.

2. While the New Testament reports miracles worked by word alone the accounts mentioned above nullify the claim that this distinguishes New Testament miracle accounts generally from 'magic'. Moreover, this claim overlooks the prominent role played by words in 'magic'. Origen's assertion (*Contra Celsum* 1.24–25, 5.45) that words could be construed as magic manipulations is illustrated by the abundant formulae for incantations and the special words or syllables in the magical papyri, cursing spells and literary texts. The power thought

to inhere in sounds is seen in the recital of mere syllables, alone or in sequence, and in foreign words or names in the magical papyri. Similarly, one finds Aramaic words preserved in the Greek text of New Testament miracle accounts (Mark 5.41; 7.34), likely for use by Christians practising healing rituals. Not surprising, then, is Tertullian's report (*Apology* 21.17) that Jesus' working of wonders by a mere word was the basis of a Jewish accusation that Jesus was a magician.

3. Another claim is that magic, in contrast to religion, seeks to compel superhuman agents, for base or mundane ends. Imperatives abound in the magical papyri but so do humble supplications and sublime praise of deity, all of which are also found in texts categorized as 'religious' (Betz, 1992). Only by defining 'religion' in ways that exclude the many (mundane) material blessings besought of deity in religious traditions can one distinguish 'magic' from 'religion' on this basis. As to 'base', cursing and binding (and often magic) texts seek to compel love or inflict harm, but closer examination of these and of African 'witchcraft' reveals how they functioned to confront and perhaps resolve social tensions and conflicts.

4. The denigrating epithets applied to magic reveal further misunderstandings: it is 'pathetic', 'silly nonsense', 'rubbish', 'decayed and decomposing religion', 'misunderstood medicine stupidly popularized' and associated with the lower social strata. In fact, 'magic' knows no social boundaries, whether in ancient or modern cultures. The epithets imply irrationality, a key component in modern treatments of magic whether in distinguishing it from religion or science. However, as various scholars have noted, rationality is relative to context. In the Ancient Near Eastern and Mediterranean worlds where a close connection was perceived between material objects and superhuman forces, it would not be 'irrational' to use that connection to achieve ends not attainable through everyday means and in language intelligible to those forces (cf. 1 Cor. 13.1; 14.2, 28). The long history of 'magic', extending to our disenchanted world (Max Weber) where books on magic abound, including those by practitioners (among them highly educated, sometimes renowned, individuals such as W. B. Yeats), points to the contingencies attending human life to which magic – and religion – are addressed.

Practices and rationalities sanctioned within a particular group may meet with disapproval in another group. In some ancient contexts 'magic' is deemed 'divine', in others it is condemned, and some kinds are declared illegal. This helps explain the occult side of magic, as does its practice as a remunerative craft, or the risks attending negotiations with awesome powers, or the safeguarding of what was considered sacred. A similar aversion to public gaze is seen in biblical texts in which healers closet themselves with those to be healed.

The relational definition of 'magic' is succinctly captured in Robert Grant's aphorism, 'Your miracle is my magic, and vice versa.' Common to the various activities condemned in Deut. 18.9–12 is that these are what 'the nations' (non-Israelites) are said to practice; Deuteronomy sets them off from Israel with the social classifier 'abhorrent practices'. Another social classifier associated with 'magic' is 'witchcraft' which, applied predominantly to women, had baleful consequences in Western history. Some students of religion and anthropology situate 'magic' and 'religion' on a continuum rather than in antithesis. Other scholars eschew the term 'magic' altogether as ambiguous and misleading. For them, it functions, rather, to reveal the speaker's attitude to beliefs and practices that he or she for various reasons does not sanction: 'magic' is opposed to 'religion'; magic devolved from religion; magic preceded religion and then science; magic is superstitious belief characteristic of the uneducated. That the allure of magic will persist is evident. How one assesses that allure depends on the assessor (Remus, 1999). [*H. Remus*]

MALE PSYCHOLOGY
Distinctive personality characteristics attributed to masculine gender.

At least in Northern European and Northern American contemporary culture, males are generally regarded as more likely than females to be aggressive, to prefer hierarchical relationships to relationships of parity, to suppress affect, to value independence, to give high priority to performance and achievement. It is unknown and disputed how accurately all males in these cultures are so characterized. It is also unknown and disputed whether these are inherent or culturally acquired characteristics, and therefore how widespread in other cultures, other species, other eras, and how easily changed.

MANIPULATION
Handling a situation so as to bring about certain personally desired ends.
Since it is unusual for human beings to be fully aware of their motives, some manipulation is likely to be present in all pastoral situations and counselling settings. For example, any request for advice will probably contain some element of seeking approval of actions already taken or contemplated. The client is likely to present the situation in order to manipulate the counsellor into offering that approval. If a counsellor fails to be aware of manipulation, collusion with it on his or her part may be the outcome. There will also be a failure to offer the client the opportunity to recognize the manipulative component in the way in which he or she has presented needs. Such awareness can lead to a clearer grasp of real needs and the options available for meeting them.

While 'manipulation' generally carries with it a negative evaluation, it is in fact an appropriate response to situations where demands are unlikely to be met or satisfaction of needs likely to be denied. The child–parent relationship is an ideal school in manipulative techniques; the child is powerless against a refusal by parents to meet a demand, and therefore seeks, and quickly learns, forms of behaviour or ways of voicing demands that can circumvent that refusal. Where this means of obtaining satisfaction is not replaced in later years by negotiation and compromise, the manipulative pattern becomes set and emerges in any situation where it appears that the straightforward voicing of a demand will not produce the desired end. Hence in the pastoral situation the client knows that certain ends will not be acceptable and therefore does not bring them to expression or even to consciousness. This is particularly likely where the pastor has some other role, such as responsibility for a local church; the client may try to use the confidentiality of the pastoral relationship as a means of securing an alliance or the pastor's willingness to take responsibility for aims that in fact belong to the client. *[Peter Selby]*

MARRIAGE
The socially, and in most cases legally, acknowledged union, usually between a man and a woman, such that the resulting children are recognized as the legitimate offspring of the parents.
Marriage can be a divisive issue for the churches and for society because its decline as a social institution in modern society is viewed by some as positive and others as problematic. Marriage has without doubt enabled patriarchal and abuse practices, but it also remains something 95% of English and American adults desire or are glad to have. The churches have a pivotal role to play in rethinking the culture of marriage today so that marriage can be at once a substantive and sacred institution and an egalitarian one as well (Browning *et al.*, 2000).

Marriage has been defined in a variety of ways in the Christian tradition. In the early Jesus movement, marriage was held up as an egalitarian institution between 'children of God' in opposition to Graeco-Roman patriarchal family structures (Balch and Osiek, 1996). In the Middle Ages, it required only the consent of the two parties and their having been baptized, with church canon law not being necessary for the contract to take place. Augustine, and later Aquinas, developed the influential notion that marriage has three unique 'goods': children, fidelity and sacrament. The Reformation introduced the idea of civil law as governing marriage, especially around Calvin's concept of marriage as a public 'covenant' between the couple and their broader society, an idea that dominated North American views of marriage up until the early twentieth century. Anglicans tended to view marriage instead as a domestic 'commonwealth' embedded in the larger commonwealth of the state. Post-Reformation Catholics embraced the idea of marriage as primarily a 'sacrament', meaning a sign of Christ's union with humankind, a sacred bond akin to baptism (Witte, 1997). Contemporary Catholics have also understood marriage under the idea of 'the principle of subsidiary', so that marriage should be supported by the larger society but with the freedom to fulfil its own special functions.

Today, marriage in the USA and the UK is generally viewed as having more or less separate theological and legal dimensions. English national law has secularized traditionally religious injunctions so as to require the parties to a valid marriage to be biologically male and female respectively, over sixteen, and not within prohibited degrees of relationship or lawfully married to other persons. In the USA, marriage is regulated primarily by the states, and involves similar prohibitions to those in England, except that the parties in most states must be eighteen years old.

Anglican ecclesiastical law is part of the national law in the UK and a parishioner of whatever religious belief has the right to be married in the parish church. Nevertheless, the minister may legally (1) refuse to solemnize a marriage of any person whose former marriage has been brought to an end by divorce and whose former spouse is still living, or (2) refuse to permit the marriage of such a person in the church or chapel where he or she ministers (Bursell, 1996). Roman Catholic canon law today recognizes the competency of civil authorities over the civil effects of marriages, but requires that marriage between two Catholics take place within the church, rather than in a civil ceremony or in some other religious setting (Coriden, 1991). In addition, the Roman Catholic Church does not recognize the ecclesiastical efficacy of divorce, but either party may seek a marital annulment from the Church on the grounds of canonical impediment, defect of consent, or lack of canonical form. In the US, Protestant perspectives on marriage are resurfacing in state law in the option in select states for a 'covenant' marriage governed legally by stricter entry and exit requirements than ordinary 'contractual' marriages.

Churches of all denominations are playing a vital role in the emerging 'marriage education' movement in North America, England, and many other parts of the world. While churches have always played a significant part in preparing couples for marriage, especially the pre-Cana programme of the Roman Catholic Church, they are now increasingly helping couples take advantage of new psychological research into effective marriage 'communication skills' (Stanley, et al., 1998). Churches typically teach these skills to couples in combination with more traditional Christian marriage education activities like exploring the meaning and value of marriage, providing couples with already married mentor couples, and sustaining a community of friends and family committed to supporting the couple's growing relationship in all its sacred and social dimensions. [Christopher Clulow/John Wall]

MARRIAGE COUNSELLING
The process of addressing marital problems through a counselling relationship.

Marriage counselling is a generic term covering different approaches to helping couples with marital problems. Its defining function is to focus attention on the adult heterosexual couple relationship when responding to problems that one or both partners present for help, an orientation that is sometimes described as regarding the 'marriage as patient'. The process is constructed of three interacting variables: the setting within which counselling takes place, the clients who use the service, and the counsellors who provide it.

Marriage counselling is available from different practice settings. The most frequently approached are specialist organizations offering counselling and/or psychotherapy services, medical settings and private practice. The United Kingdom is unusual in having specialist marriage counselling organizations that are staffed mainly by trained volunteers who are accessible to couples in every part of the country. Although the largest of these is secular, it has historical roots in the established Church and operates co-operatively with marital agencies run by the Catholic and Jewish faith communities. Some hospital departments offer marital psychotherapy (see the discussion of counselling and psychotherapy below), and it is becoming increasingly familiar for general practitioners to employ clinic-based counsellors. Many counsellors and psychotherapists working in private practice will also see couples. While these are the most commonly used settings, marriage counselling activities are not exclusive to them. Employee assistance programmes, student counselling services and counsellors in legal practices are examples of other settings in which marital help may be available.

Different settings will appeal to different couples according to how they see their problems. Couples may take a sexual problem to a medical setting, or to an organization that they know specializes in treating sexual dysfunction. They may unconsciously 'designate' a partner to present a medical symptom at a general practice surgery, or to go to a counsellor for help with relationship problems that may not, at first, be understood as such. Parents seeking help for disturbances in their children may receive marital help as part of a family therapy programme. When things go well there will be an exchange between client and selected agency that fashions a shared understanding of the nature of, and the most effective response to, the problem for which help is sought.

Marriage counselling does not require that couples be married (couple counselling), nor do both partners always need to be directly involved in the process. Changing family patterns regarding marriage mean that many couples seeking counselling help will be unmarried. Also, women are more likely to initiate the search for help and involve themselves in the counselling process than men, although this pattern is changing.

The third variable influencing the process of marriage counselling is the counsellor. The counsellor takes responsibility for formulating the nature of the problem that, in turn, indicates the kind of therapeutic response required. In doing this she or he will depend on the way couples or partners present their problems and on her or his own theoretical orientation. There are well-established theoretical schools of thought (Crowe and Ridley, 1990) offering perspectives on marital problems and informing practice. Each has its own professional training. The psychological 'maps' provided by different theories will, to some extent, reflect the personalities of the counsellors who are drawn to them. They will provide more or less suitable guides to the actual territory that they and their clients must traverse in the course of their work together. The main purpose of counselling will vary according to the relative emphasis given to support, prescription and exploration; feelings, thoughts and actions provide the raw material to be worked upon.

There is debate as to whether and how to distinguish marriage counselling from marital or couple psychotherapy. In the United Kingdom this has been crystallized by attempts to map counselling and psychotherapy in terms of 'outputs' that demonstrate competent practice, as distinct from training 'inputs' that lead to professional recognition. The purpose of this exercise is to establish a framework of practice standards to be used in awarding National Vocational Qualifications.

Therapeutic approaches in marital work have much in common: for example, adopting a couple focus, having a non-judgemental approach, and fostering the capacity for self-help. Different theoretical frameworks for understanding marital problems result in different styles of intervention. Differences are likely to be more defined across these modalities than within them, whether practitioners are described as counsellors or psychotherapists. For example, psychodynamic marriage counsellors and psychoanalytical marital psychotherapists are likely to have more in common with each other than either group will have with behaviourally oriented marriage counsellors or sex therapists. Differences within the same modalities are most likely to exist in terms of therapeutic focus, the settings within which practitioners work, their status, and the problems with which they are typically confronted. Hooper and Dryden (1991) assert that the terms 'counselling' and 'therapy' are likely to become increasingly interchangeable as techniques and training develop. Outcome research suggests that practitioners using different modalities may be less different from each other than is commonly supposed; what they actually do may converge more than what they say they do. It also indicates that outcomes to therapy for relationship problems are positively related to what the various approaches have in common (for example, the capacity to form a therapeutic alliance), not to what differentiates between them.

Insofar as marriage counselling has been understood as a response to the general instability of marriage, it has been open to one fundamental criticism. By focusing on the private troubles of couples, attention can be diverted from relevant public issues that have dominated the social agenda in the second half of the twentieth century. Inequitable divisions of material resources, redrawn boundaries between work and family life, upended assumptions about gender and the restructuring of family life are some of the public issues that have been cited as impacting on the private world of couples and destabilizing the institution of marriage. Where the institution has been equated with patriarchal interests and traditional demarcations between the roles of men and women, it has been seen as part of the problem, rather than part of the solution, to contemporary socio-economic dilemmas. Marriage counselling is not the most effective way of addressing these social concerns, nor is it intended to be. However, by focusing on questions of identity, communication, responsibility and interpersonal behaviour at the microscopic level, it is likely to influence the ways individuals relate to the macroscopic issues that are of concern to society as a whole. [*Christopher Clulow/John Wall*]

MARRIAGE, INTERCHURCH
See: INTERCHURCH MARRIAGE

MARRIAGE, INTERFAITH
See: INTERFAITH MARRIAGE

MARRIAGE, MIXED
See: MIXED MARRIAGE

MARRIAGE PREPARATION
See: WEDDING PREPARATION

MARRIAGE, THE LAW OF
The rules relating to marriage in England, both nationally and in the Roman Catholic and Anglican Churches.

Both marriage and divorce affect the manner in which the parties to the marriage, and their children, are treated by their own and other national laws. For example, they affect the rules as to inheritance. Christian churches regard marriage as a sacrament, but accept that the civil authorities are competent themselves to regulate matrimonial status even when not all such churches accept the religious validity of divorce. Pastoral tensions are inevitably caused by these conflicting approaches, in addition to those caused within the matrimonial relationship itself and upon its breakdown.

English national law requires the parties to a valid marriage to be biologically male and female respectively and over sixteen. They must not be within prohibited degrees of relationship, neither may they be lawfully married to other persons. Other prerequisites relate to publicity, location and the officiant's qualifications (either a superintendent registrar or an Anglican cleric). In the absence of these requirements the marriage is automatically void. Marriages may also be voidable on the decree of a competent civil court, for example on the grounds of impotency. Apart from any such annulment a marriage may be brought to an end by divorce on the grounds of irretrievable breakdown.

Anglican ecclesiastical law (canon law) is part of the national law and a parishioner of whatever religious beliefs has the right to be married in the parish church. Nevertheless, the incumbent may legally (1) refuse to solemnize a marriage of any person whose former marriage has been brought to an end by divorce and whose former spouse is still living, and (2) refuse to permit the marriage of such a person in the church or chapel where he or she ministers. A similar exemption arises in relation to the marriage of persons within certain otherwise permitted degrees of relationship. Such a refusal often causes pastoral difficulties, which may be exacerbated by the fact that different ministers adopt different approaches to the marriage of such people (Bursell, 1996).

Roman Catholic canon law adopts different criteria for the religious validity of a marriage, although at the same time it recognizes the competency of the civil authorities over the civil effects of any marriage. Certain of the impediments to marriage in Roman Catholic canon law are, however, subject to ecclesiastical dispensation. Roman Catholics are 'required by the canon law to be married within the church, rather than in a civil ceremony or in some other religious setting' (Coriden, 1991); this may, however, be dispensed with in relation to a marriage with a non-Roman Catholic. Such mixed marriages may only be entered into after dispensation and subject to condition, including a promise on the part of the Roman Catholic party 'to do all in his or her power to have the children baptized and brought up in the Catholic Church' (Coriden, 1991). Such a promise may itself cause pastoral tensions. If a marriage fails, the Roman Catholic Church does not recognize the ecclesiastical efficacy of divorce but either party may seek a declaration from the Church that the marriage was canonically invalid by reason of canonical impediment, defect of consent or lack of canonical form. After such a declaration the parties are usually free to remarry. As the grounds for such a declaration of annulment are different from those in civil law, additional pastoral problems may arise especially in mixed marriages. [*Rupert D. H. Bursell*]

MARY, BLESSED VIRGIN
The honorific title accorded to Mary, mother of Jesus, by Catholics and others.

Mary's status has been a bone of contention between Christian denominations. Marian dogmas (such as her perpetual virginity and immaculate conception) are rejected by

Protestants as post-scriptural, along with her veneration as Theotokos (God-bearer) and Queen of Heaven. Feminists reject the oppressively impossible ideal: virgin as well as mother!

Yet Mary might have a significant pastoral and ecumenical role. A gender-inclusive symbolism could emerge from the ancient claim that as Christ reversed Adam's fall, so Mary was the antitype of Eve. The *Pietà* as 'type' of suffering has enabled some women to find meaning in the midst of anguish.

MASCULINITY
The qualities, attributes or condition of the male sex that constitute men's gender role and identity.

While men have long reflected upon and given expression to their sense of male role and identity, the challenge of ideological feminism has subverted the notion of male experience as universal, so that masculinity is now understood as an aspect of gender relations, always in conjunction with, and in opposition to, the roles and identities of women. As Virginia Woolf commented, 'masculinity has become self-conscious'. The influence of the women's movement and the development of gay identity among male homosexuals have led men to reconsider themselves as men. Since the 1970s in Britain and the United States local men's groups have formed for mutual support and reflection, resulting in publications, conferences and national networks that some commentators have called a 'men's movement', though numbers of men actively involved remain small. This focus on masculinity has given rise to a range of therapies and self-help literature for individuals and groups that has won considerable attention in the USA. More influential in academic circles has been the development of Men's Studies, which are historical and psychosociological and tend towards reforming social practice. Broadly, approaches to masculinity fall into two camps.

1. *Essentialism.* Influenced by Jungian psychology, essentialist writers such as Robert Bly offer a critique of contemporary Western masculinity arising out of therapeutic practice. Bly (1991) suggests that men are grieving for masculine qualities such as wildness, inner strength and solitude, which are suppressed by the commercialism and militarism of post-industrial America. While women have found an appropriate and healthy self-understanding, men are alienated from the creative sources of masculinity deep within themselves and have no initiation into mature manhood. Drug abuse, violence, emotional dysfunction and spiritual lethargy among men are the products of this severance from the 'deep masculine'. Mainstream Christianity is seen to be offering an asexual and docile model of masculinity in which the saviour figure has been emasculated by the Church. In story and myth men have access to timeless masculine archetypes that offer a complete and fruitful manhood. Much of this work of rediscovery is to be undertaken via psychotherapeutic encounter one-to-one or in groups.

2. *Constructionism.* This approach understands masculinity as a social construction in which men's identities are not biologically determined nor an expression of ontological make-up, but the product of a particular historical culture or society. Masculinity is not a fixed set of values and behaviours innate within all men, but differs according to race, sexuality and social class as these factors interact with biological and physical conditions, so that there is no universal masculinity but a plethora of masculinities. Increasingly this approach comes to view these masculinities as shifting social practices that embody the exercise of power within patriarchal society in and through the politics of gender and sexual orientation. Connell (1995) explores a range of masculinities within a single city, and having analysed these as social constructions, sets out an agenda for change towards greater social justice in the relations between men and women, gay and straight.

While constructionists and essentialists differ in their analyses of masculinity, both approaches suggest a crisis in male identity and self-understanding that has arisen since the arrival of feminism and sexual liberation, further complicated by a transformation in the nature and pattern of work. Both approaches express dissatisfaction with prevailing masculinities among men in the post-industrial West and suggest that male dominance is harmful for men as well as women and children. Both approaches see the roots of male violence, homophobia, paternal inadequacy, emotional inarticulacy, drugs/alcohol/work dependency and men's incapacity for intimacy as the products of distorted masculinity rather than intrinsic masculine qualities. However, some feminist commentators and constructionists have criticized the essentialist approach and the Men's

Rights lobby in the USA as a conservative attempt to shore up male power, which is enjoyed at the expense of women, black men, gay men and children.

Theology and spirituality have been influenced by both perspectives. The Jungian basis of essentialism has inspired attempts to constitute a specifically masculine spirituality, and Evangelical Christians have embraced aspects of the North American men's movement in initiatives such as Promise Keepers, which offers men a clearly defined set of practices and values deemed to embody an authentic, biblical manhood. The sense of a crisis in masculinity has been mirrored in evangelistic strategies aiming to win over men and boys to the Church as a place for 'real men', while constructionist masculine theology challenges conventional models of masculinity in the light of feminism, homosexual liberation and men's experience. Nelson (1992) presents a reconstructed masculinity sustained by a practical men's body theology in which sexuality and spirituality are integrated. The manhood of Jesus is highly representative within this discourse for both traditionalists and radicals as a model of ideal masculinity and perfect humanity.

Awareness of masculinity can assist the Christian community in attending to issues of power, gender and sexuality within the Church and the practice of pastoral care. The modes of youth work, evangelism, liturgy, and the general conduct of the Church's life, together with issues such as work and unemployment, family and parenting, physical and sexual abuse, health and well-being, loss and grief, will have particular – though diverse – implications for men and boys. The pastor is also enabled to develop a level of personal self-awareness in terms of gender and sexuality that will impact upon the nature of the pastoral encounter and on his or her role and function as an agent of care. [Mark Pryce]

MASOCHISM
The tendency to derive pleasure (often sexual) from experiences of domination, humiliation, pain or suffering.
The word 'masochism' comes from Leopold von Sacher-Masoch, who first discerned this condition. Psychologists treat masochism as one pole of a disorder that generally includes sadism, the desire to master, control or humiliate another person. In masochism,

aggression is turned inward, often as a way to deal with unconscious guilt. The masochistic person has little sense of his or her own power, autonomy or self-worth, and finds satisfaction in total submission to, and identification with, an idealized partner. This partner's abusive behaviour may be construed either as deserved punishment or as an expression of love.

MASTURBATION
Stimulation of one's own sexual organs for pleasure.
Masturbation has historically been seen as a sin and the Church has disapproved of it. Today, however, it is widely recognized even by many Christians as a normal activity from early childhood to adult maturity. It is also believed that the psychological context matters more than the act itself. It can range from being comforting in the absence of a partner to a neurotic avoidance of intimacy with another. Pastors should, therefore, beware generalizing, not least because if the subject is raised with them there is almost certainly an accompanying sense of guilt.

MATERNAL DEPRIVATION
When a child is deprived of a warm, caring and continuous relationship with his or her mother.
It is useful to consider maternal deprivation in a relative sense, following John Bowlby (1985a), whereby a child may experience to a varying extent inadequate psychological care from the mother or permanent mother substitute. Extreme emotional neglect can engender serious developmental disorders in children, but healthy emotional development can be impeded by lesser degrees of deprivation, as when a mother can care for her child's physical needs but may be emotionally unavailable due to persistent depression. The effects of maternal deprivation can continue into adult life. Pastors may need to be alert to this possibility.

MATURATION
The process of reaching full growth and development.
Physical and psychological development do not always proceed hand in hand. Particularly in adolescence, physical and emotional maturation may be unsynchronized, with emotional maturity fluctuating considerably in both directions. Unlike physical and physiological development, which is

normally fully completed by the early twenties, emotional and intellectual maturation continue to progress throughout life, and require constant endeavour if they are to be sustained. In this respect they differ from the involuntary maturation imposed by the normal processes of physical development.

MATURITY
The state of fullness of growth or development.

Full height and weight, and full physiological and sexual functioning, are normally completed in late adolescence, although not necessarily accompanied by an equal or stable maturity in emotional or intellectual development – in Freud's terms, the capacity 'to work and to love'. In ordinary usage, maturity refers to emotional and cognitive wisdom built upon a good grasp of external reality. It represents a considerable achievement of the individual against pressure from regressive factors and forces – fatigue, stress, alcohol, overwork, conflict, illness and loss.

MEDIA
A channel that enables communication to occur.

Media, the plural of medium, can refer to different modes of communication. These include: primary, secondary or electronic media:

1. *Primary media*: spoken words, facial movement, and other non-verbal gestures. It normally involves the communicator being present. If the words are not consistent with the speaker's actions, then the intended communication may be undermined. It is important for pastoral theologians to recognize that 'the message of a person's life seems usually to carry more weight than the message of a person's words' (Kraft, 1991).

2. *Secondary media*: writing, painting, tapestry and architecture. The communicator does not need to be present for these media to be effective.

3. *Electronic/technical media*: telephones, computers, films, radio and television. By using these media, the communicator can appear to be present while crossing barriers of time and space.

These are not three distinct categories, as the different media are frequently connected. For example, a Gregorian chant, a Wesleyan hymn or a song by Madonna can be personal media, secondary media, and then broadcast via the electronic media. The term 'media' is increasingly used to refer solely to the third category, the electronic/technical media. It has evolved into an expression that is now used in two ways. First, it is sometimes linked with a specific means of communication: 'print' or 'broadcast' media. Second, and more commonly, it is used to refer in a more general sense to television, radio, film and newspapers: the mass media. In public discourse 'the media' has almost become synonymous with 'the mass media'. This linguistic shift points towards the increased significance of the electronic media. Pastoral theologians cannot afford to ignore the increasingly media-saturated environment in which they now operate. The rapid evolution and proliferation of media technologies has serious implications in a range of pastoral spheres.

For example, preachers are now attempting to speak in a highly competitive communicative context. Congregations are exposed to an array of electronic media. The result is that, through the mass media, audiences have become accustomed to greater visual stimulation. Viewers are regularly confronted in their living rooms with mediated images of tragedy. With the 'fireside chats' of radio, listeners have come to expect public discourse to be more conversational and intimate in style. Preachers who fail to adapt to this changed communicative environment will struggle to hold the attention of their listeners.

Many pastors are beginning to engage critically with the stories that, coming from the media, feed the imaginations of their congregations. Pastoral theologians, therefore, need to promote theologically informed media literacy, while also asserting the continuing place of primary and secondary media in an electronic age. This means going beyond teaching the practical skills of using electronic media to developing a critical awareness of the mass media's role in shaping, reflecting and interpreting our world. [*J. Mitchell*]

MEDIATING STRUCTURE
A relationship between people that is shaped by certain conditions and that mediates the psychological experience of being 'held' or 'contained'.

The importance of a mediating structure has been especially discussed by Winnicott (1961), who termed it 'holding', and Bion (1962), who used the word 'contain'. Such a structure is an aspect of the relationship between therapist and client, pastor and people, liturgy and worshipper. It can be important in supporting people through periods of crisis, dependency or regression. In pastoral activity it provides a powerful justification for regularity in such activities as visiting.

MEDIATION

The peaceful resolution or compromise of disputes, legal or otherwise, between individuals through the impartial intervention of a neutral mediator.

Mediation is most often used in solving marital disputes, although it is becoming more widely used as local arbitration or conflict resolution to avoid recourse to the courts (Goodman, 1994). The two or more parties in conflict meet in a neutral, secure environment. The role of the mediator is to smooth relations and communication between the parties by acting as an objective intermediary. The aim is for the warring parties to settle joint decisions that had proved difficult to achieve due to a lack of successful communication between the parties in question without assistance. For instance, in cases of divorce or separation, the mediator can assist couples in deciding on living arrangements, child access, division of capital and other financial issues. In addition to working as sole mediators, mediators can also work as co-mediators. Co-mediator teams often consist of a lawyer and a professional from a therapeutic background. Mediation is intended to complement the legal system and it offers a more rapid and cost-effective alternative to legal recourse. [L. Ratna]

MEDICINE

The art or science of the prevention or cure of disease or illness.

The term 'medicine' is also used more specifically to describe: (1) that area of speciality, that relies mainly on drugs or other therapeutic materials rather than opening the body; (2) a substance used to treat disease. Medicine is practised by those who have undertaken a formal training along scientific, empirically based lines. The practice of medicine draws on two main ideologies. The first contains assumptions about life and death and the place of disease in human experience. Frequently this draws implicitly or explicitly on a philosophical or spiritual tradition. Disease is understood as a dislocation of the natural state of affairs or even occasionally as punishment for wrongdoing.

The second strand, developed since the Renaissance but influential in, for example, traditional Arab medical practice, stresses the need for observation of disease patterns in an attempt to establish systematically what treatments are effective.

Medicine traditionally attempts to hold these principles together by means of close observation of the process of sickness, undergirded by reference to a theoretical framework. Medical training is thus rooted in the biological sciences and, to a lesser extent, in the social and psychological sciences. Medicine has developed a pre-eminence during the twentieth century as the profession perceived to have control over disease and presiding increasingly over the beginning and end of life. Consequent upon this development has been the organization of the profession, both in defining medical practice and training and developing its scientific rationale. The success of the traditional 'medical model', the application of skills and resources to cure or mitigate the effects of a disease process, are self-evident. Many diseases that were previously seen as incurable or intractable are now well within the range of effective medical care. However, many of the successes achieved in the containment of disease, e.g. the decline of tuberculosis and the eradication of smallpox, have had more to do with improved living conditions and preventative programmes of vaccination than with direct clinical intervention. The recent speciality of palliative medicine stresses the importance of properly based care for people whose life expectancy is short and whose illness is not 'curable'. Psychiatric practice has drawn heavily and to great effect on a scientific understanding of mental illness in that many people with severe mental illness can now be treated with medication. But practice and effective treatment may be adversely affected by poor social and economic circumstances.

Medicine has become identified as a stabilizing authority, not merely to alleviate individual disease and distress, but also in the face of events which threaten to be overwhelming. Doctors play a prominent part in the definition of illness and the formulation of health policy, both nationally and internationally, and thus form a significant power group. The power of medicine has been underlined by social and economic changes. A decline in formal religious belief and practice in many areas has led to medical professionals laying claim to an authority not simply in the area of illness, previously exercised by priests and religious leaders. Definitions may be made, for example, of what makes for a good and healthy life and what is right or wrong behaviour, e.g. about smoking, alcohol consumption or 'healthy eating'. Some diagnoses, as has been pointed out by feminist and other 'user' groups, contain implicit judgements of value on particular behaviour or lifestyles. Some human behaviour, e.g. grief, is conditioned strongly by religious and cultural factors and makes what is 'abnormal' difficult to define. Illness, which is a central concept of medicine, may sometimes not be so much a matter of scientific fact as a deviation from a theoretical or generally agreed norm.

Doctors have privileged physical and psychological access to a group of people who are typically vulnerable and not able to question. However the details of practice may vary, the trust placed in doctors is deemed to have been abused if, for example, a patient's confidentiality is breached or he/she is submitted to an unproven treatment for no good reason. Some forms of medicine which rely heavily on technology, a sophisticated economy and developed specialist skills, may be of less value in countries where these are not present. The growth of interest in 'alternative' therapies may reflect the disquiet felt by some at the de-personalizing effects of conventional medicine. There is an increasing contact between the systems in some areas, despite being hampered by difficulty in establishing common assumptions, reference points and methodology.

A number of forces are at work in medicine, which do not always point in the same direction. One view is that medicine has been increasingly 'de-professionalized' as part of a general reaction against a perceived professional paternalism and distancing. In many respects the decreasing knowledge gap between doctors and patients may imply a changed relationship. Patients and users of care may increasingly wish to define what treatments they hope for and what they find acceptable. Roles and boundaries in practice between doctors and colleagues in related disciplines are becoming more flexible; some duties, for example, that were traditionally 'medical' are now performed routinely by nurses and others. The management of health resources by politicians and professional managers at a time when potential treatments and consequent public expectation may be increased illustrates a changing

role for medicine. Equally, advances continue to be made not only in the treatment of disease but redefining crucial points of life. Assisted conception, the development of organ transplantation, possibly between species, and genetic therapies have implications which may affect future generations and not just an individual. The application of these treatments and ethical questions about their use require consultation outside the strictly medical area. At the same time increasingly sophisticated demands, such as those made on junior doctors working in hospitals in the 'developed' world, represent some of the complex medical and social decision-making faced by doctors. The appropriate allocation, and the establishment of priority, for resources of necessity involves a careful balance of what is scientifically possible, what a society deems it can afford and what is desirable for the good of individuals and communities. [Ian Ainsworth-Smith]

MEMBERSHIP OF CHURCH
Theologically almost universally defined by baptism in the name of the Trinity.
Most Christian churches baptize infants born into the Christian community, with the noted exceptions of the Quakers and the Salvation Army. Orthodoxy regards baptism with chrism as conferring full membership. The Western tradition has tended to have a second stage when full membership is endowed and personally accepted, i.e. confirmation (Roman Catholic, Anglican etc.) or reception (many Protestants). Faith, which also defines being a Christian, is present vicariously in baptism and appropriated at the age of discretion. The pietistic/evangelical tradition, however, lays emphasis on conscious personal faith as necessary for being a Christian. Baptists and similar groups bring this together with baptism, which thus becomes a witness to, as well as a sacrament of, faith.

However, it is difficult to know, in a post-Christian society, how to tell the realistic strength of the churches. There is increasingly a tendency to assume that it should only include those who actively identify with them. The Free Churches have only ever included full members, though within a wider body of adherents. Anglicans and Roman Catholics, modifying their tradition of using baptismal figures, will turn to other means, e.g. Easter communicants, registered voters or attendance registers (Brierley, 1991). How church membership is manifested is, therefore, increasingly complex. The inherited patterns are further complicated by other developments (Davie, 1994).

1. The rapid decline of 'cultural' Christianity means that belonging is increasingly a deliberate and personal, yet public, choice. Yet there are still many who identify with Christianity in some form, as a cultural reality, using for example the rites of passage. Similarly there is a strong civic religious tradition that marks national and community life (e.g. Remembrance Sunday).

2. Ecumenism has eroded the received patterns of denominational allegiance. One identifies with the Christian community that is convenient (e.g. nearby) or amenable. This is reinforced by the slow but clear convergence among Christians in forms of worship as well as other activities.

3. Paradoxically, this collapsing tradition also means that there is a greater variation in practice. It is possible to choose a congregation whose mode of worship or style of theology or area of concern attracts. The primary form of Christian belonging has always been through a local fellowship. Today there are signs of an increasing parochialism, mobility and willingness to set up new groups together, with a loss of the sense of belonging to the Church of God universal across the ages and in every place.

In this fluid situation the pastor faces many diverse expectations: from maintaining the tradition to creating the new. Perhaps the most crucial task is to maintain that tension that is at the heart of Christianity: of belonging to the universal community of faith yet being responsible to the particularity of one's own time and place. This is not easy in the fragmented, postmodernist, consumerist society of today. *[Paul Ballard]*

MEMORY
See: AMNESIA, HEALING OF MEMORIES

MENTAL HANDICAP
An old term for learning disability.
From the 1959 Mental Health Act the term 'mental subnormality' meant a delayed or arrested development of the mind. That term was used until the 1970s adoption of 'mental handicap'. As a general term it deals with the emotional and social consequences of an individual's intellectual or mental impairment. The World Health Organization (WHO) defined impairment as any loss or abnormality of structure or function. A disability is defined as a restriction resulting from an impairment and a handicap is the disadvantage to an individual resulting from the impairment or disability.

The word 'handicap' probably derives from a seventeenth-century game called 'hand in cap', in which a player gained either a reward or a forfeit – a concept that seemed accurately to reflect chance.

However, in the last decade in the UK the term 'learning disability' has now taken over. 'Handicap', 'disability', 'retardation', 'subnormality' – it seems that whichever word we use cannot hold the difficulty of being different. There have been more changes of terminology for this subject than for almost any other.

'Secondary handicap' is a psychoanalytic concept coined by Sinason. It refers to a defence mechanism used by some learning-disabled people. Through this, the pain of the original difference is hidden through exacerbating the handicap. For example, a patient with a slight speech defect might exaggerate that organic problem in order to hide shame and hurt at having a voice that is different. In a similar way, there can be excessive smiling. *[Valerie Sinason]*

MENTAL HEALTH AND MENTAL ILLNESS
The ability to co-operate or not with others, thus sustaining a loving relationship and making as objective as possible an estimate of one's self in relation to the rest of the world.

Contemporary definitions of mental health tend to refer to a capacity to cope with the problems of everyday life. While it is clear that other cultures and times have favoured different understandings, this approach emphasizes two important considerations: first, human mental functioning must always be understood in a social context and, second, mental health is much more than merely absence of mental disorder.

Mental disorder is now considered to be a preferable term to either mental illness or mental disease, owing to the even greater problems of defining illness and disease. However, the term 'disorder' is also imprecise. In practice it is used to refer to a recognizable set of clinical signs and symptoms, usually associated with personal distress and impaired functioning. Social deviance or interpersonal conflict alone are specifically excluded. However, mental disorders frequently include social as well as psychological and behavioural signs and symptoms.

Two major systems for classification and diagnosis of mental disorders are employed internationally. The tenth revision of the International Classification of Diseases includes a chapter on 'mental and behavioural disorders'. The fourth edition of the *Diagnostic and Statistical Manual of Mental Disorders* (DSM-IV; American Psychiatric Association, 1994) focuses solely on mental disorders. These systems differ in the detail of their overall classification of mental disorders, and their diagnostic criteria. However, both include sections for organic disorders (including dementia and delirium), disorders due to the use of psychoactive substances ('drugs'), mood disorders, schizophrenia and other psychoses, personality disorders, and disorders of childhood. The World Health Organization's ICD-10 classification retains use of the older term 'neurosis', which is not found in DSM-IV. DSM-IV is a multi-axial system which recognizes the need to assess domains of life such as psychological and social functioning, personality and psychosocial circumstances alongside, and independently of, clinical diagnosis.

Personality disorders are diagnosed from the end of adolescence, and are considered to represent extremes of personality rather than 'illness'. (In DSM-IV this is recognized by means of their allocation to a separate axis of the diagnostic system.) Adult mental illness arises after a period of normality in adult life. The neuroses, many of which are characterized by anxiety, arise in a setting of unaltered contact with reality and are associated with symptoms that are close to normal experience. The psychoses, which are major mental illnesses, are usually characterized by severe signs/symptoms, such as delusions and hallucinations, and by a lack of insight. These are further divided into the organic psychoses, with a demonstrable physical abnormality, and the functional psychoses (e.g. schizophrenia), which in theory have no underlying physical cause. However, in practice, research is increasingly demonstrating a biological basis for the so-called 'functional' psychoses.

Mental disorder is determined by the genetic makeup inherited from parents (or, more rarely, resulting from new mutations) and also by environmental influences of all sorts. Genetic factors include both abnormal genes which directly cause a disorder (e.g. Huntington's chorea) and also genes which confer a vulnerability or predisposition to certain disorders. Environmental factors include a wide range of events, many of which concern relationships with other people. These may be stresses that precipitate an episode of illness (e.g. divorce, unemployment, bereavement, or marital disharmony), or developmental influences which confer a vulnerability to a disorder (e.g. loss of a parent in childhood, or childhood sexual abuse). Biological influences, such as physical illness or drugs, may also precipitate, predispose to, or directly cause mental disorder.

In the Western world, mental disorders have traditionally been approached from a perspective of the medical model, where a diagnosis is made, and treatment offered, by a doctor (psychiatrist) within a health service framework. Today, the approach tends to be much more multidisciplinary, involving social workers, psychologists, occupational therapists and other health professionals. Treatment is likely to include psychological and social measures where possible, and not simply a reliance on medication. However, innovation in pharmaceutical research has resulted in the development of a range of effective drugs, which include antidepressants, tranquillizers (which relieve anxiety) and neuroleptics (used in the treatment of psychosis).

The various schools of psychotherapy have tended to see mental disorder as virtually universal (although differently construed to ICD-10 or DSM-IV) and mental health as a goal of perfection towards which everyone might aspire, but which few will reach. Thus the focus of concern has been more upon symptoms such as depression or anxiety, and relational issues such as family or marital disharmony, and less upon biological factors. Drug treatments are similarly often eschewed.

Christian spirituality involves the relationship between the whole person and a God who reveals himself uniquely in the person of Jesus Christ. This relational perspective on human experience has much in common with the understanding of mental health outlined above. In spirituality the relationship of concern is the human/divine, as well as the human/human, but in an incarnational faith such as Christianity these can hardly be separated. Different approaches to spirituality have parallels in the different schools of psychology and psychotherapy. Thus, for example, Peter Morea (1997) notes the similarities between Carl Jung's analytical psychology and the 'interior journey' of Teresa of Avila.

For Freud, religion was a neurosis, arising from the 'wish fulfilment' associated with the longing for a protective and powerful father figure. The notion of 'spiritual health' was thus, for him, the exact opposite of that conceived by Christianity, and Christian faith in his view was incompatible with mental health. A more recent tendency has been to see some forms of religious observance as a type of 'addiction'. While it would appear likely that, for some people, religious faith may be a sign of mental disorder, a contemporary understanding of spiritual and mental health would be likely to find many more themes of common concern, and fewer reasons for perceiving any conflict. There is clearly a need to develop a more thoughtful theological basis for an understanding of mental health and mental illness. [Christopher Cook]

MID-LIFE
See AGEING

MIND–BODY
See: BRAIN, BODY

MINISTER
A person formally recognized as performing a particular spiritual service on behalf of a church or congregation.
In common usage the term is still used generally to designate clergy of all denominations, and in the secular term 'minister of religion' official representatives of any faith. Within the Church, however, the development of lay ministry has led to a general shift in usage which has uncovered more of its traditional meaning. The word derives from the Latin *minister* (servant), *ministerium* (service); which in turn is used to translate the New Testament Greek *diakonos, diakonia*. Individual ministry is an outworking of the corporate fellowship (*koinonia*) established by Christ's own service on the cross and his service is taken as the norm for all ministry,

individual and corporate (cf. John 13.1–15; Matt. 25; Phil. 2.1–11; 2 Cor. 3.6; 2 Cor. 11.15; Rom. 15.8). Anyone who performs a particular function which is needed by the whole Christian community for the completion of its service (cf. Ephesians 4.12) can be recognized as the 'minister' of the particular function they have been called to perform, as in the term 'welcoming ministry', for example, or 'ministry of the word'. Sometimes the occasion itself demands a 'minister', without there being any formal recognition of the individual, simply the need for that ministry, e.g. nurses performing emergency baptism. In a similar sense individuals entering Christian marriage are regarded as its ministers, both formally in the exchange of vows and in terms of their continued life together. Sometimes it is the function itself which defines the minister (e.g. in the Book of Common Prayer the usage denoting whoever is conducting a service). Or, as in modern liturgical usage, a priest 'presides' at a Eucharist, but other individuals, lay and ordained, may be ministers of different parts of the service and every member of the congregation may be regarded as a minister of the sacrament, by virtue of their participation in the offering of prayer and worship.

Thus the term can be used to denote any person performing a service on behalf of the whole community, lay or ordained. However, this still recognizes a distinction between the ability of any individual to exercise a particular gift (*charism*) and those who can be regarded as its ministers on behalf of the whole community. For example, an individual might claim a gift of healing and yet not be recognized as its minister. The latter term is a statement of their relationship to the whole Christian community and its service (*diakonia*) as well as their particular gifting as an individual. This distinction is almost invariably given substance within different denominations by some kind of commissioning, ordaining, training or accreditation. This validation of individual ministry may occur at various levels, from the local congregation upwards and vice versa depending on differences in church tradition and theology, but the recognition by the whole community of its need for a particular form of service (call or commissioning) and its acceptance of an individual for such (validation, ordination), is always implied by the use of the term 'minister' of any individual. [Christopher Moody]

MINISTRY, LAY
The exercise of particular gifts and functions on behalf of the whole Church by lay people.

The adjective 'lay' in secular society carries the connotation 'not expert' or 'not professional'. Discussions about lay ministry may, therefore, unconsciously import the question 'How can we make it more professional?' without questioning how far any spiritual ministry, lay or ordained, which derives ultimately from the corporate experience of worship, can be termed professional in the usual sense. On the other hand, the root of the term 'laity' in the *laos theou*, i.e. people of God, is gaining increasing importance in thinking about all ministry, lay and ordained (Marriage, 1995).

Thus, on one level the term 'lay ministry' simply describes the development of voluntary, trained and accredited ministries among the non-ordained in many churches, including the Roman Catholic Church, widely undertaken out of necessity (e.g. the use of catechists in rural areas of Africa) without too much theological reflection. But on another level it is one of the most contentious terms in use in the Church today, (1) because it points to an area of change and development in the internal structure of many denominations, and (2) because it indicates the influence that changes in secular society generally have had on how the Church sees itself and its mission in the world. Lay ministry is a specifically modern term that reflects the process of transition from a Christendom to a post-Christendom model for the Church and society, which began, in the Western Church at least, with the Reformation. In the Christendom model any citizen might be regarded, potentially, as a member of the faithful, and the Church was usually defined more narrowly in terms of its ordained hierarchy. There was no such thing as 'the laity', at least as a term that people might apply self-referentially to define their own role within the Church. In a post-Christendom model, however, the Church and its membership, lay and ordained, is largely defined over against society in general. Membership of the laity thus becomes more self-conscious and is usually defined by active participation in church life (Schillebeeckx, 1985).

Historically, the development of lay ministry has been influenced by a number of factors, positive and negative. While in many

denominations, the ability to attract and support paid clergy has declined, the increase in general education, training and leisure among large sections of the population means that they are still able to draw on wider resources of lay involvement and expertise. From the Methodist Sunday schools, classes and lay preachers of the eighteenth century, to the house groups, catechumenate and locally based training courses of today, many are drawn into active ministry of various kinds. Increasingly, churches draw their ordained ministers from those already drawn into active lay involvement. On the other hand, some argue that this has clericalized some lay people while disabling others, and has been largely managed, institutionally, without questioning the professional status of the clergy. According to this view, the focus has been on co-opting lay people into the internal life of churches rather than outwards into the world, traditionally the area in which the ministry of the laity was most clearly to be known and appropriate. A renewal of missionary studies and the insights drawn from sources as various as 'every member ministry', the charismatic movement, biblical scholarship and liberation theology have led more recently to an emphasis on the corporate nature of all ministry, lay and ordained, and the attention that needs to be given to the development of the Christian community in ministry as well as individual training.

The nature of New Testament thinking about ministry is corporate throughout. It knows no hard and fast distinction between lay and ordained ministry. Instead there is a variety of different patterns involving local and peripatetic ministries. The only time the term 'priesthood' is used of the Christian Church is in relation to the vocation of the whole community to be built up into a spiritual house (1 Pet. 2). The same chapter makes it plain that this is part and parcel of the call to become God's people, his *laos*. The vocation is most clearly revealed in the life, death and resurrection of Jesus Christ, into which all are incorporated through baptism. Though it may be anticipated already in the life of individual congregations through the indwelling Spirit, their final nature and fulfilment as the people of God will be known only in the coming of the Kingdom, a new reality inclusive of the world as well as the body of believers. Thus the ministry of believers, lay or ordained, is not undertaken for the benefit

of the Christian community alone, but for the benefit of all creation. Service is connected with the alternative word 'stewardship' in the parables (cf. Luke 19.11ff; Matt. 25.14ff) and thus with God's plan of salvation for all humanity, not just the Church. Paul uses the same association of words and ideas to describe his own apostolic task in 1 Cor. 4.1ff, and in 1 Pet. 4.10 it is applied to the ministry of every Christian. The 'in-house' nature of much modern thinking about lay ministry and how it fits in to church structures does less than justice to the eschatological character of the term 'people of God' as the servant of creation following the example of Christ, the second Adam (1 Cor. 15), the nature of whose fellowship is already a sign of the reality of the age to come (Zizioulas, 1993).
[Christopher Moody]

MINISTRY, ORDAINED
The exercise of particular gifts and functions by authorized persons on behalf of the whole Church.
The New Testament knows no hard and fast distinction between lay and ordained ministry. Instead there is a variety of local and peripatetic ministries, serving a single congregation or groups of churches. Direct reference is made to the ministries of the bishop, or 'overseer', and the deacon, or 'servant' of the community (e.g. Acts 6.1–6; Acts 20.28; Phil. 1.1; 1 Tim. 3.1–8). But, notoriously, it is impossible to extrapolate from the pages of the New Testament, and especially from the corporate function of the elders, or 'presbyters' of the community (1 Tim. 4.14), the figure of the single ordained minister of a local congregation – the way in which the ordained ministry is still most commonly exercised and experienced in churches today. This particular way of structuring the ordained ministry is something historically associated with the development of a parochial system. Some argue, therefore, that the return to a more 'missionary' context for ministry in modern conditions severely questions and undermines such a position and blurs once again the distinction between lay and ordained.

It is also true that the title of priest in the New Testament is reserved for the exalted Christ alone (cf. Heb. 4.14ff and the whole Epistle). This is a priesthood established by Christ's obedience to the Father and his one, perfect sacrifice, and mediated to the world

through the ministry of the Church in all its members, lay and ordained (Moberly, 1897). Two points flow from this which have been reflected in modern discussion: (1) it is impossible to give absolute scriptural validity to any single form of church order, e.g. the threefold order of bishops, priests and deacons, or a presbyterian form of government, though the differing weight given to conformity with church teaching and tradition as well as Scripture in the different church traditions also affects the argument; (2) a renewed emphasis on the mutual and corporate, relational aspect of all ministry, known in such terms as 'collegiality' or 'collaborative ministry'. Attention needs to be given, not only to how the ordained ministry functions and derives authority, but how it is received by the whole people of God, the laos, in a variety of circumstances, described in terms of its common mission as well as pastoral and spiritual needs.

On the other hand, there is general agreement that order itself is a gift of the Holy Spirit to the whole Church (Eph. 4; 1 Cor. 12), and that this is reflected particularly in the relationship between the local congregation and the wider church which finds its focus in the ordained ministry. A further distinction can then be made between the individual gifts, or *charisms*, which are distributed to all God's people, without discrimination, and 'the grace of orders' by a formal invocation of the Holy Spirit and the laying on of hands (ordination) through which the ministry of some individuals is recognized and dedicated for the benefit of the whole community. Originally the need for pastoral oversight (Greek: *episkope*) to keep the Church in the way of faith was binding on all members of the Church (Heb. 12.5ff). But it quickly became the function of a special office. This need for 'oversight' still constitutes the core function of the ordained ministry. The Lima document states: 'Every church needs this ministry of unity in some form in order to be the Church of God, the one body of Christ, a sign of the unity of all in the Kingdom' (para. 23, p. 25).

Ordained ministry is known in a variety of ways in different churches and different circumstances, via the authority to preach and teach, to preside at the celebration of holy communion, the pastoral care and 'discipling' of the church and individuals, the ministry of reminding the church of its own task and representing it in various ways, and the discernment and enabling of the gifts of individuals. This does not mean that these functions are reserved exclusively to the ordained, as long as the principle of order is maintained. How this is done, for example in presiding at the ministry of word and sacrament, the exercise of charismatic gifts in teaching, prophecy and healing, and the role of the local congregation in receiving and structuring the ministry, lay and ordained, is the focus of much modern discussion (Carr, 1989).

If one imagines a square divided vertically by a line between two poles, functional and representative, and horizontally by a line between two poles, collaborative and hierarchical, one can see how various descriptions of the ordained ministry, modern and traditional, more or less fit into the different quadrants. As a very crude generalization, traditional views of the ordained ministry have concentrated either on its hierarchical and representative aspect within a sacramental model (Catholic/Orthodox), or its hierarchical and functional aspect in a magisterial one (Protestant), while modern discussions concentrate on either its collaborative and functional aspect as a profession helping to energize and organize local congregations (evangelical models), or its collaborative and representative aspect in relation to the changing social and cultural world beyond the Church (liberation models). All these lines of argument tend to justify themselves within their own terms, but none of the poles can be entirely neglected. The Church knows its own true nature only as it is called into the mission of God to the world, as well as the way it embodies the life of Christ in its own fellowship. This argues for the continued existence of an apostolic and pastoral ministry which points beyond the needs of individual congregations and immediate church structures (Moody, 1992). How far actual patterns of ordained ministry reflect this is a different question. Modern representatives of the Catholic and Orthodox positions, such as Schillebeeckx and Zizioulas, argue that within the pattern of relationships set up by the call of God to be his people and the continuously renewed gift of divine life in worship, teaching and sacrament, the different ministries, 'lay' and ordained, depend on each other for their fulfilment and realization, but without one being derived from the other. They both help to constitute the nature of the Church as the sacrament of the unity of all people in the life of the Kingdom. *[Christopher Moody]*

MIRACLE
An event in which God is believed to act in order to reveal himself and further his purpose.
Every definition or attempted explanation of miracles presents its own difficulties. A 'stronger' definition might include the idea of change in the course of nature which observers believe would not have happened without a direct or indirect act of God. Christians can agree with David Hume that miracles are not historically or empirically verifiable, while still rejecting his formal denial of God and miracles. Whether faith precedes perception of God's work or follows it, miracles are reported by persons of faith, though not all persons of faith have observed miracles nor believe that they occur. The fundamental feature of any notion of miracle is 'God' and God's activity: not the outcome. So long as one believes that God has created and sustains the cosmos, there is always the possibility of actions which would be termed 'miraculous'. Virtually every theistic religion affirms miracles. Yet, since neither God nor faith are part of nature, divine acts ascertained by human faith elude scientific observation. The popular view of miracles, the one that pastors will chiefly encounter, is a long way from theological sophistication. Individuals frequently observe aspects of folk or common religious life and perceive miracles. Belief in a miracle (especially, for instance, deliverance from death, or healing) can be deeply rooted in a person's experience, and cannot be proven otherwise.

Even when theists accept miracles, theological hurdles remain. For example, many biblical and claimed contemporary miracles appear unjust, trivial and meaningless. Though the Bible promises that God's power is available to believers, Christians seem to experience divine silence and unrelieved suffering as often as anyone. Counter-intuitively, in fact, God often works miraculously in the lives of the unrighteous leaving the righteous to suffer. And Jesus' teaching, following the wisdom tradition of the Old Testament, flatly denies that God is good only to the righteous. Moreover, the recipients of miracles do not seem to have been blessed in order to accomplish some great work for God.

More problems emerge if God is believed to perform miracles clearly and regularly. Most theologians recognize that if God were to rescue individuals whenever they faced the painful consequences of their own or others' misdeeds, it would so radically alter human freedom as to call it into question. In this fashion miracles can subvert responsibility and negate freedom. Also, if God were consistently to grant the faithful person's requests, what mortal could resist the temptation to have faith in God in order to receive the gifts of God? Self-interest would triumph. Routine miraculous deliverance would mute God's universal call from the midst of suffering to repent and do good works (Lewis, 1947). God does not do miracles clearly, regularly, or with obvious intentionality.

Most believers will conclude that God does miracles, but rarely and ambiguously so as not to undermine human freedom or divine purpose. Nevertheless, it is extraordinary how often people will claim to a pastor that they have experienced a miracle. The minister has to listen: the story will often give a clue to other aspects of the person's life. It is usually unhelpful to address the issue directly. But the pastor may gently indicate the potential consequences for the treatment of others, the understanding of God, or whatever seems to be the next point of interpretation, thus encouraging the person who believes that he or she has encountered a miracle to develop their faith and their sympathy for others. The public claim to miraculous events, usually a cure, as proof or evidence of the work of God may even result in a charge of false advertising. The idea of miracle provokes faith and thought rather than proves anything. This occasions the pastor's opportunity (Kushner, 2000). [Paul Plenge Parker]

MIRRORING
A care-giver's empathic interaction with a young child.
Object relations theorists have stressed the importance of a nurturing and empathic environment for healthy childhood development. If an adult responds empathically to (or 'mirrors') the child's self-ambitions and idealization of its parents and the feelings and sensations of the child within their care, then the child is more likely to develop a sense of self-esteem and autonomy. Occasional failure by the care-giver to be empathic can help the child to develop a realistic sense of themselves and others. A chronic lack of empathy from a carer, however, can cause longer-term psychological damage to a child.

MISCARRIAGE
See: PERI-NATAL DEATH

MIXED MARRIAGE
Marriage in which the partners come from different national, ethnic or religious backgrounds.
Increasing geographical mobility and social tolerance have made mixed marriage common in contemporary Western societies. Very occasionally, cross-national marriages will be contracted to secure the right to live and work in a foreign country (marriages of convenience). More commonly, they reflect the realities of pluralistic societies. Sometimes they will be contracted because they embody 'otherness'. Mixed marriages are most vulnerable in times of national, racial or religious conflict. It has been wryly observed that every marriage is a mixed marriage in the sense that each encompasses differences of gender and family culture.

MONASTICISM
A religious way of life lived outside the normal structures of society and church, that aims to establish conditions favourable to personal sanctification through a common life based on a rule and the 'counsels of perfection' – poverty, chastity and obedience.
While monasticism exists in traditions other than Christianity, most notably Buddhism, this entry focuses only on Christian contexts. In origin monks were drop-outs, the form of whose faith led them to despair of finding salvation in the world. They therefore established an alternative world, the monastery. Monastic life was not seen as one vocation among a spectrum of possible vocations, but as the only way to be seriously committed to discipleship. The prologue to Benedict's *Rule for Monks* defines a monastery as 'a school of the Lord's service'. From it the monk might emerge only to run away, or to become a hermit after long years of disciplined communal life. The monastery, then, is the alternative to a world that is inimical to salvation. It provides an environment in which priorities seen as worldly are put into reverse and distractions from the service of God minimized.

The history of monasticism is kaleidoscopic. Monks and nuns continue to engage in a remarkable variety of tasks and to assume very diverse responsibilities. But monasteries have never entirely lost the originating impulse to be a world over against the world. A monastery is an attempt to implement eschatological values: in an otherwise time-bound world monasteries are islands of people aiming to live already in the eternal. The possibility of the encumbrance and complication of marital and familial entanglements is removed by the simple but drastic expedient of excluding members of the opposite sex. In Benedict's Rule status-seeking and the accumulation of possessions are strongly discouraged. The three key aspects to monastic life are prayer, work and reading. Together these provide a basic pattern by which to live, thus creating a stable structure for the monk or nun. Humility and obedience are the characteristic monastic virtues, silence is crucial and the monks' only indispensable work is the direct praise of God in the monastic liturgy.

The predominant contemporary Christian ethos is self-consciously pastoral, with the emphasis on doing good in one form or other. This mental world is poles apart from the monastic project, which is therefore easily seen as an escapist fantasy. A powerful case can be made against the monastery as an institutionalized refusal to engage with and take responsibility for our world with a view to changing it from within. A counter-argument would be that in such a Church above all there is need for a living sign of the transcendent. From this standpoint it is a strength that the aims and purposes of monasteries cannot be defined by the immediate and empirical. A monastery could even be described as an environment explicitly designed to promote soul-searching and consequent self-transcendence. The persistence of the monastic aspiration in a world and a Church startlingly different from the period of its origins may reflect an appropriate discontent. Whether any actual monastery either does or could provide the necessary witness is a different question. [Nicholas Peter Harvey]

MONOGAMY
A condition of marriage allowing for only one spouse.
Monogamy can be interpreted differently. Some faith communities recognize only one valid marriage in a lifetime. Civil laws governing marriage are likely to legitimate remarriage providing a prior marriage has been legally ended; this condition is described as serial monogamy. Differences between church and state in the interpretation of monogamy can be a source of tension for individuals who use both institutions as a reference point for deciding what constitutes legitimate behaviour.

Monogamy is also sometimes used as a synonym for fidelity, incorporating the aspiration of most married couples to remain together as a sexually exclusive couple until one partner dies. There is evidence to suggest that while the monogamous ideal receives widespread support, it often does not correspond with actual behaviour in marriage.

MOOD DISORDERS
Mental illnesses characterized by excessively low moods, or both low moods and great highs.
There are two primary types of mood disorder: (1) *depressive disorder* includes periods of hopelessness, self-loathing and apathy, changes in sleep and appetite, fatigue, and social withdrawal; (2) *bipolar disorder* includes depression as well as mania, which is a period of euphoria, inflated self-esteem, reduced sleep, and racing thoughts. A vulnerability to mood disorders is often familial. Optimal treatment usually involves both psychotherapy and medication (Goodwin and Jamison, 1990). [Susan Dunlap]

MORAL DEVELOPMENT
Growth in moral understanding, character and behaviour over the course of a person's lifetime.
Recognition that moral development is a significant aspect of human life has a long history in Western thought. In ancient Greece, Plato suggested that it was linked with intellectual development, as humans struggle for knowledge of goodness and truth. In a different way in ancient Israel, the prophet Jeremiah described his moral development as part of his growth in faith and understanding of God's will for his life and for his society. Similarly, St Paul wrote of his growth from childlike understanding into adulthood, as he contemplated the nature of love (1 Cor. 13.11). It is affirmed that Jesus too developed as a human being (Luke 2.40).

Therefore the Church has always acknowledged its responsibility for encouraging and enabling moral development. It has been concerned with appropriate education and moral teaching, and for the nurture of the individual conscience. In some churches this responsibility has rested primarily with the priest; in others the entire community of faithful people has shared in the tasks. The Christian spiritual tradition has emphasized the connection between spiritual growth and moral development, describing life as a pilgrimage, or a journey, through various stages.

In the twentieth century several theories of moral development were proposed by psychologists. Freud emphasized the connection with biological growth. As the body changes in response to the demands of life so individuals develop from the pre-moral stage of infancy, into the stage of ego-centred behaviour, and finally into the socially acceptable life of the morally mature person. Piaget emphasized the link with cognitive capacities. Growth in moral behaviour occurs with the acquisition of different skills in perceiving and interacting with the world. The most comprehensive theories of moral development are to be found in the work of Lawrence Kohlberg and Carol Gilligan. Kohlberg (1984) describes six developmental stages, from being led by the will of other people, to being self-centred in decision-making, and finally to being guided by universal principles. In a hypothetical seventh stage, Kohlberg suggests that we may begin to question the very basis of morality by asking why we are moral at all. Gilligan (1982) challenges this theory for its gender bias, proposing that the moral development of women is different. Since women understand themselves to be living within networks of relationship, their moral development is linked with increasingly complex and intricate negotiations with others. The most mature stage is one in which mutual care and connectedness can be most fully realized.

Theories of moral development are helpful in considering the pastoral care of women and men of all ages. We may also come to understand those factors which contribute to, or which may inhibit development into, the fullness of our humanity. [Susan F. Parsons]

MORAL JUDGEMENT
How moral decisions are made.
The long-standing natural law tradition holds that a set of universal principles can be read off with certainty from the nature of things. The task of moral judgement is to apply these principles in particular situations.

A characteristically modern emphasis is that much behaviour and thinking result from social conditioning. People are all products of their culture, family of origin, socio-economic circumstances and so forth to an extent that leaves them with very limited freedom. Even principles are an aspect of a particular human environment.

Meanwhile psychological theories draw attention to the extent to which unconscious factors can determine attitudes. This insight need not be taken fatalistically. Like the social conditioning argument, it is a salutary corrective to the rationalistic view that it is adequate to describe human actions entirely in terms of conscious choices. The reluctance of systematic and moral theology to take seriously psychological and sociological perspectives has been unhelpful to pastoral studies, where questions of responsibility, culpability and guilt, all relevant to moral judgement, loom large. In this respect pastoral theology finds itself unduly isolated.

Kierkegaard (1843, 1985) saw that if morality is governed by universal principles then ethics is God. In stark contrast he recognized the creativity of decisions taken in faith, meaning trust in awareness against all odds. A connection can be made with the themes of social conditioning and the unconscious. Human action can only be called moral when it transcends the inertia, conformism and alienation from spontaneity which always threaten to prevail. A faith-based morality generates actions performed in hope, the stubborn conviction against sometimes overwhelming empirical evidence that this world is heaven in the making.

Situation ethics argues that in all circumstances we must do whatever is most loving. It resembles faith-based morality in eschewing rules but diverges radically from it in enshrining a principle. In practice 'the most loving thing' tends to be recognized by means of a calculation of advantageous outcomes. Thus utilitarianism appears in the guise of love.

In theory, Christians have tended to look for moral guidance to something oracular, whether the Bible itself or some version of tradition. In practice there is a largely unexamined assumption that the allegedly revelatory source confirms and makes explicit those principles available to reason. Revelation clarifies what is obscured by sin as people pay attention to principles. Yet the notion that the moral teaching to be found in the Bible and/or other authoritative church documents forms a coherent, transcultural whole bears no scrutiny. It therefore cannot be the case that either the Bible or tradition as such founds moral judgements. An unacknowledged process of selection and reconstruction is going on. When ready appeal is made to principles, or to biblical morality or tradition, the suspicion must be that social control, not faith, predominates. [*Nicholas Peter Harvey*]

MORTIFICATION
The practice of freely abstaining from certain habits or patterns of lifestyle in order to live at a deeper level.
The biblical justification for mortification (literally 'putting to death') appears in two texts (Rom. 8.13; Col. 3.5). In each of these the call to 'put to death' certain activities is only a part of the call to live by the Spirit and to share the life of the resurrection: a means, not an end. But the terminology used ('the deeds of the body', 'what is earthly in you', etc.) later helped to encourage the idea that the body and all things physical were inherently sinful for Christians: mortification, in whatever form it was practised, thus became a particularly intensive manifestation of a way of life to which all Christians were called.

Modern feminist historians have shown that this understanding led to a pervasive depreciation of women, who were especially associated with the 'sins of the flesh' in early and medieval Christian teaching. Some women felt obliged to adopt forms of mortification (such as extreme fasting), which in turn led to the experience of visions (often centred on the sufferings of Christ) of overwhelming power and intensity, and thereby attained an inner spiritual freedom in a sternly patriarchal society (Jantzen, 1996). Broadly speaking, however, monastic writers (of both sexes) sought to encourage a carefully controlled pattern of personal mortification, not only in order to redirect the promptings of the flesh towards the desire for God, but also as a form of loving and costly response to the sufferings of Christ; and this approach was adopted by many Protestant writers as well.

Religious people sometimes interpret mortification as requiring self-mutilation. This has been a mark of extreme religious behaviour. Few spiritual teachers, however, have held this to be a desirable aspect of mortification. It is more than likely to represent some psychological disturbance for which therapeutic treatment is advisable.

Mortification is an attempt to apply to one's own life Christ's injunctions about wealth and self-denial (thus Harton (1932) defines it as 'the necessary condition of living the gospel life'). The weakness of Christian teaching on the subject, apart from its suspicion of all things bodily, may be felt to be its narrowly individualist emphasis. Its strength, however, lies in its recognition that Christ-centred self-denial is integral to the Christian life, not least as a form of active identification with the poor; and in this respect it has clear parallels with recent critiques of self-indulgent consumerism, and with the insights of liberation theology. [*Gordon Mursell*]

MOTHERING
See: PARENTING

MOURNING
The public side of personal grief.
To grieve following a bereavement is widely recognized as important. Part of that process is mourning. Here the personal loss is given public recognition, thus enabling the mourners to begin to reintegrate their lives. When mourning is for some reason not completely possible, as seems to occur, for example, when the deceased's body is not recovered after a war or disaster, mourning may become pathological. Thus in many (probably all) cultures rituals of mourning have been developed and are usually well defined. Special behaviour and distinctive clothing are expected and boundaries are set. However, in Western societies such customary mourning has become less significant. The long-term effect of this change remains unclear. Freud's classification of normal mourning at loss, pathological mourning (where the person cannot let the deceased go) and melancholia, in which the person identifies with the lost object, has been very influential this century, not only in psychoanalysis but also in the understanding of bereavement (Freud, 1917).

Yet even if social mourning on the grand scale has declined, there are outstanding exceptions which seem to require major response. Examples would be at the death of a monarch or president, or a catastrophe involving many people. It still seems necessary to mourn in some fashion. Bowlby (1985a) refers to studies of the different courses that mourning may take for widows and widowers. Men were less likely to report their feelings and tended to be more matter-of-fact than women, less fearful of breakdown and less given to rehearsing the events leading to their spouse's death. Men also expressed anger less frequently, and in general were reported to be more in control of their feelings. One consequence of the loss of profound public mourning can be that people do not appreciate that extended mourning is natural. It is reckoned that the process normally lasts as long as between 12 and 18 months, and until such time has elapsed the possibility that mourning has become pathological should not be considered. But if the bereaved person shows signs of not being able to resolve their sadness, the possibility of some deeper counsel should be considered. [D. Murray]

MUSIC
Motion in the dynamic fields of tone and time.

There are many theories about what music is. Budd (1985) distinguishes two distinct schools of thought: one holds that music as beauty of form has little to do with the world of feeling; the other regards music as having everything to do with the expression of feeling.

Zuckerkandl (1956) draws together important dimensions from the many theorists by seeking to uncover the core of music. He describes this core as motion in the dynamic fields of tone and metre and holds music to be symbolic of the dynamic flow of life itself. In particular he writes that this tonal motion, an 'away from' and 'towards', is a flux between the tones themselves and forms the structure of scales, the elemental structural dynamic patterns underpinning all music.

If music is a symbol of the dynamic core of life itself then music in pastoral studies and in pastoral care in particular is of importance. From a symbolic perspective music may be thought of as a way of approaching the dynamic core of life which, in religious language, is called God.

Music traditionally has had an important place in the Church's liturgy, both in performance and shared hymn singing. Celebrations such as marriage and the funeral service are further occasions when music is evident. How this powerful dynamic flowing symbol of God is understood is of interest here. Music may be described as a holding flowing phenomenon in which people experience the creation and resolution of tonal and rhythmic tensions. From the perspective of pastoral care, the listeners or participants in music could be said to be caught up into this dynamic flowing space which is shaped by tone and metre. They may then experience some resolution of their conflicting mental states as they are held in the right ordered dynamic symbol of the ebb and flow of life itself. This interpretation of the power in music demands that the choice of appropriate music for any religious event must be exercised with sensitivity and care.

Music in the concert hall may also offer a containing, transforming function as it does in church. The listener's/performer's inner mental tensions are temporarily met and held in this flowing space. Music, this sounding story of the ebb and flow of tensions, may pattern a resolution for the listener/performer which they then embody. This process may provide some mental space for further peaceful reflection.

The same dynamic principles described above inform and govern the musical engagement of client and therapist in the therapeutic context. Music here becomes a flowing playground in which a right ordering of ebb and flow of the core of life itself may be experienced. [Mary Butterton]

MUTILATION
See: MORTIFICATION

MYERS-BRIGGS TYPE INDICATOR (MBTI)
A self-completion questionnaire designed to identify with Jungian personality types.

The Myers-Briggs Type Indicator was originally developed by Isabel Myers and Katharine Briggs to assess Jungian personality types by identifying preferences between introversion and extraversion, sensing and intuition, thinking and feeling, and judging and perceiving. The MBTI employs two types of forced-choice questions: a choice between phrases and a choice between word pairs. Form G of the MBTI is the version most frequently used. This is available as a self-scorable booklet containing 94 scored items, and a form scored by the test administrator containing an additional 32 items not generally scored. Sale and use of the MBTI is restricted to qualified test-users. A good review of the test is provided by Bayne (1995).

MYSTICISM
The usual – but in some ways unhelpful – term for those experiences by which religious doctrine and imagery are 'internalized' by the believer.

The study of 'mysticism' is surrounded by a lot of conceptual confusion. For many traditional exponents of religious studies, it describes experiences of union with the divine or transcendent; and there have been many attempts to identify some kind of core experience in all traditions – and indeed in the lives of people apparently not connected with any formal religious tradition at all. Quite often, this core experience has been identified as a profound sense of 'unity', with God and with the creation, or simply with the sheer thereness of being. For some scholars, a distinction may be made between 'theistic' and 'monistic' mysticism – between the experience of <u>love</u> and communion and an experience that can better be thought of as 'absorption' in its object.

Writing on the matter has become increasingly suspicious of these categories and increasingly sensitive to the huge variety of ideas and narratives that have been lumped together as 'mystical' (Woods, 1980). The words 'mystical' and 'mysticism' in the sense of referring to specific kinds of experiences are relatively modern and exclusively Western. Far more attention has been devoted lately to the ways in which 'mystical' texts, texts discussing or evoking direct experience of the divine, are noted in their own traditions. While accounts of experiencing the divine or transcendent in different traditions may from time to time converge, we fail to understand the way these texts work if we fail to see how the experiences are interpreted and structured as what one writer has called 'exemplifications' of the doctrines and images of a faith community. The extraordinary experiences often recorded are not seen as significant except as showing how the deepest patterns of reality as set out in the teachings of a <u>religion</u> are made real in the lives of particular individuals (McGinn, 1991). The 'mystic' lives out what the religious language and images describe. The Buddhist meditator realizes the transitoriness and illusoriness of all impressions; the Christian contemplative's story reflects the patterns of self-emptying, cross and resurrection; the Sufi enters into the depths of obedience or submission (the literal meaning of 'Islam') to

find there a totality of bliss, a kind of erotic joy; and so on.

To be able to respond effectively to experiences of unusual intensity and religious fulfilment requires not only familiarity with the 'phenomenological' accounts of mysticism (descriptions of what seems to happen), but sensitivity to the entire belief system of the person involved. Sometimes it is important to reassure people that these intense and disorienting experiences have happened to others and are not necessarily signs of insanity or imbalance. But it is always desirable to help people integrate any such experiences into how they see the world and themselves – and God – overall (Lash, 1988). *[Rowan Williams]*

MYTH
Symbolic narratives which explain the origins of the tribe and cosmos, and which locate the values of a group or society in a large frame of reference – cosmic, historical or societal.

Myths are common in oral or written form to almost all known cultures. They include accounts of natural events, stories of heroic or paradigmatic individuals or groups in the past, and narratives of the actions of supernatural beings. Mythic narratives are often placed outside normal human time in a supernatural realm. But they may refer to events which oral tradition or textual record place within the realm of human history. The Jewish and Christian traditions include both mythic styles in their Scriptures.

N

NARCISSISM
Obsessive self-preoccupation.

Narcissus was a youth who, according to Greek legend, mistook his own reflection in a pool for another person and fell in love with this image. Narcissism in common usage is therefore simply used to mean love of the <u>self</u>, and has usually a negative connotation. Narcissistic relationships are those in which an image of the self gets in the way of seeing the other person. Narcissus was also wooed by the nymph Echo, but would not look up from his own reflection to see her. She therefore dwindled away to a mere auditory reflection. Narcissistic relationships are therefore those in which something, usually fear, prevents the individual from risking looking at the other person. When the other person refuses to be ignored or impinges in some way which might often be unintentional, the result is often what is known as narcissistic rage.

Because these sorts of relationships have to be carefully controlled to keep the awareness of the other at bay, the narcissistic person tends to feel that something is missing, as of course it is. The result of this is that the narcissistic person has a great need for something more to put in the place of what should be another person, but the something more that is acceptable must be carefully controlled. It might consist of positive reinforcement, approval or good feelings, which will be eagerly sought. These positive reinforcements are known as narcissistic supplies.

Narcissus was brought up by a single-parent nymph and psychoanalytic theory would suggest that narcissistic relationships come about sometimes because of impingement in infancy or because the primary carer and the infant could not together arrive at a satisfactory mutual interchange of food, care and love.

Counsellors and psychotherapists are often consulted by people with excessively narcissistic tendencies because they have very counterproductive relationships characterized by outbursts of anger and a sense of injury over a feeling that they have been deprived of something that is rightfully theirs – hence the problems with narcissistic entitlement. Therapeutic work in this area will need to bring about an awareness of the existence of the other that is not too threatening or frightening, but that allows for gradually more acknowledgement that the other exists. This can be a long slow process, requiring great skill and patience.

Symington (1997) has moved on from Freud's (1914) paper on narcissism. He puts great emphasis on the refusal implied in narcissism and calls it 'turning away from the lifegiver'. The lifegiver in this sense can be seen as initially probably the mother, but may also be seen as a more fully functioning part of the self, or as the individual's concept of God. [*Lesley Murdin*]

NARRATIVE THEOLOGY
Theological perspectives that emphasize the central role of imaginative language, including the use of stories, metaphors, and symbols in peoples' religious faith and traditions.

Narrative is characteristic of Scripture and the Christian tradition: it is told in stories. Biblical theologians study different types of narratives and use them to reconstruct early Christian ideas about Jesus, the Trinity and other doctrines (Wright, 1988). A narrative hermeneutic can be used to understand how stories, metaphors and symbols shape what truth is for people of religious faith. Narrative theology has enabled people with different beliefs and from various disciplines to enter into dialogue with one another around the story. Similarly, these perspectives are useful in developing contextual pastoral theology, such as African-American and Asian pastoral theologies (Wimberley, 1997).

NARRATIVE THERAPY
An approach to therapy using philosophy and literary theory to describe the social construction of reality.

Narrative therapy was formulated in the 1990s by two family systems therapists, White and Epston (1990). These therapists help people, first of all, to use particular strategies to recognize how their personal/family narratives are problem-oriented and shaped by cultural narratives. This process, called externalizing the problem, allows people, then, to develop new stories about their lives – this is called re-authoring. Pastoral counsellors who use narrative therapy value its congruence with liberation theology.

NATURAL DISASTERS
See: DISASTERS

NEIGHBOUR
Any other human being as encountered in the here and now.

In Christian understanding all human beings share a relatedness as sisters and brothers in Jesus Christ. This relatedness becomes relationship when others are met in any concrete situation. Once encountered they become the neighbour whose needs must be responded to with practical love. Unlike English, French helpfully distinguishes between *voisin*, as in 'next-door neighbour' and *prochain*, as in biblical usage, notably the story of the Good Samaritan (Luke 10.25–37). The parable contains a twist in that the reader expects Jesus to define neighbour as 'someone in need', whereas he turns round the question to ask who has behaved most as neighbour (most compassionately) to the person in need.

In the Old Testament neighbour can mean 'one another' (Jer. 23.27) but generally refers to a fellow-member of the covenant people. It implies moral obligation, e.g. in the Ten Commandments: 'You shall not bear false witness against your neighbour. You shall not covet your neighbour's house' (Exod. 20.16–17). It occurs frequently in Deut., but most famously at Lev. 19.18: 'You shall not take vengeance or bear a grudge against any of your people, but you shall love your neighbour as yourself: I am the LORD'. This is the passage Jesus used to summarize the law in Luke 10.27.

In Christian eyes, love of neighbour lies at the heart of both morality and spirituality, since someone in need is both an icon of God and a means towards God; in showing compassion I encounter Christ (Matt. 25.31–46). In recent decades the notion of neighbour has been threatened by a macro-economic approach to problems. It is precisely the perspective on human beings most in danger of being lost by the dehumanizing consequences of international transfer of capital or the downsizing of an organization to fit in with shifts in the global economy.

There is a pastoral issue around the relation of loving one's neighbour and loving one's self. Modern psychology recognizes the indispensability of self-esteem and the interdependent nature of all human relationships. Browning (1987) discusses this tension in relation to Freud, humanistic psychology, Reinhold Niebuhr, Skinner, Jung, Erikson, Kohut and others. He argues that the modern psychobiological theories of the non-moral good offer basic frameworks for the definition of health and illness. They tell us what human beings naturally and regularly want and need. They are not able to prescribe how human needs should be organized morally to match the love of my neighbour. The need for healthy self-esteem does not deny the human freedom for agape and sacrificial love. However, Browning's analysis does criticize sharply some understandings of self-sacrifice within Christian tradition, especially those which have led to the exploitation and oppression of women and others. Self-abnegation is not self-giving. He suggests an ethic of equal-regard whose sacrificial love is designed to restore life to mutuality rather than be the goal of Christian life. [Nicholas Bradbury]

NEURO-LINGUISTIC PROGRAMMING

A behavioural technique concerned chiefly with how people think, communicate and behave.

NLP originated during the 1970s and is a learned technique through which practitioners are able to recognize the ways in which their clients think and communicate and then to respond in a similar way. For example, we make contact with the world by seeing, hearing, feeling, tasting and smelling. We all use language to articulate our experiences, but each expresses this in his or her own unique way. Each person is predominantly visual, auditory or kinaesthetic. For example, one client may say: 'I hear how sad you are'; others may say: 'I can see how sad you feel', or, 'I can feel your sadness'.

The therapist learns to respond and mirror the client. It is almost a Rogerian reflective listening technique, but taken to extremes. The therapist may 'pace' their client by speaking at the same speed, copying the tone of voice or speed of breathing, by body movements such as blinking, moving face muscles, using the same words and ideas. This enables the client to relax and trust. But unlike the pure Rogerian, the therapist may then 'lead' and positively direct a client. NLP is very much therapist-led, teaching the client new skills in order to achieve the required outcomes and aims. It has learned which skills and techniques are used by people excelling at many different subjects. The programme then teaches these same skills to help others. It was noticed, for example, that people who are good at spelling raise their eyes to the top left corner of the room while thinking, and that bad spellers look at the ground. By changing the way people behave, their brains are enabled to work more efficiently (O'Connor and Seymour, 1990).

NLP claims to be scientific: it studies how individuals structure their own unique experiences. But it is also practical. It teaches skills to help people change. For example, desensitization may be used when working with people who have a phobia or who are distressed by a scary incident. Clients are encouraged to distance themselves from their fear by imagining the event happening on a cinema screen, and then repeatedly describing the event on an imaginary screen which goes progressively further and further away. [W. Weston]

NEUROSIS

A term used in psychoanalysis and analytical psychology to denote a psychological condition in a person who is considered sane but more or less troubled.

Neurosis is very likely an eighteenth-century term first used in Scotland by William Cullen. Neuroses were originally thought to be solely related to the nervous system. In late nineteenth-century Paris, the neurologist Jean-Martin Charcot (1835–93) drew up a map of the nervous system. This convinced Freud that it was possible to begin to think about means of easing the appalling suffering he saw in his patients. This was the suffering caused by 'neurosis', and particularly, at that time, hysteria.

Nowadays the term neurosis describes a psychological illness which colours the personality in a particular way. A neurotic person suffers from emotional symptoms which generally originate in early childhood and are the result of unresolved unconscious conflict. Neurotic symptoms are often expressed symbolically as 'fixations'. A neurotic person, for example, may always be drawn to talk about the same subject. Psychosomatic conditions often have their origins in an unresolved neurosis.

A neurotic person, one who possesses a neurosis, is very different from a person troubled by a psychosis, and can be treated effectively in psychotherapy and psychoanalysis.
[Heather Formaini]

NEW AGE MOVEMENTS

An imprecise term describing 'alternative' spiritualities in contemporary Western culture.

The New Age is the astrological Age of Aquarius, and historical antecedents for the movement can be found in theosophy, spiritualism and, further back, Gnosticism, Catharism, the Knights Templar, etc. Most New Age beliefs and practices are not new, but represent the resurgence of ideas from different contexts, applied to the problem of human identity in a postmodern world. New Agers typically believe that modernity displaced spiritual values with a mechanistic, rationalist, reductionist world-view, and a new paradigm for the future will reverse that, with a rediscovery of spirituality. 'Spirituality' here means first-order experiences of the 'other', though the nature of such experiences is exceedingly diverse and generally defies logical analysis. New Agers are as likely to be dualistic – emphasizing communications with angels, extraterrestrials or lost civilizations – as monistic, pantheistic or panentheistic.

1. *Sociologically*, the New Age is an attempt to maintain stability in the face of uncertainty. This explains its popularity among both business people and the disadvantaged, for in the face of declining privilege it provides a chance to be part of an elite with access to secret power denied to others.

2. *Theologically*, the New Age is eclectic, adopting anything that offers the possibility of transformational experiences. Four dominant sources regularly recur: (a) *non-Western world-views*: if modern Western thinking is the source of the problem, things ancient and Eastern are the corrective – hence the popularity of, for example, a westernized Buddhism; (b) *'first nation' beliefs*: Western imperial expansion displaced native cultures that were more spiritually orientated. Reviving these may provide new hope for the future – hence the popularity of, for example, native American spirituality; (c) *creation-centred spirituality*: Western culture had a spiritual base in paganism before Greek and Enlightenment values took over. Re-establishing pre-Christian Western spirituality is therefore another option (Goddess worship, neo-paganism, etc.); (d) *person-centred therapies*: various psychotherapies claim to provide 'mystical' transformational experiences but without religious dogma.

3. *Pastorally*, Christians need to know that New Agers believe the Church has had its chance, and failed: it turned out to be merely a projection of the rationalist/materialist tradition into the world of religion, and is to be rejected along with the rest of the Enlightenment heritage. New Agers are more interested in personal meaning than rational certainty (though many claim that recent scientific theory validates spiritual experience). They prefer to construct their own spirituality rather than accept ready-made answers. Belonging to a faith community offering space for meaningful do-it-yourself ways of expressing the spiritual search will be more helpful than hierarchical structures. For this reason, the New Age challenge is bound up with issues relating to the nature and identity of Western Christianity: questions of power, control, the nature of ministry, the role of women, etc. It also raises questions

about the nature of theology: how do affective experiences of the numinous/mystical relate to dogma? How can the gospel be both story and theological abstraction? And what will Western churches learn from the world Church? [*John Drane*]

NEW TESTAMENT
The collection of 27 writings that comprises the second portion of the Christian Bible.

The name 'New Testament' distinguishes these writings from the Jewish Scriptures, which Christians call the 'Old Testament'. The name may derive from Jer. 31.31–4, which speaks of 'a new covenant' (or 'testament') to be effected by God. Christians maintain that the newer Scriptures witness to this new covenant of grace that came through Jesus Christ (1 Cor. 11.25; Heb. 8.8–13). The term is not meant to disparage previous revelation, for the Old Testament is also a witness to God's grace and its writings are deemed by almost all Christian groups to be equal in authority to those of the New Testament (Moule, 1962).

The writings are arranged chronologically with regard to their content, not their composition. The first four books are the Gospels, or narrative accounts of the life, ministry, death and resurrection of Jesus. Of these, the first three (Matt., Mark, Luke) are identified as 'the Synoptic Gospels' because there is much overlap in the material they relate. The fourth Gospel, John, bears less similarity to the first three. The fifth book, Acts, has traditionally been regarded as an early account of Church history. Many modern scholars, however, view Acts simply as the continuation of Luke's Gospel: Luke–Acts is construed as a single book.

Twenty-one epistles follow, including thirteen attributed to Paul, the missionary whose work is described in the latter half of Acts. Nine of these are written to congregations. Four are written to individuals. Both the letters to congregations and those to individuals are presented in order of length. An anonymous epistle follows, addressed to the 'Hebrews'. Some traditions have attributed this letter to Paul, but this has never been generally accepted, otherwise the letter would have been placed earlier, grouped by length with the other Pauline missives. Seven more epistles are commonly called the 'catholic' or 'general' epistles. Unlike the others, these are named after their supposed author rather than their recipients. The final book is called either Revelation or the Apocalypse. It presents a vision of the last days, including the final judgement and the consummation of God's victory over evil.

The writings of the New Testament were originally composed in Greek during the latter half of the first century CE (some scholars think 2 Peter was written in the second century). The actual authors of most of these writings are disputed or unknown. All four Gospels are anonymous; the popular attributions to Matthew, Mark, Luke and John derive from later tradition. Modern scholarship also regards many of the epistles as pseudonymous, that is, written in the name of a prominent individual by someone unknown. The authorship of seven letters attributed to Paul, however, is mostly accepted without question: Rom., Gal., 1 Cor., 2 Cor., Phil., 1 Thess., Philem.

The 27 writings have been accepted as Scripture with a minimum of controversy since at least 367 CE, when they appeared in a list prepared by Bishop Athanasius of Alexandria. Prior to that date certain other writings such as the Apocalypse of Peter seem to have been regarded as Scripture in certain locales at certain times. Even after Athanasius, some New Testament books (especially 2 Pet. and Rev.) were sometimes excluded. Criteria for inclusion and exclusion of writings are difficult to ascertain, In some cases, the presumption of apostolic authorship was a factor, but more often fidelity to an emerging understanding of the gospel was dominant. In a basic sense, the books that came to be most revered were simply those that were used the most, those that proved most helpful in nurturing the faith of common people. In the Roman Catholic Church, the Council of Trent ruled decisively on the canonical status of the current 27 books in 1546. Most Protestant groups have preferred to accept the New Testament canon on a practical level without making acceptance of the definitive list a matter of doctrine. This has allowed for anomalies. Martin Luther argued that Heb., Jas, Jude and Rev. warrant a lesser status than the other 23 books. While not excluding the four lesser books from the canon, he did rearrange the traditional order of books in the New Testament so that these four appeared at the end. Lutherans have not followed him in this practice. Many apocryphal writings from ancient times were lost and some have only been discovered in the last century. Some of these, such as the Gospel of Thomas and the Gospel of Peter, are deemed important for Christian scholarship even though they are not regarded as part of the New Testament itself.

The New Testament is typically used by Christians in at least three ways: (1) *historical*: the New Testament serves as a resource for reconstructing the life and teaching of Jesus and the development of early Christianity; (2) *theological*: the New Testament is mined for its religious ideas, which are typically deemed normative or authoritative for Christians; (3) *liturgical/devotional*: the New Testament is read as transparent divine revelation, such that congregations or individuals receive its words as spoken directly by God to them.

The second of these three uses has given rise to the science of exegesis (Conzelmann and Lindeman, 1988). Various methods attempt to interpret New Testament texts within their historical or literary context in order to identify theological messages applicable to modern concerns. All of these factors yield a rich but sometimes confusing panoply of meaning. The New Testament itself evinces diverse literary forms and gives expression to disparate views. When these writings are put to a variety of uses and studied with a multitude of methods employed by readers with different hermeneutical goals, sundry interpretations are bound to ensue. Accordingly, pastoral leaders need to realize that contradictory understandings of the New Testament may appear equally 'scriptural' to persons who espouse them. Indeed, for pastoral ministry, to point away from oneself to the New Testament is not usually helpful. The pastor embodies the Scripture so far as those with whom they are dealing are concerned. Hence he or she is expected to know the New Testament rather than just use it.
[*Mark Allan Powell*]

NON-DIRECTIVE COUNSELLING
Counselling which reflects here and now interventions to the clients and avoids any direction.

As a therapy, non-directive counselling became prominent in the research and clinical practice of Dr Carl Rogers after the Second World War. Indeed, the approach is sometimes called 'Rogerian'. His research

added much to understandings of health and wholeness. But similar stances can be traced back as far as Greek and Asian philosophies. The latter particularly find the practice consistent with Asian views of harmony. It is often linked with client-centred therapy, but though related the therapies are not identical. Non-direction is always client-centred. Other therapeutic approaches may also centre on the client but are directive in questions and observations (Rogers, 1951).

The theory begins with the view that the resources for healing lie within the individual or the group. Therefore, this therapy has been used in work with individuals and groups in matters of dysfunction, education and administration. The medical model for all healing is rejected in favour of a 'systems model' of social process. As a practice, non-directive therapy holds that a basic thrust of the ego to health and wholeness comes alive when the care-giver helps the client (or group) do his or her work. This 'help' comes from providing an accepting/caring context for the person as a person and from reflecting to the individual or group what happens in the 'here and now'. Diagnosis of the past, blaming, or focusing on others play no part in non-directive therapy. The client corrects, sharpens and moves on from the comments of the care-giver, who then reflects the movement of the client. A further theory of this practice is that the ego will not go further than it can handle at any given time. As healing takes place at one level, the ego allows itself to move to another level. As more and more unresolved data come to the surface and are integrated into the individual or the group, healing and wholeness result.

Empathy is key to the counselling. This refers to a process of participant observation by the therapist that allows for self-understanding, self-confidence, and freedom from overdependence on the part of the client.

From the Christian perspective this approach takes seriously the work of the Holy Spirit in the individual or the group. The care-giver sees his or her role as facilitating a process in which the Spirit heals and guides. Some would note a lack of a theology of the fall, but most theologians would applaud the view that only the Spirit can serve as the personal director. The care-giver offers a practice of love (agape) that becomes the context in which all healing by the Spirit takes place. Critics of this therapy hold that the process fails to take seriously the effect of neurosis on the client's ability, or the validity of interventions such as guidance, diagnosis and interpretation from an outsider. [*J. G. Emerson*]

NON-STIPENDIARY MINISTRY
Lay and ordained ministers who receive no direct salary or stipend for their work.

Non-stipendiary ministers (NSMs) play an increasingly important part in the life of Anglican parishes, as well as in Methodist and United Reformed Churches in Great Britain. The decrease in the number of stipendiary clergy and the prospect of not being able to afford them has meant that dioceses are coming to rely increasingly on the involvement of non-stipendiaries for the maintenance of their parish ministry. At the same time, there is greater mobility between different forms of ministry – Readers being ordained, NSMs becoming stipendiary or being introduced to parishes under 'house-for-duty' agreements. Formal and informal team arrangements are also increasingly common. The development of regional theological training schemes and diocesan courses makes it more possible for people with family and work commitments to train for all kinds of ministry. Increasing numbers of older people are taking this route into stipendiary and non-stipendiary ministry. The time may be approaching when NSMs will be as much a part of the parochial system as stipendiary clergy. Meanwhile, the Roman Catholic Church is beginning to experiment with various forms of unpaid ministry, such as that of the permanent deacon.

Non-stipendiary ministry includes those directly ordained or accredited to such a ministry and those who were originally ordained to stipendiary ministry but have moved to other employment and hold a licence from their church. There are two main categories of NSMs: 'those in secular employment whose chief area of ministry is in the context of their employment, commonly called "ministers in secular employment"' (MSEs); and 'those ... whose chief area of ministry is in the context of a parish or a chaplaincy' (ACCM Paper number 23). The two categories are justified theologically in slightly different ways: the former by an incarnational doctrine of the 'ministry of pre-sence' signified by a representative person in a secular institution like a school, hospital or business; the latter by a Spirit-focused approach to collaborative ministry within the church fellowship. In practice, except in situations where there is already a tradition of chaplaincy, MSEs often feel neglected by a Church which is focused on its own institutional needs. Meanwhile, the churches increasingly seek to make their NSMs more deployable, but without paying attention to their need for fair treatment and terms of work. Much depends on the attitudes of individual (stipendiary) incumbents, who may be jealous of their own professional status. It is unfortunate that such an important area of ministry should be defined by a negative. What has not yet been established is 'an acceptable title which both recognizes the status of non-stipendiary ministers as part of the ordained ministry of the Church, and at the same time acknowledges the distinction between those whose ministry is financially supported by the Church and those who have other support' (ABM Report, 1993). [*Christopher Moody*]

NURSING
The work of a nurse, someone who has undergone a recognized course of study and is subsequently employed in a health setting.

The word nurse (and nursing) derives from the Latin *nutrire*, to nourish. One image of a nurse is that of a young woman in a uniform dress with a white apron and cap who is to be found in a hospital ward caring for the sick. However, nursing, as an integral part of the health-care system, encompasses health promotion, prevention of illness and the care of the physically ill, mentally ill and disabled of all ages in all health-care and other community settings.

The World Health Organization definition of nursing states that 'the unique function of nurses in caring for individuals, sick or well, is to assess their responses to their health status and to assist them in the performance of those activities contributing to health, recovery or dignified death, that they would perform unaided if they had the necessary strength, will or knowledge, and to do this in such a way as to help them gain full or partial independence as rapidly as possible'.

Given such a widely based definition, it is not surprising to find nurses in a variety of situations, such as in industry and commerce, schools, the armed forces and prisons. Nurses work with children and the elderly, and as health visitors and midwives. Nursing, and the management of nursing, provides a good background for other and wider responsibilities. Nurses can be found as chief executives and chairs of health trusts, in senior appointments and in policy-making positions. They are usually the largest group of health-care workers in any country, and many governments have a nurse to advise them on nursing and midwifery issues.

Obviously whether the work of nurses is worth doing or otherwise depends on the importance or unimportance assigned to human life itself. Much of Jesus' public ministry was concerned with the healing of the sick, and there was as unqualified a commission to his followers to continue this work. His saying, 'as you did it to one of the least of these who are members of my family, you did it to me' (Matt. 25.40), has encouraged many nurses in the practice of their profession. The Christian Church kept alive the duty of compassion towards sufferers for many centuries. Monastic institutions provided accommodation for the aged and sick poor in infirmaries, and hospitality for travellers. Although monks often offered this care, nuns also looked after the sick and dying. Some nursing titles reflect this history: the mother superior of a religious house was sometimes known as matron, and those who worked with her were called sisters (Gliddon and Powell, 1952).

Living from 1820 to 1910, the British nurse Florence Nightingale was described by John Stuart Mill as more universally admired than any other living person (Woodham-Smith, 1951). In her era, nursing emerged to become a respected vocation extending to most parts of the world. Until then nursing had been seen either as a vocation, like a religious calling, or as a service provided by Sarah Gamp characters who were uneducated, coarse, and with a predilection for gin. There was a strong movement to introduce training and so to overcome these two extremes. But Miss Nightingale held that a nurse should have both a vocation and training. In this belief she stood between the extreme views of the old religious orders and those of some of the moderns of her time.

From the late nineteenth century, nurses' training focused on the meticulous acquisition of clinical skills in an institutional environment and in a strongly hierarchical setting. It was designed to produce a disciplined workforce which did not question orders or established practice. This approach resulted in what many regard as the traditional nursing role, including that of being handmaiden to the doctor. By 1920 many countries around the world had enacted legislation regulating nurses' education and securing state examinations and public registration. The carnage of the First World War brought sweeping changes in nursing practice, and throughout the twentieth century, particularly in the latter half, and into the twenty-first century, developments and changes in education have had a far-reaching impact on nursing practice. In many countries, education moved from the hospital to academic establishments, resulting in the award of a diploma or degree. The modern syllabus includes, in addition to clinical skills, subjects such as psychology, physiology, social studies and health promotion. Experience is gained of a wide range of health-care settings, not just hospitals. Qualified nurses may develop a particular speciality. In many of these, nurses now work as autonomous practitioners. In the hospital they work in close co-operation with other colleagues in the caring team, which may include the hospital chaplains.

Much of the work of nurses (Clay, 1987) is about coping, getting through the day, giving one's self to someone else and denying (or managing) one's own feelings and needs so as to create confidence and calm in others.
[Heather M. Bond]

NURTURE, CHRISTIAN
Means of nourishment in the Christian life.

In Scripture, two kinds of communication can be distinguished, though not separated. One is *kerygma* – the preaching of the story and saving acts of Jesus Christ's life, death and resurrection. This is proclamation that calls for conversion and new birth. Often such preaching is experienced as an appeal to the heart. Its aim is transformation: for the hearer to become a Christian. The second kind of communication is *didache* – the teaching that elucidates the significance of the story and the saving acts of Jesus Christ in the form of instruction for the believer to bring about growth towards maturity. Often this teaching is an appeal to the head. The aim is the formation of the person as a Christian.

The gospel speaks to the whole person. Both preaching and teaching, therefore, will address a person's thinking, feeling, willing and doing. Preaching and teaching are thus complementary. Nevertheless, their functions are distinguishable. Nurture is generally understood to include the process of teaching and formation.

In the New Testament and early Church, there was a strong emphasis upon *kerygma* – the proclamation of the gospel. The aim was conversion. Nurture was a subsequent and dependent activity, located in the life and worship of the Christian community. As Christianity became officially established in the Empire, and a culture of 'Christendom' developed, the emphasis moved towards nurture, since to be born into Western society was to be born a Christian. This legacy is still powerful in both the Catholic and Protestant traditions in Europe and North America. Thus in the modern age, since the Enlightenment, and with moves towards making education universally available, churches have become increasingly conscious of the need to offer their own programmes of teaching. This has become especially pressing in the last century with the realization that a more consciously secular culture contributes very little to any Christian formation, and may well be undermining of Christian values and aspirations. These forces, combined with new and more sophisticated approaches to teaching and learning, particularly through participatory programmes that take individuality seriously, have led to notable innovations in Christian nurture. Local churches have begun to organize a range of teaching programmes, often supported by resources and personnel from their parent bodies, to help the formation of their members across a wide area – including spiritual growth, personal awareness, intellectual understanding and pastoral skills.

However, this is only part of the picture. Nurture has been the priority of liberal Western churches. At the same time there has been a renewed emphasis in evangelical Christianity for the need for proclamation and conversion. This gives rise to an important debate. Nurture assumes that people need to be educated into the faith, and then led towards maturity. This assumption accords with early twenty-first-century culture. It assumes that the Christian community provides a context to offer resources for, and to harmonize, these individual journeys. Pastoral practice assumes a foundational role of ensuring that all nurture involves socialization into a community of faith. Liturgy has tended to become pastorally orientated with an emphasis upon fellowship, participation and wholeness. Worship is seen as formational experience. Baptism and Eucharist are significant occasions of nurture, giving basic direction to formation and to the teaching needed to enhance it. Moreover the presuppositions about growth, change and maturity as process demand pastoral care as the link and lubricant of nurturing activity. There is no set curriculum – all persons need an environment of love and encouragement in which to become more fully themselves as children of God. All are held to be involved in such a journey, and God is seen as the ultimate source of nourishment. On this model there needs to be continuing reflection upon the implications of Christian faith for individuals and for community. Such a pattern of nurture depends upon pastoral care and theological reflection, and provides a key ingredient of pastoral studies.

However, the importance of nurture is limited. Critics argue that it can promote a sense of journeying in the Christian life without necessarily providing the challenge to conversion – i.e. the transformation that changes lives and challenges the more harmonious negotiation with the world that nurture generally presupposes. This view holds that there is a sense in which the gospel is counter-cultural. Christians are not made through nurture: this is a second stage. Conversion as a change of attitude and behaviour in response to the proclamation of the story of Jesus Christ is primary: nurture will follow. In this model, priority is given to evangelism, and nurture becomes the deepening of the transforming experience of conversion. Nurture in this sense requires a strong and continuing element of *kerygma*, rather than an ongoing exploration of the teaching (*didache*) of the gospel.

These two models of nurture exist side by side in the same denominations. Each has different implications for pastoral studies: one is liberal and open-ended, the other is more properly evangelical and firm about ingredients and implications. The outcome in terms of pastoral practice is similarly contrasting.
[*Alastair Redfern*]

O

OBEDIENCE
Total engagement with present reality through respect for the will of a lawful superior.
In its derivation 'obedience' has overtones of listening. It suggests full attention and response to whatever happens. Yet the word is most commonly used to mean simply doing what you are told. This is why many women object to the promise in the old wedding service to obey their husband. More soundly based is the objection to this promise as a one-way requirement. For mutual obedience is essential to every serious relationship. Readiness to honour the other person in the mystery of their otherness and of the relationship itself is foundational to a marriage. Obedience treats with due reverence the irreducible, and not infrequently taxing, particulars of each person, relationship and situation.

In monasticism, obedience is linked with the other moral virtues of poverty and chastity. But even in Benedict's *Rule for Monks*, in which constraints on the abbot's power are minimal, a monk who is told to do something that he regards as impossible is encouraged to take the matter further with the abbot. Elsewhere the Rule says that 'the brethren are to strive to obey one another out of love'. Authentic obedience is always a functional quality of relationship. To the extent that the relationship is minimal or deficient, so will obedience be, whatever the lip service or seeming compliance. Immediately to do what any other person says in all circumstances is compulsive behaviour, and as such a caricature of obedience.

Distorted versions of obedience are widespread. 'I was only obeying orders' has become a familiar defence of soldiers or police accused of torture or murder. Yet obedience is not about the imposition of one person's will upon another. Proper human obedience may have to resist a particular command. In traditional Christian terms a command to sin must not be obeyed. Obedience always has a context, and therefore cannot be reduced to rules. At the outset of what became a famous victory for the British navy, Horatio Nelson put his telescope to his blind eye to avoid seeing his superior officer's signal to disengage from the impending battle. Nelson clearly thought he could recognize possibilities in this situation that the admiral either could not see or did not take sufficiently seriously. This response, while obviously contrary to orders, has not been stigmatized as disobedience. Nobody can know in advance what true obedience will entail. It is a matter of becoming sensitively attuned to all that is going on, which in Nelson's case included knowledge of his commanding officer's strengths and limitations. His behaviour is properly called obedient in the light of all the circumstances.

All churches include some concept of obedience when ministers are authorized. Within the Roman Catholic tradition, canonical obedience is due to the pope from all cardinals and bishops, and from all priests to their bishops. In the Church of England every priest before institution to a living is required to take an oath of canonical obedience to the bishop of the diocese. But in line with what has already been stated, this is only 'in all things lawful and honest'. The appeal to obedience has been used, not least within churches, to sustain particular forms of power or identity. The abuse of obedience by Christian leaders has a long pedigree. It may even be discerned in St Paul, who at times seems to have demanded that members of those churches that he had established should obey him on the grounds that he had seen the risen Lord. But such tendencies have been, and may be, countered by reference to the obedience of Jesus Christ to his Father (Phil. 2.8; Heb. 5.8). *[N. P. Harvey]*

OBJECT
The term used in psychoanalysis, not to refer to a thing, but as the counterpart of 'subject'.
In the early phase of the development of his theory, Freud described the vicissitudes of the instincts, each instinct having an object to which it was primarily directed, although it could deviate from its primary aim. Thus the baby's first desired object, to which his or her most basic instincts are directed, might be considered to be the mother's breast. In development the original (i.e. primary) objects are replaced by substitutes that stand for the original object but are understood as being distinct from it, and in this way interest spreads from the mother to the family, to people and things in general.

The term 'object' underwent a major transformation in meaning when Freud described the process of internalization and identification with lost objects. For example, he described (Freud, 1917) how a lost external object becomes internalized and so, although the external relationship is lost, it is maintained internally. Though at first he thought of these processes as pathological, internalization was subsequently viewed as constituting an important part of normal development. The self or ego is constituted by the internalization of objects that have been lost. Freud's work shows a vivid sense of an inner world or psychic reality, but in the earlier part of his work he lacked a theoretical framework within which to locate this conception. With *Mourning and Melancholia* (1917) and *The Ego and the Id* (1923), where the processes of internalization and identification are described in detail, Freud established the basis for a full object relations theory that was subsequently developed by Anna Freud, Melanie Klein, Ronald Fairbairn, Michael Balint and Donald Winnicott. *[David Bell]*

OBJECT RELATIONS
The theory that the inner world is populated by primitive objects which are felt to be in relation to each other, and which can become the basis of the processes of projection and introjection.

The object relations perspective is one of the dominant models of contemporary psychoanalysis. In *The Ego and the Id* (1923) Freud describes the ego as 'the graveyard of abandoned object cathexes'. By this he means that the ego, roughly speaking 'the self', is constituted by internalized lost objects which become the basis of identification. A particularly important internalization takes place, according to Freud's theory, as the outcome of the resolution of the Oedipus complex, and results in the formation of the superego – an internalized version of parental authority. He regarded this internalization as having profound consequences for the formation of character, and understood various types of psychopathology as having their roots in the fear of and submission to the superego. An example would be the unconscious sense of guilt that characterizes melancholia and obsessive-compulsive disorders.

The main contributors to object relations theory include Anna Freud, Donald Winnicott, Michael Balint and Ronald Fairbairn. But the most substantial contribution came from Melanie Klein who, although building upon Freud's idea of internal objects, made a fundamentally new departure based upon her work with very young children (Klein, 1921, 1963). She described how the infant's internal world of objects is established through a continuous and complex process of projection and introjection. Essentially the child in phantasy projects both 'good' and 'bad' aspects of himself and then re-introjects them, now altered by experience. She laid great stress on the need of the infant to be able to establish within him- or herself a 'good' internal object that provides a sense of security and integration. Where this capacity is lacking (e.g. as a result of emotional deprivation in childhood), this becomes the basis for later mental illness and restriction of interest in the world. She also described in detail how internal objects are projected and introjected in the process of psychoanalytic treatment, and this laid the foundation for a deeper understanding of the transference.

Sometimes the term 'object relations theory' is used to refer only to the actual relations between people. This is confusing and detracts attention from the focus on the internal world and its relation to its objects internal and external, which is fundamental to contemporary psychoanalytic theory. *[David Bell]*

OBSERVATION
Careful and attentive examination of phenomena to gain understanding.

It is now widely recognized in training programmes that the skill of observation underlies the capacity to engage in therapeutic work. It is necessary to be able to maintain an open and receptive attitude in order to observe carefully and to reflect upon the kinds of relationships people make with those who offer support and help (L. Miller, 1991).

Observation requires a quiet state of mind, which facilitates listening and seeing what seems to be of significance in a communication. In the context of pastoral work it does not involve keeping a cold distance, and it does not preclude engaging actively in conversation.

OBSESSION
A stream of repetitive and irresistible thoughts.

Such streams of thought can be recognized in lives organized on the basis of anxiety or a locked, trance-like fixation on someone or something. Characteristics such as secretiveness, doubting, indecisiveness, low self-esteem, inhibitions and social isolation can develop. Obsession takes many forms: a panic over sinning (scrupulosity), fascination with experiencing symptoms of illnesses (hypochondriasis, which is different from being hypochondriac); or a horror of harming others (as with a mother aghast at her preoccupation with the thought of harming her baby). Obsessions usually bond with compulsions for seeking relief–repetitive actions ('rituals') such as going from priest to priest or doctor to doctor. This combination is termed 'obsessive-compulsive disorder' (OCD) (Collie, 2000). Such obsessions have a neurological and biological basis and readily mingle with other, more visible disorders that have a similar basis (e.g. anxiety attacks or bulimia). Obsession is often obscured by a consequent depression. The 'rituals' have been compared to religious ceremonies. Moreover, OCD is the disorder most characterized by religious concerns, although atheists obsess and can be scrupulous.

OCD often exaggerates the 'normal'; clinical definition begins when symptoms interfere with social and work life. Approximately 2.5% of occurrences have this degree of intensity. Its scale ranges from psychotic to mildly disruptive and varies with stress levels. It occurs earliest in males, but by adulthood there is little differentiation according to gender or socio-economic background. Culturally there are differences in predominant symptoms, but worldwide similarities are striking.

The obsessions and compulsions of OCD can be distinguished from fixations such as alcoholism, gambling and sex, in that these initially give pleasure whereas OCD never does. There can, however, be overlapping, as when sufferers with OCD relieve themselves by drinking. Contamination is a common source of anxiety, but sex and violence are also frequent themes. An obsession may be on a 'serious matter' (mortal sin), although unwilled, as in blasphemous or bizarre thoughts. But obsessions can be non-religious: for example, popular superstitions such as 'If I touch, count, hoard or check, then magically disaster will not hit me'.

The murky origins of obsessions can be analysed, but not helpfully. A traumatic event, thought or sensation seems to etch itself in the brain. One helpful theory, however, is that if an EEG were graphing brainwaves, obsessing would begin as an unusual 'spike',

a thought readily dismissed by most brains. But with a brain vulnerable to anxiety – maybe a chemical imbalance that contributes to a 'defective conscience' – a loop in a circuit begins and there is little to curtail it. The causes of compulsions can sometimes be traced to medical conditions, but probably OCD is an interaction between genetic 'memory' and individual social histories. The issue is accessing a power to get out of a 'rut'.

John Bunyan produced a record of obsessions in the autobiographical first chapter of *Grace Abounding to the Chief of Sinners*. Another account of almost obsessional doubt may be that of Christian imprisoned in Doubting Castle in *Pilgrim's Progress*. Seemingly without cure – especially by advising, lecturing, nagging or reassurance – management of an obsession is nevertheless possible. From his personal experience Ignatius of Loyola developed an approach to treatment that is still highly regarded. Roman Catholics have Scrupulous Anonymous honouring St Alphonsus Liguori. There are twelve-step support groups. And in psychotherapy specific behavioural techniques have been used, combined with cognitive therapy and frequently use of serotonin re-uptake inhibitor medications. A holistic approach of individual therapy, pastoral consultation, therapeutic reading, medication, family therapy and support group might be considered. [Robert Collie]

OCCASIONAL OFFICES
See: BAPTISM, WEDDINGS, FUNERALS

OCCULT
Magical and secretive religious practices and belief systems.

Occult practices involve the attempt to manipulate natural, cosmic and supernatural forces for particular ends. All the major religions have spawned occult beliefs and practices, including astrology, alchemy, divination and magic. Occult knowledge systems frequently trace relationships between cosmic events or processes, such as the movement of the stars or the cycles of the moon, and parts of the human body, or the human psyche. Occult practitioners seek to use this knowledge to heal sickness, to predict the pattern of a person's life or to influence a person's destiny. Occultists also frequently call upon an array of intermediary supernatural beings, including demons and departed spirits as partners in their cere-monies and magic.

Occult practices have traditionally been in conflict with established religious authority. Such conflict has at times been violent, as in the persecution and burning of witches. Certain women were labelled witches because of their practice of healing arts, including herbalism, massage, manipulation and midwifery. These skills were thought by official religionists to indicate familiarity with unseen, and anti-Christian, spiritual forces. Conflict between shamanism and offi-cial religion is still common in many develop-ing societies. Occult practices are also a continuing source of conflict in Western societies. Some occultists are said to practise devil worship and are accused of practices such as child sexual abuse and bodily mutila-tion.

Occult practices experienced a revival in nineteenth-century Europe, reflecting the growing influence of esoteric Eastern reli-gious philosophies. The related revival of spir-itualism – the attempt to communicate with the spirits of the dead – led to the establish-ment of spiritualist churches in many Western cities. The theosophical movement founded by Madame Blavatsky was another source of occultist revival in the nineteenth century. The hippy counter-culture and the 'New Age' movement in the twentieth century also drew on esoteric doctrines, including Blavatsky's belief in reincarnation.

Occult ideas and practices are now wide-spread in the contemporary West, partly through the influence of the New Age move-ment. Belief in reincarnation is growing, while resort to divination boards, communi-cation with 'channelled' spirits, astrological consultations, and attempts to deal with sick-ness by manipulating crystals, precious metals or spiritual emanations are increas-ingly popular.

Occult practices are said to meet an endur-ing psychological need for power and control over the larger forces which determine indivi-dual circumstances such as chance and inheri-tance. The mainstream religions, including Christianity, have generally sought to channel this need for control into the formal ritualized magic of sacraments, blessings, relics, pilgrimage, exorcism and anointing. The Reformation swept most of these prac-tices away in Western Europe and among the Puritans of the New World. But rationalist, anti-magical religion never eradicated

magic or shamanism in Europe or in the colo-nies despite the enthusiastic and sometimes violent efforts of rationalist clergy and mis-sionaries. Its re-emergence in secular Europe, and its continuing significance in post-colonial contexts, indicate the tenacity of human belief in a world beyond the physical senses, and of the desire to manipulate that world for good and sometimes for ill. [*Michael Northcott*]

OCCUPATIONAL PSYCHOLOGY
See: APPLIED PSYCHOLOGY

OEDIPUS COMPLEX
The set of loving and hating wishes that a child feels towards its parents.
The Oedipus complex is one of the most well-known and popularized of Freud's ideas. He developed it early in his thinking, taking the term from the story of King Oedipus, who unwittingly killed his father and married his mother. The rivalry between the child and the parent of the same sex leads to a wish for that parent's death, so that the child can express its sexual desire for the other parent. Freud located the Oedipal period in children about the ages of three and five and noted that it re-emerged at puberty (Freud, 1905). The theme is central to much psychoanalysis and is a topic that is regarded as having uni-versal significance. Indeed, Freud argued that the primitive desire of the sons to kill their father lay at the heart of the origins of religion, and applied this through his histor-ico-cultural theories (Freud, 1913).

OLD AGE
Two phases of life arbitrarily defined as beginning at the age of 65:
(1) a time of fulfilment;
(2) a period of failing health, increasing dependence on others, and often a time of bereavement and loneliness.
During the twentieth century in Western countries, there were spectacular advances in medical and other sciences that led to a significantly prolonged expectation of life; so that now, in contrast to a century ago, the great majority of people will survive into their seventies, and many into their eighties and nineties. Furthermore, their quality of life is higher than ever before, their health better, their economic circumstances more prosperous. So for many, 'old age' may consist of two phases – a sustained period of good health, reasonable physical and mental

activity, a time of fulfilment; and then a period of failing physical and mental health, increasing dependence on others, and often a time of bereavement and loneliness.

During the time of good health, people should be encouraged to maximize their contribution to society, not only for society's sake, but for their own sense of achievement. This is the time in life when, after years of experience, they may have, perhaps for the first time, an opportunity to develop their interests and hobbies; to take a university degree; to participate in voluntary bodies; to care for grandchildren and the dependent elderly. For many people, these can be the most fulfilling years of their life.

But old age is also for many a time of sadness – sadness at the loss of loved ones, loneliness, regret at lost opportunities and broken relationships. There may be a sense of inability to keep up with the ever-increasing pace of change, and a feeling of uselessness and futility that may lead to depression. Depressive illness in old people is easily missed, being attributed to other factors; and yet it responds to standard medical treatment as well then as at other ages. More sinister, and as yet without satisfactory treatment, is the menace of senile dementia (Alzheimer's disease), which may affect up to a quarter of those in their eighties. This is a steadily progressive condition, characterized by a failure of short-term memory which may lead ultimately to a state of complete confusion and dependence on others.

For those involved in pastoral care, the principles of management should be: (1) to encourage the mentally and physically able to maximize their opportunities for an active mental and physical life; (2) to be on the alert for early signs of both mental and physical disease – which usually respond to treatment as well as in younger people, though the elderly often take longer to recover from illness. There are no diseases that are specific to older people, though the incidence of many illnesses increases with age; (3) to care for the lonely, the bereaved, the housebound. None of these conditions is peculiar to old age, though each is commoner among the elderly. Many people say that loneliness is harder to bear than physical disability. It is important that the wishes of the dependent elderly should be respected; thus their desire to maintain an independent existence for as long as possible, even when to an observer this appears perverse, should not lightly be overruled. Conflicts within families over the care of the dependent elderly are frequent, and call for the exercise of much tact. Many old people are reluctant to accept help, for instance with transport or money problems. [John Leonard]

OLD TESTAMENT
The pre-Christian section of the Christian Bible, identical with the Jewish Bible except for the order of the books.
In the Roman Catholic Church and some other denominations, the Old Testament is used in a form expanded by the Apocrypha. On the whole, Old Testament study and pastoral studies have continued as separate disciplines within an academic field. Occasionally such large concepts as 'well-being' (*shalom*) have been incorporated into pastoral thinking. Yet careful and critical study of the Old Testament can inform pastoral studies (Peterson, 1980; Capps, 1981). Pastoral studies also have the capacity to draw attention to aspects of the Old Testament's own concerns. Among the themes and insights for which the Old Testament can provide pastoral studies may be included: (1) *fundamental insights on humanity*: e.g. men and women as created equal but doomed to hierarchy, communal and individual, working and resting, responsible and needy, living and on the way to death, enjoying youth, maturity and old age; (2) *fundamental concepts for the shaping of human life*, such as blessing, well-being, decisive judgement, right/rights/rightness/ righteousness/justice, faithfulness/constancy/ truth, integrity/wholeness/innocence, compassion/mercy, commitment/steadfast love, love, trust, hope, grace, covenant/contract/ relationship; (3) *stories of God's activity as pastor to individuals* (e.g. Abraham, David, Job, Jeremiah, Jonah) and communities (e.g. in Exod., Num.), which as stories recognize the narrative form of human experience and resource the narrative aspect to the pastoral task; (4) *stories of human pastors at work*, both negative and positive models (e.g. Eli and Hannah, Nathan and David, Job's friends); (5) *stories of people facing the interwoven issues* raised by human involvement in sex and violence (Judges) and in power and wealth (David, Solomon); (6) *stories of people taking responsibility* for their destiny and their relationships, often despite contemporary cultural norms (e.g. Hagar, Joseph, Ruth, Esther); (7) *stories which subordinate 'pastoral' concerns* to the perceived priorities of the

community and of God's purpose (e.g. Ezra–Nehemiah); (8) *anthologies* emerging from God's pastoral/prophetic ministry to the people of God and to other peoples, in sin and in need, confronting both confidence and gloom (e.g. Isa., Jer., Ezek.); (9) *models of pastoral ministry*, such as prophet, priest and sage; and a subverting of the image of the 'pastoral' by an understanding of the pastor/shepherd as a person of power and authority as well as provider and carer, and one who thinks socially not merely psychologically, and corporately not merely individually; (10) *material and models for the pastor* to enable individuals and communities to express their grief, loss, anger, hurt, doubt, enthusiasm, joy, and gratitude, and to relate these to God, in pastoral and liturgical contexts (Pss., Lam., Eccles.); (11) *specific insights for everyday life* in connection with matters such as friendship, sexual relationships, relationships with God, and possessions (Exod., Deut., Prov., Song of Sol.). [*John Goldingay*]

OMNIPOTENCE
See: THEODICY, SUFFERING, GRANDIOSITY

OPEN SYSTEM
A system with inputs, a conversion process (something done with these inputs) and outputs.
This deceptively simple model can be applied to an individual, a group or a complex organization. The essential characteristic of an open system is that it survives by interacting with its environment. It is also useful in identifying ways in which a group or organization may be acting as if it is a closed system – not taking account of the world outside, with which it has to relate – and working with the problems that result.

ORDINATION
The public recognition and celebration of a person's movement from one order in the Church to another.
The twentieth-century ecumenical international debate about the nature of the Church raised many as yet unanswered questions about ordination. The emphasis on baptism into the community of faith as the basis for all ministries, combined with a trinitarian undergirding of the nature of the Church, affirms the different but equal ministries of all, rather than the professional separation of bishops, priests and deacons. Ordination may be said to be fundamentally about the particular place within the Body of Christ to which an individual accepts the call to be a representative and distributing focus of the whole Church's gifts for mission and ministry.

ORGANIZATIONS FOR PASTORAL CARE
National and international organizations whose primary purpose is the furtherance of pastoral care and counselling.
The second half of the twentieth century saw a phenomenal growth of interest in various forms of counselling. A concomitant development in the United Kingdom, North America and throughout the world has been renewal of the Church's traditional pastoral ministry through encounter with the philosophies and practices of the emerging secular psychotherapies. The development of pastoral care and counselling has been furthered in the establishment of a number of pastoral organizations, both through the debates which have taken place within them and in their interaction with one another (Lyall, 1995).

Founded in 1959, the aim of the Scottish Pastoral Association was 'to promote an exchange of ideas and a basis of co-operation among all who regard themselves as exercising a pastoral function'. Perhaps its most important legacy was the journal *Contact*, which is now published as an interdisciplinary journal of pastoral studies sponsored by all the main British pastoral organizations. Likewise concerned with interdisciplinary dialogue, the London-based Institute of Religion and Medicine was formed in 1962 to promote co-operation between doctors and ministers of all denominations. The Institute set up two consultations (in 1966 and 1968) on Practical Training in Pastoral Care Ministry whose recommendations were subsequently reflected in new approaches to pastoral education in theological colleges and divinity faculties.

A number of organizations came into being committed to the advancement of pastoral care and education. In 1962 the Clinical Theology Association was founded by Dr Frank Lake. Deeply influenced by the psychoanalytic perspectives of Harry Guntrip,

Lake, at the request of the English bishops, began to offer clergy courses on pastoral care and counselling. These sought to integrate traditional theological insights with a particular understanding of human personality known as the Dynamic Life Cycle. The courses introduced ministers to a range of concepts, practical tools for ministry and a possibility for self-understanding which they had never previously encountered. Since its inception, many thousands of people, in fact mostly lay, have participated.

In 1965, Bill Kyle, a Methodist minister, proposed the setting up in London of 'a church-cum-centre in which the whole ministry of the church would be concerned with pastoral counselling'. This proposal was embodied in the Westminster Pastoral Foundation, which has become a national centre of excellence both in the extent and quality of its counselling. It has also established a sophisticated training programme with its own certification. A national network of about fifty affiliated and associated counselling centres has come into being, each one working to standards of accreditation established by WPF.

Father Louis Marteau, a Roman Catholic priest, set up the Dympna Centre in 1971. Besides providing counselling for those whose emotional problems arise in the context of their faith, it saw itself as having a distinctive role in the pastoral care of priests and members of religious orders. Although a Catholic foundation, its influence was ecumenical and its early participants were instrumental in setting up counselling centres within other religious traditions. Irene Bloomfield was co-founder of the Jewish Raphael Centre, and Harry Dean became director of the Salvation Army Counselling Centre. Within the Catholic tradition Jim Christie, a Jesuit, established the Garnethill Centre in Glasgow, and the Dominican Michael O'Regan became director of Eckhart House in Dublin.

There were other important initiatives. Some universities were introducing diploma or certificate courses in pastoral studies, some dioceses were appointing directors of pastoral care and counselling, and hospital chaplaincy was becoming more professional (in the best sense of that word). It is not surprising, therefore, that before long moves were afoot to set up a national pastoral organization which would at least facilitate communication between these diverse enterprises. This was not to happen, however, without searching questions being raised by Robert Lambourne. He warned against any hierarchical, accrediting organization based upon what he perceived as the psychoanalytic, individualistic, problem-solving perspectives of North America. In the event, its ethos arguably shaped by Lambourne's intervention, an Association for Pastoral Care and Counselling (later a division of the British Association of Counselling) came into being.

Parallel developments were taking place in other countries. In the USA two organizations acquired national importance. The Association for Clinical Pastoral Education brought together a number of separate bodies to become the controlling and accrediting agency for supervisors offering CPE in hospitals and prisons. The Canadian Association for Pastoral Education fulfilled a similar purpose. The American Association of Pastoral Counsellors initially provided a professional home for many counsellors in private practice, and later extended its membership to include parish ministers, though in contrast to the British movement, not laity (Holifield, 1983). In both the German Federal Republic and the German Democratic Republic (as they then were), in Holland and in the Scandinavian countries, and later in Italy, Poland and other European countries, pastoral care organizations were formed.

The inevitable next step was the formation of European and International Organizations. Preliminary international seminars were held in Arnoldshein, GDR (1972) and Ruschlikon, Switzerland (1975), bringing together delegates from North America and Europe. The first 'official' European Conference was held in Eisenach, GDR (1977), followed by gatherings in Lublin, Poland (1981), Turku, Finland (1985), Assisi, Italy (1989), Debrecen, Hungary (1993) and Ripon, England (1997). The first International Congress was held in Edinburgh, Scotland, in 1979, bringing 400 people from around the world and prompting the then Moderator of the General Assembly of the Church of Scotland to compare it to the great ecumenical gatherings of 1910 and 1937. Similar gatherings followed in San Francisco (1983), Melbourne (1987), Amsterdam (1991) and Toronto (1995). There is a vibrantly self-conscious pastoral care movement in Asia which, since 1982, has found its focus in four Asian Conferences. The African Association for Pastoral Studies and Counselling came into being in 1985 and Ghana hosted an International Congress in 1999. More recently, a Latin American organization has come into being. *[David Lyall]*

OSCILLATION
In both childhood and adulthood, alternation between autonomous activity and contact with sources of renewal.
In the individual such behaviour is normal. Its application, however, to the Church as an institution is chiefly associated with the work of Bruce Reed (1978) and the Grubb Institute. He argues that oscillation is a characteristic of everyday life, but one which particularly manifests itself in religion. The process involves switching from seeking for someone or something on which to depend; through acknowledgement of helplessness; to the emergence of new ideas about and responsibilities for the self and its place in the world, which are the new basis of action.

OVERDOSE
The intended or accidental result of the intake of licit or illicit drugs in higher quantities than the body can assimilate.
An overdose is generally associated with the effects of stimulants, narcotics, amphetamines or hallucinogens which affect the central nervous system, causing paranoia, delirium, hallucinations, unconsciousness, vomiting, convulsions, as well as damaging the organs of the body. In lethal quantities, cardiac seizures, renal failure, brain damage and coma may result in death. Both addiction and mental illness may lead to overdose; however, depending on one's body's chemistry, physiology, and the drug, fatal effects may occur from a single dose. Whatever the apparent psychological aspect of an overdose (whether claimed or actual), medical help should always be first sought.

OWNING
To take responsibility for a feeling, attitude or action.
The term is widely and loosely used in counselling and in everyday language. It has become almost a jargon word, but has no specifically technical meaning.

P

PAEDOPHILE (PEDOPHILE)/CHILD SEX ABUSER
An adult who is sexually attracted to children and not to other adults.
The word paedophile (pedophile) comes from two words – *paedo* from the Greek for child and *philia*, meaning love. Paedophiles are attracted only to children. There are also adults who may have sexual relationships with other adults and sexually abuse children. They are typically called child sex abusers. Both groups abuse children, though they may use different excuses to justify what they do. It is correct to refer to both groups as child sex abusers.

Practically all information known about child sex abusers comes from prison studies. Since relatively few abusers are sent to prison, knowledge is limited to those who are caught, convicted and imprisoned. The vast majority of reported abusers are men, though women sexually abuse children as well. Abusers come from all classes, professions, racial and religious backgrounds. Contrary to the popular stereotype of child sex abusers as sinister strangers, most abusers are known to their victims and include family members, neighbours, friends, teachers, coaches, scout leaders, bank managers, vicars, police officers, etc. About one third of reported cases involve teenage abusers.

Some studies show that a high percentage of paedophiles were themselves abused as children and may be repeating what happened to them. What is not clear is why so many children who have been abused do not become abusers. Most child sex abusers delude themselves into believing that they are loving the child and that it does no harm. In fact, abusers often claim that all children have the 'right to sex with adults' and that the laws should be changed to permit this.

Those who work with child sex abusers say that power is a major motivation. Since it is impossible for a child to give informed consent to sex with an adult, the adult has complete control. The power over the child combined with the sexual abuse becomes a compulsive, addictive behaviour which is difficult to change. Abusers are adept at convincing themselves that they are not responsible for the abuse and that the child really wants to be involved. For a small minority, violence and/or killing the child also becomes a part of their compulsive mentality.

Abusers contact and control children in various ways. They make friends with children and appear to be kind, trustworthy and caring; use fear, threats and violence; live in or join families to abuse children; look for jobs which put them in contact with children; hang around places where children play or go; offer a combination of games, gifts, outings, bribes or threats to entrap children; tell the child that he or she is special and say the abuse is a secret between them. Abusers will tell a child that their mother knows and has given her blessing to the abuse. They may tell children they are teaching them what grown-ups do. Often they make children feel guilty by saying the child 'enjoyed it or wanted it', or they flatter the child, saying he is handsome or she is pretty. Therefore 'it is the child's fault' for attracting the abuse. Using guilt is a powerful tool with children, and often children say that they were told they would be in trouble or go to prison, or the family would be broken up if anyone found out.

Children need to be protected from sex abusers. It is vital that effective treatment programmes be combined with prison sentences to ensure that sex abusers are no longer a threat to children. Unfortunately there are few such programmes available. Some abusers are motivated to change their behaviour and can be helped with intensive therapy and ongoing supervision. For them and others who are fantasizing about abusing children, but have not yet acted on their impulses, it is essential that help be forthcoming. The problem is finding treatment programmes that work and getting the funding to introduce them. The reality is that this is an unpopular use of public funds, but it makes sense to prevent the abuse whenever possible.

What has to be faced is that there is no known cure for child sex offenders and that many child sex abusers continue to be a danger to children for their entire lifetimes. Most will need continued support to prevent them reoffending. Various solutions have been suggested: castrate them; lock up child sex abusers and throw away the key; register them and follow their movements; keep them under lifetime supervision; inform communities when they move into a neighbourhood; ban them from being around children in any capacity; label their driving licences and all records with a symbol indicating their crime. All of these ideas and others have been used with varying degrees of success in different countries.

The insurmountable problem is that there are thousands of child sex abusers who are not caught and convicted. There should be a way for them to get help if they want it and for society to be protected from those who are determined to abuse children. Perhaps the only other solution is to ensure that children are taught to get help if approached by anyone who tries to abuse them, and parents, teachers and others are given information about child sex abusers which will alert them to people intent on harming children.

The dilemma underlying the problem of child sex abusers is that they, too, can be seen as victims, given the abuse they suffered as children. Should they be forgiven and given a chance to prove they will not reoffend? Should they be allowed to be involved in their religious communities? If so, does the community have the right to know about their past offences? Can this chance be taken when children may be put at risk? And for Christians how does the question of forgiveness reconcile in this case with Jesus' harsh words in Matt. 18.6 that 'if any of you put a stumbling-block before one of these little ones who believe in me, it would be better for you if a great millstone were fastened round your neck and you were drowned in the depth of the sea'? [Michele Elliott]

PAEDOPHILIA
See: PAEDOPHILE

PAIN
An unpleasant sensory and emotional experience associated with actual or potential tissue damage or described in terms of such language.
This definition was offered in 1980 by the International Association for the Study of Pain. It also refers to pain being subjective and related to the person's mood, their morale, and the meaning of that pain for the individual. Thus an abdominal pain following removal of an appendix is recognized as being due to cut muscles knitting together and so is associated with healing. However, the pain created by the spread of a malignant tumour into the skeletal frame may 'speak of' an incurable state, of decay and death.

For people who possess a belief system the experience of pain can challenge that belief. 'If God is all-powerful and good then how can such things be allowed?' This can lead to a sense of unfairness and anger, which in itself can enhance the pain being experienced. The Greek word *poinē*, meaning penalty, implies pain is a consequence of sin, and this still lingers in the minds of some. The cause of much of the pain we experience, however, is more to do with accident, ageing, disease process, interpersonal relationships, emotional state, etc., rather than God. Pain may be classified as (1) acute – a well-defined onset, clear physical signs, responding to treatment with analgesia ranging from aspirin to morphine; (2) chronic – pain that persists for more than three months, a less well-defined onset, fewer objective signs to back up the person's statements. There are often changes in lifestyle, personality and functionality leading to a cycle of pain, depression and anxiety, requiring a multi-faceted approach; (3) emotional and spiritual; such pain links more to a life experience that has shaken one's trust in self or others and that may create a degree of hurt, abandonment or anger. This may result from bereavement, divorce, redundancy or other loss. The feelings of helplessness and vulnerability are especially painful at such times and the experience will shape how we cope (or not) with any similar experiences in the future.

If pain comes to dominate a person's life it has become usual to talk of 'total pain' (Saunders, 1967) encompassing physical, social, psychological and spiritual factors, requiring careful assessment.

Various methods have been produced to improve assessment of perceived pain, using both verbal and visual scales, but it remains important to believe the patient's complaint of pain, take careful history of the patient's experience, assess the psychological state, examine both medically and neurologically and formulate a treatment plan.

The treatment may use drugs, techniques to physically alter pain pathways between receptor and brain, or approaches to modify the way of life to reduce factors which exacerbate pain. These may include cognitive behavioural techniques, rational emotive therapy, peer group support, massage or relaxation. The ministry of healing with laying on of hands and anointing can be helpful in achieving a sense of inner peace which can reduce the subjective experience of pain. *[Peter Speck]*

PAIRING
One of the three basic assumptions influencing the unconscious behaviour of small groups.
The other two basic assumptions are dependence and fight/flight. They were identified by Wilfred Bion (1961) in work with small groups during and after the Second World War. They derive from a hypothesis that there is a group mentality, that the group acts collectively at an unconscious level.

Pairing refers to an underlying belief in the group that its survival will be achieved through some magical fusion with an ideal. In this sense it has a messianic quality. Hope is invested in one or more members of the group and their ability to create new life. Sometimes two members of a work-group will be encouraged to work together, as if the relationship is a sexual one and there is a fantasy that they will produce a child. In the group mentality, what matters is having an idealized future, rather than addressing and overcoming contemporary problems. Everything will be better when we have new premises/funding/organizational structure, etc.

PALLIATIVE CARE
The active total care of patients and their families by a multi-professional team when the patient's disease is no longer responsive to curative treatment.
This definition by the World Health Organization (1990) may be expanded to focus on the quality of life and integration of the physical, psychological, spiritual and social aspects of care.

Palliative care is frequently associated with the term hospice care. In recent years this term has come to be used to refer to an underlying philosophy which informs the palliative care approach and not solely that provided by an inpatient hospice unit. The palliative care approach is seen as a vital part of all clinical care whatever the illness or its stage. Therefore most professionals would be expected to have acquired some basic understanding of these key principles whether they work in primary care or hospital care: (1) a focus on quality of life, including good symptom control; (2) a whole person approach, seeing the individual in the context of their total life experience; (3) care which encompasses both the dying person and those who are important to that person; (4) respect for patient autonomy and choice (e.g. over place of death, treatment options). This can raise difficult ethical issues for care-givers if the person wishes to end their life prematurely, or to cease treatment; (5) open and sensitive communication, extending to patients, informal carers and professional colleagues.

In addition there are also specialist palliative care teams who either provide 'hands-on' care or act as a specialist resource to others. Access to palliative care depends on where the person is at the time.

If they are at home or in a nursing home then care will usually be provided by the primary care team (district nurses, family doctor, supported perhaps by a specialist palliative care team). The person may also attend for day care at a local hospice or other inpatient unit.

In hospital many of the carers should have familiarity with the palliative care approach and/or have access to a specialist palliative care team or palliative medicine consultant within the hospital or local inpatient unit.

If it is not possible to provide the required level of care for distressing symptoms or complex needs at home or in hospital, then the person may be transferred to a specialist palliative care inpatient unit. The person may remain there for a brief period while particular problems are addressed or, if death seems imminent, may stay through the terminal phase of their illness if they and the family wish them to die there.

At all stages the spiritual needs of the person should be taken into account as an integral part of the palliative care. There is research evidence to show (Speck, 1997) that in the absence of specific religious need a broader spiritual need may remain and that access to spiritual resources and support is very important. [*Peter Speck*]

PARANOIA
A mental disorder marked by delusions and sometimes hallucinations.
Paranoia (from the Greek for madness, dementia) usually appears in early adulthood. With little or no evidence, paranoid people assume that other people will exploit, harm or deceive them. Unjustifiably, they are suspicious about the trust and loyalty of friends or loved ones, responding with anger, argumentativeness or complaining to per-

ceived insults. Paranoid people do not forgive insults, slights or injuries easily. They may exhibit grandiose fantasies. The features described influence all intimate relationships pastoral care-givers will encounter. Pastoral care to paranoid individuals is very difficult and should not be taken towards counselling. Rather it should be characterized by establishing a trustful, supportive relationship, refraining from rational argumentation about the beliefs; usually referral to a trained professional.

PARANOID PERSONALITY
See: PERSONALITY DISORDER

PARANOID-SCHIZOID POSITION
In Kleinian thinking, the infant's earliest stage of development, to which individuals and institutions may revert.
Melanie Klein's psychoanalytic work with children led to thinking of childhood development as a shift from the paranoid-schizoid position to the depressive position (Klein, 1963). These terms carry technical meanings that are not self-evident. The infant's early emotional life is populated by objects, of which one is mother's breast. These objects are experienced as both good (gratifying) and bad (frustrating). The child locates feelings chiefly of love and hate in them and explores contradictions by projection. Infants also resolve what seems unmanageable anxiety by assigning different feelings to the different characters that populate their world. Klein calls this state 'paranoid' because badness is felt to come from outside, and 'schizoid' because emotions are coped with by splitting. The word 'position' is used rather than 'phase' because this behaviour is not confined to childhood but recurs throughout life (Hinshelwood, 1991). Development consists in moving to a second position – 'depressive'. Splitting and projection are also ways in which institutions and families cope with anxiety. They may unconsciously create a paranoid-schizoid system to cope with emotions that participants are unwittingly using to undermine or avoid working at the task, especially if this involves change (Obholzer and Roberts, 1994).

PARAPSYCHOLOGY
The scientific study of the paranormal.
Parapsychology has occupied a place on the fringes of psychological study. More recently, however, it has gained greater credibility.

Parapsychologists try to set up experiments in a scientific fashion in order to test whether there are unseen and as yet unknown links between minds, such as in telepathy and clairvoyance. They may also explore such areas as spiritualist beliefs and the effects of hypnosis. Alongside these studies a parallel exposé by magicians and conjurors is frequently offered. New Age thinking and postmodernism have both encouraged wide-ranging beliefs and brought back to the fore views of the world that had been largely discounted through nineteenth-century science. These have given parapsychology a renewed lease of life. For the pastor, the paranormal is more often encountered in requests for deliverance or even exorcism than in the scientific examination of what may be there.

PARENTING
To be or act as the father or mother of someone and therefore to be responsible for the care and nurture of that person.

Until the latter half of the twentieth century, in the post-Enlightenment world of the developed West, it was taken for granted by the majority of people that parenting, particularly of the very young child, was primarily a woman's job and that she would know by instinct how to do this. Few manuals existed and those that did concentrated on manners and discipline ('spare the rod and spoil the child') rather than on any discussion of how to nurture any potential in a child or guide that child's spiritual or moral development. In this, the Church was no exception. Children themselves were not expected to take part in worship, except in so far as their silent presence was tolerated, and parents were not expected to need help with the duties and responsibilities of parenting, beyond the examples of the previous generation. Although the education of a child had for many centuries been taken seriously by the Church, the education of parents in their role of nurturing and caring for their children, let alone providing any form of support for parents, was deemed by most church men and women to be not only unnecessary but an intrusion into the private territory of the family – whether by 'family' is understood the nuclear family, as developed in the latter half of the twentieth century, or the more extensive household of earlier generations. This attitude was supported by the law in Britain until as recently as the 1989 Children

Act, which, for the first time, formally places upon the court the duty of putting the best interests of the child over and above any wishes or needs of a parent. However, despite this, it is still the 'gut reaction' of many, including many church people, that the care and nurture of a child is something that is best left to the natural instincts of those who have borne the child or who have, either by adoption or through the action of the courts, been charged with that duty.

The structure and authority of the Church of England and therefore of the Anglican Communion, in the first instance, is not conducive to the development of what have been seen as peripheral activities. Bishop Gerald Ellison, sometime Bishop of London, once said, 'The Church, by itself, has never opened a school, trained a missionary or founded a hospital. These have been the actions of individual committed Christians, acting in obedience to their understanding of the teaching of the Gospel.' The first person to be concerned with teaching the skills of parenting was Mary Sumner, wife of an incumbent in the Winchester diocese, who founded the Mothers' Union in 1876. One of her principal objectives in founding the Society was to help mothers to train their children in the service of Christ and to teach them the faith. 'Train up a child in the way he should go' was in fact the first motto of the Society. To that end Mary Sumner held meetings at which she spoke, among other topics, of the importance of parenting in all its aspects. One indication of how novel and essential a theme this was may perhaps be gained from the speed and enthusiasm with which the Society spread throughout the Anglican Communion.

Today the Mothers' Union is no longer the only organization offering training in parenting skills, though it is still one of the leaders. It is active in over 260 dioceses worldwide, and in every diocese in which the Society works it seeks to support family life in the best way suited to that diocese, whether this be through the direct enabling of parental skills, literacy programmes for women and girls, or the kick-start funding of a variety of projects that enhance the quality of life for the whole family. In the British Isles, in recent years, several organizations have been set up with the specific object of offering training in parenting. Some of these are Christian-based, founded by practising Christians, though they may not actively seek to spread the faith directly through their work; others owe no allegiance to any faith, but nevertheless are successful in providing for the needs of parents.

Parenting is both a lonely and a stressful occupation, though it undeniably also brings great satisfaction and joy. Ever since the demise of large households and the loss of the close proximity of both kin and well-known neighbours, to which has been added an ever increasing desire for family privacy, the isolation and potential stress of anyone in charge of young children has increased. As well as the confidence which can be generated by skills, most adults in this situation need the support and companionship of others similarly placed. It is surely here that the Church can be most effective. The Church is spoken of as a family and, where this is genuinely so, it can be very caring and supportive. However, it will be essential for the Church as a whole to apprehend that parenting is not something that can wisely be left to the mere instincts of parents, but needs knowledge, skill and the devoted support of the whole community. [Rachel Nugee]

PARISH
1. A geographical area having its own church and minister.
2. A body of people associated for Christian worship and work in connection with a particular church.
Although the parish has become progressively less important as an administrative geographical unit, it still retains its importance in the Church of England as an 'idea in the mind' (Ecclestone, 1988). The root of the word is the Greek *paroikos* meaning neighbouring, the neighbour, implying those not of your own family or 'house' (= *oikos*). Later it came to have the meaning 'district', and it was in this sense it was first used in the Church to denote the diocese, and then the subdivisions of the diocese delegated by the bishop to resident presbyters. In England it also had roots in pre-Christian times when the landowner was bound to provide a place of worship for his dependants and a priest as his agent for this purpose. In the medieval Church this helped to ensure the independence of the parish priest against both his patron and his bishop. 'Parson's freehold' – a privilege enjoyed by a decreasing number of clergy today – was an expression of this. The 'parson' was the legal 'person' by whom the property of God (i.e. the church and the parsonage and any land belonging to them) was actually held. This focus on one representative person identified with the people of a particular area irrespective of church affiliation has bitten deep into the English psyche and helps to explain some of the resistance to modern arrangements in group ministries, teams, combined benefices as well as church 'plants' which are taken to undermine the notion of 'one church, one parish'.

The parish was also an important unit of civil administration. This is still remembered in the rural parish council, which is a civil unit totally independent of the parochial church council (which only arrived on the scene in 1919). The parish system was very slow to adapt to the impact of urbanization and industrialism. Two things happened as a result: (1) whole populations were left effectively unchurched; (2) a split began to occur between people's domestic environment and the world of work. Today the mission of the parish church and parson is overwhelmingly identified with the domestic and residential, and hardly takes into account the thousands who flow in or out of an area every day. In some urban areas, the parish church may never have really taken root as an 'idea in the mind' of a particular locality. This is sometimes forgotten in Anglican discussions about the parish system as a ministry of presence in every area. The freeing of other denominations from legal restrictions, and their subsequent setting up of their own parishes, districts and circuits, also severely modified the sense of the importance of the parish in relation to different denominational allegiances. Today the provisions under the Pastoral Measures of 1968 and 1983 for dioceses to make their own arrangements and revisions make the Church of England much like any other denomination in the way it runs its own affairs. Parish boundaries are rarely referred to except in the matter of baptisms, marriages and funerals, which many, including an increasing number of clergy, find irksome.

Thus the secondary meaning of the parish as 'the body of people associated for Christian worship and work in connection with a particular church' (*Shorter Oxford Dictionary*) has now become, practically speaking, the most important. This has gone hand in hand with a growing sense of congregationalism. 'The concern to build up a lively worshipping community of committed Christians equipped to serve God in their daily lives and to bring others to faith, has taken priority over the concern for the whole of life within the area of the parish' (ABM Report, 1993). This has led, in turn, to a discounting of older notions of 'church', still prevalent in the wider community, based on relatedness to a particular church, locality and God, rather than the actual time spent in church and in relationship with other church members. The Church of England is still seen, both inside and outside its own membership, as having a general responsibility towards the population of its parishes, and this is reinforced by the requirement to baptize, marry and conduct the funerals for those families which require it within the parish boundaries. But though the demands of the community are welcomed at one level, they are often deeply resented at another. The congregation can effectively 'unchurch' many on the fringes of its life by the way it draws boundaries around its worshipping life (e.g. in liturgical changes and the demands it makes on those requiring baptism, etc.) and the priority it gives to different activities.

This is all reflected in the ongoing debate about the future of the parish system and general strategies for mission. In this debate, the conflict between a 'communal' or 'parish' model of ministry and an 'associational' or 'evangelistic' model are often emphasized. Thus, the notion of the parish is still crucial to the self-perception of parish clergy and church members. It raises the question of what sort of church they think they actually, or wish to, belong to. The commitment to a parish system is seen as reflecting God's participation in the world and the Church's commitment to catholicity in the service of the Kingdom. 'God's active presence is offered [through worship, the sacraments, service and pastoral care] in ways which suggest that God is equally available to all, no matter what the social setting or circumstance' (ABM Report, 1993). The new awareness of the importance of particular local contexts in determining the shape of a local church and its mission has helped to break down the polarity between 'parish' and 'associational' models. It is often true that a particular context demands the presence of both models. A greater appreciation is needed of how the missions of different churches interact in a locality. At a time when the concept of society itself has been severely tested, wholehearted commitment to the notion of being church for a specific locality or local community is still needed, however it is managed or expressed (Moody, 1992). In the Bible the word *paroikein* carries the meaning 'to sojourn', 'to live besides strangers'. Truly social as well as Christian values are tested, in one sense, by how far they promote this ability. One way of revising and reapplying the notion of 'the parish' would be to pay closer attention to this dimension of belonging in the company of strangers. [*Christopher Moody*]

PASTOR
A shepherd of souls: one who cares for a congregation.

The biblical symbol for a pastor is a shepherd. Pastors are God's under-shepherds, are exalted to tend the flock of God (1 Pet. 5. 2–4). They are to work freely and not compulsively. They are not to do this work for money: it is not a job for pay, but a calling from God. A labourer deserves to be paid (Luke 10. 7). Nor are they to be motivated by the love of power over others. The desire to be an example, a role-model and a mentor is to be their main motivation. The New Testament also includes the Pastoral Letters, which are written under the name of the apostle Paul and contain extensive instructions for the churches and their leaders, who are variously called bishops, deacons and elders.

As the church developed, the pastor became known as 'priest'. He (for they were male) administered the seven sacraments: baptism, confirmation, eucharist, penance, unction, holy orders and matrimony. But like pastors, priests were called to care for people in times of adversity and celebration. After the Reformation, the notion of 'pastor' returned, and in some churches ministers to this day are called 'pastors'. In the Anglican tradition, the minister, as in the Roman Catholic Church, is called both priest and pastor. But in all these traditions there is a common agreement that being a pastor is one of the gifts of Christ. The task is 'to equip the saints for the work of the ministry, for building up the body of Christ' (Eph. 4. 10). The pastor's objective is that all should attain to the unity of faith and knowledge of the Son of God.

This biblical and historical stance remains the key factor in contemporary understanding of the meaning of 'pastor'. But population growth, the increasing complexity of religious organization, and the new tasks laid upon pastors have made this work far more complex. H. Richard Niebuhr (1956) affirms the historic meanings discussed above. But he adds that functionally the pastor is director of many dimensions of the congregation. He names the shepherd of the flock the 'pastoral director', and defines a pastoral director as one who oversees the single church. The pastor is head and overseer of this household of God, and his or her functions are:

1. *The building or edifying of the church* as its members serve the local community and the world. This is done by pastoral preaching, instruction, persuasion and counselling;

2. *Pastoral care and counselling* with a view to reconciling people to God and to one another;

3. *Teaching*, including the training of teachers as competent Christian educators;

4. *Administration*, so as to call out the gifts of members to increase their love of God and neighbour.

This description is that of an overseer of the flock of God, who leads by example but not by domination. Smaller churches may each have a sole pastor, often a local person. Larger churches may have several pastors under the leadership of a senior. In the USA, for example, such a church may have a pastor who cares for children, one for youth, and even one for the elderly. They may also have a pastor in charge of pastoral care and one in charge of administration, funding or stewardship.

Especially since the Second World War, newer forms of pastoring have come into prominence. Among the most obvious is the chaplain in an institution other than the church. The military chaplain, for example, played a vital part during both world wars, and hospital chaplains become a spiritual guide for the patients, doctors and nurses. Training for hospital chaplains in the USA is provided by the Association for Clinical Pastoral Education. Pastoral counselling is another form of pastoring that has recently become more well known. Extensive education supervision is required for responsible activity in this field.

In the current ecumenical climate, words for ministry carry particularly strong overtones. However, in much writing the term 'pastor' seems to be coming back into use as an appropriate model. *[Wayne Oates]*

PASTORAL CARE
Those activities of the Church which are directed towards maintaining or restoring the health and wholeness of individuals and communities in the context of God's redemptive purposes for all creation.

In a classic study of the history of pastoral care, Clebsch and Jaeckle (1967) identified four main strands of healing, sustaining, guiding and reconciling, and described pastoral care's distinctiveness from secular acts as the provision of care to troubled persons by 'representative Christian persons' working within the context of 'ultimate meanings and concerns'. This provides a comprehensive description which allows a range of activities to contribute to pastoral care, including skilled advice and counselling, sacraments and healing rituals, charitable work and social action, and simple acts of comfort, support and encouragement. This wide scope enables neglected elements of the tradition to be rediscovered and reinstated in subsequent eras.

Limitations of the Clebsch and Jaeckle definition include its somewhat vague religious reference and its linking of pastoral work to specific representatives (though not necessarily clergy). Alternative ways of describing the specifically Christian aspects of this form of care include Pattison's (1988) reference to 'the elimination and relief of sin and sorrow and the presentation of all people perfect in Christ to God'; Wilson's (1988) description of Christians in secular life rebuilding communities in accordance with the biblical concepts of shalom and the Kingdom of God; and Campbell's (1986) use of New Testament accounts of Christ's steadfastness, vulnerability and seeming foolishness to portray the uniqueness of Christian caring.

However, no definition is likely to be fully adequate to describe, as Wilson puts it, the 'coat of many colours' of pastoral care. It may be more important to recognize its diversity, and encourage continuing debate about its theological grounding and Christian distinctiveness. At different epochs some aspects of pastoral care have gained greater prominence (for example, the pastoral counselling emphasis which dominated the American literature from the 1960s until recently). In recent American, as well as British writing, the limitations of the counselling model are now widely perceived, and historical (Oden, 1984), hermeneutical (Capps, 1984), moral (Browning, 1976) and socio-political (Clinebell, 1984) dimensions of pastoral care have been given fresh prominence.

Despite this wholesome diversity, the following essential features of pastoral care may be identified:

1. *Transcendent aims*. Pastoral care must be set within a theological context which attempts to describe God's purposes for humanity and for the whole of creation. Thus it must encompass social justice, harmony with the environment, and personal well-being and fulfilment. Pattison's use of perfection in Christ and Wilson's use of the Kingdom recognize this transcendent reference, as does the phrase 'health and wholeness in the context of God's purposes for creation' contained in the definition section of this entry.

2. *Recipients*. In some eras and some traditions, an emphasis on ecclesiastical concerns (discipline, spiritual direction) has been dominant, but in common with its other activities, the Church cannot restrict its pastoral mission to its membership alone. Pastoral care is not merely chaplaincy to the religious, but should be offered as widely as possible, in an effort to combat the forces of destruction and despair in the lives of all individuals and communities. Justification for this comprehensiveness is found in the ministry of Jesus, which broke through the religious barriers of his day and offered healing and hope to the socially outcast and to those perceived as outside the Covenant. Indeed, if the revolutionary work of Christ is taken as a standard, then many churches and local congregations seem to be trapped in an inwardness and pettiness which seriously disables their pastoral ministry.

3. *Providers*. The term 'pastor' derives from the biblical image of the shepherd, and so may be thought to refer (as in Clebsch and Jaeckle's definition) only to church leaders or 'representative Christian persons'. Clearly, ordained clergy or other selected church workers have specific pastoral responsibilities, both to the congregation and the wider community. But given the broad scope of pastoral care and its transcendent aims, every Christian has a pastoral role to play both in everyday life and in the Christian community. Pastoral care must never be over-professionalized, though specific professional skills in counselling or in community development can play a part in the overarching task. When confronted by sin or sorrow, we each have a part to play if we are committed to God's plan for creation. The guiding passage is the parable of the good Samaritan, in which help comes from the least professional, most unexpected, source.

4. *Limits*. Finally, pastoral care is practised in conditions of human fallibility and with no escape from sin's pervasiveness. Often people cannot or will not be helped, and unjust institutions are highly resistant to change. The Church has frequently colluded in the injustices of society, and individual Christians easily lose vision and hope as they struggle with their own weaknesses and doubts. This means that ecclesiastical triumphalism and delusions of omnicompetence must both be eschewed in a spirit of true Christian humility. Often, if we are honest, we are closer to Good Friday than to Easter morning, vulnerable, afraid and feeling defeated, not at all victorious. Perhaps an awareness of such limitations is the best contribution of pastoral care to God's final purposes, since it offers the sensitivity of the wounded healer, and the strange wisdom of the fool. [*Alastair V. Campbell*]

PASTORAL COUNSELLING
**1. Counselling by clergy with advanced training in pastoral psychotherapy.
2. Crisis intervention by ministers.
3. Popularly often confused with 'pastoral care'.**

Pastoral counselling is an essential part of the total ministry of pastoral care. The uniqueness of pastoral counselling is derived from the training of pastors that equips them to integrate insights from contemporary psycho-social sciences and psychotherapeutic methods, on the one hand, with the healing resources of the Jewish and Christian heritages and the resources of gathered communities of faith, on the other.

This modern expression of the ministry of pastoral theology and care was stimulated in North America by the Clinical Pastoral Education movement flowing from the pioneering ministry of Anton Boisen in the 1930s. Pastoral counselling theory, training and practice flowered profusely in the period after the Second World War. It has now become a significant ministry in many countries where post-seminary academic and clinical training are available at universities and from organizations for pastoral care. A series of International Congresses on Pastoral Care and Counselling over recent decades has been a significant influence in globalizing the modern pastoral counselling movement, giving it a multicultural awareness and orientation in an increasingly pluralistic world.

The blossoming of pastoral counselling reflects the growing recognition that training in psychology and counselling skills is essential for ministering to troubled people in a world where rapid social change, urbanization, high-tech depersonalization and violence proliferate.

The theories and methods of pastoral counselling have evolved continually since the movement had its post-war renaissance in the late 1940s and 1950s. Primary early sources of theoretical models in North America were the approaches of Sigmund Freud and the American psychologist Carl R. Rogers, together with some influence from the work of Carl G. Jung. Four Americans who made pioneering contributions in establishing the field were Carroll Wise, Paul Johnson, Seward Hiltner and Wayne Oates. In England, Frank Lake's development of what he called 'clinical theology' had a significant impact. On the European continent, pastoral theologians emphasized the importance of recovering the theological roots of the pastoral counselling movement, thus giving it a stronger religious foundation.

In subsequent decades, a wide variety of psychosocial, psychotherapeutic and theological theories and methods have been integrated into models for practising pastoral counselling. These include relationship orientations, crisis intervention and grief-healing approaches and, more recently, social systems therapies. The latter have provided the foundation for the introduction of a prophetic dimension into the field, enlarging the horizons of healing. This involved the use of methods of pastoral care in and through social institutions with the aim of changing them to enhance their constructive impact on the well-being of all those whose lives are affected by them.

A recent significant development has extended the circles of pastoral care-giving further to include the natural environment as well as the social environment. This approach, developed by Howard Clinebell, is called 'ecotherapy'. It assumes that healing individuals and relationships must also involve healing the earth on which the well-being of all living things depends. The focus is on making pastoral counselling and teaching (and all other dimensions of ministry, as well as all the other healing, growth-nurturing arts) instruments for helping to save a healthy earth on which all future generations of children can live healthy lives. Pas-

toral counsellors have a crucial role in that the root causes of the destruction of a viable earth are spiritual and ethical pathologies. These are problems for which clergy have special training for understanding and becoming instruments of healing.

As the human family moves into the new century and millennium, with all its challenges and opportunities, the need for well-trained counselling pastors and specialized pastoral counsellors clearly is great. Fortunately, contemporary clergy have more abundant resources for this healing and growth-nurturing ministry than ever before in the long history of pastoral care-giving. They have more insights and better methods for use in walking in the footsteps of the one who, through most of church history, has been called 'the Great Physician'. Pastoral counselling is an effective means by which clergy can become channels for the healing, growth-enabling power of God's liberating love in the lives of suffering, oppressed, burdened human beings. [*Howard Clinebell*]

PASTORAL EDUCATION
The art and craft of preparing women and men, ordained and lay, for ministries of pastoral care and/or counselling.

The development of special courses of pastoral education is a comparatively recent phenomenon. Historically, men (and it was only men) were trained for the pastoral aspects of the ordained ministry on an apprenticeship model. They learned their academic theology in the universities and then, as curates or assistant ministers, encountered the demands of their calling to respond to the heights and depths of human experience. Sometimes they were all too aware of their unpreparedness for these tasks, but under the benevolent direction of more experienced ministers they increased in skill and confidence.

Modern approaches to pastoral education have their roots in two separate but related series of events. First, Clinical Pastoral Education, originating in North America, has had a significant international influence. In 1925, the Revd Anton T. Boisen, a Congregationalist minister who was then chaplain at Worcester State Hospital, Massachusetts, was recovering from a psychotic breakdown. Distressed that it was possible to become a minister without having studied the human personality either in sickness or health, he invited a number of theological students to work with him in the hospital over the summer. He believed that there was no better laboratory for the study of people in crisis than the mental hospital and no better library than the 'living human documents', a phrase which has become a watchword of the movement. There are now over four hundred institutions in North America offering training in pastoral care in hospitals and prisons, using an approach involving the practice of pastoral care and careful reflection upon that practice under skilled supervision that leads to personal and professional growth. Clinical Pastoral Education has made its international impact in at least three ways. Pastoral educators from other countries have experienced CPE in North America and returned home to incorporate its insights into their own training programmes; the vast American literature was for many years all that was available and the main texts have been translated into many languages; and in the last quarter of the twentieth century, there was an American influence in the international development of organizations for pastoral care.

The second main influence upon pastoral education has been the growth of training and education in other helping professions. The twentieth century witnessed both radical change in old professions (such as psychiatry) and the appearance of new disciplines, such as social work and the many varieties of psychotherapy and counselling. Each of these has been supported by new approaches to education and/or training. These have included elements particular to the discipline and an underlying commonality of approach. The common element has been, as in CPE, controlled exposure to the practice of the discipline and competent supervision of that practice. The growth of other disciplines, sometimes indeed taking over tasks previously undertaken by the clergy, has had an inevitable impact upon the training of ministers and, more widely, upon the pastoral ministry of the Church.

The twentieth century also witnessed new (or recovered) understandings of the Church and its ministry which have important implications for pastoral education. First, a recovery of the insight that ministry belongs to the whole people of God, not to the ordained ministry alone, has had the practical outcome that lay ministry involves more people in the Church then ever before in pastoral care.

Second, the admission of women to the ordained ministry has introduced a new dimension into ministry itself. This has raised such questions for pastoral education as whether the approaches developed for male clergy are relevant for women and what implications the insights that women bring to pastoral care may have for the way in which all are trained to be pastors.

Pastoral education takes place in a variety of settings. First, in theological colleges and divinity faculties courses seek to equip men and women to exercise competently the traditional ministries of pastoral care within churches and communities. Both theoretical input and supervised exposure to practice are common. Field education in a variety of settings is now regarded as mandatory for ordinands, and there is an increasing concern to provide training for those ministers charged with the task of supervision. Second, there are courses, often part-time, which offer a qualification in pastoral counselling. Those who enrol on them are predominantly women and lay people. Such courses are often of a very high standard, offering nationally recognized qualifications in counselling. Their graduates can be a resource for the Church. Third, with increased emphasis upon an 'official' pastoral role for lay people within congregations, attention is being given to their selection, training and support. This, in turn, demands a fresh understanding of the role of the ordained ministry in relation to pastoral education (Ballard and Pritchard, 1996).

Pastoral education uses a variety of training methods. Certain underlying issues which have implications for pastoral education continue to be a matter of debate. Lambourne (1974) warned against the 'medicalization' of pastoral care, and one must always seek a balance between helping individuals to cope with life crises, and building up communities of faith, hope and love. Again, there is a question relating to the theological content of pastoral education. Some pastoral counsellors are content that their own faith remain implicit and unspoken in their pastoral relationships, while those who are happy to be identified as Christian counsellors are more explicit in their use of religious language and ideas.

The final question relates to professionalism (Foskett and Lyall, 1988). While there have been great gains both in a more professional understanding of pastoral care and pastoral education, there are also dangers. In identifying and training those with specific pastoral responsibilities it may be forgotten that much caring is a spontaneous outflowing of love and compassion from one human being to another. For such caring no special education is needed, and it could in fact be counter-productive. The few need to be skilled without de-skilling the many. *[David Lyall]*

PASTORAL LITURGY
See: RITUAL, BAPTISM, WEDDINGS, FUNERAL

PASTORAL PSYCHOLOGY
A general, and imprecise, term that refers to the application and use of psychological knowledge in pastoral practice, including both pastoral care and pastoral counselling.

In the twentieth century, the term came into its most popular usage during the 1950s and 1960s and a professional journal of that name began publication. The general field of knowledge to which the term refers, and to which *Pastoral Psychology* addressed itself, was the development and search for more general acceptance in both the Church and the scholarly world. During that time much effort was devoted to the integration of psychology and theology in the interest of making wider knowledge available to pastors, as well as professional chaplains and counsellors working in a religious role. Programmes of study seeking to address this integrative approach varied in their choice of titles. Some used pastoral psychology, but others chose pastoral theology, psychiatry and religion, clinical pastoral theology, and other similar terms. The psychology of religion, which also was used as the title of some graduate departments, sought similar integration of theory and practice, although the discipline of the psychology of religion in its more formal sense addressed itself to the psychological analysis and explanation of religious phenomena.

Pastoral psychology, though not the universally accepted title, emerged with great popularity in the middle of the twentieth century. Prior to that emergence, training in pastoral skills for times of crisis was viewed by many as somewhat superficial because of the absence of any sophisticated understanding of the dynamics of human behaviour and

change. The field of psychology, most popularly known first through the work of Freud, had been viewed with suspicion by many religious professionals. Theological seminaries did not include the study of psychology in their curricula prior to the middle of the twentieth century. Consequently, many pastors and chaplains learned about the clinical usefulness of psychology by studying in university departments of psychology or working with psychiatrists and psychologists in clinical settings.

As both interest and pressure increased to incorporate the insights of psychology into the training of ministers, faculties raised basic questions about the danger of sacrificing the supremacy of theology to this new and 'secular' discipline. No doubt the term pastoral psychology was chosen to allay such fears and to convey the idea that the knowledge of psychology would be used in the service of pastoral tasks and be subject to theology as the 'controlling' discipline. Others addressed the problem by making a distinction: theology was understood as the source of beliefs about God and the human condition; psychology provided disciplined observation, description, and explanation of human behaviour. Pastoral psychology was a useful discipline, bringing these two different, but complementary, fields of knowledge into a valuable and co-operative relationship. While the term still does not automatically reveal one's particular method of correlating theology and psychology, it does identify an underlying commitment to the use of these sources of knowledge for the sake of the ministry of the Church and synagogue. *[William Arnold]*

PASTORAL PSYCHOTHERAPY
An interpersonal response to human distress and dysfunction by one who understands this practice as a religious ministry.

The pastoral psychotherapist is usually a person who holds a formal office of leadership in the Church such as ordination or consecration. Psychotherapy has been described in a classic text as a form of personal influence that is characterized by (1) a healing agent, typically a person trained in a socially sanctioned method of healing, believed to be effective by the sufferer and by at least some members of his or her social group; (2) a sufferer who seeks relief from the healer; and

(3) a healing relationship – that is, a circumscribed, more or less structured series of contacts between the healer and the sufferer in which the healer tries to bring relief from the symptoms (Frank and Frank, 1991). Because psychotherapy may be more often identified with psychology or psychiatry than with ministry, and includes a formal therapist – patient type of relationship, it has sometimes been seen as involving a different kind of relationship from that which usually exists between pastor and parishioner. 'Pastoral counselling' has, therefore, more often been used to describe this form of religious ministry. The term 'counselling', however, is not without its problems. It has been defined generally as a mutual exchange of ideas and opinions, and advice resulting from such an exchange. Understood in this way the term has been used to include a wide range of relationships, involving such types of counselling as nutritional, vocational, financial, and a variety of others that may also seem quite different from ministry.

One of those in the USA who argued persuasively for the use of the term 'pastoral psychotherapy' rather than 'pastoral counselling' has insisted that in using the term 'psychotherapy' a religious practitioner is returning to the roots of Christian religious tradition, because the Greek words from which the term 'psychotherapy' is derived are New Testament words (Wise, 1980). *Psyché* suggests meanings such as the principle of human life or the centre of the inner life of the person. *Therapeuō* includes meanings of serving, healing and worshipping, and suggests healing over against the forces that diminish or destroy life. Such healing can be understood as a healing of the life force which is central to humankind both in earthly existence and beyond. Psychotherapy understood in this way can certainly be seen as an enterprise of the religious community.

The issue of pastoral psychotherapy's or counselling's connection with or separation from the religious community remains, whichever term may be used. One of Britain's major contributors to the understanding of pastoral counselling has argued that it is separated from its very life unless it is substantially concerned with the larger service of the Church and the development of community rather than 'being preoccupied with the ego-formation, identity righteousness, or salvation of its individual members'.
[*John Patton*]

PASTORAL STUDIES
An academic discipline which is a subset of practical theology, with distinct subject matter but a shared methodology.

'Pastoral studies' is a term that is mostly found in the UK (though it occurs occasionally in Roman Catholic and Anglican seminary education in the USA). Comparable developments in the USA were occurring at the same time, if not somewhat earlier, but went by various names, the term 'pastoral theology' being perhaps the closest equivalent.

As an academic study, pastoral studies emerged in England and Wales during the 1960s in two interrelated forms.

1. Pioneered in Birmingham (1964), there were soon courses in Cardiff, Manchester and London (Heythrop). Characteristically they took the form of postgraduate, post-experience diplomas and master's degrees (roughly equivalent to the D.Min.) aimed at clergy and other practitioners. In Scotland the same development was possible through the restructuring of the traditional departments of practical theology in the ancient universities, notably at Edinburgh. At the same time research degrees (MPhil and PhD) became available. The distinguishing mark of such courses was to bring together the academic study of theology and pastorally relevant disciplines in the context of theological reflection and informed pastoral practice. Emphasis was more on personal development and deeper insights into the nature of pastoral action than on the acquisition of techniques or skills.

2. From about 1969 pastoral studies were introduced in the theological colleges (seminaries) and began to transform ministerial training, but not in such a highly professional way as sometimes found elsewhere. The new courses mainly provided an introduction to human socialization and counselling skills. They became mandatory in Anglican colleges; and in some universities pastoral studies were related to ministerial training, though usually on a wider basis which included sociology and other fields. In Scotland the Diploma in Ministry was introduced. Free Church colleges, however, tended to follow a different line, moving towards an integrated internship training.

Since 1970 there has been an annual conference of those engaged in the subject with the aim of engendering some kind of coherence and norms for an embryonic field. It has steadily grown as the subject has expanded. A further important step was for the conference to establish itself as the British and Irish Association for Pastoral Theology (1993), associated with the International Academy for Practical Theology (1991). There has also been a significant growth of literature in the field, not least discussing the bases of the discipline.

In the academic field, the emergence of pastoral studies heralded and has been caught up in a wider interest in practical theology. This, has, however, tended to be somewhat haphazard and eclectic, reflecting not least the pressure on universities and theological colleges to diversify into serving the wider constituency, including lay training, and to provide accreditation for different initiatives. Pastoral studies, therefore, are part of the wider activity better called practical theology. Sometimes the terms are synonymous. But pastoral studies can be distinguished as having their focal interest in theological reflection on the concern for specifically pastoral care.

What was happening in the academic context was paralleled by the appearance of ecclesial and para-ecclesial organizations in the wider Church. The denominations sponsored a number of pastoral, training and educational initiatives. More important for pastoral care was the emergence of a number of organizations for pastoral care and voluntary associations such as the Scottish Pastoral Association, which initiated what is still the only journal in the field, *Contact*, the Irish Pastoral Association, the Westminster Pastoral Foundation, Clinical Theology and the Association for Pastoral Care and Counselling. This clearly mirrored similar developments elsewhere, notably in the USA.

As an academic discipline pastoral studies has its own defining characteristics both in relation to its subject matter and its methodology.

1. The subject matter is, basically, *reflection on the pastoral, caring ministry of the Church* in the widest sense. That is, it will be concerned with the aims, skills and practices involved in working with people not only at points of need but also in creating personal and communal health. It thus is directed at those offering pastoral care, both to individuals and corporately, whether authorized so to act, as clergy or professional workers, or exercising an informal caring role in congregation or neighbourhood.

2. Pastoral studies is, therefore, *a practical discipline*. As such it draws on the insights, skills and wisdom from its own past in the Christian tradition, and from the cognate human sciences and related professions, to equip pastoral practitioners to the highest level. Learning will be closely conjoined with practice, whether through placements and fieldwork or reflection on personal pastoral experience.

3. Pastoral studies, however, is *a reflective discipline*. Practice constantly comes under critical scrutiny in the light of theological and other perspectives in order to fulfil its task of serving the mission of the Church with integrity and understanding.

4. Pastoral studies is *interdisciplinary*. The original intention was to find for theology new dialogue partners (other than the traditional ones of history and philosophy) from among the newly emerging human sciences. There is, therefore, common ground with the 'critical correlation' approach of much North American practical theology. But such a dialogue, while exciting and creative, has to be sustained with care, patience and determination.

5. But, above all, pastoral studies is a theological discipline. Theology, as a second-order activity, takes the experience of faith and life and enquires how it relates to and illuminates the understanding of the faith and the demands of the gospel. Pastoral studies, with its focus on pastoral practice, sets up a dialogue between the working out of faith in the life of the world and our understanding of God in Christ found in Bible and tradition. From it will come both new insights into the human condition and a deeper understanding of how God is open to and cares for the world. [*Paul Ballard*]

PASTORAL THEOLOGY
1. The theology and practice of pastoral ministry (Roman Catholic).
2. The theology and practice of pastoral care and counselling (Protestant).

Pastoral theology is often related to practical theology, the theology and practice of everyday Christian life. Within the Roman Catholic Church, pastoral theology is a broad term that refers to the theology, training and practices of ordained priests working in parishes, including liturgy, sacraments, preaching, teaching and counselling. Sometimes called 'practical theology', this discipline attempts to develop programmes, skills and theological reflection that are consistent with the other branches of theology. For example, if philosophical and moral theology emphasize the sanctity of life and the importance of enhancing life and opposing death, then the ministries of the local church are likely to focus on the moral education of children and parents around issues such as birth control and abortion. The theology and practice of such life-enhancing ministries would be called pastoral or practical theology (or, sometimes, applied theology).

Within Protestant churches, pastoral theology usually refers to the theology and practice of pastoral care and counselling. Seward Hiltner (1958) defined pastoral theology as the branch of theology that focuses on the caring ministries of the Church and engages in theological reflection based on these ministry experiences. This places pastoral theology as a sub-discipline of practical theology, alongside homiletics, religious education, liturgical studies and administration. In the Protestant sense, pastoral theology attempts to include several tensions within the daily life of Christians:

1. *Pastoral theology and the clergy–laity tension.* Since Martin Luther, Protestants have struggled to define the theological basis for lay-centred ministries. The priesthood of all believers is a respected doctrine, but often the work of the laity is overshadowed by professional clergy. If pastoral theology is a ministry of care for God's people and the world, then lay people have a central role to play in its theory and practice. Pastoral theologians have attempted to define the theological basis for care in such a way that its practice is possible for all baptized Christians. In this sense, pastoral theology is the basis for the caring ministries of Christians. For example, deacons who visit the sick and care for those in need have been the focus of reflection in pastoral theology.

2. *Pastoral theology and the theory–praxis tension.* Modern pastoral theologians since 1920 have been intrigued with the revelations of God that come from the experiences and witness of suffering people. Originally located in hospitals, prisons and agencies for the poor, pastoral theologians such as Anton Boisen and Russell Dicks listened for the challenges to official theologies. Verbatim accounts and supervised live interviews provided occasions for theological reflection on how God is working in the lives of persons threatened by illness, punishment and poverty. This empirical principle has been strengthened in recent years with the development of liberation and feminist theologies that call Christians to listen to the witness of the world's poor and oppressed. Theologically, God's Spirit is revealed in the everyday witness of people, and then brought into dialogue with the established wisdom of Scripture and tradition. Theology as theory is not the only source of knowledge about God. Praxis is also a source of revelation that must be respected in its own right.

3. *Pastoral theology and the social sciences.* Pastoral theology since 1920 has been interdisciplinary, especially in relation to psychology, sociology and anthropology. In fact, a critique of pastoral theology can be seen in the perennial question: 'What is pastoral about pastoral counselling?' or 'What is the difference between pastoral and secular counselling?' Because of the many interconnections across disciplinary lines, the boundaries have not always been clear, and some scholars have suspected that pastoral counsellors are only psychologists trying to use their religion as a justification for their trade. Sometimes these questions have been sharply debated within the movement of pastoral theology itself. Accrediting organizations in pastoral counselling and clinical pastoral education have evaluated and changed criteria for competence as understandings of pastoral theology have changed. Interdisciplinary areas of study include: psychology and sociology of religion (the study of religious experience using the methods of social science); pastoral psychology (the application of social science to the caring ministries of Christians); pastoral care, counselling, and psychotherapy (the development of cross-disciplinary theories and practices of care).

According to Seward Hiltner, pastoral theology becomes theological when it brings insights about God from its practice with people to the debates with other religious leaders and theologians. Constructing genuine theological insights about Scripture and theology is the defining mark of pastoral theology. Along the way, pastoral theologians engage in disciplined practices of care, interdisciplinary dialogue with social sciences, and theological reflection. [*James N. Poling*]

PEAK EXPERIENCES
Transient moments of self-actualization.

In humanistic psychology, moments of profound change are called 'peak experiences' (Maslow, 1971). They may be associated with music, art or religion. But they cannot be sought or guaranteed: they just are. These experiences are also crucial for our development into human beings. The idea has a mystical, quasi-spiritual quality and is connected with the notion of being 'fully human'. The theme was especially prominent in the 1960s and 1970s.

PENANCE
An obligation undertaken as a sign of sorrow for sin.

The root of the word 'penance' is the Latin 'poena', meaning punishment. In the early history of the Church the penalties imposed as a public sign of sorrow for sin were severe, and absolution was delayed until the obligation was completed. Penitents were excluded from communion and stood in a special place in the church. After a severe course of prayer, fasting and almsgiving they were readmitted to the community but certain conditions remained: they could not serve as a soldier; the process of penance could not be repeated again, and they were committed to lifelong continence. As a result, it became common to delay the process until the point of death.

The voluntary undertaking of penances is a feature of early monasticism. One way of describing the monastic life was as a life of penance. One of the principal motivations was to escape eternal punishment in the life to come by accepting a penitential ascetic regime in this one – not, however, as an attempt in any way to manipulate God, but as the outward expression of a fundamental attitude of humility and acceptance of God's grace. In the early Middle Ages a more flexible penitential practice was introduced which allowed for confession of sins in secret, but still postponed absolution until after an often long and arduous penance had been completed. But it was not until the Lateran Council of 1215 that private confession and absolution became the norm, followed by a light, formal penance. Lengthy pilgrimages were often undertaken as a form of penance for serious offences, and penance continued to be seen as a form of 'heavenly medicine'

which shielded the penitent from sin and prevented further temptation.

The Protestant Reformation swept the whole penitential system away, stressing that Christ's atonement on the cross was the only perfect satisfaction for sin. God's forgiveness could not be made conditional on human effort. Penance was regarded as a form of justification by works and therefore condemned. However, true repentance, the intention to amend and lead a new life, were still recognized as necessary for the reception of God's forgiveness. Penitential self-discipline might therefore remain a feature of Christian living, but as a regular aspect of the spiritual life, rather than a temporary practice or obligation. In recent secular discussion on the rehabilitation of offenders, there has been more emphasis on the place of community work or some other transaction as a form of satisfaction for the hurt done to individuals or society as a whole. The Truth and Reconciliation Commission in South Africa could be seen in one light as a public form of penance in the higher interests of reconciliation. As a form of individual religious practice, penance may have virtually disappeared. However, the communal demand for some form of penance, seen as a voluntarily undertaken sign of a change of heart rather than a punishment, contains more than an echo of early Church practice.
[Christopher Moody]

PERFECTIONISM
The theory that people are morally perfectible.

The concept that Christians can become morally perfect has been a controversial aspect of the Christian tradition since the time of the apostles. It seems generally to accompany the early stages of conversion. The texts about it in the New Testament are ambiguous and disputed. The result has been the notion of grades of perfection, the highest belonging to God alone. Perfectionism played a major part in the development of Methodism. John Wesley held that the newly converted Christian immediately embarked on the way of perfection. The 'Perfectionists' were a group established at Oneida, NY, in 1848. They insisted that sinlessness was achievable when one was in communion with Christ.

The 'counsels of perfection' (poverty, chastity and obedience) are the foundation of the religious life.

Perfectibility is also implicit in the secular understanding of human nature and belief in progress.

PERINATAL DEATH
The death of a child of less than 24 weeks' gestation, where it is born alive, and from the twenty-fourth week of pregnancy to 28 days after the birth.

A stillbirth is the death before birth of a foetus of more than 24 weeks' gestation. A neonatal death is one occurring within 28 days of birth. Perinatal death encompasses both categories. Thirty years ago the effect of perinatal death on the immediate and more distant family as well as those responsible for medical care was a subject on which there was little published literature and apparently little interest. There was little appreciation of the fact that this was a significant pastoral area where there was need for understanding and help and where problems and difficulties were being ignored.

The problem is two-fold. First, unacknowledged loss. Support and sympathy of friends and neighbours traditionally available to mourners are usually absent for a family suffering perinatal loss. Nothing is perceived to have happened; nothing has been lost. Second, there is the impact on the mother, the father, the siblings and the grandparents. This is both varied and complex but common to all is the fact that memory facilitates the normal mourning process essential to recovery and that here there is no memory. Mourning is normally retrospective, a remembrance of a person's past; perinatal bereavement results in prospective mourning, relinquishing wishes and hopes about one who could have been but never was.

Why was the problem ignored for so long? To a significant extent this was because the medical profession demonstrated a lack of understanding, sensitivity and responsiveness to the traumatizing effect of perinatal birth. There have been considerable advances in pastoral care in recent years although there is still very little published literature on the subject other than in specialized journals (Leon, 1990). Much of the research has been inadequate. Credit for improved pastoral care can be traced to the pioneering work of the Stillbirth and Neonatal Death Society (SANDS) and to the support of midwives reflected in the pressure they applied within hospitals to change and improve practice and procedures. Current medical training and practice are now guided by a greater appreciation of parental grief for perinatal loss. Hospital staffs now help bereaved parents to accept the reality of their loss and to mourn their child. There has been a reversal of the former prevailing medical wisdom from denying the loss to facilitating its complete expression and thereby promoting its resolution. Practice often lags behind theory, however, and it is doubtful whether doctors always recognize the caring burden that falls on midwives (Kohner, 1995). Outside the pastoral care now offered by hospital chaplains and maternity departments, one of the main sources of social support and understanding for perinatal loss has been self-help groups where bereaved parents reaffirm for one another the fact that grieving is a normal reaction and find a place where those feelings may be freely expressed. *[David Bond]*

PERSON-CENTRED COUNSELLING
Counselling in which persons seeking care are seen as unique human beings to be treated with unconditional positive regard and empathy.

Often associated with the humanistic psychology of Abraham Maslow, Carl Rogers and others, this theory treats individuals with attention to their differences more than their similarities. It is theologically rooted in the belief that the image of God is present in each person in a special way. Pastors following this method seek to listen carefully, respond authentically, and seek solutions that are unique, with genuine respect for the autonomy and integrity of each person.

PERSONA
The part-self or favoured social role behind which the real and more personal self gets used to hiding.

Jung took the term from the Latin for an actor's mask. Examples of such 'masks' are a person's profession, gender, and stage of life. They are all collective factors, not necessarily inappropriate in the right setting. The persona has the quality of an archetype.

PERSONALITY
The dynamic organization of an individual's thinking, feeling, desiring and behaviour into a coherent whole that gives direction and stability to a person's life over time.

Personality refers to the characteristic pattern of an individual's interaction with the environment. It describes the active integration of all the various aspects of human psychological functioning into a system that gives a discernible, unique shape to a person's life.

Personality develops through the interaction of inherited and environmental factors. Nature and nurture, biology and society, maturation and learning all interact to form a personality. Theories of personality vary in the emphasis they place on each of these factors, but all except the most radical recognize some interplay between unfolding of inherent tendencies and response to the environment.

Although personality develops through the lifespan, there is recognizable continuity in the personality of individuals over time. There is also consistency in personality across situations. A friendly person, for instance, is likely to be friendly towards most people in most situations. We come to know and relate to people through the unique patterns of their personalities. Pressures from the environment, however, and especially from the social environment, can be powerful enough to make people act in ways contrary to their personality.

Personality theories vary widely in their views of the concept of the unconscious. The Freudian tradition has attributed great influence to unconscious forces in personality. Consequently, Freudian theory is sceptical of people's descriptions of their own thoughts and feelings. Other theorists focus on conscious states and activities, placing greater trust in self-reports and observable behaviour.

The health, or pathology, of the personality is a central concern of personality studies. All four of the basic psychological processes in personality – cognition, affect, volition and behaviour – have been implicated in psychopathology. At the same time, given the interconnectedness of the four, therapeutic intervention on any one process can yield beneficial change in the whole personality.

Research into personality has been carried out in three distinct traditions: the clinical, the correlational and the experimental (Maddi, 1980). The clinical method draws on the observations of therapists to build theories about personality. It benefits from the intense, extended contact of therapists with research subjects. The uniqueness of each therapeutic encounter, though, makes it hard to generalize from clinical experience to theory. In correlational research, statistical analysis of measures of difference is used to reveal relationships among a few elements of personality. Experimental approaches attempt systematically to manipulate variables to establish causal links among them. This approach produces the most reliable information, but the narrow focus on a few variables of personality and the artificiality of the laboratory setting limit the usefulness of experimental data in the real world.

As one of the most encompassing concepts in the psychology of the individual, personality is particularly significant in pastoral studies. Preferences in types of spiritual experience, interpersonal relationships within communities, tendencies towards pathology, and modes of repair are all shaped by personality. [*D. M. Thorpe*]

PERSONALITY DIMENSIONS
Hans Eysenck's dimensional model of personality.

The model of personality developed by Hans Eysenck and his associates (Eysenck and Eysenck, 1985) argues that individual differences can be most economically and efficiently described in terms of a small number of higher order personality dimensions. According to this mathematically derived model, these major dimensions of personality are orthogonal or uncorrelated. Eysenck's original model, in the Eysenck Personality Inventory (EPI), proposed two major dimensions characterized as extraversion and neuroticism. Eysenck's more recent model, in the Eysenck Personality Questionnaire (EPQ) and the Revised Eysenck Personality Questionnaire (EPQR) proposed three major dimensions characterized as extraversion, neuroticism and psychoticism. These instruments also contain one further index known as 'the lie scale'. Various editions of this family of instruments contain between 24 and 100 items. The Eysenck Personality Profiler contains 440 items in order to produce seven subscales within each of the three major dimensions.

Eysenck's use of the language of psychopathology to describe aspects of normal personality is deliberate. The model suggests that neurotic and psychotic disorder is not discontinuous from normal personality but located at one extreme pole of a normal personality continuum. At the same time psychotic and neurotic disorders are seen to be unrelated to each other. One dimension of normal personality moves from stability through emotional lability to neurotic disorder. Another dimension of normal personality moves from tender-mindedness through tough-mindedness to psychotic disorder.

Eysenck's extraversion scales measure sociability and impulsivity. The opposite of extraversion is introversion. The higher scorer on the extraversion scale is characterized by the test manual as a sociable individual, who likes parties, has many friends, needs to have people to talk to and prefers meeting people to reading or studying alone. The typical extravert craves excitement, takes chances, acts on the spur of the moment, is carefree, easy-going, optimistic, and likes to 'laugh and be merry'. Eysenck characterizes the high scorer as sociable, lively, active, assertive, sensation-seeking, carefree, dominant, and venturesome. The low scorer on this dimension is characterized by the opposite set of traits.

The neuroticism scales measure emotional lability and over-reactivity. The opposite of neuroticism is emotional stability. The high scorer on the neuroticism scale is characterized by the test manual as an anxious, worrying individual, who is moody and frequently depressed, likely to sleep badly and to suffer from various psychosomatic disorders. Eysenck suggests that if the high scorer on the neuroticism scale 'has to be described in one word, one might say that he was a *worrier*; his main characteristic is a constant preoccupation with things that might go wrong, and with a strong emotional reaction of anxiety to these thoughts'. Eysenck characterizes the high scorer as anxious, depressed, tense, irrational, shy, moody, emotional, suffering from guilt feelings and low self-esteem. The low scorer on this dimension is characterized by the absence of these traits.

Eysenck's psychoticism scales identify the underlying personality traits which at one extreme define psychotic mental disorders. The opposite of psychoticism is normal personality. The high scorer on the psychoticism scale is characterized by Eysenck as being 'cold, impersonal, hostile, lacking in sympa-thy, unfriendly, untrustful, odd, unemotional, unhelpful, lacking in insight, strange, with paranoid ideas that people were against him'. In the test manual Eysenck draws particular attention to the characteristic absence of certain emotions from high scorers on the psychoticism scale: 'empathy, feelings of guilt, sensitivity to other people are notions which are strange and unfamiliar to them'. The low scorers are empathic, unselfish, altruistic, warm, peaceful and generally more pleasant, although possibly less socially decisive individuals.

Eysenck's dimensional model of personality has been applied to three main areas of pastoral studies. First, a number of studies have located individual differences in religiosity within this dimensional model of personality. The general conclusions are that religious people are neither more nor less stable (on the neuroticism scale), and neither more nor less introverted (on the extraversion scale) than people who are not religious; and that religious people tend to be more tender-minded and less tough-minded (on the psychoticism scale) than people who are not religious. Second, a number of studies have explored the personality profile of clergy within this dimensional model. The general conclusions are that male clergy project a much more feminine personality profile than men in general, while (at present) female clergy project a more masculine profile than male clergy; that clergy who score high on the dimensions of neuroticism and psychoticism are likely to experience more difficulties in ministry and are more likely to leave the clerical profession; and that clergy who are influenced by the charismatic movement are more stable (on the neuroticism scale) than other clergy. Third, several studies have explored the implications of this model for lay adult education programmes. The general conclusion is that many churchgoers are introverts who sit uneasily with adult learning programmes which put an emphasis on group processes. [*Leslie Francis*]

PERSONALITY DISORDER
One of the three categories of diagnostic classification in psychiatry.

The diagnostic classification of psychiatry distinguishes three broad categories: psychosis, neurosis and personality disorder. In neuroses there are typical symptoms or constellations of symptoms, such as occur in the various anxiety disorders and depression. In psychoses there is a break with reality and, typically, delusions and/or hallucinations. The term 'personality disorder' refers to enduring states which are pervasive to the extent that they colour the whole personality and are present at least in embryonic form from childhood onwards. In all personality disorders there are character traits which, though recognizable as aspects of normal human experience and behaviour, are exaggerated, inflexible, associated with a marked degree of limitation of emotional development and very often involve considerable distress. In these disorders there are disturbances in thinking (e.g. ideas of reference (see below)), emotion (e.g. marked emotional lability or flatness) and behaviour (e.g. poor impulse control). In all personality disorders there is marked impairment of interpersonal functioning. Typical personality disorders would include the schizoid, psychopathic, hysterical and borderline personalities.

However, it should be noted at the outset that from a psychoanalytic perspective the distinction between 'personality' and 'illness' is by no means clearly demarcated. The various neurotic and psychotic conditions that might appear to arise *de novo* really emerge from already established personality structures. Thus at a deeper level, there are more continuities between personality and illness than might be apparent on superficial enquiry. For example, when a patient who has a manic breakdown recovers he or she will still show typical manic depressive features that form part of a more enduring personality structure. These deeper continuities become very clear when such patients undergo psychotherapy. Although it is conventional to classify personalities in a typology, it should be borne in mind that this is to some extent artificial as, in reality, there are many overlaps. Nevertheless the pattern that dominates is often fairly clear. With these riders in mind it is still helpful to distinguish the principal personality disorders, and below are listed the commoner types.

Paranoid personality. People with this type of personality are excessively sensitive and like to misinterpret the actions of those around them as having reference to themselves – for example may easily imagine that someone laughing in the pub is laughing at them. Such phenomena are termed 'ideas of reference'. They are excessively suspicious and over-preoccupied with themselves and easily slighted. Emotional experience of others is very limited and often confined to fear as to what the other person is thinking. Such people often easily become jealous without foundation in reality.

Schizoid personality disorder. In this disorder there is marked limitation of any emotional responsiveness and detachment from social relations. Such persons often feel themselves to be empty of feelings and experience themselves and/or the world in a quite mechanical manner. The work of Franz Kafka gives a very vivid account of a schizoid world. Although those suffering from this disorder may appear to be affectless, at a deeper level they are frequently persecuted by very primitive anxieties of an existential type (e.g. fear of disintegration). In other words, their apparent cold aloofness is really a defensive structure which, while protecting them from these deep anxieties, results in considerable restriction of emotional life.

Borderline personality disorder. This is today a frequent diagnosis and a very broad category, sometimes meaning different things to different people. However, most would agree that the following features are typical. There is a severe disturbance of identity and such individuals are prey to very primitive (infantile) anxieties. Emotional life is highly labile and the world tends to be described in very 'black and white' ways. For example, a person of emotional significance will at one moment be highly idealized and the next be thought of as hateful and persecuting. Behaviour is often impulsive and may include sexual promiscuity, drug addiction, self-mutilation (e.g. cutting wrists) and suicidal acts. Sometimes there are experiences of inner deadness. Interpersonal relationships also carry this extreme quality reflecting central claustro-agorophobic difficulty. Feeling close to an 'object' brings feelings of engulfment and loss of identity, whereas feeling too far away from their 'object' causes feelings of disintegration.

Histrionic personality disorder. Here there is marked emotional lability and dramatization. Such individuals have a very low tolerance of frustration and need to experience themselves as being in the centre of attention. Despite the intensity of affect, its shifting quality conveys a certain lack of emotional depth. There is a tendency to act impulsively and sometimes this is reflected in sexual promiscuity. [*David Bell*]

PERSONALITY FACTORS
Raymond Cattell's sixteen factors model of personality.

The Sixteen Personality Factor Questionnaire (16PF) developed by Raymond Cattell identifies the above number of distinct personality factors (Cattell, Eber and Tatsuoka, 1970). Each factor is characterized as a bipolar continuum and identified by a letter or letter and number (e.g. factor A or factor Q4). Many of these personality factors are linked with one another. This model of personality has been widely used in programmes of personal and professional formation for clergy.

The factors measured are: emotional orientation towards other people; mental capacity and general ability; emotional stability and ego strength; the submission to or exercise of control; enthusiasm, lack of inhibition and impulsiveness; the superego; psychological insulation or independence; contrasting modes of evaluating experience; identification with others; contrasting ways of perceiving the world; self-presentation in social situations; feelings of self-worth and self-esteem; orientation towards change; the progression from dependence to self-sufficiency; strength of concern about self-concept and social image; physical sensations associated with nervous tension. [Leslie Francis]

PERSONALITY TYPES
Rooted in Jungian psychology, the theory contrasts introversion and extraversion, sensing and intuition, thinking and feeling, judging and perceiving.

Jung's theory of psychological type identifies two main mental processes. The first concerns the ways in which we gather information. This is the *perceiving* process. Some people prefer *sensing* (S); others prefer *intuition* (N). According to the theory these two types look at the world in very different ways. Sensing types focus on the realities of a situation as perceived by the senses. Intuitive types focus on the possibilities, the 'big picture', that goes beyond sensory information. Individuals who have a preference for sensing develop keen awareness of present experience. They have acute powers of observation, good memory for facts and details, the capacity for realism, and the ability to see the world as it is. They rely on experience rather than theory. They put their trust in what is known and in the conventional. Individuals with a preference for intuition develop insight into complexity. They have the ability to see abstract, symbolic and theoretical relationships, and the capacity to see future possibilities. They put their reliance on inspiration rather than on past experience. Their interest is in the new and untried. They trust their intuitive grasp of meanings and relationships.

The second process concerns the ways in which we make decisions. This is the *judging* process. Some people prefer *thinking* (T); others prefer *feeling* (F). These two types come to decisions about the world in very different ways. Individuals who prefer thinking make decisions by objective, logical analysis. Individuals who prefer feeling make decisions by subjective values based on how people will be affected. Individuals with a preference for thinking develop clear powers of logical analysis. They develop the ability to weigh facts objectively and to predict consequences, both intended and unintended. They develop a stance of impartiality. They are characterized by a sense of fairness and justice. Individuals who prefer feeling develop a personal emphasis on values and standards. They appreciate what matters most to themselves and what matters most to other people. They develop an understanding of people, a wish to affiliate with people and a desire for harmony. They are characterized by their capacity for warmth, and by qualities of empathy and compassion.

Jung also suggested that individuals differ in the *orientation* in which they prefer to employ these two processes. Some people prefer the outer or extraverting world (E); others prefer the inner or introverting world (I). These two types are energized in different ways. Extraverts draw their energy from the outer world of people and things, while introverts draw their energy from their inner world. Introverts like quiet for concentration. They want to be able to shut off the distractions of the outer world and turn inwards. They often experience trouble in remembering names and faces. They can work at one solitary project for a long time without interruption. When they are engaged in a task in the outer world they may become absorbed in the ideas behind that task. Extraverts like variety and action. They want to be able to shut off the distractions of the inner world and turn outward. They are good at remembering faces and names and enjoy meeting people and introducing people. They can become impatient with long, slow jobs.

When they are working in the company of other people they may become more interested in how others are doing the job than in the job itself.

Finally, the theory of psychological types suggests that individuals differ in their *attitude* to the outer world. Both introverts and extraverts need to deal with the outer world and both may prefer to do this with a *judging* (J) or a *perceiving* (P) process. These two types display a different attitude to the outer world. Individuals who prefer to relate to the outer world with a judging process present a planned and orderly approach to life. Individuals who prefer to relate to the outer world with a perceiving process present a flexible and spontaneous approach to life. Judging types schedule projects so that each step gets done on time. They like to get things finished and settled and to know that the finished product is in place. They work best when they can plan their work in advance and follow that plan. Judging types use lists and agendas to structure their day and to plan their actions. They may dislike interruption from the plans they have made and are reluctant to leave the task in hand even when something more urgent arises. Perceiving types adapt well to changing situations. They make allowances for new information and for changes in the situation in which they are living or acting. They may have trouble making decisions, feeling that they have never got quite enough information on which to base their decision.

Personality types can be assessed by various self-completion questionnaires. The two best known questionnaires are Myers-Briggs Type Indicator and Keirsey Temperament Sorter.

By taking seriously the ways people differ, type theory has a number of practical applications in the Christian life. For example, type theory has been applied to Christian living (Goldsmith and Wharton, 1993), prayer (Duncan, 1993), religious leadership (Oswald and Kroeger, 1988) and preaching (Francis, 1997).

By helping people understand themselves, the theory promotes personal development. By helping people to understand others, the theory promotes interpersonal relationships and team building. By respecting individual differences, the theory helps in understanding preferences in ways of studying Scripture, praying or participating in church services. While the introvert may prefer the silent retreat, the extravert may be more likely to experience spiritual growth through group processes and role play. While the sensing type may prefer studying the detail of Mark's Gospel, the intuitive type might be much more enthused by the ideas of John's Gospel. While the thinking type may prefer to follow the theology of the head, the feeling type may respond much more to the Christian way of the heart. While the judging type may expect the church service to be organized and disciplined, the perceiving type may long for spontaneity and freedom. [*Leslie Francis*]

PHANTASY
An imaginary scene in which the subject is active, it being an unconscious wish-fulfilment.

The spelling 'phantasy' has been proposed and to some extent used in order to emphasize the technical importance of fantasy. 'Fantasy', with an 'f', was regarded as too much associated with eccentricity and trivia. The suggestion has not on the whole survived and the term is usually spelled with an 'f'.

PHENOMENOLOGY
The study of how meaning is founded in human activity and relations.

The term 'phenomenology' is used in sociology, psychology and philosophy. The core idea in all settings, however, is the focus on the description of the contents of human, conscious, subjective experience of phenomena (Sokolowski, 2000). There are no presuppositions or assumptions about the phenomena, but rather the phenomena under investigation are allowed to speak for themselves. The phenomenologist is subjectively and intuitively open to and aware of the essence of experience. Sense data, therefore, are important for the way in which something is perceived by the individual's conscious awareness. Neither is he or she concerned about what other people may think about a particular phenomenon. Rather, the phenomenon is allowed to have its own impact on the intuitive, subjective and experiential aspects of the individual's conscious awareness.

PHOBIA
A fear, horror or aversion, usually morbid.

Phobias are technically classified among the anxiety disorders (DSM-IV, 1994). Besides phobias, anxiety disorders include obsessive-compulsive, post-traumatic stress, acute stress, generalized anxiety and panic disorder. There are three major classifications of phobias.

1. *Agoraphobia* is anxiety about, or avoidance of, places or situations from which escape might be difficult (or embarrassing) or in which help may not be available in the event of a panic attack or panic-like symptoms.

2. *Specific phobia* is characterized by clinically significant anxiety provoked by exposure to a specific feared object or situation, often leading to avoidance behaviour. The most frequently experienced specific phobias include fears relating to animals or insects; other natural environment fears such as fear of storms, heights or water; fears stimulated by the sight of blood, experience of injury, or receiving an injection or other invasive medical procedure (e.g. dental work); and situational fears such as use of public transport, tunnels, bridges, elevators, driving, flying or enclosed places (claustrophobia).

3. *Social phobia* is a marked and persistent fear of social or performance situations in which embarrassment might occur. Individuals with social phobia recognize that their fear is excessive or unreasonable, and the feared situation is one that is typically avoided, often to the detriment of personal happiness and/or professional effectiveness and reward (Heimberg *et al.*, 1995).

The three types of phobia are distinguished by the normal age of onset. *Specific phobias* typically emerge in childhood, *social phobias* form in adolescence (though children who are temperamentally shy are at greater risk of developing social phobia); and *agoraphobia* tends to develop in the mid to late twenties. In general, specific phobias are the most responsive to treatment, while social phobia is the least responsive. Persons with specific phobias may use avoidant behaviour with better effect than persons with social phobia and agoraphobia; this is partly because specific phobias, such as fear of snakes or heights, may have little impact on normal social functioning. Agoraphobia differs from social phobia in the fact that agoraphobics fear they may experience a panic attack in any of a wide range of situations outside the home, whereas social phobics experience anxiety (and occasionally panic attacks) in certain situational domains (e.g. formal speaking and interaction, informal speaking and inter-action, assertiveness interaction, and situations where one is under observation). Social phobics may experience anxiety in one of these domains but not in any of the others.

Among the three types of phobia, social phobics are the least likely to seek treatment. There are many different types of treatment for each type of phobia, and treatments that are effective with one type (e.g. exposure therapy for specific phobias) are not necessarily effective with others (e.g. cognitive-behavioural and social skills therapies are generally more effective with social phobia than is exposure therapy). Gender, ethnicity and culture influence susceptibility to certain phobias; genetics may also play a role (e.g. shyness, which is a strong determinant of future social phobia, is passed down from one parent); and phobias are often accompanied by other problems (e.g. depression and alcoholism may accompany or even disguise social phobia). There is some evidence to suggest that social phobics may be attracted to worship services because this affords the opportunity to participate in a relatively low-risk social activity (in contrast to other more demanding social functions like informal parties and eating in up-market restaurants). [*D. Capps*]

PIETISM
1. A specific historical movement.
2. A type of Christian expression of faith.

1. *Pietism as a historical movement.* Pietism is a Northern European development starting in the seventeenth century. Germany was its birthplace and the University of Halle was its centre. Two men stand out as representative leaders, Philip Jacob Spener (1635–1705) and August Herman Franke (1663–1727). Pietism spread to the Scandinavian countries and was imported to North America through immigration. Rooted in the Lutheran lands, its features reflect older and broader dynamics.

Spener and Franke wanted to recover a more practical person-centred approach to Christian faith. Reacting to the Scholastic and formal expressions of faith prominent in their day, they stressed a transforming, personal relationship with God that touched the whole person. The Bible was the key resource for transforming life, and lay involvement in its study was essential. God's gift of salvation was celebrated as the central message of the Bible and seen as providing the recognizable pattern of faith's generation and repeated recovery. Humans could not meet God's expectations adequately, and when sufficient performance was seen as impossible this would drive people to hear the good news of God's gift of unmerited forgiveness. Often lay people could get a hold of this message even better than the clergy who had been indoctrinated in more academic and formal expressions of faith. To complement large-scale liturgical worship, small groups were fostered for studying the Bible and prayer. Non-ordained people could exercise leadership there.

Pietism saw the practical transformation of this life tied directly to a human destiny beyond it. When the otherworldly issue of salvation was settled by God's forgiveness, freedom to change and serve came along with it. The result was a persistent interest in improved personal behaviour and the development of social institutions to help the needy. Schools, children's homes and hospitals sprang up in Northern Europe and then in North America among the immigrants.

2. *Pietism as a Christian expression of faith.* Pietism erupted in other places where the problems of rationalistic and formal Christianity were evident. While the label was not used in these other movements, the term has come to characterize certain ways of living out the Christian faith.

In England, Methodism was an early parallel movement. Since the seventeenth century pietistic emphases have become pervasive. Today the fastest growing churches (such as Pentecostalism) manifest many of the pietistic characteristics. Mainline churches have also tried to make faith personal, relevant and contemporary.

In pastoral studies the pietistic emphases are evident, both as constructive means for integrating and invigorating human life and as excesses that bring predictable problems.

The characteristics of pietism as a type of Christianity include: (1) personalized Christianity; (2) Bible-centred stress on salvation as God's gift; (3) emphasis on heaven and hell; (4) lay involvement in witness and service; (5) strong desire to help people change and to minister to the unfortunate; (6) a missionary concern.

The excesses of pietism include: (1) legalistic expectations; (2) individualistic, otherworldly preoccupation; (3) emotionalism; (4) anticlerical and anti-institutional dynamics. [*Lyman T. Lundeen*]

PLAUSIBILITY STRUCTURES
The framework of human organizations necessary to make a tradition or belief system seem worthy of faith and trust.
'Plausibility structures' is a sociological term used to describe the dialectical relationship between a system of belief and the persons in an organization who trust in that belief. The term is grounded in the sociological assumption that persons both produce religion and are products of religion. All religious traditions require 'specific communities of believers for their continuing plausibility' (McGuire, 1992). In pastoral studies, a plausibility structure could be a local congregation or a denomination.

PLEASURE PRINCIPLE
One of the two principles that according to Freud govern mental functioning.
The other principle is the 'reality principle'. All natural impulses, according to this theory, seek their own satisfaction quite apart from all other considerations. Freud refined this thinking and argued that the pleasure principle rules the individual from the start of his or her life and remains the guiding principle at work in the unconscious.

PLURALISM
1. The fact of diversity, especially religious or cultural.
2. The theological view that all religions are equally valid ways to God.
The first meaning is common in the USA. As people travel more, nations become more religiously and culturally diverse. This is called the fact or problem of pluralism. But the second meaning is becoming increasingly prominent. It is especially associated with the work of the theologian John Hick. He believes that all the major religions of the world hold facets of the truth, each sustaining a dimension of the larger truth which other traditions are discovering without realizing that they are so doing (Hick, 1989).

Pluralism used in the first sense raises a number of complex issues. The first is whether it is something destabilizing or to be welcomed; the second is the impact that this diversity has upon pastoral activity. Pluralism used in the second sense raises the question of the metaphysical status of those who are not Christian.

On the whole the Christian tradition finds diversity difficult to cope with. The diverse languages of the world are viewed as God's judgement on human hubris. In the New Testament there are repeated exhortations to 'unity' and pleas that Christians should be 'of one heart and one mind'. Historically, the Christian tradition has not encouraged or welcomed pluralism: from Augustine's attack on the Donatists to the Inquisition, strong tendencies to deny and reject diversity are displayed. In political theory, Hegel, Hooker and Burke all inclined to the view that the nation state is defined in terms of one unified culture. Too much diversity within a nation undermines the state: in short, people cannot cope with other people who are too different.

However, during the twentieth century, there was a change. Instead of seeing pluralism as a threat to Christianity, many Christians have come to believe that it is intended by God. Despite the Bible's ostensible opposition to diversity, in actual fact it embraces considerable argument and disagreement. The picture of the Bible emerging from critical scholarship exposes the different positions taken by different groups: Chronicles disagrees with Kings; Matthew was written to correct the errors of Mark; and Paul disagreed with Peter. And in the modern world there is a growing sense among Christians that our obligation to love each other should extend to the respecting of difference and diversity. It has been argued that God has intended pluralism as a way of teaching us humility and mutual respect (Markham, 1995).

On the second matter, pluralism has enormous implications for pastoral theology. Most importantly, it requires an awareness of the different pastoral needs of each culture. On the mundane level, some religious cultures are much more strict about the conventions surrounding the interaction between men and women. So while in a Christian setting a male counsellor might be appropriate for a female, this would be considered inappropriate in an Islamic one. On a theological level, encouraging a person to 'affirm the self' might be an important part of (at least contemporary) Christian pastoral support; it is considered less appropriate for a Muslim. Traditionally, Islamic spirituality has stressed the importance of self-negation; ideally the self should disappear in God (ultimately the only reality). Here a sensitivity to the theology should lead to an entirely different approach.

Finally, the second meaning of pluralism raises the whole question of the metaphysical assumptions which operate when we encounter different cultures. Those who believe that salvation depends on the recognition of the truth of Christianity tend to treat the pastoral as secondary to the overall goal of conversion. In the end, what is the point of helping a person from another faith tradition to cope with his or her immediate predicament, if that person is still entering eternity without God? In addition the exclusivist will tend to assume that a person from another faith tradition is still under the judgement of God and in the grip of sin and Satan. In both outcome and approach, one will find the exclusivist being very distinctive.

For the inclusivist (i.e. those who, like Karl Rahner, believe that the Triune God is active in other religions), the pastoral can be an important area for the grace of God. In other words, the creator God is active in all human lives, even before encountering the visible Church; it is the duty of the pastor to be sensitive and alert to this activity. In terms of approach, one should assume that the person encountered has already had the grace of God active in his or her life; in terms of outcome, one might hope for recognition of the truth of Christianity, although one is unlikely to require this.

Pluralists would be critical about the hidden assumptions in terms of approach and outcome made by the inclusivist and exclusivist. They would not want to make any ontological assumptions about the other. Despite its obvious attractions, there are problems here. How does one make sense of wickedness? By what criteria should one distinguish more constructive traditions from less constructive ones?

The need for pastoral theology to come to terms with pluralism (in both senses of that word) is one of the most important requirements at the beginning of the twenty-first century. *[Ian Markham]*

POLITICAL CONTEXT OF PASTORAL CARE
The political and social context, beyond the individual or family, in which pastoral care is offered.

Pastoral care, like all human activities, has a political and social context. Human potential and suffering are profoundly and directly affected by socio-political factors. On a micro level, human relationships within the family or between couples may be characterized by inequalities of power and opportunity. At a societal level, politically influenced factors like poverty and injustice may have an enormous influence on individuals and groups of all kinds in terms of their health and well-being. In so far as pastoral care ignores or recognizes these factors, it has social and political effects and implications. It can function, wittingly or unwittingly, as a politically conservative or a radical force. While it may ignore inequalities of race, class, power, status or gender, it cannot remain entirely politically neutral (Pattison, 1997).

Throughout its history, Christianity has held in tension the concepts of love and justice, of concern for individuals and concern for whole communities. However, modern pastoral care in Western countries has mostly been blind to the socio-political context and implications for justice of its theory and practice. Building upon nineteenth-century individualistic pietism in Protestantism, the modern pastoral-care movement has been reinforced in its primary concern for troubled individuals by its more recent encounter with dynamic and humanistic psychology. This has provided many new insights and tools for understanding and improved care of the distressed person. The techniques of counselling have been married to the existentialist and personalist themes of much modern Western theology. This has ensured the growth, particularly in the USA but also in Britain, of a flourishing, psychologically informed and equipped pastoral-care movement. This has probably raised the standard of pastoral ministry to individuals. It has, however, failed to place that ministry in its proper socio-political context. Social and political factors have been marginalized, ignored, even hidden by an individualistic focus and the use of therapeutic methods.

A main purpose of pastoral care is the alleviation of suffering and the facilitation of growth for all people as interdependent members of communities and of society as a whole. There must, therefore, be awareness of social and political factors which impinge on that goal. Pastoral methods must not be exclusively determined or limited by the needs that individuals have for personal adjustment and therapy. Selby asserts that 'to presume to care for other human beings without taking into account the social and political causes of whatever it is that they may be experiencing is to confirm them in

their distress while pretending to offer healing' (Selby, 1983).

Arguably, since Jesus proclaimed a corporate Kingdom of God pastoral care has always had an important social and political dimension. This has sometimes been overt and radical. More often, it has been hidden and implicitly conservative. From a variety of perspectives, since the 1960s pastoral theorists on both sides of the Atlantic have begun to explore this dimension more thoroughly. Feminist and other kinds of liberation theologies have also challenged pastoral care to recognize its political context and implications and to acknowledge that the pastoral is political as well as personal (Pattison, 1997). [Stephen Pattison]

POLITICAL THEOLOGY
Theology that interacts consciously with the political dimension of life.

Political theology has taken a multitude of forms down the ages. In the ancient world it was the counterpart of civil religion and commonly provided the ideological underpinning of government, identifying piety and patriotism and inculcating the politically important virtues of obedience and loyalty by way of affirming that the political order is sacrosanct. Augustine emphatically rejected this kind of political theology as making no claim to truth, and in developing his own account of 'true' (that is, Christian) theology, he produced a new kind of political theology. This related to the political order in a more complex, critical and sophisticated way than the ancient political theologies had been capable of. This new theology endeavoured not so much to sustain and legitimate the political order as speak truth to power and interpret what was happening in the light of the gospel. For Augustine and many later Christian political theologians, Christianity made the old kind of political theology impossible and demanded a quite new style of political theological thought. Eschatology, the sufferings of Jesus at the hands of an unjust ruler, and the understanding of God as Trinity between them forbade any simple supportive analogy between the Kingdom of God and earthly kingdoms.

The political theologies of Christendom sometimes resolved the tensions between Augustine's two cities too simply. But the duality was always there and easy accommodations to the structures of political power regularly evoked protests and opposition. In the first half of the twentieth century political theology gained a bad name, partly because of the attempts of Carl Schmitt and others to justify the Nazi movement through the development of a conservative and conformist political theology that assimilated secular and pagan elements in the Nazi ideology without apparent difficulty. With the 1960s there came a rehabilitation of a very different account of political theology from J.-B. Metz, J. Moltmann and others. They argued that politics was a major sphere for the expression of faith, and saw theology as reflection on political practice. What Metz called the 'subversive memory' of Jesus challenges established orders and disturbs complacency (Forrester, 1988).

The liberation theology that emerged in the 1960s, initially from Latin America, shared much with the new wave of political theology in Europe and the USA. Both were concerned to relate theory and practice, and saw theology and Christian faith as necessarily involving political commitment; both were radical. But liberation theologians saw the political theologians as excessively abstract, detached and academic in their theologizing; they needed to give concrete content to their talk of solidarity with the oppressed, and to enlist the help of social analysis in seeking to analyse theologically structures of oppression. In famous words Gustavo Gutiérrez (1973) suggests that Western theology concentrates on the problem of the non-believer and how unbelief calls religion and its institutions into question. For liberation theology the starting point is the problem that poverty and oppression have condemned multitudes to a non-human existence: 'The question ... is no longer how we are to speak of God in a world come of age; it is rather how to proclaim him Father in a world that is not human and what the implications might be of telling non-humans that they are children of God.' Latin American liberation theology has been immensely significant and has stimulated similar theological movements throughout the world. Political and economic and ideological changes, in particular the collapse of the communist dictatorships of eastern Europe, have prompted some fundamental rethinking, but it is clear that this variety of political theology has far from lost its impetus or its ability to challenge (O'Donovan, 1996).

In pastoral matters liberation theology has insisted that the pastoral and the political should be held together, rejected the individualism characteristic of much modern pastoral care, stressed the role of the Church, questioned the oppressive elements in institutional structures, and insisted on the need to take sides with the victims and the oppressed. [*Duncan B. Forrester*]

POLYGAMY
A condition of marriage allowing for more than one spouse at a time.
Polygamy is the generic term encompassing polygyny (permitting a man to have more than one wife simultaneously) and polyandry (permitting a woman to have more than one husband simultaneously). Polyandry is a much rarer practice than polygyny, which, for example, is sanctioned by Islam and was evident in the early Mormon church. The social and economic functions of marriage are underlined by polygamous practices. That polygyny occurs more frequently than polyandry may reflect the usual tendency for societies and faith communities to be structured on patriarchal lines. Within polygamous societies it is also common for monogamous marriage to be a widespread practice.

PORNOGRAPHY
The portrayal of the human sexual organs, copulation and other sexual activity in various cultural forms (paintings, carvings, literature, and modern audio-visual media) with the intent to stimulate erotic rather than aesthetic and emotional feeling alone.
The viewing of pornography for pleasure is evidenced in various cultures and has a long history. In the Western world, however, under the influence of Christendom such viewing has been a source of anxiety and disagreement. The term 'pornography' is derived from the Greek word referring to prostitution and illicit sex. Thus pornography in the West chiefly bears illicit connotations and has to one degree or another been secreted away. For example, the medieval erotic poem *Carmina Burana* was hidden in a monastery for centuries. Boccaccio's *Decameron* has been treated as forbidden literature. Many religious carvings and paintings in early Renaissance Europe have pornographic elements, particularly in some resurrection scenes – a story long forgotten in art history.

Following the sexual revolution of the 1960s public access to pornography has been more widely tolerated. There has also been much research, especially into the implicit power relationship between the reader or viewer (historically a man, but less so exclusively today) and the people portrayed. Arguments have also attempted to distinguish theoretically between erotica and obscenity. The former celebrates sexuality while the latter deliberately offends current beliefs. A further distinction is often drawn between 'soft' and 'hard' pornography. But none of these distinctions is absolute. The link between pornography and malignant forces in the culture, such as rape and violence particularly, but not solely against women, has been persistently explored but has not been decisively demonstrated (Malamuth and Donnerstein, 1984). It may be that Japanese culture, with its low rate of violence against women coupled with its tolerance for pornography, might demonstrate the obverse. Nor does Tantric Hinduism appear to have promoted violence in spite of the candour of its temple carvings, many of which are stunning in their polymorphous frankness.

The intermingling of pornographic images and religious worship also has a long and complex history. Ancient and modern Hinduism, for instance, and the Dionysian cult in ancient Greece extensively used phallic representations. Within the Jewish and Christian traditions the Song of Solomon has posed problems. Its frank dialogue is sexually explicit and erotic – some would say, pornographic.

Pornography generates anxiety and dispute among religious people, especially in the West. Pastors, whatever their personal views, need to recognize that it is an artefact of the culture that for some may have an educational function. For example, someone referred for sexual counselling may find pornographic material used in treating a sexual problem. It is important that pastors do not allow a moral stance to hinder their ability to listen and respond to a person's anxiety. [*Raymond Lawrence Jr*]

POSITIVE DISCRIMINATION

Discrimination in favour of a member of a particular group, on the grounds that this group has been unfavourably discriminated against in the past and that therefore the balance needs redressing.

Sometimes the term 'reverse discrimination' has been used for the same thing. In the USA, the term in favour is 'affirmative action'. American law allows quotas to be set for racial or ethnic groups. If a quota is set for, say, five minority members to be employed in a firm and it has fewer than five, affirmative action may be used to prefer a minority candidate for a post. In Britain quotas are illegal and so is positive discrimination. Under the Race Relations Act 1976, however, positive action is permitted in the limited field of training. The Act provides that if members of a particular racial group have suffered from racial discrimination or if the group is under-represented in some field of work, members of the group may be preferred to others for training courses. There must be no discrimination in their favour at the point of recruitment or promotion.

In European Community law, there has always been provision against sex discrimination. A recent judgement by the European Court of Justice stated that if two candidates for a job, a man and a woman, are equally well qualified, and if there is no special reason why a man should be employed, the woman may lawfully be preferred for a job in the public service.

There has been much debate over the principle of positive discrimination (Dworkin, 1977). To some, it seems obviously fair that a serious imbalance should be corrected and access to favoured jobs be made easier for groups which have suffered adverse discrimination in the past. Another group which may benefit is that of disabled people. Others claim it is unfair, since the present generation cannot be held guilty of the sins of the fathers, and the best candidate if not from a minority will be passed over. In practice it is often difficult to say exactly who the best candidate may be.

In California in the 1990s the Indian minority was doing better in school than the white majority, but was also benefiting as an ethnic group from affirmative action policies in admission to higher education. Other ethnic minorities, however, e.g. African-Americans, were still far behind in school. There were complaints of unfairness, from both white people and African-Americans, that Asians were being given an unfair advantage over them. The rights and wrongs of such a situation are difficult to resolve.

Most countries have no provision for positive discrimination and many have little effective protection against unfair racial discrimination at all. In recent years, however, women have gained in protection from direct discrimination against them in many countries.

Pastoral care needs to be sensitive to the difficulties that can arise from positive discrimination, for instance when the relative positions of different groups have changed over time. [*Ann Dummett*]

POSITIVE REGARD
An affirmative valuing of persons, including their experiences, feelings and beliefs.
A consistently positive regard towards self and others is known as 'unconditional positive regard'. Positive regard entails a valuing of persons and their experiences as such. It is a basic stance of Rogerian or client-centred therapy or counselling. The key themes are warmth and respect, liking as well as sympathy and acceptance, but it does not imply approval of particular behaviours. The concept has influenced pastors and laity to become more person-centred and process-oriented in their ministry.

POSTMODERNISM
A general term for various styles of contemporary critique of unifying and universal discourses.
The term 'postmodern' is being increasingly used in a variety of contexts without reference to or awareness of its origins. Postmodernism can be viewed as a (not entirely) new critique of reason. Modernity, which has dominated the intellectual scene for about three hundred years, sought and found universality and necessity in human thought. The postmodern emphasis is on particularity and contingency. Thus, for example, 'postmodern' architecture breaks with the 'international' style in favour of a variety of local styles. But postmodernism is technically a series of philosophical and literary-critical theories growing out of Nietzsche and Heidegger and developed in French thinkers such as Derrida, Foucault and Lyotard.

Two closely related themes are the 'death of the author' and the 'death of the subject'. The first claims that authors cannot preside over their texts to ensure that they mean only what the author intends: texts inevitably escape such control. Similarly, the subject of knowledge is not the final arbiter of truth. Rather, the decentred subject is conditioned by processes to which it belongs but over which it does not preside; its judgements are limited in their perspective. Human understanding is partial, not just because there is always more to know, but because what it does know it only knows from a particular point of view.

The radical implications of this approach emerge in perhaps the most widespread expression of postmodernism: deconstruction. This is a holistic theory of meaning and reality that finds all meanings and facts to refer to other meanings and facts essential to them. The fundamental incompleteness of human understanding stems from the non-atomic character of meanings and facts. These require for their full determinacy the completion, impossible for human understanding, of the infinite chain of references. In other words, to know things as they really are, it would be necessary to see them from every possible 'angle'. But this is never possible for human understanding.

The churches' pastoral theology is largely based, like much theology, on engagement with modernity. One effect of the developing debate on postmodernism is to bring into the forefront of thinking dimensions of spirituality and metaphysics that were thought to have had their day. This may encourage a return to uncritical superstition. The phenomenon of the New Age and its eclectic approach to spirituality and belief is an instance that the pastor is likely to encounter. There are those, however, who also believe that the importance of experience within the postmodern scheme may also open up more freedom with the gospel. [*Merold Westphal*]

POST-TRAUMATIC STRESS DISORDER
A psychiatric disorder following the experience of being involved in life-threatening events.
Survivors from natural disaster, a serious accident, war or personal assault relive the distress through dreams and flashbacks, find sleep difficult, feel detached and find it difficult to function socially. PTSD often accompanies another disorder, such as depression, substance abuse or problems of memory. It is a matter for physical and psychiatric diagnosis and treatment.

Distinctive physiological and psychological changes are associated with it. Chronic PTSD may have periods of remission, although in some it may persist unremittingly. There is no single treatment or cure. It is usually treated by a combination of psychotherapy and drugs.

POTENTIAL SPACE
The area of separation which exists, both physically and emotionally, between a growing child and his or her mother.

D. W. Winnicott remarked that most mental health colleagues focused their energies on elucidating only the unhealthy aspects of aloneness and of being alone. He noted that although people who spend much time on their own might be clinically unwell and possibly unable to form satisfying relationships, aloneness need not necessarily be an indication of psychopathology. Indeed, the state of being on one's own might be a manifestation of active creativity.

Potential space is also called the 'transitional space', or the 'third area', or the 'intermediate area' (Winnicott, 1971). It is the physical and emotional gap that exists between a mother and a baby, in which a variety of exciting possibilities can occur. Only when the mother reduces her extensive involvement with the growing child, will he or she have the opportunity to learn how to explore and to play alone, without needing mother's vigilant ministrations at every turn. Infants can only develop their own creative capacities if mothers permit them a potential space in which possibilities for psychic development and expansion may take root.

The newborn infant exists in a state of absolute dependence, unable to function without continual care from the mother. Assuming that the primary care-giver, usually the mother, has worked hard at responding to the baby's needs, then mother and baby can begin to separate from one another through a gradual withdrawal process. This stimulates the development of the youngster's sense of autonomy. The mother decreases her preoccupation with her child and a potential space between mother and child is created. Transitional objects, such as teddy bears and toys, help the child to cope with separation and to enjoy his or her own company. Gradually, in the healthy scenario, play and creative acts will emerge, especially when the infant feels confident that mother will reappear when needed.

The potential space or transitional space of early childhood serves as a template for more sophisticated creations in later life. As the child becomes an adult, the potential space of infancy eventually becomes transformed into what we regard as culture, whether music, or art, or dance. The joy of listening to a piece of music, for example, stems from the pleasure of being alone, and yet simultaneously engaged with one's own inner world and with the outer world of the music makers. Creativity (for example, the making of music, or the enjoyment of music) occurs in the potential space; and as Winnicott reflected, such creativity gives meaning and richness to life, and makes life worth living. [*Brett Kahr*]

POVERTY
A state of being poor, either physically or spiritually, voluntarily or involuntarily.

Poverty has been interpreted variously in the Jewish and Christian traditions. The Hebrew Scriptures range from seeing poverty as a sign of God's judgement for sloth and disobedience, e.g. Prov. 6.6–11; 23.21, to the prophets who condemn exploitation of the poor as a violation of God's covenant, e.g. Amos 2.6–7. The prophets and the psalms affirm that God takes the side of the *anawim* – the 'little ones' of the world – against the wealthy and powerful. In the New Testament this prophetic siding with the poor is echoed in Mary's Magnificat (Luke 1.46–55). The incarnation of God in Jesus of Nazareth is a sign of God's identification with the poor and outcast. However, Jesus' poverty appears to have been primarily voluntary, a sign of the inbreaking Kingdom of God which he preached. St Paul builds on the voluntary poverty of Jesus by speaking of the radical self-emptying (*kenosis*) of Christ (Phil. 2.5–8). Voluntary poverty is expressed in the apostolic Church by holding all possessions in common (Acts 2.44–47) and in the willing offering of oneself in martyrdom. Voluntary poverty finds its most radical expression in the asceticism of the desert fathers and mothers, many of whom forsook lives of wealth and privilege, desiring to grow in holiness, simplicity and self-awareness. Monastic identification with the poor Christ continued through the centuries, particularly with the mendicant orders exemplified by Francis of Assisi and his devotion to 'Lady Poverty'. Monasticism has included poverty as one of the three 'evangelical counsels' along with chastity and obedience. Such voluntary material poverty was seen as an expression of one's spiritual poverty (Metz, 1968).

In contrast to this voluntary understanding of poverty, liberation theology emerged in the 1960s in Latin America, reaffirming the biblical theme of God's preferential option for the involuntary poor who are victims of political and economic injustice (Gutiérrez, 1988). Because God's love is universal, God sides with the weak and powerless who otherwise would be voiceless. As the poor reflect on their experience of poverty and read the Scriptures in local base communities, they become more than worthy causes for others' charity: they become a special revelation of God's utter otherness which judges the world's status quo. True liberation is not only economic and political, however. It involves the embodiment of God's reign in history in which all persons are loved and respected as interdependent equals. In a postmodern world where the proportion of the world's population living in poverty is increasing with frightening speed, all pastoral ministry must place the needs of the poor and dispossessed at the heart of Christian life and mission. [Phillip C. Bennett]

POWER
The dual, or bipolar, capacity to influence and to be influenced.
Every entity, to exist as real, must have both the capacity to exercise power, or influence, as an agent, and the capacity to be a receptor of the influence or agency of others. Agential power helps us create, overcome obstacles, and engage the world with strength. Receptive power enables us to engage empathetically with others, be transformed by new knowledge, and receive healing and blessing in our lives. God's power is also characterized in much contemporary theology and philosophy as the capacity to be influenced by, as well as the capacity to influence, the life of each entity in the world, and the cosmos as a whole.

When people seek the assistance of a pastor, it is usually related to a power imbalance of some sort. For example, people who are depressed or struggling with spiritual malaise are experiencing an acute loss of agential power. A depressed person may feel that they do not have adequate agential power to be truly themselves, to realize their goals, and to live as vitally as they once were able to live. They may feel powerless to accept God's love and care, or to feel the

support of their loved ones and of their religious community. In these circumstances, persons may reach out to pastors or counsellors to regain their own power as agents, as well as the capacity to be nurtured and empowered by others, as receptors (Graham, 1992).

A major challenge to pastoral ministry arises in the face of the abuse of power in social relationships. Feminist, womanist and other forms of liberation theology have provided tools by which religious communities have been able to discern pervasive unjust power imbalances generated by oppressive social arrangements. Oppression by definition exists when one social or cultural group unjustly dominates the conditions by which another group lives. The dominant group is able to act primarily as agent to the oppressed group while the oppressed group is primarily relegated to the role of receptor. Power is acutely imbalanced, and unjustly arranged. Agency without receptivity becomes tyranny and sadism; receptivity without agency becomes victimization and masochism. When these dynamics of domination–subordination emerge in pastoral care, they often are connected with forms of sexual and physical violence against women and children, and heterosexist oppression of gay, lesbian, bisexual and transgendered persons. Racism and its negative consequences also derive from inherently unjust power dynamics. In the pastoral situations arising from oppressive dynamics, those in a powerless position need to be empowered as agents to resist, recover from, and to co-operate with others to restructure the social order. Those in dominant power relationships need to be helped to find ways to be more genuinely receptive to those who are disadvantaged by their agency. In addition to working with individual participants in oppressive systems, pastoral ministry should mobilize liberating forms of power that will contribute to the creation of new forms of just power arrangements in the social order. Caring, in this sense, responds to more than the immediate needs of those coming for help. It also seeks to arrange the power dynamics within social systems by means of resistance, advocacy, coalition building, conscientization and organic transformation.

Power is the basis for pastoral identity and authority. The pastoral representative, whether lay or ordained, is both a receiver and an agent of divine and ecclesial power.

This power gives a sense of identity as a representative of a historic community of faith, and the training by which to exercise pastoral authority on behalf of that community. Power therefore is accountable, available and viable when united in the identity and function of agents of the Church. This is the redemptive and transformative arrangement of power in pastoral ministry. However, there have been a significant number of cases in which the power and role of the pastoral office are abused, and power becomes unbalanced in destructive ways for parishioners or others dependent upon the minister for nurture. Pastoral power becomes abusive when the line between pastor and parishioner is crossed, and ministers sexualize the pastoral relationship, or use it for their own economic and personal gain. In such cases, there is no genuine mutual consent, no equal negative consequences, and those who are in more vulnerable power relationships (as receptors) become abused victims of the minister's relatively greater (agential) personal, symbolic and relational power. To prevent the tragic consequences of this unjust use of pastoral power, it is critical that ordained ministers understand the power of their role and office, and use that power to set limits and to maintain appropriate boundaries so that their call to ministry may be properly fulfilled (Ramsay, 1998).

Finally, the question of power becomes a central issue in circumstances involving loss and tragedy. The question of responsibility for tragedy is a question of power as agency. A frequently asked question is, 'Why did God allow this to happen?' or, 'Why did God not prevent this?' Underlying the question is, 'Did God have the agential power to prevent or stop this from happening, or is God too a receptor of life's power to harm and inflict evil?' The question of the relation of God's power to evil and suffering is a complex question of theodicy, and is the core issue in much pastoral care. If power is bipolar, then God is a receptor of the world's power, even when it works against God's agency. But if God is also 'a bulwark never failing' who has power to endure and to offer redemptive possibilities in every tragic circumstance, then God's agency is never removed. While God may not have all the power there is to have, God has all the power necessary to be God, and to make divine power mediated by love available in all necessities and circumstances. *[L. K. Graham]*

PRACTICAL THEOLOGY
The part of theological education or ministerial formation that deals with pastoral and practical matters.
Historically pastoral studies courses included, with different emphases in the various churches, four components: (1) homiletics: discerning and proclaiming the word; (2) liturgics: understanding and leading worship; (3) catechetics: the educational dimension to ministry; and (4) poimenics: pastoral guidance and care for individuals. Much of this is still taught. But there is a greater emphasis on experience and learning through action, especially on placements (Ballard, 1986).

PRAXIS
Ideas that indicate action to change the world.
Karl Marx coined the term to indicate the difference between those philosophies or ideologies that are implicated in the oppression of humanity, and political and social ideas that have the power so to critique social conditions and economic structures as to liberate people from oppression. The term has been adopted in Western political theology and Latin American liberation theology to indicate the kind of social analysis and theological beliefs that together are said to generate human liberation, or the realization of the Kingdom of God on earth.

PRAYER
The communion of an individual or group with God, expressed in adoration, confession, thanksgiving and supplication.
Prayer is the moment when the aspirations and regrets which constitute every human life are focused in the desire for assistance or blessing from some outside agency. For Christians this comes through the person of Jesus Christ, in the power of the Holy Spirit, connecting the natural praying of human beings with the power and purposes of God. The role of the Church is to root prayer within the resource and guidance of Scripture, the tradition (accumulating wisdom of Christianity), the experience of others, and the corporateness of the Kingdom. Thus prayer is both an individual and a collective activity, which can be formal or informal, silent or expressed in words, music and action, and which brings together (1) acknowledgement of God's saving acts in history; (2) awareness of the

choices and issues which constitute the present; (3) a desire to receive and fulfil the promise of glory which is offered to all who are truly willing to receive it.

For pastoral studies the activity of prayer is based on the awareness of three factors: (1) the sense of gap and distance between God as ultimate and fulfilment, and humankind as penultimate and incomplete; (2) the potential for experiencing a sense of union with God despite such differences – often in moments and glimpses, but sometimes in more sustained mystical encounter; (3) the confidence that in and through Jesus Christ this sense of separation can be overcome so that a real and enduring oneness can be achieved.

In the Old Testament, prayer is rooted in remembering God's saving actions and promises, to provide a sense of hope and direction for individuals and for the community. But increasingly, personal conversation with God becomes subordinate to the rules and rituals of communal worship, and to the power of priestly intermediaries.

In the New Testament, Jesus reaffirms the centrality of a personal, childlike trust in God as Abba, Father – a parent separate from yet at one with his children. However, he also continues to observe the disciplines of synagogue and temple worship – the wider context for personal prayer. The Lord's Prayer (Matt. 6.9–13) provides a definitive outline: (1) the priority of the corporate (*our*) and of the otherness of God (*Father in heaven*); (2) the foundational attitude of worship – *your name be hallowed* – as the means of connecting what is hitherto separated (*heaven and earth*); (3) the process of such connection: seeking God's Kingdom and God's will, owning human dependence and failings, asking for aid against temptation and evil; (4) the acknowledgement that all these things belong to God and are in his gift alone – *yours is the Kingdom, the power and the glory*.

Paul helps Christians after the resurrection to recognize that it is the Spirit of the Lord Jesus which enables prayer, and which unites the many different kinds of prayer – private, corporate, charismatic, eucharistic, mystical, inarticulate. Now the remembering of God's saving actions and promises is focused on the life, death and resurrection of Jesus: the story of the new covenant. The same element of repetition and key stories remains central to the enterprise of prayer: providing connection between past acts, present issues and future promises. Prayer is made in the name of Jesus, and thus can only contain petitions and praises that can genuinely be offered in the spirit of Christ, who himself is at God's right hand to make intercession for humankind. This prevents prayer being selfish or too subject to human foibles.

Throughout Christian history there have been a variety of approaches to prayer. But an enduring theme has been the struggle to connect the largely inarticulate instinct to pray, which constitutes the human ability to want and to regret, with the sophisticated understanding of this activity held by the Christian churches. This challenge to connect constitutes the heart of the pastoral task.

In classical Christian thinking a means of facilitating a deeper connection between the human soul and the gospel of Christ has aimed to isolate and highlight the constituent parts of prayer, usually recognized as the following:

1. *Adoration* – owning the holiness, transcendence and majesty of God. Such prayer often exceeds the limitations of human language and leads to silence, the use of symbol, and a sense of being lost in wonder and awe. Adoration draws persons out of themselves, and thus is a means of growth.

2. *Confession* – acknowledging sins so that there can be forgiveness and healing. This is another seed of potential change and growth. Confession can be made privately before God, in the context of public worship, before a fellow-Christian or before a priest, depending upon the particular Christian tradition and the needs of each person or community.

3. *Thanksgiving* – for what God has done in Jesus Christ, for the power and presence of God in this life, and for the promises to which humankind is called. The basis of thanksgiving is that of Jesus at the Last Supper, in relation to bread and wine being his body and blood: this is the new covenant. Thanksgiving is an important antidote to sin and to selfishness, since it places life in a larger context.

4. *Intercession* – articulating human needs before God, in the spirit of Christ, seeking his fulfilment and wholeness: 'If you abide in me and my words abide in you, ask for whatever you wish, and it will be done for you.'

Each of these ingredients provides a key part of pastoral ministry. In a world orientated towards success and wholeness, many people carry burdens of guilt and failure that they long to confess: the gospel of repentance and forgiveness is given to encourage this type of prayer. Similarly the desire for more is the energy of much intercessory prayer in human hearts, which again needs focus to become connected with God's grace and call to his creatures. At times of creativity and joy, such as birth or marriage, prayers of thanksgiving can be given a focus to better shape human endeavours with the divine purpose. Adoration has become the most esoteric of the forms of Christian prayer, yet the pastor has great opportunities to encounter awe and a sense of the transcendent in people's lives. The art of public worship is to provide models whereby all these ingredients of prayer can be articulated and nourished. [*Alastair Redfern*]

PRAYER COUNSELLING
Counselling which culminates in prayer.
This is a specifically Christian form of counselling which brings God into the dyad as a third party through a period (sometimes for hours) of extended prayer at the end of the session. The prayer may be vocal or silent. It is claimed that the counselling procedure conforms to the usual aspects of therapy, but that is not the case if there is always the expectation of prayer to come. Dangers, such as that of manipulation, whether deliberate or not, are obvious, and some who practise this approach recognize these.

PRAYER FOR THE DEAD
Prayers offered for the repose of those who have died.
These prayers have been a contentious issue in Christian history. There is little guidance given in the New Testament, and the practice first came to prominence in North Africa in the second century. Despite the theological debates, highlighted at the Reformation, it has become an increasingly accepted practice in the West since the world wars of the twentieth century. This is a significant example of pastoral need providing the impetus towards the churches' beginning to articulate in prayer an instinct deep in many people. Theology may need to be the handmaid of prayer.

PREACHING, PASTORAL
The occasion when by its dimension, its strategy or its subject a sermon addresses or impacts on the personally invested concerns of its hearers.
When preaching is spoken of as 'pastoral', one or more of three meanings is typically intended: (1) one dimension of the sermon is its negative or positive pastoral *impact or consequence* in the response of the hearer, regardless of its intention; (2) preaching is designed with a pastoral *strategy or intention* of relating to the life experience or need of the hearers, involving or touching their personal concerns, regardless of its actual topic; (3) preaching is about a *subject* of pastoral import – e.g. grief, conflict, family issues, depression, community disaster and the like – regardless of its homiletical method.

PRECONSCIOUS
Unconscious material that is ready to become conscious.
The word refers to aspects of the unconscious mind which are available to become conscious. 'Preconscious' also refers to an area in the mind which lies somewhere between consciousness and the unconscious. For Freud it was an important concept, although it was always difficult to define. It is perhaps most helpful in beginning to overcome any excessive duality between the 'conscious' and the 'unconscious' mind.

PREJUDICE
Strongly held opinions or bias, often preconceived and not based on knowledge.
Prejudice directed to specific groups and individuals, leads to their idealization or denigration. It can therefore be positive. Prejudging, as a routine part of perception and cognition, requires placing people and things in general categories, as long as these are then adjusted to correspond with reality. Prejudice normally refers to the denigration of groups and individuals through labelling and stereotyping. Such beliefs are not tested against reality, but relate to people's own feelings and attitudes. Labelling based on race, nationality, religion or gender degenerates into racism, anti-Semitism, ethnocentrism and sexism. Damaging effects of prejudice vary from acts of avoidance and discrimination to mass extermination as in Bosnia and Rwanda. It therefore violates social norms, including: *rationality*, by overgeneralization, prejudgement, refusal to take account of individual differences, and thinking in stereotypes; *justice*, by placing individuals and groups at a disadvantage which is not merited; and *tolerance*, because it involves intolerance of others, and violates human dignity.

Loyalty to groups can reflect positive prejudice to members. As search for identity and self-development, it includes promoting and defending moral and religious principles. It is only morally legitimate if it is tested by the facts of the situation, and does not degenerate into religious and political fundamentalisms. Such loyalty to groups implies unfavourable prejudice against outsiders. It produces double standards, with identical actions called by different names, depending which group has undertaken them: 'One person's act of liberation is another's act of terrorism.' It becomes a consequence of and reinforcement for the existence of in-groups and out-groups, for the distinction between 'us' and 'them'. It derives identity from opposition to the other – groups magnify the enemy's vices, ensuring that reason, justice and tolerance no longer apply.

Such stereotyping may result from tendencies to authoritarianism found in some psychoanalytic theories and the matching personalities of their practitioners. These theories became increasingly public in the 1920s. In the USA they were connected with attitude theories and growing concern with racial discrimination. In Europe the link was with anti-Semitism. After the Second World War more social perspectives corrected excessive individualism. It demonstrated that the authoritarian type is more likely to hold inflexible attitudes associated with prejudice and anti-democratic beliefs.

The persistence of prejudice in the contemporary context is epitomized by the tension between the universalizing tendencies of the global economy and the particularism of tribalisms. Three pastoral strategies combat such prejudice: (1) promoting loving reason, by re-establishing rationality as central to Christian decision-making; complementing analysis and self-analysis to meet others in face-to-face dialogue; realizing we have more in common with our neighbour than we have differences; (2) developing an understanding of God encompassing gender, other faiths and environment, holding identity and dialogue together; (3) promoting justice, recognizing that prejudice cannot be eradicated by the facts of the situation and moral principles. It will always demand policies to combat its harmful consequences, through legal compulsion in race relations, sex discrimination, and war-crime tribunals. [*John Atherton*]

PREMARITAL COUNSELLING
An intervention aimed at preparing couples for marriage.

Premarital counselling is a generic term covering a range of activities. At one end of the spectrum are formal programmes of instruction about marriage, while at the other are responses to requests for counselling from engaged couples about issues or problems that concern them in their relationship. In the UK and in the USA, two-thirds of all marriages take place in church. It is therefore not surprising that much premarital counselling is a church-related activity. It focuses on either or both of the processes of 'getting married' (the wedding and its meaning) and 'being married' (the vicissitudes of the couple relationship). A discussion with the marriage celebrant, and/or attendance at a marriage preparation class, may be conditions of marrying in church. At their most restricted these interventions will focus on the logistics of the wedding ceremony, but they are also likely to explore the religious significance of the event and to underline the responsibilities partners will have towards each other in the future. The work will be undertaken as part of the wider mission of the church community to demonstrate its faith and uphold its values.

Marriage education programmes generally encompass a broader field than this, and they are likely to employ less didactic methods. Typically, the aims will include: (1) raising awareness about expectations of and needs within the relationship; (2) expressing and reviewing values; (3) fostering better communication and articulating feelings; (4) reducing areas of ignorance; (5) developing awareness of the effects each partner has on the other, and those that the couple have on their immediate circle; (6) developing problem-solving and conflict-management skills; (7) informing couples about services or specialist knowledge that may be helpful to them; (8) providing couples with a good experience of discussing their relationship with a third party so they can ask for help in the future if they need it; (9) following up the programme shortly after the couple are married.

Methods may include quizzes, questionnaire analyses, role plays, video presentations and small-group discussion. Groups will vary in how far they provide a lead for discussion or follow the agenda of the members. Leadership is likely to be non-directive when conducted by those with counselling skills. In the UK, the Catholic organization Marriage Care, the Anglican organization FLAME, the Jewish Marriage Council and the national secular counselling organization Relate are the key bodies providing marriage education.

In the USA, the first documented effort at premarital intervention was a course taught in 1924 at Boston University by Ernest R. Groves, entitled 'Preparation for Marriage and Family Living'. About the same time, the medical community awakened to the benefits of premarital counselling for emotional and physical health, as first described in a 1928 article in the *American Journal of Obstetrics and Gynecology*. The role of the physician as premarital adviser was at the forefront of the literature on the subject until the 1950s, when clergy, led by pastoral counselling pioneers such as Charles Stewart and Paul Johnson, began to develop ideas about pastoral responsibility for evaluating a couple's readiness for marriage and for encouraging marital growth (Stahmann and Hiebert, 1997). Today, in addition to courses offered on the subject of marriage and family life at most colleges and universities, premarital counselling is available in various forms through physicians, pastors, and professional counsellors.

Couples who refer themselves for counselling prior to marriage will receive different responses according to whom they turn to for help. The roles of priest, doctor and therapist all have counselling components, but the nature of the counselling given will be heavily influenced by the setting. The choice of setting is important information about how couples see their problems. Given the rapidly growing practice of cohabitation before marriage, and for periods that may last a long time, the boundary between couple-initiated premarital counselling and couple counselling is becoming increasingly blurred.

A recent national opinion poll conducted in the UK indicated that only one in five couples have any form of marriage preparation. Given the high rate of marriage breakdown there is considerable pressure to extend marriage education programmes as a preventive measure. There is evidence that communication and problem-solving skills can be taught, but these do not necessarily illuminate understanding of why conflicts occur and recur in marriage. Measuring effectiveness is not a straightforward matter, given the captive audience or volunteer nature of the subjects and their control groups. While some longitudinal, controlled studies of the effectiveness of marriage education programmes have been carried out in the USA, the overall long-term effectiveness of these interventions remains unclear.

The term 'premarital counselling' raises important questions about how marriage is understood and the paradigms used to inform supporting interventions. The plurality of family structures in contemporary society allows no easy assumptions of linear development in the forming of marriage. Many cohabiting couples regard themselves as married and see no reason for a church or register office wedding. A high proportion of couples live together between marriages and are in very different circumstances from the never-married. It is common for cohabiting couples in either of these situations to consult counselling agencies when things go wrong in their partnerships, and the question of whether they should marry or not is frequently raised. The helping process in such situations is likely to be identical to that of marriage or couple counselling. Further, couples come from families with a variety of marital arrangements and have varying marital histories themselves. Recent studies in the USA show that between 30 and 40% of people seeking premarital counselling have been married previously (Stahmann and Hiebert, 1997).

Premarital counselling is firmly endorsed as an 'upstream activity' (Egan and Cowan, 1979). The image is one of communities spending all their resources fishing casualties out of the river downstream when all it takes is a walk up the river bank towards the source to stop people falling in in the first place. Prevention is better than cure, but some caution must be taken in applying the metaphor. For example, divorce could be prevented by blocking marriage. While screening for potential high-risk marriages is possible, and might even be effective in terms of bolstering marital stability, it would carry considerable risks if policing of this kind was to become the focus of premarital counselling. Screening and prevention are medical as well as policing activities. Yet the analogy with medicine has its drawbacks. Viewing ordinary life events such as marriage as if they are potential precipitators of illness distorts experience. This would be the case even if there was an effective vaccine against marital distress, which there is not. If policing and medical paradigms have their draw-backs, there is always education. Unfortun-ately, even education cannot always be relied upon to disseminate information effec-tively. It assumes people are rational beings, and takes no account of the universal ability to screen out unsettling or unwelcome in-formation, or of the power of the heart to override that of the head.

These cautionary observations do not negate the potential value of good premarital counselling. Timing and motivation are central to the capacity to learn. The best pre-marital counselling relates to the current pre-occupations of couples, follows their cues, and does not cut short their tentative explora-tions with explanations. In this respect the boundary between educational and thera-peutic processes, and between preventive and remedial work, may be considerably more permeable than is often believed. *[Christopher Clulow]*

PRESBYTER
A local church elder (Greek *presby-teros*).
This leadership title is derived from the Jewish synagogue, which was administered by a council of elders who were respected members of their local community. The New Testament Church inherited this model (Acts 15). At first there was no distinction between the bishop or 'overseer' of a congre-gation and the body of elders from which they were drawn (Titus 1.5–7). These shared collegially the responsibility for teaching, administration and sacramental functions, including the laying on of hands (1 Tim. 4.14). This pattern is still preserved in presby-terian forms of church government. In English the word 'priest' comes from this root, although the significance of this obser-vation is disputed. *[Christopher Moody]*

PREVENTION
Action taken in advance, to stop some-thing from happening, e.g. disease or crime.
Preventive medicine traditionally includes diet, personal hygiene, exercise, sanitary and other measures to control communicable disease. Today it also concerns health and safety at home and work, prevention of road traffic accidents, population screening and antenatal diagnosis, health promotion and education, and political action to relieve poverty, a major cause of ill-health. Prover-bially better than cure, its effectiveness may be more difficult to demonstrate, especially when patients, politicians or the public are not motivated to take a long view.

PRIDE
Arrogant desire to be superior to others.
Pride is one of the seven mortal sins and is often considered the supreme vice. It is anti-social (along with envy and wrath) and not, as is sometimes assumed today, an individual failing. Pride is the essence of sin, according to many writers, because it is the desire to be superior even to God. Self-aggrandizement is always at the expense of others. This is a theological and pastoral problem, calling for repentance and absolution, rather than something that can be dealt with by counsel-ling. The sin of pride is not to be confused with an individual's appropriate self-valuing and assertiveness.

PRIEST
One of two orders of episcopally ordained ministry.
This English word is used to cover both the sacerdotal functions of the elder ('presbyter') in the New Testament and those of the 'priests' of the sacrificial system of the Old. In the New Testament the Old Testament term was applied only to Christ or to the Christian body as a whole (1 Pet. 2.5). But by the end of the second century the words 'elder' and 'priest' became more interchangeable. This was true particularly of those functions delegated to local ministers by the bishop, especially presiding at the Eucharist. The word still derives its most powerful meaning from a 'high' or sacrificial theology of the Eucharist. In pastoral studies the Protestant emphasis upon the 'priesthood of all be-lievers' has to some extent combined with the traditional Catholic notion of priest in a recognition that the pastor holds a represent-ative function that he or she embodies on behalf of others. This has resulted in an increasing recognition of the priestly style of ministry offered by the Church to the world.

PRIMAL THERAPY
A form of psychotherapy derived from theories of Arthur Janov.
Primal therapy involves the theory of primal trauma and the therapeutic agent, the primal scream. The primal scream

occurs when the client is able to get in touch with their primal trauma that is believed to be a childhood trauma involving the parent that is the root of their adult neurosis. The scream unleashes their emotions concerning this event.

PRIMARY CARE
The first point of contact for people seeking health advice, support and treatment.
The responsibilities of primary care are 'to allow and encourage people to participate in the planning, organization and management of their own health care in home, school, work and community'. It is thus distinguished from secondary and tertiary care, which are mostly undertaken in a hospital or other specialist setting.

Access to health care through a general practitioner rather than direct consultation with a specialist clinician is a feature of many health-care systems, e.g. the United Kingdom and New Zealand, and has an important role in developing countries. In North America, by contrast, the person seeking help is more likely to refer themselves to a specialist on the basis of their perceived needs. However, in the USA most insurance systems are now requiring patients first to see a primary-care physician before they move on to specialist care. In all these countries rising costs, ageing population, and pressure on scarce health resources are promoting primary care's role as a gatekeeper to specialist treatment. Many symptoms are in fact still dealt with by self-care.

Goals are: (1) the management and treatment of 'presenting problems'; (2) help in modifying the behaviour which contributed to the problem; (3) appropriate treatment and support including referral if necessary when a problem continues; and (4) developing opportunities for health promotion, frequently working in alliance with other groups (WHO, 1978).

A primary-care team may be drawn from a number of disciplines including medicine, nursing, midwifery, professions supplementary to medicine, e.g. dietetics and administrative staff. High-quality care is responsive to the community which it serves and is best planned, at least in part, in consultation with it. The assessment of need in primary care has to allow for the differences between countries and areas whose health-care systems are relatively sophisticated and complex and those where basic health requirements such as adequate nutrition and safe water have still to be attained. Needs can be defined in four ways: *normative* as determined by experts; *comparative* as defined by one group or person compared with another's standards and needs; *felt* needs, those to which the person in need lays claim; *expressed* needs when these are implemented and provision has to be made (McIver, 1993).

Pastors may be in a position to work effectively with primary health workers when common community needs are identified and appropriate professional boundaries, e.g. confidentiality, understood. This can be particularly true where a community has been affected by a disaster or crisis. Health workers and pastors may be equally aware of the established links between poverty and ill health. Both may concern themselves with the relationship between individual, family and community distress. Many primary-care systems use a 'holistic' model which pays attention to physical, psychological, social and spiritual needs.

Some ways of working that have developed in primary care have been taken up by pastors to develop and enhance their work. One example is the way in which Balint's method of mutual consultation, which he developed with general practitioners in mind to enable them to care for distressed people more effectively without recourse to immediate specialist help, has been adopted as a way of making pastors more aware of their distinctive role (Balint, 1968). Many ministers have found the comparison between their work and that of the general practitioner clarifying. *[Ian Ainsworth-Smith]*

PRIMARY PROCESS
One of the two modes of functioning characteristic of the unconscious mind.
The other term is 'secondary process'. Freud used 'primary process' to refer to his theoretical elaboration of the unconscious processes of which he was becoming aware. It is the process that produces in the unconscious those phenomena that operate in dreams – e.g. displacement and condensing. It is paralleled with secondary process which occurs when dreams are retold. The contrast is typical of the dualism in Freud and matches, for example, that between the pleasure principle and the reality principle.

PRIMITIVE
Refers to early stages in evolution.
There are two main uses of this adjective:

1. The first refers to early stages of civilization, especially those which have no recorded history. In that sense the word is today used less frequently than hitherto. It may also refer to an early stage of evolution.

2. The second use is more prominent in pastoral studies: it refers to early stages in psychological development. Technically it is a value-neutral word, but it is always worth watching for an implicitly pejorative sense.

PRIORITY SETTING
Deciding what activities take precedence, when resources are limited, e.g. for health care.
Scientific advances continually make available new forms of medical treatment. But development costs often make new drugs expensive, innovative therapies can be labour intensive, and funding must also be found for less dramatic, but no less essential, health-care needs. Deciding which therapies should have priority requires research into their relative effectiveness and efficiency, the severity and spread of the needs they meet, and public preferences. Ultimately, priority setting is a complex political process, involving political, cultural, economic and scientific considerations.

PRISONS
Places of confinement (for convicted offenders and sometimes for accused persons on remand) and of punishment.
Prisons are a comparatively modern institution. Transportation to the colonies was a British practice from Tudor times until well into the nineteenth century, when the 'internal exile' of imprisonment took its place. Early prisons were designed on a Christian and monastic model: the regime was, through solitude, labour and the offices of religion, to encourage the offenders to a thoroughgoing repentance. Even convicts confined prior to execution were encouraged and indeed pressured to repent. The chaplain, along with the governor and the medical officer, formed the triumvirate that controlled the prison as a place of punishment and a vale of soul-making, and were present at executions.

More secular ideologies of imprisonment emerged in France and in the English-speaking world with the growth of utilitarianism. The prison was now seen primarily as an institution of social control and rehabilitation. It was like a barracks or the strictest of workshops. In these 'complete and austere institutions' isolation and solitude together with hard work were still seen as necessities if the offenders were to be reformed, the inner roots of rebellion curbed, and the conscience retrained. Utilitarians designed prison buildings such as Bentham's famous 'Panopticon' to serve their purposes. The prison at this time was to be 'the microcosm of a perfect society, in which individuals are isolated in their moral existence, but in which they come together in a strict hierarchical framework, with no lateral relation, communication being possible only in a vertical direction' (Foucault, 1979).

In more modern times there has been considerable uncertainty about what prisons are for. With secularization, the role of religion and therefore of the chaplaincy in the life of the prison has been greatly reduced. Although chaplains remain, they have less status and influence than in the past and there is considerable confusion about their role. Earlier ideas that the function of imprisonment was to engage with the roots of offending in the soul re-emerged in 'treatment' or 'rehabilitation' theories of custodial punishment (Ignatieff, 1978).

Argument continues as to whether offenders are sent to prison *as* punishment or *for* punishment. Liberals suggest that the deprival of freedom is the punishment, and that prison regimes should be made as constructive and forward looking as possible. The more punitively inclined suggest that prison conditions should be bleak and austere so as to deter offenders from a life of crime. Fashions change, and currently the idea that imprisonment is for the sake of rehabilitation is displaced by the so-called 'justice model'. This is interpreted in various ways, but at its heart is the idea that imprisonment should be regarded as punishment apportioned according to desert, and there should be no uninvited invasion of the offender's inner space or questioning of the offender's values. There remains a great deal of confusion about the functions of imprisonment, and policy tends to swing erratically. Meanwhile in some Western countries, particularly the UK and the USA, prison populations soar and a system which is seriously under-resourced lurches from crisis to crisis. [*Duncan Forrester*]

PROFESSIONALISM
Quality of conduct of those belonging to a profession.
The word 'profession' derives from the Latin *profiteri*: to make a public declaration. Hence its usage in relation to religious vows made in front of colleagues. Professionalism was first mentioned in 1856 in relation to conduct in general which shares the qualities of those who belong to a group calling themselves a profession. To qualify as a profession, more is required of a group than that they share a common training that is based on a body of knowledge and techniques and governed by codes of ethics and practice. Three components are essential: accountability, responsibility and autonomy. Medicine, for example, has had the status of a profession since the Greeks evolved an oath under Hippocrates which established the doctor's responsibility for patients and the principle of doing no harm. It was not until the end of the nineteenth century that the doctors began to band together and added accountability to responsibility via the foundation of such national bodies as the General Medical Council in the UK. Autonomy is safeguarded in that such bodies take responsibility for actions of members not only in their working lives but also to some extent in their personal lives. Ethical codes of most professions include a clause which forbids bringing the profession into disrepute. This could limit scandalous personal behaviour.

Professionalism is a broader term in that it extends the attributes of those belonging to a profession into areas of activity that are not necessarily known as professions and may not have formal codes of practice. Thus in the churches, the ministry would have all the attributes of a profession but it would be perfectly possible for lay members who are carrying out any form of work to do so with professionalism, if they work within the confines described above.

The helping professions, particularly, involve relationships, and these can stray over the lines of formality into an intimacy which could be exploitative and harmful. Another important quality of professionalism is, therefore, the use of boundaries.

A worker who is in a position of power could seduce or exploit the weak or vulnerable who come for his or her service. This vulnerability brings with it the necessity for the imposition of limits to the kind of contact that will be allowed. Professionalism implies not only that there should be limits on exploitative relationships but also that the professional should know how to determine what limits are appropriate. Lawyers in particular have codes which spell out how much the lawyer may use his or her own initiative in helping a client. The client's interest is a vital concept and will predominate in any view of professionalism as the price that must be paid for autonomy.

Not all agree with professionalizing if that means achieving the status and organization implicit in the idea of a profession. For example, psychotherapists in the UK are wary of the public accountability associated with professionalization and its impact on their practice. *[Lesley Murdin]*

PROJECTION
1. In a series of general senses projection describes the displacing of a psychological aspect of the self outside the self.
2. A defence whereby aspects of the self are located in another person or thing.
Projection is a widely and loosely used term. Its general use describes the way in which people interpret a situation by reading into it their own feelings. In a more analytic use it is sometimes almost a substitute for transference. An example of projection was early suggested by Freud to be at work in paranoia. Paranoid people put their intolerable ideas out of themselves into others, from whom they return as a reproach, although the material itself remains unaffected.

PROJECTIVE IDENTIFICATION
A psychological mechanism through which the individual seeks to manage uncomfortable experience by dissociating from it and inducing such feelings in another.
Projective identification was described by Klein (1946), since when it has become increasingly significant in psychiatry and in organizational studies (Shapiro and Carr, 1991). It is based upon an initial empathic feeling for the experience of others. The disavowal of an uncomfortable aspect of the self joins the discovery of another who has an attribute that corresponds to this aspect. If that person is willing (usually unconsciously) to accept the projection, an unconscious collusion follows that sustains the projections. This person or other group is consciously identified as unlike oneself and manipulative behaviour ensues that is unconsciously

designed to elicit behaviour to support the idea that the projected attribute belongs to him or her. The relationship is usually collusive in that both participants project.

Projective identification (as will be obvious) is often discerned in couples and is a key theme in much marital therapy. The couple is a small enough unit to see this behaviour clearly. It also provides a way of thinking about organizations. A church, for example, may seek to survive by projectively defining itself over against its environment (Carr, 1997).

PROMISE
An agent's voluntary self-binding commitment.

Promises may sometimes have a conditional or contractual character ('I promise to do A in the event of B'). Promises are distinguished from statements of intention, which make no formal commitment to performance. The distinction is generally marked by a phrase (e.g. 'I promise ...') which constitutes the making of a promise. Pastoral issues may arise from (1) contextual incapacity to distinguish intentions from promises; (2) the claim that promises can be inferred even when unstated; (3) questions of when and how release from promissory commitment is possible.

PROPHECY
Prediction and proclamation of the Word of God.

In St Luke's account of the trial of Jesus he reports, 'Now the men who were holding Jesus began to mock him and beat him; they also blindfolded him and kept asking him "Prophesy! Who is it that struck you?"' (Luke 23.63–65). This picture represents a popular understanding of prophecy – the ability to discern what is happening in human affairs. In the Christian tradition prophecy is discerning what God is doing in human affairs. This distinction is crucial.

In Scripture the line of prophets runs from Moses to John the Baptist. The initiative in making a prophet rests with God (Exod. 3—4), whose word and wisdom through the prophet provide a proper understanding of history as it unfolds. The message varies from encouragement to warning, and is delivered by word, signs and symbolic actions.

Often the prophet confronts the institutional expression of God's people with new possibilities, or the need to remain faithful to its founding principles. The proclamation of future wrath or blessings is always linked to a call to a renewed seeking of God's mercy in the present. There is a call to worship rather than to mere organization or reform in human terms. This call to deeper knowledge of God's working in history is rooted in an awareness of God's holiness, the set-apart vocation of God's people, and principles of judgement and mercy. There is a consistent emphasis upon God's justice as concern for those in whom God's image is defaced.

A key debate concerns distinguishing true from false prophecy. The Books of Jeremiah and Ezekiel make clear that false prophecy proclaims peace without a prior call to holiness and repentance of sin. True prophecy is concerned with the process of discovering God's peace, by challenging sin, recognizing the reality of judgement and seeking a more holy life. Ultimately the prophet is right because he is right. Testing is in the fruits, though these will only emerge from true worship. Thus there is a way of preparing in the present for the unfolding of God's will. Prophecy links true worship with attaining a proper sense of direction.

In the New Testament every Christian is potentially a prophet (Acts 2.18), but there was a special category of person called 'prophets', mentioned after apostles in the list of ministries (1 Cor. 12.28–29). The prophets in Scripture remain key teachers for Christian practice, since the proclamation and prediction given through them has been vindicated in the person of Christ.

In recent times Max Weber highlighted the contrast between prophet and priest – representing respectively charismatic and institutional models of church. There is an inevitable and necessary tension between these two models, since the strength and stability of the institution can become complacent and self-centred, thus requiring challenge from outside to conform more fully to the vocation as God's people by self-criticism (recognizing the reality of sin), making worship central, and depending upon God's mercy and holiness. This analysis is helpful in understanding conflict throughout church history between charismatic individuals and movements and the institution, the latter usually enforcing immediate conformity, but the truth of prophetic utterances coming to fruition eventually. Examples would range from the Franciscan movement to the debates about the place of women in the Church.

In pastoral terms this introduces the important debate between the need for security and dependence, which values an institutional expression of Christianity, often focused in key ministerial figures (priests), and the danger of this mode becoming a human construct subject to the weaknesses and sins of those who control it. Prophecy is a reminder that all human institutions, especially churches and Christian communities, need to be challenged by a Word from outside – which proclaims and predicts judgement, mercy, and the centrality of worship. Thus dependence upon God is held to be prior and primary. The dynamic between priestly and prophetic ministry is essential to the health of pastoral practice. Prophecy is openness to interpretations that do not conform with the current institutional norms, but which are clearly rooted in humble worship and quest for the gift of renewed holiness. In this sense, looking to the future will require changes in attitudes and behaviour, rather than the simple dependency which acts as a reinforcement of prevailing practices. Prophecy usually comes from unlikely sources and moves the focus from a desire to discern what is happening in human affairs to a desire to discern what God is doing, and wills to do, in human affairs. [*Alastair Redfern*]

PROSTITUTION (FEMALE)
Providing sexual services in return for a fee.

Prostitution occurs among people of both heterosexual and homosexual orientation. Heterosexual, female prostitution is probably the most common and occurs worldwide. It is controversial, since it appears to threaten sexual norms and calls into question the basis of gender relationships. Prostitution occurs in a number of settings – street work, legal and illegal brothels, hotels, homes, escort agencies, etc. Varying personal circumstances mean that women may work in a number of these settings during their careers.

Female prostitution must be understood in the context of patriarchy. This restricts women's access to resources, devalues their experience and defines them primarily in terms of their sex and gender roles. Women can earn more in the sex industry than in almost any other occupation. Where families and individuals have few other choices, prostitution can be a way of rejecting poverty. The appearance of being able to break traditional patterns and norms leads to prostitutes (often called 'sex workers') being defined as aberrant women. However, their relationships largely follow traditional lines. In their work and in their personal lives women service the needs of men and support families. The definition of prostitutes as aberrant allows the denial of their human rights. For instance, forced medical examination has occurred historically and in the present day. Legal responses to prostitution, predicated on patriarchy, claim to protect women but may in fact increase their vulnerability.

In the UK many women prostitutes have been in local authority care or have experienced manipulative relationships during childhood. A proportion have been sexually abused. This pattern occurs elsewhere and the resulting lack of self-worth makes women especially vulnerable to exploitative relationships and repeated self-harming behaviour. Prostitution before the age of sexual consent is common and the prostitution of a minor is increasingly recognized as child abuse. Prostitution is part of a subculture around which other illegal activity clusters, but there has been an increase in the number of women prostituting themselves in order to support a drug habit. This subculture, and the responses of 'respectable' society, may make it difficult for women to change their lifestyle. It is a culture that any pastoral worker must learn carefully and move through with great caution. Mistakes can have physical repercussions for women and can prevent pastoral work developing.

Prostitution affects women's physical, psychological and social well-being. However, women develop coping mechanisms and are not only victims but survivors. Women's issues are the same for women sex workers as for all women, including access to safe housing; access to education; information on health care; the well-being of their children; relationships with partners; information on legal rights and safety at work.

Pastoral care needs to avoid repeating traditional gender patterns. 'Saving fallen women' so that they become 'respectable' only moves them from one area of patriarchy to another. Rather, pastoral involvement is about increasing self-worth and developing women's control of their lives. For some this might mean leaving prostitution; for others it might involve keeping the money they earn.

Key elements of pastoral work include facilitating women's access to reliable information and specialist resources; demonstrating consistent commitment; and a willingness to be where women are and to share something of their experience of vulnerability.

The Church has been ambivalent about prostitution. On the one hand there is the radical association by Jesus of the Kingdom of God with social outcasts, among whom notably were prostitutes. On the other hand there are the Old Testament denunciations of prostitution, which have both religious and social overtones. These have been largely taken over into the Church's teachings. However, whatever the clergy or rulers did and said had little impact on the social mores that allowed prostitution to continue.

It must not be forgotten that the act of prostitution involves both a sex worker and a client. Research indicates that many clients of women sex workers are married men or men in stable relationships. Most do not require unusual sexual services. A proportion use prostitutes when their partners are temporarily sexually unavailable through pregnancy, ill health or absence. Some men state that paying a prostitute is preferable to an affair as there is no relationship involved. A small proportion of clients have particular sexual needs or, for various reasons, find it difficult to establish intimate relationships. Pastoral work with users of sexual services will need to explore these issues sensitively and referral may be appropriate. [B. Hayes]

PROVIDENCE
God's creative and sustaining care of the universe; sometimes specifically an event or circumstances of divine interposition.

Greek philosophers used the word *pronoia* to describe a power which rationally guides the world and human destiny by a fixed set of natural laws. This idea also links with the biblical understanding that in various ways the creator remains directly involved with creation. The Old Testament records a gradual development of the belief in such providence. It is dynamic: God guides history, but in such a way that independent and free human actions are not annulled. Unlike the less personal Greek concept, this understanding requires the creator's continuing and intimate involvement with humanity. The New Testament develops this approach, but not as a theoretical explanation of God's relationship in the world. The incarnation, for example, is God's ultimate providential intervention in the world.

Early patristic literature was again strongly influenced by Greek philosophy, particularly cosmology. Clement of Alexandria expressed the intimate relationship of God and providence. He also contended that to deny providence was to be atheist. Later, the Church Fathers explored the biblical idea of freedom with responsibility under God's provision. During the Middle Ages, the scholastic theologians further developed thinking on the nature and meaning of providence. The Council of Trent designated divine providence as a doctrine of the Church. The Reformers also presented renewed views on this theme. Returning to the practicalities of faith in the New Testament they focused less on an explanation of the universe and more on realizations of faith and practical living. John Calvin's teaching on predestination provides an extreme example: God's providence was restricted and human free will restrained. Popular expressions of the Protestant belief in providence were sustained in devotional literature and hymns. In the eighteenth century scholars of the Enlightenment viewed providence from a more rationalistic position. As a result, it became the fulcrum of natural theology. G. W. Leibniz, for example, described providence as the rational and meaningful order of both human history and the cosmos. But any systematic explanation of providence raises the problem of theodicy – questions about the goodness and fairness of God given the evil and suffering in creation. The magnitude of suffering in the twentieth century – world wars, concentration camps and genocide – has made the question again acute (Ward, 1990).

For pastors the issue of providence arises chiefly in terms of whether (and if so, how) God intervenes in the life of an individual, group or even nation. There are two aspects of providence that may be distinguished: (1) God's guidance to individual believers and God's assistance in ordering their life; (2) more general providence, which is God's activity in the social and political context within which the Church and Christians live. Belief in providence also introduces a moral dimension: God provides not just for survival but for human growth in righteousness, which is both individual and social. The idea of providence, therefore, is both a theological profundity and a key source of hope for human development (Ward, 1990). [David MacBeth Moss]

PROZAC
A medication for the treatment of depression and several other psychiatric conditions.

Released in the USA in January 1988, Prozac attracted a great deal of attention because it was the first of the so-called 'new antidepressants'. Prior to 1988, a number of effective medications were available for treating depression, but these were likely to cause unpleasant side effects. They were also potentially toxic for patients with heart disease and lethal if taken as a suicidal overdose. The depressed individual was often faced with the dilemma of either living with difficult side effects or refusing the medication and remaining ill.

Prozac, which works by a different chemical mechanism, offered equally effective treatment with less probability of side effects. It was safer for cardiac patients and less likely to be fatal in an overdose. Because of these factors, many more people were able to tolerate antidepressant treatment and benefit from it.

In the first few years of its use, Prozac produced many dramatic cases of successful treatment, and was in great demand. It was touted as a 'wonder drug' and by 1990 about two million people in the USA were taking it. But in 1990 psychiatrists began to report instances in which patients taking Prozac developed intense suicidal preoccupations. Even more disturbing was the highly publicized 1989 case of an individual taking Prozac who went on an armed rampage in his workplace, killing eight others and then himself. These cases represented only a tiny fraction of all Prozac patients, and experts offered plausible alternative explanations for these bad outcomes. But there was damaging publicity, the public was frightened, and the use of Prozac declined.

Then, in one of the more curious examples of the interaction of religion and psychiatry, the Church of Scientology became involved. This sect, known for its antipathy towards psychiatrists, labelled Prozac a 'killer drug' and sponsored an all-out media attack and intense lobbying of the US government, pressing to have the medication banned. In response, the US Food and Drug Administration (FDA) held extensive hearings and, in July 1991, denied the petition of the Scientologists. The FDA concluded that there was no convincing evidence that the incidents of violence or intense suicidal feelings were caused by Prozac rather than the patients' underlying depression or other psychiatric conditions. This helped restore confidence, and by 1992 Prozac was back in use.

Since 1990, a number of new, low side effect antidepressant drugs have been developed, and Prozac has lost its unique position. But it is still widely prescribed for depression, and its usefulness in combating bulimia, panic disorder and obsessive-compulsive disorder has been demonstrated. One side effect of Prozac which has proven most troublesome is inhibition of sexual functioning, and this leads a good number of patients to request a change to a different medication. Fortunately, other medications exist for these individuals.

By the late 1990s an estimated 38 million people worldwide were being prescribed Prozac, and in 2000 concern about suicidality resurfaced in the UK. The Medicines Control Agency required that, owing to evidence of a causal link between Prozac and suicidal behaviour, a warning about suicide should be added to the patient information leaflet. The manufacturers of Prozac continue to maintain that the drug is safe, and at the time of writing opinion remains divided. [Dana Charry]

PRUDENCE
One of the cardinal virtues – practical wisdom.

This virtue approximates to the modern notion of 'common sense'. It is foresight, the ability to manage one's behaviour with consequences in mind.

PSYCHIATRY
The medical specialism concerned with the diagnosis, treatment and prevention of mental illness.

A psychiatrist is a medically qualified doctor who has added this specialty to the basic clinical qualifications. They are trained to discern, interpret and treat disturbed behaviour and minds. They may also treat people with, e.g., personality disorders, substance abuse difficulties, or family and other group dilemmas. There are also further specialisms within psychiatry, e.g., forensic and child psychiatry.

Psychoanalysts until recently had to be

psychiatrists, although this requirement has now been relaxed. Treatment of mental disturbance today is through procedures which require medical qualification such as Electro-Convulsive Therapy (ECT) or medication. By contrast, a psychologist is not necessarily medically trained and he or she cannot prescribe medication.

PSYCHIC
1. Relating to non-material powers, often occult.
2. Aspects of our mental life.
'Psychic' has several meanings.

1. It is a popular term for someone with the capacity to invoke forces. These may be good – e.g. dowsing, natural prophecy and inner seeing. They may also become occult (Perry, 1996).

2. In the study of the paranormal, a phrase like 'psychic force' describes the possible cause of something like telekinesis or mind reading.

3. A psychic may also be another way of describing a spiritualist medium.

4. The adjective is sometimes found. For example, Freud spoke of 'psychic determinism' to mean that all aspects of our mental life are as determined as are events in the world.

The pastor, therefore, needs to be careful about how the term is being used and pay attention to the context.

PSYCHOANALYSIS
1. A technique to investigate mental processes using free association, dream analysis and interpretation of transference.
2. A theory of the mind and psychopathology developed by Freud from the study of his patients.
3. A form of treatment for mental illness, established by Freud and developed by those that followed.
Psychoanalysis is a discipline founded by Freud (Freud, 1933). It involves the interpretation of behaviour in terms of subconscious desires rather than conscious thoughts, using free association, dream analysis and interpretation of transference. Freud believed that the conscious manifestation of subconscious wishes was mediated by certain mental processes that he termed defence mechanisms. He postulated that human development is driven by the libido

(sexuality). He gave primacy of place to childhood sexuality, especially in his description of the Oedipus complex, where the male child desires his mother and is jealous of his father.

Freud first used his theories in the treatment of hysterical patients. His consultations involved the patient lying on a couch while the doctor sat out of sight. In this environment, Freud reckoned that, if no prompts were given, the patient's conversation would reflect their subconscious. This was known as 'free association'. As the patient free-associates, the analyst offers interpretations. Another important dimension is transference, the feelings of the patient towards the analyst and what these represent. Counter-transference refers to the feelings awakened in the analyst by the patient.

Psychoanalysis as a theory of psychology and (as psychotherapy) a method of psychiatric treatment has been developed and reinterpreted by several key figures since Freud, including, for example, Carl Jung, Alfred Adler and Melanie Klein. Jung emphasized the collective unconscious, which derived from the memories of our ancestors and which led to the development of archetypes. Adler evolved theories around the human need for power, and his writings have been influential in the development of educational reforms. Klein developed theories to do with object relations which have become particularly important in, for instance, family therapy. While Freud emphasized instinct, modern practitioners have focused on the role of the ego or the adult self.

Psychoanalysis has been criticized as being an elitist form of treatment available only to the rich, and ineffectual in the treatment of more severe mental disorders. The lack of clinical evidence in support of its claims as well as the cost and time involved have led to a decline of its influence and availability in mainstream psychiatric services. Reactions to its perceived exclusivity have led to variations in forms of therapy, such as group therapy and counselling. Nevertheless, psychoanalytic ideas pervade the fields of psychotherapy and counselling.

The term psychoanalysis is now used with reference to a range of theories, practices and techniques. Its rapid assimilation into Western culture, especially in the USA, and its impact on theories of human behaviour have given psychoanalysis a social identity of its own. It is significant in literary, historical and social studies. [*Lawrence Ratna*]

PSYCHODRAMA
The practice of using dramatic material from a counsellee's own life experiences in order to empower the healing process.
In practice, psychodrama, as classically understood in the tradition of Jacob L. Moreno, is a narrowly defined discipline. It involves using many of the techniques and conventions of traditional theatre: a stage, specially trained actors to play designated roles in the client's life, props, and so on. The therapist/director typically assists the client in setting up the psychodrama. Scenes may be repeated until some sort of catharsis happens for the client. Alternatively, the client may try out imaginary options in life, by creating such scenes on the stage, and thus use the process to work through a difficult life crisis. For Moreno, psychodrama was both a theory of self rooted in the concept of spontaneity and a therapeutic practice. His development of psychodrama contributed to the shift in therapy from a focus on individual and intrapsychic dynamics to the consideration of the interpersonal perspective.

As a young man in medical school in Vienna early in the twentieth century, Moreno began working informally with children, as well as with groups of prostitutes. This was the origin of his psychodramatic method. Out of these experiences came a first book on the 'theater of spontaneity' (1947). In this work, Moreno shared his concerns about traditional forms of drama, which he condemned as a worship of death, because it did not engage people at the level of their spontaneity. Spontaneity was the key concept, by which he meant what happens in the 'here and now'. In the psychodramatic situation spontaneity allows the protagonist/counsellee to break out of rigid personality moulds and fully engage the present.

Psychodrama, in both its theoretical and practical aspects, has many merits. Through its use, Moreno and his followers were successful in reaching people with whom other methods had failed. Many informal ways of working in pastoral counselling have grown out of psychodrama, for example, role play or other forms of rehearsal in the therapeutic process. However, other approaches to the use of drama in pastoral counselling have arisen. One approach involves the recogni-

tion of the therapeutic value of completed works of drama, valued as works of art, rather than dramatizing material from the client's life. [*Ronald Baard*]

PSYCHOLOGY
The scientific discipline concerned with the study of human behaviour.
Sociology and anthropology, among other disciplines, would also define themselves as the study of human behaviour. What is psychology's uniqueness? Whereas anthropology studies human behaviour cross-culturally, and sociology studies human behaviour within society, psychology focuses on intrapersonal determinants. These differences become somewhat blurred, and many universities teach social psychology in both sociology and psychology departments. All three fields are known as the social sciences.

Psychology focuses primarily on the internal dynamics of human behaviour. These 'internal dynamics' are as old as Aristotle's concept of the *psyche*, from which the word 'psychology' is derived. The term is often translated as 'soul' or 'mind'. Aristotle thought of it as the breath or essence of life. Plato thought of psyche as a non-substantive reality that was immortal. While modern psychologists no longer use the term in the way the ancients did, they remain interested in the same inner processes that lie behind the thoughts, words, feelings and actions (i.e. behaviour) of human beings (Lahey, 1988). Defining psychology as the study of human behaviour does not exclude those who do research on animals – a type of investigation that would never be done by sociologists or anthropologists. These researchers investigate behaviour in lower forms of life in order to infer that similar processes occur in human beings. That is why they are called 'comparative' psychologists.

In the above paragraph, behaviour was defined in four ways: thoughts, words, feelings and actions. Typically, human behaviour is understood only in the last sense, i.e. actions – those overt, observable movements of people from one place to another. However, psychologists take seriously the thesis that actions are motivated by non-observable thoughts and feelings. The measurement and investigation of all forms of behaviour as well as their internal determinants are encompassed by psychology. In this regard, psychology uses the basic formula B: P + E (behaviour is a function of Person plus Environment). Although basically concerned with the P (or Person) variable, psychologists acknowledge that behaviour always occurs in interaction with the environment. The first major 'person' distinction made by psychology is between sensation and perception. Sensation refers to the electrical impulses sent to the brain by the body's sense organs. Known as sight, sound, taste, smell and touch, these five sensations are uniquely and distinctly comprehended by the brain even though the nerves which transport them are of similar composition. Perception is the term applied to the activity of the brain as it combines, interprets and makes meaning of these sensations. This process assumes the integrity of the sense organs as they transmit sensations, an assumption which is not always correct, as any who have suffered loss of sight, hearing or any similar handicap attest. Psychology's studies of reaction times has focused on these differences in sense-organ functioning.

Perception is also based on prior experience, as the research of Wilhelm Wundt in psychology's first laboratory at the University of Leipzig in 1874 illustrated. In assessing subjects' responses to red lights he conjectured that the meanings they gave were based, in part, on the 'apperceptive mass' of their memories of personal and cultural experiences. Psychologists have spent much time investigating the effect of people's learning histories on their behaviour. The meaning of present experience is grounded in what has happened in the past. Memory is the core of perception, and perception is the prime determinant of thoughts, words, feelings and actions. In the late nineteenth century, Hermann Ebbinghaus studied the memory of nonsense syllables and found that people forget them very quickly. However, memory of meaningful events becomes the basic stuff of perception and mental life. This was the prime discovery of Sigmund Freud, who coined the term 'unconscious' to stand for that part of the mind which retains the interpreted meaning of the past. Freudian thinking dominated psychological thinking in the twentieth century. He reckoned that there were no innate ideas but that the content of the mind was, as John Locke stated, a blank tablet on which experience writes. This understanding of perception provides a segue into discussing applied psychology.

The twentieth century saw the rise of a new profession, clinical psychology. This exemplifies the intent of psychology to become a social science that not only understands but predicts and changes behaviour. Emerging during the First World War as a form of psychology that could predict adjustments to certain types of assignments, clinical psychology has developed into a helping profession alongside the medical speciality of psychiatry. Whereas psychiatry has become increasingly biophysical in its approach to changing perception, clinical psychology has retained the Freudian-based goal of altering past memories of catharsis and reflection. Even client-centred counselling, the approach made famous by Carl Rogers, was based on the presumption that recovering forgotten memories that clouded perception would result in healing if it occurred in a permissive atmosphere that replaced the harmful past with a supportive present experience.

Contemporary psychology is a worldwide, cross-cultural social behavioural science and profession that involves scholars and practitioners in both basic and applied studies of human behaviour. Associations exist in almost every country and continent. An International Congress of Psychology is held every four years and the International Council of Psychology meets yearly. Among the largest national groups are the British Psychological Society (BPS) and the American Psychological Association (APA) – this latter association having over 100,000 members. Of special interest to those in the pastoral field has been the appropriation of psychological knowledge into the understanding of religious experience and pastoral work. William James' *The Varieties of Religious Experience* stimulated the study of the psychology of religion. A division of the APA is devoted to the psychology of religion and the APA recently published *Religion and the Clinical Practice of Psychology* (Shafranske, 1996). [*H. Newton Malony*]

PSYCHOLOGY OF RELIGION
The application of psychological theories and methods to the study of religion.

The psychology of religion needs to be distinguished from religious psychology. Religious psychology is rooted in religious traditions and may take two forms. In the first it draws on religious data (e.g. revelation or sacred texts) to construct a model of the human mind or to account for human functioning. Examples include the Enneagram or psychological healing through divine intervention. In the second form religious psychology is driven by the agenda of the religious community. Instances include the use of psychological techniques in promoting religious conversion. The psychology of religion, on the other hand, is rooted in the theories and methods of the academic discipline of psychology.

The psychology of religion has developed within two academic contexts: departments concerned primarily with the study of religion and departments of psychology. There are strengths and weaknesses to both traditions. When conducted within departments of religion, the psychology of religion may suffer from employing poor psychology. When conducted within departments of psychology, the psychology of religion may suffer from misunderstanding or misinterpreting religious phenomena. At its best the psychology of religion is an interdisciplinary activity.

The major literature in the psychology of religion can be divided into two streams. The first is driven by psychological theory, and may be rooted in forms of clinical experience. The second is driven by measurement and mathematical models, and may be rooted in forms of social psychology.

Examples of classic theoretical perspectives in the psychology of religion are found in Freud and Jung. In *Totem and Taboo* Freud linked his psychoanalytic theory regarding the 'Oedipus complex' with the 'totemism' observed in primitive groups to account for the origins of religion. His speculative theories about the origins of religion are developed further in *The Future of an Illusion, Civilization and its Discontents*, and *Moses and Monotheism*. He regarded religion as an obsessional neurosis from which humankind needed to be released. Jung, on the other hand, took a more positive view of religion in books like *Modern Man in Search of a Soul*. For him the absence of religion was the chief cause of adult psychological disorders.

Classic empirical perspectives on the psychology of religion are to be found in the work of William James and Edwin Starbuck. James set out to describe the varieties of religious experience through the qualitative organization of personal documents. Starbuck concentrated on understanding religious conversion through the quantitative analysis of questionnaire data.

One major contemporary empirical perspective concerns attempts to characterize and measure different ways of being religious or different religious orientations. Gordon W. Allport developed measures to distinguish between 'extrinsic' and 'intrinsic' ways of being religious. The extrinsic orientation values religion as a means to self-serving ends, while the intrinsic orientation values religion for itself. Bernard Spilka used the terms 'consensual' and 'committed' religion to make a similar distinction. C. Daniel Batson added a third orientation which he characterized 'religion as quest', which is open-ended and questioning. Scales measuring these orientations have been employed in a large number of independent studies (Batson, Schoenrade and Ventis, 1993). Other contemporary empirical interests in the psychology of religion include attitudes towards religion, conversion, faith development, gender differences, mysticism, personality and religion, prayer, religion and death, religious experience, religious judgement, religious thinking, and spirituality (Spilka, Hood and Gorsuch, 1985; Wulff, 1991). [*Leslie Francis*]

PSYCHOLOGY, PASTORAL
See: PASTORAL PSYCHOLOGY

PSYCHOPATHOLOGY
A psychiatric and psychoanalytic term meaning the study of 'abnormal' psychological behaviour or functioning.

Freud brought psychoanalysis into respectable prominence at the end of the nineteenth century. He (1901) wrote about the psychopathology of everyday life, being convinced that it was possible to discover all of the mental processes which led to disturbances and prevented everyday, or 'normal', functioning. His conviction suggested that psychoanalysis could reveal all the subtleties as well as the difficulties of mental functioning. Jung (1946) wrote that 'the unbalanced state affords the investigator a very favourable opportunity of gaining an almost exaggeratedly distinct view of certain psychic phenomena, which are often only dimly perceptible within the boundaries of the normal'. Otto Gross, who knew both Freud and Jung, also published research into psychopathology.

All three theorists believed that certain manifestations of psychopathology lay beneath the surface of ordinary everyday behaviour.

PSYCHOPATHY
A general term used to refer to mental disorders or diseases for which there is no specific, recognized or discernible aetiology, making more exact classification or diagnosis difficult or unattainable.

The term 'psychopathic' is now seldom used, partially due to the fact that it has become an increasingly stigmatizing label used in medico-legal arguments and in the media to denote an unfeeling and violent individual. Psychopathy is rarely used within psychiatry and the term 'psychopath' has been replaced by 'anti-social personality'.

PSYCHOSIS
A psychiatric and psychoanalytic term referring to severe mental illness.

Unlike neuroses, which can successfully be treated in psychotherapy and psychoanalysis, psychoses are much more difficult to treat. This is because a psychotic person is much closer to unconsciousness than consciousness: that is, consciousness has been overwhelmed by the unconscious. This may be due to an unbearable trauma, such as sexual or physical abuse, or experience of war. Psychosis can bring on periods of temporary or longer-term 'dissociation' when a person seems to vanish from everyday reality. Schizophrenia, manic depression and paranoia are all psychoses and all bring enormous suffering.

Psychosis is understood differently by the various psychiatric and psychoanalytic orientations to describe a lack of functioning in relation to everyday reality. Some psychoanalysts find it possible to work with psychotic individuals, challenging the generally accepted opinion that it is not possible to form a transference relationship with a psychotic person.

PSYCHOSOMATIC PROBLEMS
A vague term applicable to distinct sets of ideas about actual or supposed relations between bodily and psychological (mental) events, processes or factors.

1. *Causation.* Certain diseases with obvious manifestations based on physical pathology – for instance asthma, ulcerative colitis and rheumatoid arthritis – have sometimes been supposed to be caused in some fundamental sense by psychological disturbances often formulated in psychoanalytical terms such as 'unconscious conflict' or 'repressed anger'. It is now recognized that emotions play little part in the initial causation of these illnesses, so this usage of 'psychosomatic' is obsolete.

2. *The course of established medical illnesses.* The course of many physical illnesses, once established, may be affected for good or ill by psychological and social circumstances, stresses, events and processes. This includes the illnesses already mentioned, and also many forms of cancer, multiple sclerosis and epilepsy, chronic renal failure, HIV infection and AIDS – and indeed some responsiveness to external stressors is to be expected in every kind of chronic illness. Responsiveness to environmental stressors (stressor means 'event making demands on the individual') and to the demands on bodily adaptation brought about by serious physical disease, are both mediated by hormonal and immunological mechanisms, and also involve the evocation and consequences of autonomic arousal (see below). Hence, all these kinds of process may be implicated in the manifestations and progress of physical diseases once established, and also in the adaptation of the person to stressful events.

3. *Responsiveness to stressful events.* The impact of an environmental event on a person depends on the degree of physical threat arising from the event itself (e.g. being involved in a serious road accident, or being in conditions of starvation or water deprivation, would involve a high degree of such threat) and also on what the event signifies to the person. Healthy people are more often disturbed by what an event or experience means than by the degree of danger or damage involved in the event itself. Different patterns of meaning tend to evoke characteristic patterns of response: 'loss' events tend to sadness or depression; threat ('the possibility of something adverse happening') to anxiety or fear; frustration to anger; and reward to joy. Every emotion-coloured experience is a composite of bodily responses which increase with the intensity of the feeling, and cognitive and subjective features (thoughts, beliefs, intentions) which give the experience its characteristic content. In one meaning, 'psychosomatic' concerns this area of the bodily and psychological patterns of experience, including emotional experience, which 'connect' people to their external surroundings and also to bodily changes arising from disease.

4. *Psychiatric disorders.* Not infrequently, individuals consult doctors with any or many of a wide range of bodily symptoms which on

due assessment turn out not to be due to physical disease. These symptoms can be understood in terms of the inevitability of bodily perturbation of some degree being part of all emotions, perceived and experienced as accompanied by cognitions suggesting bodily illness, rather than a psychological state.

Individuals who experience multiple bodily symptoms not explicable in terms of physical pathology are often resistant to psychiatric referral and consultation and may request and receive multiple sets of medical investigations. Sometimes, there is a focus on symptoms associated with a particular body system, for example the gastro-intestinal tract, the heart, or joints, or skin; or with symptoms referable to a particular variety of experience, for instance pain. When 'somatic symptoms unjustified by somatic pathology' are widespread and intense, the diagnosis is 'somatization disorder'; when the focus is restricted, the diagnostic label reflects this, as for instance in 'somatoform pain disorder', 'irritable bowel syndrome', 'psychogenic hyperventilation' (overbreathing), 'chronic fatigue syndrome', and others. In all these disorders, depressive and anxiety symptoms may coexist, but do not necessarily do so (Rees *et al.*, 1997).

In all circumstances where psychosomatic (i.e. mixed physical and psychological) symptoms are troublesome, the primary task of any clinical, counselling or pastoral involvement must be to accept the person's distress as real and troublesome, and to try and understand their personal view of the natures, causes and prognosis of their problems. Simply to deny the reality of the person's distress, for instance by saying after tests that 'there is nothing wrong', tends to strengthen ideas that no one understands and the consequent determination that a more adequate medical approach is essential. *[James Watson]*

PSYCHOTHERAPY

A general term for approaches that use the interaction between patient and therapist as their focal point for healing. The word is derived from the Greek *psyche* (mind or soul) and *therapeia* (healing). Psychotherapy occupies an area of healing for the mind which is very broad. Freud is generally credited with laying most of the foundations for recent thinking about how to provide relief of mental suffering by psychol-

ogical means. From Freud's lifetime of work have come so many ideas that it is impossible to convey them all briefly. All his work was based on the hypothesis that there is an area of mind which is not available to consciousness or to a deliberate effort to recall but which nevertheless affects the thoughts, feelings and behaviour that are conscious.

Many psychotherapies have developed since Freud was writing: some are based on his ideas and some are in reaction against them. Psychoanalysis is the most intensive form of the work that has developed from Freud's ideas, usually involving meeting four or five times per week and placing more emphasis on understanding the patient than on cure. Counselling is another more recent development in which greater emphasis is placed on problems in the present circumstances of the client than is usual in psychotherapy and meetings would typically be once a week or less frequent, and might be for a short period such as a few weeks. There is considerable debate about the distinctions between these areas of the therapeutic field and no one has succeeded so far in fencing them behind definitions other than that different trainings offer a qualification in one or other of these areas: for example, a psychoanalyst is someone whose training says he or she is a psychoanalyst.

Generic psychotherapy. In all psychotherapies there is a therapist or therapists and a client or group of clients. In all psychotherapies there is an attempt to bring about change by applying a particular model of the mind and its functioning. The direction of change that is desired by therapist and by client will be associated with a particular value system. This will need to convey not only that suffering is bad, but also that for some people some kinds of suffering may be worthwhile or even necessary, depending on what form of good is regarded as predominant.

A model of the mind is an essential prerequisite for a discipline to be known as a form of psychotherapy. Generally there will be an academic study of the rationale for a particular way of understanding mental functioning. This will lead to technique and the consequences that follow clinically. Models of the mind used in psychotherapy are generally not well established by quantitative research, although this area of research has increased greatly in recent years. Traditionally, psychotherapy has been based on the qualitative studies of individuals and this has been tested clinically in terms of establishing what is helpful pragmatically in working to understand and relieve mental suffering.

Specific models of psychotherapy. These models have tended to fall into three broad categories of the dynamic, the cognitive/behavioural and the humanistic. Dynamic models are usually based on psychoanalytic theory and emphasize the way in which we can recognize distinct parts of the self which may co-operate or conflict with one another. In this model the therapist will seek to help the client to identify and as far as possible resolve conflicts that are damaging. Psychoanalytic theory and technique emphasize the paradoxical importance of the unconscious. We are always haunted by the 'it' which lurks beneath the conscious surface of the rational mind. On the one hand, by its very nature, the 'it' is not consciously known; on the other hand, as more of the unconscious becomes conscious, so a person has more of themselves available and is stronger and able to live more fully.

Cognitive behavioural models emphasize counter-productive thought patterns or schemas and help clients to modify their behaviour by identifying self-limiting thought patterns. The humanistic therapies emphasize the potential wholeness of the self and the human being that could develop if he or she were unlimited by the constraints that have been imposed by upbringing, culture, society and developmental deficits. Personal experience is the highest authority. These therapies seek to enable the client to function with genuineness and congruence of feeling and thought.

Other psychotherapies emphasize particular techniques, as for example hypno-psychotherapy where hypnosis may be used as an adjunct to the technique of a psychotherapist. Hypnosis used by a practitioner who is not a psychotherapist would not be considered to be a psychotherapy.

Values and ethics. As psychotherapy is a powerful tool with the potential to do good, it also has the potential to do harm, and practitioners need strong and well-enforced codes of ethics and practice. So far, in 2001, there is in the UK no statutory regulation of psychotherapy although several of the existing regulatory bodies are working towards statutory regulation and would welcome it. Currently there are three main bodies registering practitioners in the UK: The United Kingdom Council for Psychotherapy is the largest and most inclusive. The British Confederation for Psychotherapy registers only some psycho-analytic psychotherapists and the British Association for Counselling and Psychotherapy so far registers only counsellors. This situation is fluid but members of the public seeking psychotherapy are advised to find practitioners who are accountable to a relevant professional body. This advice is also relevant in the US. [*Lesley Murdin*]

PSYCHOTHERAPY, PASTORAL
See: PASTORAL PSYCHOTHERAPY

Q

QUESTIONNAIRE
A self-report instrument used for gathering information.

Two main types of questions are employed in questionnaires for data gathering: open-ended and closed. The open-ended question invites respondents to write in their own discursive answers. The problems with this method are that many external constraints influence the amount different people will write (e.g. how much time they have available and how good they are at writing). The investigator may also experience difficulties in interpreting and categorizing what has been written. The closed question invites respondents to choose between alternative answers, to tick boxes or to assess intensity of agreement or feeling on precoded rating scales. The problems with this method are that some respondents may feel constrained by the limited opportunities for response; that only a limited amount of information is derived from each question; and that the investigator must invest a great deal of time in designing and piloting each individual question in order to ensure that it is understood consistently and unambiguously by different respondents.

Closed or precoded questions may come in a number of forms. Six frequently employed types are: forced choice, multiple choice, dichotomous, Likert, rating scales, and semantic differential. Forced choice questions make the respondent choose between options: 'Would you rather: (1) stay in and read a book; or (2) go out to a party?' Multiple choice questions invite the respondent to choose one or more options from a list: 'Which of the following newspapers do you read? (1) *The Times*; (2) *Express*; (3) *Telegraph*, etc.' Dichotomous scoring asks respondents to choose between the answers Yes and No: 'Are you a worrier: Yes or No?' Likert scoring invites respondents to indicate their level of agreement with statements, usually on a five-point scale of: agree strongly (AS), agree (A), not certain (NC), disagree (D) and disagree strongly (DS): 'I think church services are boring' – AS A NC D DS. Rating scales invite respondents to assess frequency or intensity according to a predetermined list of qualifiers: 'How often do you attend church?' (1) never; (2) occasionally; (3) at least once a month; (4) at least once a week. The semantic differential invites respondents to assess their response to key ideas or concepts within a calibrated space anchored by contrasting descriptions: the following rating grids might be proposed to assess responses to a church service:

traditional	1 2 3 4 5 6 7	modern
lively	1 2 3 4 5 6 7	dull
high church	1 2 3 4 5 6 7	low church
too long	1 2 3 4 5 6 7	too short

Good questionnaires are often developed by interviewing individuals who belong to the group to whom the instrument will be sent in order to listen to the way in which they express themselves (designing a questionnaire for 11-year-olds should begin by talking with 11-year-olds); by pilot testing the instrument; and by making modifications in light of the pilot test. Pilot testing will pay particular attention to the language used (Can everyone understand it?), to the sensitivity of the issues raised (Do many people object to answering certain questions?), to the time taken to complete (Do many people stop before the end?), to the design, layout and typography (Do many people experience difficulty reading it?).

Questionnaires should to be tested against ethical considerations. Respondents need to be properly informed about the purposes of the questionnaire. The right not to participate needs to be respected. Matters of confidentiality and anonymity need to be properly faced. If personal data is stored on a computer alongside respondents' names the requirements of the Data Protection Act must be observed (Oppenheim, 1992). [*Leslie Francis*]

R

RACE
1. A group of people of common ancestry, history or geographical origin.
2. The fact of belonging to such a group.
All people are descended from a common ancestor, and have a high level of genetic similarity with one another while being distinct from other species. Faith traditions sometimes emphasize what people throughout the world have in common so that, say, Christians may believe that everyone is a beloved child of the same heavenly Father. So humankind may be referred to as the 'human race'.

However, physical differences have arisen in response to climatic and other conditions. For instance, people originating from hot countries often have more melanin in their skin, making them darker and less likely to suffer sunburn. Groups of communities originating broadly from the same geographical region, and with similar physical characteristics, have sometimes been described as belonging to a particular race. However, history is full of instances of migration, intermarriage and change within and exchange across 'racial' communities. Political and religious alliances and divisions have led communities to merge or split to become different ethnic groups. Most people cannot easily be described as belonging to a biologically and culturally distinctive 'race', unchanged for generations.

Sometimes ethnic communities in conflict, for instance over land, have ascribed negative features to their neighbours, from moral weakness to physical inferiority. Past political and military leaders have sometimes passed into legend as heroic and pious champions of their 'race'. This has sometimes fuelled unpleasant racial prejudice and ethnic nationalism. Occasionally, particular communities within a nation or empire have been allocated an inferior status and restricted to certain occupations, and sometimes they and their descendants have been forbidden to mix socially and intermarry with other communities (for instance apartheid, abolished in the late twentieth century in South Africa, and the caste system in parts of South Asia).

During the last millennium, several European nations – made up of different ethnic communities within a geographical area – conquered and colonized much of the world. A large number of African people became slaves and were deported to the Americas as a source of cheap labour, while many of the original inhabitants there and in Australasia died through deliberate design or damage to their environment. While small élites within the colonies were encouraged to imitate the culture of their rulers, given some privileges and used to help manage the administration and economy, most people found themselves relatively powerless, their own traditions undervalued. Sometimes evidence of past achievements was looted, destroyed or allowed to fall into disrepair. The idea that humankind was made up of several races, with white 'Caucasian' people as the most advanced and African people at the lowest level, became widespread. This world-view was used to account for imbalances in power, wealth and status in the world on the basis of racial characteristics.

Attempts were made to justify even the worst cruelties, since those who suffered were supposedly less sensitive to hardship and on balance benefited from having their lives controlled by people who were more capable and virtuous, though others believed that white ruling-class men had a duty to treat their inferiors humanely. In some instances, even white people who were regarded as 'imperfect' specimens of the 'master race' (for example physically and mentally disabled people in Nazi Germany) were sterilized or sometimes killed.

Not surprisingly, some people rejected the notion of a hierarchy of races and, as anti-imperialist and anti-racist movements gained ground, the concept was increasingly discredited. However, even when most countries had won formal independence, they largely remained economically dependent on the West, which appeared more culturally and economically advanced. Minorities of African, Asian and Latin American descent, and the descendants of those of the original peoples of Australasia and North America who survived, were largely in jobs with low pay or poor working conditions or unemployed, and many – though not all – of these ethnic communities tended to have fewer educational opportunities and worse health on average than their white neighbours. To racists, the disadvantage faced by these ethnic communities was evidence that they were inferior, not that society was unjust. Partly in reaction against this, some members of underprivileged communities and nations claimed that they were racially superior and that, for instance, the cruelty of the slave trade showed that European people were innately inhumane.

The ideology that some people are fundamentally different from, and inferior to, others on grounds of race is still widespread, so that even people opposed to it can occasionally make racist assumptions. Sometimes claims that race is irrelevant can be used to gloss over ongoing differences in the way that people are treated (and regard themselves) because of their 'race'. Nevertheless, in many parts of the world there is greater awareness than in the past of what people have in common, and the importance of racial justice.

Though the early Church was a community made up of people of different nations and cultures, for whom 'there is no longer Greek and Jew, circumcised and uncircumcised, barbarian, Scythian, slave and free: but Christ is all and in all' (Col. 3.11), it later often aligned itself with the socially powerful who sought to justify their quest for dominance by using the concept of race. However, Christians have also sometimes been at the forefront of opposing racism.

While it is healthy for people to feel positive about their own culture and heritage, hostility or contempt for others or self on the grounds of 'race' can be psychologically and spiritually damaging to individuals and relationships. Dealing constructively with issues of race is likely to be a major challenge for humankind in the twenty-first century. [*Savitri Hensman*]

RACE RELATIONS
The relationships between groups defined by race or ethnicity or colour.
The term is broad and vague and means different things in different countries. As definitions of 'race' vary, so do concepts of 'race relations'. In South Africa in the early twentieth century, it was used for relations between British and Boer. Yet one might speak of race relations between Hutu and Tutsi in Rwanda, although the two black groups are physically hardly differentiated. But most commonly it has been used of the relationship between white and non-white. It generally deals with the relationship between a dominant group and one or more subordinate ones.

It is usual for the dominant group, e.g. in the UK and the USA, to speak of 'race relations' while the subordinate group speaks more of anti-racism or the need for equality or justice. Nobody demonstrates in the streets for 'good race relations'. In the USA, the struggle for racial equality in the 1960s was in terms of civil rights within an existing political framework, while advocates of Black Power, like Stokely Carmichael, stressed the need for new economic relationships rather than use of an existing political process.

Calls for 'good race relations' may mean a harmonious situation unmarred by violence, yet remaining in many respects unequal, or may look to the complete abolition of all forms of unjust racial discrimination. Because of the essential vagueness of the notion, it is always difficult to answer questions like 'Are race relations improving in your country?' Philip Mason's study (1970) remains a helpful guide to the great complexity of the situations and attitudes involved, dealing with dozens of countries around the world. The term 'community relations' came into vogue in the 1970s to describe a broadening of the race relations concept, the involvement of whole communities in improving their internal relationships.

A major survey of race relations in the UK (Rose, 1969) was conducted by the Institute of Race Relations, an unofficial body. A series of Race Relations Acts in 1965, 1968 and 1976 outlawed unjust racial discrimination and eventually required the promotion of 'equality of opportunity and good relations between persons of different racial groups generally'. The 1976 Act is still in force.

The term 'race relations' is not now used much in the USA because of the diversity of ethnic groups there claiming special attention and their rivalry with each other. What was seen as a black–white issue up to the 1970s is now far more complex. Pastoral work needs to distinguish between different meanings given to 'race relations'. *[Ann Dummett]*

RACISM
1. A doctrine which classified human beings according to their descent.
2. A set of practices which unjustly treats racial or ethnic groups differently.
3. Expressions of racial hatred or contempt.
Racism is difficult to define with precision, partly because it is irrational. The brief definitions above may be expanded. (1) Descent may be from the race or nation

people are deemed to belong to. The doctrine believes a person's character, intelligence, culture and/or other non-physical attributes are determined by that race or nationality. (2) The most powerful group in a society determines these practices, which may include segregation, denial of opportunities, social stigmatizing or systematic unfair discrimination in any area of policy. (3) These expressions may be in speech or writing, violence of one group against another, and in extreme cases genocide.

Definitions of 'race' vary widely between countries and cultures and also over time. Anti-Semitism is one form of racism; so is hostility between ethnic groups which differ little from each other physically but between whom hatred has led to horrific massacres (e.g. in Bosnia, Kosovo and Rwanda in the 1990s). Racism may be interwoven with cultural prejudices, religious hostilities or economic factors. It has been a major political issue in the world in the twentieth century.

Institutional racism is of two kinds. An institution may be racist without saying so openly if it is designed to exclude unwanted groups in practice. Or it may discriminate unintentionally if it was set up in such a way that unwanted groups will in fact be excluded or treated unequally. In either case, individuals working for such an institution need not themselves be racist but the institution will still need to review its practices to make them fair. A 'racist society' need not be composed of individuals who are all racists. It is one where racial discrimination is institutionalized.

Christians have often been guilty of racist behaviour. But racism is contrary to Christianity because it is unjust. It denies the personal dignity of the individual, the natural right to be respected as a human being and the unity of human society in the sight of God. People may 'vary widely in knowledge, virtue, intelligence and wealth, but that is no valid argument in favour of a system whereby those who are in a position of authority impose their will arbitrarily on others'; rather, they have a greater responsibility to help others (Pope John XXIII, 1963).

An individual's racist beliefs and actions may often seem trivial or unimportant, but they can still produce great damage for others, ranging from refusal of a job or a place to live to social isolation or wounding remarks. Pastoral care needs to take account of the cumulative effects of racist words and behaviour on individual victims. It should also understand the roots of an individual's racism and help the individual to understand the great harm it can do. Some people are racist less from ill-will than from muddled thinking and an over-ready acceptance of widespread assumptions. [*Ann Dummett*]

RAPE
An act of violence in which sexual penetration is used to overpower someone.
Rape occurs when there is no consent to sexual contact, or inauthentic consent because the person raped is a child or the perpetrator is in a position of authority (for example, the father, teacher or minister of the person who is raped). Date rapes occur when one person withdraws consent to sexual intimacy and then is forced to have intercourse.

It is difficult to determine how frequently rape occurs (especially among boys), because it often goes unreported. Random surveys in the USA have indicated that one out of three women will be raped within their lifetime, and one out of six boys will be sexually assaulted before the age of eighteen. In both the UK and the USA it is reported that the number of rapes continues to rise. But statistics about the extent of crime are based on police records which necessarily include only reported crimes. There is a higher incidence of non-reporting in the case of rape than in any other crime. Since rape is not primarily about sexual desire but about someone exercising complete power over another person, survivors often experience rape as life-threatening (Poling, 1991). Afterwards, they may alternate between feeling numb and re-experiencing being raped in nightmares and flashbacks (vivid and intrusive memories), especially in the six to eight weeks immediately after the assault. This alternation is called post-traumatic stress. It increases when aspects of the rape are especially disturbing (for example, when perpetrators are sadistic). Survivors with histories of violent experiences that have not been processed may also experience more intense post-traumatic stress (Herman, 1992).

Survivors need support and often crisis intervention in order to process the fear, anger and shame that surface when they re-experience the violence of rape. They also need support during times when they feel numb and unable to trust others and enjoy aspects of their lives.

Religious traditions can be used either to enhance or to destroy the life of survivors and their communities of faith. When they maintain silence about sexual violence, these traditions are being used destructively. With such silence religious leaders are experienced as protecting perpetrators and blaming survivors. Religious meanings given to women's sexuality (e.g. that women are temptresses) and homosexuality (e.g. that men who sexually assault boys are motivated by homosexual desire) can damage or even destroy survivors' religious faith, their relationship with God, and their communities of faith (Doehring, 1993). For religious traditions to be life-giving, rape must be named as a sin, and justice must be enacted by making perpetrators fully responsible for their acts of violence. In addition, the meanings given to sexuality, and particularly women's sexuality and male and female homosexuality, must help survivors reclaim and reconstruct a life-giving relationship with God, and a trust in the goodness of others and the goodness of their own sexuality (Cooper-White, 1995). [*Carrie Doehring*]

RAPPORT
Professional intimacy between a pastor or counsellor and a client.
Rapport is a wide-ranging word which refers to the privileged relationship that may develop between two people who share a high level of common interest, thought and feeling. It is sometimes claimed that rapport can be deliberately generated. This is true of another use of the term – to refer to the connection between a hypnotist and his or her subject. But in most circumstances rapport emerges as a working relationship develops. The idea of rapport, however, stresses the professional aspect of this relationship and is therefore a helpful concept in resisting confusion of roles and person.

RATIONAL EMOTIVE THERAPY
A system of therapy built on the belief that one's interpretations of, and beliefs about, events greatly influence one's feelings and behaviours.
Rational emotive therapy (RET) was developed by Albert Ellis (1975), beginning in the late 1950s. He found that, as people encountered events in the world, they would often become distressed. Consequently, they often blamed their feelings on that event. These

activating events he labelled 'A' in the RET model. The consequences – both feelings and behaviours – he labelled 'C'. Ellis proposed a step between the A and C in causality. He labelled this step 'B' for the belief about the activating event. Traditionally, people had thought that A caused C. Ellis suggested that an activating event (A) occurs. People then have thoughts and beliefs (B) about that event, which bring about certain consequences (C).

The beliefs that people have about events may be either rational or irrational. Rational beliefs (rBs) are those which further happiness and well-being. Irrational beliefs (iBs) are those which bring pain or distress. These iBs tend to revolve around making demands on ourselves, others or the world. People think things or people must act in certain ways for life to be worth living. To bring about better consequences (feelings/behaviours), people vigorously dispute their irrational beliefs. They challenge their validity and replace them with more rational beliefs. This leads to new emotional and behavioural consequences.

Basic principles for RET include: people's cognitions are a primary cause of their feelings; people are limited or fallible; there is no valid way to assess the worth of people, only their specific behaviours; beyond survival needs, there are no pure 'musts' or 'needs' for people; people are best served functioning as long-range hedonists. A case may be made that all of these principles are appropriate for pastoral care and counselling (West, 1992).

RET can be a brief counselling style, which would be effective for pastors who do not have limitless time to spend in pastoral counselling. Furthermore, it is helpful in challenging the misconceptions that misused or mislearned religious beliefs may have fostered in people's lives.

RET is not free of controversy in religious circles. Notably, Ellis has been vocal in his attacks on religious belief. Because of this, some people of faith have chosen to say that none of his theory is usable. While Ellis' complaints about religion have generally tended towards religiosity rather than faith itself, tension continues. Other criticisms include the idea that there is no room for belief in the unseen (or non-intellectual) in this therapy and that it is self-centred and hedonistic. Further, to practise RET requires a certain intellectual level in the person receiving the therapy. [Gordon West]

RATIONALIZATION
Justifying one's behaviour by reasoning after the event.

Psychologically people rationalize acts, and sometimes feelings, that, after the event, they wish to discount. To do this they shift an account of their motivation from one level of consciousness to another. Indeed rationalization is often merely a defence mechanism against accusing oneself and against the accompanying guilt. In management studies it can also describe the so-called scientific restructuring of an industry or series of companies.

REALITY PRINCIPLE
One of the two principles that according to Freud govern mental activity.

The other principle is the 'pleasure principle'. The reality principle refers to the constraints that are imposed by physical and social contexts on attempts to gratify the pleasure principle. As a result people revert to indirect attempts to satisfy the pleasure principle by making psychological detours or postponing attainment of its goal, depending on the conditions that the outside world imposes.

REASSURANCE
The provision of comfort and encouragement through consolation, compassion, and/or reminders of past experiences which lead to the restoration of faith and stability.

Pastoral studies, in the classical religious traditions, has defined its forms in four different ways: healing, sustaining, guiding and reconciling. Each of these expressions intends the restoration of a hurting person, or persons, to some improved level of acceptance and functioning within life's circumstances. Goals for the restoration process may include learning new skills, new ways of understanding, renewed commitments, renewed health, and/or the building of new relationships. Virtually all approaches, at some point, assume that the helper must offer reassurance along the way.

The concept of reassurance assumes several things about human nature and the person being helped: (1) there has been a time of confidence, assurance and more stability in the person's past; (2) when suffering, one is likely to forget resources and past experiences of consolation and recovery; (3) genuinely caring relationships increase the likelihood of remembering and recovering former sources of comfort; (4) genuinely caring relationships foster openness to new sources for comfort and recovery. In pastoral studies, reassurance is most commonly discussed in relation to grief and loss. In the Judaeo-Christian tradition, the classic model for grief and recovery has been identified in the Psalms of Lament. In most of those psalms (e.g. 22, 64 and 102), there is a predictable movement. The sufferer moves from awareness and recitation of the suffering, or complaint, to apparent memory of God's faithfulness in the past. Throughout the movement, there is an implicit assumption that the recitation is being heard. The sufferer is not alone. The result is an ending of the psalm in a spirit of praise. In much the same way, modern descriptions of normal grief and recovery include similar experiences. The role of reassurance is critical in the overall process of recovery and/or stabilization. Reassurance takes the form of reminding the person(s) that resources, old and new, are present and available in the midst of the pain. Hope is encouraged, along with the belief that a return to stability and confidence is possible.

It is also important to note times that reassurance may be out of place. For example, it is sometimes used in an effort to silence a person who is giving expression to the pain of loss. When used to silence, reassurance may indeed prolong and even damage the recovery process. Reassurance may also be used prematurely, not in an effort to silence, but in a genuine desire to comfort. Nonetheless, premature reassurance lacks the perception that there is not yet a 'readiness' to be comforted. The sufferer is not likely to be comforted in the absence of full realization and acknowledgement of the nature and extent of the loss.
[William Arnold]

RECONCILIATION
Making harmony after estrangement.
There is a tendency in pastoral work to think of reconciliation as being about making whole, and bringing together people or parties who are irreconciled. That may be true, but for Christians the point about reconciliation is not what it involves, but how it happens: 'While we were still sinners, God reconciled us to himself' (Rom. 5.12). In Christian theology reconciliation means atonement through the death and resurrection of Jesus Christ.

Reconciliation is about human oneness in God, in a common creator, sustainer, redeemer. It may not always be possible to appreciate or construct this oneness in human terms. It is a gift – to be received and owned, not made and measured by human endeavour. Similarly, reconciliation for Christians is rooted in the crucifixion and resurrection of Christ: it is made manifest in human living by self-giving, sacrifice, going beyond 'justice' for the sake of inviting others into that deeper oneness in which all creatures are made. Its energy is love. Thus reconciliation does not simply reside in those popular activities of the late twentieth century, arbitration and advocacy. Such activities need to be related to the Christ-like self-giving and deeper sense of oneness that is at the heart of the Christian gospel. The aim is wholeness that can be tasted in this life, but failure to realize tangible signs does not undermine the achievements of attempts at reconciliation. The basis is prayer: (1) exploration of oneness with God and with others; (2) willingness to receive this gift; (3) a desire to be forgiven and to forgive; (4) openness to trusting without seeing. Such a spirituality is the seed of the realization of any reconciliation.

In the Christian tradition reconciliation is essentially with God, from the position of estrangement in which humanity finds itself. However, reconciliation with God necessarily includes reconciliation with others, and with the self. The paradigms are the Exodus and the Eucharist, wherein the love of God takes the initiative in providing a means of owning estrangement and accepting a new union with God and, in God, with each other. Reconciliation in human situations needs to be understood within this defining context. The process involves repentance, remembering the definitive story of reconciling salvation, and in the act of remembering, receiving new life which offers to enflesh oneness with God and with others. More recently in history there has been an emphasis on being reconciled with one's true self as integral to this process. The danger for pastoral practice in a Western culture so dominated by therapeutic practice is that this latter aim (being reconciled with one's true self) can be exalted at the expense of the prior need for a greater oneness with God and with creation.

Although the cost is paid by God's defining act (in the death and resurrection of Jesus), the Christian tradition teaches that accepting this gift of new life will embrace recipients in sharing the way of the cross in this world – being ready to play a particular role in the difficult work of confronting human estrangement with the possibility of atonement. Often the attractions of selfishness and the small-scale provide a powerful and resistant force not only in those who reject the gospel of oneness in God, but also as a continuing feature in the lives of all who seek to respond more positively. In this sense, although reconciliation as atonement in Christ is a once-and-for-all action, it needs constantly to be received and appropriated. This truth gives pastoral practice a particular realism about illusions of progress in the search for reconciliation, and alerts practitioners to the fact of a continuing struggle in this life to own the tendency and temptation to estrangement and the need to receive the gift of oneness. Human attempts to express the gift are important signs of the potential for reconciliation that summons all creatures, but such endeavours need to recognize their dependence upon God's grace and a continuing discipline of acknowledging failings, desiring wholeness and rooting these things in the new covenant in Jesus Christ. Reconciliation can never be a purely pastoral matter: it must be pursued within a theological and liturgical context. The tendency to separate these things has been damaging throughout Christian history to both individuals and churches. This explains why those who exercise ministry in and on behalf of Christian churches need careful training and linking to appropriate systems of apostolic oversight. *[Alastair Redfern]*

REDEMPTION
The deliverance of human beings, and ultimately of all creation, from all forms of bondage.
Often used as a synonym for salvation to speak of the whole work of God in fulfilling the purposes of creation, redemption has important roots in the ancient world which give it a more precise meaning. In the Hebrew Bible it is often used to speak of God's action in freeing Israel from slavery in Egypt. But it also refers to the ancient social institution of the kinsman who avenges murder, buys a relative out of slavery or releases alienated property. In the Greek world the word was used more generally to refer to buying individual slaves out of bondage. Freedom is the goal of redemption in both Testaments (Exod. 3.8; Gal. 5.1).

Christ delivers us from bondage to sin, death and the law (Rom. 5.12; Gal. 3.13), but we also hear of redemption from 'futile ways' (1 Pet. 1.18).

For the early Church the metaphor of redemption was a key to understanding Christ's work. It was often described in vivid mythological language in terms of the deception of the devil. Anselm criticized this idea on the ground that the devil had no rights, but the imagery continued to be used through the Middle Ages and appealed to Luther. After a long period when it receded into the background, Gustav Aulén sought to rehabilitate it, describing it as 'the classic theory' (Aulén, 1931).

The rehabilitation of a theology of redemption is the fruit both of growing sociological and psychological understanding and of reflection on various forms of mass alienation in the twentieth century. Walter Wink has explored the language of 'the Powers' in a trilogy (Wink, 1992). Developing the hints of earlier theologians he argues that this language refers to the determining forces of physical, psychic and social existence. The Powers are the interiority of earthly institutions, structures and systems such as capitalism, militarism or patriarchy, which represent an idolatrous focus of human systems of domination. The sin from which we need to be delivered is not just personal but takes on structural form because it is, in a classic formulation, 'in each the work of all, and in all the work of each'. The Powers operate according to a set of 'delusional assumptions', the 'futile ways' of 1 Pet., according to which only violence, control, strength and possessions can ward off chaos. Christ redeems us by exposing these assumptions for what they are. The Powers are 'unmasked', above all on the cross, where their reality is made plain. He calls into being a movement based on a domination-free order, committed to the discipline of forgiveness and non-violence. The aim of this movement is not just the redemption of individuals but of the Powers as well, for human beings need to live within structures. Thus the work of God within history moves towards their transformation. In this process redemption means being liberated from the oppression of the Powers, being forgiven for one's complicity, and being involved in liberating the Powers from their idolatry.

The contribution of depth psychology to our understanding of redemption is illustrated by Wink's use of Jungian analysis to understand what is involved in learning to love our enemies. Hatred, this analysis argues, feeds on the shadow in ourselves. We condemn most vehemently what we most dislike in ourselves. Redemption is to learn to 'see the log in our own eye', accepting and dealing with that before dealing with the splinter in our neighbour's eye. A similar argument, independently proposed by the French cultural anthropologist René Girard, has argued that Christ's mission was to reveal the secret of violence, which consists in the scapegoat mechanism (Girard, 1987).

Paul speaks of redemption not only from sin and death but from the law. The background of this assertion was a situation where fellowship was denied and community destroyed by insistence on the strict observance of the kosher laws. 'Law' thus stands for all cultural codes which justify and reinforce apartheid of any kind; whether between man and women, different races, or classes (Gal. 3.28). To be redeemed from the law means to understand that all cultural codes are made to serve humanization, not the reverse (Mark 2.27).

For Paul the Powers were cosmic forces, and it was not just human society but the whole of creation which was 'in bondage' to 'corruption' – meaninglessness and ultimate decay. The resurrection of Christ allows us to hope that the whole creation will ultimately be 'freed' and realize its true destiny of glorifying God without the shadow of death hanging over it (Rom. 8.18–25). We are returned to the Patristic images of 'Christ the Victor' and the reality of being 'saved by hope', the promise of redemption, or deliverance from all that destroys and diminishes which is the ultimate promise of the gospel. [*Timothy Gorringe*]

REFERRAL
The introduction by a pastor or therapist of a client or patient to another helping professional.
Pastors may be among the first to learn of people's crises or distress. They are likely, therefore, to be involved in referral to another professional person. In so doing they are not sending people away. Rather they are engaged in a 'ministry of introduction', as Wayne Oates called it. Other professionals may on occasion similarly pass a client on to another therapist with special skills. In both cases the work is an alliance in care.

Pastoral referral has developed in direct proportion to increased professionalization and specialization among the helping professions that has, in turn, led to refinement in professional role definition and sensitivity to role conflict. In an earlier time a pastor might have no question about being intensely involved in the pastoral care of a lay leader of the congregation. Today, however, the pastor will more likely ask how a role in intensive pastoral care might conflict with the leadership roles of the two parties. Increased professionalization of the minister's role has led to a division of labour in the helping process in which pastors provide co-ordination and support for persons in crisis and introduce them to one or more other professionals.

Recent developments in biblical studies (Crossan, 1994) and in psychotherapy (Monk, 1997) provide useful theological guidance on referral. Studies of Jesus that stress his challenge to domination systems (Wink, 1992) raise the pastor's awareness of practices among the helping professions that may tend to pathologize individuals, diminish their sense of agency, and foster a debilitating dependency. Jesus' attitude towards the religious institutions of his day revealed both his appreciation for their power to help and for their power to do harm by putting people into categories that diminished and marginalized them. A theological reference point in making referrals, therefore, is the agency of persons being referred. *Agency* is 'the extent to which individuals can act for themselves and speak on their own behalf', and it is often established in the face of powerful social forces that work against that agency (Monk, 1997).

Referrals that enhance parishioners' agency, preserve their relationship to the pastor, and build a bridge to the new relationship depend on pastors' attention to these considerations. (1) Know and maintain an ongoing relationship with people to whom you make referrals. (2) Educate parishioners about the different roles of pastor and the person being referred to. (3) Help parishioners clarify their expectations in seeking help. (4) Discuss the probable cost of help from the person to whom you are referring. (5) Protect parishioners' confidentiality by getting specific permission to share or receive information about them. (6) Support parishioners' sense of agency whenever possible by keeping the initiative for getting help with them. Make referrals to persons you know support and nurture the agency of their clients. [Richard L. Hester]

REFUGEES
People fleeing from their homeland and needing to find a place of refuge where they will be safe.

There has probably never been a time in world history when no one has been driven from their native community and forced to seek refuge elsewhere. Some historians called the twentieth century the age of total war. Partly for that reason it was also the age of the refugee. The reasons for the persecution of individuals and significant minorities are many and complex: political, religious, racial, ethnic, tribal, ideological, and often a combination. Jews have seldom felt safe in Christian Europe. This has resulted in a Jewish presence throughout the world. In 1685 the statute of religious toleration was revoked in France; the Huguenots fled to neighbouring countries. Many early white settlers in North America had fled from Europe because of the widespread intolerance of religious nonconformity. The word refugee has not been used to describe economic migrants, though they have frequently fled from intolerable conditions. There are, for instance, more people of Irish origin outside Ireland than at home. This is largely the product of extreme poverty and hunger. Economic migration is likely to remain a major cause of world population movements.

Large populations are forced by civil strife to leave their homes without crossing a national frontier. Generally described as 'displaced persons', these are not technically refugees. But they face similar problems and need comparable help. The term 'ethnic cleansing' describes the attempt to eliminate a particular group of people from a region or nation. This may lead to killing on a large scale and invariably to the flight of the survivors. Refugees who have fled to another country are today described as 'asylum-seekers'. Granting asylum is a matter of acute political sensitivity. The ancient privilege, by which places of worship offered sanctuary to those fleeing from persecution, has recently been revived. In Europe and the USA refugees who are threatened with expulsion are on moral grounds being offered sanctuary by churches and religious institutions. This, while not recognized in law, is often accorded some measure of official respect, enabling particular cases to be reconsidered.

The last years of the twentieth century saw wave after wave of refugees and displaced persons, and this is not likely to diminish. In 1920 the League of Nations appointed Fridtjof Nansen as the first international commissioner for refugees. In the inter-war years Jews were fleeing Nazi rule in Central Europe. Many eventually perished because they could not find asylum. In Europe alone German invasions made at least 12 million people homeless. In the Far East Japanese aggression had even more devastating consequences. Allied agreements at Potsdam after the Second World War led to the forcible expulsion of more than 12 million ethnic Germans. The partition of the Indian subcontinent produced a bloody confrontation between Hindus and Muslims and mass migrations. Some 700,000 Palestinians fled after the creation of Israel, and civil wars in many parts of Africa led to a vast, uncounted number of refugees. The break-up of Yugoslavia led to a series of ethnic persecutions in Europe. Six million Afghans fled from their country as a result of the Soviet invasion, and more are likely to do so in response to war and famine.

To aid in refugee settlement, in 1950 the United Nations established the Office of the High Commissioner for Refugees (UNHCR). Other concerned bodies include the Red Cross Societies, Amnesty International and international religious agencies, as well as national bodies. International agreements (most importantly the 1951 United Nations Convention Relating to the Status of Refugees and its 1967 Protocol) commit most nations to accepting those who qualify as genuine refugees. Whereas in Africa and parts of Asia many poor nations are flooded with refugees, the wealthier nations of the USA and Europe are restrictive in their interpretation of international human rights law. Immigration quotas in the USA make it possible to accept limited numbers. This is also true of Australia and Canada. The member states of the European Union, while meeting minimum humanitarian standards, accept only a small proportion of asylum-seekers, leaving many in long-term insecurity and deporting others to their country of origin, occasionally with tragic consequences. In 1997 the UNHCR estimated that there were 12 million refugees in need of resettlement. This figure is likely to be an underestimate.

Social history suggests that in most cases refugee movements have significantly influenced for the good the social and cultural climate of their new homeland. The ordered and ready acceptance by the UK of Asians expelled from Uganda was exceptionally successful. Comparable has been the absorption in Western Europe and the USA of refugees from central and Eastern Europe during the Cold War. Hungarians and later Czechs were readily welcomed as, comparably, were Chilean refugees from the Pinochet regime in Eastern Europe. In these instances generosity combined with political expediency. But the majority of the world's refugees benefit from no such circumstances and depend on the very limited resources of international and national refugee agencies.

The pastoral care of refugees falls into three categories: (1) political; (2) social; (3) personal.

1. *Political.* All concerned persons and social institutions, including churches, national and local, need constantly to monitor refugee policy, both legislation and its day-to-day administration. International obligations, fair and humane treatment, access to competent advice in their own language, housing and subsistence, the grounds and conditions of detention are in a civil society all matters that do not concern professional agencies and carers alone.

2. *Social.* Social groupings and organizations, especially religious ones, can act corporately to meet refugees' needs when these are not met by statutory agencies. This may include providing clothing and furniture and other needs of daily life, language tuition, special help for women, who are often severely isolated, and advice on health care. Children especially can be isolated and their parents helpless. If asylum-seekers are threatened with expulsion and there are good reasons for believing this to be unjust, it may be right – and then require strength and the solidarity of a whole group – to offer sanctuary. This will also require help from sympathetic legal experts.

3. *Personal.* This does not depend on social organization; it is the response of heart and mind to new neighbours in need of friendship. It calls for sensitivity and openness to need, which can be costly and even be rejected or misunderstood by people who may have had

no experience of openness from strangers. Yet more often it is highly rewarding. It is the practice of the art of hospitality. *[Paul Oestreicher]*

REGRESSION
Return from one stage of a process to an earlier one.

The idea of regression is found widely in modern psychology. It describes a reversion (or sometimes retreat) to earlier forms of or moments in a person's development of thought or structure of behaviour. It is, for example, a familiar aspect of dreaming. The regression is often to a state of dependence such as is characteristic of childhood. The term originally tended to be given negative connotation, but it has progressively been seen in a more positive light. It is a normal facet of human behaviour, both in individuals and in groups (Bion, 1961). Pastorally, for example, worship may be thought of as the managed regression of a group. Worshippers are offered the opportunity to regress in a structured way (the liturgy) from their current life demands to their primary relationship with God (Reed, 1978) in order to be able to resume their adult functioning.

REHABILITATION
The rehabilitation of offenders and their restoration to the community.

From Cain, the fratricide, to Jesus, the executed convict, the Bible has had a particular interest in the well-being of criminals. Jesus enjoined his followers to visit those in prison (Matt. 25.38), and on the whole they have followed this injunction.

In modern times Christians – Quakers in particular – have been in the forefront of penal reform and the advocacy of more humane punishments. As early as the eighteenth century both in the UK and in the USA prisoners were visited, prisons were improved, and capital and corporal punishments were condemned as ineffective and immoral (Potter, 1993). Deterrence and retribution were the prime motives for punishment, but it was increasingly thought that punishment should not preclude, but rather promote, rehabilitation. Christians perceived that offenders against human laws were little different from the rest of sinful humanity who offended against divine laws. They should and could be redeemed rather than just eradicated. Monks lived in cells, so should miscreants; Quakers kept silence, so should criminals. Utilitarian philosophy tended towards the same conclusion: criminals were sick but treatable; they were defective machines but could be mended. Thus arose the penitentiary system whereby felons were locked in single cells, secluded from the contamination of their peers, often enjoined to work in silence the more to reflect on their sinful ways and repent. Chaplains – 'technicians of guilt' – worked on the pliant consciences of their charges and tried to induce change. Many felons went mad.

Though the 'silent system' was soon abandoned in England, rehabilitative ideas were not. Attempts were made to remove bad influences and instil virtues. Youngsters were segregated from more hardened adults by being sent for borstal training rather than to prison. Education, physical health and the work ethic were emphasized. Older offenders were given education and employment. Probation officers were appointed to try to assist in rehabilitation on release.

In the USA 'treatment' models were to the fore in the 1960s and 1970s. Felons could be kept from one to ninety-nine years depending on their response to treatment. The more recalcitrant the offender the longer would be his or her stay. In the UK, Grendon, the first psychiatric prison, was built in the 1950s. A doctor was made governor. Group work and individual therapy were provided for sex offenders and the seriously violent.

Making people better has rarely worked; allowing them to return to normality has. One of the greatest bars to rehabilitation is the inability of ex-offenders to find work and regain their position in the community. Pariah status tends to recidivism. In the UK the Rehabilitation of Offenders Act 1974 addressed this problem by treating past convictions as 'spent' after the expiry of a certain number of years (Forrester, 1997).

Rehabilitative ideas, while still strong in Europe, have been discounted to a large extent in the USA and to some extent in the UK, where more purely retributive and punitive policies have been adopted. While rehabilitative attempts have been bedevilled by pseudo-science, inadequate resources, rising crime rates and the whims of politicians, the rehabilitative ideal persists. The maintenance of dignity within prison, the prospect of employment without, and the support of a tolerant community willing to welcome back and assist the rehabilitation of its outcasts are crucial factors in this (Morris and Rothman, 1995). [Harry Potter]

RELATEDNESS
Being influenced as much by our idea of the other as by the reality.
Relatedness is not dynamic in the way relationship is. It is enough that we are aware of the other, a person, a group, an organization, a nation, so that our perception of the world and hence our behaviour is affected. We may expect to see relatedness wherever there is a context in which there is projective identification, the psychological mechanism where individuals and groups may ascribe to others characteristics of themselves which are unwanted and denied.

RELATIONSHIP
To be connected to or with another person, through blood, marriage or affectional ties.
Human beings are born with an innate readiness to seek out and attach themselves to others. From the earliest hours, the infant seeks a state of physical and emotional connectedness with his or her primary care-taker, investing her with immense significance as a provider of both good and bad experience. The nature of the experiences infants receive at the hands of their primary care-takers will profoundly affect their adult life: first, the capacity – or lack of it – to form durable loving relationships in turn; second, the capacity, or lack of it, to develop their own mental (intellectual) capacities fully and productively. Children born to a couple who succeed in staying together within a reasonably good relationship will have a better chance of moving on in adolescence to form good durable relationships of their own, eventually leading to a choice of partner and the birth of a new generation. In the same way, children who are grossly ill treated, or who suffer multiple changes of care-taker, may come as adults to re-enact their own traumatic experiences by doing to other children what was done to them. Rarely, some infants are born with a primary deficit in the capacity to relate to others, a condition known as *autism*.

A capacity for true relationships with friends, partners and children is not easily come by. It involves the recognition of others as separate beings, with minds and motivations of their own. It also involves the capacity to tolerate that knowledge without attempting, consciously or unconsciously, to restrict or unduly influence others' minds, feelings or behaviour in the service of one's own needs or desires. This capacity is achieved only gradually during the course of early development, and can involve young children in painful feelings of loss and rage as they realize their mother does not belong to them alone, or exist solely for their needs. Coming to terms with the fact that the good mother who loves and cuddles them is also the bad mother who leaves them to attend to father, or to their siblings, or even to herself, is an essential part of growing up. It leads to a recognition of ambivalence: that in all significant relationships there are both positive and negative feelings about the other. However, without an eventual recognition and respect for the essential separateness and difference of others there can be no real relationship. Narcissus, who fell in love with his own reflection rather than with another being, was doomed to live and die essentially alone. Real relationships are fundamental to our social, emotional and intellectual well-being and are the fabric of our society. Individuals who have difficulty in establishing lasting, intimate relationships may seek analytic psychotherapy, which addresses these difficulties within the context of a therapeutic relationship on either an individual or a group basis. [Caroline Garland]

RELIGION
A generic term referring to all conceivable religions, formal or informal.
It is virtually impossible to provide a one-sentence definition of 'religion'. Confucianism, for example, is primarily an ethical system, while Islam stresses belief in the One. Finding a definition that manages to embrace both these religions is very difficult. Ninian Smart has suggested that religion is best understood through seven dimensions: the mythological, ethical, social, experiential, ritual, doctrinal, and symbolic. However, the problem here is that the emphasis given to these dimensions varies so much from religion to religion that it is almost distorting. This, coupled with the fact that certain movements (e.g. Marxism) share many of these dimensions yet clearly would not view themselves as a 'religion', makes Smart's seven dimensions problematic. Perhaps the best way forward is to take the route suggested by Byrne and Clarke (1993). These take Wittgenstein's insight that definitions should not

aspire to be all-inclusive, but instead should identify those different strands which link religions in different ways. So there are many threads which make up the religious rope: for some, belief in God is central and this can link some religious traditions together; for others, it is a strong sense of the ethical. No single thread covers all religions, but overlap of some sort is found between all religions.

A sense of the diversity of religious life is crucially important for those interested in pastoral theology. For the Christian Church, the pastoral has in large measure become part of the professional duties of the priest or minister. The Christian bishop is required to be a shepherd to his or her flock and carries a pastoral staff (crook) to symbolize this role. Hospital chaplains are defined in terms of their pastoral responsibility for those sick in hospital. In addition, the Church believes that the chaplain should be trained in psychology and counselling as an essential precondition of this pastoral role.

Although most religions stress co-operation and care, the professionalization of pastoral theology is vary rare outside Christianity. In addition, the 'pastoral' is rarely considered the principal responsibility of a religious leader. Care for each other is still firmly rooted in the family and community. In Islam, an Imam attached to a mosque (not to be confused with the initial twelve leaders of Islam, which are often called the Twelve Imams) derives from the Arabic word meaning 'to head', 'to lead in prayer'. The primary role is therefore prayer leader. The religious duties are central. The role should not involve the pastoral. Even in Judaism, pastoral care is not considered a central role of the rabbi. Originally the title applied to first-century ordained members of the Sanhedrin. It then extended to those who were exceptionally educated and to the 'spiritual head' of large Jewish communities. The primary role was teacher; they were often responsible for the religious instruction of the community. It was only in the twentieth century that a pastoral role arose at all; even now, it is still secondary to the teaching role. In both Islam and Judaism, the 'laity' are largely responsible for the pastoral or, to be more precise, family and friends are the people who should be there in the first instance.

Coupled with this tendency to make the pastoral less important as a duty of a religious leader, we also find a strong suspicion of 'pastoral training'. Training should be located in families; it is in childhood that a person discovers those skills of care, compassion and support. To imagine that people cannot help other people until they have read Freud is viewed as a gross distortion of what the 'pastoral' really should be. It is much more natural and spontaneous.

The other major concern for pastoral theology raised by the fact of different religions is the need for alternative pastoral models. A pastoral model is the framework of assumptions which lead to a certain pastoral approach. Many assumptions central to a Christian pastoral model are not relevant to other religions. For example, talk of 'affirming the self' makes perfect sense in a Christian context, but can seem highly inappropriate in Islam and Hinduism. In addition, different religious traditions require different conventions – for example, gender conventions vary widely and it is very easy to behave inappropriately (Markham, 1996).

The whole area of 'comparative pastoral theology' is relatively neglected. This is a pity, for the interfaith perspective provides an interesting challenge to many assumptions about the significance and role of the pastoral in Christian theology. [Ian Markham]

RELIGIOUS EDUCATION
The teaching of the history and traditions of various religions, of moral and ethical codes, with attention to the spiritual development of pupils.

In most countries religious education is not a part of the school curriculum. However, in the UK it is by law part of the basic curriculum of every maintained (or state) school. It is also included in the curriculum of most independent schools. Religious instruction, as opposed to religious education, was first defined by Thomas Arnold (1795–1842) of Rugby School. He saw that religious instruction included no more than the learning of creeds, catechisms and hymns by rote. Religious instruction seemed concerned with the head, and not with the whole person. Since then religious instruction has also become identified with evangelism and nurture and is seen as the preserve of faith groups.

The 1944 Education Act laid down for the first time that religious instruction was to be taught to all pupils. The act did not specify that the religion was to be Christianity, though this was almost taken for granted. Some safeguards were built in for those who wished to withdraw from the instruction, and the measure allowed for the creation of locally agreed syllabuses for religious instruction. The churches would determine their own syllabuses.

By the 1980s, however, religious education, rather than instruction, was seen as more suitable for a multicultural society. Religious education encouraged pupils to explore different faiths: to gain knowledge about a variety of cultural and religious traditions; and to experience (albeit at second hand) what it was like to be a member of a faith group. Religious education also encouraged pupils to explore their own beliefs and faith systems, and to engage in moral and spiritual development. Pupils were taught to retain an independent perspective on the subject.

The Education Reform Act of 1988 defined its purpose as promoting the 'spiritual, moral, cultural, mental and physical development of pupils at the school and of society' (Section 1, 2a). Religious education was to be a part of the basic curriculum because of its contribution to the development of all pupils and ultimately of society. Behind this undoubtedly lay the belief, prevalent in much folk religion, that religion had to do with social and moral issues rather than doctrinal belief. Perhaps also was the feeling that there may be more to the world than could be discerned by the scientist, and pupils should have experience of that unseen world, which might loosely be called the spiritual.

The question of what it means to be religiously educated has still to be answered. Early syllabuses concentrated on the phenomenological aspects of the subject, before shifting towards the experiential. Issues concerning the time allocated to religious education, the appropriate manner in which to store and handle artefacts, the need for specialist teachers, and the way in which pupils can be assessed continue to surface at different times. [Sharon Swain]

RELIGIOUS EXPERIENCE
Specific or general experience of the numinous, spiritual or divine.
The study of religious experience has received relatively little attention in Christian theology, and could justly lay claim to being a Cinderella subject within pastoral studies. Part of the problem can be traced to the ambiguity and elusiveness of the category itself. It can refer to any number of moments or disposi-

tions: mystical, numinous, born-again, converted, paranormal or transcendental, to name but a few. Furthermore, there are some fundamental philosophical questions behind the identification of significant phenomena that may be initially identified as a 'religious experience'. For example, what is the difference between a religious experience and an experience you give religious significance to? Religious experiences, like 'miracles', are not descriptions of events, but rather interpretations of them, albeit rooted in an immediate historicizing of phenomena. Such an account may be the most valid interpretation, but is clearly still only one point of view among a number of possibilities. The study and discernment of religious experience traverses the lines of ascription and description, which in turn raises necessary questions about the extent to which religious experiences are partially constructed through our social or psychological contexts (Bowker, 1985).

William James is probably the first modern scholar to use the phrase 'religious experience' in a technical sense. However, his *Varieties of Religious Experience* (1902) does not define 'experience' so much as it attempts to classify various modes of religion. In common with other writers in the nineteenth and early twentieth centuries, James was concerned with the 'essence' of religion. For him, the core of religious experience was bound up with intensity, mysticism and states of consciousness. Rudolf Otto (1917) identifies the essence of religion as the experience of the numinous.

Prior to the twentieth century, a number of philosophers had separated 'experience' from 'reality' in their reflections on the nature of religion. From earliest times, Greek philosophers had distinguished rationality from the experiential. Schools of thought that stressed the empirical and experimental were primarily concerned with reflecting on the experiential, whereas other schools stressed logic and reason. From these initial divisions, the history of religious studies can be traced.

A key figure in the theological study of religious experience is Friedrich Schleiermacher, who, like Kant, was nurtured within German Pietism. He was disenchanted with Christianity as he saw it, believing it to have capitulated to dogma, ethics and ecclesiastical polity. Schleiermacher's response to this was *On Religion: Speeches to Its Cultured Despisers*

(1799), in which he argued that the heart of religious faith lies in affections and distinctively honed religious feelings (and therefore not in constructed doctrines), such that religion could be described as 'the feeling of absolute dependence'.

Social science has studied religious experience more systematically since the end of the Second World War, partly with a view to testing theories of secularization. Indices of religious belief have been collated, which have shown that while people may go to church less frequently, they nevertheless perceive that they have had religious or spiritual experiences, and regard these as significant. The Religious Experience Research Unit in Oxford identified a sizeable body of persons who believed that they had encountered 'a presence or a power, whether or not you call it God, which is different from your everyday self' (Hay, 1992). This work has led to other studies that have explored out-of-body experiences, altered states of consciousness, charismatic or ecstatic experience, and parapsychological phenomena, dealing with ghosts, poltergeists, angels or apparent manifestations of evil (e.g. demons or malign spirits).

While contemporary social scientists would, by and large, be more cautious about constructing reductive accounts of religious experience, there are nevertheless a number of consistent factors that have been identified as significant in the formation of religious experience, which may partially account for subsequent behavioural patterns. For example, psychological accounts of religious experience examine contexts alongside specific forms of facilitation. Meditation may be enhanced by drug use or by sensory deprivation: altered states of consciousness can be induced. Sociological accounts may explore the extent to which an agreed 'grammar of assent' in worship or teaching actually preconstructs the subsequent religious experience of adherents. Anthropological studies may stress ritual, boundaries and other constructions of reality that shape and delimit the horizons of religious imagination in individuals or groups.

Whether or not religious experience is constructed or revealed, it is often nonetheless completely real to the person or group who claims it. In pastoral studies, therefore, it is important that religious experiences, when they are claimed, especially if they are ecstatic, exotic or apparently disturbing, are neither deconstructed through reductionism nor, equally, read literally and taken at face value. There are no 'pure' religious experiences – everything that comes from God is mediated through something temporal and tainted. Religious experiences need to be treated with the utmost seriousness, as they will often be utterly foundational for the individuals or groups claiming them. However, in treating the experiential with due respect, it should not be forgotten that experience should be both tested and discerned. [Martyn Percy]

RELIGIOUS LIFE
Particular way of living out the baptismal vows by the single-minded devotion of oneself to the worship and service of God through specific additional vows.
These solemn promises to God traditionally include the adoption of a way of life that is simple, celibate and obedient to a rule that is specific to an individual or a particular religious community.

There is wide diversity of ways of living the religious life. Among the earliest practitioners was St Antony (c. 251–356) who towards the end of the third century gave away all his possessions and retired to live as a solitary ascetic at Pispir in the Egyptian desert. In 305 he came out of solitude to organize his followers, who had fled from the big cities they considered to be full of corruption, into a community of hermits. In the desert, living alone, but in association with other ascetics, these devotees of God witnessed the primacy of God in their lives through their alternative and often startling lifestyles. Every founder of a religious community or congregation since the fourth century has used Antony's original example as a foundation upon which to build diverse ways of living the religious life. The Master, author of an ascetic rule in the fourth century, St Basil (330–379 CE), St Benedict (480–550) and St Augustine (354–430), or his immediate followers, all produced their own styles of religious life which their disciples followed strictly with varying degrees of success.

Living in community has been the most usual way of living the religious life since the time of St Benedict. This offers its adherents a common rule of life and a degree of companionship and support that is helpful to those adopting a difficult way of life that is similar to, but different from, the traditional family life of married people. In recent times religious communities have developed in which married people and celibates live together under a common rule of life. The benefits of this arrangement are offset by the difficulties, but small communities of this kind are appearing and disappearing all the time.

The solitary form of religious life is gaining ground, either in its traditional form where life-professed 'religious' live apart from their cenobite communities, but linked through prayer with them, or where people decide to live alone a life of prayer in vows of religion without any prior formal religious training. The vows of these hermits, anchorites and anchoresses are often held by their local bishop.

Members of all other faiths may also adopt similar ways of life, either for a time, or in perpetuity. They have much in common with Christian 'religious', and denominational and interfaith boundaries are relatively easy to cross between such 'religious'. [Una Kroll]

RELIGIOUS PSYCHOLOGY
See: PSYCHOLOGY OF RELIGION

RELIGIOUS TOLERATION
See: TOLERATION, RELIGIOUS

REMARRIAGE
A marriage in which one or both partners have been previously married.
People have married more than once throughout history. There have been many whose partners met untimely deaths through war, childbirth or epidemic. The ancient Jews insisted that a childless widow should be remarried to her husband's brother so children could be raised in the dead man's name. On the other hand, the ancient Hindu custom of *Suttee* meant that widows followed their dead husbands into the funeral pyre. In Christian Europe there has been more ambivalence: the medieval Roman Church disapproved of remarriage but did not forbid it, and many accepted social penance as a price worth paying. The same ambivalence persists today in relation to remarriage in church.

Remarriage continues to form a high proportion of all marriages in most Western countries, accounting for approximately one-third of marriages in England and Wales. In the USA over 40% of all marriages are remarriages for at least one of the adults. High divorce rates have replaced high mortality rates as the predisposing factor. This affects both the dynamics and structure of remarried family life, and may account for the fact that remarriages are statistically more vulnerable to divorce than first marriages. Remarriage is rooted in the experience of loss. Also, when there are children from the previous marriage, a hybrid family form is created with which society and the individuals concerned may not adequately have come to terms.

Loss. A dominant feature of remarriage is the shadow(s) of the previous spouse(s). When she or he has died, memories and associations may be hallowed by the surviving partner and any children they may have had together. This 'Rebecca Syndrome', after Daphne du Maurier's eponymous novel, is symptomatic of uncompleted mourning. Unresolved loss can make it very difficult for a new partner to establish an appropriately differentiated place in the family from her or his predecessor.

The situation following divorce is likely to be quite different. Here, memories of the previous marriage may be predominantly negative, and every encouragement may be given to consigning them to history, if not to obliterating them altogether. The new partner may be heavily relied upon to support, comfort and protect the previously married partner in the face of conflicts associated with the aftermath of the earlier marriage. The previous history of death or divorce may be of less significance for the incoming partner in relation to the task of establishing a relationship with any children from the previous marriage.

A controversial view of remarriage proposes that, whether preceded by death or divorce, new partners are unconsciously chosen in relation to the previous marriage. The relationship may be one of likeness or difference. Partnerships formed 'on the rebound' are the most obvious example of this process. Unresolved loss can result in psychological preoccupations that continue to work themselves out in and through later attachments. While it would be surprising if choice of partner was unrelated to earlier family relationship patterns, whether identified with or repudiated, it is too narrow and pernicious a view to explain the instability of remarriages as the consequence of the remarried obsessively 'repeating their mistakes'.

Hybrid. When there are children, the structure of remarried family life in a step-family differs from that of first-time marriages. There may be more than two adults who act as parents for the children. The boundaries of the immediate two-generation family unit may not correspond with any one particular household. There are likely to be visiting relationships with non-resident parents. There may be children growing up under the same roof who are not biologically related. Different hybrid forms face family members with work in common on two fronts: (1) issues of inclusion and exclusion; (2) matters associated with authority, power and hierarchical difference. This is uncharted territory for many people, and there are few social guidelines to point the way forward. Add the financial pressures, logistic problems and emotional conflicts associated with step-family life and the relative vulnerability of remarriage is unsurprising. *[Christopher Clulow]*

REPENTANCE
The reorientation of one's entire life and person from sin to God.

Repentance is often expressed in the Old Testament by words such as turn and return. It may mean simply a change of mind or a change of action. The term finds its fullest Old Testament expression in the writings of the prophets. Here it means much more than a change of mind. To repent is to turn away from understandings and actions that are reprehensible and unjust and turn to a life of ethical and just conduct. To repent is to forsake sin and turn to righteousness. While repentance is a human action, ultimately it is God who gives the power for individuals and nations to repent. The end to which repentance leads is conversion to a new life and new behaviour.

In the New Testament, the presence of John the Baptist, his demand for repentance, and his joining of this to a baptism for the forgiveness of sins, form the context for Jesus' preaching and teaching. Jesus' Galilean ministry in the first three Gospels centres on the theme of repentance. He makes the prophetic emphasis on sincere repentance a requirement for inclusion in God's kingly rule. He also emphasizes the connection between repentance and belief. One is called to turn from sin and turn to belief in the good news.

In his teaching, Jesus draws a contrast between the outward legal observances of the Pharisees and true repentance. His most compelling teaching on the subject is in the parables of the prodigal son, the lost coin, and the lost sheep. Here Jesus emphasizes the divine joy that results from human repentance.

Following Jesus' example, the preaching and ministerial practice of the early Church centred on repentance (Acts 2.38). Here repentance is undergirded by mutuality, community support and community discipline. St Paul seldom uses the specific word 'repentance' in his correspondence to the churches of this period. But his pastoral focus is on dying to sin, being transformed, new creation, and walking in newness of life, phrases which add up to the same vision as the word suggests.

Repentance was an important part of the pastoral activity of the post-apostolic Church. Here its character and practice began to shift, moving from an emphasis on change and transformation lived out in community, towards the penitential disciplines of contrition, confession and satisfaction. This shift became increasingly prevalent up to and through the Middle Ages. Then the pastoral emphasis centred on the penitent's naming a range of particular sins, coupled with repeated acts of penance. At this time, clergy became expert, both in hearing individual confessions and in setting out the guiding penitential practices. Significantly, confession, which previously had been made voluntarily in the midst of the gathered congregation and was deed-specific and relatively infrequent, became private, frequent and eventually obligatory.

In the late Middle Ages the rise of the universities and growth of towns brought with it commerce, education and the beginnings of modern secularism. However, repentance continued to focus on individual confession and penance. Gradually the process became corrupted by casuistry with regard to sin and veniality with regard to absolution. For example, the sale of indulgences (which so offended the Reformers) developed into a business, whereby in exchange for money people bought what they believed to be forgiveness of some sins and remission from the penalty of purgatory.

The Reformation rejected much that had been built up by the Catholic penitential tradition. In its place the focus was on the priesthood of all believers, a doctrine which emphasized the direct personal access of every believer to God and the common responsibility and privilege of all Christians to provide care for each other in the Church.

Martin Luther stated in his Ninety-Five Theses that 'the whole life of believers should be repentance'. He believed that the word repent had little to do with sacramental penance. Luther had searched the New Testament and discovered that the Greek word for repentance involved a change in one's heart prompted by God's grace. This led him to continue to recommend strongly the act of individual confession, but to emphasize personal trust in the promises of God as the basis for repentance and renewal. John Calvin understood repentance more broadly. He spoke of it as a spiritual regeneration which would both restore God's image and bring forth a process of moral transformation in the believer. Calvin, like Luther, strongly recommended confession. He believed that its goal was to confirm and seal the grace of the gospel in the minds and hearts of the faithful.

Since the time of the Reformation much of the Church's effort in the areas of repentance has centred on pastoral care. Clebsch and Jaekle (1983) name healing, sustaining, guiding and reconciling as the four historic functions of pastoral care. They place repentance under the province of reconciling. Reconciliation is the pastoral function which seeks to help 'alienated persons to establish or renew proper and fruitful relationships with God and neighbour' (p. 56). More specifically, they speak of 'discipline' as that specific pastoral mode of reconciling that is directed towards confession, repentance and amendment of life. Oden (1983) speaks of this as 'pastoral admonition'. He notices that it is conspicuously absent in modern pastoral writings, and affirms its necessity for the work of ministry. He points out that whether done publicly in preaching or privately in pastoral care, 'the task must be approached with great care, concern, sensitivity, and delicacy – and is fraught with hidden dangers' (p. 207).

As a critical activity which seeks to return persons to God, to themselves and to their neighbours by moving them from sin to faith, repentance has been and remains a central component of and challenge for pastoral ministry. [J. Paul Balas]

REPRESENTATION
Doing something or being someone on behalf of others.

Representation lies at the core of the Christian tradition because of its belief that Jesus

Christ acted on behalf of (not in place of) the world. In contrast to the notion of a delegate who can only express explicitly pre-agreed views, a representative can speak more generally on behalf of others. A barrister is briefed by a client and then uses this data in what seems to him or her the best way to represent the client in court. The barrister does not have to refer back to the client between each point but is entrusted with the role of representative.

The idea of representation starts to become difficult when, as since the 1960s, popular assumptions about the nature of individuality are so tightly construed that the sense develops, 'no one except me can speak for me'. For both theological and psychological reasons pastoral studies holds to a view of the individual that has room for representation. The biblical picture chimes with a modern psychological understanding that we carry others within us, a mother her children, siblings their siblings, and so on. Family therapy, for example, has much profited from the insight that when you meet one member of a family there is an important sense in which you meet the whole family. A family breadwinner does so on behalf of all the others. In doing this they represent the family. In the same way a local church's *intercessory prayer* represents its local community. It prays on behalf of others, expressing needs and hopes.

Pastoral care is a ministry performed by representative Christian persons who stand for the wisdom and authority of the tradition. Representation is a crucial concept in the work of the ordained ministry. The minister represents God as a walking symbol. Ministers interact with their environment. Part of their representative role is to enable others to interact across the boundary between their existential confusion and their sense of direction and destiny. This requires a skilful reading of the expectations ministers raise and the responses they receive. Part of their task is to interpret appropriately the feelings involved, which may have a powerful meaning. For example, if I have unresolved feelings of anger towards a parent they may transfer to God and so to a minister. Recognition of what she or he represents to others is therefore important.

Requests for baptism, marriage and funerals are instances of a minister being asked to do something representative. Around these rites of passage it is not appropriate for the minister to collude with the fantasies of those involved but rather to represent certain truths on their behalf. The minister may have to stand in a place where temporarily the people she or he serves cannot stand. In a funeral, for example, the minister articulates on behalf of the bereaved. The minister is able to manage a ritual process which bereaved people, in the disorientation of their grief, cannot do for themselves. [*Nicholas Bradbury*]

REPRESSION
A defensive process that repels unwanted feelings or impulses from consciousness to the unconscious.
One of Freud's earliest and most pervasive concepts, repression was the heart of the 'talking cure'. The patient was encouraged to relate memories and thus consciously come to terms with them and the following symptoms. He or she is not aware of the repressed material, even though it affects their lives. But the defence may not be complete: dreams or so-called 'Freudian slips' may partially lift the repression and allow access to the underlying material. It is a universal process lying at the root of the unconscious.

RESEARCH IN PASTORAL STUDIES
The academic study of pastoral practice and thinking, resulting in theses, books, articles and other occasional literature.
The aims, level and content of such research and writing can be varied. Fundamental research examines the nature of the discipline, its foundational perspectives, methodologies and tasks. Perennial concerns have been the nature of theology and of practical theology as normative of theology or as one of the theological disciplines; the relations between theory and practice; the scope of pastoral theology in relation to ministry, Church and world; and the possibility of doing (practical) theology in the light of philosophical and scientific developments (e.g. in a postmodernist era). Practical theology reflects on pastoral practice, its aims, methods and structures. It thus clarifies, refines and strengthens practice in the light of foundational theology. Conversely, from the demands and insights drawn from practice, practical theology invites the exploration of new ways of understanding how God in Christ is with and for the world. As an inter-

disciplinary field there is constant dialogue between the changing forms of theological understanding (e.g. liberation, process, hermeneutic theologies, missiology or spirituality) and the other disciplines that inform pastoral action (e.g. psychology, sociology, education), which themselves are always developing. As a practical discipline there is a continuous exploration as to how the insights and skills of various approaches to caring, therapy, community development, etc. can be appropriately used in the pastoral context. Concern for practice means understanding society. Thus pastoral studies will be interested in empirical data concerning socio-economic realities, social attitudes and religious practices. Here it will be allied with, among others, economics, social psychology and sociology of religion.

At the same time, as a practical discipline, in order that pastoral action, mission and service can be better planned and executed, there will be investigation into specific issues and concerns. This can range from the national or regional scale (e.g. *Faith in the City* (1985)) to the local (e.g. a parish audit). Pastoral wisdom also depends on listening to and reflecting on pastoral practice. An important type of pastoral literature, therefore, tries to make accessible to a wider audience stories and experimentation done in working, for example, in and for the local community. Much of this is necessarily in the form of occasional papers and reports, more of which needs to be in more permanent forms. [*Paul Ballard*]

RESISTANCE
In counselling and therapy and, by extension, in all ministry, a tendency to avoid self-disclosure and change and to oppose the process of healing.

Especially in Freudian thought, it is normal and universal for a person, even though genuinely committed to self-discovery, candid expression and personality change, also unconsciously to adopt strategies (such as changing the subject or 'forgetting' appointments) that impede such progress. Such defensiveness is evidence that the process is approaching important and anxiety-provoking affect or memories. Though it appears an obstacle to therapy, confronting the resistance directly becomes occasion for therapy to proceed.

RESOURCE ALLOCATION
Deciding where, and to benefit whom, society's finite resources should be located.

The human, material and financial resources with which society provides care for its members are always scarce in proportion to perceived needs and expressed wants. Rising expectations of modern medicine make this problem especially acute. Common decency and prudent management demand that the distribution of health-care benefits should not be left simply to market forces. The problem is to find an alternative that is efficient, effective, equitable and politically feasible. Traditional medical triage provides this in war or major emergencies: it gives priority to those who will survive only with immediate treatment over both less serious and 'hopeless' cases. But even hopeless cases can benefit from labour-intensive palliative care, non-treatment of the less serious may lead to more expensive complications, and medical need or the prospect of medical success are too prevalent to serve alone as allocation criteria. Many 'objective' methods of determining the relative effectiveness of different therapies (e.g. 'evidence-based medicine'), or their comparative benefits in terms of healthy life expectancy (e.g. QUALYS – 'quality adjusted life years'), are no more adequate: they are either too controversial theoretically or too limited in what they can measure. Broader-brush proposals, such as 'age-based rationing', which would limit therapies available to the elderly in the interests of 'inter-generational equity', are equally open to philosophical and medical objections (e.g. such rationing would be morally acceptable only if social goods generally were fairly distributed; overall health status, not age in itself, is the best predictor of likely medical benefit).

This does not mean that no use of 'objective' evidence in prioritizing is feasible. The relative effectiveness and potential benefits of many forms of treatment, care or prevention can be sufficiently demonstrated to secure agreement among professionals. This evidence can then be used in the essentially political process of resource allocation. Many local and national health authorities are now seeking to refine this process through public consultation, in which basic principles of resource allocation (e.g. efficiency, effectiveness, equity, beneficence, non-maleficence, respect for autonomy) and their practical implications can be identified and agreed. But will such agreements hold when individual cases which breach them attract media attention and public sympathy, or when particular loyalties or interests (e.g. to a local hospital or less-effective service) conflict with principle-based decisions? Will an electorate, concerned to limit taxation or to spend more on education, transport or defence, agree to any increase in health expenditure which may be needed to ensure equity? In these political debates, those with pastoral concerns or theological insight into the deeper roots of human solidarity have a difficult responsibility. They must acknowledge that the cost of allocating finite resources at one point is the missed opportunity to allocate them at another. But they must not then leave the field to those who know 'the price of everything and the value of nothing'. [Kenneth Boyd]

RESPONSIBILITY
Being answerable or accountable for expectations growing out of relationships.
Human beings are answerable or accountable to: (1) God. God in the Bible invites humans into a relationship that includes expectations. 'What does the Lord require of you but to do justice, and to love kindness, and to walk humbly with your God' (Mic. 6.8)? (2) Others. Social systems are built upon expectations of certain behaviours of its members. (3) Self. Growing into maturity means accepting certain kinds of responsibility for oneself.

The standards to which people are held accountable are found, for example, in the Ten Commandments (Exod. 20) and in Jesus' statement of the greatest commandment (Matt. 22.36–40). The Torah, as well as Jesus, calls persons into a community of discipleship. This is a moral community, which both fosters and requires accountability and responsibility (Niebuhr, 1966). The word 'responsibility' has the same root as 'respond'. To be able to respond a person must be free. Historically the Church has debated that freedom in relation to the issue of God's sovereignty. Now, the context has shifted. Three considerations influence one's answer to this question. First, culture, gender, power, race and roles are being examined for their influence on responsible behaviour. Persons in power, for example, have different kinds of responsibility from those who have less power. Roles also shape responsibility. A father has obligations to his daughter which go beyond those he may feel towards other six-year-olds. In terms of gender, many women are undergoing a profound re-examination of roles and responsibility. Second, psychology has shown the impact of dysfunctional families and stages of human development upon the shape of human responsibility. Persons with defective notions of responsibility may take too much responsibility for themselves, others or the world. This results in burnout. On the other hand, persons may take too little responsibility, where responsibility is seen as a constraint to be free of. One's faith community can provide a balanced perspective that may help correct one's self-perception. Growing maturity results in a more balanced view of one's own responsibility, including possibilities and limitations. Third, vision and loyalty are linked to responsibility. What people see as worth attending to shapes what they feel responsible for.

A pastor will relate to persons who have varying perceptions of their own responsibility and of the Church's. A pastor can have empathy for the particular shape of that person's perceptions, while at the same time calling for selfhood that is grounded in God's covenant and grace. Then that self is open to looking at her or his responsibility in a situation, without blame or criticism, knowing that patience and forgiveness of oneself and others are the path of true responsibility (Farley, 1983). A pastor's task can include the following: to find his or her own balance of responsibility; to call a faith community to its rightful sense of responsibility, under God; to help individuals to see their proper responsibility in a given context. [J. Bill Ratliff]

RESURRECTION
The act of God in raising the dead, especially the raising of the crucified Jesus.
In the two centuries immediately before the Christian era, the idea began to take root among the Jewish people that, when God intervened to free his people, he would vindicate those who had suffered for their faithfulness to him by raising them to life – as well as raising those who had persecuted them so that they could be humiliated and punished (Dan. 12.2). By the lifetime of Jesus, many Jews, particularly the Pharisaic party, looked to a general resurrection of (at least) the righteous in the coming age. Jesus' resurrection was clearly seen as a first moment of

the new age and a foretaste of what was to come for faithful believers.

But the Gospel narratives of the resurrection and Paul's reflections on it take in a number of further themes. The risen Jesus is presented as returning to confront those who had betrayed and abandoned him, re-establishing table fellowship with them (especially in Luke and John). His resurrection thus becomes not only a demonstration of the new age, but a specific assurance that God's faithfulness in Jesus is not to be deflected by any human falling-away. In the Fourth Gospel, the risen Jesus proves his identity to Thomas by displaying his wounds; so that the risen life is not to be seen as a happy ending, cancelling out the memory of suffering and defeat. And the emphasis on the material nature of the risen body likewise affirms that the new age is not a negation of the material and creaturely order of the present. For Paul (e.g. Rom. 6.5ff), to share Christ's risen life *now* (not just in the new age when it has fully arrived) is to be free from the compulsions of sin, from the treadmill of self-destructive patterns of life and the inexorable cause-and-effect of the processes of sin and punishment. The body is in one sense as if already raised from death because the behaviour of the Christian in his or her bodily life reflects the love and liberty of Christ, who is alive with indestructible life (Barton and Stanton, 1994).

Belief in the resurrection, then, is more than belief in life after death, more even than belief in the victory of Christ. It is a confidence in Christ's divine freedom to forgive and restore, in the body's capacity to show and signify Godlikeness, in the possibility that the memory of injury and failure is not cancelled but transfigured (Hoskyns and Davey, 1981; O'Donovan, 1986). Resurrection faith is not a triumphalist belief that the righteous will be proved righteous at the expense of their enemies, but a hope that divine meanings and divine promise can be manifest in the vulnerable bodies of humanity, and that God loves and welcomes the entire spectrum of human experience as worthy of an eternal regard (Williams, 1982). *[Rowan Williams]*

RETIREMENT
That period of the adult lifespan that follows the active working years and continues until death.

Retirement is often characterized by certain degrees of freedom from the responsibilities of full-time work. Retirement offers, in many cases, opportunities for life enrichment, life review, and the quest for a depth of spiritual meaning, which encompasses the whole of life. Persons in this span of life may be referred to variously as older adults, seniors (or senior citizens), or elders.

From a cross-cultural perspective, retirement is a concept of the developed world, where positive and productive economic realities allow for its existence. In less-developed regions of the world, where the average lifespan of adults is generally much shorter, the active work of adults may continue until death; and/or, elders may be integrated into the total life of the community through other traditions such as the 'wise elder' role of many native or aboriginal peoples.

The retirement years of adult life can be thought of as unfolding in three more or less distinct phases – the 'active' retirement years, the 'cautious' retirement years, and the 'reflective' retirement years. In the active years, seniors are often eager to travel, pursue hobbies, or undertake new educational adventures that may have been postponed until this time of life. If grandchildren are part of their lives, active seniors have much to gain by forming deep connections with this younger generation. In the cautious years, the limitations of an ageing physical body may mean curtailment of some, though not all, of these chosen pursuits. New interests (especially those which place fewer demands upon the body) may arise at any time and develop rapidly if nurtured. In the reflective years, the focus often turns to the business of life review and the need to ascertain deeper meanings regarding the whole of the life journey. Religion and spirituality may take on new and more significant levels of importance, if that has not already happened at an earlier time.

Retirement is often a time of great challenge for seniors, both from without and from within. Ageism, the prejudice against persons based solely upon the fact that they are older, is very real in many cultures. Many modern cultures in the developed world place the highest value on youth so those older adults may often feel devalued both in the workplace and in family life. Challenges from within are very often health-related. One of the most devastating health concerns for seniors deserves special mention: Alzheimer's disease. This disease affects the mind and the body in such a way that memory gradually deteriorates and physical health declines as well. Family members of older adults with Alzheimer's disease suffer too, as their loved one slowly fades away in terms of significant capacities for relationship and remembering. The reflective work of the senior years is disrupted to the detriment of all concerned. [*Ronald Baard*]

RETREATS
A temporary retirement (whether physical or merely mental) for religious exercises and spiritual development.
Retreats are again becoming popular. The style varies. They may involve withdrawing to a retreat house for a few days, a week or longer. They may be a retreat in daily life, in which retreatants undertake exercises and regular prayer during their everyday activity. Retreats may be wholly silent or only have silence as a component. They may be directed by a leader or be self-directed. They may be made as a member of a group or in solitude. But most retreats have in common a withdrawal from the external stimuli of daily living and from some of the customary courtesies of the world in order to rediscover relationships with God through silence, reading and prayer.

There are different types of retreat. An individually guided retreat, often within or dependent on the Ignatian tradition (after Ignatius of Loyola, sixteenth-century founder of the Jesuits), encourages the use of retreatants' imagination in discerning the will of God. This type of retreat has a connection with psychotherapy and a retreat has a relationship with confession. Other retreats consist of pure silence, the retreatants seeking to be immersed in the love of God with as little human interference as possible. In the USA the term 'retreat' is used also for an in-house residential in-service training event. [*Martin Israel*]

RIGHTS, ANIMAL
See: ANIMAL RIGHTS

RIGHTS, HUMAN
See: HUMAN RIGHTS

RITES OF PASSAGE
Rituals giving cultural recognition to transitions in the life-cycle of individuals or groups.
Nineteenth-century anthropologists, turning attention to praxis in small-scale societies, concentrated on the origins and evolution of customary rituals. In *Rites de Passage* (1909) Arnold van Gennep, who originated the expression, turned attention to the structure of the rites themselves. He divided the process into separation from the old status and grouping; a period of liminality (living at the boundaries); and concluding with incorporation into the new category. A significant development in the field was Victor Turner's (1969) specific study of 'liminality'.

The need for some such concept as rites of passage was apparent from its ready acceptance. However, the subsequent absence of serious development suggests the need for caution in using it in pastoral studies. Certainly it focuses attention on the biological and social dimensions of human behaviour in times of crisis and change, such as adolescence and marriage, which contemporary thought might otherwise overlook. However, it is by no means clear that these aspects ever exhausted the meaning of, say, confirmation, even in those teenage contexts in which it was once the norm.

Rites that speak to and for such times are inevitably both mysterious and sacramental. No doubt they were once overvalued, as being automatically, mechanically and magically efficacious. However, the need for a humane understanding is underestimated when they are described as 'mere' rites of passage. The use of this term in churches has probably contributed to society's loss of faith in the loss of a sense of efficacy of any rite. Since ritual reaches areas that are inaccessible to rationality, this has meant the substitution of less orderly rituals, which offer less opportunity to contemplate the paradox and richness of life. [*Edward Bailey*]

RITUAL
Certain bodily and linguistic practices which are repetitive, stylized or formal in character and to which any instrumental purpose cannot easily be ascribed.
Precisely because ritual seems to differ from the instrumental and apparently economic behaviour of everyday life scholars have largely agreed that it is an easily identifiable

phenomenon, even though they disagree over matters of interpretation. The concept of ritual as a distinct, universal, substantive or definable operation entered the English language in the middle of the seventeenth century. But rituals, in the sense of particular practices, scripts or rites, appeared as early as the ninth century. The term 'ritual' is still occasionally used to denote particular liturgical practices. But this meaning has largely been displaced since the late nineteenth century onwards by the modern conception of ritual as an active symbol. This semantic alteration of the concept of ritual as symbolic, expressive or non-rational activity has a variety of connotations. These depend upon a particular interpreter's view of symbol: either (1) as an essential component of all meaning as such; or (2) as relegated to the innocuous realms of the aesthetic, magical or religious. This change in the concept is itself a manifestation of a broader transformation which, from the Reformation onwards, has tended to separate ritual from everyday life. It has also made instrumental activity more significant than assumed knowledge as the representation of hidden meanings. Following Descartes, the dichotomy of interior essences and exterior forms has been assumed, as has the contingency of individual experience versus public and systematic structures. This transformation has tended to encourage two apparently disconnected views of ritual, as either (1) a curious, quaint, ethnic or primitive custom which requires sophisticated, exhaustive and authoritative analysis by objective exegetes; or (2) on account of its concealed symbolic content, bodily configurations and lack of immediate instrumental purpose, a dangerous and manipulative tool whose formalistic operations are oppressive and authoritarian devices. These force participants to surrender (a) their creative freedom of will through the hypnotic effects of automatic or repeated actions; and (b) their perception of the available choices, so that they become (c) locked into superordinate or subordinate positions, and (d) unwittingly collusive in a self-perpetuating exercise of power. The enactment of such ritual does not merely express a hierarchy of power but makes it actual. In so far as both interpretations, whatever their differences, emphasize the mechanical, automatic and recursive aspect of ritual behaviour, they effectively liken such action to texts or objects of a reading.

Later anthropologists have attributed the supposed symbolic meanings of ritual action to quite different structures. They have traced them to attempts at: (1) dealing magically with the natural environment; (2) maintaining certain social structures; (3) creating a common experience and social solidarity by means of a restricted code; (4) communicating cultural messages or memories; (5) shaping communal memory through the commemoration or representation of prototypical actions, events or persons; (6) attaining religious experiences which transcend cultural specificities and channel powerful atavistic emotions; (7) creating illusions which can be believed in and marking periods and occasions of cosmological significance; (8) releasing dangerous tensions through the expression of politically subversive emotions. But all these scholars, despite their differences, share a fundamental interpretation of ritual as: (1) a distinct object of a general theory; (2) which comprises signifying acts which can be deciphered; (3) and which are present in the religious, rather than the technological life of all culture.

The symbolical reading of ritual has gained widespread appeal and has influenced recent interpretations of Christian ritual. Thus the sacraments are seen as representational vehicles of a particular culture's root metaphors; or monastic rites become ways of repressing socially dangerous psychic forces or inculcating new values. However, a recent approach to medieval monastic and liturgical ritual has stressed that such operations do not encode or communicate special messages in an enclave which is remote from ordinary activity. Rather they seek to reform or re-form moral dispositions or virtues through the exercise of certain disciplines which are embedded within and constitutive of ordinary activity and form a whole way of life which is ritual in character (Pickstock, 1997). The liturgical rituals of St Benedict and Bernard of Clairvaux, for example, are not species of enacted symbol classified from activities that are defined as useful or technical. They are practices among others that are essential to the acquisition of Christian virtues. On this analysis, rituals do not evoke or release, coerce or inculcate isolatable values or universal human emotions. Rather they seek publicly to reorganize certain distinctive and historically specific emotions, such as charity, humility and contrition. Each task in the programme was to be accomplished in order to make the self approximate more closely to a saintly exemplar. Such an order refuses any disjunction therefore between inner motive and outer form, personal contingencies and public ritual, symbolic expressive acts and technical useful ones, and between soul and body.

The modern conception of ritual as non-rational behaviour sees such operation as valid, irrespective of its lack of economic or instrumental method or intentionality. Nevertheless it tends to classify such activity as marked, peripheral, occasional and residual, according to a presupposition that authentic or true work begins where formalistic ritual ends. The ritual character of many medieval institutions has been shown to be based upon fundamental attainment of social peace through the creation of kinship bonds. Later civil peace substituted codes of manners and courtesy for these and was held in place by a more empty formalism of arbitrary rules of conduct which were detached from any determination of the good. The false civility of such a mannered peace, moreover, depended upon its ability to dissemble and detach outward sign from inner meaning. From this it is a short step to the notion of 'mere ritual', seen as a pointless excrescence concealing possibly dubious purposes.

As a result, it may be precisely where ritual appears to be absent that one might begin to look for the kind of ritual that is now identified by modern scholars. The marks of such ritual are: (1) it sunders outer from inner; (2) it reduces perception of available choices; and (3) it catches people off-guard, so that they cannot recognize the exercise of power in isolation from the reasons why it is exercised. In the face of such assumptions as the unquestioned authority of instrumentality, the Church has through its use of ritual much to contribute. One approach would be to recover the medieval virtues, i.e. practices involving the whole person and forming the self to the service of God. Ritual would then no longer be seen as something one does but as something one perpetually enters into, a discipline of praise for which no ordinary routines are too mundane to be included. For they will all be offered to God as worship. It is here that the ritual aspects of pastoral care, both in care in the community, care for the individual and care for the world, become prominent (Ramshaw, 1987). Such ritual offering, acquired and practised communally, forms a self which retains the authority to pose a living critique of those many other hidden rituals which are deployed in the service of the state and in an instrumental economy. [Catherine Pickstock]

ROLE
1. The part a person plays (as in the theatre).
2. The function of an individual in relation to the task of an organization.

Person and role are intimately connected. How a person takes up a role will be affected profoundly by the kind of person they are. But there are also expectations of what someone may do in role. These expectations, which are not defined formally as in a job description, help to define what is appropriate to a role. The individual, keeping in mind the task of the enterprise in which she or he is involved, takes up ownership of their responsibilities in relation to that task, and chooses the actions and behaviour that is appropriate to that task.

But this choosing may be problematic. There may be things that someone would like to do but feels inhibited by their role. Or someone may be influenced to behave out of role. Often this will be an unconscious process, where there is a dynamic in the enterprise to subvert its task, possibly because the task is too difficult or too painful. When we talk of wearing this or that hat, we are acknowledging that we have different roles in life, and what is appropriate to one may be inappropriate to another. The concept of role is also used to provide individual consultancy to managers. Role analysis focuses on the relationships that the individual has to others in order to explore how the person manages herself or himself in relation to the enterprise.

Taking up a role is integral to our experience and the meaning we put on our actions. It is in no way superficial and is not to be confused with role-play, which is a way of exploring the experience of another as if it is one's own. It is instead a way of putting the individual in context, as a member of this or that system and engaged with the task of that system. It is also a holistic concept – having an awareness of the whole context. For example, it is possible to learn some of the skills of an appraisal interview, but to be effective it is essential at the same time to be the manager, to have an understanding of oneself in that role.

This understanding is open for exploration and development. How far is one going along with myths and assumptions about the social institutions of which one is a part? What is the nature of the deference – or lack of it – being shown to authority? Managing oneself in role implies working to discover one's own reality rather than taking on the supposed realities of a wider society in an uncritical and unexamined way. *[Tim Dartington]*

ROLE-PLAY
The enactment of a life situation in the presence of another in order to gain insight or to learn new behaviours or skills.

The use of role-play in counselling originated with Jacob Moreno who created psychodrama for use in group therapy in 1925. Moreno's theatre-like re-creations of a client's life situation focused primarily on increased insight about one's own feelings and the impact of one's behaviour on others and on one's life story. Similar aims have prompted the use of role-play, including role-reversal, in counselling families, couples and individuals in conflict or at an impasse (Sandbek, 1990).

Role-play has also been extensively used as an educative tool in behavioural counselling. It is often appropriate for the short-term assistance that pastors provide to help careseekers change self-sabotaging behaviours to more fitting functioning. This includes social and personal skills, communication skills, conflict management, and anxiety reduction. Various organizations also use role-play as a means of teaching new skills, such as a local church instructing their lay care team in listening skills.

Although it looks simple, there are basic boundaries that have to be kept in using role-play, most notably being very clear when someone is in or out of role. It is not a technique that should be used without some training or teaching from an experienced person.

RURAL THEOLOGY
The interface between theology and issues of importance to rural church and society.

The notion of rural theology has been actively promoted by the Rural Theology Association (RTA) and the association's journal *A Better Country*. Unlike rural sociology, the activity of rural theology has not yet established a particularly solid tradition or literature. It is a growing discipline which is developing two main strands. One strand is rooted in the practical needs of the rural church; the other in theological illumination and critique of issues salient within the social, political and economic life of rural society. Both strands are represented in major church reports of the 1990s including the Archbishops' Commission on Rural Areas (1990) and the Rural Commission of the Church in Wales (1992).

Looking inwardly towards the Church itself, rural theology has been concerned with such issues as ministry, spirituality and worship, education and youth, mission and evangelism, and structures and finance. Theological reflection on ministry has needed to face the consequence of declining vocations and dwindling resources in all churches. Multiparish benefices have changed the nature of rural ministry. Questions have had to be faced regarding the expansion of lay ministry and eucharistic presidency. Theological reflection on spirituality and worship has examined the competing priorities for tradition and for change in patterns of services in light of the competing expectations of indigenous population and incomers. Theological reflection on education and youth has faced the closure of smaller rural church schools and the appropriate resourcing of voluntary activities for young people. Theological reflection on mission and evangelism has needed to assess the appropriateness of models developed in suburban environments within rural communities. Theological reflection on structures and finance has indicated alternative strategies for pastoral oversight, the best response to medieval buildings and the appropriate development and deployment of financial resources.

Looking outwardly towards the rural community, rural theology has been concerned with such issues as change in the rural community, environmental concerns, rural economy and the rural social conditions. Reflection on change in the rural community involves assessing the implications of new technology, the pressures faced by the farming community, the expectations of incomers, and the development of the countryside as a leisure activity. Reflecting on environmental concerns includes contributing to the debates on ecology and animal rights. Reflecting on the rural economy goes beyond the farming community to face issues like unemployment and quality of employment, small-business initiatives, problems of accessibility and training, the conversion of buildings for new businesses, affordable housing and the impact of second homes. Reflecting on the rural social condition confronts the problems of housing, education, transport, shops and post offices, health provision and community development. [*Leslie Francis*]

S

SACRAMENT
The outward and visible sign of an inward and spiritual grace, ordained by Christ as a means of grace and an assurance of it.

The definition is adapted from that in the Anglican Book of Common Prayer. But the precise definition of a sacrament and its efficacy has been one of the most divisive aspects of Christian faith. The basic belief is that sacraments convey grace objectively, which is in turn apprehended by faith. For this to occur, proper form is required, as is (in most churches) an ordained minister or priest, although his or her worthiness does not affect the effectiveness of the sacrament. However, it has always been accepted that in emergencies lay people may baptize.

In the catholic tradition there are seven sacraments, two of which (baptism and Eucharist) are recognized by the Protestant churches as dominical (given by the Lord) and scriptural, although the other five are also to varied degrees acknowledged. The Orthodox churches have never officially adopted this medieval list. The seven are: (1) baptism, the rite of initiation; (2) confirmation, the completion of baptism (in the West by the bishop); (3) penance, confession with absolution administered by a priest; (4) Eucharist, celebrated by a priest and offered to the baptized (and usually also confirmed); (5) holy orders, the bishop laying on hands to confer orders, e.g. deacon or priest; (6) holy matrimony, the ministers of which are the couple themselves; and (7) unction, the anointing of the sick which is sometimes (and erroneously) spoken of as the last rites.

There is a strong connection between sacraments and pastoral work. In particular the power of Christ present in the Eucharist is central to pastoral ministry, especially of churches in the Catholic tradition, where it has even been called 'the medicine of immortality'. [*Wesley Carr*]

SACRAMENTAL HEALING
Use of the sacraments, specifically in the context of prayer for healing.

The main Catholic sacrament of healing is anointing. But the other sacraments also have their place (Maddocks, 1990). First, Holy Communion may provide a context for prayer for healing. The ancient idea of 'medicine of immortality' shows how long the connection has been made. And whether sick or not, many people find their spiritual 'sickness' removed through participation. Second, the laying on of hands is a key facet of sacramental ministry and healing. The psychological importance of touch has been increasingly acknowledged in recent times, especially as a form of communication with those who apparently cannot see, hear or speak.

SADISM
Delight in mental or physical cruelty of any kind.

The term was derived from Comte Donatien Alphonse François de Sade (1740–1819) who, while in prison for prohibited sexual practices, wrote a book in which he described fantasies of sexual violence which led to sexual gratification. Sadism is not confined to fantasy, however. The fantasy is acted out. And the term has come to denote an abnormal condition in which a person obtains sexual gratification from inflicting actual pain and humiliation on animals or people.

SADO-MASOCHISM
A condition in which an individual gains sexual pleasure from both inflicting pain and submitting to pain.

In its mild forms it is not necessarily harmful. Sado-masochistic fantasies are common in both sexes and may facilitate orgasm. During actual sexual intercourse many people enjoy being treated roughly. 'Love bites', 'holding down', and quite forceful penetration are common. The condition becomes pathological when sexual arousal can only occur if an unusual degree of pain is inflicted and received, such as violent beating, partial strangulation, cutting and burning. Role-reversal between sado-masochistic individuals is common.

SALVATION
1. Deliverance from everything which is life-threatening.
2. The fulfilment of purposes of the God of life.
3. The sum of the gospel.

In the Hebrew Bible the verb 'to save' (*yeshua*, from which Jesus' name derives) refers primarily to God's deliverance of Israel from her enemies, paradigmatically at the Exodus (Exod. 14.30). In the Psalms the individual frequently cries for deliverance from personal enemies (Ps. 7), and God is said to save 'the children of the needy' (Ps. 72). Jesus' very being is defined in terms of salvation (Matt. 1.21). He characterizes his healings as salvation (Mark 3.4) and his enemies acknowledge that he 'saved others' (Mark 15.31). In Acts, and for Paul, salvation signifies everything accomplished in Christ (Acts 4.12; Rom. 1.16). Salvation is a present reality (2 Cor. 6.2) but also an eschatological promise (Rom. 8.24). It is something to work out with fear and trembling (Phil. 2.12).

From the third century on it was proposed that there was no salvation outside the Church. The eschatological emphases of the epistles led to the view that salvation referred above all to life after death. Baptism and the other sacraments, channels of grace, were the necessary, though not sufficient, road to this. A virtuous life was essential, but in Augustine's view the best virtues of good pagans were nothing but splendid vices since they were not founded on grace. The task of the Church was to extend the numbers of those saved through conversion. Though Protestantism changed the theology of grace, the notion of salvation remained individual and otherworldly with an emphasis on the experience of assurance. Both the liberal theology of the nineteenth century and the existentialism of the twentieth at bottom represented variants of this view, though neither confined salvation to the Church. The recognition that grace is not confined to the Church also characterizes Vatican II (*Lumen Gentium*) with the corollary that salvation, known in human openness to God and to others, extends beyond it. Liberation theology has gone further towards restoring the breadth and this-worldliness of the biblical concept (Gutiérrez, 1974). If salvation refers to health, wholeness and deliverance from enemies then it has personal, social and political dimensions which together comprise a spiritual reality.

Salvation refers to wholeness of life, the realization of integrity through other-directedness rather than ego-centricity (Mark 8.35). This can only be achieved within community because 'no one can be fully human until all are fully human' (Jenkins, 1976). Thus the restoration of right relationships is part of salvation. This in turn has a political dimension because politics is the structuring of human community within which alone right relationships can be established. Jesus' use of the political metaphor of the Kingdom of God points in this direction. Prayer for the establishment of God's Kingdom on earth is prayer for salvation. All three dimensions of salvation are oriented to, and embraced by, the promises of God's final healing of all historical reality (Rev. 22.2) when the glory and integrity of creation, no longer threatened by death, will be its realization. [*Timothy Gorringe*]

SATAN
See: DEVIL

SCAPEGOATING
The process whereby one person is blamed for the behaviour or offences of others.

The term derives from the role of the scapegoat in the Hebrew Day of Atonement rituals described in Lev. 16. It is a psychosocial phenomenon involving an active, destructive and largely unconscious dynamic whereby individual, family or group cohesion is maintained by disavowing unacceptable aspects of the self. These aspects are located in another person who is then persecuted for having become the repository for the repudiated parts. The underlying mechanisms are primitive ones of splitting and projection, often involving a sado-masochistic bind of the mind which characterizes the phenomenon of bullying and victimization. [*Caroline Garland*]

SCHIZOID
1. A personality type.
2. A component of the paranoid-schizoid position in Kleinian theory.

The term is often used loosely to describe splitting or division. It describes the personality that tends to separate the person's emotional life from the mind or intellectual aspect. It has been widely used in discussion about schizophrenia and is particularly associated with R. D. Laing (1962). The second sense is found in Kleinian thinking. The paranoid-schizoid position is the infant's earliest stage of development and one to which individuals and institutions may revert.

SCHIZOID PERSONALITY
See: PERSONALITY DISORDER

SCHIZOPHRENIA
A term used to describe the progressive disintegration of the personality.
The term 'schizophrenia' was coined by Eugene Bleuler in 1907 and displaced 'dementia praecox', a term first developed by Emil Kraeplin in 1896, because of the condition's early onset in adolescence.

Bleuler emphasized the splintering of the components of the personality and coined 'the four As' – autism, ambivalence, association and affect. Schizophrenia is marked by deterioration in social, interpersonal or vocational functioning associated with the presence of psychotic symptoms, disturbed experiences and behaviour. The symptoms include delusions, hallucinations (which are usually auditory), incoherence of thought, blunting of affect and disorganized behaviour. Symptoms are also classified into 'positive' (such as hallucinations and delusion) and 'negative', for example, self-neglect, loss of feeling, social avoidance, or incapacity to manage a job or finances.

Schizophrenia is treated with a variety of measures including drugs, psychological and behavioural interventions, and support both social and classical or atypical; the classical drugs are effective against both positive and negative symptoms and have fewer side-effects, but they are expensive.

Psychological interventions include education, cognitive behaviour therapy and family therapy to improve communication and reduce the level of expressed emotion. One third of patients recover completely, one third make a partial recovery, and one third run a deteriorating course. Treatment reduces the risk of relapse. Schizophrenia remains one of the main causes of hospital-bed occupancy worldwide. *[Lawrence Ratna]*

SCHOOL ASSEMBLIES
In the UK the daily act of worship held in state and independent schools.
Schools assemble for different reasons, e.g. a fire drill or to hear a match report. In the UK the phrase 'school assembly' has come to mean that part of the assembly properly called collective worship, whereas in the USA this meaning is affected by the constitutional separation of church and state. On the whole public or 'state' schools are required to maintain a clear policy of nonsectarian and non-religious assembly. Private schools may form their own policy.

The 1944 Education Act ordered all maintained schools in the UK to hold a collective act of worship at the beginning of the school day. The 1988 Education Reform Act laid down some changes, but retained the concept. Acts of worship could now be held at different times during the day, by different groups and in different places within the school (Hull, 1987). The rights of teachers and pupils were safeguarded. Teachers could refuse to conduct an assembly, and the overall control of the assembly was given to the head teacher and to the chairman of governors. Parents could choose to withdraw children if the act of worship was felt to conflict with the dictates of their own faith. Local Standing Advisory Councils for Religious Education, established by each Authority, would advise on all matters and make recommendations regarding religious education and collective worship.

In church voluntary-aided and church voluntary-controlled schools (Church of England, Methodist and Roman Catholic schools), material of a denominational nature could be used during worship. In other maintained schools worship had to be 'wholly or mainly of a broadly Christian character', defined as worship of a broad Christian nature, without being characteristic of one denomination. In effect at least 50% of the worship had to be of a Christian nature; the rest could be of a moral or ethical tone.

The Education Act of 1992 introduced the notion of a unified inspection for all schools, to include the spiritual and moral education of all pupils. Assemblies were also to be inspected by the Ofsted (Office for Standards in Education) inspectors and church authorities were to be allowed to inspect assemblies in church schools.

The difficult question of how an act of

worship was to be assessed was not explored, neither was the nature of any worship that might be deemed suitable for a multi-faith educational establishment. Professor John Hull of Birmingham University carried out much of the initial thinking concerning collective worship, and helped to define the kind of worship suitable for schools; he also explored the notion of taking pupils to the 'threshold of worship', of offering pupils a climate in which worship might occur (Hull, 1989).

Questions still being debated include: What is worship? How is it possible to know if a pupil is worshipping? What helps pupils to worship? What distracts from worship? How can schools cope with different faiths worshipping together? How is it possible to separate the act of worship from other aspects of the assembly like the giving of notices? These questions, though specific to Britain, apply to sectors throughout the USA, as the meaning and relevance of worship in school assemblies continues to be tested. [*Sharon Swain*]

SCHOOL, PASTORAL CARE IN
Pastoral care concerned with sustaining personal, social and psychological development.
With its roots in Christian ministry and theology, pastoral care in schools is part of a broad secular culture. It retains much of its original meaning from the practice of ordained ministry including care, nurture, guidance and leadership. In all schools and particularly in residential schools, pastoral care values the experience of being at school as important in itself and in application humanizes institutional life. The pastoral care in a school is usually a formal structure and may have scheduled periods assigned to the 'pastoral needs' of the students. In secular, materialistic, educational settings spirituality is not normally considered a part of pastoral care which is instrumental in ensuring the 'general well-being' of students. However, pastoral care still offers an opportunity for less fashionable but nevertheless bolder ideas of enriching both the individual and the community as a model of communication and sharing of experience.

Teachers, chaplains and counsellors are given specific responsibilities to 'carry out pastoral duties'. In application the theoretical basis of pastoral care is drawn from the psychology of counselling but it is not considered a clinical treatment model. Although

pastoral care derives meaning from Christian ministry, it has its own status as an expression of a duty of care towards the students. Thus in schools pastoral care harbours the ideas of responsible and caring relationships upon which lives need to be built. Pastoral care attends to the interrelated needs of emotional and intellectual fulfilment. In this sense the teaching role is quasi-parental and always contains aspects of pastoral care. However, the theory of pastoral care also distinguishes between personal need and academic requirements. There is a duty of confidentiality both in pastoral care and in teaching and this can cause conflict of interests. Such conflicts can be partly resolved structurally in a school by separate provisions of a professional school counsellor and/or an ordained minister who are not teachers (Barwick, 2000).

Pastoral care is essentially an activity that is 'about the person' and encourages self-awareness. It is contiguous with learning and supporting individual growth. Pastoral care may be interpreted as extending beyond the strict confines of the school and sometimes involves home support. The increasing importance of pastoral care is part of the movement from coercive models of education towards consultative models involving democratic principles. These include 'buddy schemes', 'student care line', 'peer support and peer counselling', which in themselves express a pastoral attitude in a school that endeavours to achieve better support, communication and understanding of the needs of young people. [*Philip Hewitt*]

SCRUPULOSITY
Habitual and unreasonable hesitation, anxiety and indecisiveness in making moral judgements.
Derived from the Latin diminutive, *scrupulus*, meaning a small sharp stone, scrupulosity makes the journey through life as painful as if one were walking in pebble-filled shoes. Scrupulosity is normally related to moral decisions and seems most severe in adolescents. It often reflects a faulty conscience, a harsh God-image, a sense of perfectionism or a form of neurosis.

Freud put scruples in the category of obsessions or nervous compulsions which need not be religious in character. Pastoral care of scrupulous persons requires the following attitudes and skills: respectful listening to the person, recognition that the problems are not really conscience problems, patient enabling of the person to make decisions and to develop trust.

SECONDARY PROCESS
One of the two modes of functioning that according to Freud is characteristic of the unconscious mind.
The other mode is 'primary process'. Secondary process is the way in which the narrative of, for example, a dream is reconstructed as a defence against the power of primary process.

SECRECY
Withholding information or binding a pastor or counsellor to withhold.
Secrecy should not be confused with confidentiality. The latter is a condition of any professional pastoral relationship. Secrecy, by contrast, is often an extra request that may be made before a so-called 'secret' can be mentioned and the client or penitent tries to lay down further conditions about its use, even within the counselling context. The pastor or counsellor needs to resist the natural response of agreeing and to examine what the reasons for the attempted secrecy might be. It is more than likely that this exploration will yield data and move the working relationship along.

SECT
A group of dissenters from an established religious tradition.
In popular parlance the term sect is frequently used as a term of opprobrium for any religious group of which the user does not approve. This popular usage is linked with the historical Christian intolerance and persecution of dissenters as heretics.

The nineteenth-century theologian and sociologist Ernst Troeltsch developed a formal theory of religious organizations which divided them primarily into churches and sects according to certain characteristics. Identifying the early Christian movement as a Jewish sect he described a recurring pattern of sectarian breakaway from established churches in Christian history. He also identified a historical process by which sects mutate into churches over time, as did the early Christian movement by the fourth century.

Sociologists have refined a set of characteristics of sects which distinguish them from church-type organizations including: lower class origins of their members and egalitarian or anti-clerical tendencies; a distinctive doctrine or teaching said to be uniquely revealed or understood by the founders of the sect; protest or dissent against established religious leaders, dogmas and social practices; membership by choice, not inheritance; strong bonds and requirements of commitment; alternative moral values and lifestyle; unwillingness to accommodate to established or mainstream social styles or mores.

Sects sometimes arise as protest movements against the religiously sanctioned status quo. They more often arise in societies experiencing rapid social change, such as nineteenth-century Europe and North America, or twentieth-century Japan or Southern Africa. Most modern European or North American sects, such as the Mormons, Christian Scientists, Jehovah's Witnesses and Seventh-Day Adventists, have their origins in the nineteenth-century industrial and urban revolutions. The other condition for the emergence of sects is religious tolerance and pluralism, which is why they are more numerous in Protestant than in monopoly Catholic societies (Wilson, 1970).

The largest and fastest-growing style of sectarianism in the twentieth century is Pentecostalism, whose adherents are estimated at around 600 million. From their origin in urban North America, Pentecostal sects have sprung up on every continent and are growing fastest among Catholic and mainstream Protestant believers in Latin America, Africa and Asia. Pentecostalism combines some of the classic features of sects with a strong emphasis on physical healing, on spiritual experience, including glossolalia, or speaking in tongues, and spontaneous prophecy. Pentecostalism also combines features of primal and magical religious systems – such as belief in spirits and physical or psychic manifestations of possession by the divine Spirit – with aspects of established Christian belief and practice.

Sects often sustain patterns of belief and behaviour which are at fundamental variance with mainstream society as well as established religion. This can result in conflict with state authority in relation to such issues as the education of children in secular schools, acceptance of conventional medical practices, or military and jury service (Beckford, 1975). Some sects refuse to use certain modern technologies such as cars or telephones. Other sects are highly organized global movements with centres in most major cities connected by satellite and jet plane. The decline in the monopoly authority of established churches in most Christian countries has led to increasing toleration of sects despite their alternative value and belief systems. Muslim countries, however, remain very intolerant of sectarian activity, as seen in the fierce persecution of Baha'is in Iran and elsewhere in the Middle East. [Michael Northcott]

SECULARIZATION
Decline of the social significance and practice of religion.
Secularization names a cluster of phenomena which together indicate declining participation in religious institutions and the declining influence of religion. These phenomena include: (1) reductions in church attendance and in use of religious rites of passage such as church weddings and baptisms; (2) diminishing religious belief and diminishing authority of traditional religiously sanctioned moral values; (3) reduced religious practice or private prayer in the home; (4) growing pluralism of belief- and value-systems; (5) reduced social status of clergy, and in some contexts anti-clericalism; (6) diminishing social role and influence of religious institutions in areas of public life and civil society, including education, local and national government and the administration of justice; (7) reduced public authority of religious leaders; (8) demolition or sale of religious buildings for secular usage.

These phenomena have become manifest in the nineteenth and twentieth centuries in all Protestant countries in Northern Europe (Chadwick, 1975). They are also becoming evident in Southern European Catholic countries, in Australia and New Zealand, and in North America. Most observers believe that secularization is linked with certain features of modernization, including urbanization and industrialization. The rapid modernization of European societies since 1945 is particularly strongly linked with religious decline. Only 10% of the population of many Northern European countries now regularly engage in public worship, whereas participation was between 30% and 40% in most European countries before 1939 (Martin, 1978).

Three clusters of explanations are advanced by sociologists to explain secularization. The first is social differentiation. This refers to the separation of Church from State, of political economy from religious authority, and to the division of modern industrial society into distinct sectors of life experience including work, residence, education, culture and religion.

The second explanation is rationalization, which operates in at least three distinct ways: sacred accounts of the origins of life and the cosmos are undermined by the physical and the human sciences; rational cause–effect relations in modern technological and bureaucratic societies remove magical and spiritual explanations of most life events; cost-benefit procedures rationalize human production and exchange relations.

The third explanation is societalization. The organic, local and face-to-face relations on which religious communities rely are replaced by societal, statist, industrial, systemic and organizational relations in modern societies. This massification of the social world also gives rise to growing individualism which again subverts religious belonging and community.

The link between modernization and secularization is, however, hotly contested (Harvey, 1989). Societies in Asia, the Middle East and Latin America have experienced rapid modernization in the last 30 years. But in many of these countries modernization has been accompanied by religious resurgence, most notably that of Islam in the Middle East and Southeast Asia, and of fundamentalist or Pentecostal Christianity in Latin America. The USA has also sustained much higher levels of churchgoing and religious practice and belief than modern European Protestant countries.

Some sociologists argue that religion uniquely fulfils certain emotional and ecological functions for individuals and societies, including the provision of cosmic meaning, personal identity and social integration. They argue that competition between different churches in the USA, or between religions in Asia and parts of the Middle East, provides a religious economy in which individuals can find organizations which effectively meet these needs, hence the higher social value placed on religion. Correlatively the traditional monopoly of established and state-supported churches is advanced as the cause of declining interest in religion in many European countries. [Michael Northcott]

SELF
The subject of personal experience.
The self is a key notion in psychology and in the modern and postmodern worlds. It

approximates to what theologians called 'the soul', although the correlation is not perfect. No single definition, however, can be applied universally: the word has always to be examined carefully in its context. Chief among associations are the following: (1) the unique personal self with his or her specific identity; (2) the self as responsible agent; (3) psychoanalytic senses – in Freud the ego and in Jung an archetype; (4) in postmodern thought a subject which is always in relation – its identity is discovered and created within a maelstrom of political, economic and cultural forces (Graham, 1996).

The term is often attached to another to produce a particular meaning: e.g. selfhood, self-actualization, self-orientation, self-image, self-determination. In pastoral studies there is a discernible shift of emphasis from concern for the self as an individual in need to seeing and responding to the self as a being who lives self-aware amid social challenges in a politically unstable and economically uncertain world (Pattison, 1993, 1994).

SELF-DENIAL
The practice of denying oneself the gratification of a legitimate desire or comfort such as food, sleep, warmth, pleasure and sexual intimacy.
Such practices may be undertaken for the sake of a beloved child or partner, but some people deny themselves in order to gain control over their bodies and minds.

Self-denial is also practised by people of all religious faiths in the belief that such asceticism is pleasing to God. In particular, fasting from food and sleep produces altered states of consciousness in which the awareness of God or the numinous is heightened.

SELF-DESTRUCTIVE BEHAVIOUR
Actions that are harmful to self and potentially to others.
Self-destructive behaviour can take many forms: alcoholism/drug abuse, cigarette smoking, self-mutilation, eating disorders, reckless driving, unsafe sex, accident-proneness, compulsive gambling, and medical non-compliance. The ultimate self-destructive behaviour is suicide. Self-destructive behaviour can be both conscious and unconscious. Miller (1994) states that it can be a re-enactment of childhood trauma, thus distracting a person from unbearable thoughts and feelings. Religious traditions and spiritual beliefs may contribute to acts of self-

destruction and the pastor should be alert to this possibility.

SELF-ESTEEM
A term drawn more from contemporary feminist, humanistic and interpersonal psychology than from classical psychoanalysis and psychotherapy.
Self-esteem is one of the objectives of feminist, humanistic and interpersonal psychotherapists. Counsellors and therapists from these and associated schools work towards achieving a true understanding of the 'self' (personality) and with a deep respect and esteem for every individual and every individual's personal situation.

Self-esteem has been a particular psychological difficulty for women who have experienced social exclusion and social oppression, often the consequence of misogyny. Women's identification as 'inferior' has also come about through traditional church teaching which said that Eve, the female partner of the first human couple, was a temptress. Thus in Christianity women have been made to suffer the indignity of that teaching and only since the women's movement of the 1970s and 1980s have they been able to relativize such inaccurate portrayals of themselves.

Without self-respect and self-esteem it is not possible to relate straightforwardly to other people.

SELF-WORTH
A term associated with the psychological value of the 'self' or personhood of an individual.
Self-worth, the real valuing of oneself, stems from having an internal world which is secure. Such security is the consequence of good early care-giving which allows for internal boundaries to be established. Once these boundaries are in place they stay there for the whole of life unless a trauma occurs and interferes with an individual's continuous narrative. A feeling of self-worth gives individuals a sense of agency and creativity. They are able to act and speak for themselves. Such individuals are able to love and forgive themselves and to act in the same way towards other people.

Some distorted strands of Christian teaching have contributed to the sense of worthlessness which many people feel; this sense can lead to depression and, at worst, suicide. At the heart of all true psychological and religious teaching lies the belief in the value of every human person.

SENILE DEMENTIA
An obsolete term for dementia.
The term 'senile dementia' is obsolete, because 'senile' is pejorative and stigmatizing. The subject is better referred to as 'dementia (or dementing illnesses) in elderly people (or in later life)'.

SENSORY IMPAIRMENT
The complete or partial loss of one or more of the senses such as sight or hearing.
It is distinguished from both physical impairment and mental or cognitive impairment. The need to create more inclusive pastoral care has led to changes in nomenclature (Hull, 2001). People with a sensory impairment may be described as 'differently abled' or 'visually challenged'. It is important to remove from the language references to blind and deaf people which disparage them, such as 'not taking a blind bit of notice' (Hull, 1997).

SENTIENCE
In the study of groups, the aspect that reflects the affective dimension.
In any group, how it organizes itself is influenced not only by the requirements of the task but also by the sentient relationships between the different members of the group. The sentient system has as its task the maintenance and promotion of feelings of good will and love. But it may threaten to take over the task of the group. Then decisions may be taken on the basis of personal affection and group survival rather than on competence at the task. However, the sentient group is also important to the success of a project, in that it focuses and receives the loyalty of all members of the group.

SEPARATION
In human development, the act of separating or the state of being separated.
The capacity to separate, and to maintain a state of mind of being separated, is essential for individual human development. But the achievement of a mature separate identity can be hard won.

Developmental problems arising from separation anxiety are usually understood as stemming from premature or prolonged separations between mothers and infants.

When a baby or small child is separated from the mother or the parents in a manner which is unmanageable for the immature psyche, acute anxiety states can arise which may result in emotional difficulties in making and sustaining relationships in later life.

Studies on the adverse effects of separation have focused upon physical separation, as when a parent dies or is absent for long periods of time from the baby or small child. More recently, separation has been studied in a more subtle sense, as when a mother can be physically present but emotionally absent, as in cases of severely and persistently depressed mothers.

Winnicott (1965) has written of the importance of allowing a baby gradually to come to realize that he or she is separate from mother. He writes of the need for a mother to maintain for her baby an illusion of non-separateness in the early weeks of a baby's life. Yet it is essential that the mother gradually disillusion her baby, helping him or her to realize that she is a separate person who cannot meet every need the moment it arises.

Weaning plays a pivotal role in this gradual process of achieving a separate identity. Babies may be deeply attached to the breast, yet mothers must help them to relinquish this and to move forward in their development. Winnicott's concept of the 'transitional object' is of relevance here, and an example would be a baby's strong attachment to a soft toy which facilitates the transition from feeling in possession of the mother, to perceiving her as a separate person with whom the baby has an intimate and loving relationship. The possession of a transitional object permits an intermediate state of mind.

However, when early experiences of separation are abrupt, unexpected or prolonged, the infant may try to cling to the mother, unable to manage the temporary loss of her, or turn away from her after an absence in anger, or even despair.

The moving films made by James and Joyce Robertson convey vividly the effects of adverse separations upon small children. Generated by the work of John Bowlby (1985), and increased public awareness of the implications for children's emotional development of being subjected to sudden or long separations from their parents has given rise to changes in institutional practice.

In special-care baby units, parents are now allowed more contact with their premature or at-risk infants, within the restrictions of life-saving medical procedures. Paediatric hospital practices have changed so that children admitted to wards for short- and long-term stays can often be accompanied by a parent with overnight provision. It has also been recognized that in day-care nurseries, children need to find a substitute parental figure if they are to manage many hours in the week apart from their working parents. This has led to professional rethinking about the importance of consistency of staffing.

A consideration of issues related to separation also raises questions about whether or not it is conducive to young childrens' development for mothers to engage in full-time work, and this is a contentious area. It is sometimes the case that the quality of childcare available to working parents is far from ideal.

Attachment theory is perhaps the best-known conceptual basis for addressing issues related to separation. It is proving to be a valuable research tool in studies of the parent–child relationship. John Bowlby's theory of infant attachment to the mother was created in order to understand better the behaviour of infants in the family setting. It is centrally concerned with the tendencies observable in young children to seek security on the one hand, and to explore and master the environment on the other hand. This polarity is most obvious in small children but remains central in psychological development throughout the life-span.

Bowlby's research focused initially on the effects of physical separation of young children from their parents. More recent attachment research has investigated the quality of the mother's emotional availability to her child when she is present; her sensitivity and her responsiveness, or her lack of these qualities. It is now understood to be this factor which is of significance in enabling a child to cope well, or not, with separations.

Recent research has also shown that the infant's relationship to the father cannot be predicted from the nature of the relationship to the mother. The quality of the relationship between the young child and each parent has its own history. Thus a parent who is sensitive and responsive to the infant can provide essential qualities of relationship, even if the other parent is unable to do so. For example, when the child's attachment to the mother is insecure, the father may be the preferred attachment figure – the one from whom the child will seek comfort when tired, ill or frightened.

It is important to note that whereas an inse-cure attachment pattern can derive from an early experience of prolonged separation from the parents, or from the emotional unavailability of one or both parents, problems in children can also be generated by the parents' inability to separate appropriately from their child. When, for example, a mother has had difficulties in her own childhood, she can unwittingly impede her child's development by avoiding situations which require separations between herself and her child.

If early experiences of separation have been successfully negotiated, adults will be better equipped for parenthood, and indeed for managing painful separations which arise in later life, such as the death of a spouse or close friend. In pastoral work, an understanding of the literature on separation can be of great assistance when dealing with people suffering loss and bereavement. [*Lynda Miller*]

SERVANT
One of the cluster of New Testament images used both of the Church and of ministry.

The present quest to discover what has continuing validity and what can be abandoned in the Church's life has been largely resourced through a re-examination of the New Testament foundations of the Church's task and life. This has led to an increased awareness of the number of complementary understandings of ministry that have existed from the earliest times. The titles first used by Christians of the Church's ministers have clear links with the person and work of Jesus Christ. As Jesus was described as a servant, so too were ministers. As he was called apostle, evangelist, prophet, teacher and shepherd, so too were the servants of the Church.

Throughout the New Testament, leadership is service (1 Cor. 16.15f; 2 Cor. 3.7–9; 2 Tim. 4.5; Col. 4.17). When leadership is prominent (1 Pet. 5.1–4) the warning is sounded to obey God's will by not using leadership as a vehicle for domination. The radical cutting-edge of the Greek word *diakonos* (deacon) is blunted by the overtones of the English translation 'servant'. Although the word does describe serving at table (Mark 1.31; 15.41; Acts 6.2) it has a particular reference to caring service among the poor and the needy (Rom. 15.25, 31; 2 Cor. 8.14–19). This is more than charity, and different from slavery. At heart, it is being available to those at table and fulfilling their needs. Thus one who is leader within the community of faith may be recognized as having a service (1 Cor. 16.15f). As Jesus was a servant, so every Christian is called to be available as modelled in Jesus' own life (Mark 9.35; 10.42–45; John 13).

Service is more than helping. The key to serving lies in the mutual regard spelled out in the words, example and relationships of the gospel. For a Christian community to remember and be formed by both Israel's and Jesus' stories is to be nourished as an alternative or exemplary community – rooted in service – which takes time to care and nurture friendships, and to be an instrument of peace in a divided world. It is worth noting that as well as the pattern of Jesus' life, the theme of the suffering servant in Isaiah (e.g. 42.6–7 and 61.1) has clear links with a Church dedicated to serving God's desire to build the Kingdom of God on earth.

In the international ecumenical debate about Church, mission and ministry of the last three decades, the model of Church as servant has featured strongly. Official statements of the churches reflect the way in which churches and theologians – for example Teilhard de Chardin, Harvey Cox, John A. T. Robinson and Dietrich Bonhoeffer – had been developing the theme of servanthood. So, a servant understanding of the Church undergirded the Presbyterian Confession of 1967, the Uppsala Report of the World Council of Churches in 1968, the Conclusions of the Second General Conference of Latin American Bishops at Medellín in 1968, and the document on Justice in the World issued by the Roman Catholic Synod of Bishops in 1971. Rather than the Church confronting society with its own demands, the attitude of serving suggests that God's final purposes can be achieved by companionship and dialogue between the Church and other groups and organizations. Not only in proclamation, but in listening, in compassion, and in many forms of service, the Church can be for others a sign and sacrament of the coming Kingdom.

After the Second Vatican Council, the theme of _kenosis_, the self-emptying of Christ, has been a significant element in the Roman Catholic ecclesiology, which itself has had a major effect on worldwide consideration of the nature of the Church. In particular this moves the emphasis of church concern away from itself and its own perpetuation towards the Church's roles in keeping alive and nurturing the hopes and aspirations of humanity in relation to the whole creation.

Distortion occurs when one paradigm of Church and ministry is allowed to take up so much space that others are obscured. While the notion of serving must be fundamental to any approach to responding to God's call, without a sense of mutuality an unhealthy element of patriarchy, manipulation or omnipotence can set in. A clear example is a papal ministry, dedicated to serving, yet demanding in return inflexible obedience. To a lesser degree this has been true of dedicated clergy and laity who have served others intensively in isolation and who consciously or not put others down. The renewed recognition of the value of a trinitarian understanding of God's life and activity, together with the recovery of New Testament insights about the body of Christ and the people of God working in a correlative manner, and in companionship with the whole of society, provide the tools for dealing with such problems. [_Robin Greenwood_]

SEX
In human beings, the distinction according to type as male or female.

The distinction, as with any other to do with sex, is controversial at a number of levels. First, the basis for establishing sex-type is debatable. Second, there is controversy over the extent to which difference of sex goes beyond the role one may play in reproduction. This may include questions of the relation of sex to gender distinction, and the claimed objectivity of sex-difference. It also points towards questions of whether sex-type is fixed or alterable.

Sexual difference is often afforded the status of a biological truth. Determination of sex may be associated with a range of criteria, such as chromosomal make-up, external genitalia, gonads, reproductive organs, hormonal states and secondary sexual characteristics. Even the first of these is problematic, although it has been used as a test of the sex of athletes in sporting competitions. The standard expectation for human beings is two X chromosomes in female and an X and a Y in male humans. This leaves open what determination is to be made in cases of chromosomal abnormality, or where other sex-indicators give a different answer to the question of whether a person is 'male' or 'female'. In biology and medicine it appears that the gonads, or producers of gametes and sex-hormones, are regarded as definitive indicators.

A person's sex, however, is rarely interpreted on the basis of information about a person's gonads. Instead, there are a variety of public 'cues' of various kinds, such as appearance. These may in part depend upon some list of sex-indicators, but need not do so absolutely; indeed they may not do so at all. These cues are often self-consciously drawn from the stock of gender associations which determine what is to count as masculine and feminine. Gender appears to be relative to the cultural interpretation of the significance of sex. Sex has at least a degree of apparent objectivity, of givenness, compared with the admittedly 'constructed' typology of gender.

The interpretation of a human being as belonging to one or other sex is a matter of construction out of biological data. Classification according to sex might be itself a construction, although not an arbitrary one. The central biological phenomena relating to reproduction appear to be a given fact of human experience. Our conception of sexual difference is obviously related to this. Controversy is unlikely to be located here. It is the further claims that styles of thought and aptitudes for tasks are related to biological factors (rather than forms of social conditioning through family and education, media and marketing) which are much more hotly contested. In assessing claims of the putative sex-relatedness of physical strength, spatial awareness or numerical reasoning, the forms of thinking are abstracted from the particular existence of individual persons. Individuals may provide exceptions to any general claims. Such exceptions are likely to undermine the utility of these claims, and even make them appear to be means for suppressing the capacities of individuals. In contrast, it may be possible to posit an assumed 'common human nature', which is masked behind the division of human beings into male and female.

Some contemporary writers claim that belief in 'sexual difference' is a modern conception. It may be allied with the rise of pervasively biological interpretations of human existence. However, it is worth recalling the extent to which quasi-biological claims (such as the differing ages of a male or female foetus at 'ensoulment' according to some ancient, including Christian, writers) may be a reverse version of precisely the same entrenching of sexual difference. If such authors desired a biological account to explain and 'objectify' their perceived gender distinctions, this might point to a presumption of a more thoroughgoing sexual difference.

The claim of a sex-neutral common human nature might be challenged by the observation that bodily sexual identity is not the only level at which sex (as opposed to gender) identity may be known. One version is belief in sex-differentiated 'souls' which may find themselves united to bodies of a different sex, such as a male soul with a female body. Where the existence of souls as constituents or components of humanity is rejected, one may still encounter a strong belief in the capacity of the individual's consciousness of self to constitute a fixed truth about sexual type. This might be distinct from the biological–physical sexual identity of the body. The nature and status of truth-claims in this area becomes the concern of a variety of parties: for pastoral ministers, medical practitioners and policy-makers and legislators. The language of 'sex-change' is sometimes used to characterize the surgical, cosmetic and pharmacological reassignment of physical and hormonal characteristics. However, in some countries medical practitioners have been more inclined to speak of 'gender-realignment'. They may regard the question of true sex type as either unanswerable or absolutely determined by physical characteristics at birth. In keeping with the latter view, in some legislations it is not possible to change one's legal sex-type as determined at birth. This clearly has consequences for access to employment or legally sanctioned forms of relationship where sex-type is legally significant.

In relation to the nature of sex and sexual difference, an understanding of the disputes detailed above relates to questions in the philosophy of language and of mind. It seems clear that no individual can have a pure self-knowledge unaffected by the conceptual categories of gender expectation. Even self-knowledge is dependent upon matters (such as language and meaning) which are public rather than private. So it is not surprising that biology becomes the key arena for determination of the truth of sex-type. The truth of the extent of biological sex-difference cannot be investigated independently of empirical investigation. Questions of truth concerning the plasticity of sex-type in the individual, and critical conceptual interpretation of the empirical data, are more obviously philosophical and theological. [David Leal]

SEXISM
A form of injustice affecting relationships between men and women.

Sexism is behaviour that denies the dignity of women. Such actions prevent or discourage women from being free, autonomous persons. Women thereby are meant to feel inferior and to become dominated by the judgements of men. Sexism is located in social institutions, practices and customs, resulting in inequalities of opportunity, recognition and prospects for women.

Sexism is also any form of thinking which categorizes people according to preconceived notions of gender identity. These stereotypes inhibit the full expression of the human potential of women and men.

SEXUAL COUNSELLING
A combination of psychotherapy and teaching, with homework assignments, designed to help couples, or individuals, who experience sexual dysfunction.

Sexuality lies at the heart of human identity as female and male. Sexuality and spirituality are related, in that each involves a longing which can be satisfied only outside one's self. Ministers will find the two areas closely related in working with members of faith communities (Nelson, 1994).

The four stages of the sexual response cycle are the following: (1) desire phase, where thoughts, fantasies and actions produce sexual arousal; (2) excitement-plateau phase, where sexual behaviour is engaged in, with growing intensity; (3) orgasm phase, where sexual excitement peaks in orgasm, resulting in ejaculation for the male and rhythmic pelvic contractions for the female. This phase is brief and intense, with one's attention pulled inward; (4) resolution phase, where the partners are relaxed, a sense of well-being is felt, and their bodies return to a pre-aroused state.

Difficulties can occur at any of the four phases. In the desire phase, either partner may experience inhibited sexual desire, although it is more usual for the woman to feel this. This is the most common problem. Among couples, one partner often desires sexual contact more frequently than the other. In some cases, there is a compelling fear of sex, so desire is avoided.

In the excitement phase, most persons are not responsive all the time, given other preoccupations and tensions of living. For women this often shows in lack of lubrication, while in men it shows in difficulties in getting and maintaining erections.

During the orgasm phase, premature ejaculation for the man and inhibited orgasm for the woman are the most common sexual problems. The man may also have difficulty with inhibited ejaculation. Usually the man is able to ejaculate through masturbation or with manual or oral stimulation from the partner; in extremely rare cases a man may never have experienced an orgasm. A few women have never experienced orgasm, with or without coitus, while others have difficulty experiencing orgasm during coitus but can do so manually. Difficulties in this area can lead both men and, more commonly, women to fake orgasms. For a variety of reasons, intercourse may be painful for both men and women.

Difficulties in the resolution phase are the result of problems in the previous phase. If orgasm has not occurred, or has occurred too quickly for one partner, both partners may be left feeling frustrated and with a heightened sexual tension not discharged.

For any of the above difficulties, a person or couple may seek sexual counselling. Such counselling may be intensive, so that it occurs for several hours each day for a period of usually two weeks, or it may occur once or twice a week over a longer period of time. It may include the following: physical examination, careful sexual history, dealing with any communication problems between the couple, providing information in needed areas, and giving homework assignments designed to meet the need of the particular couple. This often includes sensate focus exercises, where partners take turns in giving and receiving touch. Both partners are asked to focus on their pleasure, whether in giving or in receiving. At the beginning, the couple is explicitly prohibited from proceeding to sexual intercourse, even if there is strong desire.

Deeper problems, having to do with sexual abuse or rape, or woundedness from the past, may surface and need attention. The sexual counsellor may be professionally equipped to provide this therapy or she or he may refer the person.

Some people do not seem to fit the usual categories of female and male, for a variety of anatomical, genetic and other reasons. Transgender is the term increasingly used to refer to individuals who cross or transcend culturally defined categories of gender. This includes persons who have undergone hormone therapy and/or sex-change operations, persons who wear clothing associated with the other sex, female/male impersonators, and others. Such persons may seek sexual counselling in dealing with the social stigma or before 'coming out' in dressing like the other sex. Sexual counselling is required before sex-change surgery.

Homosexuality and bisexuality, and even more so transgendered persons, are controversial in most churches around the world today. As a result, the Church and ministers have tended to shy away from serious discussion of any sexual topics or from sexual education in the Church. Ministers need to be aware of their own sexuality, feelings and needs, and be reasonably comfortable with them. When persons come to talk, the minister should be open to discussing the sexual area and using sexual words, as any other area of a person's life might be shared. A sexual relationship on the minister's part with a member of the faith community is *always* unethical, given the minister's professional role and the resulting power difference. Ministers needs to know the position of their Church on such issues as abortion, homosexuality, premarital sex, etc., and should have come to their own reasoned position. In providing pastoral care with a person dealing with one of these difficult areas, the job of the minister is not to provide the answer but to assist the person in coming to a position that is right for them, after considering the position of the Church and of society (Arnold, 1993).

People need to know that Matt. 5.28 does not mean that a sexual feeling and acting on that feeling are the same thing. Indeed, they may need sometimes to be reassured that the text concerns the protection of women in the context of the law on adultery. People often need to be given permission to enjoy sexual relations with their partner, given the prohibitions that many people have received from their childhood and in some cases from the Church. Sometimes sexual misinformation can be corrected or books containing appropriate material can be loaned. Beyond that, people need referrals to trained, competent sexual counsellors. Ministers need to know professional persons in the community to whom they can make such referrals. [*Bill Ratliff*]

SEXUAL DEVIATION
Sexual behaviour that diverges from society's accepted norm – also called sexual perversion.

Sexual deviation is often used as a milder, more acceptable term to refer to sexual perversion. The difference in meaning is subtle but important. *Deviation* is defined (in the Oxford English Dictionary) as a 'turning aside from a path or track'. *Perversion* (also in the OED) carries a more sinister meaning of 'turning the wrong way; turning aside from truth or right; diversion to an improper use; corruption, distortion'. Whether one is concerned simply about turning aside or about turning wrongly, both definitions presume the existence of a standard of normal sexual behaviour from which one turns away. Thus, sexual deviation or perversion refers to behaviour that is habitual, that leads to sexual excitement, and that deviates from society's norms (Gillespie, 1956).

An additional important feature is that these physical behaviours are accompanied by fantasy, either conscious or unconscious. The content of these fantasies can reveal a great deal about the meaning and etiology of the behaviour. Freud (1905) initially viewed deviations as persistence into adult life of infantile forms of sexuality, involving oral and anal rather than genital areas of the body. Later, he came to view them as defences against anxiety, particularly castration anxiety. For example, a boy might turn his sexual interest to the safer arena of a fetish, such as a shoe, to defend against anxiety engendered by a fantasy that his penis would be cut off if he engaged in genital sexuality.

Currently, hypotheses about perversions centre more on problems in central relationships. Difficulties in separation from the mother are sometimes seen as contributory. Stoller (1975) suggests that perversions result from childhood trauma that subsequently gives rise to hostility and a wish for revenge. An example of this could be a man who was psychologically traumatized as a boy by his mother. As an adult, he comes to view women only as potential sexual conquests, dehumanizing them so that they are no longer unique individuals. Thus, he converts trauma to triumph over the female figure that hurt him.

Some personality features associated with perversions include aggressiveness, narcissism or self-preoccupation, and avoidance or twisting of reality. These features indicate the psychological severity of perversions. Far from being benign, they are indicators of serious psychological difficulty. Often, the perversion serves to contain personality diffusion that would otherwise occur. For this reason, individuals with perversions should be referred to specialized practitioners for assessment and treatment.

Some examples of perversions include: (1) exhibitionism, the need to reveal one's sexual organs to others; (2) voyeurism, the need to look at others' sexual organs; (3) sadism and masochism, excitement generated by the experience of pain; (4) transvestism, the wish to behave as the opposite sex; (5) fetishism, sexual attraction to an inanimate object or a non-genital part of the body. The question of whether or not to include homosexuality as a deviation or perversion is highly problematic. Current opinion ranges from viewing homosexuality as a normal variant to viewing it as a destructive psychological disorder. Perhaps the safest position is to consider that there is a range of homosexual behaviours and that, as in heterosexuality, they represent a variety of levels of psychological health.
[*Judith Freedman*]

SEXUAL HARASSMENT
Unwelcome sexual attention, verbal or physical.

Unlike rape or sexual assault, harassment does not constitute a criminal offence but rather a misdemeanour which, when reported, normally requires investigation. An upheld claim of such harassment can lead to the perpetrator being formally rebuked and/or dismissed from the place of employment or public office. Concerted moves to eradicate forms of such behaviour, now formally undertaken by a number of public institutions, have been accompanied by considerable public debate. The US Army, for example, set up a special task force in 1997 to examine this problem, concluding it to be endemic across 'gender, rank and racial lines'.

Questions as to what the term can be accurately said to consist of, and how serious a problem it is, remain highly disputed. Also of particular concern to pastoral thought and practice is an underlying question: what does the problem itself, along with the high profile

it has come to assume, signify about male/female relationships in our society?

A number of social changes have combined to bring this issue to the fore. First, there is women's entry into the workplace (where the majority of reported cases occur) in significantly larger numbers over the last thirty years. Men and women who would formerly have either never met or done so only in a limited and defined social context, now spend extended periods of time together and, with increased professional and educational opportunities for women, are more often doing so as equals. Second, their stronger more visible presence in public life, combined with the emancipatory egalitarian ideals promulgated by twentieth-century feminism, has made women less willing to 'fit in' with a predominantly male 'workplace culture'.

Most incidents of sexual harassment occur within what the plaintiffs, mainly women, experience as an ethos/atmosphere which demeans and trivializes them. For example, the public display of 'girly' or nude pictures in office or canteen, while not themselves constituting sexual harassment, appears to give out an intimidating message to women. Thus it has become appropriate to speak of a spectrum of abuse/harassment, i.e. of a female-hostile atmosphere where hostility can, both in the workplace and in wider society, lead to the kind of abusive behaviour – 'groping' and 'propositioning' – which constitutes the misconduct of 'sexual harassment' and in extreme cases the criminal offences of assault and rape. Pleas of mitigation still sometimes include assertions that 'she was flaunting herself' or 'she was asking for it'.

The high correlation between those seeking to minimize the extent, nature and significance of sexual harassment with those opposed to social change is significant. Punditry, such as 'if you don't like the heat, stay out of the kitchen', is presently given credence and even respectability in the media. Such a position can be reinforced by some forms and expressions of Christian thought. An unease about women deserting their 'proper sphere' is detectable across the denominational and doctrinal spectrum – from the 'headship'-oriented theologies emanating from Protestantism to the 'special sphere'-oriented theologies we see in more traditional forms of Christianity and Judaism.

The above uncertainties are clearly outweighed by Christianity's common understanding of the dignity and integrity of the human body and that of human personhood itself, which suggests that pastoral theory and practice can, and must, go on to address the enduring question this issue has exposed, namely how, in a changing context, men and women can build up a genuine, heartfelt and non-exploitative interest in one another. [*Susan Dowell*]

SEXUALITY
Those physiological, psychological, behavioural and spiritual dimensions of being a male or female human being which may or may not be given expression in sexual feelings and activity.
The word 'sexuality' is often used loosely as an umbrella term to cover, variously, sexual gender, identity, orientation and drive. It is, however, a more complex, but fundamental, part of our human nature in the same way as is our mentality, rationality or spirituality. We are all sexual creatures, and this 'sexuality' forms and informs the way we think, feel and behave, whether or not we choose to be sexually active.

Sexuality is woven into the fabric of all human relationships. In both conscious and unwitting ways our sexuality motivates the way we act, react and interact with other men and women – with family members, friends and strangers as well as with sexual partners. Since we cannot escape the fact that we are sexual beings, this inevitably influences and inspires our thought, feeling and creativity.

Our earliest relationships will root within us the way we relate to people of the same and opposite genders. From our parents, as infants, we ideally learn trust and reliability, closeness without fear, and intimacy without manipulation; we learn to receive love and to feel good about ourselves. Each person has elements of male-ness and female-ness within them, and how we integrate and use these will depend on whether our sexuality was affirmed by our parents. From siblings and significant others we learn who and what we are sexually. All these early relationships will determine how easy we are with our sexuality, whether it becomes integral to our personality. This in turn will affect our adult relationships, how we cope with sexual drive, and how we balance the instinctual desire for gratification with a capacity for self-giving.

If we are healthily integrated in this way it means we shall be able to give ourselves and of ourselves. In other words we shall be able to love. But if our early parental relationships have not satisfied us, we shall need more than we can give. Sexuality may then seek its expression purely for pleasure or for power, for affection or exploitation. The integration of sexuality into our personality is necessary for psychological wholeness, and is the foundation of what Christian tradition means by chastity. Since human sexuality is such a powerful force – it can affirm and heal, but also destroy – Judaeo-Christian teaching has surrounded it with explicit rules.

The psychosociological changes of the second half of the twentieth century, with an increasing emphasis on self-fulfilment (hand-in-hand with advances in fertility control and the changing role of women), saw a shift towards *individual* sexuality – expressions of gender and orientation – as a means of defining oneself. Sexuality has been given an inflated significance, especially in the media and popular arts and entertainment, and is often seen now as a commodity, or as a vehicle for self-expression and means of self-fulfilment in an age which considers these to be rights. Paradoxically this has led to a trivialization of personal sexuality.

The Church may often have given the impression that sexual sin is the most heinous, and bears some responsibility for this emphasis on sexuality over all the other factors which make up a person. Such an accentuation may lead people whose sense of self as a sexual being is fragile either to use sex exploitatively, or to feel devalued and worthless if they do not consider they live up to peer standards of attractiveness, or to the norms and codes of the society in which they move.

Christians recognize that human sexuality comes from the creator, and is thus good. However, the Church holds out the ideal of chastity, which is generally taken to mean either living in continence, or expressing our sexuality genitally only within marriage, as a sign of Christ's self-giving love for his people. In previous ages of fragile mortality, sexual intercourse was seen as primarily for the procreation of children. Church teaching draws biblically mainly on what St Paul wrote, and has often given the impression that continence is the better way. Some later teachers, preachers and writers saw the 'flesh' as corrupt and contact with women as a distasteful necessity. Their fear, or misunderstanding, of sexuality has served to induce in some Christians a sense of shame and guilt at what are natural feelings and responses.

In the late twentieth century, scientific advance affected social practice. Fertility control has separated pleasure from procreation, and contributed to the increase of uncommitted sexual relationships. We also know now that a homosexual orientation is unlikely to be solely a psychological aberration (and thus 'curable'), but probably of genetic origin, and therefore may have to be re-evaluated within the total pattern of human sexuality.

The Church must address the pastoral care of all those in relationships which fall outside the ideals of continence or lifelong marriage. Because people need time and space to grow and change, especially to integrate their sexuality, it is entirely right that there should be a dissonance between the way people are handled pastorally and a strict interpretation of Scripture and tradition. Good pastoral practice puts people foremost, with sensitivity, openness, understanding and compassion.

This will not be the case unless those in ministry have resolved the issues of their own sexuality. Selection boards increasingly address these issues as part of their assessment of a candidate's personality and suitability. If the minister has not fully integrated his or her own sexuality while growing up, or this has not been achieved by therapy or counselling, then it will affect all pastoral relationships, and jeopardize both proper detachment and the maintenance of boundaries.

In a pastoral context ministry teams also need to be aware that some people, because of early experience, will be more comfortable being ministered to or counselled by someone of their own gender, while others will respond better to someone of the opposite sex. [Mary Kirk]

SHADOW
The dark side of the human psyche.
The inferior or unpleasant or shameful parts of a person which he or she tries unconsciously to hide. As the shadow is an archetype, it carries much affect. It can manifest either collectively in the various 'isms' and persecutions, or in the individual in irrational attitudes to other people.

SHAME
A painful emotional state of humiliation caused by the exposure, or the fear of exposure, of failure or deficiency.
Although this definition would be widely agreed, interpretations of shame vary according to the view taken of its relationship to guilt. Some writers regard shame as an aspect of guilt. Others hold that shame and guilt are distinct emotional states. The anthropological tradition has tended to emphasize the element of public exposure in shame, and to define guilt in terms of the internal disapproval of conscience and shame in terms of the external disapproval of the group. On this basis it has distinguished between shame-cultures and guilt-cultures. Primitive societies, village communities and the Eastern world are held to be shame-cultures, and advanced societies, urban communities and the Western world to be guilt-cultures. However, this view has been challenged from within the anthropological tradition itself on the grounds that guilt as well as shame is found in primitive societies, that shame can be internalized like guilt, and that the criteria for identifying shame-cultures and guilt-cultures are insufficiently precise (Piers and Singer, 1953).

The psychoanalytic tradition, while including the fear of exposure in the concept of shame, focuses on the doer rather than the deed and stresses the element of failure. Shame arises from failure to achieve, whereas guilt springs from transgression. Shame is related to internalized ideals and guilt to internalized prohibitions. The sense of shame is inculcated by loving and admired authority figures, the sense of guilt by those who are harsh and feared. Shame anticipates contempt and rejection; guilt expects punishment (Lewis, 1991).

The disadvantage of the psychoanalytic exposition is that the very neatness of its contrasts disguises the extent to which the two emotional states overlap. A single act may be seen as both a transgression and a failure. For example, an extra-marital affair is simultaneously a transgression of the prohibition against unfaithfulness and a failure to maintain faithfulness. High ideals are imposed by harsh parents and prohibitions enforced by loving parents. Those who transgress are often treated with contempt and rejection, and those who fail to achieve are often punished.

Nevertheless, the value of the psychoanalytic distinction between failure and transgression is that it directs attention to those failures caused by excusable factors like inability and inadequacy rather than by culpable factors like laziness and cowardice. Those who are persistently shamed, that is humiliated, for inability to achieve at all or for failure to achieve idealistic standards, frequently develop false feelings of guilt, believing themselves to be blameworthy. If these feelings become excessive or pathological, pastoral care involves explaining the difference between culpable failure and failure through inability, establishing realistic standards, affirming achievement however modest, and building appropriate self-esteem. [*Howard Gordon*]

SHEPHERDING
A movement to bring about whole-of-life commitment among members of house churches.
This movement is found chiefly in house churches. Adult Christians are shepherded by group leaders, accountable to church elders, supposedly into spiritual maturity. All decisions must be sanctioned by the leader. Although some leaders are aware of the risks, the movement may sometimes lead to false dependence on the leaders, manipulation and spiritual immaturity.

SHYNESS
A tendency to shrink from the notice of others and a reticence in approaching them.
Shyness is considered a temperament in that it is an inherited personality trait and is present in early childhood. Recent research suggests a distinction between early-developing, fearful shyness and later-developing, self-conscious shyness. The former typically emerges in the first year of life and is influenced by temperamental qualities of wariness, emotionality, and behavioural inhibition; the latter appears around ages four to five, has a cognitive component of self- and other-perception, and reaches a peak in mid-adolescence. While little psychopathology is attached to shyness as such, shy children are at greater risk of developing social phobia in adolescence (Jones, 1986). Research studies show that while children are born with a biological predisposition to shyness, early home environment plays a decisive role in developmental outcomes of shyness in adults, the child's relationship to the mother having a strong effect on whether the shy adult develops feelings of insecurity and/or excessive loneliness owing to temperamental shyness. Pathological forms of shyness seem more pronounced among men than women, but this may be attributed to

social expectations of male assertiveness in social and occupational performance (Daly and McGroskey, 1984). [*Donald Capps*]

SICK, CARE OF THE
To offer appropriate treatment and support for the person who is dis-eased in order that they may return to a state of wellness (absence of disease) or, wherever possible, health and wholeness.
This care may be offered in a variety of settings by a variety of people. Hospitals are increasingly the places where acute, intensive, short-stay treatment is offered and the community (specialized units and nursing homes) is becoming the preferred place for convalescence or long-term care. The early or less acute stages of disease, as well as the terminal phase of life-threatening illness, may be cared for in the patient's own home. Changes in the pattern of care have implications for those offering care, as, for example, the moving of long-term care of the elderly from hospital to community care has widespread consequences for patients with chronic disease or mental incapacity as well as the emotional and financial toll on family/lay carers. Apart from emergency situations, more sick people will initially be cared for by their family and the Primary Care Team, led by the family doctor/general medical practitioner. The family doctor will then refer the individual to the hospital for more specialized investigation and/or treatment, which the patient will receive as an outpatient or inpatient, subsequently returning home to community care.

Various people will be involved at different stages. They will identify and respond to discerned needs, often in accordance with their role. The doctor will identify any disease processes and prescribe treatment, the nurse may additionally pay attention to the patient's subjective feelings and responses as well as act as an intermediary between doctor and patient. The physiotherapist will primarily focus on the person's mobility and any necessary exercises pre- or post-operatively to enhance the recovery. Often non-professional carers, paid and unpaid, will attend to the need for a clean environment, the arrangement of flowers, the feeding of incapacitated patients, the voluntary transporting of patients to outpatient clinics and day-care centres. Some of this care will be non-clinical and focus more on the person than the disease. The rather impersonal nature of some high-technology medicine, and the desire for a more person-centred approach, has been a key factor in the growth of complementary therapies such as acupuncture, aromatherapy, osteopathy, homeopathy, etc.

When a person becomes sick, various questions will arise in their minds as to why this has happened: 'Why now?' and 'What have I done to deserve this?' The person will usually refer to their belief system or philosophy of life to answer these questions and begin a quest for satisfactory answers which is a search for existential meaning and purpose within the experience (Speck, 1988). Spirituality is to do with the search for existential meaning and purpose with reference to some power other than the self which may or may not be referred to as God. For some this will take a clear religious pathway, but for others the search will be more philosophical. Pastoral care of the sick is to do with accompanying the individual on this search as a resource. Journeying in this way may lead to the need for a more specific ministry according to the person's faith tradition or for a more general sharing. The focus for pastoral care is existential and relates to the individual's relationship with God, but the way and the timescale for achieving this will vary greatly with each encounter.

If the sick person has a religious belief then they may wish to continue to express that while in hospital or elsewhere. Thus they may value having access to the religious writings/Scriptures of their faith, to uninterrupted times for prayer or meditation, opportunities to worship with others at the bedside or in a hospital chapel, or to receive the sacraments in the Christian tradition. At various points in the progression of the disease the faith tradition may have specific rituals to provide strength and meaning. For example, the emergency baptism of a very sick baby, the sacramental anointing with oil and/or the laying on of hands as part of the ministry of healing, and the commendatory prayers at the time of death.

Alongside such specific religious ministry there may be a need for pastoral counselling to enable the sick person and family to examine and perhaps reaffirm or restructure their understanding of their faith. In the absence of a religious faith we should beware the assumption that there will be no spiritual need. The search for existential meaning and purpose will still be taking place for most people and represents a broader spiritual need. Whether in the context of religion or broad spirituality, the causality of sickness is a common theme and possible links between the sickness and perceived past 'wrong-doing' will often be explored. In some traditions this can be experienced quite punitively and can become built into the thought patterns of some forms of mental illness.

The object, pastorally, of care of the sick is to enable the individual to come to a more harmonious relationship with their own body, mind and spirit, with other significant people in their lives, and with God. This may entail modifications to their lifestyle and behaviour, and implies the need for a good working relationship between the pastoral care-giver and the other professional and non-professional givers, some of whom may also be recognizing and meeting the sick person's spiritual needs. [Peter Speck]

SICKNESS
The result of the manifestations of symptoms indicating disease processes within the body of the individual.

Sickness, as the result of disease, is defined by doctors and based upon the observation of biological pathology. It therefore has objectivity and a scientific basis (the biomedical model of pathology), which is the foundation of modern Western medical thought. Earlier doctors had mainly dealt with the verbally expressed concerns of the sick person and provided advice on physical treatment of conditions. The biomedical model of health likens the human body to a machine which is to be restored to health (more accurately to symptom-free 'wellness') through treatments which arrest, or reverse, the disease process. Some treatments may have side-effects, usually short-term, which can lead to new episodes of sickness. Medical technology has made new forms of treatment possible – heart surgery, transplants and genetic manipulation – which have increased expectations of a disease-free life. In recent years there has been a development of overdependence on health-care services, with a consequent reduction of the individual's responsibility for their own health care. The over-medicalization of life events (birth, childhood, ageing, dying) has contributed to this 'social iatrogenesis', which was criticized by Illich (1991). Recent developments in health promotion and complementary medicine have sought to restore the balance.

Modern medicine has moved its focus to scientifically defined disease processes which occur within the body of the individual and create 'sickness', rather than deal with the whole person. Any verbal report of believing oneself to be sick must therefore be substantiated by other evidence *or* discounted in subsequent treatment. In contrast, the experience of the sick person is listened to and taken into account within palliative care and other health-care approaches. While symptoms of sickness may be treated, the focus in palliative care is more on quality of life for that whole person. The subjective experience of ill-health links more to the word 'illness' than 'sickness', since illness goes beyond the biological consequences of disease to encompass the person's subjective well-being and social functioning.

The term 'sick role' was developed by Parsons, who suggested that sickness creates problems for the sick person and for society and that this aspect of sickness gradually becomes regularized into a social role. The sick role is complementary to that of the clinician and it has been criticized (Friedson, 1972) for being too consensual a model for doctor–patient relationships. However, it does provide a bridge between the definitions of sickness and of illness. Having symptoms (being sick) does not necessarily lead to someone defining themselves as ill. Many chronic diseases may not produce symptoms for a long time, so that the individual does not perceive themselves as being ill, e.g. diabetes, held in check by insulin, may not restrict the individual's life. [*Peter Speck*]

SILENCE
The absence of speech or noise so that the full attention of the person can be completely focused in the present moment.

Absence of speech or silence between persons is never wholly negative. It might be comparatively empty, e.g. between two strangers sitting beside each other in a bus, or comparatively full, e.g. between two lovers alone together. Because silence is meaningful, it has pastoral significance. There is a relationship between the amount of talking which takes place between persons and the amount of deep communication. At a certain stage of intimacy, the more talk, the less communication; the less talk (i.e., the more silence), the

more communication. Two strangers on meeting have to keep talking to each other because silence between them is a breakdown in communication. Later, however, friends may communicate better when not speaking. In the intensity of love, people may find themselves in situations when they cannot speak because the use of words would actually prevent adequate communication: they find themselves literally and emotionally speechless.

There are at least four pastoral and spiritual aspects to silence:

1. In counselling, silence plays an essential part. By remaining silent but in touch, a counsellor gives the person room to speak about his or her problems, room to express emotions and space to reach his or her own conclusions. The absence of words enables the counsellor to be more effective when the time comes for speaking. A chattering counsellor will get nowhere in therapeutic listening and will fail to draw out the other person. Silence may indicate trust and acceptance. Equally it may indicate restlessness. Often, however, it points to hostility, anxiety, withdrawal or simply bewilderment. Silence is rarely if ever simple or unambiguous, and the pastor must therefore rely on some understanding of non-verbal communication.

2. In preaching and teaching silence may also be used. Strategically placed, it enables the speaker to establish a rapport with the audience and gives that audience time to think.

3. Silence plays an important part in worship, especially in the sacraments. There are many communications through movement, lights, colours and so on. Amid these a careful balance between interpretation, explanation and silence is an integral part of sacramental experience.

4. Silence is a major factor in prayer, especially contemplation. It is increasingly being used by individuals, not least in retreats. Corporate silence for prayer is also becoming a normal part of the liturgical life of many churches. [*John Dalrymple/Martin Israel*]

SIN
The condition of relational brokenness and estrangement which exists perpetually between God and all humans, and the destructive human actions which result from this separation and brokenness.

In the Hebrew Bible, a variety of words and phrases pictures sin and its consequences.

Their meanings include: deviation from what is right; the missing of a prescribed target; moral and spiritual failure; wilful rebellion; and defiance and disobedience towards God. In the Old Testament, sinful people are seen as wicked, immoral and guilty. Sinful actions are viewed as abnormal, and destructive of the self and others.

Israel's prophets view sin as a violation of one's personal relationship with God. It is a disobedient breaking of God's covenant resulting in both separation and judgement from God. The prophet Jeremiah emphasizes that sin originates in the heart, the centre of human life and home of the will. The heart is wilfully deceitful and corrupt. As a result, humans continually break the covenant God has made with them. One sin leads to another, establishing a perennial personal, interpersonal and social pattern. All humanity is involved and guilty. All come under God's judgement.

The story of Adam and Eve illustrates these points definitively. Here wilful disobedience of God leads to family turmoil and death. This begins a pattern which corrupts the whole earth. It is filled with such violence that God destroys all its inhabitants, save Noah and his family and their charges. Remedies for sin include repentant liturgical rituals, faithful obedience to God's law and, ultimately, trusting one's self to the soul-restoring mercy and forgiveness of God.

The Christian Scriptures emphasize not only sin and its consequences, but also and most importantly the role of Jesus as God's answer to sin. Jesus, as portrayed in the first three Gospels, displays a deeply penetrating understanding of both sin and sinner. He names sinful motivations as well as actions. Even the outwardly righteous are subject to his judgement. Jesus takes seriously the Hebrew prophetic view that sin grows out of the corrupt human heart. He draws from intertestamental Judaism the role of Satan as the prime source of human temptation. Jesus also confronts sin in a personal way, calling sinners to repentance and offering personal forgiveness as if it came directly from God.

Sin is a central theological and pastoral concept for St Paul. While observant of individual sins and sinners, Paul focuses on sin as a consuming power, a cosmic principle, which works constantly in human life against faith in God and Christ. For Paul, 'Whatever does not proceed from faith is sin' (Rom. 14.23). Death is his comprehensive term for the physical and spiritual results of sin's rule among humans. No one is innocent. Through Adam all humans are under the power of sin, all fall short of God's intent, and all are subject to God's judgement. Obedience to the law is no remedy. The law only reveals and emphasizes the presence and power of sin.

Paul's answer to sin's rule is Jesus, who died, was raised from the dead by God and made Lord and Christ. Through baptism and faith in God's graceful action in Christ, one is freed from the power of sin, is forgiven and restored to a right relationship with God, and receives the gift of new life and a new future. Never very far from the grasp of sin, the Christian struggles with it constantly under the guidance and help of the Holy Spirit.

Traditional Christian theology has defined sin as unfaith, a denial of the reality and faithfulness of God. This basic understanding has been complemented throughout history with terms such as pride (meaning the human tendency to make one's self ultimate and absolute), and concupiscence (the selfish desire to have and control all that is). Common distortions of this understanding of sin include identifying human finitude, and therefore creation itself, as the basic source of sin (Manichaeism), and seeing sin as only a matter of human choice, and therefore denying its inevitable and systemic character (Pelagianism).

Sin has been the focus of pastoral concern in the Christian Church since the first Jerusalem congregation began the task of ordering its life together following the experience of Pentecost. Holifield (1983) points out that by the second century the Church had developed standard pastoral methods of private guidance and public penance for sin. Following the Protestant Reformation at the end of the sixteenth century, Roman Catholics, Lutherans, Anglicans and English Puritans had all developed pastoral traditions for the care and cure of souls. In all four traditions pastors regarded the cure of souls primarily as a way of dealing with sin.

Beginning with the Enlightenment, the validity of sin as a defining concept for humanity's relationship with God has been challenged from both within and without the Church. This critique has become particularly acute with the knowledge explosion in the natural and human sciences, especially psychology, since the Second World War. As a consequence, many pastoral practitioners and care-givers have replaced their traditional religious understandings of humans with non-religious, therapeutic understandings. These approaches often remove the category of sin from ministry, and replace it with various theories of causality and therapeutic cure. Here circumstance replaces sin as the defining factor in human life.

With this development, pastoral ministry may be facing the most fundamental challenge ever to its understanding of the human and to the centrality of sin in that understanding. It has yet to be determined what part sin will play in future pastoral definitions of the human, in pastoral diagnosis of the human condition and of human problems, and in the pastoral ministries of healing, sustaining, guiding and reconciling. [*J. Paul Balas*]

SINGLE PARENTS
Lone parents who reside with and have principal day-to-day responsibility for their dependent children.

There are three principal routes into single parenthood. First, there are parents, almost exclusively women, who choose to bring up children on their own. The choice may follow an accidental pregnancy occurring in the context of a casual sexual relationship, or where a longer-term relationship comes to an end. Faced with the alternatives of abortion and adoption these (often young) mothers will opt to bring their children up alone. The fortunate ones will have help from family and friends, but there are others who struggle to manage alone. Poverty and social disadvantage are likely to be features of these families.

There are also more deliberate pathways to single parenthood. In the past, informal surrogacy and adoption-cum-fostering arrangements were the only means by which women who did not want a male partner could have children. Today, there are tight legal controls on adoption that reflect, among other things, the social values of the community. Informal surrogacy remains an option, but rapid advances in assisting conception through medical technology (and the practical demonstration that cloning is possible in non-human animals through the manipulation of genes) have opened potential new horizons for aspiring single parents. They have also raised substantive ethical and moral issues that attract fierce debate.

Second, there are parents who are left on their own following the death of their partner. Historically, this was a common route to single parenthood. Wars, disease, famine and childbirth were just some of the misadventures that deprived children of one of their parents. That situation remains unchanged in some parts of the world. Studies of family life in England have indicated that the rate of remarriage 300 years ago was similar to that in many contemporary Western societies (around one marriage in every three being a remarriage for one or both partners); the difference is that then remarriage was almost always preceded by the death of a partner whereas today it is usually preceded by divorce.

The third route into single parenthood is, as indicated, through separation and divorce. It is by far the most common pathway for parents living in affluent Western countries, where high rates of divorce have been prominent features on the social landscape in recent times. For England and Wales, lone-parent families now constitute around one in five of all families with dependent children, and the proportion is increasing. It is commonly a transient state, terminated by parents forming other partnerships or remarrying. While it lasts, it is often associated with poverty and material hardship.

The term 'single parent' is a less than accurate description of lone-parent family life. It implies the absence of another parent or adult functioning in a parental role. While this absence is accurate in terms of physical residence and principal care-taking responsibilities, it can be misleading. At the very least, a fantasy of the absent parent is likely to persist in the minds of children and adults that may influence their feelings about themselves, their sense of identity and where they and others belong in the family unit. This can be true even when there has been no contact with the absent party, as when conception has relied on the anonymous donation of egg or sperm. An absence caused by death may instate an image of an ideal parent with whom family members must come to terms, even when memories are at odds with the image. In any event, bereavement is often accompanied by a measure of idealization that masks complicated feelings about a departure for which no one can usually be blamed. Conversely, an absence owing to divorce may invoke negative parental images when the departure has caused pain, rejection and insecurity among remaining family members.

It is in the context of separation and divorce that the term 'single parent' is most likely to be a misnomer. While between one-third and one-half of parents (notably fathers) are said to lose contact with their children after divorce (and for reasons that are often more complex than the irresponsibility commonly ascribed to them), they are still in a minority. Non-resident parents frequently maintain an active relationship with their children. Through visits, staying contact, telephone calls and letter-writing they can remain an influential, if not always welcome, presence. They are likely to provide material support for the upbringing of their children and may share legal responsibility for them with the resident parent. For these reasons many social scientists have substituted the descriptor 'lone parents' for 'single parents' as being a more accurate statement about their condition.

Single parents are currently the subject of much social and political criticism. Images of young women becoming pregnant to secure social housing, of the state standing in for errant fathers in providing for the children they have spawned, and of children roaming the streets out of control, represent lone parents as social pariahs. They reflect anxiety about the public costs of private choices, waning economic certainties, rapid changes in sexual roles and relationships, high levels of juvenile crime, the erosion of traditional authority and changing moral values. In this context lone parents can become the scapegoat for a range of concerns that cause social disquiet. Their politicization overrides the diversity of lone-parent family life and affects not only how they are seen but also how they are treated.

A central issue of debate is how lone parent family life affects the well-being of children. Some research (Burghes, 1994; Clulow, 1996) suggests that the quality of family relationships (process) is more important in this context than how families are structured (form). This research also recognizes that process and form are highly interdependent, and that the economic burden of bringing children up single-handedly, or the logistical complexity of maintaining relationships when family members are living in different households (form), are likely to have an impact on the quality of a child's life. Other research (McLanahan and Sandefur, 1994; Wallerstein *et al.*, 2000) points to various possible effects of single parenting on children including economic instability, decreased overall time with adults, lower performance in school, and higher rates of depression, anxiety, and ill-health both in childhood and on into adulthood. [*Christopher Clulow/John Wall*]

SINGLE PERSONS
Those who are not part of a couple, unmarried, frequently living alone.

There is a significant group of single people within society. The housing market has had to take this into account; there are more people living alone now than ever before. Despite this, there is still a considerable pressure on individuals to become part of a couple. Anthony Giddens says, 'To be in a couple is now more important than being married, if one wants to avoid loneliness and social disapproval' (*Observer*, 11.02.96). At the same time, individualism is increasingly valued. The single person today can be the focus for pity, envy and a whole range of false assumptions.

The primary assumption is always that a single person will experience overwhelming loneliness. While it is true that being alone is inescapable for the single person, it is debatable whether loneliness must always follow. It could be argued that those who are single have faced isolation at an early stage and learned to live with it and to explore the freedom it can bring. Those who have gone directly from a family to a couple have never had the opportunity to be alone for any length of time. They will certainly have to confront their own aloneness at some point in their lives. To have to do this for the first time in old age can be very frightening.

The fact is that no one can escape being alone for ever. The isolation of old age, illness and bereavement is part of life. For the single person, aloneness can be traumatic and the pitfall of loneliness is ever present. But it is not an inescapable trap and strategies to avoid it can be developed.

In the longer term it is the development of self-esteem and self-value which will have the greatest impact on loneliness. Confidence grows by learning to like oneself and enjoy one's own company. It is therefore essential to spend time exploring individual interests and enthusiasms. The temptation to immerse oneself in work or in a borrowed social group must be avoided. To learn to value the peace of one's own home and to realize the freedom which is there is an antidote to society's assumption that single always equals sad.

Selfishness is often seen as an inevitable part of the single life. It is thought that anyone who only has themselves to consider and look after will inevitably become self-centred. But personality is often set long before singleness becomes an issue and selfishness develops early on in life. It is not selfish to run a home, do the washing and cooking for one person, or even to plan enjoyable pursuits for oneself. It is selfish to show lack of consideration for others and to think only of one's own comfort, but there is no evidence that single people have a monopoly on those attitudes.

It is often the case in church communities and charities that a high proportion of those who are able to give of their time are single. When this is founded on a desire to help and to make a difference it can be enormously valuable. But any single persons who find themselves filling up every spare moment with activity might question their motives. The need to be needed is a strong one and it can become distorted. Charities or church work cannot be a substitute for having a partner. Single people can also be prone to what Martin Israel (1982) terms 'officious interference in other people's lives', tempted to monopolize the time of their friends under the guise of being helpful. They can depend too heavily on the telephone or on the Internet as an escape from reality.

Friendship is of paramount importance to many single people, forming part of their identity and some of their personal story. Support groups of friends who can be relied on in a crisis are a lifeline, but the friendships which are there for fun are valuable too. Sharing memories and laughter and interests in common can be transforming. It is in friendships that many people will discover the greatest love in their lives – not romantic love but selfless, giving, generous charity.

Many single people will abstain from sexual relationships, whether or not there is a calling to celibacy. This creates its own tensions and most people will find it stressful at some point in their lives. The desire to procreate and to be a parent is one of our strongest impulses. For many, if not all, there will come a time to acknowledge childlessness and to recognize the hurt that can exist as a result. Acknowledging that it is something missed out on begins the process of acceptance.

In pastoral terms there are a number of points to consider in relation to the single.

(1) There are few generalizations that can easily be made about the individual single person, any more than about all married people. (2) Singleness can be a gift, a positive experience, if the projected bad press is resisted. (3) Singleness is not a sign of an un-fulfilled person. Often there are greater opportunities for fulfilment because of the consequent freedom. (4) Single people should not be at the beck and call of others. Their own lives and activities have as much validity as any family responsibility. (5) For Christians in particular, being single may be a route to deeper faith. Dietrich Bonhoeffer (1954) wrote: 'Alone you stood before God when he called you; alone you had to answer that call; alone you had to struggle and pray; and alone you will die and give an account to God. You cannot escape from yourself, for God has singled you out.' *[Belinda Barwick]*

SLEEP
A basic, physiologically complex state of human life characterized by periodic and easily reversible sensory disengagement from environmental stimuli. Sleep appears necessary to refresh the mind and body, occupying nearly one-third of a person's lifetime. Investigations of more specific possible physiological and psychological functions of sleep remain inconclusive, but speculations include conserving energy or body heat, enhancing attention in waking, erasing extraneous memories, assisting in the maturation of the nervous system, and testing and reinforcing the brain's neuronal circuitry (Kryger *et al.*, 1989; Dement, 1996). Since its inception in the mid-twentieth century, however, scientific sleep research has generated a wealth of knowledge concerning sleep, dreaming and sleep disorders that has contributed, beginning in the 1970s, to a burgeoning field of sleep medicine.

Pivotal in this regard was the discovery that human sleep consists of two highly distinctive components, classified as Non-Rapid Eye Movement (NREM or Non-REM) and Rapid Eye Movement (REM) sleep. In healthy adults, sleep onset normally occurs through NREM, identified by relatively quiet brainwave activity (measured with an electroencephalogram or EEG) and an active, moveable body. The first NREM period generally progresses through four deepening stages, each distinguishable by subtle EEG markers. A person easily awakens from transitional stage 1 NREM sleep, sometimes with a spontaneous jerk and a sensation of falling; arousal from stage 4 sleep – the usual locus, especially in children, of sleepwalking, sleeptalking, night terrors and enuresis – becomes much more difficult.

Following an initial 30- to 45-minute period of deep sleep, stages 3–4 sleep, an ascent to stage 2 NREM begins. This in turn signals a transition into REM sleep, associated with a vigorous EEG pattern similar to that of wakefulness but accompanied by bursts of rapid eye movements in an otherwise immobilized body (Kryger *et al.*, 1989). In 80% of REM awakenings, subjects report vivid dream narratives, whereas in NREM awakenings they typically recall only vague, fragmented images or nothing at all (Cooper, 1994). A complete NREM/REM cycle lasts approximately 90 minutes and repeats itself four to five times throughout the sleep period, stages 3–4 NREM predominating in the first one-third and REM in the latter one-third of the night.

Abundant artificial lighting and heating, shift work, electronic media and other developments impinge on sleep and contribute to the detrimental, often tragic consequences of widespread sleep deprivation in contemporary life. Polysomnographic monitoring and bio-medical advances have led to improved treatment options for persons suffering from various sleep disorders, including insomnia (difficulty in falling asleep), sleep apnea (cessation of breathing during sleep), and narcolepsy (unrelenting daytime sleepiness with sudden attacks of muscle weakness). Caregivers alert to the integral role of unencumbered sleep in physical, emotional and spiritual health may assist those in their care by routine inquiry into sleep patterns and difficulties. [*Robert C. Dykstra*]

SOCIAL CONTEXT OF PASTORAL CARE

The understanding of pastoral care in its wider societal setting in contrast to one which is purely individualistic in nature.

The development of pastoral care and counselling in the twentieth century has been highly dependent upon the philosophies and practices of the secular psychotherapies such as psychoanalysis and the person-centred approach. From a pastoral perspective, these therapies have sometimes been perceived as focusing too much upon the client–therapist relationship, thus distorting a more tradition-

ally Christian understanding of pastoral care as located within the community of faith. Robert Lambourne has argued that to build pastoral counselling upon a psychoanalytic, individualistic, professional, problem-solving approach 'would be a disaster, because not only is it not what is wanted but also because it will be an obstacle to what is wanted'. He believed that a pastoral care which was 'lay, corporate, adventurous, variegated and diffuse' was required. Howard Clinebell (1981) has expressed reservations about the work of Carl Rogers on the grounds that 'he does not emphasize the fact that every personal problem is rooted in and fed by its social context'.

Lambourne was one of the pioneers of pastoral studies in Britain, with a formative influence upon the development of the discipline in Birmingham and beyond. Originally a general practitioner, he was also a psychotherapist. Yet he sought to locate the practice of both therapy and pastoral care in wider social networks. For him, health care involved more than the 'elimination of defect'. It was concerned with the restoration of total well-being: emotional, communal and spiritual as well as physical. He understood pastoral care as an activity which took place within a worshipping, caring community concerned as much with the social pressures which led to disease as with intrapsychic conflict. In a paper entitled 'With Love to the USA' (1970) he noted two significant, but apparently separate, developments in practical theology in North America. On the one hand, clinical pastoral education, heavily influenced by psychology, was flourishing within hospital chaplaincies but was usually insensitive to political issues either within or outside these institutions. On the other hand, in depressed urban situations ministries, undergirded by sociology but sometimes insensitive to issues of personality dynamics, were becoming significant. He saw a danger in 'the separation of the theory and art of loving from the theory and art of justice'. He also discerned a hope that these two diverse approaches to ministry might be brought into dialogue by means of what was then the comparatively new discipline of medical ethics, if it could find the courage to say anything prophetic about medical structures. How far this has in fact come to pass is a matter for debate.

One of Lambourne's successors at Birmingham, Stephen Pattison, has continued to focus attention on this issue. He seeks to integrate the insights of liberation theology into pastoral theory and practice (Pattison, 1994). His 'bias to the poor' leads to an exploration of the care of the mentally ill. Commenting on the number of reported cases in which hospital patients have been ill-treated, he criticizes the churches 'which have shown relatively little interest in fundamentally changing the injustices of society or in the situation of mentally ill people'. In particular, hospital chaplains have been so seduced by an individualistic counselling approach to ministry that they have been disabled from doing all that they might have done to prevent abuse or to support staff who were prepared to 'blow the whistle'. While Pattison has rightly set pastoral care in its wider social (and political) context, not everyone, and certainly not all hospital chaplains, would accept his negative critique of their role.

The social context of pastoral care is reflected in the use of a much wider range of placements in theological field education. As well as placements in parishes and hospitals, students may be placed in prisons, in industrial mission or in a range of organizations, both statutory and voluntary, working in areas of multiple deprivation where the socio-political dimension of ministry cannot be avoided. In a seminal American study, Hunter (1977) described placements in ministries among oppressed minorities and ministries working for political change. In Britain placements under the auspices of the Urban Theology Unit and similar agencies serve the same purpose.

The tension between individual pastoral care and a concern for factors in the social environment which interact with that care will continue to be central within pastoral practice. Peter Selby (1983) maintains that pastoral care and political involvement are mutually dependent and that the tension between the two can be creative and that an encounter with the limitations of one side of this ministerial polarity can awaken an awareness of the importance of the other. Pastoral carers can move from counselling the unemployed to a political involvement which seeks to tackle the roots of unemployment; from caring for the victims of injustice to fighting the causes of injustice. Martin Luther King began as a pastor of a black congregation but was assassinated fighting racism itself. The movement can also be in the opposite direction, social activists becoming aware of individual pastoral need in the midst of social distress (and sometimes of needs generated by the response to the distress). Whether or not ministries of pastoral care and social action are separate or complementary, there is no doubt that each is deficient without an appreciation of the importance of the other. [David Lyall]

SOCIAL NETWORKS AND SUPPORT
The role of social groups, both formal and informal, in the alleviation of human distress and in the support of those who care for others.
The primary human grouping is the family. Families where there is love, acceptance and appropriate boundaries tend to nourish individuals with a positive sense of their own identity and worth, capable of functioning within and contributing to society. Where these qualities are lacking, or where abusive relationships predominate, whether physical or emotional, families tend to produce damaged people. Demographic factors, such as smaller families and greater geographical mobility, render families less capable than hitherto of providing practical and emotional support. With the diminished importance of such natural support groups other networks are coming into being.

1. *Self-help groups.* In parallel with the changing place of the family has been the emergence of many self-help groups within the community. Whether this is a consequent or merely a concurrent phenomenon is open to debate. Such groups may exist as alternative forms of support independent of institutional structures. Indeed they may be a judgement upon the failure of institutions to provide needed support. Their constituencies are wide-ranging, encompassing alcohol and drug-related problems (Alcoholics Anonymous is one of the best-known of the self-help groups), HIV/AIDS issues, women's concerns and support groups for cancer patients and their families. Relationships between self-help groups and professionals working in the relevant field may be ambivalent. While needy people may see professionals as remote and authoritarian, the professionals may see such groups as a threat. At their best, however, both parties can come to appreciate one another as partners in care. Apart from the response to the specific need, participation in a self-help group has

been a source of empowerment and personal growth (Clouette, 1995).

2. *The local congregation as a social network.* Writing from the perspective of social psychiatry and in a North American context, E. Mansell Pattison has highlighted both the reality and the importance of 'systems pastoral care'. Drawing upon general systems theory, he sees the local congregation as having a major preventative function in relation to mental health. Churches are agencies of moral dialogue, as a context for learning and growth, as a place of human support and as a centre for restoration and renewal amid the crises of life. He perceives local congregations as providing primary prevention through their modelling of good human behaviour, through their identification and early response to dysfunctional behaviour and through the rehabilitation of those who have dropped out of society. Although this picture is to an extent idealized, it is undoubtedly true that for many participation in a local congregation can be an important source of personal meaning and social support. Commitment to a shared task, even as mundane as the annual fête, can bring a sense of belonging as a by-product. There is also some evidence that it is through belonging that many come to believe. In congregations where lay people are deeply involved in pastoral care, support groups are more than desirable. They are necessary as a setting for shared learning, for monitoring progress and for mutual support.

3. *Social networks and support for the clergy.* It is a sad fact that many who spend their lives providing support for the vulnerable and broken can find themselves isolated and lacking in support. As in other caring professions, burnout has been diagnosed among the clergy. Irvine (1997) conducted research into isolation with a study involving 200 ministers of the Church of Scotland. He found that isolation was evident in three areas, although none of them related primarily to geography – ministers can feel isolated in a big city. First, professional isolation reflected ministers' inability either to seek or to receive support from fellow ministers or other professionals in the community. Second, social isolation was a function of their lack of social interaction apart from the ministerial role. And third, spiritual isolation was related to the fact that ministers (and their spouses) had no one to minister to them. The extent to which those in the ordained ministry experience work-related stress is difficult to quantify, though most denominations recognize it as a problem which can impair the personal and professional functioning of many clergy. While ministers may be members of local fraternals, anecdotal evidence indicates that their value as a social network varies enormously from a deeply personal support to a highly destructive competitiveness. *[David Lyall]*

SOCIAL PSYCHOLOGY
The branch of psychology concerned with individuals in relationship to their social environment.

Topics of current relevance in social psychology include: social interaction between individuals in or outside group settings; intergroup relations; the application of psychological knowledge to social issues and problems; individual differences and personality in relation to social cognition and social behaviour; self and identity; social influence; social aspects of affect; emotion; social judgement; attribution; pro-social and anti-social behaviour; prejudice and discrimination; socialization and the acquisition of attitudes and values; the dynamics of attitude change; interpersonal perception; social exchange; language and social communication; nonverbal communication; group characteristics and functioning; conformity and nonconformity (Pennington *et al.*, 1999).

SOCIAL SCIENCE
The scientific study of human relationships, groups and societies.

Social science applies to the study of human behaviour and social life the methods of controlled observation, experimentation and statistical analysis that are the hallmarks of the 'hard sciences' (chemistry, physics and biology). The academic fields include sociology, anthropology, social psychology, political science and economics. Broadly speaking, sociologists study the dynamics of modern industrial societies, often using sample surveys and sophisticated techniques of data analysis, as well as statistics and demographic studies. Anthropologists customarily study societies and subcultures using participant-observation and other field research methods. Social psychologists conduct small-group experiments. Political scientists and economists employ a variety of research methods to study people's political and economic behaviour.

Social scientists strive for objectivity in their researches. The potential conflict between the perspectives of theology and social science is minimized when social scientists focus their investigations on the empirical world of observable facts and leave the non-empirical issues of divine causation to the theologians. Nevertheless, it has become clear during this century that no study is completely value-free and devoid of ethical implications.

Three areas of social science have special relevance for pastoral studies,

1. *The sociology of knowledge.* This investigates the everyday assumptions and knowledge about reality, behaviour and community shared by the members of a society. Understood as a total package, this knowledge makes up people's world-view. Every world-view is a social construction, based on selective perceptions of reality, and depends for its maintenance upon constant social reinforcement in daily interaction. Why, the sociologists of knowledge ask, have religious world-views become so precarious and unstable today? Because, they answer, the social reinforcement of those world-views, their 'plausibility structure', has become so weak. The pluralism of modern urban environments and the hegemony of 'science' undermine religious approaches to spiritual reality. The reigning world-view, modernism (which is now itself under challenge from postmodernism), claims to be superior to all pre-existing world-views. The sociologists of knowledge, however, challenge this, claiming that it too is a complex of selective perceptions. The sociology of knowledge 'relativizes the relativizers' (Berger, 1969). Pastoral studies may learn from the sociology of knowledge the importance of the social conditions needed to sustain religious world-views including liturgy and worship, small groups, and intense social interaction of believers. They also discover in it a corrective to the anti-religious bias in some psychological counselling, the so-called 'triumph of the therapeutic'.

2. *The analysis of social systems.* Sociologists and anthropologists view societies, organizations and groups as social systems. These are composed of subsystems that make outputs to the other subsystems and receive needed inputs from them. Social subsystems are analogous to the organs of the human body whose biochemical exchanges keep the total physiological system in stable equilibrium. At the level of the social group, the subsystems are termed 'roles'. Borrowed from the theatre, this concept refers to the social norms that govern the occupant of a position. Pastor, hospital chaplain and theological student are all roles with complex sets of expectations. Role conflict is the troublesome situation in which someone's role-partners disagree on that person's proper actions. Family systems theory, familiar to most pastoral counsellors, represents one part of this larger social scientific perspective. Exemplifying the group systems approach is research on 'double-bind' communication as a contributing cause of schizophrenia. A parent is found to give conflicting signals to a child, for example saying verbally 'I love you very much' while communicating a non-verbal message of rejection by pulling away in disgust, thus creating a psychological dilemma for the child that may contribute to psychosis. Social scientists also view whole societies as social systems. The subsystems there comprise many roles, groups and organizations that collectively make a needed societal output. These outputs, termed 'functions', determine whether the society will survive and prosper. Four major analytical subsystems of a society have been identified (Parsons, 1977): the economic, the political, the integrative and the fiduciary. The latter's function, that of maintaining a strong value system and engendering people's sense of trust, is fulfilled by religion, its personnel and organizations. By means of social system analysis, pastors and pastoral caregivers assess the optimum functioning of groups (families, church boards) and organizations (congregations). Some needed function may be lacking, thus creating disequilibrium, conflict and impaired performance.

3. *The sociology of religion.* This investigates the interaction between a society's religious (fiduciary) subsystem and the other subsystems. Karl Marx, Max Weber and Emile Durkheim, pioneers of modern social science, all made important studies of religion. Marx, whose understanding of social dynamics undergirds conflict sociology, saw religions as ideologies legitimating the interests of particular economic classes. Weber traced how Calvinistic religion with its value of worldly asceticism (strong economic activity and non-consumption) created preconditions for the modern Western economy. Durkheim, although questioning the scientific truth of religion, concluded from his

researches that the integrative and fiduciary functions of religion are indispensable to a vital modern society.

Two studies in the sociology of religion offer examples of the process of social scientific research. A study of American denominations (Kelley, 1972) presented data showing the membership growth of more conservative, evangelical and fundamentalist churches and the decline of the so-called mainline liberal churches. Kelley attributed the growth to 'strong' religion (unambiguous theology, stringent membership requirements and strong social reinforcement) and the decline to 'weak' religion (tolerant theology and minimal demands of members). A subsequent study (Hoge, Johnson and Luidens, 1994) tested the thesis using a research design that was carefully controlled for denomination and generation. They interviewed two age-cohorts of adults who had been confirmed as adolescents in Presbyterian churches. The latter study confirmed Kelley's thesis yet found that other factors, especially weakened community ties, contributed to the decline of mainline churches. The field of such congregational studies brings the sociology of religion directly into connection with pastoral studies. In the UK such work as that by Robin Gill (1989, 1993), with its careful analysis of statistical data, is of direct importance to any strategy for ministry. Similarly influential has been the overall study of the religious situation in the UK with the theme of 'believing without belonging' (Davie, 1994). [George M. Furniss]

SOCIAL STRUCTURES AND PASTORAL CARE
Activity which is concerned with changing social structures in order to facilitate the pastoral care of individuals living within these structures.

If individual counselling once tended to dominate pastoral care, today its wider context receives as much, if not more, attention. The stronger form of this emphasis is to insist that the pastoral care of individuals has little or no value if it does nothing to change the economic and political structures responsible for oppressing those individuals. The weaker form contends that even ad hoc actions of pastoral care take place within specific social contexts, raise specific social expectations and require wider networks and communities to make them properly effective.

The stronger form is particularly found in liberation theology. Its exponents share a common critique of economic, global capitalism and modernity and a common conviction that theology must side consciously with the marginalized and oppressed in an attempt to bring about social and political change. Concern about the physical environment and ecology has also become increasingly important. The emphasis is upon changing social and physical structures rather than upon helping individuals to live within existing structures. On this understanding, the pastoral care of the oppressed, and even of the oppressors, requires socio-political action rather than individual counselling. There is, however, considerable debate within liberation theology itself about whether or not it is legitimate to use violence as a means of changing violent and oppressive socio-political structures and about how far liberation theology is to be identified with Marxist ideology.

The weaker form of this contention is evident in those who have attempted to use insights from the sociology of organizations or from the sociology of communities. In Britain, R. A. Lambourne (1979) increasingly came to stress the communal aspects of pastoral care: psychotherapy was practised in an 'artificial situation' of professional and middle-class seclusion, and churches should not model their pastoral care too closely on it. Stephen Pattison's (1994) work has built upon this and explored political and social contexts of pastoral care. In the USA, E. Mansell Pattison (1977) and in the Netherlands Mady Thung (1976) both used the social sciences to construct communal models of pastoral care. Thung produced a blueprint of a future church which might combine pastoral and prophetic functions. With more attention to structures churches could become more effective agents of pastoral care within society. E. Mansell Pattison advanced a model of systems pastoral care which emphasized that someone in need must always be considered in a social context. Support for a social dimension to pastoral care can also be found in some comparatively conservative theological approaches. Thurneysen (1962), for example, argues that pastoral care occurs within the realm of the church. Preaching, worship and public confession and absolution can therefore be seen as forms of pastoral care. Pastoral care is done for and by local churches.

Once social structures are taken seriously within pastoral care, the discipline becomes very much more complex than it might have seemed in the past. Graham (1996) argues that the shift from an individualistic to a more communal approach to pastoral theology can be seen, at least in part, as a shift from modernity to postmodernity. For her, postmodern perspectives portray the self as a subject-in-relation, whose identity is forged within the complex interplay of economic, cultural and political factors. She takes the familiar feminist critiques of patriarchy and relates these to pastoral theology. Lartey (1997) directs attention to the complexities produced when radically different cultures interact. He used his personal experience of British, African and British-African cultures to challenge pastoral theology to recognize the pluralism of the social, religious and cultural contexts in which it is set. [Robin Gill]

SOCIAL WORK
An applied science concerned with enhancing the level of psychological, social and political functioning among individuals, groups and larger communities.
Oriented principally towards the person-in-environment situation, the goal of social work is the amelioration of problems in living brought about by personal psychological dysfunction and by the interrelation of individuals, groups and communities with oppressive social, economic and environmental systems and structures. Intent on empowering its recipients (clients) to help themselves, social work employs a wide-ranging knowledge base and numerous conceptual theories and methods of practice. It also looks to the social sciences, particularly psychology, sociology and social policy, to inform its research, methods and policy-making initiatives.

Social work was established as a profession in the late nineteenth century, although its philosophy is grounded in religious and social systems of caring for the poor, particularly the Elizabethan Poor Law in seventeenth-century England. Historically, social workers have been principally concerned for the poor and have also been at the forefront in challenging the structures that oppress and dehumanize human beings both individually and collectively. Since the 1950s, however, social work has to a large extent moved from its traditional orientation to identify more strongly with psychological counselling and psychotherapy. Neverthe-

less, competent social work continues to demand substantial knowledge of human development and behaviour, organizational structures and functioning, social and economic policy, and legislative processes. It also requires an ability to think globally and to employ a wide range of vision in order to understand the various complexities of contemporary human life. Schools of social work evolved during the twentieth century and developed a vigorous programme of formal professional education which is now required for social work practice.

With this professionalization, social work has become increasingly diverse and has expanded both its methods and fields (settings) of practice. The same has occurred with regard to the population it serves. Its four primary methods include clinical practice, generalist practice or social casework, social work policy, and social work research.

Clinical practice describes work directly with individuals and groups (couples, families or others) that is often psychosocially oriented. Thus, clinical social work is usually informed by behavioural science theories, systems theory, or other theories relating to emotional or mental dysfunction.

Generalist practice (or generic social work) is more broadly conceived. While still involving work with individuals, groups and communities, it is frequently less specialized but requires more of an ability to work eclectically with regard to both theory and models. It also calls for an aptitude for working collaboratively with other human service professionals to assist mutual clients. Generalists often serve as 'case managers' for social service agencies, and are responsible for coordinating a wide array of resources and services to their clients, which may include referrals to other resources. Generalists also organize, oversee and evaluate agency- or community-based programmes designed to address particular needs of those they serve.

Social work policy is a method that involves working at a macro-level to solve problems through policy and legislative initiatives. This often is closely linked to political action, and may involve working with grass-roots organizations, community or civic groups, or the various levels of local, state or national government to enhance public welfare. This also entails policy analysis, formulation and implementation.

Social work research describes investigation and analysis for establishing and enhancing the knowledge base, methods, fields of practice and programmes of professional training for social workers. Those working in research are concerned with evaluating the outcomes and characteristics of specific problems, populations and programmes. Such research most frequently occurs in the context of social agencies, schools of social work, political and public-policy 'think tanks', at various levels of government, and increasingly in the public 'for-profit' sector (Compton and Galaway, 1994).

In the UK the emphasis is somewhat different. There have been two distinct approaches to the practice of social work, namely generic and specialist. The generic approach has advocated the benefits of a broad-based training, with practitioners operating across a wide spectrum of social need. The specialist approach follows a practice base which is more narrowly focused with an emphasis on developing specialist expertise in a particular social work field. Since the 1980s the specialist approach has predominated, as the field of social work has become more complex and more subject to regulation.

Generally, social work services are divided between the statutory sector (comprising those services operating under local government management or the probation service operating within the judicial field) and the voluntary and independent sector (comprising voluntary and charitable agencies and private companies).

Local government statutory social services are currently divided between Children and Family Services and Adult Services. Children and Family Services comprise Child Care and Protection Services, Fostering and Adoption Services, Child and Adult Psychiatric Services and Residential Services. Adult Services include Services for Elderly People, People with Mental Health Problems, People with Learning Difficulties and People with Physical Disabilities. During the last fifteen years there has been a trend within local government services to split the functions of commissioning or purchasing services from the function of providing direct services. More recently this has led to local authorities transferring more and more direct services to the independent sector in order to reduce expenditure. This trend is likely to increase as local authorities strive to meet the demands of central government's 'Best Value' regime.

Within Adult Services, social work practice is becoming increasingly focused on meeting the needs of more highly dependent people who choose to remain living in their own homes within the community, as opposed to moving to a residential home environment. This moves towards 'care in the community' rather than 'care in institutional settings' places a greater emphasis on the need for social services to work in partnership with primary care and other health services at both a strategic planning and a service delivery level.

A field of practice designates the context in which social work occurs, the problems it is involved in solving and the population it intends to serve. The profession continues to expand its fields of practice in order to keep pace with the constantly new and complex problems, populations and settings encountered in a rapidly changing world. Current fields of practice include: health and mental health (hospitals, community clinics, psychiatric and drug treatment centres, disabilities), education (schools), employment (employee assistance programmes and departments of human resources), immigration (international social work), geriatrics (the aged and their care-givers), corrections (prisons, jails, juvenile detention centres) and contemporary social problems such as homelessness, AIDS, substance abuse and domestic violence (Meyer and Mattaini, 1995).

Social work is related to the pastoral disciplines in several ways.

1. Both professions share a concern for the 'whole' person and their environment and seek to provide assistance with problems experienced by individuals, groups and communities of people. Included in this is the common goal of mitigating oppressive social, economic and environmental systems and structures.

2. Both ministers and social workers often are involved in working with the same populations in a given community. This is particularly true in urban settings, and in other areas in which poor and disadvantaged persons live.

3. Professional pastoral counsellors and clinical social workers draw their theories and practice methods from common social scientific sources, and may share similar approaches to solving a given problem in living.

4. Social workers and ministers may serve as vital resources for each other as they often

have entry into different aspects of people's lives and therefore may work collaboratively to maximize human welfare.

5. Social work and the pastoral professions are grounded in a set of common core values and ethical standards. These include a regard for individual worth and dignity, acceptance, honesty, responsible behaviour, confidentiality and a commitment to provide the best possible care to those they serve. Pastoral care-givers could benefit from adopting more of the person-in-environment focus embraced by social work. A challenge for both professions is to explore ways in which their respective areas of expertise can be used conjointly in order to effect positive change in both the individuals and communities they serve. [Allan Hugh Cole, Jr/Phil Cowley]

SOCIOLOGY
The academic discipline concerned with analysing social phenomena and processes.
Sociology is increasingly used in pastoral theology as more attention has been paid to social structures. This development can be set into a broader context of ongoing dialogue between theologians and interested sociologists.

Among classical sociologists, Max Weber showed a profound interest in theology. Mutually influenced by the theologian/historian Ernst Troeltsch, Weber exhibited this interest in several ways. His early work, *The Protestant Ethic and the Spirit of Capitalism* (1904–5), advanced the possibility that theological differences may have been socially significant. He argued that notions within popular Calvinism may have been important in developing within Europe the culture that assisted the rise of rational capitalism. Unlike Karl Marx, who tended to see theology as either epiphenomenal or as a dependent social variable, Weber argued that theology might also become an independent variable within society. His later work explored other theological interests – notably in charismatic prophecy – and demonstrated a considerable knowledge of contemporary biblical scholarship.

Weber's writings had a major influence upon several theologians in the first half of the twentieth century. In America, H. Richard Niebuhr's *The Social Sources of Denominationalism* (1929) was influenced by both Weber and Troeltsch. They also had a similar impact on Dietrich Bonhoeffer's

Sanctorum Communio (1930). However, the growing dominance of theologians such as Karl Barth, with his radical stress upon revelation and the Word of God, limited this influence. Sociology came to be seen as dangerously 'secular' and a force for relativization.

In biblical studies these fears may have delayed the use of the social sciences, although there were always some scholars who attended to them. Radical thinkers such as Rudolf Bultmann used ideas with many affinities to the social sciences, especially in his development of form criticism, which tried to identify the ways that particular communities shaped stories and sayings that eventually appeared in the Gospels. However, these scholars tended to make little direct use of social theory. Students of the Old Testament often treated Weber as an amateur; textual, historical and exegetical issues tended to predominate.

However, during the last two decades of the twentieth century there has been a new focus upon social origins and upon hermeneutics. Both have raised sociological questions more directly. For example, John Gager (1975) made direct use of cognitive dissonance theory to understand the millennial expectations of parts of the New Testament. Richer still in sociological nuance is Wayne Meeks (1983). He made considerable use of anthropological and sociological theory to understand the shift between the rural world of Jesus and the urban world of Paul. In Germany, Gerd Theissen has extensively employed sociology and psychology.

In modern theology there has also been an increasing use of the social sciences. Liberation theology has been a major influence. Gutiérrez (1973) seminally argued against understanding theology as being concerned with timeless orthodoxy. Instead he argued for the notion of 'orthopraxis', stressing that the way Christians behave and whether they argue for the rich and powerful or for the poor should be central theological concerns. This understanding of theology has frequently seen Marxism as an ally rather than as a foe. Within modern theology its influence has now extended into feminist and postmodern theology. All these approaches tend to give the social sciences an important role, both in identifying more accurately the nature of modern culture and in understanding theology as a social reality within that culture.

This increasing emphasis upon social context and praxis has begun to blur traditional distinctions between systematic, pastoral and moral theology. For Barth systematic or dogmatic theology attempted to establish the doctrinal framework within which pastoral and ethical decision-making could then be done. Within many forms of liberation and contextual theology, ethics, practice and belief constantly interact, so that rigid divisions between them seem no longer viable. Influential Christian ethicists, such as Stanley Hauerwas (1981), have championed instead a stress upon the formation of Christian character that is directly relevant to pastoral theology. Theological ethics attempts to identify the ways that Christian living is distinctive in a pluralistic world. Heavily influenced by Alasdair MacIntyre (1981), some have argued that an emphasis upon character and community should lead to a renewed attempt to apply sociology more rigorously within modern theology. [Robin Gill]

SOCIOLOGY OF RELIGION
The sociological study of religious behaviour, beliefs and institutions.
The human sciences, including sociology, have their origins in the Enlightenment. The Enlightenment placed a premium on the discovery of truth through observation of the natural order and its laws, rather than on received wisdom or religious authority. Sociologists sought to apply the same principles of scientific observation to the rational discernment of the underlying laws of human behaviour.

The sociologist is fundamentally concerned with human interaction. Individuals are nurtured in social groups. Their languages, customs and roles are acquired in relationships with other persons and groups of persons including the family, the school and the workplace. Social structures, knowledge and religion are viewed by the sociologist as the products of social interaction. Humans create artefacts. They also create class and caste distinctions, conceptual and belief systems, forms of monetary exchange, patterns of governance, and ethical codes. As well as studying personal interaction, sociologists study the interaction between persons and the social structures and processes that persons in groups create and sustain.

The sociological study of religion is one of the oldest sub-disciplines of sociology (Wilson, 1984). Three of the founding fathers of sociology, Emile Durkheim, Karl Marx and Max Weber, all developed theories of religion drawing on diverse data, including empirical studies of Australian Aboriginals and historical studies of European Protestants. Durkheim found that religion exercised certain fundamental social functions in tribal society. Religious totems and ceremonies were sacred representations of the tribe, its origins and its location in the cosmos and the landscape. Participation in religious rituals affirmed the identity of the tribe and cemented tribal solidarity. It helped all individuals to identify with the shared values of the tribe, and to commit to the survival and collective good of the group. Durkheim speculated that in post-revolutionary France, the state would need to create analogous civic rituals and symbol systems to those of the totemic tribe in order to generate commitment to shared values, and solidarity in the new republic. Examples of such civil religion – veneration of the flag, or the building of shrines for founding political leaders such as Lincoln or Lenin – are common in republican societies.

Karl Marx regarded religious beliefs, hierarchies and rituals as a smoke screen laid down by the dominant classes to legitimize their power to the peasants and workers. Religion both hides the social roots of class oppression and acts as an opiate for the oppressed classes, promising deferred joys in heaven as reward for earthly suffering, thus subverting popular challenges to the status quo.

Max Weber's theory of religion exercises a mediating role between the metaphors of religion as social cement and religion as social smokescreen. Using comparative case studies of religious traditions in different periods of history, Weber contended that religion was both a product of society and an independent social force. Religion at times sustained social cohesion in the context of rapid social change. At other times religion cohered with the forces of change in the creation of new social patterns and ideas. He argued that Protestantism played this latter role in early modern Europe in the birth of capitalism.

In explaining religious beliefs and practices as social constructs, and viewing God or gods as cosmic representations of social hierarchies, sociologists may be said to be committed to debunking religious belief. There is some truth in this claim. Most Western sociologists predicted the demise of religious influence and social significance in modern societies. Many sociologists tend to overlook evidence of the tenacity or resurgence of religions in the late modern world. The re-emergence of religion as a significant factor in international relations in the light of the resurgence of Islam, the role of religion in the overthrow of communism in Eastern Europe, the political influence of fundamentalism in the USA, have taken most social scientists by surprise.

But there is no inevitable connection between the social study of religion and the debunking of religious belief and practice. Rather than debunking the reality of unseen or supra-empirical forces, the sociologist *qua* sociologist attempts to bracket out the existence of such forces for the purposes of their research. Judgement as to the existence or non-existence of such forces is not strictly part of the sociological enterprise. The sociologist is rather concerned with the examination of the interplay of psychological, economic or social forces in the micropolitics of a congregation or in the waxing and waning of religious belief or practice. Such study enhances understanding and theorization of the social world. It also provides theologians or clergy with an independent referent in their deliberations on the character of religious believing and community, or the prospects of religious institutions, in particular social contexts. Many churches and religious institutions now employ social statistics, qualitative and quantitative survey techniques and congregational studies in designing their mission and organizational strategies.

Sociologists have drawn particular attention to the changing role and character of religion in the modern or late modern world. Sociologists have made numerous studies of new religious movements such as the Unification Church (the 'Moonies') and the Children of God. They have explained these new movements variously as evidence of the internal collapse of official religion in the light of secularization or as social or psychological responses to the effects of rapid social change (Kurtz, 1995).

Some sociologists discern a quasi-religious tendency in the emergence of single-issue social movements in late modern societies. New social movements concerned with animal rights, the environment, human rights or gender issues are said to represent popular efforts to resist the dehumanizing and corporatist tendencies of late capitalist societies. Beliefs, values, rituals and cultural or tribal identities in these movements are often constructed and pursued with religious fervour and may be seen as new styles of immanent or civil religion.

Sociologists are also examining the origins and impacts of religious resurgence, including Christian and Islamic fundamentalism, on modern rational, bureaucratic and corporate social structures. The resurgence of religion in non-Western contexts is often linked with efforts to resist the global reach of Western culture and Western-dominated capitalism. Some Islamic fundamentalists have lent support to a jihad against Western culture and Western capitalism because they are said to threaten the integrity of Islamic civilisation and the putative purity of certain forms of Islamic economy, law, polity and society. This jihad may take violent form as evidenced in conflicts in the Middle East, and in the terrorist attacks on the USA in 2001. The sociological study of religious resurgence is therefore an important element in the larger post-Enlightenment project of the human sciences to discern the true character and sources of human flourishing, and to critique that which subverts it. [*Michael Northcott*]

SOCIOPATHIC PERSONALITY
See: MOOD DISORDER

SOLITUDE
The state of being on one's own, away from all social engagement.
Solitude is one of the fundamental traditional disciplines of the spiritual life. The practice of intentionally disengaging from social intercourse for a period of time by separating oneself from the world has been associated with prophets, mystics, the desert mothers and fathers, contemplatives and monastics. However, it is not a practice reserved for holy orders or mystics. As a spiritual discipline, it is a habit essential for any person who wishes to pay attention to the spiritual dimension of human life – attention to God, to oneself, to neighbour and to the world (Nouwen, 1991).

As a discipline, solitude differs from privacy, isolation, loneliness and escapism. Privacy is time and space alone for the sake of protecting oneself from intrusion. Isolation is a seclusion from others that is not necessarily freely chosen, the goal of which is separateness. Loneliness is lack of human company even though one desires to be in relationship; it connotes sadness or bleakness. Escapism is a turning away from engagement for the sake of non-involvement. Solitude is intentionally chosen time and space alone for the purpose of finding a silence in which to listen for and attend to God, oneself and the world of human need. The attentiveness of solitude, paradoxically, is to lead to deeper community, more compassionate service, and more holistic and just relationships. The spiritual discipline of solitude includes an emptying of one's space and time of noise, clutter, distractions, busyness and self-justifying props. This emptying and disengagement is for the sake of spiritual awakening, awareness and focus.

The implied rhythm in the discipline of solitude is aloneness and community, withdrawal and engagement, separation and solidarity. Jesus' ministry was a demonstration of this rhythm. He was often in solitude before and after events of engagement and ministry (e.g. Matt. 4.1–11; Mark 1.35). Solitude without engagement can lead to self-focused pietism. Engagement without solitude can lead to shallow and self-interested action.

Solitude as a spiritual discipline is important to pastoral studies because ministry involves encounter between God and people (Jones *et al.*, 1986). Solitude is a focused place of attentiveness to that encounter. In pastoral ministry, because of incessant demands on the pastor's time and energy, busyness can replace reflective action, and shallow entanglement can replace clarifying solitude through which compassion is born. Without the practice of solitude, the spiritual life is an impossibility. Without the spiritual life, ministry becomes hollow. Solitude provides space for attentiveness to God within one's life and within the world. Solitude becomes a time and place for personal conversion, deepening compassion, and spiritual transformation (Merton, 1975). *[Victor L. Hunter]*

SOUL
1. The vital, non-material principle of life.
2. The spiritual aspect of human existence.
3. A person's total self.

The Hebrew *nephesh* and the Greek *psyche* are often translated in the English Bible as 'soul'. When God breathed the breath of life into the formed clay, it became a living being, *nephesh*. *Nephesh* is the livingness of human being. To be human is to be an embodied soul, a soul-filled body. Hence, the Hebrew understanding of *nephesh* stressed both the unity of human existence and its paradoxical nature. In the Christian Scriptures, *psyche* is understood sometimes as life itself, the expression of personality, and as the religious root in human life. While these understandings are consistent with the Hebrew *nephesh*, the understanding of the meaning of salvation and life itself is radically new. *Psyche*, therefore, is sometimes understood as the seat of supernatural life and the object of salvation. Salvation, however, is of the whole person, body and soul, within the context of the faith community (Childs and Waanders, 1994).

Philosophical and theological understandings of what it means to be human underlie concepts of soul prevalent in any given age and culture and influence the way in which pastoral issues are addressed. In Plato's philosophy, the soul was a pure spiritual principle, pre-existent, immortal and distinct from the body. Platonic thought influenced dualistic notions of body and soul that carried over into neo-Platonism, the church fathers and Cartesian philosophy. Soul became identified with mind and its functions, reinforcing the hierarchical dominance of spirit over flesh, mind over matter, male over female, man over nature that pervade Western patriarchal culture. If the eternal soul is primary, then the body or matter can become dispensable, disdained, and the object of abuse, exploitation, violence and genocide. This is especially true for women, who are frequently identified with the body, and for races deemed to have inferior souls or no souls at all. Incorporating Aristotelean philosophy, Aquinas reclaimed the living unity of the human being and considered the soul the animating principle, the consciousness and life of the body. Such reclaiming, however, did not alter the political, racial, gender biases embedded in the culture.

Whenever such dualisms are operative, the 'cure of souls' often becomes the Church's domain, while care for the body becomes the domain of science. However, feminist philosophy and theology, the emerging scientific studies in faith and health, and the renewed interest in spirituality, are providing the impetus to reclaim a wholistic understanding of soul. Embodied soul reflects the totality of the person open to its mysterious depths and transcendent source and goal in God as it relates to one's body/self, others, the natural world and God. To recover soul is to reawaken a reverence for transcendent immanence – the sacred in everyday life – and to deepen one's capacity for full-bodied responses to life. *[Martha A. Robbins]*

SOUL FRIEND
A non-technical term for one who directs and/or guides persons in spiritual reflection and the development of spiritual practices and disciplines.

As the practice of spiritual direction has moved into popular experience, a variety of descriptive terms has been used, including: spiritual conversation, spiritual sharing, spiritual guidance and spiritual mentoring. Use of the description 'soul friend' for a guide or spiritual companion has both ancient and modern usage (Leech, 1977). It connotes maturity, depth, intimacy and trustworthiness. The spiritual quest is often described as a pilgrimage. The soul friend accompanies the 'pilgrim' figuratively, providing counsel, caution, comfort and encouragement (O'Donohue, 1997).

SPIRIT
1. An energizing force, creative power of life and vital activity, efficacious presence.
2. The human spirit.
3. Evil spirits or other spirits.
4. God's spirit.

The English word, the Hebrew *ruach* and the Greek *pneuma* carry multiple meanings. As wind, *ruach* denotes a moving force that effects change (Gen. 1.2). As breath, *ruach* is the energizing life that Yahweh breathes into formed clay resulting in a living being, *nephesh* (Gen. 2.7). Yahweh's breath is both the creative power of life and the created capacity to live that all living beings enjoy. Although inseparable, a distinction is thus made between spirit and soul: *ruach* is the vitalizing force and *nephesh*/soul is the enlivened being just as breath and the organ/process of breathing are distinguishable but found together. The divine spirit confers and authorizes special gifts (e.g. wisdom, understanding, counsel, knowledge of God) and bestows a clean heart (conscience) and steadfast will to follow its guidance. The biblical understanding of human being as *ruach* can only be fully understood in its dynamic relationship with God, as human receptivity to God's efficacious Holy Spirit.

In the Christian Scriptures, these inherited Old Testament anthropological understandings and the promise of the universal Spirit are given new content and meaning with the reception of the Spirit. The reception of the Spirit is the fruit of Christ's life, death and glorification. The same Spirit that filled Christ is poured into the hearts of Christians, uniting them to one another and forming the Church. The Spirit liberates, transforms, endows with special gifts, and empowers humans to live in word and deed the gospel message of reverence, justice and love for all life (Moltmann, 1992).

Pastoral ministry is a participation in the Spirit's work of healing and transformation of the world. Such ministry is enhanced by the development of a capacity to be attentive and responsive to the movements of the divine Spirit in all dimensions of life, along with an ability to discern and facilitate this development in others individually and communally. One must also become aware of underlying assumptions about the nature of the transformed life as shaped by sacred Scriptures, religious or spiritual traditions and practices that are historically and culturally mediated. These human capacities to be attentive, responsive and critical become more complex and richly textured as we mature. If our capacities are underdeveloped or are blocked, pastoral counselling may be helpful. Spiritual direction or companionship, however, assists in discerning the direction in which a person's vitality flows as led by the Spirit. As an energizing force, the Spirit initiates and capacitates a full-hearted response to what brings about fuller life. For Christians, this fuller life becomes embodied through ongoing participation in the Paschal Mystery in which dying and rising become paradoxically related. *[Martha A. Robbins]*

SPIRITUAL HEALING
The practice of healing using spiritual as opposed to physical means.

Spiritual methods of healing have been used in every culture and religion from tribal religion to our own. Western society itself knows a variety of spiritual healing practices based on belief systems that are current today. Outside mainstream Christianity spiritual healing is practised by such groups as Spiritualists, Christian Scientists and followers of what are broadly known as New Age ideas. Spiritualism shares ideas with other alternative religious cultures but places a special emphasis on the role of discarnate beings in the healing process. Christian Science claims considerable success over illness by inculcating a belief system which denies lasting reality to pain or illness. New Age beliefs about healing broadly cluster around the way that certain meditational techniques can release healing energy. Such beliefs and techniques are for the most part shared with Spiritualist practitioners. Healing energy is believed to promote and enhance self-healing or allow another person to receive this energy through touch.

The Christian tradition of healing has been reluctant to identify with the expression 'spiritual healing' on the grounds that it might be confused with Spiritualist ideas and beliefs. But in any examination of Christian healing, whether by individuals or groups, spiritual training and preparation is important (Parsons, 1986). Many ministries have been influenced by charismatic renewal and this style is important for two reasons. First, the charismatic/pentecostal tradition has created a climate in which prayer is experienced in a corporate way; prayer is a means of bonding Christians together. Such spiritual bonding with its emphasis on love has clear therapeutic significance. Second, charismatic spirituality has brought into prominence the idea of 'gifts'. This has raised Christian awareness of the possibility that Christians can and should pray for one another with the expectation that there will be a positive outcome. In summary, charismatic spirituality would appear to have the potential for releasing in certain individuals a hitherto little understood human capacity for affecting the course of illness in another person. The discovery of such an ability within a Christian context will not absolve an individual from using the utmost wisdom in the exercise of such a ministry, particularly against abuse of power.

Healing ministries are also rooted in a more contemplative, meditative tradition (Reddie, 1966).

Spiritual healing is a term which reminds healing practitioners of all religious traditions of the spiritual component involved in what they do. For Christians involved in healing prayer in whatever tradition, the term recalls them to the discipline of prayer and spirituality which is the only healthy basis for the exercise of a Christian ministry of healing. *[Stephen Parsons]*

SPIRITUALISM
A religious system devoted to study and involvement with psychic phenomena, especially the spirits of the departed.
Spiritualism (sometimes disparagingly called 'spiritism') originated formally in the USA in 1848. It accepts parapsychological data, especially manifestations of the spirits of those who have 'crossed over' – i.e. the dead, but who are able to be contacted by mediums in this world. The mass deaths of the First World War gave an impetus to the movement and correspondingly to charlatans. Christians have adopted various attitudes towards Spiritualism, ranging from condemnation of it as witchcraft to careful acceptance of some of its claims.

SPIRITUALITY
An umbrella word used in connection with people's subjective experiences of their personal relationship with God.
Spirituality is difficult to define. It covers a multitude of meanings. And, since these intimate relationships with God, mediated through human experience, relate to a person's cultural background, religious beliefs and practices, the term covers a wide variety of experiences and practices. It is used in all religions.

Among Christians the word, *spiritualis*, dates from the fifth century when it was used to describe the quality of life that should result from Christian belief and devotion. By medieval times spirituality was associated with the interior life of a person and the devotional practices used to foster that life, such as prayer, meditation, contemplation, and mystical union with God. Many of these spiritual practices grew up around a monastic founder such as St Basil, St Benedict, St Francis of Assisi, St Teresa of Avila, St Ignatius of Loyola. Followers of the founders knew what they meant when, for instance, they referred to Carmelite spirituality, derived from the desert tradition, Benedictine spirituality, used about the stable life of monks living in community, Franciscan spirituality, which emanated from the Franciscan love of poverty, simplicity and love of nature, and Ignatian spirituality based upon the Spiritual Exercises devised by St Ignatius for his companions.

These kinds of spirituality were thought to be the province of specially called and fervent believers, rather than of everyone who was a Christian. This led to attitudes that tended to be élitist. The spiritual life in its fullness came to be associated with monks, nuns, hermits and holy people who lived a form of the religious life in the world rather than in a religious community or a hermitage.

By the twentieth century, however, such élitist attitudes were dying. Spiritual experiences were seen to be a gift of God rather than achievable by human effort. This means that lay people who try to live their Christian lives in families and secular communities can live as devoutly as any monk, nun or hermit.

A huge literature has grown up around the different forms of Christian spirituality. People can pick and choose according to temperament and opportunity. In the latter half of the twentieth century, and the beginning of the twenty-first century, Western Christianity has been influenced by adherents of other religions, notably Hinduism, Buddhism, Sufi mysticism and New Age forms of mysticism.

Spirituality has become a growth industry. Its principal dangers are those of pietism that privatizes spiritual experience, and preoccupation with personal holiness that may lead to relative indifference to the problems of people who are struggling to survive in near impossible conditions of poverty, hunger and oppression. Its principal advantages are the growth of self-understanding, compassion and tolerance of other people's ways of approaching God. *[Una Kroll]*

SPLITTING
A primitive defence against anxiety by splitting an object into good and bad parts and using it for projection.
Splitting is a key notion in the Kleinian thinking about psychoanalysis (Klein, 1963). The early developmental stage is paranoid-schizoid, which gives way to the depressive position. As part of that process, the infant discovers that what he or she had split off in order to cope with anxiety can, albeit with a struggle and not always total success, be reintegrated. This process – especially splitting and projective identification (i.e. a case of seeing the mote in one's brother's eye but not the beam in one's own) – can be observed in many institutional settings (Obholzer and Roberts, 1994).

STEP-FAMILY
A step-family is formed when a parent takes a new partner.
Step-families were once most likely to have been formed following the death of a partner; nowadays they are frequently the consequence of separation and divorce. Children growing up in step-families may have more than two adults acting towards them as parents, and the boundaries of family life may straddle more than one household. These structural factors may combine with dynamic processes associated with feelings of loss and exclusion to generate tensions that may be relevant to the mythology of the 'wicked stepmother/father'. They also create opportunities for constructing generous and innovative family relationships (Salisbury and Walters, 1997).

STERILIZATION
Any medical procedure by which persons are intentionally rendered incapable of reproduction.
For sterilization to be undertaken the person to be sterilized must, in normal circumstances, be a mentally competent adult and able freely to decide the matter as defined by the legal jurisdiction in which the procedure takes place. Note, however, that sterilization may also result from life-saving medical procedures such as chemotherapy or radiation therapy, or be caused by illness or genetic accidents. In the case of adults who cannot decide freely, protection must be provided from various notions of eugenics that may be applied in a biased or prejudicial manner. Historically, 'normal' society periodically demonstrates difficulty in accepting the enjoyment of, or even participation in, sexuality by the 'mentally defective' or 'developmentally disabled'. Pastoral care-givers should be aware that whenever interest in genetics and reproductive technology increases, misinformed eugenic notions threaten to affect public policy.

Sterilization is normally considered to be irreversible. If sterilization is sought for birth control, all other (less permanent) methods must be considered and understood as options. Since both male and female sterilization procedures involve surgery, inherent medical risks must be presented and understood to be warranted. As irrevocable decisions are discussed with the physician, the situations of sterilized persons who have later sought reversal of the procedure should be explored.

When female sterilization is undertaken at the time of childbirth, hormonal changes in the mother following the birth need to be explained sufficiently for the woman and her family to understand that any post-partum depression most likely results from sudden, though normal, hormonal shifts. Pastoral care-givers who become aware of a new mother's sadness should be sensitive to the possibility of post-partum depression and not assume that the sadness is caused by the sterilization. (Yet grief over the loss represented by sterilization cannot be discounted, however unexpected.) Pastoral recognition of post-partum depression can result in encouraging appropriate medical care along with continued pastoral support. When the birth was desired and a planned-for event, the contrast between anticipated joy and the desolation of depression can be overwhelming. If the sterilization decision was well thought out and carefully considered, it usually does not need to be revisited in any depth. All possible causes for the sadness should be explored and the persons involved supported as they traverse this valley of shadows.

Any warranted pastoral conversations will take place, it is hoped, before a decision for sterilization is reached, particularly if the man or woman wants to explore the procedure's moral and ethical dimensions. Broadly speaking, Christian traditions that allow or encourage artificial birth control have few qualms about sterilization if the person considering this step is an autonomous and competent adult operating within the realm of informed consent. On the other hand, Christian traditions that prohibit artificial birth control usually look askance at sterilization. Yet, with regard to sterilization, it must be noted that significant numbers of persons within any Christian tradition often choose options that vary from that tradition.
[William M. Clements]

STIGMA
A characteristic which causes a person or persons to be regarded as different, inferior or dangerous.

Goffman's (1963) classic study divided stigmas into three categories: deformities of the body, blemishes of character, and attributes of large groups. Within each of these categories some characteristics are stigmatized only if found outside their usual context, whereas others are considered unusual in any context. For example, to have a black skin is unusual only in those societies where most individuals are born white, but to have a large birth mark on the face would be regarded as abnormal in any society. Reactions to those who are stigmatized range from uncertainty how to respond, through fear of being adversely affected or contaminated, to serious hostility and even violence.

The process of stigmatization depends on stereotyping and prejudice, and the stigma becomes the defining feature for that person and the person's contacts. There is no agreement on the origin of the tendency by humans to stigmatize. It is possible that it derives from an instinctive and unconscious drive to ensure the survival of the fittest which, like the drive for self-preservation, can militate against other individuals in society. Illness and disabilities of body and mind are potent sources of stigmatization.

Various approaches are employed to deal with the problems of stigma. Some involve action by those who are stigmatized. Others require a positive response from those who are not. In the former category, the stigmatized may attempt to remove or at least conceal the stigma. Inevitably in many cases this is difficult, or even impossible. The stigmatized may seek the company, either secretly or openly, of those who share their stigma. To do so openly is to risk a negative reaction from the non-stigmatized. The decision by a homosexual to 'come out' is an illustration of this approach. The stigmatized may seek the company of those who, though not stigmatized, will hopefully be sympathetic, understanding and accepting. This approach always presents a challenge to the Church and its pastoral leaders.

In the latter category, those who are aware of the problems of a particular stigma may campaign for changes in public attitudes. This has been the policy, with some positive results, of those working with leprosy patients. Others may advocate changes in terminology. It was for this reason that the 'mad houses' of the eighteenth century were called 'asylums' in the nineteenth century and 'mental hospitals' in the twentieth century. However, the new terminology tends sooner or later to attract the old stigma. At the national level, legislation is essential to control discrimination against the stigmatized, to provide social support, and to offer opportunities for employment. *[Howard Gordon]*

STILLBIRTH
See: PERINATAL DEATH

STRATEGIC LEADERSHIP
Leading a church or other institution in the carrying out of its strategic plan.

Once a church has agreed its strategic plan, with clear objectives, ways of putting them into practice, and moving resources from one area to another, the next step is implementing it. If it is difficult to agree a strategic plan, then putting it into practice is a test of strategic leadership. There is a temptation, common to all institutions under pressure, to expect someone else to do it: the bishop, the minister or priest, anyone but the congregation. For a church as a whole to put its plan into practice, there has to be a general sense of ownership. This in turn can only be created through the debate, despite its inevitable disagreements, that precedes the adoption of the plan. Only when all those involved accept that the proposals are the best that can be achieved will they be prepared to act upon them.

That is the time for leadership. Perhaps the first test of strategic church leadership is to resist the temptation for the leaders to think that only they can carry it out. It is essential to pick able men and women, who share the vision and to whom considerable responsibility and authority must be given. Every leader must also be prepared to live with the consequences of delegation; for mistakes are inevitable and some changes of emphasis will appear. Delegation means explaining carefully what is expected, how much freedom of action each person has, and then leaving them alone. Strategic leaders do not need to look over people's shoulders, because there is a shared vision.

In the next stage, the objectives for the institution, split into the different years, must be matched with the available budget, specific budgets allocated for each project, and handed over to those who have been given the leadership. Complaints will be heard, and this is the moment for the leader to stand firm. Everyone will have less than they hoped or expected, but if the plan has been agreed by all, then the consequences are inevitable. This is the second test for strategic

church leadership: being prepared to face conflict.

But churches are not just about budgets; their objectives are spiritual and strategic leaders must be able to share that spiritual vision and be themselves people of real spirituality. That is a third test for the strategic church leader: to keep the congregation firmly focused on the vision that lies behind the objectives.

All this is quite different from the understanding of church leadership that is customarily encountered. The strategic church leader is concerned with vision rather than harmony and balance, with priorities rather than with equality of distribution, and with accountability rather than maintenance (Gill and Burke, 1996). *[Derek Burke]*

STRATEGIC PLANNING
The process through which institutions can determine future objectives.

All institutions, including churches, face a period of unceasing change with declining resources. The many changes occurring in society put pressure on all churches which wish to witness to a historic faith in a way that meets the needs of contemporary society. New initiatives are needed. But when there are inadequate resources to meet existing commitments, let alone start new ones, churches need to be able to prioritize. In such situations, churches, which value consensus decisions and depend heavily on volunteers, tend to avoid difficult decisions in order to avoid hurting anyone's feelings. The inevitable outcome is that all existing commitments are scaled down and no new ones initiated. Such institutions wither and die. The alternative is to come to terms with the future through a process of strategic planning.

A good way to start is to analyse the current situation and to test how well the church is responding. One technique is to use a SWOT analysis: a particular Strength of an organization is set alongside a corresponding Weakness; these are both matched to relevant external Opportunities and Threats. The aim is to create better self-knowledge. The next step is to decide what are the church's main objectives. One way of deciding is to agree on the essential reasons for the institution's existence. All institutions accumulate all sorts of additional tasks. These are no doubt worthy, but not necessarily essential for the institution to fulfil its central function. Every activity must therefore be questioned and only those that are essential retained. It is often useful to arrange them in order of their importance, and see if the allocation of money and time are in the same order. Often they are not, a relatively unimportant activity taking a disproportionate amount of resources. Such activities must be stopped if any new ones are to be started; it is a great mistake to spread the available time, money and energy over an ever-increasing list of activities. All of them are likely to fail.

This process often involves much debate and difficult decisions, but it should lead to a limited number of objectives for the church. There should be testable, i.e. in, say, five years' time it should be possible to determine whether the objectives, often broken down year by year, have been reached or not. Bland, untestable objectives are no use to any institution.

Agreed objectives can lead to agreed strategies. The setting of priorities means that some objectives are more important than others. To put this approach into practice, the resource allocation must be selective, so that high priority areas receive more than low priority areas. That is a real test of leadership (Gill and Burke, 1996). [Derek Burke]

STRESS
The psychological and physiological product of reaction to change.
'Stress' refers both to the pressure connected with change and to the result of such pressure – the feeling of being stressed. It is caused by the actual or believed excess of factors which make the person feel, or actually be, unable to cope. Pastorally it is important to recognize that stress that feels real has a basis and is not just a figment of the imagination. There is also some evidence that a person's personality type affects the capacity to cope with stress. Physiological changes resulting from stress may produce chronic stress, sometimes called 'burnout'. Symptoms are varied, but may include disturbed sleep, loss of application at work or at home, reduced or loss of sex drive and general crossness. The pastor or counsellor needs to recognize that stress is an inevitable component of human existence, without which there would be a limited drive for change and little excitement (Wilkinson, Moore and Moore, 1999). Post Traumatic Stress Disorder is recognized by the law. It may follow an extremely traumatic incident, such as an accident or a violent attack (Kinchin, 1998). Treatment is often by behavioural therapy and medication to relieve depression.

SUBCONSCIOUS
Often used for 'unconscious'; also a technical designation of processes that are scarcely conscious.
In popular use the word is frequently confused with 'unconscious'. It is still used in a technical sense, mainly by French psychologists, to refer to processes which are parallel to conscious processes but which occur outside the individual's personal awareness.

SUBLIMATION
The unconscious process by which sexual energy is expressed in non-sexual activity.
This was a key theme in psychoanalytic thought. Freud suggested that, for instance, artistic creation and intellectual endeavour were the result of the sublimation of the basic sexual instinct into other more socially acceptable channels. These are valued and non-sexual. Today the term is used in a looser sense to refer to the replacement of what appears to be a basic desire with a more highly valued satisfaction.

SUFFERING
Experiences which are felt to be painful or negative.
The everyday meaning of the word generates the principal issue raised in modern theology: how to explain the presence of suffering in nature and human life if we inhabit the creation of a good God.

This key problem is also unavoidable in the context of pastoral studies, since sufferers often pose the question, rebelling against their situation. The effect of suffering is paradoxical: some respond by turning to religion for help and comfort. But many abandon religion on the grounds that they cannot believe in a good God when such bad things happen. The latter argument lies at the root of the atheist critique.

In the twentieth century the issue was brought into sharp relief by the event known as 'the Holocaust'. If there is a God and God chose the Jews, how could God allow their extreme suffering at the hands of the Nazis? 'If I were God,' a Professor of Jewish descent once said, 'I would not let my children do to each other the things they do.'

Earlier in the modern period the question was sharpened by the Lisbon earthquake of 1755. The destruction was indiscriminate: many who died must have been decent, good people. This event shattered the widely held view that God had created the best of all possible worlds. Now people thought that God must either be not omnipotent or not good. In the modern period, some have argued that God does not exist; others that, supposing there is a God, God must be a demon. The word 'theodicy' was coined by Leibniz (1710) to express the endeavour to justify God's ways with the world and defend divine goodness in the face of suffering and evil. It has remained a central issue in philosophical theology.

Intellectual history apart, ordinary people react to everyday situations of hardship and pain by raising the question. Few are now afraid to challenge God. As the influence of religion wanes, the question may lose force, suffering simply confirming for the majority God's irrelevance and non-existence. Yet for believers the puzzle will remain.

Ordinary people in earlier centuries also suffered. Indeed, high infant mortality, brief life expectancy, inability to alleviate many medical conditions, epidemics and unrelieved famine meant they suffered far more than most people who are now troubled by the question. Once there seems to have been more general acceptance of suffering, and indeed death, as a natural part of human life. This contrast between modernity and the past is worth exploring. Why was the atheist response not so powerful in past centuries? It was, of course, partly that the culture was dominated by Christian 'truths' which were socially unchallengeable. But there were other factors.

One was the widespread belief, encouraged by many passages in the Bible, that suffering was God's punishment for sin. Even Jesus (Mark 2.3–12 and parallels) forgave the paralytic's sins before healing him, apparently endorsing the connection. 'The parents have eaten sour grapes, and the children's teeth are set on edge' (Jer. 31.29): this saying suggested that sin and judgement passed from generation to generation. The same view lies behind the question posed to Jesus: 'Who sinned, this man or his parents, that he was born blind?' (John 9.2). Jesus is reported as refusing to blame either. But that did not prevent the idea sinking deep into the Christian tradition. It is still true that people with

disabilities and their parents are made to feel guilty for their situation by some people with beliefs of this kind.

A more humane version of this idea is that suffering is God's way of disciplining people, like a father punishing his sons in order to improve their behaviour. So God's anger and God's love are two sides of the same coin. This too had biblical backing (e.g. Heb. 12.5–11), and was once very common in the preaching traditions of the Church. One example would be a sermon delivered in the fourth century after a community in Cappadocia (Eastern Turkey) had suffered a devastating hailstorm. The message was that they should amend their ways.

Another fourth-century work suggests that people should distinguish moral and physical evils. It was thought appropriate that people suffer from wrongs they had done. As for physical suffering, it came from the human bodily condition, and provided a testing ground of moral character. When souls reached heaven all sorrow and sighing would be taken away.

Perhaps modern anxieties about the problem of suffering arise from two factors: the loss of the sense that earthly life is meant to be tough and temporary, and the loss of expectation that it is a preparation for another life. Both were once deeply entrenched in the Christian tradition.

What modern discussion often fails to notice is the difficulty of understanding the death of Christ on the cross if you begin with the issue of theodicy. If justifying the ways of God is the problem, then the central Christian story is the biggest problem of all. Jesus is understood to be innocent – indeed the very Son of God. The cross is presented as his destiny – indeed as an act fulfilling the prophecies and accomplishing God's intention. So shouldn't the crucifixion be seen as unfair and cruel, and God be placed in the dock?

In fact, however, Christian tradition understands the cross as a redemptive act, and has celebrated the sufferings of martyrs as an imitation of Christ's sacrifice. Some modern theologians have even advocated the idea of a suffering God. Christianity's celebration of suffering has been criticized as psychologically unhealthy. Yet suffering lies at the heart of Christian faith.

Maybe we need a revolution in theological thinking which begins not with the problem of suffering but with its positive and redemptive value. Can we grasp the love of God in the act of atonement which the cross represents? Should we not see the cross as God entering the suffering and darkness of the world so as to bring light and healing? *[Frances Young]*

SUICIDE
Self-killing.
The act of suicide was regarded with peculiar horror by Christians until the Second World War. Suicides were buried in unconsecrated ground. Attempted suicide was a felony in the UK until 1961. The offender might be imprisoned or bound over to a psychiatric hospital. Once the law was changed it was easier for those contemplating suicide to seek help. One notable organization was the Samaritans, founded by Chad Varah in 1953, to befriend the suicidal. The Samaritans are also active in the USA, along with other similar organizations. In the ensuing decades many studies of suicidality have been undertaken both in the USA and in Europe.

There is no such person as a 'suicidal type'. Almost anyone can become suicidal as their circumstances become intolerable and apparently devoid of any possible happy outcome. At this point escape from life appears to be the only solution to misery. The state of the potential suicide becomes one of 'helplessness-hopelessness' (Schneidman, 1986). Only where the depression appears to be caused by chemical changes in the brain is it a simple matter of saving a life; doctors may prescribe antidepressant medication. The trend in state laws governing suicide in the USA has been to eliminate or not exercise criminal sanctions, regarding those who have attempted suicide as being in need of treatment rather than punishment. However, in many states, a person who has attempted suicide may be required to undergo involuntary treatment.

The first serious study of suicide was made by Emile Durkheim (1952); he demonstrated that the suicide rate in a society is related to its entire ethos and culture. For example, the suicide rate of Indo-European nations is half that of Hungary and Finland. Durkheim thought that the rate of suicide could not be changed by merely picking up casualties. Only war and social upheaval would have significant impact in altering numbers, although there appeared to be a link in suicide reduction to the growth of a well-publicized international network of Samaritan branches.

A marked increase of young suicides, especially in the last two decades of the twentieth century, led to increased attention, not only to suicide prevention which is the hallmark of the Samaritans, but to survivors of suicide. Counsellors must consider the family, spouse, children, friends and colleagues of anyone exercising their 'right' to die. Survivors experience universal shame, guilt, anger, grief and loss brought by suicide. Legal questions aside, this need may be especially pressing if the family is being asked to help with the suicide as in assisted dying. Even if suicide is rational, it is still suicide. While persons who kill themselves are beyond help, their survivors are not (Lukas and Seiden, 1997). *[Chad Varah]*

SUNDAY SCHOOL
The section of the local church community involved in teaching the Christian faith.
Sunday schools are usually composed of small groups of children working under adult leaders. The first such school was established in 1780 by Robert Raikes in Gloucester, England. By the 1790s, Sunday schools patterned after British programmes began to appear in North America, often inspired by the goal of providing basic reading skills and religious knowledge for poor working children, while encouraging appropriate Sunday behaviour (Boylan, 1988). The emphasis is on nurture and learning as a preparation for the children's entrance into the adult life of the Church. The term 'Sunday school' is falling into disuse. There is today in many churches a greater emphasis on pilgrimage rather than school as a way of learning, and on association with the body of believers as an experiential way of introducing the Christian faith.

In some churches, notably within the evangelical tradition, the term 'Sunday school' has been applied to adult learning programmes. This use is found both in the UK and in the USA.

SUPEREGO
In psychoanalytic thinking, the judge of the ego, which eventually produces conscience.
The superego develops in the unconscious through a build-up of early experiences. These are mainly those of the child's relationship to his or her parents. An overactive superego may be the result of excessively

strict parenting. The superego functions as a kind of conscience that judges and criticizes the thoughts and acts of the ego. This may produce feelings of guilt or anxiety.

SUPERSTITION
Irrational fear, belief or practice.
Superstition is a belief or fear which most people regard as irrational. Such beliefs or fears may be acted out in certain practices or conventions, or through the wearing of charms, bracelets or religious symbols. Superstition indicates a belief in unknown forces, and in the capacity of certain objects or events to ward off or attract evil or beneficent forces. Superstition is also related to common-sense perceptions of risk and danger, as for example in the common superstition of walking under ladders.

Superstitions are strongly associated with religious practices. The association between bad luck and black cats is related to the practice of witchcraft in early modern Europe. Hospital chaplains are often asked to baptize an infant who has died at or shortly after birth by parents with no affiliation to any Christian church. The ancient fear that an unbaptized child would be damned is rarely voiced but lives on in such practices.

Superstitious beliefs and practices are often condemned by official religious representatives. The Protestant Reformation and its Puritan inheritors condemned popular devotion to relics, statues or sacred wells. Clergy of all religions often seek to limit the physical channels by which people approach unseen powers to prescribed activities such as the Christian sacraments, or the Kaaba of Muslim devotion and pilgrimage at Mecca. As in the case of the Kaaba, a building associated with Abraham, superstitious associations are often linked with religious practices which have been supplanted by a new religion. Thus in Scotland there are many sites of sacred interest associated with pre-Christian Celtic practice which the official Church sought to suppress.

In modern secular societies rational and mechanical controls and processes, such as traffic lights or computer banking, regulate a growing number of personal and social interactions. The place for unseen forces in such societies is diminished and superstition tends to decline. In such contexts official religion itself may increasingly be regarded as superstition. Attachment to unseen forces whose existence is no longer part of the conventional laws, principles and assumptions by which society is ordered appears irrational to a growing percentage of the population. However, in contemporary North America and Northern Europe, the popularity of New Age practices, beliefs and therapies may indicate a resurgence of superstition and belief in unseen forces both spiritual and extra-terrestrial, and a reaction to the modern dominance of secular rationality. [*Michael Northcott*]

SUPERVISION
Pastoral ministry, the aim of which is to facilitate the development of pastoral identity and competence in a person engaged in ministry.
Pastoral supervision takes place in many contexts, in theological education, in preparation for specialized ministries such as chaplaincy, pastoral counselling or spiritual direction, and in lay training for ministry. Pastoral supervision is diverse. It includes certified supervisors for those engaged in specialist ministries and supervisors of field education for students at a theological school. The parish pastor may be seen as a supervisor of the ministries of the members of the congregation. Bishops or others in similar roles exercise a ministry of supervision for their clergy. Pastoral supervision may take place in individual or group modes or a combination of both.

The origins of pastoral supervision in the twentieth century can be traced to Anton T. Boisen (1876–1965). In the summer of 1925, Boisen led one of the first courses of Clinical Pastoral Education (CPE) at Worcester State Hospital, a psychiatric hospital in Massachusetts. The rationale for this training was articulated by Richard Cabot, an early supporter of Boisen and prominent medical educator. In a 1925 essay, 'A Plea for a Clinical Year in the Course of Theological Study', Cabot argued that in addition to classwork, theological students needed to spend time in supervised pastoral ministry with people in crisis. Such experience would acquaint the student with the real struggles and pain of the people they would serve and help them develop pastoral skills to respond to those needs.

Around this time in the USA, other programmes of supervised pastoral ministry with similar aims were being developed. Within a few years several organizations had emerged to foster the development of these programmes. These organizations established standards for the accreditation of training programmes and for the certification of those who supervised them. In 1967 these different organizations came together forming the Association for Clinical Pastoral Education. A similar pattern of pioneering efforts in supervised pastoral ministry and later organizational development can be traced for many other nations.

In pastoral supervision the student is an adult learner and to a greater or lesser degree invited to identify their goals for the supervisory experience. The learning cycle begins with the student doing ministry. In supervision the student reflects on that ministry with the aim of better understanding and more effective subsequent ministry. Verbatim reports of pastoral conversations and case reports are two common ways students bring their ministry to supervision.

Relationships are a key component in pastoral supervision. The pastoral supervisor often serves as a role model for beginning students. By developing a supportive, empathic relationship with the student, the supervisor provides a model for the student's relationships with those with whom they minister. The security of the supervisory relationship plays a key role in helping the student face the anxiety of undertaking new pastoral duties and critical reflection on themselves and their ministry. Some supervisors also encourage students to reflect on their experience in the supervisory relationship itself to develop increasing self-awareness.

Pastoral supervision, particularly as practised in CPE, focuses both on the student's personal and professional identity and on professional competence. The goal is to help him or her become more self-aware. This includes becoming aware of their own gifts and growing, and how these manifest themselves for good or ill in this practice of ministry. It also involves becoming aware of their own needs and how to maintain appropriate boundaries in their pastoral relationships. It includes an opportunity to integrate a pastoral identity into a personal identity. The goal of addressing professional competence is to help students increase their ability to form caring empathic relationships with people in crisis and to integrate knowledge from the behavioural sciences with theological insights in order to minister more effectively.

The dual focus on personal growth and professional competence has created a tension in pastoral supervision between education and psychotherapy. Some supervisors emphasize the importance of personal growth, others emphasize professional skills. Some supervisors distinguish their work from psychotherapy by only addressing the personal issues of a student that contribute to or detract from their pastoral effectiveness. The best balance may be different for each individual student.

Pastoral supervision is a key place for students to examine the relationship between theological knowledge and the joys and sorrows of people with whom they minister. Most programmes of supervised pastoral ministry include an emphasis on theological reflection. Theological reflection is designed to help students discern the theological themes in the stories people tell about the joys and sorrows of their lives, the sacred dimensions of coping both with daily life and extraordinary crises. This enables students to help people reflect on the theological themes in their own stories, to discern where they are in their relationship with God.

Theological reflection in programmes of supervised pastoral ministry differs from theological discourse in seminary in three ways. First, in supervised ministry, theological reflection begins with the story or experience of a person to whom ministry has been offered rather than with tradition. Second, the reflection often must deal with the story or experience of a person who is experiencing a serious crisis. Third, due to the interfaith nature of many programmes of supervised pastoral ministry, students will encounter the beliefs and practices of many faith traditions. Theological reflection in such a setting can be challenging for many students. Hopefully it will aid them in developing a mature faith from which they can provide more effective companionship and ministry to people in need.

In recent years more women and people from different faith, racial and ethnic groups have become pastoral supervisors. This has helped supervisors become aware of the role gender, race, ethnic and cultural background, and faith play in pastoral supervision. An important challenge for the years ahead will be learning what constitutes effective pastoral supervision in different cultures and faith traditions, and in the context of cultural and religious diversity. [George Fitchett]

SUPPORT GROUPS
See: BURNOUT, STRESS

SURVIVOR
One who outlives others who have died or suffered.

From the fifteenth to the eighteenth century the term 'survivor' meant someone who continued life and living after the death of another or after the occurrence of some event. It often had a legal meaning in terms of one person outliving another and therefore gaining some right or privilege.

From the end of the Second World War an additional meaning was added. As a result of Nazi concentration camps in particular, the term designated individuals who experienced time in such camps. In keeping with the original meaning of the term, camp 'survivors' had outlived others who died as a result of camp life. Additionally, the 'survivor' had managed to carry on living despite life-threatening experiences and memories. Within schools of therapy and social science the term could then be applied to those who experienced similar ill-treatment in other war or genocidal situations.

The term took on a further meaning in the 1980s. The growth of awareness of the extent of child abuse and domestic violence in the USA and UK in the 1980s led to the term 'survivor' being applied to women who had managed to carry on living after the physical, sexual and emotional violence they had endured previously. Within the women's movement this term was increasingly seen as an aid to moving away from rigid concepts of woman as 'abuse victim'. To survive an abusive experience is seen as implying greater personal agency and resistance rather than the stereotyped 'passive' accepting.

This newest use of the term is widespread in feminist psychotherapy but not yet in other schools. Those who have witnessed state-allowed torture of citizens (in concentration camps) have concerns that applying the term too widely loses impact. For example, whilst abuse and violence in the home corrode in the same way as camp violence, if not more, it is still possible to phone the agencies of law and order. Where the law of the country is also on the side of abuse there is no recourse.

Linguistically, we are likely to see the use of the term become more acceptable with the addition of a describing word. 'Camp survivor' and 'abuse survivor' allow the shared important concept of 'survivor' to be considered while delineating the different contexts of human suffering that gave rise to them.
[Valerie Sinason]

SYMBOLS
Objects, sounds, actions and words in which we find a 'surplus of meaning'.

Symbols are instruments of communication in which we find a 'surplus of meaning'. Humans learn to communicate with ever greater specificity, whether that communication be by means of gesture, action, sound or language. The place in such communication of actions and of objects, both natural and fashioned, is central. When such communication takes place without ambiguity and with maximum clarity, we speak of a 'sign' or 'signal' being employed. However, in some contexts actions or objects 'speak' to us and for us in ways we can only partially articulate linguistically. We recognize their symbolic import. By close attention to the symbol in its context, we may explicate its meaning, but such explication can never be exhaustive. The adequacy of such explication will always be a matter of debate (Dillistone, 1986).

Sensitivity to symbols is vital for Christian worship and pastoral care. It is of major importance for counsellors and therapists. In symbolic communication, we articulate our experience of birth and death, love and hate, trust and aggression. The role of memory, both individual (Freud) and corporate (Jung), is vital to such communication (Proust explores this magnificently). Within a community the use of certain symbols is a matter of tradition, though it can also be manipulated artificially (as did the German Nazi party). The extent to which there may be transcendent symbols, which communicate similar meaning in all human communities, is a matter of debate. The sharing of a common fund of symbols holds together human communities.

For Christians the determinative symbol is Jesus Christ, who in his perfect humanity communicates an infinite 'surplus of meaning', such that Christians speak of his 'divinity' (Tillich, 1951). Within the Church, focused attention is paid to Jesus Christ in worship which often takes place in a building of symbolic significance (church) and usually makes extensive use of symbols. Such worship includes celebration of the sacraments, study of the Scriptures, teaching and learning of the Christian tradition. The faith of the Church is articulated in 'symbols' (creeds) which 'bring together' (the root meaning of the Greek term symbols is 'throw together') the beliefs of the Church in such a way as to preclude errors of doctrine. The creeds are useful summaries; their 'surplus of meaning' is studied in more extended theological commentaries (Coulson, 1981; McIntyre, 1987).

In the incarnation, flesh communicates the Word. In the life of the Church, the Word is communicated by means of water, bread and wine, through the words of the Scriptures, in ritual, music and art (for example icons), in the lives of the saints. Through the active participation of Christians in the Church, the symbols that are significant in their daily lives gain or lose power, or come to communicate new meaning. Christian pastors seek to promote this process as one of 'conversion' (change and renewal) and transformation towards a closer realization of the image of Christ (cf. 2 Cor. 3.18). [*Nicholas Sagovsky*]

SYMPATHY
The natural human sense of shared feelings.

The idea that human beings can share one another's feelings seems both natural and part of being human. Logically, however, such an expression as 'I know how you feel' is difficult to sustain. Yet people do believe with some justification that they can experience at least similar feelings as those being manifested around them and, more importantly, as a result make a contribution to the developing well-being of the other person. It may be that passive sympathy – just allowing feelings to affect us – is a primitive part of human life. Active attempts to sympathize by seeking to share another's feelings may be less altruistic than sometimes appears. The pastor or counsellor needs to be wary of sympathy. Their own feelings in the interpretative context are data and should better be reflected on in terms of empathy and countertransference.

SYSTEMS PASTORAL CARE
An approach that emphasizes the significance of the local church's social system as the key area for pastoral ministry with individuals and the community.

The approach to pastoral ministry through systems theory emphasizes the local church as a social system to be understood and worked with on this basis. The theory is chiefly associated with E. M. Pattison (1977).

In the UK, Reed (1978) and Lawrence and Miller (1993) provide examples of systemic thinking about the church and its ministers. The pastor sees himself or herself first in role rather than as a person, and works with the idea of the series of systems that make up a church. There has been much discussion about how such a system is to be discerned and in particular where the pastor is located in relation to its boundaries and centre. Since an open systems approach stresses that every social system exists through interaction with its context, to some extent this question is determined by that context (Carr, 1985; 1997). So, for example, a parish priest in an Anglican church may be in a different relationship to the system's boundary from that of, say, a Free Church colleague. An Episcopalian in the USA will be in a different relationship to the community than a vicar in the Church of England. But whatever the detail, the approach remains the same: to see the system as a whole first and then determine tasks and responsibilities in the light of that. This approach locates the pastor firmly in the church and as a worker with the confusion, and discourages reliance on a therapeutic model.

SYSTEMS THEORY
A scientific approach to the proposition that, the whole being greater than the sum of its parts, meaning is found in the connectedness and interdependence of apparently discrete and separate experiences and actions, and therefore of different structures, concepts and meanings.

The concept of an 'open system' draws attention to the relationship of a system to its environment. A system is thought to have a permeable boundary, through which it interacts with the outside world. It receives inputs from its environment, processes them in various ways, and produces outputs. A system thus survives and thrives according to its success in this import–export business.

In this very general sense, we may think of a person as a system, managing oneself in relation to the world we live in. We can also apply this template for understanding to large and complex systems, like hospitals or multinational companies.

A 'closed system' in contrast would be self-contained and interact only with itself. Sometimes organizations may be thought to act as if they are closed systems, not having to bother with external relations. A theatre company may be dismayed and angry that it is to be closed down, although everyone knows that it hardly has any audiences. In fact, closed systems may be thought to have a tendency to deteriorate and run down.

A systemic approach to the understanding of groups and organizations therefore emphasizes the interdependence of all those working in the system. Making an intervention in one part of the system has an impact on other parts. This helps us to understand how there may be resistance to change, but – rather like referred pain – not always where we would expect it.

A system has a recognizable boundary. This boundary cannot be entirely arbitrary, though it may at times be controversial in what it includes or excludes – much like territorial boundaries. There are bounded (sub)-systems within systems, and systems are themselves a part of wider systems. Thinking in this way therefore allows us to move between microscopic and macroscopic perspectives on what we are observing and experiencing.

This concept of boundary then draws attention to the need for there to be management of that boundary, a mediation of what transactions are to take place between what is inside and outside of the system. In the individual, seen as a system, this management may be thought of in terms of ego function. The individual has to understand and manage the boundary between his or her own inner world and the realities of the external environment. In enterprises of different kinds there is a need also for its management to provide the boundary conditions necessary to carry out the task, the conversion process that is necessary for the system to do well in practical, social, psychological and economic terms.

The concept of the open system is attributed to a biologist, Ludwig von Bertalanffy, writing from the perspective of the natural sciences, and wanting to make connections between different scientific disciplines. His general systems theory was taken up by social scientists who wanted to think of organizations not simply as pieces of technology with people neither as inefficient cogs, nor as groups of people acting without reference to the technology. It was open systems theory that led them to a socio-technical understanding of work enterprises, with recognition of the interaction of the human and technical

aspects of an enterprise (Miller and Rice, 1967).

Later systemic descriptions of an enterprise sometimes also make a distinction between the operating and the management or maintenance systems in the conversion process. These may be seen to be interdependent, each impacting on the other – a dynamic that may be observed, for example, in the relations between professional and managerial leadership in human service organizations.

Another influential strand derives from the work of Maria Selvini Palazzoli and colleagues in family therapy. Systemic family therapy emphasizes the interaction between family members and seeks to intervene in a way that draws attention to this internal dynamic. It proposes that the family is operating according to implicit rules, in order to maintain homeostasis in relation to external pressures. One rule that is always present is that these rules cannot be challenged.

The meaning that those in a system put on a problem facing the enterprise gives an insight into what can be thought about and what cannot. By framing the problem the system has the capacity to transform itself and make changes to its internal structures. A paradoxical injunction involves identifying a behaviour that is symptomatic of what is dysfunctional in the family system and then encouraging that behaviour. This is intended to make an involuntary symptom into a conscious choice, which can then be rejected. Systemic approaches to consultation in an organization also aim at making such re-framing possible. This is done, for example, by using the consultancy relationship for mutual feedback and the development of alternative hypotheses about the meaning that informs actions. Circular questioning, which focuses on the patterns of connectedness between people, beliefs and actions is different from the kind of diagnostic questioning that is looking for a root cause of difficulty or dysfunction. Change in itself is not regarded as the problem, but work is to be done on the meanings that change may have for relationships between people and the pressures it puts on their existing rules of engagement (Obholzer and Roberts, 1994).

Although systemic and psychodynamic thinking about the family and other groups are sometimes seen as very different, with dissimilar therapeutic trainings and loyalties, it would be in the spirit of systems theory to explore the interrelatedness of these conceptual transitions. This is attempted, for example, in the 'Tavistock' model of group relations training. The systems approach to consultancy has proved applicable and effective in a variety of situations and organizations, including religious, voluntary and business organizations (Miller, 1993). [Tim Dartington]

T

TABOO
Sacred, prohibited or restricted actions or objects.

Taboo marks off certain kinds of artefact, natural phenomena and social discourse as special, privileged, sacred or prohibited. Diet, gender, certain bodily functions, sexual relations and death are the commonest areas of taboo in most societies ancient and modern (Douglas, 1966). Taboo may sometimes serve a biological function. The Jewish proscription on keeping or eating pigs goes back to the ancient Hebrews. Pigs are genetically close to humans. Consequently they are effective carriers of viruses and infections between other animals and humans. It is possible that the ancient Hebrew taboo on pigs as unclean animals reflected some indigenous biological wisdom about the dangers of cross-infection. Similarly, taboos concerning incest and sexual relations between close cousins have a long history in most societies. They are still adhered to in modern societies, often with the force of law, because the progeny of such relations suffer from a high incidence of genetic and developmental defects.

The regulation of sexual relations illustrates the moral function of taboos. Taboos proscribe behaviours or interactions which may cause harm to other persons or which show disrespect to tribal leaders. Taboos also mark out and protect relationships, such as marriage, which is essential to the survival and stability of the tribe. Residual taboos may still be discerned in certain wedding customs and rituals in modern industrial societies.

Taboos are strongly associated with religious ritual in traditional societies. They mark out the realm of the sacred from the realm of the secular. They highlight the loca-

tion of spiritual qualities, of great holiness, or of magic or evil power, in certain locations, or in certain individuals or classes of person. By demarcating the boundaries of the sacred from ordinary life they provide a visible focus for religious awareness and worship. They provide physical pathways from the world of bodies and sense impressions to the unseen world of spirits.

Modern industrial societies have fewer external taboo markers than tribal societies to indicate danger from safety, right from wrong and sacred from secular. Appropriate and non-harmful behaviours must be learned and internalized by the individual, or are represented in extensive legal and bureaucratic systems. But the absence of physical taboo markers or face-to-face feed-back on taboo behaviours generates social and psychic tensions not found in small-scale societies.

Death is the strongest taboo in most Western societies. Mental illness is another, though weaker, taboo area. Such modern taboos may be said to mark out the sacred boundaries of modernity. Subjection to unseen or uncontrollable forces in death or mental illness is counter-intuitive in a civilization whose sacred myth – progress – sets much store on the mechanical and rational control of nature and the body. Consequently modern taboos, though fewer, may be more dysfunctional than primitive taboos. Fear and taboo in relation to death may encourage denial, and hinder a person from making a 'good death' or prevent effective grieving. [Michael Northcott]

TEAM MINISTRY
A formal structure in the Church of England to enable churches in an area to collaborate in worship, community life, mission, service and ministry.

Preparations for the establishment of a team ministry take account of the entire neighbourhood and ecumenical relationships. In the Church of England a team ministry consists of a team rector and a number of team vicars. The team rector is appointed by a patronage board established under the terms of the pastoral scheme. The team vicars are usually appointed jointly by the bishop and the team rector. Appointments are normally term appointments (often seven years) and may be renewable. Other clergy and laity can be part of the team even though they are not named in the scheme and not of incumbent status. A team ministry normally covers a benefice, and the parishes can either be separate or united. Most team ministries cover one parish, but since the Pastoral Measure 1983, provision has been made for some parishes to remain distinct.

Team ministries are established through procedures identified in the Pastoral Measure 1983. New proposals developed in a collaborative process between the deanery pastoral committee and the diocesan pastoral committee are submitted to the Church Commissioners. Draft proposals are then expressed formally and copies sent to interested parties. Comments and objections are considered and, when the Commissioners are satisfied, they submit the scheme to the Privy Council. In due course the scheme is published in the *London Gazette*. A team ministry can only be altered or dissolved by a further scheme under the same measure.

Advantages: it offers mutual support, especially where the alternative might be daunting in terms of isolation or a sense of being overwhelmed by the task; (2) it combines resources to achieve a greater strength than the sum of the separate parts; (3) it avoids duplication of effort, so that a more efficient use of time is achieved; (4) it provides a wider area for the exercise of particular gifts in an individual person or group. Conversely, it may relieve others of tasks for which they are not well suited.

Challenges: (1) loss of autonomy by individual churches and often a need to compromise on some vital issues; (2) a need for wholehearted commitment to collaborative ministry by all the team; (3) it demands clarity about the aim of the team together and of its individual members.

Teams thrive best when they enlist the help of an outside consultant who regularly meets with the whole team to listen and facilitate the process of creative reflection. A pastoral scheme establishing a team ministry will probably include a paragraph to the effect that the bishop may establish District Church Councils for the various churches in the team. With the approval of the Bishop's Council, the bishop can also make provision for separate representation on the deanery synod. Parishes will, in the first instance, decide whether they wish to have distinct District Church Councils or whether they wish to operate under one Parochial Church Council with local church committees. The ABM Occasional Paper No. 39 (January 1991) sets out elements of good practice in team and group ministry. [*Robin Greenwood*]

TEMPERAMENT
The general nature of an individual.
The word is used in two senses: (1) a loose and general description of a person's attitudes and desires; (2) a sense derived from the ancient world, according to which four temperaments were recognized as depending on the dominant humour of the body. These were sanguine, melancholic, choleric and phlegmatic. This would be of antiquarian interest but for the revival of interest in such ideas in contemporary alternative therapies.

TEMPERANCE
Self-control as
(1) a Platonic virtue, and
(2) a mark of Christian character.
Whereas for the ancients temperance was a model of a way of life that moderated the passions, for St Paul and the Christians it was a characteristic of Jesus and a fruit of the presence of the Holy Spirit. The precise nature of temperance depends upon the particular conditions in which actions or thoughts are occurring. In the nineteenth century the word became associated with teetotalism, the movement against the use and abuse of alcohol. It therefore came to mean 'abstinence', which is not at all the original virtue or grace.

TEMPTATION
Feeling enticed to do something that is wrong or forbidden.
Temptation is to do with the human ability to know the call of 'ought' but to be free to ignore or contradict it, and thus to offend against God. The only remedy is God's mercy.

In Scripture the Hebrew words for temptation can also mean testing. From the story of Adam and Eve onwards, human beings have been tested both by the environment in which they are set, and by their inherent weaknesses. In the Old Testament God tests his chosen people (e.g. Exod. 15.25 or Judg. 2.22) and particular individuals (e.g. Gen. 22.1 or Job 1.11). This is sometimes understood as a means of purification and education, revealing the true quality of faith. There is another sense in which human beings test God, by asking him to prove his justice and promises (e.g. Exod. 17). By the time of the New Testament, prominence is also given to the notion of the Tempter, the

Devil or Satan (Mark 6.13; 14.38; 1 Cor. 7.5), though it is made clear that God can help overcome such testing. There are a number of theories as to the source of the possibility of wrongdoing.

Thus temptation, as the freedom to do wrong, is part of the human condition, but God's grace is available to offer a remedy and a restoration. In pastoral terms this requires honesty in recognizing the reality of the attraction to do wrong in the sight of God (repentance) and a turning to God's grace and the teaching of Christ as the means and the method of learning to choose the right path. Traditional marks of this turning are prayer, self-examination, seeking direction, and the exercise of the will.

The measure of temptation can be the individual conscience, the teaching of the Church, the insight of a prophet, or the consensus of the community. Pastoral studies confronts this issue in exploring the respective claims of these factors, and in reminding those involved that temptation includes the possibility of both good and evil. The gift of free will brings temptation, i.e. the possibility of choosing less than God desires.

The key can be seen in the teaching of Jesus in the garden of Gethsemane, 'Watch, and pray that you may not enter into temptation; the spirit indeed is willing, but the flesh is weak' (Matt. 26.41). For this reason it is dangerous to isolate temptation as an individual issue. The point of the temptations of Jesus is that he was invited to choose to use what God gives for himself, or for God's greater purposes. This is true of all temptation – it involves exercising a choice about what God gives, either for selfish purposes or for ends that involve and enhance the true well-being of others. For pastoral practice temptation needs to be confronted with prayer, not just with counselling. [*Alastair Redfern*]

TERMINAL ILLNESS
The final stages of any illness before death, most usually applied to the final weeks and months of life of someone who is suffering from a definably mortal disease.

The term is a shorthand term that is sometimes used to assist surgeons and physicians to alter their approach from that of trying to effect a cure or containment of a disease to one of trying to improve the quality of a person's life during the remaining time of that life. It is a realistic phrase if used in this way,

but it is not always helpful to use it for two reasons: it is notoriously difficult to predict when a person is going to die, yet once the phrase is used it alters the medical team's and family's perceptions of the future life and well-being of the person who has a serious life-threatening illness. Using this phrase unwisely can sometimes be taken to be equivalent to the dread phrase 'there is nothing more we can do'. Since there is always something that can be done to help people with life-threatening illnesses it may be a phrase that can destroy the morale of patients, relatives and friends.

Although there are conflicting views in the medical, nursing and caring professions about the wisdom of informing patients that they are suffering from a life-threatening illness, and may be approaching the end of their lives, there are good precedents for explaining the nature of an illness to those who quite obviously want to know where they stand. In doing that it is important to stress the impossibility of accurate predictions and the good quality of life that can be provided by medical and nursing care during the final stages of anyone's life.

Good management of terminal illness is an art. The hospice movement has enhanced medical understanding of the management of physical and emotional pain during the ends phase of people's lives. Hospice chaplains who are well trained can provide support in a variety of ways, not always overtly religious. There is still need for the insights provided by such experts to filter into community care of the dying. Dying at home can be managed as skilfully as dying in a hospice, but good training in pain management is required as well as good attentions to the emotional and spiritual needs of dying people. Immense benefit can be gained from people who are willing to visit those who are dying and to provide them with sufficient time and opportunity to talk about their feelings about approaching death. It is important to realize that the good management of terminal illness depends on effective professional team work and adequate support for the whole team, including relatives and close friends. [*Una Kroll*]

TERMINATION OF COUNSELLING
The planning and effecting of the end of a counselling contract.

A significant part of the process of counselling is the ending of the therapeutic relationship and the counselling contract, since endings often have particular poignancy for clients. The date (approximate or exact) of the ending of counselling is normally reckoned to be one of those features which is arranged with the client at the outset, so that it can be prepared for, although sometimes the contract is open-ended, or open to review. Even if a counselling contract is open-ended, with no date fixed for its termination, counsellors usually ensure a period of time between the decision on the part of the client to end, and the actual termination. This period of time is sometimes reckoned as being about one quarter of the total length of the sessions as required. It provides sufficient time for the different issues involved to arise, and for working them through.

Not only does this period provide the opportunity for client and counsellor to review progress, to look at issues of not coming to counselling any longer, and to identify the helpful and unhelpful features of their work together; the termination also evokes feelings in the client (as well as in the counsellor) which are associated with other losses and endings. For example, the ending of counselling may remind a client of the death of a parent, or the break-up of an intimate relationship, or of leaving home as a young adult. Feelings associated with loss and grief can be expected to show themselves in relation to the counsellor, especially if the counselling has been intense, as well as to be re-experienced in relation to earlier losses: feelings such as anger, sadness, being unable to imagine what it will be like no longer to come for counselling, relief at the ending because of the inconvenience or financial outlay, gratitude for feeling better, anxiety at being on one's own, the wish to go on, or in some way to cling to the counselling – all these and other feelings may be evoked.

The working through of some of these feelings can therefore be extremely beneficial for the client, even if loss was not part of the initial presenting issue. But since losses very often are part of the main presenting issue, the termination may even be related to these issues from the very beginning of counselling, so that someone who has experienced a recent loss can be reminded how the end of counselling will also involve further loss. In short-term counselling one of the features which is emphasized throughout is the termination of the counselling relationship. Making links to termination appears to be one factor that increases the efficacy of short-term work.

Inevitably there are clients who wish to bring their counselling to an end immediately, once they have made up their mind to stop. This can sometimes be related to their desire to avoid the painfulness of the ending. Counsellors respect the client's wish in these matters, while at the same time suggesting that at least one more session might be helpful, in order to review how the counselling has gone. *[Michael Jacobs]*

T-GROUP
'Training group': an educational methodology for studying group and interpersonal dynamics.

In T-groups, a small number of people (6–12) observe and reflect on their attitudes and behaviour for the purpose of learning about effective human relationships. They pay attention to: group formation and development; leadership and followership; and productive co-operation, including satisfactory working through of conflict. The T-group was created in 1947 by the National Training Laboratories Institute in the USA. Historically, it relates to 'encounter groups' (initiated by progressive churches during the 1960s to 1970s) and to 'group relations conferences' (created and developed by the Tavistock Institute in the UK, also since 1947).

THEODICY
To speak of God in a way that is just, especially in light of the problems of evil and suffering.

The term theodicy is an English combination of two Greek words: *theos* (God) and *dikē* (just). The problem of the presence of evil and suffering in a world created by an almighty God who is also loving, good and just is one of the oldest and most persistent challenges to faith in God in the Hebraic/ Christian tradition. Simply put, if God is all-powerful, how can one, in the presence of the experience of evil and suffering, speak of God as being good, loving and just; or, if God is good, loving and just, how can one, in the presence of the experience of evil and suffering, speak of God as all-powerful? Theodicy is the task of vindicating God and the divine attributes in face of the existence of evil, where such faith seems most doubtful.

In pastoral studies, the importance of developing a theodicy which has integrity cannot be overstated (Oden, 1983). The pastoral vocation is one that is lived in and with the terrible sufferings of people and in confrontation with the existence of evil. The first stance of pastoral care is not to defend or vindicate God, but to enter into the sufferings of others, acknowledging their pain, confusion and anger. To do otherwise is to belittle suffering and, therefore, to belittle the sufferer.

Various approaches to theodicy have been made from the patristic period on in Christian theology. Some have concentrated on the incompleteness of human beings: in order for them to become what God intends, they are confronted with free choice between good and evil; the misuse and abuse of human freedom results in evil and suffering. Others have argued that the concept of the omnipotence of God is an import from Greek philosophical thought into Christian theology and must be questioned or abandoned. Still others have argued that the central Hebrew/ Christian conception of God is of a God who suffers and joins humanity in its suffering. This constitutes a protest theodicy – a protest in which God participates against pain, suffering and evil.

From a Christian perspective, especially in relationship to pastoral studies, two confessions undergird a meaningful theodicy: (1) suffering is real and is the existential condition of our fallen humanity; and (2) suffering is not the last word about our human condition (Hall, 1986). A theology of the cross demands that we move our thinking from a preoccupation with the power of God to the woundedness of God. Omnipotence as sheer almightiness is the exaltation of power in and of itself. The God of the Hebrew/Christian tradition is not the God of sheer almightiness but the God of supremely powerful love who suffers and engages suffering for the purpose of conquering sin and suffering and bringing redemption and liberation to the suffering world. [Victor L. Hunter]

THEOLOGICAL REFLECTION
In pastoral studies, a hermeneutical process concerned with action.
Theological reflection in pastoral studies has gone through a huge shift in method (Anderson, 1993, 1997; Browning, 1991; Hiltner, 1958). Previously, the goal was the application of theology. But without a theological theory of pastoral practice, pastoral studies became increasingly connected to non-theological perspectives on the human

situation. The question became: What is theological about pastoral studies?

The concern is to develop a theological method for pastoral studies that allows for a mutual, critical conversation between theology and ministry leading to practical theological knowledge and wise practice by the Church. A new discipline of practical theology has emerged, the immediate task of which is the development of its identity as a theological discipline.

Theological reflection in pastoral studies brings two theological affirmations into a mutual, critical conversation. (1) From Scripture, God is known as a God who acts for the salvation of humankind. As such, Jesus Christ is the mission of God to and for the world. (2) God is active in situations of ministry and experience. A two-way relation exists between knowledge of the acting God and reflection on the ministry of the Church. The ministries of the Church and the Church's continuing interpretation of Scripture interpret each other. Thus theological reflection in pastoral studies is a hermeneutical process. It leads to a practical knowledge of God in our action (theology), and the ability to engage in wise practice (*phronesis*), knowledge for action rooted in God.

Theological reflection in pastoral studies proceeds through conversation between knowledge of the acting God and critical reflection on what that knowledge calls forth and makes possible as the Church's ministry. This is a conversation between the confessional and descriptive moments of practical theology. It forms an ongoing hermeneutical process concerned with action (see Hermeneutic Circle). The confessional moment is the Church's naming of the action of God, which is the mission of God in and through Jesus Christ in obedience to the Father (John 6.38), attested by Scripture. This is the actuality of God's history of salvation in Jesus Christ brought to speech. The descriptive moment is reflection on the Church's participation through the Holy Spirit in this mission of God. This is understood as participation in Christ, for there is no other basis for ministry than our sharing in the continuing ministry of the Son to the glory of the Father (John 15.5). The descriptive moment is reflection on some specific practice of the Church in its life in Christ.

The result of this conversation between the confessional and descriptive moments of churchly practical theology is twofold. First, it is knowledge of God illumined and clarified by the study of situations and events. Second, the practice of the faith is enriched by an ever deeper practical wisdom rooted in participation in God's mission.

The two-way movement between the confessional and descriptive moment is conversational, i.e. mutual, relational and open to discovery on both sides. Theology refers only to a God who acts. Church practice is participation in the continuing ministry of God. Thus, God is the subject and the verb in the conversation. Just as the Church's practice of the faith depends upon a deep practical wisdom rooted in a graced participation in God's mission in and through Jesus Christ, so also knowledge of God is illumined and clarified by the study of situations and events.

The bipolar method for theological reflection in pastoral studies is a hermeneutical process concerned with action, both God's and the Church's. It involves the movements from God's practice to churchly practice as participation in Christ in situations and events, and from reflection on situations and events to illuminate and confirm our understanding of God's mission in and for the world in and through Jesus Christ. It is a hermeneutical process insofar as it interprets situation and event in the light of the living God, and the truth of God is understood ever more deeply through the Church's interpreted reflection on ministry.

In theological reflection in pastoral studies, neither an understanding of the mission of God, nor reflection on churchly practice as participation in Christ, is satisfactorily identified without the other, or resolved into the other. For theological reflection to identify God's ministry apart from the corresponding ministry of the Church leads to abstraction. To identify the Church's ministry apart from God's ministry leads to pragmatism. God has called the Church to be the Body of Christ, in which there is knowledge of the mission of God. Yet the Church has neither identity nor function apart from the action of God in Christ.

There is an ordering in theological reflection in pastoral studies. First, as a hermeneutical process concerned with action, we move from God's practice and the Church's knowledge of it, to churchly practice. This is the move from God's ministry to theology to the Church's ministry. There is a theological priority to this ordering, for the Church has

no ministry apart from participation in Christ's ministry. The movement from (God's) action to (the Church's) knowledge of and participation in that action, is from God's actuality to the Church's possibility for ministry. This is not the movement from theory to practice, but a sharing in the practice of God.

Second, we move from churchly practice to theological reflection. Critical reflection on churchly practice as participation in Christ, which includes an understanding of situation and action in the fullest way possible (a 'thick' description), illuminates and confirms the knowledge of God. The movement is from participation in God's ministry to description of experience to knowledge as a deeper awareness of God's action. [Andrew Purves]

THEOLOGICAL VIRTUES
Faith, hope and charity: the marks of Christian living.
These virtues are not attainments but ways of living. To have faith is to commit oneself fully to the Christian pilgrimage. But this virtue has sometimes been degraded to mean doctrinal correctness. Hope is aspiration with joy. The old, and simpler, notion that it means desire for heaven has declined in significance. Charity, once freed from the idea of a superior giving to his or her inferiors, becomes love. But since that term also has been debased, it may be that in English 'charity' may be reclaimed. These three, coupled with the four cardinal virtues, make up the so-called seven virtues which contrast with the seven mortal sins.

THEOLOGY AND PASTORAL CARE
Theology: the systematic study of God. Pastoral care: the disciplined expression of God's love in relation to persons within social systems.
Care has been a central focus of Scripture and theology since the formation of religious communities. To love God and to love one's neighbour as oneself (Lev. 19.18; Mark 12.31) are among the oldest texts in Hebrew and Christian Scriptures. Indeed, God is love. Every world religion teaches some version of loving self and others as a principle of the good life. Learning what such love and care means in actual situations is one of the central challenges of faith.

The term 'pastoral care' comes from Hebrew and Christian images of the shepherd. Religious leaders are admonished to be like shepherds who love their sheep, sometimes even risking their lives to save the sheep from dangers. While the shepherd image has been criticized in recent years for its implicit hierarchy and inequality, pastoral care has retained its meaning of genuine care that respects the image of God in persons. Theologians, however, have differed over the meaning of God's love and its mandate of care for others. In critical times some theologians have justified war, capital punishment, crusades against 'heathens', slavery, oppression of women, physical punishment of children, genocide, destruction of 'pagan' cultures, poverty, and other forms of violence that seem to contradict the images of care bestowed by a loving God.

How is pastoral care rooted in the love of God? Three types of theology illustrate how theology shapes pastoral care.

1. *Begin with the love of God.* According to some theologians, we know the meaning of pastoral care when we have personally experienced a revelation from God that transforms our lives. In our natural and sinful condition, we cannot conceive of the meaning of care because our lives are filled with anxiety, competition, and trying to escape suffering and despair. However, when we encounter the living God through personal experiences, everything is transformed and we begin to see God's care for people everywhere. Such orthodox or neo-orthodox theologians rely on the sovereignty of God to break through the limitations of the human condition and teach us the meaning of caring for others the way God cares for the world. For example, after the death of his son in an accident, Karl Barth wrote a sermon on 1 Cor. 13.12: 'We see now in a mirror dimly, but then face to face.' In the midst of his grief, Barth could lament his suffering and also praise God who 'has meant and done well' with his son (Migliore and Billman, 1999).

2. *Begin with the suffering and hope of the poor.* Some theologians say that we know the meaning of pastoral care when we have lived with the faithful poor of the world who have seen the worst that can happen and know God from personal experience. The poor live without the illusions of wealth, education and security, and those poor who know God are best able to witness to the love of God that cannot be destroyed by human evil. In the suffering and hope of the poor, God's love has been revealed most fully, such as in Abraham who was a pilgrim, and in Jesus who was a peasant in Palestine. Such liberation theologians rely on God's action through the people to destroy the myths of the powers and principalities that hide God from human view. When theologians live with the poor and join in their struggles for justice and community, then God's care for the world will become a reality rather than just an abstract idea. For example, a line from an African-American spiritual gives solace during times of trial: 'We don't believe God brought us this far to leave us' (Townes, 1997). Faithful people who have endured in the past with God's care believe they can endure in the present through solidarity with one another. Religious leaders are most caring when they encourage community among suffering people.

3. *Begin with the covenant between God and the people.* A third group of theologians emphasize the covenantal relationship between God and the people. By establishing particular covenants with Abraham in Caanan, with Moses and Israel on Mount Sinai, with Jesus at his baptism, and with the disciples at Pentecost, God has revealed Godself in particular ways. Such covenants create particular histories, liturgies, theologies and practices that form Christian identity. Care is understood within particular traditions and language systems. Being a Christian means caring that arises out of one's particular identity and history, and leads to certain virtues, character and actions. For example, Christian communities with a tradition of pacifism tend to see non-violence as an important expression of care. During war, care organized among familiar communities is disrupted by violence, immigration and fear. To follow a God of non-violence creates particular images of care that are often at odds with the wisdom of other communities (Hauerwas, 1981). Religious leaders are most caring when they encourage communities to express their particular covenantal understanding of God towards one another and the world.

In summary, theologies about God have strong influence on the definitions, theories and practices of care. While Scriptures identify care as a basic expression of faith in God, theologies determine what is meant by care.

[*James N. Poling*]

THERAPEUTIC COMMUNITY
A community based on the concept of maximizing all aspects of the hospital milieu as a therapeutic tool.

The paradigm of the therapeutic community has been most extensively applied in the field of substance abuse, e.g. Alcoholics Anonymous, and in the treatment of patients with relationship problems such as autism and personality disorders. Relationships between patients and staff act as the basis for exploring and dealing with an individual's internal and interpersonal problems. Social rules and boundaries are established, and interactions within those limits are enforced and explored in a democratic atmosphere, with staff and patients working together as a dynamic social group.

THERAPEUTIC CONTRACT
An explicit agreement made between a therapist or counsellor and a client, establishing expectations, roles, and the work each will carry out in the therapy process.

The contract helps define the structure of therapy, empowers the client, and delineates the tasks involved in the process. These contracts have been extensively used in the substance-abuse field to define boundaries of behaviour and to establish a working alliance.

TIME BOUNDARY
A time limit set for consultation or therapy.

One reality condition of a counselling session or a group learning event is the setting of time boundaries – when it will begin and end. The way in which a client or a group treats time is usually an indicator of unconscious attitudes. Although strict management of such boundaries may appear odd and contrary to normal human behaviour, in the counselling and learning setting attention to and care with them is essential. Everyday pastoral activity will be less precise. But the importance of time and an awareness of what is available is a crucial part of the pastor's ministry. Although setting a time limit may sometimes feel (and be) defensive or even clinical, it often benefits the person being counselled. In his or her general confusion, a fixed point can be comforting.

TOLERATION, RELIGIOUS
The allowance of religious beliefs and practices that differ from one's own.

A topic of major concern chiefly in the modern era, it becomes increasingly important with the emergence of a global society. Whereas earlier the beliefs and values of a commonly held religion structured the various communities and countries, in contemporary pluralistic societies social order requires respect for a range of religious beliefs and practices. Thus religious toleration has a political dimension – the problem of preserving social cohesion when subgroups may not share basic beliefs and values; and a philosophical dimension – questions about whether any particular religions can claim final truth.

Religious toleration is especially challenging to the Western 'religions of the Book', namely Judaism, Christianity and Islam. Though each includes deep traditions of some respect for good people of other faiths, their beliefs in one God, divine revelation, inspired Scriptures, and their own truth work against openness towards differing religions. In contrast, Hinduism's belief in multiple gods and in many paths, and Buddhism's core commitment to personal transformation downplay proselytizing and have a different approach to issues of truth.

In Europe, the religious fragmentation of Christendom after the Reformation painfully raised the question of religious toleration. The Enlightenment mounted arguments for it, and the American Bill of Rights and the French Revolution set up constitutional states guaranteeing it. Christians lived with it for practical reasons but took centuries to justify it theologically. The Second Vatican Council, for example, reinterpreted the Christian axiom, 'no salvation outside the Church'. It proposed that 'since Christ died for all, and since all are in fact called' to salvation in Christ, grace must be 'active invisibly' in the hearts of all people of good will. Similarly, on the basis of human dignity and the sanctity of conscience, the Council supported religious freedom – not as a positive right to hold false beliefs but as a negative right not to be forced to convert.

The late twentieth century and the early twenty-first have seen a backlash of religious conservatism. Ineluctable pressures towards a global society have loosened the religious and philosophical underpinnings of Western civilization. Uncertainty and insecurity are

commonplace. A strict return to traditional religion appears to offer a simple remedy. Thus, fundamentalist movements, with exclusivist political agendas, have emerged in force. More far-sighted responses highlight commonalities among the religions – like 'global ethics' (Küng, 1996) or a 'spirituality of authenticity' (Helminiak, 1998), which appeal to a universally basic humanism, while respecting varied religious expressions of theism. Inevitably, the third millennium will witness a major transformation of Christianity. It must capitalize on the universalistic tendencies in the religion while shedding the particularities of former eras and retaining essential doctrines. To sort these out is the challenge. Pastoral ministers need to understand the historical trend and be able to inspire security through faith sufficient to allow for openness to authentic development.
[Daniel A. Helminiak]

TONGUES
Sounds, sometimes speech-like utterance, that are not consciously controlled, made during ecstasy in worship.

Tongues, known also in the Greek term *glossolalia*, are predominantly a feature of pentecostal and charismatic worship and private devotion. The Church has always had difficulty in assessing the significance and value of this practice (1 Cor. 14.1ff.), which is often associated with religious revivals. Those who experience this claim that it profoundly affects their whole being: they are ultimately calmed and suffused with a sense of love. Pastoral problems may arise with those who wish to but do not share the experience. Few churches have claimed that it is essential as an expression of faith. This provides the pastor with a basis on which to counsel any who are distressed because they feel deprived or inadequate. Glossolalia is not confined to religious ecstasy or to Christianity. It may be induced through hypnosis and is found in some pathological states of mind.

TRAINING METHODS
The form and content of courses of preparation for pastoral care and/or counselling.

Pastoral care and counselling take place at several different levels, each with its appropriate intensity of training. Three broad levels may be identified: (1) pastoral counsellors,

who may be ordained or lay, offering a professional service as accredited counsellors either on behalf of the Church or in private practice; (2) ministers and priests in parishes or chaplaincies where pastoral care is a major component of their daily work; and (3) lay people who are in some sense commissioned to exercise a representative pastoral ministry on behalf of the Church within congregations and communities. It must also be recognized that much – perhaps most – pastoral care takes place as a spontaneous outflowing of compassion from one human being to another. For such care there are no training methods – nor should we try to devise them.

The following components will feature in all training programmes, each at an appropriate depth and complexity of treatment.

1. *A knowledge base.* While training for pastoral care is more than an academic exercise, there are concepts and theories which need to be understood. Central will be some understanding of human growth and development, of what constitutes a helping relationship. Advanced students will need an introduction to the strengths and weaknesses of various psychotherapies and to own an approach which is personally comfortable.

2. *An appropriate level of skill.* Trainees need to be helped to develop basic listening skills, to recognize the limits of their own competence and develop skills of referral.

3. *A degree of self-awareness.* It is arguable that all who offer counselling to others should themselves have received counselling, not because they are sick but because they are human. People need to know something of themselves, of their own 'hang-ups' and inner motivations for helping before they are able to help others. Further, it is no bad thing for counsellors to have experienced the anxieties of having been a counsellee. For those engaged in pastoral counselling it is particularly important that they are aware of their own spiritual journey and are able to integrate their faith with their practice while at the same time respecting the individuality of those to whom they relate pastorally.

4. *Supervised experience.* Good preparation, a controlled exposure to practice and a supervisory relationship which provides a secure place in which the trainee can report back and reflect upon specific pastoral encounters are essential. Trainees commonly report to their supervisors either verbally or by the use of written documents such as verbatims or

case studies (Foskett and Lyall, 1988). A skilled supervisor will monitor progress, support and affirm the trainee and widen horizons. Supervision may take place in a group setting, and this may be the preferred setting for lay pastoral care. The supervisory relationship is the cornerstone of any training method and lays the foundation for an ability to make ongoing use of supervision and consultancy in continuing pastoral practice. [David Lyall]

TRANSACTIONAL ANALYSIS
A therapy that focuses on the transactions between people.
Based upon the ideas of Eric Berne (1964), transactional analysis focuses on three aspects to individuals. These are summed up in the mnemonic P–A–C: Parent, Adult and Child. Any encounter consists of a transaction between a stimulus and a response. The goal is to free the Adult from the Child (uncontrolled emotions) and the Parent (inhibitions). They will then make conscious choices to relate in a positive fashion. The approach was especially popular with individuals and organizations in the 1960s and 1970s.

TRANSCENDENCE
The state or action of exceeding limitation.
Transcendence may be affirmed of people who rise above their given conditions, in achievement, for instance, or in memory and hope. Such human transcendence is a positive, though finite analogue for God's state of existence beyond all external limitation (although God may voluntarily limit himself). Since God is transcendent he cannot be contained in space-time, nor in any human concept. God is therefore said to transcend all particular occasions and expressions, yet to be discerned and related to through the value and significance of finite experience in ways which cannot be adequately expressed. Since the 1960s there has been a move to express human transcendence in religious terminology, often without belief in God but retaining Jesus as exemplar, or insisting that overemphasis on divine transcendence drains the world of its own reality.

Transcendence as a single concept is essential to a doctrine of God since it reflects the quality of religious experience which goes beyond the visible and expressible, and thus provides the human perspective on divine infinity. Yet in the practice of relating to God in theology and devotion, transcendence has also acquired connotations of place. It is spatially 'up' while immanence is spatially 'in'. Ideally the two terms together express God's omnipresence, but because they have overtones of location they tend to be competing or alternating orientations for the presence of God. Each term, moreover, has its own difficulties as well as its benefits. A transcendent God may seem uncaring and remote from everyday life. Further, the above/below paradigm, especially when echoed in church structures, is currently experienced as oppressive. Conversely, immanence runs the danger of losing sight of God's otherness by domesticating God within the thought forms or social processes of the time, which themselves are ambiguous and vulnerable to upset. It seems that when the difficulties in either location are felt, there is a swing to the opposite affirmation.

The connotations of place, however, are not accidental, undesirable accretions. For a relationship to take shape and be lived with imaginatively and responsively there has to be some definition and quasi-location of God. One possible way out of the alternatives of transcendence and immanence is to change the emphatic preposition from 'up' or 'in' to 'with'. God's presence with us is not remote, yet remains independent; it expresses solidarity without removing human responsibility. The horizontal relationship would not deny God's limitless transcendence since that too may be conceptualized horizontally, radiating out from every particular 'here' rather than descending vertically from above to below. [Ruth Page]

TRANSFERENCE
A psychoanalytic term for the feelings of the patient towards the analyst.
This definition is inadequate because there is no adequate definition of transference. Yet it is one of the core discoveries of Freud. He noted that in their responses patients might treat the analyst as if he or she were someone from their past, often a father or mother. The attitude would be characterized by strong feelings of love or hate, that clearly are not addressed to the analyst as such but to what he or she may be representing to the patient during the analysis. Although at first technically confined to the analytic situation, it was soon argued that transference is also a characteristic of everyday life, although probably

in a less intense fashion. The phenomenon has been discovered in the study of groups. Although it remains somewhat mysterious, transference is one of the discoveries of psychoanalysis that has implications for the minister and his or her perception of what may be happening to them in role. The feelings generated within the analyst or minister are counter-transference (Carr, 1997).

TRANSITIONAL OBJECT
A physical possession cherished by a young child that functions to help the child engage in the essential task of separation.
This possession may be a cuddly toy or a blanket which becomes in part a mother substitute as the child begins to differentiate him- or herself from mother. D. W. Winnicott (1971) introduced the concept. As a child psychiatrist he explored human development, wondering how highly vulnerable and dependent babies mature into robust and increasingly independent adults. He came to recognize the crucial role of soft and breast-like objects, such as teddy bears, in helping the infant to break away from the full-time care-giving of the actual mother.

The development of the transitional object begins with the baby's predilection for sucking on thumbs, fingers or fists. Newborn infants often turn to their own accessible body parts for gratification during mother's absence. As the healthy child becomes older, soft toys assume increasing importance and reduce anxiety by filling a void. Developmental psychologists have discovered that youngsters often turn to those transitional objects to ease the pain of separation from parents, an inevitable feature of daily life. For example, mother may need to leave the room. The baby will either cry or suck a thumb or dummy, thus learning to turn to his or her own body for comfort. In healthy individuals, the transitional object will be used and even abused but eventually relinquished, once the individual has internalized the object.

The acquisition of the transitional object permits the healthy child to develop the capacity for illusion, and for daydreaming and creativity. By clinging to a teddy bear, for example, the young person maintains an illusion that mother has not disappeared; this ability to experience illusion is a cornerstone of healthy growing. In pathological homes, small children either have no access

to transitional objects or are not given freedom to use them. Such individuals are likely to turn to more destructive substitutes, such as alcohol, drugs or other forms of addiction.

The concept of the transitional object is of especial interest to students of pastoral studies, because transitional objects are used in religious ceremonials. For instance, important physical objects, such as the wafer and the crucifix, may serve as representations of the body of Jesus Christ, whose death may be experienced painfully by practising Christians. These transitional objects provide a sense of illusion that Jesus continues to exist, thus sparing people from an overwhelming sense of abandonment. *[Brett Kahr]*

TRANSPERSONAL PSYCHOLOGY
A broad integration of perspectives which seeks to explain human psychological and spiritual well-being and potential by focusing on experiences that transcend the sensate individual.
Originating in the 1960s as a new movement within the field of humanistic psychology, transpersonal psychology has been considered by many the fourth force in psychology (after the first force, behavioural; the second force, psychoanalytic; the third force, humanistic) because of its concern with the spiritual, mystical and transcendental aspects of self-actualization. Maslow and Grof named this movement 'transpersonal psychology' because it focuses on the transcendent capacities of human beings and the assumption that healing requires transpersonal resources. Additionally, the self may be considered less personal, but larger, more cosmic, more illuminated and more eternal than in the other three schools of psychology.

Psychology focuses its work on the human mind and on various states of consciousness. Westcott suggests that there are five such states: waking, sleeping, dreaming, entranced and released. Freud, Jung and others in the psychoanalytic tradition increased understanding of the state of dreaming. Milton Erickson and his followers deepened the appreciation of the trance state of consciousness. So transpersonal psychology seeks to describe and explain the released state of consciousness. Sometimes it is called an altered state of consciousness. In this state the body is generally at rest and passive towards the environment, but the awareness is keen and one is deeply perceptive.

Wilber (1986) has proposed a model for understanding the development of consciousness across the spectrum of psychological perspectives, including the subject matter of transpersonal psychology. Each of three primary structures of consciousness includes three sub-structures. (1) Pre-personal consciousness includes the earliest sensory and physical awareness, the emergence of the emotional mind, and the development of language and the representational mind. (2) Personal consciousness includes the personal scripting of social roles and rules, the development of formal operations or reflexive thinking, and an awareness of life's meaning amid finitude and suffering as constitutive of personal identity. (3) Transpersonal consciousness includes the psychic mind, which can inspect the mind's capacities and is the seat of inspiration and inner vision, the subtle mind, which is the seat of archetypes and illumination, and the causal mind which is the consciousness of the universal and formless self common to all humans. In Wilber's model each substructure of consciousness also has its characteristic pathology and treatment.

Some criticize transpersonal psychology for being informed primarily by Eastern religions and therefore of limited use to those in the Judaeo-Christian tradition. While it is true that no single theology underlies transpersonal psychology, it is also true that there are already diverse theological traditions within both Judaism and Christianity. Certainly both have mystical traditions which transpersonal psychology can help to understand psychologically. In religiously diverse contexts transpersonal psychology offers tools to understand the psychology of differing spiritualities. [Judith Orr]

TRANSPLANTATION
A surgical procedure whereby organs or tissue (e.g. heart, kidney, bone marrow, skin, cornea) are transferred from one body to another.

Most transplants are life-saving procedures for patients who would otherwise die. Others improve the quality of life (e.g. to restore sight). Donation from living persons is possible (e.g. for bone marrow) but the majority of transplants involve donation from a dead person. Donors of major organs are usually from intensive care units where 'life-support' machinery ensures the continuation of blood circulation until the organ is retrieved. This means that the donor's heart and lungs

continue to work after brain-stem death (brain death) tests have confirmed death. Transplant operations cannot be planned in advance because of the complexity of matching organs to recipients and the short organ storage times. Survival rates are improving but transplantation of significant organs remains a major surgical procedure. Recipients must always take immuno-suppressant medication to prevent rejection; this renders them vulnerable to infections.

Transplantation is accepted by all major world religions. However, it raises many controversial issues. Should consent to donation be assumed unless there is evidence to the contrary or should consent be sought from the next of kin? Should the wishes of the next of kin take precedence over those of the donor? What are the ethics of buying organs or tissue from the living? What are the implications of using animal organs? Are there adequate safeguards to ensure that shortage of organs does not compromise the treatment of potential donors? What criteria should determine choice of recipients (e.g. sickness, age, socio-economic status)? Is it all right to accept the status of recipient but not that of donor because of belief in the need to bury bodies intact?

Pastoral care should involve awareness of complex ethical issues. First, there are the spiritual needs of recipients. Transplantation offers hope of new life to the terminally ill but can be dependent on another person's death. Anxiety, depression, insecurity and a sense of worthlessness are common particularly if there are unresolved issues from the past or if family support is lacking. Existing faith may be shaken or existential issues newly explored. Second, there are the spiritual needs of the recipient's family and friends. In addition to the obvious causes of anxiety and helplessness there are often socio-economic implications. Relationships are strained; relinquishing the sick role may prove difficult for both, or stress may break a fragile partnership. Children can feel marginalized. Liver transplantation after paracetamol overdose includes an additional shock. Third, the spiritual needs of the donor's family must be considered. Donors are likely to be victims of sudden death. Relatives must adapt to the trauma of intensive care, the difficulty of accepting brain-stem death (the patient's chest continues to rise and fall) and also the concept of organ donation. There can be family conflict, horror at the thought of further disfigurement and denial of death. Alternatively there can be relief that something can be redeemed (one death can contribute to new life for several). Finally, there are the spiritual needs of hospital staff, where burnout is common. [Janet Bellamy]

TRANSSEXUALISM
A profound conviction that a person's sexual identity is incompatible with their external genitalia.

In psychiatric literature this condition is first mentioned by Esquirol in 1838. Krafft-Ebing (1886) described it in detail. In the DSM-IV, *Diagnostic and Statistical Manual of Mental Disorders*, edition 4 (1994), the diagnosis of transsexualism was replaced with Gender Identity Disorder. Gender identity designates a part of oneself, a set of convictions concerned with masculinity and femininity.

This pervasive and persistent sense of biological disharmony sometimes goes with the feeling of being disfigured or impaired. Such persons feel alienated from their bodies, have an overwhelming desire to live as a member of the opposite sex and seek to alter their bodily appearance and genitals to conform to those of the opposite sex. There is neither a sexual motivation for cross-dressing nor a sexual arousal. In some, transsexualism begins after many years' fetishistic transvestism. Transsexuals are greatly distressed by their predicament. Depression and suicidal attempts are common.

Transsexuals have normal sex chromosomes and there is no convincing evidence of any genetic cause, endocrine abnormality or organic brain disorder. Transsexualism is a psychological disorder but patients usually seek treatment directed to the body, not the mind.

Rejection at birth, adoption, extreme cruelty, physical and emotional neglect, denigration of masculinity/femininity shape the child's belief that he/she is neither entitled to esteem or consideration, nor is he/she acceptable, loveable as a boy/girl. This belief may lead to a narcissistically damaged self-image and may eventually lead to denunciation and rejection of his/her gender identity and anatomical reality. He/she may embark on obliterating all traces of his/her true anatomical and gender identity. He/she feels compelled to get rid of aggression which contaminates and interferes with his/her sense of being perfect. He/she may seek to alter his/her gender identity, unconsciously hoping that he/she will be recognized by his/her parents as a loveable, worthy person.

Paradoxically, transsexuals feel fear, suspicion, even conscious hatred of females. The mother is deeply feared and resented. Transsexuals' mothers seem incapable of investing in their child's masculinity/femininity with value. They neither enjoy and admire their child's body, nor try to foster the child's masculine/feminine aspirations and traits. But they explicitly or implicitly denigrate masculinity/femininity. Transsexuals' fathers appear to be equally uninterested in the child's gender identity. They do not intervene and rescue the child from the mother's engulfment and sometimes naked cruelty.

Regardless of the extreme financial, emotional, physical sacrifice and cost, a male-to-female transsexual seeks to be a woman to obtain the woman's hidden power – the right to give life and death. Sameness is not sought for merging, as some psychoanalysts have suggested, but is sought for survival and to be as powerful and invulnerable as the mother. By becoming a woman he unconsciously hopes that he will survive without needing the mother and he will safeguard himself against the sadistic and murderous attacks which he imputes to the mother. Not only women will spare him but he will also be cared for and cherished by men. A female-to-male transsexual tries to achieve the same end by becoming totally different from the mother.

Almost no information is available on the numbers of adults or adolescents who experience gender identity disorder. The main treatment seems to be psychological, which may help the individual understand the origins of his or her crisis of identity. For those who come to surgery, therapy is essential and involves meetings with doctors, psychologists and social workers. It also requires up to a year of cross-gender living and hormone treatments. The pastor who meets a transsexual person will almost without exception refer the person to someone with expertise in the field. [Elif Gurisik]

TRANSVESTISM
Heterosexual cross-dressing in which the clothing and adornment of the opposite sex are used fetishistically for sexual arousal.

Transvestism is also known as fetishistic transvestism. It is regarded as a perversion in the sense that an inanimate substitute, instead of a full relationship, is required for maximum sexual gratification (Stoller, 1978). Transvestism, a disorder of the sense of self, is manifested by distortions of both gender identity and sexuality. It has both regressive and adaptive aspects. There is no chromosomal or hormonal abnormality. The condition is neither familial nor inherited. Unresolved separation anxiety, mother's unconscious wish and her need to feminize her little boy, and father's complicity in his wife's seduction and his non-intervention coupled with associated learning may bring about this condition.

Cross-dressing usually begins in late childhood or early adolescence. It may start off simply to promote a sense of well-being or it may be sexualized from the onset. Cross-dressing may be partial or complete. The favoured garments are eroticized and used fetishistically for sexual arousal (see fetishism). It may be carried out in secrecy or in public. Sometimes female clothes are worn underneath male garments.

Transvestites paradoxically enjoy dressing as a woman but they value their maleness. In childhood they may fantasize about being girls, but assert their maleness and masculinity in overt behaviour. Adult transvestites have no doubt that they are men and have a correct conviction about their gender. They may have occasional homosexual encounters but they prefer heterosexual activity. Most transvestites are married. If they are discovered most wives express distress and disgust but a few collude, even assisting their husbands to perfect their appearance as women. The divorce rate is high among transvestites.

Transvestites use women's clothes and appearance of femininity to preserve their masculinity and potency. By cross-dressing they attempt to overcome the real or perceived childhood trauma – attempted feminization and emasculation by powerful women. Transvestism wards off the regressive pull towards passivity and bolsters a faltering sense of masculinity. It satisfies the transvestite's exhibitionistic wishes and the fantasies of revenge against powerful and hated women. The concept of splitting in the ego in the service of defence was formulated by Freud to account for the existence of two contradictory attitudes; one consonant with reality, the other with the wish to deny reality. Cross-dressing dramatizes comple-

mentary as well as contradictory roles of active–passive, mother–child, male–female. It also simultaneously affirms and negates the differences and the separateness. 'Mirror ritual' enhances and sustains the transvestite's dual identification. Gazing into the mirror allows for fusion of oneself as both a man and a woman. After gratifying a driven need for a temporary fusion with the mother, the transvestite re-asserts his masculine identity by masturbating. The cross-dressing affords the transvestite an opportunity to live in a make-believe world in which he temporarily achieves a sense of bodily and psychic completeness, self-sufficiency and self-realization. He feels compelled to repeat this fantasy whenever he re-experiences the threat of abandonment, humiliation or incompleteness. By risk-taking and surmounting it the transvestite redresses the balance. [Elif Gurisik]

TRINITY

God as understood in the Christian tradition – as three agents or 'persons' sharing a single kind of life ('substance').

Within a couple of decades after the crucifixion of Jesus, Christian communities were speaking of him as the embodiment of divine wisdom and self-communication (*sophia* and *logos*). But they were not content to see him as simply mediating transcendent power: his life had been characterized by prayer and love directed towards God as 'Abba', and this response itself comes to be seen as part of the divine life. In the fourth century CE, it is established that to ascribe honour and worship to Christ as Son or *logos* entails the belief that the divine life is fully shared between source and response, Father and Son; and following on from this, the Holy Spirit as an agent, not reducible to the identity of either Father or Son, is recognized as a third equal sharer in divine life or nature. Early Christian thought stressed that this was a unity of *action*: each subsistent agent (*hypostasis* in Greek) fully exercised divine agency, but in a mode distinguished by its relation to the other two.

In the early fifth century, Augustine of Hippo elaborated his influential image of human mind as a model of unity in diversity that reflected the trinitarian life. The acts of remembering, understanding and willing were distinct, yet unimaginable without each other: mental activity had its unity only in the interaction of these three kinds of working. Augustine certainly did not intend to minimize the distinctness of the three trinitarian agents or to suggest that God was 'really' an individual subject, though he has often been misinterpreted along these lines. Positively, his trinitarian image warned against the risks of excessive pluralism, treating the three as if they were three distinct or independent subjects; and it introduced a new subtlety into the understanding of the human mind itself, finding otherness and strangeness within the created subject.

But the more pluralist language proved more generally popular in the later modern period – partly thanks to Hegel, who regarded the doctrine as the cornerstone of all understanding of mental or spiritual reality, with its implicit movement from affirmation to counter-affirmation to reconciliation. Some twentieth-century writers developed this in a rather problematic direction, as if the three divine agents were contingent *personalities* with distinct interests and points of view (this criticism has been levelled, for example, against Jürgen Moltmann). Others, notably the Greek theologian, John Zizioulas (1985), have seen the doctrine as establishing something about the very nature of *being* as intrinsically plural and interactive: there is no abstract unity prior to the interdependence and interweaving of free action, no unity not bound up with communion and love.

Pastoral theology has made increasing use of the doctrine. Some (like Harry Williams) have seen the balance of unity and plurality as addressing the two most fundamental human fears – of isolation and of absorption. Others (like Paul Ricoeur writing about Freud) have noted how it presents an image of parenting and origination that is liberating and lifegiving: instead of the castrating Father of Oedipal myth, we have a parent whose life actually *consists* in giving life. Others again have written of how the doctrine affirms unconditional difference without rivalry, or the possibility of dependence without slavery (Thompson, 1994). Despite the risks of assimilating divine plurality too closely to human, the insights about identity, dependence and otherness offered by the doctrine rightly secure its place as a crucial resource for pastoral understanding and pastoral therapy. [*Rowan Williams*]

TRUE SELF
A term that refers to an individual's unique inner world of thoughts, experiences and needs.

Donald Winnicott suggested that, given the right psychological environment, a child would be able to develop a true self, which is contrasted to a 'false self'. This true self represents the child's capacity to be aware of its ongoing needs and experiences and to have a sense of unique personal being. While this true self becomes the basis for healthy interaction with others, Winnicott suggested that within each person there is a core of experience which is never communicated for fear that it would be exploited or overwhelmed by others.

TRUST
An emotional attachment to a person, institution or God that allows someone to have influence in one's life.

To trust someone is to believe that her or his influence will be beneficial for the self. Being receptive to such influences helps to determine one's identity and the resources that will be available for personal and spiritual growth.

Many Scriptures call on believers to trust in God, because God is benevolent, loving and just. Other Scriptures question God's trustworthiness because of suffering or injustice (Ps. 13.1). Some of the witnesses to God's trustworthiness come from those who have learned to trust in God in the midst of suffering (Rom. 8.31–39). When relationships with persons and institutions betray one's trust, many believers witness that they have found comfort by trusting in God.

Erik Erikson (1980), building on Freud's theories of attachment, believed that trust is the foundation for all other emotions. Trust develops most fully during the first years of life in relation to one's care-givers. Because a child depends on benevolent adults for physical, emotional and spiritual comfort, she or he internalizes their influence on many levels.

Betrayal of trust during early life, according to Erikson, creates a sense of mistrust that undermines human development in later stages. The struggle between trust and mistrust can contribute to problems with identity and intimacy during adolescence, as individuals decide for themselves whether the world and God are trustworthy. In adult life, most persons tend to trust members of one's family, one's intimate social group, and leaders who have been granted authority by the larger community. For example, a parishioner may trust a pastor because of ordination, education, pastoral skills, personal charisma, or a combination of these factors. Such trust enables persons to accept what the pastor says and does as authoritative. Carl Rogers (1967) believed that trust is facilitated in adult relationships by unconditional positive regard, authenticity and empathy. Conversely, betrayal of trust occurs through abusive behaviours, lack of integrity, and disregard of the inner life of the other. Religious leaders need training in how to facilitate trust in others for the sake of the gospel. [*James N. Poling*]

U

UNCONSCIOUS
The contents of the mind that are not present to the field of consciousness at a given moment.

The theory of the unconscious mind or unconscious life is the single most lasting aspect of Freud's work. He was not the first to discover the unconscious, but he began the process of systematically exploring it. There is much dispute over how the concept is to be refined. But 'the unconscious' is the collection of those hidden dynamic elements that make up the personality. The individual may be aware of some of these; others are hidden from him or her – they are the unconscious aspects. Dreams have been described as the 'royal road to the unconscious'. Through psychoanalysis and similar therapy, people may have access to the unconscious aspects of the self that may have been ignored or denied. The pastor will not be formally working in this area, but he or she can be alert to the fact of unconscious process, which at times may explain strange feelings and a sense of being lost (Carr, 1997). A major addition to the theory of the unconscious has been the idea that groups also have an unconscious life which similarly may be explored (Obholzer and Roberts, 1994). The term is in popular use often confused with 'subconscious', but technically there is a distinction between them.

UNCONSCIOUS PATIENTS
People who lack sensory awareness of themselves or the environment.

Unconsciousness may be temporary, intermittent, permanent or it may precede death. It may result from severe illness, trauma or cerebral damage or it may be deliberately induced for purposes of anaesthesia. Levels of unconsciousness vary and are measured by a scale recording eye, verbal and motor responses. Unconscious patients may require intensive-care management of cardiac and respiratory functions or may be nursed on an ordinary ward.

Controversial issues include: (1) The possible conflict between respect for patient autonomy and the health-care professional's duty to provide life-sustaining care. Knowledge of patient wishes is dependent on next of kin whose knowledge may be inaccurate or distorted by their own wishes. (2) Treatment of patients in a persistent vegetative state (PVS). For 12 months following injury the patient has total and irreversible loss of cerebral functioning but maintains involuntary breathing and swallowing reflexes. Should nutrition and hydration be withdrawn on the grounds of 'futility' of care or is there potential benefit in every life? If the patient's wishes are unknown, should the wishes of relatives determine outcome? Religious beliefs encompass a diversity of views. (3) Organ donation or transplantation.

Important issues for pastoral care include: (1) Awareness of complex ethical issues. (2) Awareness of the spiritual needs of the patient. Hearing is the first of the senses to return with consciousness and the last to disappear. It is essential to assume that all conversation can be heard and to assess the patient's likely response to speech or religious rituals were he or she conscious. If the religious needs of relatives differ from those of the patient, they should be met away from the bedside. If the patient recovers consciousness, help may be needed in adapting to 'lost' time and the implications of the event. (3) The spiritual needs of family and friends. They may experience fear, hopelessness, powerlessness, anger, guilt, denial and other signs of shock and anticipatory grief. Existing faith may be shaken or existential questions newly explored. (4) Awareness of complex dynamics. There can be a bedside meeting of estranged family members. Conflict needs to be kept away from the bedside and expressed elsewhere. Advocacy for the intimidated or vulnerable is helpful. (5) Awareness of possible ambivalence about restoration of consciousness. Death may be seen as the preferred option. It is essential to avoid assumptions or judgemental responses. (6) The facilitation of the growth of mature hope. It is important to help people let go of unrealistic hope based on denial. (7) The restoration of normality to the bedside. Within guidelines established by medical staff it can be helpful to talk to and touch the patient. Patients in coma have regained consciousness through the playing of significant music. (8) The death bed. Sensitivity to stress, group dynamics and preference for privacy is vital. Denial of death can mean the patient is cajoled to 'fight on'. If appropriate, prayers can restore dignity, initiate grieving and give a partially conscious patient permission to let go. (9) The spiritual needs of staff. [*Janet Bellamy*]

UNCTION
The last of the seven sacraments of the Latin Church.
Extreme unction was normally administered only when a sick person was nearing death and could not be repeated during that illness. From the eighth century there is abundant evidence in official documents for the anointing of the sick as part of the cycle of sacraments (penance, viaticum or last communion, extreme unction) with which life was ended, but it is unclear how frequently it was administered. It seems to have come into general use as part of the last rites in the mid-twelfth century. From the time of the Black Death in the early fourteenth century use of the rite declined, and in later centuries it was often deferred until too late because of an unwillingness to accept the possibility of death. It is still part of Catholic sacramental practice, and after Vatican II some notion of healing returned to the rite.

Defining the sacrament in 1551, the Council of Trent used proof texts from Mark 6.7–13 and Jas. 5.13–16. The effects of the sacrament were also defined: the anointing 'takes away the sins if there be any still to be expiated, and also the remains of sin; it comforts and strengthens the soul of the sick person by awakening in him great confidence in the divine mercy; supported by this the sick person bears more lightly the inconveniences and trials of his illness and resists more easily the temptations of the devil'. It was also held to restore bodily health when

expedient for the salvation of the soul. There was otherwise little expectation of healing.

The material element of the sacrament is olive oil blessed for the purpose, preferably by a bishop but in necessity by a priest. The minister is normally a priest whose thumb is dipped in the oil to perform the administration. The medieval rite involved the anointing of the eyes, ears, nose, mouth, hands and feet. The accompanying prayer asked for forgiveness of the sins committed by the use of each sense. In necessity, it was sufficient to anoint any one of the senses. The reformed Roman rite requires anointing of the head and hands only (Dudley and Rowell, 1993).

Abolished by the Reformers, it has now been restored in parts of the Anglican and Lutheran Churches in response to renewed interest in healing. Linked to the laying on of hands with prayer for healing, unction is more often called (outside Catholic circles) the anointing of the sick. There has been a tendency to employ it more sparingly than the laying on of hands and to reserve it to more serious illness. As it has a clear scriptural mandate, pastoral sense suggests that it should be available to all who need it, that it should be withheld from no one, and that it is to be preferred to the laying on of hands whenever sickness threatens the quality of life or life itself. Rites are provided in many prayer books (Dudley, 1997). [*Martin Dudley*]

UNEMPLOYMENT
The state of being 'without remunerative employment' or more simply 'out of work'.
The simplicity of the dictionary definition belies a more contested political debate about how to measure the numbers of people out of work. The 'narrow' definition of unemployment, which has conventionally been used when collecting statistics for unemployment, only includes those who are unemployed and actually seeking work. A 'broader' definition (as used, for example, in the UK Labour Force Survey) would also include those who have given up looking for work because they do not expect to find it, those who would like to work but are not available to start straight away and others who are currently outside the labour market (e.g. single parents) who would consider taking work in appropriate circumstances. 'Narrow' definitions of unemployment tend to underestimate levels of unemployment among women.

Mass unemployment is a relatively modern phenomenon of waged industrial societies. It was first linked with the depression of the early 1930s. It re-emerged in the 1970s, and rose in successive cycles until the early 1990s, reaching on official statistics to more than 20 million in the European Union countries, some 35 million in OECD countries and untold numbers in the less developed world where adequate statistics are not available.

The pastoral implications of unemployment are uneven. Up to half of unemployment, measured in person-days, is commonly experienced by less than 5% of the population. Levels of unemployment can vary enormously, not just between regions but also within individual conurbations. Ethnic minority unemployment is on average double that for the white population – but much higher still among specific ethnic communities.

The consequences of unemployment for individuals, families and wider social relationships are severe. They can include a personal sense of rejection, loss of self-esteem, a dreary daily existence, and poverty. There is also evidence of higher divorce and mortality rates for unemployed people. In many societies a strong stigma is attached to unemployment. Unemployed people regularly talk of being invisible, or being labelled as lazy and socially inferior.

In the words of one unemployed man from South Wales: 'If work brings us some measure of economic, social, psychological and spiritual security, then to find oneself unemployed means being faced with a whole range of problems which combined affect us economically, socially, psychologically and spiritually at one and the same time' (Council of Churches for Britain and Ireland, 1997).

Explanations for the growth of mass unemployment include technological change, economic globalization and liberalization, and the over-regulation of labour markets. During the 1980s and 1990s there was widespread scepticism about the possibility of ending mass unemployment. However, since the late 1990s there has been a renewed optimism in both America and Europe about the possibility of a return to 'full employment'.

Biblical studies, the early church fathers and medieval theology does not have a great deal to say about unemployment per se. However, within the context of a developing theology of work as a calling or vocation,

from Paul through to Augustine, there are regular injunctions against idleness. This strand of theology reached its apotheosis in the writings of Martin Luther and John Wesley. The duty of the individual to find work became a cornerstone of the Protestant work ethic. This characterized Protestant churches' thinking from the eighteenth century onwards. Although less common within church writings today, such ideas have been influential in legitimizing wider social attitudes to the unemployed, as morally and socially inferior people.

By contrast, Catholic social teaching since the publication of the papal encyclical *Rerum novarum* in 1891 has emphasized the right to work (Committee for the World of Work, 1995). Unemployment is understood as a denial of the dignity of the human person, made in God's image, and is in all cases an evil. A succession of encyclicals and Catholic bishops' conference statements have sought to highlight the structural dimensions of unemployment. While there is an individual duty as well as a right to work, the responsibility for tackling unemployment is laid squarely on the shoulders of governments and international bodies responsible for labour market policies.

In pastoral terms, Catholic social teaching requires the adoption of attitudes of patience and tolerance to unemployed people. No one should be written off as unemployable. Unemployed people are entitled both to social assistance and an income to keep them and their dependants out of poverty, and to special assistance in finding work.

In recent years, ecumenical thinking has tended to focus on unemployment as a social evil, and a waste of God-given talent. The Churches Enquiry into Unemployment and the Future of Work (Council of Churches for Britain and Ireland, 1997), argued strongly both on moral and economic grounds that it was both possible and desirable to create 'enough good work for all'.

Pastoral responses by the churches have been many and varied. One UK-based church agency identified 101 different project-based responses. A typology of church responses would include: (1) Congregational prayer and reflection – Unemployment Sunday has been an annual event in the churches' calendar in the UK since the mid-1980s. (2) Church-sponsored employment projects to provide support, training and advice to unemployed people in a whole host of different forms and settings. (3) Industrial mission (or mission in the world of work), although traditionally based on a workplace chaplaincy model, has sought to respond to the emergence of mass unemployment by developing alliances and providing support to unemployed workers' groups. (4) Statements and reports on social and economic policy, seeking to bring a Christian contribution to regional and national debates about how best to cope with or tackle mass unemployment. (5) Solidarity-based responses, seeking to give a public platform to or create alternative networks of unemployed activists. [Niall Cooper]

URBAN THEOLOGY
Making theological connections between the worshipping community and the analysis and proposals for change in inner-city areas of deprivation and inequality.

Urban theology is part of a vital area in the Church's ecumenical life of the last three decades. It emerged out of the turbulence of the 1960s when churches looked seriously at the need to relate the beliefs and hopes of modernity with theology and spirituality. In Britain, urban theology, as a form of liberation theology, was given a particular impetus with the publication of the Report of the Archbishops' Commission on Urban Areas (1985), entitled *Faith in the City*. Academic theologians and inner-city church ministers attempt to collaborate in a way of doing theology of great diversity, style and depth. Through reflection on narratives from inner-city neighbourhoods and faith communities, in terms of theology, spirituality and social analysis they seek to discern the presence and activity of God in situations of hope and despair. One recurring issue is the place of worship as a key activity for a community of praise. Rather than an irrelevance, urban theology practitioners regard it as a springboard for inspiration and transformation, a habitus for nurturing human dignity and growth in maturity, and a place of learning to recognize how the crucified and resurrected Christ confronts the idols of a consumerist society. Other issues include racism, unemployment, leisure, wages, the police, the National Health Service and parenting.

A further example is the concern for healthy relationships between different racial and religious groupings. There is ambiguity about the enterprise culture, on the one hand affirming the worth of each individual as a creature of God and on the other recognizing how individualism can lead to isolation. The increase in crime and violence, threatening the order of the daily life of the neighbourhood, is contrasted with the hope of building infrastructures of mutual delight, trust and interdependence that echo the transformative life of the trinitarian God.

Urban theology also seeks to discern the positive aspects to urban life. Among these are the significance of sexuality as a sacrament of the presence of God, divinely intimate, inspiring fear, fascination and fun. Another is the significance of a sense of place – the use of land and space for building personal worth and human community – as a spiritual battle with impersonal, distant and even global forces. Children are recognized as a blessing. Communities that welcome and celebrate the presence and gifts of children act as a prophetic sign to the disappearance and impoverishment of childhood in a society obsessed by money, overwork and privacy.

There is mounting evidence of the strength of purpose of many churches in urban areas being renewed through practising urban theology. Often in partnership locally or with a church in a more prosperous area, Urban Priority Area Christian communities survive. They make an audit of local needs, redesign their buildings for community use, find resources and co-operate with other bodies (voluntary and statutory) in projects with unemployed people, parents and children. Within the community they offer financial or legal advice, pastoral care, and undertake evangelism as a witness to God the creator who takes responsibility for the whole of creation and in the cross and resurrection of Christ bears the distortions and evil of the world. [Robin Greenwood]

V

VALUES
1. Commitments or principles.
2. Ideas, norms, convictions or beliefs which one holds so dear that they define one as a person.
3. An object's worth, merit, utility or price.

Etymologists trace the historical roots of 'value' back to the Latin word *valere*, to be strong, hence well. In contemporary English, the term has evolved to mean, principally, the true market price or worth of something. This meaning has, in turn, been extended, referring to anything that one holds dear, including ethical principles or convictions.

Stanley Hauerwas (1981) objects to this usage of values in ethics, arguing that it wrongly reinforces a view of the moral life as just another form of consumer choice in which each individual picks and chooses from a marketplace of ideas and principles. For him the moral life is not created through individual choice, but 'by the shaping of our thorough disciplined discovery of the good'. While the point concerning the nature of the moral life is well taken, it does not logically follow that values are inextricably linked to market prices. Yet a minority, even some economists, have argued that market prices may not always completely capture values, especially for the environment (Costanza, 1997).

Rather than being a series of options from which one picks and chooses, values are better conceived as norms and convictions that help inform one's vision of a moral life. This vision itself is developed, not in isolation from others, but rather through moral discourse with others. Frequently, this discourse occurs in what Craig Dykstra terms 'communities of conviction'. That is, a community of 'peoples who are inter-subjectively related to one another across time and space by a body of convictions, language patterns, and practices that they hold in common' (Dykstra, 1999). If we think of Christianity as forming a community of conviction, then values would be those norms and beliefs embraced through an ongoing process of discourse and exploration that helps define a person as a Christian. 'Love of neighbour' would be one of the most obvious Christian values, although how and to whom this love is expressed would be subject to continual discourse and exploration within the Christian community. Viewed from this perspective, a significant pastoral role involves engaging both individuals and the community in an ongoing exploration of Christian values.

One of the most meaningful dimensions of pastoral care is being with those parishioners who must make difficult decisions – especially decisions involving medical care for oneself or loved ones. Almost all medical ethicists agree that the decision-maker's autonomy must be fully respected under these circumstances. Yet at the same time an important form of pastoral care could include exploring with the decision-maker how Christian values might frame and inform what course of action is ultimately chosen (Wheeler, 1996). *[Richard Randolph]*

VICES
The medieval categorization of defects of character and their effect.
The list of vices matched that of the virtues in medieval thinking. Vices are dispositions rather than acts: anger, lust, greed, sloth, envy, covetousness and pride. They therefore profoundly affect the person as well as lifestyle. Most of these words carry similar meanings in modern times. 'Sloth' (sometimes called 'accidie') might today mean being bored or even masochistic. Pride is the worst vice, being self-conceit. Although it is unlikely that this medieval list will again become prominent in Christian thought, it has two valuable functions: first, it is a useful checklist when engaged in hearing confessions and talking with penitents; second, it stands today for what might be thought of as obsessional behaviour and its serious effects on others and the self.

VIRGINITY
The physiological status of a woman or man who has not known penetrative sexual intercourse; its wider connotation is a state of purity or moral innocence.
Virginity is the condition of a woman whose hymen has not been ruptured by sexual intercourse, and of a man who has not known penetrative intercourse. It is also a way of discipleship for Christians which forgoes sexual experience. St Augustine says it is possible to lose physical virginity without sacrificing the moral sort.

Many societies have prized virginity in women: for example, in Deut. 22.13–21 virginity is specifically required of a bride. An evolutionary approach to human morality would suggest that this is male insurance of the transmission of his genes. Thus for genetic reasons virginity has been desired and exalted. For similar reasons women remaining virgins felt reproach. Jephthah's daughter (Judg. 11.34–40) bewailed the fact she 'had never slept with a man'.

For Christians, virginity is both a state of mind and of life, a way of following Christ, which has been highly valued by the Church. Jesus had no sexual experience, and thus the fullness of what it means to be human was revealed in a virgin man. To imitate and follow Jesus in this way is held to be both a charism, and a calling to give oneself totally and freely to his service. It is to be distinguished from virginity which is the result of a lack of sexual experience.

Jesus himself suggested that there would be those who undertook this state 'for the sake of the kingdom of heaven' (Matt. 19.12). St Paul (1 Cor. 7, and elsewhere) seems to commend the unmarried state. Church history is full of 'voluntary' virgins, who often – in their desire to maintain this condition – were martyred. In a society which envisaged female celibacy with difficulty, the early Church protected these women by grouping them together under the aegis of older women who were themselves unmarried or widows, and by giving them the veil (the sign of a married woman) to wear. Thus originated female religious life, though then, as now, consecrated virgins could and did live in the 'world'.

Christian valuing of virginity has been enhanced by devotion to Mary, mother of Jesus, whom Catholic tradition honours as 'ever-virgin', (a doctrine ratified by the Lateran Council of 649), and as symbolizing the Church, the virgin bride united with Christ, the divine bridegroom. For all Christians she is the model of service and self-donation.

These days both virginity 'for the Kingdom' and marriage/maternity are seen as callings of equal dignity and worth. Since the churches teach that genital activity should be confined to marriage, virginity before marriage is commended.

The challenge to the Church is to recognize the needs of people who, for whatever reason, are single. Everyone needs support, tenderness and non-sexual intimacy in which to live out their sexuality and to realize their unique gifts. [Mary Kirk]

VIRTUES
A quality of living in particular moral excellence.
Medieval Christian thought brought together classical ideals and biblical principles in a scheme of virtues. Four were taken over from the classical world and called 'cardinal' (from the Latin word for 'hinge') or natural.

They were pivotal in becoming a civilized person: prudence (today meaning 'common sense'); temperance (meaning 'moderation in all things'); justice (meaning 'fairness'); and fortitude (meaning 'courage and endurance'). To these four natural virtues were added the three theological virtues of faith, hope and love (Geach, 1977). These were the gifts of God to be lived as marks of grace. Today there is less enthusiasm for such a catalogue. But the virtues are part of the tradition that informs the role of pastors. Therefore even in these 'post-virtue' days, and when there is some thought that the traditional virtues may still offer useful guidance (McIntyre, 1982), pastors need to study the classic writings on virtues and to understand how to relate these to the issues of everyday living for their congregations.

VIRTUES, THEOLOGICAL
See: THEOLOGICAL VIRTUES

VISIONS
Visual images held to be meaningful but without physical presence or sensory stimulus.
Visions are commonplace in much of the Judaeo-Christian tradition and attested in Scripture. They have often been assigned great significance, with shrines built for pilgrimages – Lourdes being an obvious example. A vision is believed to be supernatural and revelatory. Some people have been prone to visions, which those lacking that dimension have admired. Today visions may be reckoned to be induced by emotional or physical deprivation or by concentration on an object, a story or a place. They can also be a side-effect of drugs, whether medicinal or not. The Church has been ambivalent about visions, recognizing their importance for some but also alert to the danger of hysteria. In the Catholic tradition a distinction is carefully drawn between quasi-physical images, pictures in the mind and intellectual visions, the momentary grasp of some truth. The view of the later prophets of Israel has also prevailed, namely that there must be some ethical context and the vision must lead to better everyday living. These remain useful tests for the pastor when faced with someone claiming a vision, for visions may be evidence of severe psychological disturbance. While pastors cannot confidently diagnose a psychotic state, they

should be aware that a person may be suffering from this. It will be important not to join this disturbed world, least of all in the guise of religion, and to be ready to seek professional help.

VISITING
Calling on an individual, a family or a group of people in their home or temporary residence for any church-based reason.
The eighteenth-century poet George Herbert advised his parson, 'upon the afternoons in the weekdays . . . sometimes to visit in person, now one quarter of his parish now another'. Clergy visit in people's own homes to get to know them. The model is that of the Good Shepherd: 'I know my own and my own know me' (John 10.14). The New Testament word *epeskepsasthe* connects God who visits and takes care to God's creatures who care for each other by visiting: 'Blessed be the Lord God of Israel for he has visited (*epeskepsato*) and redeemed his people' (Luke 1.68). This compares with 'I was naked and you gave me clothing, I was sick and you took care of (*epeskepsasthe*) me, I was in prison and you visited me' (Matt. 25.36).

Over time this raised a strong expectation that clergy should visit: 'a house-going parson makes a church-going people' is the associated adage. A 1947 manual stated: 'Solid visiting usually achieves ten to fifteen houses in an afternoon, and two hundred a month is suggested as a minimum.' Visits are also made: to care for the sick, dying, bereaved and those in any kind of trouble; to make organizational arrangements; to do with baptisms, marriages and funerals; to evangelize. While few clergy would doubt that visiting is a significant ingredient of their job, a critical process of discernment is required. A study of the Church in rural England (Davies, 1991) showed that clergy spent 12% of their total time in visiting. Visiting fell into three categories. In addition to visiting the congregation, 97% undertook crisis visiting; 42% did communal visiting, for example, of newcomers. The study confirmed that the overwhelming majority of parishioners ascribe importance to clergy visiting.

This inheritance raises problems. Pattison (1988) questions an adequate rationale for parish visiting. He refers to the connection between visiting and discipline within a context of clergy admonition. Clergy still carry a symbolic authority. The way people leap to justify their belief suggests visiting can be experienced as oppressive and a judgement. Pattison sees visiting as, at best, unclear in aim and, at worst, as reinforcing a now outmoded model of authoritative parental shepherding rather than building shared responsibility and mutuality. Appropriate visiting needs to be based on mutual consent. It must follow the agenda of those visited, not that of the clergy, or their freedom is violated.

There are some pitfalls for the clergy. They may unconsciously develop a pattern of visiting to meet their own needs rather than those of the parish's most needy. If visits become disproportionately limited, say, to the elderly, the young or friends, it suggests a problem. Visiting can be squeezed out through apparent lack of time. A sense of not having done enough visiting is a chronic cause of guilt among clergy, suggesting a failure in clarity about their role rather than a lack of commitment. It pays to have a realistic and theologically worked out policy on pastoral care and visiting (Carr, 1989).

Since the 1960s there has been a recovery of the corporate nature of pastoral care. Visiting is now seen as the responsibility of the whole church rather than just the clergy. Local visiting teams have developed whose remit may cover the elderly and housebound, the bereaved, those requesting baptism and marriage, the sick and those in hospital and the general counselling of those in emotional need.

Such teams presuppose selection and training whose aim is to increase confidence and insight without losing skills already possessed. In training: (1) Expectations need to be examined and fantasies allowed to surface. (2) Boundaries are a major issue. They include confidentiality, punctuality and length of visit, awareness of one's own emotional limits and sensitivity to others' emotional boundaries. Visitors need to develop a sense of what to take up and what to leave unsaid. (3) The visit's purpose and effectiveness depends on a clear understanding of the visitor's role. (4) Self-awareness. Visitors need to recognize their style as an interviewer by developing a sense of their personality type and temperament. (5) The management of feelings and defences. This is a matter of learning to perceive the feelings beyond the words and to manage one's anxieties when faced with another's pain. Confronted with strong feelings a visitor may easily feel anxious or rush to judgement. But what does it feel like to be emotionally needy and distressed? And what about the visitor's own emotional needs and limits? Training helps get in touch with the often painful feelings that may surface during a visit. This helps to get beyond the natural temptation to avoid the pain by some kind of attempt at 'rescue', i.e. trying at all costs to make it feel better than it really feels. A felt understanding of the ego-defence mechanisms, depression, anger or grief helps unlock a visitor's own confusion and anxiety when faced with them. (6) Endings. Because of their inherent pain, endings tend to be avoided. This can vitiate the value of a visit. Someone being visited needs to be able to rely on a visit ending as expected. They may wish to disclose something precisely because the visit is about to end. Even an agreed series of visits must be managed with their ending in sight rather than denied.

Visiting is a fundamental building-block of Christian community, witness and work. It presupposes a willingness to accept the feelings, fantasies and expectations of others. It needs all the visitors' skills and experience in interpreting and responding imaginatively to them. Their basic trust must be in God's grace rather than their interpersonal abilities. They will never know the true outcome of their visiting. [Nicholas Bradbury]

VOCATION
A personal sense of being called to ministry and mission and the ratification of that calling by the Church.

The term 'vocation' derives from the Latin meaning 'to call'. The Church exists to enable Christians to relate to God and with one another so as to respond to Jesus' call to 'follow me' and 'to go and make disciples'. At present there is a reaction against the popular understanding that vocation is primarily concerned with ordained or publicly authorized ministry or a calling to the monastic life. A renewed emphasis on the calling of every Christian rooted in baptism is changing the centre of gravity of life in most churches. Discussion of vocation now frequently refers to the ministry of laity in the local church as well as to how Christians live at work, in the neighbourhood, and how they address current issues. The agenda to break down barriers between the roles of professional clergy and laity leads to a blurring of the notions of ministry, discipleship and vocation.

There is widespread agreement that, after a long period in the Church's history of overemphasizing a personal sense of being called, attention needs to be paid to the way in which the Christian community identifies specific needs and invites individuals to recognize a call within themselves to match them. Both the inner sense of vocation and the outward call have to be recognized in those who have a true vocation to ordained or public ministry.

A key issue for local communities of Christians today is a sense of being invigorated and given resources for the shared vocation of a people on a journey. A theology of the joy, blessings and gifts of God made known in the life, death and resurrection of Jesus Christ, through the Holy Spirit, invites the response of Christian communities as those who choose to work with God. Churches are called in joyful responsibility constantly to reproduce themselves in ways that are new and rooted in the revelation of God. The vocation of the Church to be a transforming agent, co-operating with the life and work of God in the world, is a call to be a people together in worship, ministries and order. Worship, education and prayerful reflection are its basic resources. United in holiness, catholicity and apostolicity, the main task of any church will be to interweave its own life and activity with that of God in the networks of the parts of the world that are open to its present influence.

For a local church to discern its task and to identify the interdependent roles of its members, a number of fundamental issues must be attended to over and over again.

1. *The biblical revelation.* In Abraham, God's saving purpose is focused in a nation. This work is then personified in Jesus' life, death and resurrection and is embodied in the Church, which takes on Christ's character. There is the constant danger that churches will simply continue to excavate the past in a mistaken attempt to recreate some idealized moment. Honesty demands the recognition of widely different reactions to the event of Jesus in various Christian community experiments, such as those in Antioch, Jerusalem and Corinth. Also, according to personality and spiritual preferences, churches add responses to God's work in the tradition of Benedict, Francis, Taizé or Iona.

2. *The life of the Christian community.* In the Eucharist and other forms of worship, prayer, study and gathering together, churches are open to the Holy Spirit. The Spirit creates community, inspires loving, teaches reconciliation, sustains hope, and promises guidance into new truths. Here are geographical and historical links with all other Christians – in the Anglican/Episcopalian Communication, in the diocese and in partner churches.

3. *Working with God for the wholeness of creation.* The present emphasis on eschatology – the fulfilment of God's final purposes for the whole of creation – points to the local church as a sacrament, a sign and a foretaste of God's passionate desire. Each church explores how it may be an embodiment of the Lord's Prayer – 'your kingdom come on earth as in heaven'.

4. *Engaged with society and the world.* The context in which a church is set will vary for each person, depending on the network of their everyday living. The Church is part of the context itself. But discerning vocation includes a dialogue between the local church and the pains, insights and joys of the whole of creation, of humanity and of the particular neighbourhood in which it is set. And how can churches take account of the wisdom of voluntary organizations, of educational theory, of management and organizational tools? For example, the five key principles of learning organization theory – personal mastery, seeing the whole, a shared vision, team learning and systemic approaches to planning – are relevant to churches wishing to be equipped and confident for the task of ministry and mission in the world.

This logic for working on the vocation of the local church, with most of its worshipping congregation committed to ministry in the wider world, raises questions about necessary resources, training and leadership of both laity and clergy. The ministry of vocations advisers is making a valuable contribution to this process and to addressing the 'pass' or 'fail' culture regarding selection for ordained ministry.

Jesus' ministry provides the model for considering any vocation to Christian ministry or discipleship: time in the desert, alone, living with not yet knowing and avoiding instant answers; praying alone and in secret; taking part in public worship; spending quality time with other believers in community; reflecting with others on recent events; engaging with the world and the needs of people; making connections between belief in God, faith in Christ and everyday life; being vulnerable to being prompted by the Spirit in encounters with others. [*Robin Greenwood*]

VOLUNTARY SECTOR

The voluntary commitment of people to mutual help and support, now usually compared with the state's welfare provision.

Most British social developments are fitted into a Whig interpretation of history, i.e. one which sees continuous and inevitable advance. How the voluntary sector is viewed is no exception. Indeed, the name by which it is now referred to is a give-away. The view that state welfare and state provision of services is an inevitable outcome of progress is as deeply ingrained in the country's thinking as it is misleading. The state replaced what was previously organized on a voluntary basis. And the voluntary movement was downgraded to being a mere 'sector'.

The voluntary movement was the forerunner of the welfare state, and it was because of the advances this movement was clearly making during the nineteenth century that the vote was conceded. Unlike today, the voluntary movement was run overwhelmingly by working-class people. Their friendly societies and mutual aid groups were not only miniature welfare states in action, but because of the democratic and inclusive way they were run, mini-democracies too. The English middle class conceded the vote because the working class had shown that they had earned their citizenship, and that as a group they were not to be feared.

The rise of the voluntary movement played another part in the development of democratic ideas in Britain. Unlike most continental countries people in Britain do not refer to the state. At best they speak of government as one body, albeit a powerful one, along with all those other organizations of civil society which collectively seem as the state. With the rise of more powerful governments – the state took 8% of GDP in 1914, but 40% by 1998 – a new stress was put on pluralistic ideas. Here the thinking of Maitland and his disciple, the Mirfield monk Neville Figgis, is important. Power was conceded to the centre, but individuals were to be protected from arbitrary power by the host of voluntary organizations to which they belonged and which spoke for them in negotiating how government power was exercised.

Within the rise of the post-1945 welfare state, the role of the voluntary sector was pushed to the periphery. More recently the debate has become more sensitive to the failure of government, and its most expensive function, welfare. The voluntary movement therefore has the possibility of returning to a more centre-stage position, not only as the innovatory force, an aspect of itself of great importance in a rapidly changing society, but as a major player in developing new membership organizations through which cash welfare is supplied. Similarly, given the growth in the number and proportion of elderly people, the voluntary sector will need to become a mass organizer of person care extended on the basis of friendship rather than on a cash nexus if this need is to be met. [Frank Field]

VOLUNTEERS
Children, women and men who offer to assist with defined tasks for no remuneration.
Highly trained or completely untrained, volunteers are distinguished from paid 'professionals' or 'statutory workers'. Almost all lay activity is voluntary, e.g. committees, organization of events, cleaning, training, catering, visiting, music etc. Volunteers' needs are met in their work and it is helpful when this is acknowledged. For organizational efficiency churches commonly employ professionals. Tensions can arise when jobs are done by paid workers and volunteers. The maintenance of work boundaries for paid staff is a pastoral issue as a culture of voluntarism easily leads to exploitation.

VOYEURISM
Obtaining sexual gratification through watching.
A voyeur is usually male. He obtains sexual pleasure from watching others engaged in sexual activity, although he may also find it by watching inanimate objects which act for him as sexual stimuli. Although usually harmless, the voyeur can become a nuisance and the law can be invoked. The pastor needs, therefore, to treat any confession of voyeurism with caution and beware of seeming to discount, or even inadvertently encourage, such behaviour.

W

WAR
The resort to organized military conflict as a means of settling disputes either between nation states or between national factions.
From the earliest days of the Church the Christian attitude to war has been ambivalent. The teaching of Christ in the Sermon on the Mount (Matt. 5—7) is clearly in favour of non-violence. The Great Commission of Jesus to 'Go therefore and make disciples of all nations' (Matt. 28.19) implies both a missionary imperative and an implicit acceptance by those converted to Christianity of the principle of absolute pacifism. This principle has been adopted in several parts of the Church, notably the Society of Friends, Anabaptists, etc. In a world where Christianity was universally accepted war would not exist.

At the same time an underlying theme of New Testament writing is of the war between opposing powers of good and evil, and though St Paul implies acceptance of the non-violent response (e.g. Rom. 12.14, 17, 19–21), he not infrequently uses military metaphors to make his points (e.g. Eph. 6.10–18).

St Paul also urged loyalty to the temporal powers and after the time of Constantine some interpreted this as allowing service in the Roman army. Most of the early Fathers, during times of persecution, however, espoused the non-violent position. By the time of Ambrose and Augustine (fourth and fifth centuries CE), acceptance of circumstances in which war could be justly prosecuted became more widespread. The Christian tradition of the 'just war' is derived, originally, from Cicero (106–43 BCE) and was developed by Augustine (fifth century CE) and Aquinas (thirteenth century CE) (Helgeland et al., 1985). It states five basic principles, all of which must be met in order for Christians to be able to take part as combatants. (1) The war must only be started and controlled by the legitimate authority of the state or the ruler. (2) There must be a just cause. (3) The war must be fought to promote good or avoid evil. Peace and justice must be restored afterwards. (4) The war must be the last resort; all other possible ways of solving the problem must have been tried out. (5) There must be 'proportionality' in the way the war is fought, e.g. innocent civilians should not be killed. Only enough force must be used to achieve the goals.

Kaufman (1985) argues that with the dawn of the nuclear age and the prospect of total annihilation of all earthly life, a new theological approach to war is needed. It has to be pointed out that with the end of the Cold War the nuclear threat, though arguably reduced, has not disappeared.

From a pastoral perspective, there is a noble tradition of military (non-combatant) chaplaincy to those who serve in the armed forces in the defence of their country. Chaplains seek at all times to represent Christian principles even though their ministry may be set in a less than ideal context. An interesting recent development has been the formation of military chaplaincies in the armed forces of the countries of the former Communist bloc. Ultimately the participation of a Christian in war comes down to a matter of individual, informed conscience. [Robin Turner]

WEDDING PREPARATION
The spiritual, emotional, familial, financial, legal groundwork that assists two persons in the process of becoming married within a particular culture and religious tradition.

In the Christian tradition, a wedding ceremony is a rite of passage and an act of worship that celebrates the love of God. It is, however, also culturally bound. In the USA, for example, this rite is witnessed by the covenant being made usually between a man and a woman in the presence of an ordained minister and the faith community. In order for marriage to be a sign of God's love, God's grace and the ongoing support of the faith community is needed. The wedding ceremony itself is a moment in the sacramental process of becoming married. Most churches recommend marriage preparation workshops as well as requiring couple sessions with the officiating minister prior to the wedding. If the pastoral intent is to foster Christian 'weddings that wed' (Grimes, 1995), then preparing for the wedding necessitates two major tasks: an exploration of what is involved in this particular rite of passage, and an active participation in planning the wedding ritual itself. This approach, with some modifications, is also found in the UK.

Ministers of the Church of England, however, with its established status, act as registrar, and the legal aspects of marriage are also part of any wedding preparation. In addition, whatever the minister's view, he or she is obliged to marry anyone in the parish who is eligible.

As a rite of passage, the wedding ceremony signals that a woman and man are leaving their former ways of living as single, divorced or widowed in order to make a permanent commitment to one another to move into an unknown future together. Pastoral ministry helps the couple to examine the positive and negative legacies they bring to his new relationship from their families of origin and previous relationships. Legacies are most easily accessed through sharing family stories that relate how one's family of origin dealt with important issues, such as decision-making, authority, money, parenting, careers, religious practices and conflict. The couple reflects on the positive and negative relationship patterns perceived in these stories as well as how such patterns may have affected consequent relationships. Such reflection may uncover the roles, rules and rituals for interpersonal relationships that are embedded in each one's expectations for the marriage relationship. Once made conscious, former relational patterns can be more freely discarded, modified or strengthened as the couple engages in the work of becoming married.

In some traditions the pastor may invite the couple to search for the presence and activity of God in their own storied past, present relationship, and hoped-for future together. If God is an active partner in forming the marriage covenant, then the couple will weave the divine story into their new family story and into the wedding ceremony. After the minister instructs the couple about the essential ritual elements comprising a Christian wedding, the couple chooses or composes appropriate readings, songs, gestures, promises that reflect their Christian faith, the values in their relationship, and the kind of family they would like to become. Within churches with a less flexible liturgy, there is still space for consideration of these issues, although the range of options may be more restricted. But since in any wedding the bride and groom marry each other, by enacting this wedding ritual the couple makes room for God to do a new thing in and through their becoming married. [Martha A. Robbins]

WEDDINGS
The rites marking the formal entry into marriage.

A church wedding still has a popular (although not universal) appeal. The wedding dress is usually white and elaborate, the guests wear special attire, the church is old, the organ and choir lead the singing, the bells ring out and the photographs record in perpetuity. The service is preceded by preparation and is followed by the reception and honeymoon. But the service itself is traditionally the core of the ritual process, the rite of passage. That the Church should play a part in that preparation is also often expected.

The one-off character of the event leads to emphasis upon tradition. The service in which the couple marry each other in front of witnesses has changed very little. But the peripherals constantly alter. White, usually taken to symbolize virginity, came in during Victorian times and remains fashionable, even when most couples are publicly living together. Indeed, the ceremony has returned, in the last two decades of the twentieth century, to the position it held in the first decades of the nineteenth. It is an optional extra for that majority who cohabit.

British law changed in 1995 and now conforms to the American practice of allowing weddings to take place in contexts other than churches and register offices. This coincided with clerical unease over the use of a service by those whose motives seemed more social than religious. It reverses, however, the Church's long-standing efforts to bring marriage generally under its aegis. Weddings were celebrated at the church door in the Middle Ages and eventually brought inside church at the Reformation.

The religious service customarily opens with an exposition of marriage. The couple, having ensured that each party fulfils the four conditions for marriage (exclusive, permanent, voluntary and public), make their vows to each other and exchange a ring (or two) as a token. While the priest pronounces the blessing, they remain the ministers of the sacrament. In the Orthodox tradition they are crowned as lords of creation. The inclusion of the communion service, which is general among Roman Catholics, is less common among Anglicans and Protestants.

Weddings remain part of the pastor's ministry, even though the days of mass weddings and marriage in church as a norm have gone.

It is essential that the couple understand that they are responsible adults and that it is not the minister who marries them but that they marry each other (Carr, 1994). The Church's attitude to broken marriages and divorce is today more compassionate and less judgemental than hitherto. In some churches the marriage of divorcees is allowed; in others it is still forbidden.

In the UK the Church of England priest is also the registrar, who is required to know the law on marriage. The calling of banns, licences and special licences, as well as legal age of consent and similar issues all need to be checked. The nationality of the couple may also affect their eligibility. These and similar issues may always be checked with the local registrar. [Edward Bailey]

WHOLENESS
Completeness, soundness, the achievement of full potential in every aspect of being.

The Bible begins with a strong pictorial statement of God's will for the wholeness of all that is created. The forces of wholeness are presented as being stronger than the forces of chaos (Gen. 1.1–3), and there is repeated emphasis that all that has been created is basically good (Gen. 1.4, 10, 12, 18, 21, 25, 31).

Like the rest of creation humankind is designed for wholeness. This involves our becoming one with all that is – and not least with God. Genesis 2 tells how the essence of God is breathed into Adam (Hebrew for 'man'). For we are meant to be one with our Maker (v. 7). Adam is placed in the garden of Eden (Hebrew for 'delight') to show that we are meant to be one with the good earth and to share God's joy in it (v. 15). The animals and birds are brought to Adam to be named to show that we are meant to be one with other living creatures (v. 19). God gives Eve (Hebrew for 'life') to Adam to show that life depends upon our oneness with each other (v. 23). And we are told that neither Adam nor Eve were initially ashamed of their nakedness. For we were created to be one with our inner selves (v. 25).

However, Gen. 3 tells how wholeness has been decisively lost. Adam and Eve succumb to the temptation to 'be like God' (v. 5). Self becomes the 'god' at the centre of life, and wholeness is an immediate casualty. Adam and Eve now cover their nakedness. For inner integrity is lost (v. 7). They seek to hide from the God from whom they have separated themselves (v. 8). They lose their oneness with each other (v. 12). They also become estranged from creation and no longer know how to co-operate with or enjoy the good earth (v. 17). They lose their sense of joy and are driven out of the Garden of Delight (vv. 23–24).

As the Bible continues, this loss of wholeness is shown to have physical, mental, spiritual and social implications. It affects every aspect of our experience of this life and our prospects for eternity. Scripture analyses and grieves over this fallen state but also makes it plain that the restoration of wholeness has become God's mission throughout history. To this end the nation of Israel is called to become God's agency in bringing healing and blessing to damaged humankind. The Israelites are entrusted with a sequence of experiences and a succession of gifts to assist them in doing so. They are also given a promise that one will come who will be specially anointed to fulfil God's healing purpose.

In the New Testament Jesus claims this role for himself (Luke 4.18–21). St Paul identifies him as a 'second Adam' who can restore the wholeness which the first Adam lost (1 Cor. 15.22, 45). By union with Jesus Christ we can find healing from the destructive and separative power of our self-centredness. It was for this that Jesus lived and died and was raised again. To be 'in Christ' (words which Paul uses or paraphrases 164 times) is the heart of the experience of Christian healing and our only hope for wholeness to be restored.

Wholeness is the Christian goal. The Church's ministry of healing in all its varied forms is the process by which we seek to move towards that goal. And the resource for both is union with the Christ, who promises to be with us and in us today, if we open ourselves to his presence in our midst (Matt. 18.20).
[*Roy Lawrence*]

WIDOWHOOD
The status of one whose marriage partner has died, and who remains unmarried.

There is a long tradition in the Old Testament writings that God is the protector of the weak and vulnerable, especially widows. Similar assumptions are found in the New Testament. On the whole this remained the case for widows until the nineteenth century. The former Anglo-American law of marriage was chiefly characterized by the view that the husband and wife are one legal personality

for whom the husband acts. The wife could not ordinarily make separate contracts. After the death of a spouse the survivor usually enjoyed a partial interest in the deceased's property.

By the late nineteenth century all the American states adopted 'married women's property' statutes, giving to wives complete control over their property and their contracts, and provided that a surviving spouse was entitled to a certain minimum share in the estate of the deceased spouse. The Married Women's Property Act (1882) in the UK revoked laws which had automatically transferred a woman's property to her husband at marriage. In the USA, Mississippi passed the first Married Woman's Property Act in 1839; parallel legislation followed in the other states down to the 1880s. Lifelong pensions were granted to widows in the UK in 1925, but only recently have widowers become, in some cases, eligible for pension rights accrued from their wife's employment. Movement in the direction of equal opportunity may lead to widowers and widows being treated equally in social legislation. This article assumes that the death of a married partner issues in widowhood. Increasingly we will meet partners, heterosexual and homosexual, for whom marriage has not been either a possibility or a choice, but whose grief is no less profound.

Pastoral carers need to be aware of the attitudes of society to widows and widowers. Some guides to bereavement seem to assume that widows alone are at risk and require care. Yet widowers may be under some pressure to remarry, especially if they have young children. If they are older, then they are assumed to need companionship. Such is the popular wisdom. In reality there is much more complexity.

It is, however, dangerous to generalize about the behaviour to be expected of those who have lost a spouse by death. There will be differences caused by the nature of the death. Prolonged expected death can give a couple time to prepare for the forthcoming parting and to transact some of the unfinished business of the relationship. Sudden or accidental death may leave the survivor shocked, guilty and full of regrets. The suicide of a partner will leave legacies of self-doubt, guilt and fear. Pastoral carers also need to be alert to anticipatory grief, of the process of disengaging from a still-living but perhaps unconscious partner. When death does occur grief may move through a series of stages, variously described and modified in the literature. Anniversaries are important and are often difficult times, and the knowledge that someone else remembers is important. In some churches remembrance of anniversaries is taken for granted – 'the year's mind'. In others its value is now being learned. Self-help groups such as CRUSE have been of great assistance to many, but it must be re-iterated that people must in the end find their own ways of dealing with their grief. [*D. Murray*]

WISDOM
1. A corpus of biblical books character-ized by certain literary forms and content.
2. A particular approach to life or theological perspective.
3. A movement or tradition in the ancient world.

Wisdom was an international movement or tradition in the ancient world. Mesopotamia and Egypt, for example, produced comparable literature. Israelite wisdom likely originated in the family and tribe rather than in schools associated with the royal court or temple. Contemporary scholarship identifies wisdom literature principally with Proverbs, Job and Ecclesiastes in the Hebrew Bible and with the apocryphal or deuterocanonical books of Sirach (Ecclesiasticus) and Wisdom of Solomon. Three of them (Ecclesiastes, Wisdom of Solomon and much of Proverbs) are attributed to King Solomon, the quintessential sage of Hebrew wisdom.

The identification of wisdom literature is based, first, on the use of certain literary forms. The most fundamental is the 'saying' or 'proverb', a concise statement of an apparent truth that is based on experience and endures through time. It is typically composed of two parallel lines related to each other synonymously (e.g. Prov. 4.7), antithetically (e.g. Prov. 11.1), or progressively (e.g. Prov. 25.18). The style of sayings varies. There are, for example, 'better-than' sayings (e.g. Eccles. 7.1–3), 'happy' sayings (Prov. 14.21), numerical sayings (e.g. Prov. 30.18–19), comparative sayings (Prov. 10.26), and rhetorical questions (Prov. 20.9). Other literary forms include commands (e.g. Prov. 16.3), prohibitions (e.g. Prov. 22.22–23), and longer didactic poems (e.g. Prov. 4. 1–9; 31.10–31). When read in the Hebrew, the artistry of wisdom literature (e.g. play on words and sounds) is particularly apparent.

The identification of wisdom literature is based, second, on content. Notably absent are themes found elsewhere in the Hebrew Bible – the ancestors, the Exodus and wilderness experience, the giving of the law at Sinai, the entry into the Promised Land, or the promise to David. There is no concern for covenant or salvation history. Rather, wisdom literature contains practical advice for how to get along in the world. Its aim is to enable people to cope with the complexities of everyday life. Thus, it tends to such matters as the formation of character, proper behaviour, the inequalities of life, and the finality of death. 'The fear of the Lord', or religious piety, is the starting point of wisdom and its highest achievement (e.g. Prov 1.7; 9.10). Wisdom is also attributed an independent existence, personified as a woman who is at once part of the human and divine realms (Prov. 1.9; Sir. 24; Wisd. 7.7—10.18). Finally, wisdom acknowledges that it is limited by the inherent ambiguities and contradictions of human experience and, ultimately, by the mystery of God. Wisdom is therefore not dogmatic and absolute, but tenuous and adaptable.

The general premise of wisdom is that people may discern truths through experience and observation of the world created by God. As such, revelation may come in everyday realities as well as from above (e.g. 'thus says the Lord') or from authoritative traditions. Wisdom literature thereby manifests a 'theology from below' or 'creation theology'. It begins with the human situation and affirms the authority of human experience as part of theological reflection. The theme has, therefore, been prominent in pastoral theology, especially for the way in which it links experience with universal principles of social, personal and moral behaviour, which are founded on the God of creation. [*Christine Roy Yoder*]

WOMEN'S ISSUES
Perspectives and concerns raised by women that impact on the field of pastoral studies.

The women's movement that re-emerged during the 1970s has had an increasing impact on the Church and theology (see Feminism). Questions of women's rights have intermingled with those to do with distinctively female experience and different assumptions about styles of leadership. The field of pastoral studies has been modified in recent years to include the issues specifically raised by women, both ordained and lay. There are various approaches to this field, but the general themes that emerge within diverse cultural contexts include: unity of body and soul; concern for the powerless and underprivileged (Pattison, 1994); and the importance of the maternal matrix, i.e. the feminine identification with the capacity to create and nurture.

Whereas the Christian Church has often elevated the status of the soul and devalued the body, women are reclaiming the vital unity of soul and body while underscoring the importance of the female body. Thus violence against and exploitation of women becomes a theological issue; a wound to or invasion of the female becomes a spiritual issue.

Within ecclesiastical structures and in the wider communities, concern with the less advantaged has been significantly led by women, as has the bias to the poor. This is a continuation of the struggles in the nineteenth century for social justice that were frequently led by women. It is now acknowledged that throughout history women have been accorded less power than men: this experience is now being utilized by women to network, to empathize and to encourage others who are not in positions of power.

In the Christian tradition the belief that Jesus was born of a human mother has been used to emphasize the importance of the maternal matrix. This matrix is much broader than childbearing: in a metaphorical sense, it includes the mothering process and feminine nurturing as a context for spirituality.

These three themes are well illustrated in a text which has been at the heart of liberation theology. Preceded by Elizabeth's observations, Mary's song (Luke 1.46–55), Magnificat, illustrates all three themes. (1) 'My soul magnifies ... my spirit rejoices ...' exclaims the pregnant Mary as her soul-spirit-body offer a unified model of praise. (2) 'God has put down the mighty' and honoured her, the handmaiden, typifying those of lowly estate. (3) 'Blessed is the fruit of your womb', remarks Elizabeth in a tribute to feminine fruitfulness, the capacity to carry life.

Other women's issues in pastoral studies include: a re-examination of the roles of suffering, sacrifice and selfless love as values within the Christian tradition, which has often exploited women's exercise of these values; recognition of the activity and receptivity (as opposed to passivity or dependency) that women bring to spirituality; a refusal by women to be seen as victims of pain and tragedy, and the determination to be seen as survivors; an emphasis on a theology of grace and hope, not of works and guilt; a need to experience connectedness within the family of faith and reinforcement of a primary relationship with God; an awareness of psychological abuse within the Church when women are not fully valued and treated with dignity.

There are various paradigms that illustrate the theological shift women's issues have created within pastoral studies. For example, the parable of the Good Samaritan underscores the vital interconnection among love of God, love of neighbour and love of self. Pastoral studies has always strongly encouraged the first two loves – of God and neighbour. As women have struggled with self-esteem, the valued self or the loved self, as one stands in relationship to God, becomes an integral part of the parable. Women have identified with the care-giving Samaritan and have also come to realize that the Samaritan finished his (her) journey balancing care of other and care of self (Stevenson-Moessner and Glaz, 1991). By distributing responsibility and networking, the Samaritan also relied on the innkeeper who took over the care of the wounded. Women's issues will continue to impact on the field of pastoral studies with observations such as these which bring a needed balance to the field, a challenge to traditional methodologies, and a renewed vigour to our work and life together, male and female. [*Jeanne Stevenson-Moessner*]

WORK
Productive, goal-orientated human activity.

Work is a significant and central concept in the Judaeo-Christian tradition. The stories of creation and fall in Genesis present an account of a God who works in establishing and sustaining a good creation. In the original condition the parents of the human race share in God's creative work in cultivating the garden. With the fall work becomes labour, unrewarding and demanding toil, as a sign of alienation both from God and from the earth. The New Testament, particularly in the Johannine literature, presents a God who works in redemption and in caring for human beings. Human work continues to have the dignity of sharing in the work of God, but it cannot save. As Paul in particular emphasizes, we are justified by grace through faith, not by works. When we are thus liberated from the effort to earn our salvation through our efforts, we are set free to serve our neighbour through our work. No longer do we use our neighbour to win our acceptance with God, and as a consequence we can take the neighbour's needs and our neighbours as people seriously in their own right and their own integrity.

The Greek tradition generally had a far less positive understanding of work. Work was necessary, but demeaning for a free person. Only intellectual activity and ruling had real dignity. These required repose, which was only possible if slaves, women and what Shakespeare called 'rude mechanicals' performed the work necessary to sustain a life of leisure for the privileged few. Even craftsmanship and other forms of creative manual activity were not honoured; the contemplative life was regarded as superior to almost any form of the life of action. God was understood as dwelling in serenity above all passion and activity.

In a variety of ways, Christianity consistently affirmed the importance and spiritual significance of work, including manual labour. Work was a central part of the spiritual disciplines of most forms of monasticism and the dignity of work was strongly affirmed. But it was still possible and common to draw a sharp distinction between spiritual work, which was of value before God, and the more mundane types of work which were held to have less spiritual significance. Protestantism, while rejecting emphatically any idea that works in some way earned salvation, rapidly developed a powerful ethic. This emphasized the value of hard work and austerity as spiritual disciplines which in effect were signs that one was of the elect. In all this there was a strong affirmation of the spiritual significance of ordinary life and of every kind of work. Max Weber argued that this attitude to work, particularly in its Calvinist Puritan form, was fundamental to the emergence of modern capitalism (Ryken, 1987).

The sabbath rest enjoined in the Hebrew Scriptures and observed in Judaism and in various forms of Christianity reflects the rest of God after creation, and for Christians the resurrection as the culmination of the work of redemption. The sabbath is not simply or primarily rest in order to enable one to return to work with renewed energy. It is rather the day in which the significance of work is discerned: work is to enable the sabbath to take place, for in the sabbath we delight in God, in God's creation, and in our neighbours and friends. In the sabbath we learn the limits of our own efforts, and rejoice in what has been done for us, and the love and beauty with which we are surrounded. Thus the sabbath is welcomed with joy, for it puts the other six days and the labour with which they are filled into perspective: 'This day is holy to the Lord your God; do not mourn or weep. For this day is holy to our Lord; and do not be grieved, for the joy of the Lord is your strength' (Neh. 8.9–10).

Probably the most influential modern account of work, which subtly reflects insights of the Judaeo-Christian tradition, is that of Karl Marx. Marx operates with a sharp distinction between free, creative work which is fulfilling, encourages solidarity and is an essential component of what it is to be human, and alienated labour, where the fruits of work are expropriated, work becomes brutalizing, repetitive toil, and bitterness and frustration ensue. Only in the classless society will labour as a free expression of human creativity in fellowship be possible. Marx's emphasis on the centrality of production, the relations of production in social development, and his concept of alienated labour have been, and continue to be, widely influential.

Hannah Arendt (1959) distinguishes three kinds of work: a dull repetitive toil; the more creative labour of *homo faber*, who makes things, whose work has a goal and expresses personality; and free action which is emancipated from labour and work and is essential for human flourishing and a healthy public realm. Work and worth are closely related, and the way work is organized in a society profoundly affects both individual well-being and social health.

Since work, meaning primarily paid employment, is a fundamental way in which the contribution of the individual to the flourishing of the society is recognized, and human worth is affirmed, unemployment is a deeply traumatic experience. The unemployed person may be stigmatized as work-shy, a dependant rather than a participant contributing to the life of the society. High levels of unemployment are personally and socially destructive. But work which is unfulfilling, routine and underpaid may also be

emotionally destructive. Many Western societies now have both a small section of the working population who suffer from serious overwork and associated stress-related disorders, and a large army of unemployed who suffer from poverty, stigma and a sense of worthlessness. In addition there is a multitude of older people who are still capable of contributing actively and productively to society but are denied the opportunity to do so.
[Duncan Forrester]

WORSHIP AND PASTORAL CARE
The ascription of worth (object of worship), calling forth respect, reverence, devotion. The expression of such devotion through attention, involvement, ritual.

The purpose of this article is to reflect specifically on worship as it relates to pastoral care. The relationship between them is to be found in three areas: (1) the *framework* within which pastoral care is practised and worship is celebrated; (2) the points at which the subject matter of pastoral care and worship *intersect*; (3) and the *biblical anthropology* of the rhythm of human life between the intensely personal and social/communal.

Pastoral care (that area of Christian ministry defined in the tradition as *poimenics* and the *care and cure* of souls) does not take place in a vacuum. It is practised in a social context and within a community of faith. Worship is not to be equated with pastoral care but is not to be separated from pastoral care. Worship is a framework within which pastoral care takes place and vice versa.

Analogical thinking is a useful grammatical tool in discovering resemblance in certain particulars of things that are otherwise unlike. While analogies can be taken too far when pressed to the extreme, one may be helpful in this instance to understanding something of the relationship between worship and pastoral care: worship is to pastoral care what an orchestral concert is to an individual musician. The orchestra and the concert provide a framework, a community, a ritual, and a public work for the expression of the musician's individual art, musical identity and passion.

'To worship', according to William Temple, 'is to quicken the conscience by the holiness of God, to feed the mind by the truth of God, to purge the imagination by the beauty of God, to open the heart to the love of God.' Involved in worship are the issues of ethics, confession (in both senses of the term), rational thought, pursuit of truth and truthfulness (understanding), memory, identity formation, social interaction, wonder, mystery, emotion, ordering of life, shaping of a world-view, and seeking hope for the future. All of these realities are the substance and subject of pastoral care.

The functions of pastoral care have long been understood historically to involve healing, guiding, sustaining, and reconciling. To these historic functions of pastoral care should be added liberation from bondage (being set free from domination and oppression of any sort) and transformation (those changes internally and externally which make life more human, abundant and meaningful). The purpose and function of worship addresses these same realities. Pastoral care has a much broader process and purpose than pastoral counselling, although pastoral counselling may be a part of pastoral care. Understood as *nurture toward wholeness* in human life, worship and pastoral care intersect with many common concerns.

Worship has to do with one's relationship with God, with one's own self, with one's place in the community, and with one's ethical action through that community in a broader social context. In the Bible there are seven or eight words for the concept of the single English word worship. These biblical words range in meaning from reverence, awe and devotion, to service, lifestyle, giving, and social ethical action. One worships, at least in part, to answer the question 'Who do I choose to be?' Likewise, who one chooses to be reveals the object of one's worship. Everyone worships – believers and nonbelievers alike – the question is only who or what is worshipped. The 'shaping of one's life' is involved in both worship and pastoral care. The old English word connotes 'that which is of worth' – subject-matter for both liturgy and pastoral care. That both pastoral care and worship address those realities that diminish our humanity, keep us from freedom and prevent our wholeness personally and socially was reflected early on in Christian literature: 'Give diligence therefore to come together more frequently for thanksgiving and glory to God, for when you are frequently together in one place, the powers of Satan are destroyed and his destructiveness is nullified by the concord of your faith' (Ignatius, *Ephesians*). Jesus was concerned with the 99 sheep and the one sheep – feeding, finding, nurturing, leading. Worship and pastoral care are both reflected in the shepherding image of concerns.

Liturgy (*leitourgia*) is the Church's public work of the congregation enacting its view of reality and commitments. Liturgy provides not only alternative ways of expressing certain realities, but in the use of its ritual it may provide the only way to express them. This is especially true of sacramental expressions. Therefore, the framework of worship becomes a critical part of pastoral care from a Christian perspective. It is a way of expressing who one is, who one is in relationships, and who one is coming to be – all issues addressed in effective pastoral care. Issues of judgement, challenge, forgiveness, grace, sin, shame, suffering, guilt, reverence, love, uncertainty, fear, hope and purpose – in other words, all things human – belong to the linguistic, symbolic and actual coin of the realm in both worship and pastoral care.

Biblical anthropology always connects the individual with the corporate. When one weeps, all weep. When one rejoices, all rejoice. When one suffers, all suffer. When one celebrates, all celebrate. Pastoral care takes seriously the community. Pastoral care separated from the dignity and significance provided by community involvement and the humanization through communal support of dehumanizing suffering becomes nothing more than personal and private consolation and therapy. Worship is one of the ways that individual pain or joy can become a shared experience. It takes private grief and makes it a public event. It takes personal joy and deepens it in communal celebration. This is especially true in liturgical events surrounding births, deaths, baptisms, confirmations, marriages, confessions, absolutions, anointings of the sick, and times of reconciliation.

Both the intensely personal dimension of pastoral care and the public dimension of liturgical action address the fundamental issue of human suffering. Carl Jung pointed out that a 'person over 35 cannot become well' without commitment and involvement with a cause or purpose greater than oneself. In a world where the 'principalities and powers' demand unconditional allegiance, worship becomes both a 'pastoral act' and a 'political act' – indeed, a radical act toward the humanization of life in the freeing, healing, and life-giving grace of God. [*Victor L. Hunter*]

XENOTRANSPLANTS
Organs transplanted from animals into humans.

The success of organ transplantation has created a worldwide problem of organ supply. In many countries, because deaths from driving accidents are less common today as a result of improved car and road safety and more stringent driving laws, there is now a very serious shortage of suitable organs available for ever more successful transplant surgery.

One way to meet this shortage is to increase the number of people who consent to be organ donors beyond the few people who carry donor cards (which, in any case, are invalid if objections are raised by the nearest relatives of the deceased). Logistically, if not ethically, the easiest way to increase consent is to link it to other more routine activities, such as applying for road-fund licences, making wills, etc. It would obviously be important that such consent should be renewed on a fairly regular basis and should be rational and uncoerced.

Another possibility is to move from an opt-in policy of consent to an opt-out policy. Thus it would be incumbent on those not wishing to donate their organs to specify this. However, such a policy would face some obvious difficulties. Could a health trust confidently determine that a potential donor had not made such a specification in the short time in which an organ or organs must be procured? As in any case the consent of the nearest relatives is required, there would be effectively very little difference between opt-in and opt-out.

A third possibility is elective ventilation. Here a patient who has had a stroke, say, and is near death is kept in intensive care specifically to allow time for organs to be donated. However, this option faces some very serious moral and theological objections. Even though elective ventilation may well benefit recipients of the organs, it can hardly be claimed that it is in the best interests of the stroke patient. Indeed it seems to treat the patient in a very utilitarian manner which conflicts with good pastoral care of the dying. There is also a small but real risk of turning the stroke patient into a permanent vegetative state patient.

A fourth possibility may be mechanical organs – for example, artificial hearts. To date these have not been very successful, although they are improving. Should they one day become reliable and relatively inexpensive, they may raise few moral or pastoral problems.

It is in this context that the xenotransplants –for example, hearts grafted from pigs genetically altered with human genes – become a serious fifth possibility. Yet there are still some serious physical and moral problems facing this possibility.

The physical problems of xenotransplants involve overcoming rejection and, especially, avoiding transgenic diseases (in a climate following the scare about BSE the latter may well continue to cause public unease). Moral problems concerning transplanting animal organs into human beings are significant. There are also those concerning the proper treatment of non-human animals and the mixing of distinctively human and non-human genes. For example, possibilities of rejection might be reduced if the hearts of genetically modified apes were used in transplant surgery. Yet on moral grounds the use for xenotransplants of intelligent, human-like animals, which are also endangered in the wild, is extremely dubious. [Robin Gill]

Y

YOUTH
A specific period of time in the lives of all living organisms between conception and the completion of growth into maturity.

Among human beings the maturing process lasts for a variable length of time. Youth is characterized by growth, expansion and changes in organ structure and function. Growth in cellular structure and differentiation of cells to form specialized organs is maximal during gestation. As soon as a child is born, and organs such as the lungs begin to function differently from the way they did *in utero*, the young person begins a phase of developmental growth which is not necessarily confined to organ expansion. Although

young people's hearts, lungs and kidneys function in much the same way as they will in healthy adult life, the brain and all its senses, for example, are not fully developed at birth. The child's organs and systems have to mature appropriately if the child is to learn from experience and from adults how to walk, run, read, write, think and calculate. The sexual organs mature only at puberty. The emotional and social development of a young person does not necessarily coincide with physical maturity.

Young people's bodies and personalities undergo rapid changes during their developmental years. It is not surprising that certain periods of rapid change in organ function are accompanied by emotional turbulence. Children who are learning to speak, control their bladder and bowels, and behave in ways that are acceptable to adults often become mildly disturbed. At this stage of life sympathetic understanding is all that is needed for successful maturation.

Adolescents who are subject to changes in hormonal output from their developing sexual organs are liable to emotional outbursts and erratic social behaviour. Energy peaks in late adolescence and needs to be used creatively, or it will inevitably turn to anti-social activities. Adults sometimes find adolescents difficult to understand and enjoy. Peer-group pressures, youthful defensiveness and aggression can make life difficult for all. Nevertheless youth is a wonderful time in which physical energy, mathematical, inventive and creative skills come to their peak in late adolescence. These energies harnessed to burgeoning sexual energy can all contribute to the welfare and continuation of the human race.

Societies that flourish will generally make good use of the energies and skills of young people. Adequate upbringing and schooling in a secure and affirmative environment will see most young people through to a satisfying adult life. The complexity of modern families and unusual patterns of relationship sometimes make this difficult to achieve. Human beings do, however, have a great ability to adapt to circumstances and no one, however disturbed, should be considered to be incapable of change and growth. An adult's affirmative belief in the goodness of a young person who is exhibiting behavioural disturbance can radically change the future of that young person. [Una Kroll]

BIBLIOGRAPHY

Ainsworth-Smith, I. and Speck, P. (1999) *Letting Go*, SPCK, London

Alison, J. (1998) *The Joy of Being Wrong*, Crossroad, New York

Allport, G. W. (1954) *The Nature of Prejudice*, Addison-Wesley, Reading MA

Allport, G. W. (1965) *Pattern and Growth in Personality*, Yale UP, New Haven CT

Anderson, H. and Fite, R. (1993) *Becoming Married*, Westminster John Knox Press, Louisville KY

Anderson, R. and Dartington, A., eds (1998) *Facing It Out: Clinical Perspectives on Adolescent Disturbance*, Duckworth, London

Anderson, R. S. (1993) *Ministry in the Firing Line: A Practical Theology for an Empowered Church*, IVP, Leicester

Anderson, R. S. (1997) *The Soul of Ministry: Forming Leaders for God's People*, Westminster John Knox Press, Louisville KY

Arendt, H. (1959) *The Human Condition*, Doubleday, New York

Arnold, W. V. (1993) *Pastoral Responses to Sexual Issues*, Westminster John Knox Press, Louisville KY

Ashbrook, J. B. and Albright, C. R. (1997) *The Humanizing Brain: Where Religion and Neuroscience Meet*, Pilgrim Press, Cleveland OH

Augsburger, D. W. (1979) *Anger and Assertiveness in Pastoral Care*, Fortress Press, Philadelphia PA

Augsburger, D. W. (1986) *Pastoral Counselling across Cultures*, Westminster John Knox Press, Louisville KY

Aulén, G. (1931) *Christus Victor*, SPCK, London

Badham, P. (1978) *Christian Beliefs about Life after Death*, SPCK, London

Badham, P. and Badham, L. (1984) *Immortality or Extinction*, SPCK, London

Badham, P. and Ballard, P. (1996) *Facing Death*, University of Wales, Cardiff

Bailey, E. (1997) *Implicit Religion in Contemporary Society*, Kok Pharos, Leuven

Balch, D. and Osiek, C. (1996) *Families in the New Testament World: Households and House Churches*, Westminster John Knox Press, Louisville KY

Balint, M. (1968) *The Doctor, His Patient and the Illness*, Pitman, London

Ballard, P., ed. (1986) *The Foundations of Pastoral Studies and Practical Theology*, University of Wales, Cardiff

Ballard, P. and Pritchard, J. (1996), *Practical Theology in Action*, SPCK, London

Barker, E. (1989) *New Religious Movements: A Practical Introduction*, HMSO, London

Barry, W. A. and Connolly, W. J. (1982) *The Practice of Spiritual Direction*, Seabury Press

Barton, S. and Stanton, G., eds (1994) *Resurrection: Essays in Honour of Leslie Houlden*, SPCK, London

Barwick, N. (2000) *Clinical Counselling in Schools*, Routledge, London

Batson, C. D., Shoenrade, P. and Ventis, W. L. (1993) *Religion and the Individual*, OUP, Oxford

Bayne, R. (1995) *The Myers-Briggs Type Indicator*, Chapman and Hall, London

Beck, A. (1991) *Cognitive Therapy and Emotional Disorders*, Penguin, London

Beckford, J. A. (1975) *The Triumph of Prophecy: A Sociological Study of Jehovah's Witnesses*, Blackwell, Oxford

Bellah, R. N. (1967) 'Civil Religion in America' in Cutler (1968)

Bellah, R. N., Madsen, R., Sullivan, W. M., Swidler, A. and Tipton, S. M. (1985) *Habits of the Heart*, University of California, Los Angeles

Bennett, W. and Gurin, J. (1983) *The Dieter's Dilemma*, Basic Books, New York

Benor, J. (1993) *Healing Research, Holistic Energy Medicine and Spirituality*, Helix, Oxford

Berger, P. L. (1969) *A Rumour of Angels*, Doubleday, New York

Berne, E. (1964) *Games People Play*, Grove Press, Cambridge

Betz, H-D. (1992) *The Greek Magical Papyri in Translation including the Demotic Spells*, Chicago UP, Chicago

Bion, W. R. (1961) *Experiences in Groups and Other Papers*, Tavistock, London

Bion, W. R. (1962) *Learning from Experience*, Heinemann, London

Bisbing, S., Jorgensen, L. and Sutherland, P. (1995) *Sexual Abuse by Professionals*, Michie Press, Charlottesville VA

Bly, R. (1990) *Iron John*, Addison-Wesley, Reading MA

Blythe, R. (1981) *The View in Winter*, Penguin, Harmondsworth

Bond, T. (1994) *Counselling, Confidentiality and the Law*, British Association for Counselling, London

Bond, T. (2000) *Standards and Ethics for Counselling in Action*, 2nd edn, Sage, London

Bonhoeffer, D. (ET1954) *Life Together*, SCM Press, London

Bonhoeffer, D. (1930, 1998) *Sanctorum Communio: A*

Theological Study of the Sociology of the Church, Fortress Press, Augsburg

Boorse, C. (1981) 'On the Distinction between Disease and Illness' in Caplan, Engelhardt and McCartney (1981)

Borrowdale, A. (1989) *A Woman's Work: Challenging Christian Attitudes*, SPCK, London

Bowen, M. (1978) *Family Therapy in Clinical Practice*, Jason Aronson Inc., Northvale NJ

Bowker, J. (1985) *The Religious Imagination and the Sense of God*, Oxford UP, Oxford

Bowlby, J. (1980) *Loss*, Penguin, Harmondsworth

Bowlby, J. (1985a) *Attachment and Loss*, Pelican, London

Bowlby, J. (1985b) *Child Care and the Growth of Love*, Pelican, London

Boylan, A. M. (1988) *Sunday School: The Formation of an American Institution: 1790–1880*, Yale UP, New Haven CT

Braybrooke, M. (1996) *A Wider Vision: A History of the World Congress of Faiths*, Oneworld, Oxford

Briden, T. and Hanson, B. (1992) *Moore's Introduction to English Canon Law*, Mowbray, London/Oxford

Brierley, P. (1991) *Christian England*, Marc Europe, London

Bringle, M. L. (1992) *The God of Thinness: Gluttony and Other Weighty Matters*, Abingdon, Nashville TN

Bromley, D. J. (1988) *Human Ageing*, Penguin, Harmondworth

Brown, G. and Harris, T. (1978) *The Social Origins of Depression*, Tavistock, London

Brown, P. (1988, 1989) *The Body and Society: Men, Women and Sexual Renunciation in Early Christianity*, Columbia UP/Faber & Faber, New York/London

Browning, D. (1976) *The Moral Context of Pastoral Care*, Westminster Press, Louisville KY

Browning, D. (1991) *A Fundamental Practical Theology*, Fortress Press, Philadelphia

Browning, D. S. (1987) *Religious Thought and the Modern Psychologies*, Fortress Press, Philadelphia

Browning, D. S., Miller-McLemore, B., Couture, P. D., Lyon, K. B. and Franklin, R. M. (2000) *From Culture Wars to Common Ground: Religion and the American Family Debate*, 2nd edn, Westminster John Knox Press, Louisville KY

Brueggemann, W. (1978) *The Prophetic Imagination*, SCM Press, London

Buber, M. (1937) *I and Thou*, T. & T. Clark, London

Budd, M. (1985) *Music and the Emotions*, RKP, London

Burghes, L. (1994) *Lone Parenthood and Family Disruption: The Outcomes for Children*, Family Policy Studies Institute, London

Bursell, R. (1996) *Liturgy, Order and the Law*, Clarendon Press, Oxford

Butler, G. and Hope, T. (1995) *Manage your Mind*, OUP, Oxford

Butler, J. (1990) *Awash in a Sea of Faith*, Harvard UP, Cambridge MA

Byrne, P. and Clarke, P. (1993) *Definition and Explanation in Religion*, Macmillan, Basingstoke

Callahan, D. (1970) *Abortion: Law, Choice and Morality*, Macmillan, Basingstoke

Campbell, A. V. (1986a) *The Gospel of Anger*, SPCK, London

Campbell, A. V. (1986b) *Rediscovering Pastoral Care*, Darton, Longman & Todd, London

Caplan, T., Engelhardt, H. T. and McCartney, J., eds (1981) *Concepts of Health and Disease: Interdisciplinary Perspectives*, Addison-Wesley, Reading MA

Capps, D. S. (1981) *Biblical Approaches to Pastoral Counseling*, Westminster, Abingdon TN

Capps, D. S. (1984) *Pastoral Care and Hermeneutics*, Fortress Press, Philadelphia

Capps, D. S. (1993) *The Depleted Self: Sin in a Narcissistic Age*, Fortress Press, Philadelphia

Carkhuff, R. (1969) *Helping and Human Relations*, 2 vols, Human Resources Development Press, Massachusetts

Carr, A. W. (1985) *The Priestlike Task*, SPCK, London

Carr, A. W. (1989) *The Pastor as Theologian: Integrating Theology, Spirituality and Pastoral Ministry*, SPCK, London

Carr, A. W. (1994) *Brief Encounters: Pastoral Ministry through the Occasional Offices*, SPCK, London

Carr, A. W. (1997) *Handbook of Pastoral Studies*, SPCK, London

Case, C. and Dalley, T. (1997) *The Handbook of Art Therapy*, Routledge, London

Cattell, R., Eber, H. E. and Tatsuoka, M. M. (1970) *Handbook for the Sixteen Personality Factor Questionnaire*, IPAT, Dordrecht, Netherlands

Chadwick, O. (1975) *The Secularization of the European Mind in the Nineteenth Century*, Cambridge UP, Cambridge

Childs, B. and Waanders, D., eds (1994) *The Treasure of Earthen Vessels*, Westminster John Knox Press, Louisville KY

Chilton, M. B. and McDonald, J. I. H. (1987) *Jesus and the Ethics of the Kingdom*, SPCK/Eerdmans, London/Grand Rapids MI

Chopra, D. (1989) *Quantum Healing*, Bantam Books, New York

Christ, C. P. and Plaskow, J., eds (1979) *Womanspirit Rising: A Feminist Reader in Religion*, Harper & Row, New York

Clark, D. (1977) *Basic Communities*, SPCK, London

Clark, D. (1996) *Schools as Learning Communities*, Cassell, London

Clay, T. (1987) *Nurses, Power and Politics*, Heinemann, London

Clebsch, W. A. and Jaeckle, C. R. (1994) *Pastoral Care in Historical Perspective*, Harper, New York

Clément, O. (1993) *The Roots of Christian Mysticism*, New City, London

Clinebell, H. J. (1981) *Contemporary Growth Therapies*, Abingdon, Nashville TN

Clinebell, H. J. (1984) *Basic Types of Pastoral Care and Counseling: Resources for the Ministry of Healing and Growth*, Abingdon, Nashville TN

Clinebell, H. J. (1996) *Ecotherapy: Healing Ourselves, Healing the Earth – A Guide to Ecologically Grounded Personality Theory, Spirituality, Therapy and Education*, Fortress Press, Minneapolis

Close, H. (1998) *Metaphor in Psychotherapy*, Impact, San Luis Obispo

Clouette, P. (1995) 'Self-help Groups' in Jacobs (1995), Cassell, London

Clulow, C., ed. (1993) *Rethinking Marriage: Public and Private Perspectives*, Karnac, London

Clulow, C., ed. (1995) *Women, Men and Marriage*, Sheldon, London

Clulow, C. F. (1996) *Partners Becoming Parents*, Sheldon, London

Coate, M. A. (1989) *Clergy Stress*, SPCK, London

Coleman, P. (1980) *Christian Attitudes to Homosexuality*, SPCK, London

Collie, R. (2000) *The Obsessive Compulsive Disorder: Pastoral Care on the Road to Change*, Haworth Pastoral Press, New York

Collins, J. (1990) *Diakonia: Interpreting the Ancient Sources*, OUP, New York

Colman, W. (1993) 'Fidelity as Moral Achievement' in Clulow (1993)

Compton, B. R. and Galaway, B. (1994) *Social Work Processes*, Brooks/Cole, London

Connell, R. W. (1995) *Masculinities*, University of California Press, Berkeley CA

Constanza, R., ed. (1999) *An Introduction to Ecological Economies*, St Lucie Press, Delray Beach FL

Conzelmann, H. and Lindemann, A. (1988) *Understanding the New Testament*, SCM Press, London

Cooper, R., ed. (1994) *Sleep*, Chapman and Hall Medical, London

Cooper-White, P. (1995) *The Cry of Tamar: Violence against Women and the Church's Response*, Fortress Press, Minneapolis

Coriden, J. (1991) *An Introduction to Canon Law*, Geoffrey Chapman, London

Coulson, J. (1981) *Religion and Imagination*, OUP, Oxford

Craig, Y. (1994) *Learning for Life*, Mowbray, London and Oxford

Crompton, C. (1993) *Class and Stratification*, Cambridge UP, Cambridge

Crossan, J. D. (1994) *Jesus: A Revolutionary Biography*, Harper, San Francisco

Crowe, M. and Ridley, J. (1990) *Therapy with Couples: A Behavioural Systems Approach to Marital and Sexual Problems*, Blackwell Scientific, Oxford

Cutler, D. R., ed. (1968) *The World Year Book of Religion*

Daly, J. A. and McGroskey, J. C., eds (1984) *Avoiding Communication: Shyness, Reticence and Communication Apprehension*, Sage, Beverly Hills

Damasio, A. R. (1994) *Descartes' Error*, Putnam, New York

Danforth, L. (1982) *The Death Rituals of Rural Greece*, Princeton UP, Princeton

Davey, J. (1995) *Burnout: Stress in Ministry*, Gracewing, Leominster

Davie, G. (1994) *Religion in Britain since 1945: Believing without Belonging*, Blackwell, Oxford

Davies, D. (1997) *Death, Ritual and Belief*, Continuum, London

Davies, D. J. (1990) *Studies in Pastoral Theology and Social Anthropology*, Birmingham University, Birmingham

Davies, D., Watkins C. and Winteer, M. (1991) *Church and Religion in Rural England*, T. & T. Clark, Edinburgh

Davis, S. (1989) *Death and Afterlife*, Macmillan, London

Dement, W. C. (1996) *The Sleepwatchers*, Nychthemeron Press

Demson, D. (1997) *Hans Frei and Karl Barth: Different Ways of Reading Scripture*, Eerdmans, Grand Rapids MI

Dillistone, F. W. (1986) *The Power of Symbols*, SCM Press, London

Doehring (1993) *Internal Desecration: Traumatization and God Representations*, University Press of America, Lanham MD

Dormor, D. (1992) *The Relationship Revolution*, One plus One, London

Douglas, M. (1966) *Purity and Danger: An Analysis of Concepts of Pollution and Taboo*, Penguin, Harmondsworth

Downie, R. S., Fyfe, C. and Tabbahill, A. (1992) *Health Promotion Models and Values*, OUP, Oxford

Dudley, M. (1997) *A Manual for Ministry to the Sick*, SPCK, London

Dudley, M. and Rowell, G., eds (1993) *The Oil of Gladness: Anointing in the Christian Tradition*, SPCK, London

Duncan, B. (1993) *Pray Your Way*, Darton, Longman & Todd, London

Durkheim, E. (1952) *Suicide: A Study in Sociology*, Routledge and Kegan Paul

Dworkin, R. (1977) *Taking Rights Seriously*, Duckworth, London

Dykstra, C. (1999) *Growing in the Life of Faith*, Geneva Press

Eastell, K., ed. (1994) *Appointed for Growth: A Handbook of Ministry Development and Appraisal*, Mowbray, London/Oxford

Ecclestone, G., ed. (1988) *The Parish Church?*, Mowbray, London

Egan, G. (1982) *The Skilled Helper: Model, Skills and Methods for Effective Helping*, Brooks/Cole, London

Egan, G. and Cowan, M. (1979) *People in Systems*, Brooks/Cole, London

Eilers, F-J. (1994) *Communicating in Community: An*

Introduction to Social Communication, Logos Publications, Manila

Eilers, F-J. (1997) *Church and Social Communication: Basic Documents*, Logos Publications, Manila

Ellis, A. (1975) *A New Guide to Rational Living*, Wilshire Brooks

Erikson, E. (1950) *Childhood and Society*, Norton, New York

Erikson, E. (1994) *Identity and the Life Cycle*, Norton, New York

Eysenck, H. and Eysenck, M. J. (1985) *Personality and Individual Differences: A Natural Science Approach*, Plenum Publishing, London

Faber, H. (1971) *Pastoral Care in the Modern Hospital*, SCM Press, London

Farley, E. (1983) *Theologia*, Fortress Press, Philadelphia PA

Farley, E. (1990) *Good and Evil*, Fortress Press, Minneapolis MN

Feek, W. (1982) *Working Effectively: A Guide to Evaluation Techniques*, Bedford Square Press, London

Festinger, L. (1957) *A Theory of Cognitive Dissonance*, Stanford UP, Stanford CA

Follett, M. P. (1941) *Dynamic Administration*, Harper, San Francisco CA

Ford, D. F. and Stamps, D. L., eds (1996) *Essentials of Christian Community*, T. & T. Clark, Edinburgh

Forrester, D. B. (1988) *Theology and Politics*, Blackwell, Oxford

Forrester, D. B. (1997) *Christian Justice and Public Policy*, CUP, Cambridge

Foskett, J. and Lyall, D. (1988) *Helping the Helpers: Supervision and Pastoral Care*, SPCK, London

Foucault, M. (1979) *Discipline and Punish: The Birth of the Prison*, Vintage Books, London

Foulkes, S. H. (1975) *Group-Analytic Psychotherapy Methods and Practice*, Gordon and Breach, London

Fowler, J. W. (1981) *Stages of Faith*, HarperCollins, London

Francis, L. J. (1997) *Personality Types and Scripture*, Cassell, London

Frank, J. D. and Frank, J. B. (1991) *Persuasion and Healing: A Comparative Study of Psychotherapy*, Johns Hopkins UP, Baltimore MD

Freedman, A. M., Kaplan, H. I. and Sadcock, B. T. (1972) *Modern Synopsis of Comprehensive Textbook of Psychiatry*, Williams and Wilkins, Philadelphia PA

Freeman, A., Pretzer, J., Fleming, B. and Simon, K. M., eds (1990) *Clinical Applications of Cognitive Therapy*, Plenum Press, London

Freud, A. (1937) *The Ego and the Mechanisms of Defence*, Hogarth Press, London

Freud, S. (1896) *Further Remarks on the Defence Neuro-Psychoses* (SE 3), Hogarth Press, London

Freud, S. (1900) *The Interpretation of Dreams* (SE 4), Hogarth Press, London

Freud, S. (1901) *The Psychopathology of Everyday Life* (SE 6), Hogarth Press, London

Freud, S. (1905) *Three Essays on the Theory of Sexuality* (SE 12), Hogarth Press, London

Freud, S. (1913) *Totem and Taboo* (SE 13), Hogarth Press, London

Freud, S. (1914) *On Narcissism* (SE 14), Hogarth Press, London

Freud, S. (1917) *Mourning and Melancholia* (SE 14), Hogarth Press, London

Freud, S. (1921) *Group Psychology and the Analysis of the Ego*, Hogarth Press, London

Freud, S. (1923) *The Ego and the Id* (SE 19), Hogarth Press, London

Freud, S. (1927) *The Future of an Illusion* (SE 21), Hogarth Press, London

Freud, S. (1933) *New Introductory Lectures on Psycho-Analysis* (SE 22), Hogarth Press, London

Friedman, E. (1985) *Generation to Generation*, Guilford, New York

Friedson, E. (1972) *The Profession of Medicine: A Study of the Sociology of Applied Knowledge*, Dodd Mead, New York

Fromm, E. (1977) *The Anatomy of Human Destructiveness*, Penguin, Harmondsworth

Furnish, V. P. (1972) *The Love Command of the New Testament*, Abingdon, Nashville TN

Gager, J. G. (1975) *The Social World of Early Christianity*, Prentice Hall, Englewood NJ

Gager, J. G. (1992) *Curse Tablets and Binding Spells for the Ancient World*, OUP, Oxford

Gay, P., ed. (1995) *The Freud Reader*, Vintage, London

Geach, P. (1977) *The Virtues*, Cambridge UP, Cambridge

Geertz, C. (1993) *The Interpretation of Cultures*, Fontana, London

Gelpi, D. L. (1998) *The Conversion Experience*, Paulist Press, Mahwah NJ

Gill, R. (1989) *Competing Convictions*, SCM Press, London

Gill, R. (1993) *The Myth of the Empty Church*, SPCK, London

Gill, R. and Burke, D. (1996) *Strategic Church Leadership*, SPCK, London

Gillespie (1956) 'The Structure and Aetiology of Sexual Perversion' in Sinason, ed. (1995) *Life, Sex and Death*, Routledge, London

Gilligan, C. (1982) *In a Different Voice*, Harvard University Press, London and Cambridge MA

Girard, R. (1986) *The Scapegoat*, John Hopkins UP, Baltimore MD

Girard, R. (1987) *Things Hidden since the Foundation of the World*, Athlone Press, London

Glidden, P. and Powell, M. (1952) *Called to Serve*, Hodder & Stoughton, London

Goffman, E. (1963) *Stigma*, Prentice Hall, New York

Goffman, E. (1968) *Asylums*, Penguin, Harmondsworth

Goldsmith, M. and Wharton, M. (1993) *Knowing Me, Knowing You*, SPCK, London

Goodman, A. H. (1994) *Basic Skills for the New Mediator*, Solomon Press, Rocksdale, Maryland

Goodwin, S. K. and Jamison, K. R. (1990) *Manic-depressive Illness*, Oxford UP, Oxford

Gough, T. (1990) *Don't Blame Me*, Sheldon, London

Graham, E. (1993) 'The Sexual Politics of Pastoral Care' in Graham and Halsey (1993) *Life Cycles*, SPCK, London

Graham, E. (1995) *Making the Difference*, Mowbray, London/Oxford

Graham, E. (1996) *Transforming Practice*, Mowbray, London

Graham, L. K. (1992) *Care of Persons, Care of Worlds: A Psychosystems Approach to Pastoral Care and Counseling*, Abingdon, Nashville TN

Greeley, A. (1973) *The Persistence of Religion*, SCM Press, London

Greider, K. (1997) *Reckoning with Aggression: Theology, Violence and Vitality*, Westminster John Knox Press, Louisville KY

Grey, M. (1989) *Redeeming the Dream*, SPCK, London

Grimes, R. L. (1995) *Marrying and Burying: Rites of Passage in a Man's Life*, Westview, Oxford

Guder, D. (2000) *The Incarnation and the Church's Witness*, Trinity Press, Valley Forge PA

Guenther, M. (1992) *Holy Listening: The Art of Spiritual Direction*, Cowley/Darton, Longman & Todd, Cambridge MA/London

Gunton, C. (1998) *The Triune Creator: A Historical and Systematic Study*, Edinburgh UP, Edinburgh

Guntrip, H. (1971) *Psychology for Ministers and Social Workers*, George Allen & Unwin, London

Gurman, A. S. and Messer, S. B., eds (1995) *Essential Psychotherapies: Theory and Practice*, Guilford Press, New York/London

Gutiérrez, G. (1974) *A Theology of Liberation*, SCM Press, London

Haas, L. J. and Malouf, J. L. (1995) *Keeping up the Good Work: A Practitioner's Guide to Mental Health Ethics*, Professional Resource Press

Hall, J. D. (1986) *God and Human Suffering: An Exercise in the Theology of the Cross*, Augsburg Press, Minneapolis MN

Harper, T. (1994) *The Uncommon Touch: An Investigation of Spiritual Healing*, McClelland and Stewart, Toronto

Harton, F. P. (1932) *The Elements of the Spiritual Life*, SPCK, London

Harvey, D. (1989) *The Condition of Postmodernity*, Blackwell, Oxford

Harvey, N. P. (1991) *The Morals of Jesus*, Darton, Longman & Todd, London

Hauerwas, S. (1981) *A Community of Character*, Chicago UP, Chicago

Hay, D. (1982) *Exploring Inner Space: Is God Still Possible in the Twentieth Century?*, Penguin, Harmondsworth

Healy, D. (1997) *The Antidepressant Era*, Harvard UP, Cambridge MA

Hebblethwaite, M. (1993) *Base Communities: An Introduction*, Geoffrey Chapman, London

Heimberg, R. G. et al. (1995) *Social Phobia: Diagnosis, Assessment and Treatment*, Guilford, New York/London

Helgeland, J., Daly, R. J. and Burns, J. Patout (1985) *Christians and the Military: The Early Experience*, Fortune, Bloomfield NJ

Helminiak, D. A. (1998) *Religion and the Human Sciences*, State University of New York Press, New York

Herman, J. L. (1992) *Trauma and Recovery: The Aftermath of Violence: From Domestic Abuse to Political Terror*, Basic Books, Oxford

Heyward, C. (1999) *Saving Jesus from Those Who Are Right*, Fortress Press, Minneapolis

Hick, J. (1976) *Death and Eternal Life*, Macmillan, London

Hick, J. (1989) *An Interpretation of Religion*, Macmillan, Basingstoke

Hiltner, S. (1958) *A Preface to Pastoral Theology*, Abingdon, Nashville TN

Hinshelwood, R. D. (1991) *A Dictionary of Kleinian Thought*, Free Association Press, London

Hinton, J. (1995) *Walking in the Same Direction*, WCC, Geneva

Hoge, D. R., Johnson, B. and Luidens, D. A. (1994) *Vanishing Boundaries*, Westminster John Knox Press, Louisville KY

Holifield, E. B. (1983) *A History of Pastoral Care in America*, Abingdon, Nashville TN

Holmes, J., ed. (1991) *Textbook of Psychotherapy in Psychiatric Practice*, Churchill Livingstone, London

Hood, R. W. Jr, Spilka, B., Hunsberger, B. and Gorsuch, R. L. (1996) *The Psychology of Religion: An Empirical Approach*, Guilford, New York

Hooper, D. and Dryden, W. (1991) *Couple Therapy: A Handbook*, Open UP, Buckingham

Hoornaert, E. (1988) *The Memory of the Christian People*, Burns & Oates, Tunbridge Wells

Hoover, S. M. and Lundby, K., eds (1997) *Rethinking Media: Religion and Culture*, Sage, London

Hopewell, J. (1988) *Congregation: Stories and Structures*, SCM Press, London

Hoskyns, C. and Davey, N. (1981) *Crucifixion, Resurrection: The Pattern of Theology and Ethics of the New Testament*, SPCK, London

Hull, J. M. (1989) *The Act Unpacked*, CEM, Derby

Hull, J. M. (1991) *What Prevents Christian Adults from Learning?*, Trinity Press International, Valley Forge PA

Hull, J. M. (1997) *On Sight and Insight*, Oneworld, Oxford

Hull, J. M. (2001) *In the Beginning There Was Darkness*, SCM Press, London

Hume, D. (1748, 1894) *An Enquiry Concerning Human Understanding*, Clarendon Press, Oxford

Hunsinger, D. (1995) *Theology and Pastoral Counsel-*

ling: A New Interdisciplinary Approach, Eerdmans, Grand Rapids MI

Hunter, G. I. (1977) Theological Field Education, Boston Theological Institute, Boston MA

Hunter, R. J., ed. (1990) A Dictionary of Pastoral Care and Counseling, Abingdon, Nashville TN

Hurley, M. ed. (1975) Beyond Tolerance, Geoffrey Chapman, London

Hutton, J. (2000) Working with the Concept of Organisation-in-the-Mind, The Grubb Institute, London

Ignatieff, M. (1978) A Just Measure of Pain: The Penitentiary in the Industrial Revolution, Random House, London

Illich, I. (1991) Limits to Medicine, Penguin, Harmondsworth

Irvine, A. R. (1997) Between Two Worlds: Understanding and Managing Clergy Stress, Mowbray, London/Oxford

Israel, M. (1982) Living Alone, SPCK, London

Jacobs, M. (1989) Holding in Trust, SPCK, London

Jacobs, M. (1993) Still Small Voice, SPCK, London

Jacobs, M. (2000) Illusion: A Psychodynamic Interpretation of Thinking and Beliefs, Whurr, London

Jacoby, R. and Oppenheimer, C. (1997) Psychiatry in the Elderly, Oxford UP, Oxford

James, W. (1890) The Principles of Psychology, Dover, New York

James, W. (1902) The Varieties of Religious Experience, Longmans, Green and Co., New York

Jantzen, G. (1996) Power, Gender and Christian Mysticism, CUP, Cambridge

Jenkins, D. (1976) The Contradiction of Christianity, SCM Press, London

Jenson, R. (1997) Systematic Theology, Oxford UP, Oxford

Jones, C., Wainwright, G., Yarnold, E. and Bradshaw, P., eds (1992), The Study of Liturgy, 2nd edn, SPCK/OUP, London/New York

Jones, C., Wainwright, G. and Yarnold, E., eds (1986) The Study of Spirituality, SPCK, London

Jones, L. G. (1995) Embodying Forgiveness, Eerdmans, Grand Rapids MI

Jones, W. H., Cheek, J. M. and Briggs, S. R. (1986) Shyness: Emotions, Personality and Psychotherapy, Plenum, New York

Jung, C. G. (1928) Dream Seminars in Collected Works: Seminars I, Routledge, London

Jung, C. G. (1946) Psychological Types, Kegan Paul, Trench, Trubner, London

Kandel, E. R., Schwartz, J. H. and Jessell, T. M. (1992) Principles of Neural Science, Esevier/Appleton and Lange, Amsterdam

Kaplan, H. I., Sadcock, E. J. and Scheele, A. (1996) Pocket Handbook of Clinical Psychiatry, 2nd edn, Lippincott, Williams and Wilkins, Philadelphia PA

Kaufman, G. D. (1985) Theology for a Nuclear Age, Manchester UP, Manchester

Keirsey, D. and Bates, M. (1978) Please Understand Me: Character and Temperament Types, Prometheus Nemeis, Del Mar CA

Kelley, D. M. (1972) Why Conservative Churches Are Growing, Harper & Row, New York

Kierkegaard, S. (1843, ET 1985), Fear and Trembling, Penguin, Harmondsworth

Kiernan, K. E. and Estaugh, V. (1993) Cohabitation, Family Policy Study Centre, London

Kiernan, K. E. and Wicks, M. (1990) Family Change and Future Policy, Family Policy Study Centre, London

Kilcourse, G. (1992) Double Belonging: Interchurch Families and Christian Unity, Paulist Press, Mahwah NJ

Kinchin, D. (1998) Post Traumatic Stress Disorder, Success Unlimited, Didcot, Oxfordshire

King, M., Speck, P. and Thomas, A. (1999) 'The effects of spiritual beliefs on outcome from illness', Social Science and Medicine 48, 1291–9

Klein, M. (1921) The Development of the Child: Contributions to Psychoanalysis, Hogarth Press, London

Klein, M. (1963) Our Adult World and Other Essays, Heinemann, London

Kohlberg, L. (1984) The Psychology of Moral Development, Harper & Row, New York

Kohner, N. (1995) Pregnancy, Loss and the Death of a Baby: Guidelines for Professionals, NEL, Cambridge

Kohut, H. (1976) The Restoration of the Self, International Universities Press, Madison CT

Kouzes, J. M. and Posner, B. Z. (1993) Credibility: How Leaders Gain It and Lose It, Why People Demand It, Jossey-Bass, San Francisco

Krafft-Ebing, R. von (1886) Psychopathia Sexualis, Creation Books, London

Kraft, C. H. (1991) Communication Theory for Christian Witness, Orbis Books, Maryknoll NY

Kreeger, L., ed. (1975) The Large Group: Dynamics and Therapy, Constable, London

Kryger, M. H., Roth, T. and Dement, W. C. (1989) Principles and Practice of Sleep Medicine, W. B. Saunders Company, London

Kübler-Ross, E. (1970) On Death and Dying, Tavistock Publications, London

Küng, H. (1996) Global Ethics for Global Politics and Economics, SCM Press, London

Kurtz, R. L. (1995) Gods in the Global Village: The World's Religions in Sociological Perspective, Pine Forge Press, London

Kushner, H. S. (2000) When Bad Things Happen to Good People, Schocken Books, New York

Lahey, B. B. (1988) Psychology: An Introduction, Brown and Benchmark, New York

Laing, R. D. (1962) The Divided Self, Routledge, London

Lake, F. (1966) Clinical Theology, Darton, Longman & Todd, London

Lake, F. (1981) Tight Corners in Pastoral Counselling, Darton, Longman & Todd, London

Lamb, C. and Bryant, M. D. (1999) Religious Con-

version: Contemporary Practices and Controversies, Cassell, London

Lambourne, R. A. (1970) 'With Love to the USA' in Melinsky (1970), *Religion and Medicine*, SCM, London

Lambourne, R. A. (1985) 'Wholeness, Community and Worship' in Wilson, M., ed. (1985), University of Birmingham Press

Lartey, E. Y. (1977) *In Living Colour: An Intercultural Approach to Pastoral Care and Counselling*, Cassell, London

Lash, N. (1988) *Easter in Ordinary*, SCM Press, London

Lawrence, R. (1998) *The Practice of Christian Healing*, SPCK, London

Lawrence, R. (2000) *Finding Hope and Healing through the Bible*, SPCK, London

Lawrence, R. J. (1989) *The Poisoning of Eros*, Augustine Moore, New York

Lawrence, W. G. and Miller, E. J. (1993) 'A Church of England Diocese' in Miller, E. J. (1993)

Lawson, A. (1990) *Adultery: An Analysis of Love and Betrayal*, Oxford UP, Oxford

Lear, J. (1990) *Love and Its Place in Nature*, Yale UP, New Haven CT

Leech, K. (1977) *Soul Friend*, Harper & Row, New York

Leon, I. G. (1990) *When a Baby Dies*, Yale UP, New Haven CT

Lewis, C. S. (1936) *The Allegory of Love*, OUP, Oxford

Lewis, C. S. (1947) *Miracles: A Preliminary Study*, Fontana, London

Lewis, C. S. (1960) *The Four Loves*, Fontana, London

Lewis, H. B. (1991) *Shame and Guilt in Neurosis*, International Universities Press, Madison CT

Lieberman, M., Am Yalom, I. D. and Miles, M. B. (1973) *Encounter Groups: First Facts*, Basic Books, New York

Liebert, E. (1992) *Changing Life Patterns: Adult Development in Spiritual Direction*, Paulist Press, Mahwah NJ

Lindbeck, G. (1984) *The Nature of Doctrine: Religion and Theology in a Postliberal Age*, Westminster

Linn, M. and Linn, D. (1978) *Healing of Life's Hurts: Healing Memories through Five Stages of Forgiveness*, Paulist Press, Mahwah NJ

Linzey, A. D. (1987) *Christianity and the Rights of Animals*, SPCK, London

Linzey, A. D. (1994) *Animal Theology*, SCM Press/University of Illinois Press, London/Champagne IL

Logan, P. (1996) *From Sympathy to Solidarity*, London Churches Group, London

Louth, A. (1991) *The Wilderness of God*, Darton, Longman & Todd, London

Lowen, A. (1958) *The Language of the Body*, Macmillan, London

Lowen, A. (1967) *The Betrayal of the Body*, Macmillan, New York

Luckmann, T. (1967) *Invisible Religion: The Problem of Identity in Modern Society*, Macmillan-Collier, London

Lukas, C. and Seiden, H. M. (1997) *Silent Grief*, Jason Aronson Inc., Northvale NJ

Lyall, D. (1995) *Counselling in the Pastoral and Spiritual Context*, Open University Press, Buckingham

MacIntyre, A. (1988) *Whose Justice? Which Rationality?*, Duckworth, London

MacIntyre, A. (1981) *After Virtue*, Duckworth, London

Maddi, S. (1980) *Personality Theory: A Comparative Analysis*, Brooks Cole, Holmwood

Maddocks, M. (1990) *The Christian Healing Ministry*, 2nd edn, SPCK, London

Maguire, M., Morgan, R. and Reiner, P. (1997) *The Oxford Handbook of Criminology*, OUP, Oxford

Mahler, M., Pine, F. and Bergman, A. (1975) *The Psychological Birth of the Human Infant*, Basic Books, New York

Malamuth, N. M. and Donnerstein, E., eds (1984) *Pornography and Aggression*, Academic Press, New York

Markham, I. (1995) *Plurality and Christian Ethics*, CUP, Cambridge

Markham, I., ed. (1996) *A World Religions Reader*, Blackwell, Oxford

Marriage, A. (1995) *The People of God, Royal Priesthood*, Darton, Longman & Todd, London

Martin, D. (1978) *A General Theory of Secularization*, Blackwell, Oxford

Maslow, A. (1971) *The Farther Reaches of Human Nature*, Viking, London

Mason, P. (1970) *Patterns of Dominance*, OUP, Oxford

McClendon, J. W. Jr (1994) *Systematic Theology: Doctrine Volume II*, Abingdon Press, Nashville TN

McGinn, B. (1991) *The Foundations of Mysticism*, Crossroad, New York

McGrath, A. (1995) *Evangelicalism and the Future of Christianity*, IVP, Leicester

McGuire, M. B. (1992) *Religion: The Social Context*, Wadsworth Publishing

McIntyre, J. (1982) *After Virtue*, Duckworth, London

McIntyre, J. (1987) *Faith, Theology and Imagination*, Handsel

McIver, S. (1993) *Obtaining the View*, The Kings Fund, London

McLanahan, S. and Sandefu, G. D. (1994) *Growing Up with a Single Parent: What Hurts, What Helps*, Harvard University Press, Cambridge MA

Meeks, W. A. (1983) *The First Urban Christians*, Yale UP, New Haven CT

Meissner, W. W. (1984) *Psychoanalysis and Religious Experience*, Yale UP, New Haven CT

Melinsky, M. A. H., ed. (1970) *Religion and Medicine*, SCM Press, London

Melton, J. (1992) *Encyclopedic Handbook of Cults in America*, Garland, New York

Merton, T. (1975) *Thoughts in Solitude*, Burns & Oates, London

Metz, J.-B. (1968) *Spiritual Poverty*, Paulist Press, Mahwah NJ

Meyer, C. and Mattaini, M. A., eds (1995) *Foundations of Social Work Practice*, NASW Press, Washington DC

Migliore, D. and Billman, K. (1999) *Rachel's Cry: Prayer of Lament and Recovery of Hope*, Pilgrim Press, Cleveland OH

Milbank, J., Pickstock, C. and Ward, G., eds (1999) *Radical Orthodoxy*, Routledge, London

Miller, D. (1994) *Women Who Hurt Themselves*, Basic Books, New York

Miller, E. J. (1993) *From Dependency to Autonomy: Studies in Organization and Change*, Free Association, London

Miller, E. J. and Rice, A. K. (1967) *Systems of Organization: The Control of Task and Sentient Boundaries*, Tavistock, London

Miller, L. et al., eds (1991) *Closely Observed Infants*, Duckworth, London

Miller, W. R. and Jackson, K. A. (1995) *Practical Theology for Pastors*, Prentice Hall, Ontario

Mitchell, B. G. (1970) 'Indoctrination' in Ramsey, I. T., ed. (1970)

Mitchell, J. P. (1999) *Visually Speaking: Radio and the Renaissance of Preaching*, T. & T. Clark, Edinburgh

Moberly, R. (1897) *Ministerial Priesthood*, John Murray, London

Moltmann, J. (1967) *The Theology of Hope*, SCM Press, London

Moltmann, J. (1977) *The Church in the Power of the Spirit*, SCM Press, London

Moltmann, J. (1992) *The Spirit of Life*, Fortress Press, Philadelphia PA

Monk, G., ed. (1997) *Narrative Therapy in Practice: The Archaeology of Hope*, Jossey Bass, San Francisco

Moody, C. (1992) *Eccentric Ministry*, Darton, Longman & Todd, London

Morea, P. C. (1997) *In Search of Personality: Christianity and Modern Psychology*, SCM Press, London

Moreno, J. (1947) *The Theater of Spontaneity*, Beacon House, Boston

Morris, M. and Rothman, D., eds (1995) *The Oxford History of the Prison: The Practice of Punishment in Western Society*, OUP, Oxford

Moule, C. F. D. (1962) *The Birth of the New Testament*, A. & C. Black, London

Mudge, L. and Poling, J. N., eds (1987) *Formation and Reflection*, Fortress Press

Murdoch, D. and Baker, P. (1991) *Basic Behaviour Therapy*, Blackwell Science, Oxford

Murphy, N. (1990) *Theology in the Age of Scientific Reasoning*, Cornell UP, Ithaca NY

Murray, R. (1992) *The Cosmic Covenant: Biblical Themes of Justice, Peace and the Integrity of Creation*, Sheed & Ward, London

Narramore, S. B. (1984) *No Condemnation*, Zondervan, Grand Rapids MI

Nelson, J. (1992) *The Intimate Connection: Male Sexuality, Masculine Spirituality*, Westminster/SPCK, Philadelphia/London

Nelson, J. B. (1994) *Sexuality and the Sacred: Sources for Theological Reflection*, Westminster John Knox Press, Louisville KY

Neuger, C. C. (1996) *The Arts of Ministry: Feminist-Womanist Approaches*, Westminster John Knox Press, Louisville KY

Newlands, G. M. (1980) *The Theology of the Love of God*, Collins, London

Nicholl, D. (1987) *Holiness*, Darton, Longman & Todd, London

Niebuhr, H. R. (1929) *The Social Sources of Denominationalism*, Macmillan, New York

Niebuhr, H. R. (1941) *The Meaning of Revelation*, Macmillan, New York

Niebuhr, H. R. (1956) *The Purpose of the Church and Its Ministry*, Harper, New York

Niebuhr, R. (1966) *Christian Realism and Political Problems*, Kelly

Nietzsche, F. (1990) *The Anti-Christ*, Penguin, London

Northcott, M. (1996) *The Environment and Christian Ethics*, CUP, Cambridge

Northcott, M. S. (1989) *The Church and Secularisation: Urban Industrial Mission in North East England*, Peter Lang, Bern, Switzerland

Northcott, M. S. (1996) *The Environment and Christian Ethics*, Cambridge UP, Cambridge

Nouwen, H. J. M. (1991) *The Way of the Heart: Desert Spirituality and Contemporary Ministry*, HarperCollins, London

Nuland, S. (1994) *How We Die*, Chatto & Windus, London

O'Connor, J. and Seymour J. (1990) *Introducing Neuro-Linguistic Programming, NLP*, Thorsons, London

O'Donoghue, N. D. (1989) *Mystics for Our Time*, T. & T. Clark, Edinburgh

O'Donohue, J. (1997) *Anam Cara: Spiritual Wisdom from the Celtic World*, Bantam, London

O'Donovan, O. (1986) *Resurrection and Moral Order*, IVP, Leicester

O'Donovan, O. (1996) *The Desire of the Nations: Rediscovering the Roots of Political Theology*, CUP, Cambridge

Obholzer, A. and Roberts, V., eds (1994) *The Unconscious at Work: Individual and Organizational Stress in the Human Services*, Routledge, London

Oden, T. C. (1966) *Kerygma and Counseling*, Westminster Press, Philadelphia PA

Oden, T. C. (1984) *Pastoral Theology: Essentials in Ministry*, Harper & Row, New York

Oppenheim, A. N. (1992) *Questionnaire Design: Interviewing and Attitude Measurement*, Pinter Publishers, London

Oppenheimer, H. (1973) *Incarnation and Immanence*, Hodder & Stoughton, London

Oppenheimer, H. (1990) *Marriage*, Mowbray, London

Oram, J. J. (1997) *Caring for the Fourth Age*, Armelle Press

Osborne, C. (1994) *Eros Unveiled*, Clarendon Press, Oxford

Oswald, R. M. and Kroeger, O. (1988) *Personality Type and Religious Leadership*, Alban Institute, Washington DC

Otto, R. (1917) *The Idea of the Holy*, ET 1923, Oxford UP, London

Outka, G. (1972) *Agape: An Ethical Analysis*, Yale UP, New Haven CT

Pailin, D. (1992) *A Gentle Touch*, SPCK, London

Pannenberg, W. (1977) *Human Nature, Election and History*, Westminster Press, Philadelphia PA

Parkes, C. M. (1991) *Bereavement: Studies of Grief in Adult Life*, Penguin, Harmondsworth

Parsons, S. (1986) *The Challenge of Christian Healing*, SPCK, London

Parsons, S. (1995) *Searching for Healing*, Lion, Oxford

Parsons, T. (1977) *The Evolution of Societies*, Prentice Hall, New York

Pattison, E. M. (1977) *Pastor and Parish: A Systems Approach*, Fortress Press, Philadelphia PA

Pattison, S. (1993) *A Critique of Pastoral Care*, SCM Press, London

Pattison, S. (1994) *Pastoral Care and Liberation Theology*, CUP, Cambridge

Peace, R. V. (1999) *Conversion in New Testament*, Eerdmans, Grand Rapids MI

Peddie, J. C. (1966) *The Forgotten Talent: God's Ministry of Healing*, Fontana, London

Pellegrino, E. and Thomasma, O. (1981) *A Philosophical Basis of Medical Practice*, OUP, Oxford

Pennington, D. C., Gilen, K. and Hill, P. (1999) *Social Psychology*, Arnold, London

Percy, M. (1996) *Words, Wonders and Powers*, SPCK, London

Perrin, M. (1976) *Jesus and the Language of the Kingdom*, SCM Press/Fortress Press, London/Philadelphia PA

Perry, M., ed. (1996) *Deliverance: Psychic Disturbances and Occult Involvement*, SPCK, London

Peterson, E. H. (1980) *Five Smooth Stones for Pastoral Work*, Eerdmans, Grand Rapids MI

Pfister, O. (1948) *Christianity and Fear: A Study in History and in the Psychology and Hygiene of Religion*, George, Allen & Unwin, London

Pickstock, C. (1977) *After Writing: On the Liturgical Consummation of Philosophy*, Blackwell, Oxford

Piers, G. and Singer, M. B. (1953) *Shame and Guilt*, Norton, New York

Placher, W. C. (1989) *Unapologetic Theology: A Christian Voice in a Pluralistic Conversation*, Westminster John Knox Press, Louisville KY

Polanyi, M. (1958) *Personal Knowledge*, Routledge, London

Poling, J. N. (1991) *The Abuse of Power: A Theological Problem*, Abingdon, Nashville TN

Popenoe, D. and Whitehead, B. (1999) *Should We Live Together?*, The National Marriage Project

Potter, H. (1993) *Hanging in Judgement: Religion and Capital Punishment in England from the Bloody Code to Abolition*, SCM Press, London

Powell, M. A. (1999) *The Jesus Debate*, Lion, Oxford

Powell, M. A. (1999) *Jesus as a Figure in History*, Westminster John Knox Press, Louisville KY

Pryce, M. (1996) *Finding a Voice: Men, Women and the Community of the Church*, SCM Press, London

Pryser, P. (1976) *The Minister as Diagnostician*, Westminster Press, Philadelphia PA

Rambo, L. R. (1993) *Understanding Religious Conversion*, Yale UP, New Haven CT

Ramsay, N. (1998) *Pastoral Diagnosis: A Resource for Ministries of Care and Counseling*, Augsburg Press, Minneapolis, MN

Ramsey, I. T., (ed.) (1970) *The Fourth R*, SPCK, London

Ramsey, P. (1978) *Ethics at the Edges of Life*, Yale UP, New Haven CT

Ramshaw, E. (1987) *Ritual and Pastoral Care*, Fortress Press, Philadelphia PA

Reed, B. D. (1978) *The Dynamics of Religion, Process and Movement in Christian Churches*, Darton, Longman & Todd, London

Rees, L., Lipsedge, M. and Ball, C. (1997) *Textbook of Psychiatry*, Arnold, London

Reibstein, J. and Richards, M. (1992) *Sexual Arrangements: Marriage and Affairs*, Heinemann, London

Remus, H. (1999) *'Magic', Method, Madness: Method and Theory in the Study of Religion*

Richards, J. (1974) *But Deliver Us from Evil*, Darton, Longman & Todd, London

Richards, M. (1995) *'The Companionship Trap'* in Clulow, C., ed. (1995)

Richardson, R. W. (1995) *Family Ties that Bind*, Self-Counsel Press, WA

Ricoeur, P. (1967) *The Symbolism of Evil*, Beacon Books, Boston MA

Rogers, C. R. (1951) *Client Centered Therapy*, Houghton Mifflin, Boston MA

Rogers, C. R. (1967) *On Becoming a Person*, Houghton Mifflin, Boston

Rogers, C. R. (1970) *Encounter Groups*, Harper, San Francisco

Romain, J. A. (1996) *Till Faith Do Us Part: Couples Who Fall in Love across the Religious Divide*, Fount, London

Rose, E. J. B. *et al.* (1969) *Colour and Citizenship*, OUP, Oxford

Rudy, K. (1997) *Sex and the Church: Gender, Homo-*

sexuality and the Transformation of Christian Ethics, Beacon Press, Boston MA

Ruether, R. R. (1983) *Sexism and God-Talk*, SCM Press, London

Russell, J. (1977) *The Devil*, Cornell UP, Ithaca NY

Rycroft, C. (1979) *The Innocence of Dreams*, Hogarth Press, London

Rycroft, C. (1985) *Psychoanalysis and Beyond*, Chatto & Windus, London

Ryken, L. (1987) *Work and Leisure in a Christian Perspective*, Multnomah, Sisters OR

Sacks, J. (1995) *Faith in the Future*, Darton, Longman & Todd, London

Saiving, V. (1979) 'The Human Situation: A Feminine View' in Christ and Paskow (1979)

Saliba, J. (1995) *Perspectives on New Religious Movements*, Cassell, London

Salisbury, C. and Walters, C. (1997) *All Together Now: What to Expect When Stepfamilies Get Together*, National Stepfamily Association, London

Sandbek, T. J. (1990) 'Role Play' in Hunter, R. J., ed. (1990)

Saunders, C. (1967) *The Management of Terminal Illness*, Edward Arnold, London

Schillebeeckx, E. (1963) *Christ the Sacrament of the Encounter with God*, Sheed & Ward, London

Schillebeeckx, E. (1985) *The Church with a Human Face: A New and Expanded Theology of Ministry*, SCM Press, London

Schleiermacher, F. (1799) *On Religion: Speeches to Its Cultured Despisers*

Schneidman, E. (1993) *Suicide as Psychache: A Clinical Approach to Self-destructive Behavior*, Jason Aronson, New York

Schultze, Q. J. (2000) *Communicating for Life*, Baker Academic, Grand Rapids MI

Seen, F. C. (1997) *Christian Liturgy: Catholic and Evangelical*, Fortress Press, Philadelphia

Segundo, J. (1977) *The Liberation of Theology*, Gill and Macmillan, Dublin

Selby, P. (1983) *Liberating God*, SPCK, London

Senge, P. M. (1990) *The Fifth Discipline*, Currency and Doubleday, New York

Senn, F. (1997) *Christian Liturgy: Catholic and Evangelical*, Augsburg, Minneapolis, Minnesota

Shafranske, E. F. (1996) *Religion and the Clinical Practice of Psychology*, APA, New York

Shapiro, E. R. and Carr, A. W. (1991) *Lost in Familiar Places: Creating New Connections between the Individual and Society*, Yale UP, New Haven CT

Sheldrake, P. (1987) *Images of Holiness*, Darton, Longman & Todd, London

Simmonds, I. G. (1979) *Changing the Face of the Earth: Culture, Environment and Human History*, Blackwell, Oxford

Snook, I. A. (1972) *Indoctrination and Education*, Routledge, London

Soelle, D. (1976) *Suffering*, Darton, Longman & Todd, London

Sokolowski, R. (2000) *An Introduction to Phenomenology*, CUP, Cambridge

Speck, P. (1997) *The Oxford Book of Palliative Medicine*, OUP, Oxford

Speck, P. (1988) *Being There: Pastoral Care in Time of Illness*, SPCK, London

Spilka, B., Hood, R. W. and Gorsuch, R. L. (1985) *The Psychology of Religion*, Prentice Hall, New York

Stahmann, R. F. and Hiebert, W. J. (1997) *Premarital and Remarital Counseling: the Professional's Handbook*, Jossey-Bass, San Francisco

Stanley, S., Trathen, D., McCain, S. and Bryan, M. (1998) *A Lasting Promise: A Christian Guide to Fighting for Your Marriage*, Jossey-Bass, San Francisco

Stein, E. (1969) *Guilt: Theory and Therapy*, George Allen & Unwin, London

Steinback, B. and Norcross, A. (1994) *Killing and Letting Die*, Fordham UP, Bronx NY

Stevens, A. (1998) *Ariadne's Clue: A Guide to the Symbols of Humankind*, Allen Lane, London

Stevenson-Moessner, J. and Glaz, M., eds (1991) *Women in Travail and Transition: A New Pastoral Care*, Fortress Press

Stoller, R. J. (1986) *Perversion: The Erotic Form of Hatred*, Karnac, London

Stone, L. (1992) *The Road to Divorce: England 1530–1987*, OUP, Oxford

Storr, A. (1970) *Human Aggression*, Penguin, Harmondsworth

Stott, J. R. W. (1975) *Explaining the Lausanne Covenant*, Worldwide Publishers, Minneapolis, Minnesota

Stroebe, M. S. *et al.*, eds (1993) *Handbook of Bereavement: Theory, Research and Intervention*, CUP, Cambridge

Symington, N. (1997) *New Theory of Narcissism*, Routledge, London

Tart, C. (1975) *Transpersonal Psychologies*, Harper, New York

Taylor, C. W. (1991) *The Skilled Pastor*, Fortress Press, Philadelphia PA

Taylor, T. F. (1996) *Seven Deadly Lawsuits*, Abingdon, Nashville TN

Thatcher, A. (1999) *Marriage after Modernity*, New York UP

Thiselton, A. C. (1980) *The Two Horizons*, Paternoster, London

Thompson, J. (1994) *Modern Trinitarian Perspectives*, OUP, Oxford

Thung, M. (1976) *The Precarious Organization*, Mouton, The Hague

Thurneysen, E. (1962) *A Theology of Pastoral Care*, John Knox, Louisville KY

Tillich, P. (1949) *The Shaking of the Foundations*, SCM Press, London

Tillich, P. (1951) *Systematic Theology*, Chicago UP, Chicago

Titmuss, R. (1973) *The Gift Relationship: From Human Blood to Social Policy*, Penguin, Harmondsworth

Toffler, A. (1972) *Future Shock*, Bodley Head, London

Toman, W. (1969) *Family Constellation*, Springer, New York

Tong, R. (1997) *Feminist Approaches to Bioethics*, Westview, New York

Tournier, P. (1957) *The Meaning of Persons*, SCM Press, London

Towler, R. (1974) *Homo Religiosus: Sociological Problems in Study of Religion*, Constable, London

Townes, E., ed. (1997) *Embracing the Spirit*, Orbis, Maryknoll NY

Triseliotis, J., Sellick, C. and Short, R. (1995) *Foster Care: Theory and Practice*, Free Association, London

Truax, C. B. and Karkhuff, R. R. (1967) *Toward Effective Counselling and Psychotherapy*, Aldine, Texas

Turner, V. (1969) *The Ritual Process*, Routledge & Kegan Paul, London

Valliant, G. F. (1977) *Adaptation to Life*, Little Brown, Boston MA

van Gennep, A. (1909, ET 1960) *Rites of Passage*, Routledge & Kegan Paul, London

Vanstone, W. H. (1977) *Love's Endeavour, Love's Expense*, Darton, Longman & Todd, London

Varah, C., ed. (1988) *The Samaritans: Befriending the Suicidal*, Constable, London

Veatch, R. (1989) *Medical Ethics*, Jones & Bartlett, Sudbury MA

Ven, J. van der (1996) *Ecclesiology in Context*, Eerdmans, Grand Rapids MI

Verhey, A. and Lammers, S. (1993) *Theological Voices in Medical Ethics*, Eerdmans, Grand Rapids MI

Waite, L. and Gallagher, M. (2000) *The Case for Marriage*, Doubleday, New York

Wakefield, G. S., ed. (1983) *A Dictionary of Christian Spirituality*, SCM Press, London

Walker, A. (1995) *Charismatic Renewal*, SPCK, London

Wallerstein, J., Lewis, J. and Blakeslee, S. (2000) *The Unexpected Legacy of Divorce: A 25 Year Landmark Study*, Hyperion, New York

Walter, A. (1990) *Funerals and How to Improve Them*, Hodder & Stoughton, London

Walter, A. (1994) *The Revival of Death*, Routledge, London

Ward, K. (1990) *Divine Action*, Collins, London

Ware, K. (1983) 'Apatheia' in Wakefield, G. S. ed. (1983)

Watson, J. R. (1997) *The English Hymn: A Critical and Historical Study*, OUP, Oxford

Watson, L. (1986) *Beyond Supernature*, Hodder & Stoughton, London

Webb, S. H. (1998), *On God and Dogs: A Christian Theology of Compassion for Animals*, OUP, Oxford

Weber, M., ed. Rand Wittich, C. (1922) *Economy and Society*, California UP, Berkeley CA

Weber, M. (1977) *The Protestant Ethic and the Spirit of Capitalism*, Macmillan, London

Weil, A. (1955) *Spontaneous Healing*, Knopf, New York

West, G. (1972) *The Applicability of Selected Rational Emotive Therapy Principles for Patoral Counseling*

Westerhoff, J. H. (1976) *Will our Children have Faith?* New York

Wheeler, S. (1996) *Stewards of Life*, Abingdon, Nashville TN

White, M. and Epston, D. (1990) *Narrative Means to Therapeutic Ends*, Norton, New York

Wilber, K. (1999) *Transformations of Consciousness*, Shambhala Publications

Wilkinson, G., Moore, B. and Moore, P. (1999) *Treating People with Anxiety and Stress*, Radcliffe Medical Press

Williams, R. M. (1951) *American Society: A Sociological Interpretation*, Knopf, New York

Williams, R. (1982) *Resurrection: Interpreting the Easter Gospel*, Darton, Longman & Todd, London

Wilson, B. (1984) *Religion in Sociological Perspective*, OUP, Oxford

Wilson, B. R. (1970) *Religious Sects*, Weidenfeld and Nicolson, London

Wilson, M., ed. (1985) *Explorations in Health and Salvation: A Selection of Papers by Bob Lambourne*, University of Birmingham, Birmingham

Wimberley, E. (1997) *Counseling African American Marriages and Families*, Westminster John Knox Press, Louisville KY

Wink, W. (1992) *Engaging the Powers*, Fortress Press, Philadelphia PA

Winnicott, D. W. (1961) *Human Nature*, Free Association Press, London

Winnicott, D. W. (1965) *The Maturational Process and the Facilitating Environment*, International Universities Press, Madison CT

Winnicott, D. W. (1971) *Playing and Reality*, Tavistock, London

Winnicott, D. W. (1992) *Through Paediatrics to Psychoanalysis*, Karnac, London

Wise, C. (1980) *Pastoral Psychotherapy: Theory and Practice*, Jason Aronson, New York

Witte, J. (1997) *From Sacrament to Contract: Marriage, Religion and the Law in the Western Tradition*, Westminster John Knox Press, Louisville KY

Wolpe, J. (1990) *The Making of Behavior Therapy*, Prentice Hall, New York

Woodham-Smith, C. (1951) *Florence Nightingale*, Constable, London

Woods, R., ed. (1980) *Understanding Mysticism*, Doubleday, New York

Wright, T. R. (1988) *Theology and Literature*, Blackwell, Oxford

Wulff, D. M. (1991) *The Psychology of Religion*, John Wiley, London

Young, F. (1990) *The Art of Performance: Towards a*

Theology of Holy Scripture, Darton, Longman & Todd, London

Zizioulas, J. (1985) *Being in Communion*, Darton, Longman & Todd, London

Zizioulas, J. (1993) *Being in Communion: Studies in Priesthood and the Church*, St Vladimir's Seminary Press, New York

Zuckerkandl, V. (1956) *Sound and Symbol*, Princeton UP, Princeton NJ

REPORTS AND OTHER DOCUMENTS

(1989) *Caring for People: Community Care in the Next Decade and Beyond*, HMSO, London

963 P.2d 310 (Colo 1993) *Moses v. The Diocese of Colorado*

ABM Occasional Paper 39 (1991) *Teams*, CIO, London

ABM Policy Paper 3B (1993) *Criteria for Selection*, CIO, London

ABM Report (1993) *Order in Diversity: Ordained Ministry in the Church of England*, CIO, London

ACCM Occasional Paper 23 (1987) *Bishops' Regulations for Non-Stipendiary Ministry*, CIO, London

American Association of Pastoral Counselors (1994) *Code of Ethics*

American Psychiatric Association (1994) *Diagnostic and Statistical Manual of Mental Disorders IV*, APA, New York

Archbishops' Commission on Rural Areas (1990) *Faith in the Countryside*, ACORA, Warwickshire

Archbishops' Commission on Urban Areas (1985) *Faith in the City*, Church House Publishing, London

Audit Commission (1986) *Making a Reality of community Care*, HMSO, London

British Association for Counselling (1985) *Counselling: Definition of Terms in Use with Expansion and Rationale*, BAC, Rugby

Catholic Bishops' Conference of England and Wales (1995) *A New Community of Work: A Christian Response to Unemployment*, CTS, London

CCBI (1994) *Churches Together in Marriage*, CCBI, London

CCBI (1997) *Unemployment and the Future of Work: An Enquiry for the Churches*, CCBI, London

Center for Marriage and the Family (1999) *Ministry to Interchurch Families: A National Study*, Creighton University, Nebraska

Church of England Board of Education (1992) *How Faith Grows*, CIO, London

Church of England (1995) *The Mystery of Salvation*, CIO, London

Church of England Board of Mission (1982) *The Marriage of Adherents of Other Faiths in Anglican Churches*, CHP, London

Church of England Board of Mission Inter-Faith Consultative Group (1982) *Guidelines for the Celebration of Mixed-Faith Marriages in Church*, CIO, London

Church of England Board of Mission Inter-Faith Consultative Group (1992) *Multi-Faith Worship?*, CIO, London

Church of England Board of Social Responsibility, A Working Party of (1995) *Something to Celebrate: Valuing Families in Church and Society*, Church House Publishing, London

Church of England House of Bishops (1991) *Issues in Human Sexuality*, CIO, London

CTS (1993) *Directory for the Application of Principles and Norms on Ecumenism*, CTS, London

National Society (1988) *Children in the Way*, CIO, London

Nuffield Council on Bioethics (1996) *Animal-to-Human Transplants*, Nuffield, London

Pontifical Commission Iustitia et Pax (1988) *What Have You Done for Your Homeless Brother?*, CTS, London

Pope John XXIII (1963) *Pacem in Terris*, Vatican

Pope John Paul II (1979) *Redemptor Hominis*, Vatican

Pope John Paul II (1979) *Man's Condition after Death*, Vatican

Pope John Paul II (1994) *Catechism of the Catholic Church*, Geoffrey Chapman, London

Pope Paul VI (1968) *Humanae Vitae*, Vatican

Report of the Independent Review of Residential Care (The Wagner Report) (1988) *Residential Care: A Positive Choice*, HMSO, London

Report to the Secretary of State for Social Services (The Griffiths Report) (1988) *Community Care: Agenda for Action*, HMSO, London

Rural Commission of the Church in Wales (1992) *The Church in the Welsh Countryside*

Vatican Council II (1964) *Lumen Gentium*, CTS, London

WCC (1982) *Baptism, Eucharist and Ministry* (The Lima Report), WCC, Geneva

World Health Organization (1978) *Definitions of Primary Care*, WHO, Geneva

World Health Organization (1990) *Technical Report Series 804*, WHO, Geneva